Getting Started is as EASY as 1, 2, 3 . . . . 4!

1. Sign Up

Instructors register with myBusinessCourse.com

2. Setup Your Course

Add your class details and additional materials.

3. Invite Your Students

Students register using your unique course code.

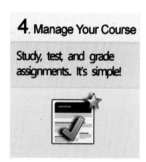

4. Manage Your Course

Study, test, and grade assignments. It's simple!

Provide Instruction and Practice 24/7

◆ Assign homework from your Cambridge Business Publishers textbook and have myBusinessCourse grade it for you automatically.

◆ With our eLectures, your students can revisit accounting topics as often as they like or until they master the topic.

◆ Guided Examples show students how to solve select problems.

◆ Make homework due before class to ensure students enter your classroom prepared.

◆ Upgrade to include the eBook and you have all the tools needed for an online course.

STUDENT SELF-STUDY OPTION

Not all instructors choose to incorporate **myBusinessCourse** into their course. In such cases, students can access the Self-Study option for MBC. The Self-Study option provides most of the learning tools available in the Instructor-Led courses, including:

◆ eLectures
◆ Guided Examples
◆ Practice Quizzes

The Self-Study option does not include homework assignments from the textbook. Only the Instructor-Led option includes homework assignments.

Want to learn more about myBusinessCourse?

Contact your sales representative or visit **www.mybusinesscourse.com**.

STUDENTS: Find your access code on the myBusinessCourse insert on the following pages. If you have a used copy of this textbook, you can purchase access online at **www.mybusinesscourse.com**.

Cambridge Business Publishers Series in Accounting

Financial Accounting

◆ **Financial Accounting for Undergraduates, 2e** by Ferris, Wallace, and Christensen

◆ **Financial Accounting, 4e** by Dyckman, Magee, and Pfeiffer

◆ **Financial Accounting for MBAs, 6e** by Easton, Wild, Halsey, and McAnally

◆ **Financial Accounting for Executives & MBAs, 3e** by Simko, Ferris, and Wallace

◆ **Cases in Financial Reporting, 7e** by Engel, Hirst, and McAnally

Managerial Accounting

◆ **Managerial Accounting, 7e** by Hartgraves & Morse

◆ **Cases in Managerial and Cost Accounting, 1e** by Allen, Brownlee, Haskins, and Lynch

Combined Financial & Managerial Accounting

◆ **Financial & Managerial Accounting for Decision Makers, 2e** by Dyckman, Magee, Pfeiffer, Hartgraves, and Morse

◆ **Financial & Managerial Accounting for MBAs, 4e** by Easton, Halsey, McAnally, Hartgraves, and Morse

Intermediate Accounting

◆ **Cases in Financial Reporting, 7e** by Engel, Hirst, and McAnally

Cost Accounting

◆ **Cases in Managerial and Cost Accounting, 1e** by Allen, Brownlee, Haskins, and Lynch

Financial Statement Analysis & Valuation

◆ **Financial Statement Analysis & Valuation, 4e** by Easton, McAnally, Sommers, and Zhang

◆ **Corporate Valuation, 1e** by Holthausen & Zmijewski

◆ **Cases in Financial Reporting, 7e** by Engel, Hirst, and McAnally

Advanced Accounting

◆ **Advanced Accounting, 2e** by Hamlen, Huefner, and Largay

◆ **Advanced Accounting, 2e** by Halsey & Hopkins

FASB Codification and eIFRS

◆ **Skills for Accounting and Auditing Research, 2e** by Collins

Seventh Edition

Managerial Accounting

AL L. HARTGRAVES
Emory University

WAYNE J. MORSE
Rochester Institute of Technology

To our families and students
— A.H. W.M.

Cambridge Business Publishers

MANAGERIAL ACCOUNTING, Al L. Hartgraves and Wayne J. Morse.

COPYRIGHT © 2015 by Cambridge Business Publishers, LLC. Published by Cambridge Business Publishers, LLC. Exclusive rights by Cambridge Business Publishers, LLC for manufacture and export.

ISBN 978-1-61853-096-7

Bookstores & Faculty: to order this book, contact the company via email customerservice@cambridgepub.com.

Students & Retail Customers: to order this book, please visit the book's website and order directly online.

Printed in the United States of America.
10 9 8 7 6 5 4 3 2 1

Preface

Welcome to the Seventh Edition of Managerial Accounting. Our book presents managerial accounting in the context of a big-picture, decision oriented, business setting. It integrates traditional coverage with contemporary topics, and does so with an eye toward the general business student because a book is not useful if it is not read. An overriding aim of our book is to engage students to read further and understand the materials presented.

APPROACH AND EMPHASIS

Managerial accounting focuses on using financial and nonfinancial information by managers and associates of a firm to make strategic, organizational, and operational decisions. Our book provides a framework for identifying and analyzing decision alternatives and for evaluating success or failure in accomplishing such organizational goals. Although accountants are important in the managerial accounting process, managerial accounting is more about managerial tools than processes. In our era of global competition, continuous improvement, process reengineering, and employee empowerment; the tools of managerial accounting are used by decision makers at all levels, rather than just by "managers." One goal of our book is to introduce students to this reality.

Our book is written for all students—not just accounting students. We place managerial accounting in a broad business context, relating it to other business areas. We also avoid details that are appropriate for advanced cost accounting books. Like the trunk of a tree, our book serves as a strong base for students' future knowledge growth and as a means of unifying the branches of business management.

We emphasize the use of managerial accounting information for decision making within the context of organizational strategy. The organization and content of our book reflect our belief that students who understand the big picture are better learners, are better decision makers, and are better able to apply what they learn.

ETHICS

Managerial ethics receives extensive coverage in this edition. For example, ethics is introduced in the context of measurement and management in Chapter 1 and discussed further in Chapters 4 and 9. "Business Insight" features and numerous end-of-chapter problems and cases in Chapters 1, 3, 8, 9, 10, and 11 include a variety of decision situations involving ethical dilemmas. The following excerpt is from Chapter 9 and discusses ethical dimensions of the budgeting process:

Ethics

Because most wrongful activities related to budgeting are unethical, rather than illegal, organizations often have difficulty dealing with them. However, when managers' actions cross the gray area between ethical and fraudulent behavior, organizations are not reluctant to dismiss employees or even pursue legal actions against them.

Although most managers have a natural inclination to be conservative in developing their budgets, at some level the blatant padding or building slack into the budget becomes unethical. In an extreme case, it might even be considered theft if an inordinate level of budgetary slack creates favorable performance variances that lead to significant bonuses or other financial gain for the manager. Another form of falsifying budgets occurs when managers include expense categories in their budgets that are not needed in their operations and subsequently use the funds to pad other budget categories. The deliberate falsification of budgets is unethical behavior and is grounds for dismissal in most organizations.

Ethical issues might also arise in the reporting of performance results, which usually compares actual data with budgeted data. Examples of unethical reporting of actual performance data include misclassification of expenses, overstating revenues or understating expenses, postponing or accelerating the recording of activities at the end of the accounting period, or creating fictitious activities.

UNIQUE PEDAGOGY

Managerial Accounting includes several special features specifically designed to engage students and help them succeed in this course.

Business Insights

Students appreciate and become more engaged when they can see the relevance of what they are learning in the classroom. We have revised and added new Business Insight boxes throughout each chapter to bring the accounting to life for students through current, real world examples. The following is a representative example:

BUSINESS INSIGHT

Using CVP for Financial Analysis and Prediction   Williams-Sonoma operates a chain of 581 merchandise retail stores in the U.S. and Canada. Their mission is to enhance their customers' lives at home. Condensed 2011 and 2012 income statements in millions follow.

	For the Year Ending	
	January 29, 2012	January 30, 2011
Net sales	$3,721	$3,504
Cost of sales and operating expenses	(3,484)	(3,304)
Operating profit	$ 237	$ 200

We can determine Williams-Sonoma's cost-volume-profit relationships and predict future profits for a given level of sales after using the high-low method to develop cost estimating equations. First determine variable costs as a percent of sales:

$$\text{Variable cost ratio} = \frac{\$3,484 - \$3,304}{\$3,721 - \$3,504} = \underline{0.8295}$$

Next determine annual fixed costs by calculating and subtracting the variable costs of either period (revenues multiplied by the variable cost ratio) from the corresponding total costs. Using 2012 revenues and costs annual fixed costs are determined as follows:

$$\text{Annual fixed costs} = \$3,484 - (\$3,721 \times 0.8295) = \underline{\$397} \text{ million}$$

Williams-Sonoma's annual cost estimating equation is:

$$\text{Total annual costs} = \$397 \text{ million} + (0.8295 \times \text{Net sales})$$

Using the fixed costs and the contribution margin ratio (1 minus the variable cost ratio) Williams-Sonoma's break-even point in sales dollars is computed.

$$\text{Break-even point} = \$397 \text{ million}/(1 - 0.8295) = \underline{\$2,328} \text{ million}$$

For 2013, Williams-Sonoma's net sales and operating profits were $4,043 million and $257 million. Using the CVP relationships developed from 2011 and 2012 data, the predicted 2013 operating profits are $292 million $4,043 − [($4,043 × 0.8295) + $397]. In this case, because of Williams-Sonoma's stable cost structure, the model error is small.

Decision Making Orientation

One primary goal of a managerial accounting course is to teach students the skills needed to apply their accounting knowledge to solve real business problems and make informed business decisions. With that goal in mind, You Make The Call boxes in each chapter encourage students to apply the material presented to solving actual business scenarios. The following is a representative example:

YOU MAKE THE CALL

You Are the Vice President of Manufacturing Your company has had a practice for many years of budgeting variable overhead costs based on direct labor hours. The managerial accountants have argued that if direct labor hours are controlled, variable overhead costs will take care of themselves since direct labor hours drive variable overhead costs. You (and your plant managers) have become very skeptical of this policy because in recent years variable overhead variances have been very erratic—sometimes being large favorable amounts and other times being large unfavorable amounts. You are beginning to plan for the coming budget year. How do you think you should budget variable overhead and evaluate managers who control these costs? [Answer, p. 366]

Research Insights

Academic research plays an important role in the way business is conducted, accounting is performed, and students are taught. It is important for students to recognize how modern research and modern business practice interact. Therefore, we periodically incorporate relevant research to help students understand the important relation between research and modern business. The following is a representative example:

RESEARCH INSIGHT

Nonprofit Donations Decrease When Donors Believe Managers Are Overpaid Over 1.4 million nonprofit organizations across the United States received more than $260 billion in donations during the year 2009. Yet with the weakening economy, contributors to nonprofit organizations are less willing to tolerate inflated salaries of the charity's executives. Specifically, donors decrease their contributions to the organization when the media reports an increase in executive compensation. On average, organizations that draw media coverage over executive compensation increases grow 15 percent less over the two years surrounding the media mention than their peer organizations. However, when this increase is reported on Form 990 for the Internal Revenue Service (IRS), only sophisticated donors reduce their contributions. Small donors may not know where to seek the compensation information out on their own, and larger donors have a greater stake in the stewardship of their donated funds. Among these larger donors, the study reports that contributions decrease by 3 percent for every $100,000 increase in executive compensation.

Source: Steven Balsam and Erica Harris, "The Impact of CEO Compensation on Nonprofit Donations," *The Accounting Review*, forthcoming.

Mid-Chapter and Chapter-End Reviews

Managerial accounting can be challenging—especially for students lacking business experience or previous exposure to business courses. To reinforce concepts presented in each chapter and to ensure student comprehension, we include mid-chapter and chapter-end reviews that require students to recall and apply the managerial accounting techniques and concepts described in each chapter. The following is a representative example:

CHAPTER-END REVIEW

Suppose the Coffee Bean has a new shop in a Cambridge village shopping center that sells high-end teas and coffees. Further, suppose they have added smoothie drinks to their product line. Below are the assumed sales and cost data for the company:

	Coffee	Tea	Smoothie
Sales price per (12 oz.) serving.................	$1.35	$1.25	$1.95
Variable cost per serving......................	0.60	0.45	0.75
Fixed costs per month $8,000			

Suppose the company sells each month an average of 6,000 servings of coffee, 3,750 servings of tea, and 2,250 servings of smoothies.

Required
a. Calculate the current before-tax profit, contribution margin ratio, and sales mix based on sales dollars.
b. Using a sales dollar analysis, calculate the monthly break-even point assuming the sales mix does not change.
c. Calculate Coffee Bean's operating leverage ratio. If sales increase by 20 percent, by how much will before-tax income be expected to change? If sales decrease by 20 percent, by how much will before-tax income be expected to change?

The solution is on page 104.

Excellent Assignments

Excellent assignment material is a must-have component of any successful textbook (and class). We went to great lengths to create the best assignments possible. We tried to include assignments that reflect our belief that students should be trained in analyzing accounting information to make business decisions, as opposed to working on mechanical computations. Assignments encourage students to analyze accounting information, interpret it, and apply the knowledge gained to a business decision. There are five categories of assignments: **Discussion Questions**, **Mini Exercises**, **Exercises**, **Problems**, and **Cases and Projects**. The following is a representative example:

LO2 **P7-31.** **Allocation and Responsibility Accounting**

TIMBERLAND COMPANY (TBL)

Assume that Timberland Company uses a responsibility accounting system for evaluating its managers, and that abbreviated performance reports for the company's three divisions for the month of March are as follows (amounts in thousands).

	Total	East	Central	West
Income....................................	$206,000	$73,000	$80,000	$53,000
Less allocated costs:				
Information Technology....................	(105,000)	(35,000)	(35,000)	(35,000)
Personnel................................	(75,000)	(28,125)	(28,125)	(18,750)
Division income............................	$ 26,000	$9,875	$16,875	$ (750)

CHANGES TO THE 7TH EDITION

Many significant changes have been made in the 7th edition, including:

- **myBusinessCourse:** This complete learning and homework program is free with new copies of the textbook. myBusinessCourse includes a complete learning path for students. Students will be able to watch eLectures, and see how representative problems are solved before proceeding to their homework. As the instructor, you can select assignments from the textbook or test bank and have students' responses automatically graded. You also have access to a robust grade book that provides many course management and diagnostic tools. Whether you teach a complete online course or just want to provide your students with additional resources to master the content, myBusinessCourse will prove to be an invaluable resource for you and your students. See the inside cover of this textbook for more details.
- Many new Business Insight boxes have replaced older ones.
- Several new Research Insight Boxes have been incorporated.
- Dozens of new, real company examples have been integrated throughout the text.
- Over two-thirds of the exercises and problems have been revised.
- All 12 Opening Vignettes have been replaced. The following companies are now featured:

Chapter 1	ModCloth	Chapter 7	Whole Foods
Chapter 2	Square	Chapter 8	Roku
Chapter 3	DuPont	Chapter 9	Pinterest
Chapter 4	Uber	Chapter 10	Southwest Airlines
Chapter 5	Samsung	Chapter 11	Volkswagen
Chapter 6	Unilever	Chapter 12	Amazon

ANCILLARY MATERIALS

Our book is part of a comprehensive and carefully prepared teaching package that includes various forms of assistance to both instructors and students.

For Instructors

- **myBusinessCourse:** A web-based learning and assessment program intended to complement your textbook and classroom instruction. This easy-to-use course management system grades homework automatically and provides students with additional help when you are not available. In addition, detailed diagnostic tools assess class and individual performance. myBusinessCourse is ideal for online courses or traditional face-to-face courses for which you want to offer students more resources to succeed. Assignments with the ✓ in the margin are available in myBusinessCourse.
- **Solutions Manual:** prepared by the authors, contains detailed solutions to all assignments.
- **PowerPoint Slides:** enhance the classroom presentation of book materials.
- **Test Bank:** a collection of problems, questions, and exercises designed to save time in preparing and grading periodic and final exams.
- **Book Website:** overseen by the authors, this password-protected site contains further instructor resources.

For Students

- **myBusinessCourse:** A web-based learning and assessment program intended to complement your textbook and faculty instruction. This easy-to-use program provides you with additional help when your instructor is not available. Access is free with new copies of this textbook (look for page containing the access code towards the front of the book). Please note the differences between Instructor-Led and Self-Study options. If you buy a used copy of the book, you can purchase access at www.mybusinesscourse.com.
- Website: Practice quizzes and other useful links are available to students free of charge on the book's Website.

ACKNOWLEDGMENTS

We are indebted to the following instructors who provided us with revision suggestions for this and prior editions of our book:

Helen Adams, *University of Washington*

William David Albrecht, *Bowling Green State University*

James L. Bierstaker, *Villanova University*

Susan Borkowski, *LaSalle University*

A. Faye Borthick, *Georgia State University*

Gary Bridges, *University of Texas—San Antonio*

Stephen Brown, *University of Maryland*

Gene Bryson, *University of Alabama—Hunstville*

Tom Clausen, *University of Illinois—Springfield*

Douglas Clinton, *Northern Illinois University*

Gary Colbert, *University of Colorado—Denver*

Vicki Dickinson, *University of Mississippi*

Paul M. Fischer, *University of Wisconsin—Milwaukee*

Benjamin P. Foster, *University of Louisville*

David P. Franz, *San Francisco State University*

Mark Friedman, *University of Miami*

Peter Frischmann, *Idaho State University*

Margaret Gagne, *Marist College*

Karen Geiger, *Arizona State University*

John Giles, *North Carolina State University*

Judith Harris, *Nova Southeastern University*

John Hassell, *Indiana University—Indianapolis*

Eleanor G. Henry, *Southeast Missouri State University*

James W. Hesford, *Cornell University*

Jay S. Holmen, *University of Wisconsin—Eau Claire*

David R. Honodel, *University of Denver*

Ronald Huefner, *SUNY Buffalo*

Eric N. Johnson, *Indiana University—Indianapolis*

Paul Juras, *Wake Forest University*

Anthony Craig Keller, *Missouri State University*

Charles Kile, *Middle Tennessee State University*

Larry N. Killough, *Virginia Tech University*

John Koeplin, *University of San Francisco*

William Lathen, *Boise State University*

Elliot Levy, *Bentley College*

Donna Losell, *University of Toronto*

Linda M. Marquis, *Northern Kentucky University*

Otto B. Martinson, *Old Dominion University*

Michael J. Meyer, *University of Notre Dame*

Dale Morse, *University of Oregon*

Ramesh Narasimhan, *Montclair State University*

Larry Paquette, *Francis Marion University*

Gordon Potter, *Cornell University*

Barbara Reider, *University of Montana*

Maryanne Rouse, *University of South Florida*

Jack Ruhl, *Western Michigan University*

Jane Saly, *University of St. Thomas*

Jeffrey Schatzberg, *University of Arizona*

Lewis Shaw, *Suffolk University*

Henry Smith, *III, Otterbein College*

Charles Stanley, *Baylor University*

Audrey Taylor, *Western Washington University*

Pierre L. Titard, *Southeastern Louisiana State University*

Leslie Turner, *Northern Kentucky University*

Sheila Viel, *University of Wisconsin—Milwaukee*

Wallace Wood, *University of Cincinnati*

Elisa Zuliani, *University of Toronto*

Appreciation is extended to the Institute of Certified Management Accountants for permission to use adaptations of problems from past Certified Management Accounting Examinations—these materials are identified as "CMA Adapted." We are also indebted to the American Institute of Certified Public Accountants for permission to use materials from the Uniform CPA exam—these materials are identified as "CPA Adapted." We are especially grateful to Vicki Dickinson for her contributions to this edition. We appreciate the tolerance and feedback of our students as we tested many of the new ideas and assignments for this book. Finally, we appreciate the encouragement, support, and detailed suggestions for improvement provided by George Werthman and his colleagues at Cambridge Business Publishers, including Lorraine Gleeson, Marnee Fieldman, Beth Nodus, Jill Fischer, Jocelyn Mousel, Deborah McQuade, and Terry McQuade. Working with them has been a pleasure. To assist us in continuously improving our book to better fits your needs and the needs of your students, comments and suggestions are welcome.

Al L. Hartgraves   *Wayne J. Morse*

About the Authors

Al L. Hartgraves is Professor Emeritus of Accounting at the Goizueta Business School at Emory University in Atlanta, Georgia. He has been a Guest Professor at Johannes Kepler University in Linz, Austria and at the Helsinki School of Economics and Business Administration and Aalto University in Finland. He is an honorary faculty member of the LIMAK Austrian Business School. He has also served as Senior Associate Dean, Acting Dean, and Director MBA Programs at Emory. His published scholarly and professional articles have appeared in *The Accounting Review, Accounting Horizons, Management Accounting, Journal of Accountancy, Journal of Accounting and Public Policy* and many other journals. Students at Goizueta Business School have selected him on six occasions to receive the Distinguished Educator Award. He is also the recipient of Emory University's highest teaching award, The Scholar/Teacher Award, and he was recognized as the Accounting Educator of the Year by the Georgia Society of CPAs. He has been recognized as an Outstanding Faculty Member in two editions of The Business Week Guide to the Best Business Schools. He is a Certified Public Accountant (inactive) and a Certified Management Accountant, having received the Certificate of Distinguished Performance on the CMA exam. He received his Ph.D. from Georgia State University, and in 2011 was granted an honorary doctorate by Johannes Kepler University.

Wayne J. Morse, is Professor Emeritis at the Saunders College of Business at Rochester Institute of Technology. An author or co-author of more than fifty published papers, monographs, and textbooks, he was a founding member of the Management Accounting section of the American Accounting Association. His most notable writings are in the areas of learning curves, human resource accounting, and quality costs. He was a member of the IMA Committee on Research and an AICPA Board of Examiners subcommittee, and he has served on the editorial boards of Advances in Accounting, Trends in Accounting Education, Issues in Accounting Education, and Management Accounting Research. A Certified Public Accountant, he received his Ph.D. from Michigan State University. Prior to joining RIT, he was on the faculty of the University of Illinois, Duke University, the University of Tennessee, Clarkson University, and the University of Alabama-Huntsville.

Brief Contents

Contents

Chapter 6

Activity-Based Costing, Customer Profitability, and Activity-Based Management 197

Chapter 7

Additional Topics in Product Costing 237

Chapter 8

Pricing and Other Product Management Decisions 267

Chapter 12
Capital Budgeting Decisions 427

Appendix A
Managerial Analysis of Financial Statements 472

1. Contrast financial and managerial accounting and explain how managerial accounting is used by internal decision makers. (p. 4)

2. Explain how an organization's mission, goals, and strategies affect managerial accounting. (p. 7)

3. Discuss the factors determining changes in the nature of business competition. (p. 13)

4. Differentiate among structural, organizational, and activity cost drivers. (p. 14)

5. Explain the nature of the ethical dilemmas managers and accountants confront. (p. 17)

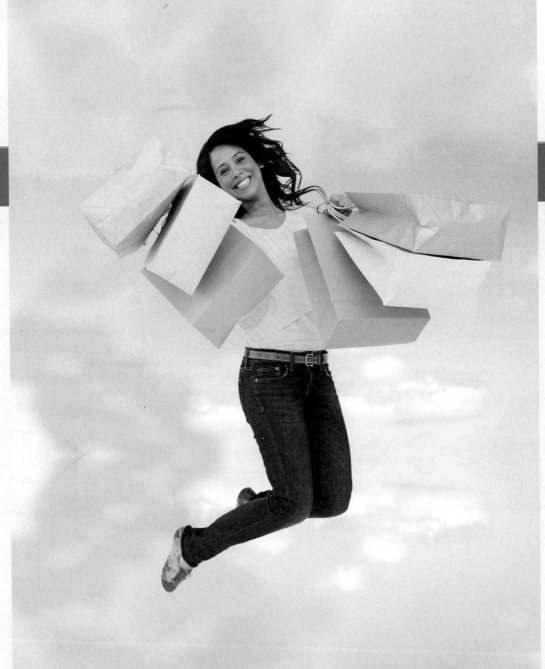

Managerial Accounting: Tools for Decision Making

Shopping for women's apparel has traditionally been a collaborative experience. Women shop with their mothers, daughters, sisters, and friends and rely on their advice in determining what styles best suit them. Yet Internet commerce has transformed what was once a social outing into an impersonal and solitary activity. One company, ModCloth, is putting the social aspect back into e-retailing.

MODCLOTH
www.modcloth.com

ModCloth is headquartered in San Francisco and sells vintage and or vintage-inspired apparel, accessories, and décor. It was founded in 2002 by husband-and-wife team Eric Koger and Susan Gregg Koger, while they were in college at Carnegie Mellon University. ModCloth was recently named "America's Fastest-Growing Retailer" by *Inc.* magazine (which also ranked the company number two for the fastest-growing private company). ModCloth's sales exceeded $100 million in 2012 and are expected to increase by more than 40 percent in 2013. The company's physical capacity is rapidly expanding both in property and staff to support planned growth. Four hundred and fifty employees now work in San Francisco, Los Angeles, and Pittsburgh.

The information provided by the managerial accounting system is critical to thriving, young companies as they build upon their corporate vision. Startup companies must search for capital while honing their strategy and making calculated decisions regarding their position in the competitive landscape. For example, ModCloth set out to target women in the technologically savvy millennial generation (18 to 31 years old). Understanding customers' demographics facilitates the company's planning activities. ModCloth's planners know that millennials are not content to be passive consumers, and they've plotted the company's growth strategy to provide increased customer participation in the shopping experience.

Nowhere is this more evident than in the company's "Be the Buyer" program, which refines product selection through crowdsourcing. To further involve the customer in the product creation process, ModCloth started a customer design contest entitled "Make the Cut" in which customers submit original designs that the company then produces and sells through the website. Customers have submitted over 4,000 designs since the program's inception in 2012. The site also contains a "Style Gallery" where customers upload photos of outfits created by utilizing ModCloth's products. Other shoppers can comment on an original poster's photos. With one click the customer can purchase the outfit components immediately.

Not only do ModCloth's managers use managerial accounting information to plan their long-run and day-to-day operations, they evaluate the feedback produced by the system to control their operations. For example, the company has found that its newly created mobile applications (for smartphones and tablets) result in, on average, more frequent visits per customer and higher purchase amounts per visit than the company's traditional website application. ModCloth managers also utilize customer comments to identify segments of their key demographic that are currently underserved. Further, the company has been

continued on following page

continued from previous page

encouraged by its customers to expand the size offerings of its merchandise. Taken together, this feedback resulted in ModCloth's newest initiative: creating a private-label collection for zero through plus sizes that utilizes customer feedback to produce sufficient inventory of each design. Throughout this book, we will learn how managerial accounting provides useful information for making informed business decisions.

Sources: Douglas MacMillan, "At ModCloth, Vintage Fashion Goes Mobile," *Bloomberg Businessweek*, August 8, 2013; Meghan Casserly, "ModCloth Hits $100 Million in Revenue, Gives Social All the Credit," *Forbes*, July 23, 2013; and Bridget Brennan, "The Retailer Winning the Battle for Millennial Women," *Forbes*, November 16, 2012.

CHAPTER ORGANIZATION

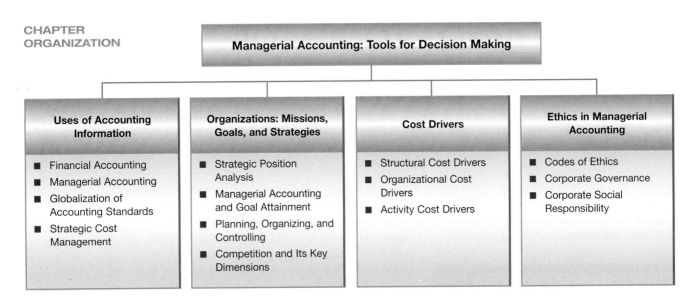

This Chapter provides an overview of the factors that make managerial accounting increasingly important to successful businesses. **Managerial accounting** is defined as the activities carried out in a firm to provide its managers and other employees with financial and related information to help them make strategic, organizational, and operational decisions. We begin by distinguishing between financial and managerial (also called *management*) accounting and by investigating how competitive strategy affects the way organizations, such as ModCloth, use managerial accounting information. Next, we explore how the emergence of global competition and changes in technology have increased the need to understand managerial accounting concepts. We also provide an overview of factors that influence costs in an organization and how these factors have changed in recent years. Finally, we examine the interrelationships among measurement, management, and ethics.

USES OF ACCOUNTING INFORMATION

Financial Accounting

LO1 Contrast financial and managerial accounting and explain how managerial accounting is used by internal decision makers.

Financial accounting is an information-processing system that generates general-purpose reports of financial operations (income statement and statement of cash flows) and financial position (balance sheet) for an organization. Although financial accounting is used by decision makers inside and outside the firm, financial accounting typically emphasizes external users, such as security investors, analysts, and lenders. Adding to this external orientation are external financial reporting requirements determined by law and generally accepted accounting principles.

Financial accounting is also concerned with keeping records of the organization's assets, obligations, and the collection and payment of cash. An organization cannot survive without converting sales into cash, paying for purchases, meeting payroll, and keeping track of its assets.

Managers often use income statements and balance sheets as a starting point in evaluating and planning the firm's overall activities. Managers learn a great deal by performing a comparative analysis of their firm and competing firms. Corporate goals are often stated using financial accounting numbers such as net income, or ratios such as return on investment and earnings per common share. However, internal decision makers often find the information provided in financial statements of limited value in managing day-to-day operating activities. They often complain that financial accounting information is too aggregated, prepared too late, based on irrelevant past costs, and not action oriented. For example, the costs of all items produced and sold or all services rendered are summarized in a single line in most financial statements, making it impossible to determine the costs of individual products or services. Financial accounting procedures, acceptable for costing inventories as a whole, often produce misleading information when applied to individual products. Even when they are accurately determined, the costs of individual products or services are rarely detailed enough in overall financial statements to provide the information needed for decisions concerning the factors that influence costs. Financial accounting reports, seldom prepared more than once a month, are not timely enough for use in the management of day-to-day activities that cause excess costs. Finally, financial accounting reports, to a great extent, are based on historical costs rather than on current or future costs. Managers are more interested in future costs than in historical costs such as last year's depreciation. While financial accounting information is useful in making some management decisions, its primary emphasis is not on internal decision making.

Managerial Accounting

Managers are constantly faced with the need to understand and control costs, make important product decisions, coordinate resources, and guide and motivate employees. Managerial accounting provides an information framework to organize, evaluate, and report proprietary data in light of an organization's goals. This information is directed to managers and other employees within the organization. Managerial accounting reports can be designed to meet the information needs of internal decision makers. Top management may need only summary information prepared once a month for each business unit. An engineer responsible for hourly production scheduling may need continuously updated and detailed information concerning the cost of alternative ways of producing a product.

Because of the intensity of competition and the shorter life cycles of new products and services, managerial accounting is crucial to an organization's success. All managers must understand the financial implications of their decisions. While accountants are available to assist in obtaining and evaluating relevant information, individual managers are responsible for requesting information, analyzing it, and making the final decisions.

BUSINESS INSIGHT

Strategic Thinking Requires a Company to Think Inside the Consumer's Sphere Emerging markets represent significant opportunities, but companies must check their preconceptions at the door when formulating their strategies. For example, a company building a mobile network in Africa will be dealing with customers who may have never had a landline telephone. Cost structures based on landline companies are outdated because building a mobile network is far cheaper than extending telephone wire to each business and home. The desktop and laptop computer market may skip Africa entirely as consumers leap to smartphones for their computing needs. And traditional brick-and-mortar banks need to rethink their functionality in a region where customers are doing the majority of their banking on their phones.

In Kenya, 40 percent of the population lives on less than $2 per day, but more and more Kenyans are purchasing low-cost smartphones. Safaricom, East Africa's telecom market leader, and the Commercial Bank of Africa have partnered in a service that allows mobile phone users to apply for and receive loans through their phones. This partnership is serving a population that is new to the entire concept of banking. The next project on Safaricom's horizon is to use cell phone technology to access and pay for health care. Managerial accounting helps guide companies like Safaricom through the myriad of growth opportunities available to them, while providing information about their costs of delivering a product or service and making a determination of what price to charge consumers for those products and services.

Sources: Eric Ombok, "Safaricom, Commercial Bank Africa Start Mobile Loan Service," *Bloomberg Businessweek*, November 27, 2012; and Tim Worstall, "Africa Might Just Skip the Entire PC Revolution," *Forbes*, August 17, 2011.

Managerial accounting information exists to serve the needs of management. Hence, it is subject to a cost-benefit analysis and should be developed only if the perceived benefits exceed the costs of development and use. Also, while financial measures are often used in managerial accounting, they are not used to the exclusion of other measures. Money is simply a convenient way of expressing events in a form suitable to summary analysis. When this is not possible or appropriate, nonfinancial measures are used. Time, for example, is often an important element of quality or service. Hence, many performance measures focus on time, for example:

- Internet vendors such as ModCloth and Amazon.com track delivery time.
- Fire departments and police departments measure the response time to emergency calls.
- Airlines, such as Delta Airlines as well as the Federal Aviation Administration monitor the number of on-time departures and arrivals.

No external standards (such as requirements of the Securities and Exchange Commission) are imposed on information provided to internal users. Consequently, managerial accounting information may be quite subjective. In developing a budget, management is more interested in a subjective prediction of next year's sales than in an objective report on last year's sales. The significant differences between financial and managerial accounting are summarized in Exhibit 1.1.

EXHIBIT 1.1	Differences Between Financial and Managerial Accounting	
Financial Accounting	**Managerial Accounting**
Information for internal *and* external users	Information for internal users
General-purpose financial statements	Special-purpose information and reports
Statements are highly aggregated	Information is aggregated or detailed, depending on need
Relatively long reporting periods	Reporting periods are long or short, depending on need
Report on past decisions	Oriented toward current and future decisions
Follows generally accepted accounting principles	Not constrained by generally accepted accounting principles
Must conform to external standards	No external standards
Emphasizes objective data	Encourages subjective data, if relevant

Globalization of Accounting Standards

As indicated in Exhibit 1.1, a major difference between financial accounting and managerial accounting is that financial accounting must conform to a set of generally accepted accounting principles (GAAP), whereas managerial accounting is not subject to any external standards. The creation of financial accounting standards in the United States, referred to as U.S. GAAP, is the purview of the Financial Accounting Standards Board (FASB), although the ultimate legal authority for accounting standards for publicly traded companies in the U.S. is held by the U.S. Securities and Exchange Commission (SEC). Over the past 25 years, a strong set of international accounting standards (IFRS) has been developed by the International Accounting Standards Board (IASB), which is based in the UK. With the emergence of IFRS, many countries, including all European Union countries, have adopted IFRS as a replacement of their domestic accounting standards for publicly traded companies.

For the past several years, the FASB and the IASB have cooperated to minimize the number of differences between U.S. GAAP and IFRS. It remains to be seen what impact this convergence of U.S. GAAP and IFRS will have on the financial reporting for privately owned companies.

Even though there is no existing regulation of managerial accounting systems, financial accounting standards invariably have some impact on managerial accounting. For example, in accounting for inventory costs, many companies use the same cost systems for both financial and managerial accounting purposes. One of the major differences between U.S. GAAP and IFRS is related to the accounting for inventory costs. It is widely anticipated in the financial accounting community that as the two sets of standards are harmonized further, some of the current inventory cost methods available under U.S. GAAP will no longer be acceptable for financial reporting purposes. This change will likely affect both the financial and managerial reporting systems in many companies.

The direct impact on managerial accounting of the convergence of U.S. GAAP and IFRS is expected to be rather limited. However, managers still need to be aware of major changes in financial accounting standards, because these standards affect how the results of their internal managerial decisions are reported to shareholders and other external constituencies. Financial reporting of managerial decisions affects earnings and earnings per share, and often affects stock valuations.

Strategic Cost Management

Most businesses are under constant pressure to reduce costs to remain competitive. A 2013 study by the accounting firm Deloitte reported that more than 75 percent of survey participants viewed an efficient cost structure as a source of long-term competitive advantage.[1]

During recent years, the rapid introduction of improved and new products and services has shortened the market lives of products and services. Some products, such as personal computers, can be obsolete within two or three years after introduction. At the same time, the increased use of complex automated equipment makes it difficult to change production procedures after production begins. Combining short product life cycles with automated production results in an environment where most costs are determined by decisions made before production begins (decisions concerning product design and production procedures).

In response to these trends, a strategic approach to managerial accounting, referred to as *strategic cost management* has emerged. Strategic cost management is a blending of three themes:

1. **Strategic position analysis**—an examination of an organization's basic way of competing to sell products or services.
2. **Cost driver analysis**—the study of factors that cause or influence costs.
3. **Value chain analysis**—the study of value-producing activities, stretching from basic raw materials to the final consumer of a product or service.[2]

We define **strategic cost management** as making decisions concerning specific cost drivers within the context of an organization's business strategy, internal value chain, and position in a larger value chain stretching from the development and use of resources to final consumers. Strategic position analysis is considered in this chapter as part of an organization's strategy. Cost driver analysis is also introduced in this chapter and examined further in Chapter 2. Value chain analysis is discussed in Chapter 8.

MISSIONS, GOALS, AND STRATEGIES

An organization's **mission** is the basic purpose toward which its activities are directed. ModCloth's current mission is to "deliver an amazing ModCloth experience in every box we deliver and with every customer interaction." Starbucks' mission is to "establish Starbucks as the premier purveyor of the finest coffee in the world while maintaining our uncompromising principles while we grow."[3] Organizations vary widely in their missions. One benefit of a mission statement is to help focus all the activities of an organization. For instance, the former chairman and CEO of Coca-Cola stated that the mission of The Coca-Cola Company is "to create value over time for the owners of our business." He went on to say:

LO2 Explain how an organization's mission, goals, and strategies affect managerial accounting.

> Our society is based on democratic capitalism. In such a society, people create specific institutions to help meet specific needs. Governments are created to help meet social needs. . . Businesses such as ours are created to meet economic needs. The common thread between these institutions is that they can flourish only when they stay focused on the specific need they were created to fulfill. When institutions try to broaden their scope beyond their natural realms, when for example they try to become all things to all people, they fail.[4]

---

[1] "Cutting Costs to Drive Growth: Trends Among the Fortune 1000," Deloitte's Third Biennial Cost Survey: Cost-Improvement Practices and Trends in the Fortune 1000, 2013.

[2] John K. Shank, "Strategic Cost Management: New Wine, or Just New Bottles?" *Journal of Management Accounting Research,* Fall 1989, p. 50.

[3] www.starbucks.com

[4] Roberto Goizueta, "Why Shareholder Value?" *CEO Series Issue No. 13,* February 1997, Center for the Study of American Business, Washington University in St. Louis, p. 2.

The CEO of Coca-Cola believed that Coca-Cola best contributes to society and helps government and other organizations fulfill their missions by staying focused on shareholder value. He believed focusing on economics keeps a company financially healthy, and a healthy company fulfills its responsibilities. Conversely, a bankrupt company is incapable of paying taxes, employing people, serving customers, supporting charitable institutions, or making other contributions to society.

We frequently distinguish between organizations on the basis of profit motive. **For-profit organizations** have profit as a primary objective, whereas **not-for-profit organizations** do not have profit as a primary objective. Clearly, the Coca-Cola Company is a for-profit organization, whereas the City of Chicago and the Red Cross are not-for-profit organizations. (The term *nonprofit* is frequently used to refer to what we have identified as not-for-profit organizations.) Regardless of whether a profit motive exists, organizations must use resources wisely. Every dollar United Way spends for administrative salaries is a dollar that cannot be used to support charitable activities. Not-for-profit organizations, including governments, can go bankrupt if they are unable to meet their financial obligations. All organizations, for-profit and not-for-profit, should use managerial accounting concepts to ensure that resources are used wisely.

A **goal** is a definable, measurable objective. Based on the organization's mission, management sets a number of goals. For-profit organizations have some measure of profitability or shareholder value as one of their stated or implicit goals. The mission of a paper mill located in a small town is to provide quality paper products in order to earn a profit for its owners. The paper mill's goals might include earning an annual profit equal to 10 percent of average total assets, maintaining annual dividends of $2 per share of common stock, developing a customer reputation for above-average quality and service, providing steady employment for area residents, and meeting or exceeding environmental standards.

A clear statement of mission and well-defined goals provides an organization with an identity and unifying purpose, thereby ensuring that all employees are heading in the same direction. Having developed a mission and a set of goals, employees are more apt to make decisions that move the organization toward its defined purpose.

A **strategy** is a course of action that will assist in achieving one or more goals. Much of this text will focus on the financial aspects of selecting strategies to achieve goals. For example, if an organization's goal is to improve product quality, possible strategies for achieving this goal include investing in new equipment, implementing additional quality inspections, prescreening suppliers, reducing batch size, redesigning products, training employees, and rearranging the shop floor. Managerial accounting information will assist in determining which of the many alternative strategies for achieving the goal of quality improvement are cost effective. The distinction between mission, goals, and strategies is illustrated in Exhibit 1.2.

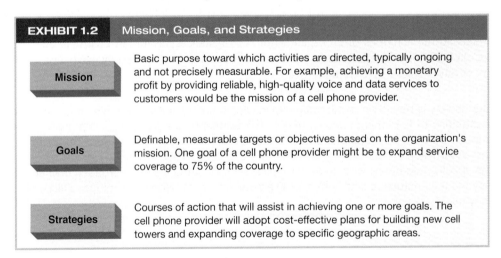

EXHIBIT 1.2 Mission, Goals, and Strategies

Mission
Basic purpose toward which activities are directed, typically ongoing and not precisely measurable. For example, achieving a monetary profit by providing reliable, high-quality voice and data services to customers would be the mission of a cell phone provider.

Goals
Definable, measurable targets or objectives based on the organization's mission. One goal of a cell phone provider might be to expand service coverage to 75% of the country.

Strategies
Courses of action that will assist in achieving one or more goals. The cell phone provider will adopt cost-effective plans for building new cell towers and expanding coverage to specific geographic areas.

Strategic Position Analysis

In competitive environments, managers must make a fundamental decision concerning their organization's goal for positioning itself in comparison to competitors. This goal is referred to as the organization's **strategic position**. Much of the organization's strategy depends on this strategic positioning goal. Michael Porter, a highly regarded expert on business strategy, has identified three possible strategic positions that lead to business success.[5]

1. Cost leadership
2. Product or service differentiation
3. Market niche

According to Porter, cost leadership

requires aggressive construction of efficient-scale facilities, vigorous pursuit of cost reductions from experience, tight cost and overhead control, avoidance of marginal customer accounts, and cost minimization in areas like R&D [research and development], service, sales force, advertising, and so on. A great deal of managerial attention to cost control is necessary to achieve these aims. Low cost relative to competitors becomes the theme running through the entire strategy, though quality, service, and other areas cannot be ignored.[6]

Achieving cost leadership allows an organization to achieve higher profits selling at the same price as competitors or by allowing the firm to aggressively compete on the basis of price while remaining profitable. One of the first companies to successfully use a cost leadership strategy was Carnegie Steel Company.

Carnegie's operating strategy was to push his own direct costs below his competitors so that he could charge prices that would always ensure enough demand to keep his plants running at full capacity. This strategy prompted him to require frequent information showing his direct costs in relation to those of his competitors. Possessing that information and secure in the knowledge that his costs were the lowest in the industry, Carnegie then mercilessly cut prices during economic recessions. While competing firms went under, he still made profits. In periods of prosperity, when customers' demands exceeded the industry's capacity to produce, Carnegie joined others in raising prices.[7]

Southwest Airlines and Costco are current examples of successful businesses competing with a strategy of cost leadership. Although Amazon.com uses the Internet to differentiate itself from traditional booksellers, its primary strategic position is cost leadership.

Conversely, while an organization might compete primarily on the basis of price, management must take care to ensure their product or service remains attuned to changing customer needs and preferences. In the early twentieth century, General Motors employed a differentiation strategy, focusing on the rapid introduction of technological change in new automobile designs to overcome the market dominance of the Model T produced by Ford Motor Company. While successfully following a cost leadership strategy for years, Ford made the mistake of excluding other considerations such as vehicle performance and customer desires for different colors. ModCloth follows a product differentiation strategy by using community collaboration to drive product design and selection that results in a unique array of merchandise compared to its competitors.

---

[5] Michael E. Porter, *Competitive Strategy* (New York: The Free Press, 1980), p. 35.
[6] Porter, p. 35.
[7] H. Thomas Johnson and Robert S. Kaplan, Relevance Lost: *The Rise and Fall of Management Accounting* (Boston: Harvard Business School Press, 1987), pp. 33–34.

The third possible strategic position according to Porter, focuses on a specific market niche such as a buyer group, segment of the product line, or geographic market and

rests on the premise that the firm is thus able to serve its narrow strategic target more effectively or efficiently than competitors who are competing more broadly. As a result, the firm achieves either differentiation from better meeting the needs of the particular target, or lower costs in serving the target, or both. Even though the focus strategy does not achieve low costs or differentiation for the market as a whole, it does achieve one or both of these positions vis-à-vis its narrow market target.[8]

BUSINESS INSIGHT

Growth Company Needs a Targeted Plan to Avoid Being Overwhelmed by Its Opportunities San Francisco startup Splunk Inc. has some seriously large customers—Bank of America, Comcast Corporation, and the U. S. Department of Defense types of customers. And you know you're on to something good when a new verb is created based on what your company does. We used to spend our time "Googling," but now we spend it "splunking." Splunk is capitalizing on the big data phenomenon by collecting and sifting through machine data.

Machine data can come from websites, cell phones, smart meters, geographic positioning system (GPS) equipment, or any other method by which data can be captured. Splunk provides the means to collect, index, monitor, and analyze massive streams of data in real time and then export the data into customers' existing systems. With a seemingly endless supply of potential customers, Splunk will have to tread carefully to use its existing capacity to serve the most lucrative customers. The tools in this chapter can help companies determine which customers should be served first when facing limited resources.

Source: Rolfe Winkler, "Splunk Looks to Be Well-Priced for Its Data with Destiny," *Wall Street Journal*, April 19, 2012, p. C12.

Splunk Inc., highlighted in the Business Insight box above, is following a market niche strategy. Other examples of organizations successfully following a market niche strategy include regional breweries that cater to local tastes and Gulfstream, which follows a focused strategy in designing and building corporate aircraft, leaving the market for larger passenger aircraft to firms such as Boeing.

Managerial Accounting and Goal Attainment

A major purpose of managerial accounting is to support the achievement of goals. Hence, determining an organization's strategic position goal has implications for the operation of an organization's managerial accounting system.

Careful budgeting and cost control with frequent and detailed performance reports are critical with a goal of cost leadership. When the product is difficult to distinguish from that of competitors', price is the primary basis of competition. Under these circumstances, everyone in the organization should continuously apply managerial accounting concepts to achieve and maintain cost leadership. The managerial accounting system should constantly compare actual costs with budgeted costs and signal the existence of significant differences. A simplified version of a *performance report* for costs during a budget period is as follows:

Budgeted (planned) Costs	Actual Costs	Deviation from Budget	Percent Deviation
$560,000	$595,000	$35,000 unfavorable	6.25

Frequent and detailed comparisons of actual and budgeted costs are less important when a differentiation strategy is followed. This is especially true when products have short life cycles

---

[8] Porter, pp. 38–39.

or production is highly automated. In these situations, most costs are determined before production begins and there is little opportunity to undertake cost reduction activities thereafter.

With short product lives or automated manufacturing, exceptional care must go into the initial design of a product or service and the determination of how it will be produced or delivered. Here, detailed cost information assists in design and scheduling decisions. A simplified version of the predicted costs of producing one batch of a specialty product is as follows:

Engineering and scheduling (12 hours @ $70).....	$ 840
Materials (detail omitted)	3,500
Equipment setup (2.5 hours @ $100)	250
Machine operation (9.5 hours @ $90)...........	855
Materials movement	150
Packing and shipping	675
Total	$6,270

When a differentiation strategy is followed, it often pays to work closely with customers to find ways to enhance the perceived value of a product or service. This leads to an analysis of costs from the customer's viewpoint. The customer may not want a costly feature. Alternatively, the customer may be willing to pay more for an additional feature that will reduce subsequent operating costs.

Planning, Organizing, and Controlling

The process of selecting goals and strategies to achieve these goals is often referred to as **planning**. The implementation of plans requires the development of subgoals and the assignment of responsibility to achieve subgoals to specific individuals or groups within an organization. This process of making the organization into a well-ordered whole is called **organizing**. In organizing, the authority to take action to implement plans is delegated to other managers and employees.

Developing an **organization chart** illustrating the formal relationships that exist between the elements of an organization is an important part of organizing. An organization chart for Crown Department Stores is illustrated in Exhibit 1.3. The blocks represent organizational units, and the lines represent relationships between the units. Authority flows down through the organization. Top management delegates authority to use resources for limited purposes to subordinate managers who, in turn, delegate to their subordinates more limited authority for accomplishing more structured tasks. Responsibility flows up through the organization. People at the bottom are responsible for specific tasks, but the president is responsible for the operation of the entire organization.

A distinction is often made between line and staff departments. *Line departments* engage in activities that create and distribute goods and services to customers. *Staff departments* exist to facilitate the activities of line departments. In Exhibit 1.3, we see that Crown Department Stores has two levels of staff organizations—corporate and store. The corporate staff departments are Purchasing, Advertising, Operations, Treasurer, and Controller. Staff departments at the store level are Personnel, Accounting, and Maintenance. All other units are line departments. A change in plans can necessitate a change in the organization. For example, Crown's plan to discontinue the sale of hardware and add an art department during the coming year will necessitate an organizational change.

Controlling is the process of ensuring that results agree with plans. A brief example of a performance report for costs was presented previously. In the process of controlling operations, actual performance is compared with plans.

With a cost leadership strategy and long-lived products, if actual results deviate significantly from plans, an attempt is made to bring operations into line with plans, or the plans are adjusted. The original plan is adjusted if it is deemed no longer appropriate because of changed circumstances.

With a differentiation strategy and short-lived products, design and scheduling personnel will consider previous errors in predicting costs as they plan new products and services. Hence, the process of controlling feeds forward into the process of planning to form a continuous cycle coordinated through the management accounting system. This cycle is illustrated in Exhibit 1.4.

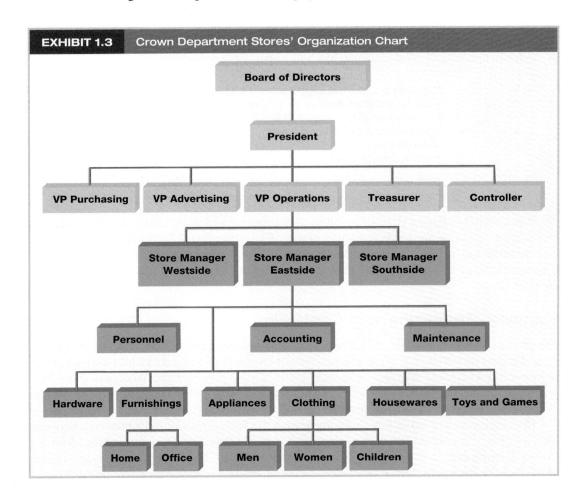

EXHIBIT 1.3   Crown Department Stores' Organization Chart

EXHIBIT 1.4   Planning, Organizating, & Control Cycle

MID-CHAPTER REVIEW

The previous discussion has focused on understanding the difference between financial and managerial accounting and the broader context of managerial accounting within a company.

Required

Identify the statements and phrases from the following list that are primarily relevant to managerial accounting, as opposed to financial accounting:

1. Preparing periodic financial statements
2. A company's strategic position
3. Calculates earnings per share for stockholders
4. Summarizes information about past events
5. Is not based on generally accepted accounting principles
6. Must conform to external standards
7. Helping managers make decisions is its primary purpose
8. Encourages use of selective data, if relevant
9. Is tailored to the needs of the company and its managers
10. Cost driver analysis

The solution is on page 28.

Competition and Its Key Dimensions

The move away from isolated national economic systems toward an interdependent global economic system has become increasingly pronounced. International treaties, such as the North American Free Trade Agreement and the General Agreement on Tariffs and Trade, merely recognize an already existing and inevitable condition made possible by advances in telecommunications (to move data), computers (to process data into information), and transportation (to move products and people).

LO3 Discuss the factors determining changes in the nature of business competition.

The labels of origins on goods (Japan, Germany, Canada, Taiwan, China, and so forth) only scratch the surface of existing global relationships. Behind labels designating a product's final assembly point are components from all over the world.

The move toward a global economy has heightened competition and reduced selling prices to such an extent that there is little or no room for error in managing costs or pricing products. Moreover, customers are not just looking for the best price. Well-informed buyers routinely search the world for the product or service that best fits their needs on the three interrelated dimensions of price/cost, quality, and service; hence, these are the three key dimensions of competition.

To customers, *price/cost* includes not only the initial purchase price but also subsequent operating and maintenance costs. To compete on the basis of price, the seller must carefully manage costs. Otherwise, reduced prices might squeeze product margins to such an extent that a sale becomes unprofitable. Hence, price competition implies cost competition.

Quality refers to the degree to which products or services meet the customer's needs. *Service* includes things such as timely delivery, helpfulness of sales personnel, and subsequent support.

Managers of successful companies know they compete in a global market with instant communications. Because the competition is hungry and always striving to gain a competitive advantage, world-class companies must continuously struggle to improve performance on these three interrelated dimensions: price/cost, quality, and service. Throughout this text, we examine how firms successfully compete on these three dimensions.

COST DRIVERS

LO4 Differentiate among structural, organizational, and activity cost drivers.

An **activity** is a unit of work. To serve a customer at a restaurant such as Fleming's Prime Steakhouse, a server might perform the following units of work:

- Seat customer and offer menu
- Take customer order
- Send order to kitchen
- Bring food to customer
- Serve and replenish beverages
- Determine and bring bill to customer
- Accept and process payment
- Clear and reset table

Each of these is an activity, and the performance of each activity consumes resources that cost money. To manage activities and their costs, it is necessary to understand how costs respond to **cost drivers**, which are the factors that cause or influence costs.

The most basic cost driver is customer demand. Without customer demand for products or services, the organization cannot exist. To serve customers, managers and employees make a variety of decisions and take numerous actions. These decisions and actions, undertaken to satisfy customer demand, drive costs. While these cost drivers may be classified in a variety of ways, we believe that dividing them into the three categories of structural, organizational, and activity cost drivers, as summarized in Exhibit 1.5, provides a useful foundation for the study of managerial accounting.

EXHIBIT 1.5	Structural, Organizational, and Activity Cost Drivers
Structural Cost Drivers	Fundamental choices about the size and scope of operations and technologies employed in delivering products or services to customers. For example, Apple Computer's decision to enter the online music distribution business.
Organizational Cost Drivers	Choices concerning the organization of activities and the involvement of persons inside and outside the organization in decision making. Authorizing lower-level employees to make decisions to solve problems is an example of an organizational cost driver.
Activity Cost Drivers	Specific units of work (activities) performed to serve customer needs that consume costly resources. Assembling a product is an example of an activity cost driver.

Structural Cost Drivers

The types of activities and the costs of activities performed to satisfy customer needs are influenced by an organization's size, its location, the scope of its operations, and the technologies used. Decisions affecting structural cost drivers are made infrequently, and once made, the organization is committed to a course of action that will be difficult to change. For a chain of retail stores such as Target, possible structural cost drivers include:

- *Determining the size of stores.* This affects the variety of merchandise that can be carried and operating costs.
- *Determining the type of construction.* While a lean warehouse type of construction is less expensive, it is not an appropriate setting for selling high-fashion clothing.

■ *Determining the location of stores*. Locating in a shopping mall can cost more and subject the store to mall regulations but provides for more customer traffic and shared advertising.

■ *Determining types of technology to employ in stores*. A computerized system for maintaining all inventory and sales data requires a large initial investment and fixed annual operating costs while providing more current information. However, the computerized inventory and sales systems can be less expensive at high sales volumes than a less costly system relying more on clerks taking physical inventory.

One of the most important structural cost drivers for many companies is the decision to reach out to a global marketplace. The following Business Insight illustrates how some companies have successfully weathered the current economic downturn as a result of their globalization strategy.

BUSINESS INSIGHT

Globalization as a Structural Cost Driver The Coca-Cola Company has operated internationally since the 1920s. It operates in more than 100 countries with about 75% of its sales coming from abroad. The Wall Street Journal recently reported that within the last year, Coca-Cola has announced plans to invest $27 billion in developing countries over the next decade.

In today's recessionary economic environment, it is companies with a global focus that are experiencing the greatest revenue growth. The Journal reported that among the 30 companies in the Dow Jones Industrial Average, the 10 companies that get the largest share of their revenues from abroad saw revenue growth of 8.3%; whereas, the 10 companies with the least global revenues saw only a 1.6% growth. In tough economic times, with a weaker American economy, companies that have made structural cost decisions to go global are realizing significant payoff from those decisions.

Source: Justin Lahart, "Divided by a Two-Track Economy," *The Wall Street Journal Digital Network (WSJ.com)*, September 7, 2010.

Organizational Cost Drivers

Like structural cost drivers, organizational cost drivers influence costs by affecting the types of activities and the costs of activities performed to satisfy customer needs. Decisions that affect organizational cost drivers are made within the context of previous decisions affecting structural cost drivers. In a manufacturing organization, previous decisions about plant, equipment, and location are taken as a given when decisions impacting organizational cost drivers are made. Examples of organizational cost drivers at a manufacturing organization such as **Harley-Davidson** include making decisions regarding:

■ *Working closely with a limited number of suppliers*. This can help achieve proper materials in the proper quantities at the optimal time. Developing linkages with suppliers can also result in suppliers' initiatives that improve the profitability of both organizations.

■ *Providing employees with cost information and authorizing them to make decisions*. This helps improve decision speed and reduce costs while making employees more customer oriented. Production employees may, for example, offer product design suggestions that reduce manufacturing costs or reduce defects.

■ *Reorganizing the existing equipment in the plant so that sequential operations are closer*. This more efficient layout reduces the cost of moving inventory between workstations.

■ *Designing components of a product so they can fit together only in the correct manner*. This can reduce defects as well as assembly time and cost.

■ *Manufacturing a low-volume product on low-speed, general-purpose equipment rather than high-speed, special-purpose equipment*. Assuming the special-purpose equipment is more difficult and costly to set up for a new job, this decision can increase operating time and operating cost while reducing setup time and setup cost.

The following business insight illustrates how an innovative hospital in the suburbs of Seattle managed a key organizational cost driver to bring down costs and achieve profitability.

BUSINESS INSIGHT

Managing an Organizational Cost Driver at Providence Hospital A key costing challenge for any hospital is how to manage the traffic flow of patients as they go from one level of care to another, from the patient room to laboratory, radiology, or testing location and back to the patient room, or to and from physical therapy or other treatment locations. Just as in any production environment, how the processes are organized is a key cost driver. Providence Hospital in Everett, Washington radically changed its patient movement practices resulting not only in significant cost savings, but also greatly improved patient satisfaction. In their "single stay" section of the hospital, the patient remains in the same room at all times as the level of care changes, or as testing or therapy takes place. Instead of moving the patient around, equipment is moved in and out of the patient room depending on the required level of care, the testing, or treatment to be performed.

Source: Based on Catherine Arnst, "Radical Surgery," *Bloomberg Business Week*, January 18, 2010.

Activity Cost Drivers

Activity cost drivers are specific units of work (activities) performed to serve customer needs that consume costly resources. Several examples of activities in a restaurant were mentioned previously. The customer may be outside the organization, such as a client of an advertising firm, or inside the organization, such as an accounting office that receives maintenance services. Because the performance of activities consumes resources and resources cost money, the performance of activities drives costs.

The basic decisions concerning which available activities will be used to respond to customer requests precede the actual performance of activities. At the activity level, execution of previous plans and following prescribed activities are important. All of the examples of structural and organizational cost drivers involved making decisions. In the following list of activity cost drivers for a manufacturing organization, note the absence of the decision-oriented words.

- *Placing a purchase order for raw materials*
- *Inspecting incoming raw materials*
- *Moving items being manufactured between workstations*
- *Setting up a machine to work on a product*
- *Spending machine time working on a product*
- *Spending labor time working on a product*
- *Hiring and training a new employee*
- *Packing an order for shipment*
- *Processing a sales order*
- *Shipping a product*

In managing costs, management makes choices concerning structural and organizational cost drivers. These decisions affect the types of activities required to satisfy customer needs. Because different types of activities have different costs, management's decisions concerning structural and organizational cost drivers ultimately affect activity costs and profitability. Good decision making at the level of structural and organizational cost drivers requires an understanding of the linkages among the types of cost drivers and the costs of different activities.

YOU MAKE THE CALL

You are the CEO How can you use information about structural, organizational, and activity cost drivers to help you in implementing the organization's strategy? [Answer, p. 20]

ETHICS IN MANAGERIAL ACCOUNTING

Ethics deals with the moral quality, fitness, or propriety of a course of action that can injure or benefit people. Ethics goes beyond legality, which refers to what is permitted under the law, to consider the moral quality of an action. Because situations involving ethics are not guided by well-defined rules, they are often subjective.

Although some actions are clearly ethical (working a full day in exchange for a full day's pay) and others are clearly unethical (pumping contaminants into an underground aquifer used as a source of drinking water), managers are often faced with situations that do not fall clearly into either category such as the following:

- Accelerating or decelerating shipments at the end of the quarter to meet current earnings forecasts.
- Keeping inventory that is unlikely to be used so as to avoid recording a loss.
- Purchasing supplies from a relative or friend rather than seeking bids.
- Basing a budget on an overly optimistic sales forecast.
- Assigning some costs of Contract A to Contract B to avoid an unfavorable performance report on Contract A.

LO5 Explain the nature of the ethical dilemmas managers and accountants confront.

Many ethical dilemmas involve actions that are perceived to have desirable short-run consequences and highly probable undesirable long-run consequences. The ethical action is to face an undesirable situation now to avoid a worse situation later, yet the decision maker prefers to believe that things will work out in the long run, be overly concerned with the consequences of not doing well in the short run, or simply not care about the future because the problem will then belong to someone else. In a situation that is clearly unethical, the future consequences are known to be avoidable and undesirable. In situations involving questionable ethics, there is some hope that things will work out:

- Next year's sales will more than make up for the accelerated shipments.
- The obsolete inventory can be used in a new nostalgia line of products.
- The relative or friend may charge more but provides excellent service.
- A desire to have more confidence in the sales staff.
- Making up for the cost shift by working extra hard and more efficiently with the remaining work on Contract B.

When forced to think about the situation, most employees want to act in an ethical manner. The problem faced by personnel involved in measurement and reporting is that while they may question the propriety of a proposed action, and the arguments may be plausible, they want to be team players, and their careers can be affected by "whistle-blowing." Of course, careers are also affected when individuals are identified as being involved in unethical behavior. The careers of people who fail to point out unethical behavior are also affected, especially if they have a responsibility for measurement and reporting.

Major ethical dilemmas often evolve from a series of small compromises, none of which appears serious enough to warrant taking a stand on ethical grounds. WorldCom is such a case, in which managers deferred expenses inappropriately over several periods to meet profit forecasts, expecting to recognize them at later time when sales improved. Unfortunately, these small compromises establish a pattern of behavior that is increasingly difficult to reverse. The key to avoiding these situations is recognizing the early warning signs of situations that involve questionable ethical behavior and taking whatever action is appropriate.

Codes of Ethics

Codes of ethics are often developed by professional organizations to increase members' awareness of the importance of ethical behavior and to provide a reference point for resisting pressures to engage in actions of questionable ethics. These professional organizations include the American

Bar Association, the American Institute of Certified Public Accountants, the American Medical Association, and the Institute of Management Accountants (IMA).

Many corporations have established codes of ethics. A summary of GM Corporation's 20-page code of ethics, "Winning with Integrity" is presented in the following Business Insight box. One of the important goals of corporate codes of ethics is to provide employees with a common foundation for addressing ethical issues. These codes provide a summary of a company's policies that define ethical standards of employee conduct and they often include broad philosophical statements about behavior. A basic rule of thumb used by GM is that employees should never do anything they would be ashamed to explain to their families or to see in the front page of the local newspaper.

BUSINESS INSIGHT

GM Code of Ethics: "Winning with Integrity"

- GM hires, promotes, trains and pays based on merit, experience, or other work-related criteria and strives to create work environments that accept and tolerate differences while promoting productivity and teamwork.
- GM endeavors to protect the health and safety of each employee by creating and maintaining a healthy, injury-free work environment.
- All GM employees have an obligation to protect GM's assets, including information, and to ensure their proper use.
- Use the Internet only for work assignments and all email and voice mail messages become GM records. Posting anonymously on social media should be avoided and identify yourself as a GM employee. Do not tarnish the image, damage the reputation or infringe on the rights of others. Providing false or misleading information in any GM business record is strictly prohibited.
- As a general rule, GM employees should accept no gift, entertainment, or other gratuity from any supplier to GM or bidder for GM's business.
- GM employees must immediately disclose any situation that could result in an actual or potential conflict of interest, involving the employee or any member of his household, such as investing in a supplier, dealer, customer, or competitor.
- GM and all its employees must comply with all laws, including the U.S. Foreign Corrupt Practices Act, competition laws, and export control laws.
- To protect GM's reputation for integrity, it must communicate clearly and accurately to the public.

Source: http://www.gm.com/content/dam/gmcom/COMPANY/Investors/Corporate_Governance/PDFs/Winning_With_Integrity.pdf

---

Corporate Governance

Corporate governance refers to the system of policies, processes, laws, and regulations that affect the way a company is directed and controlled. At the highest level, the system of corporate governance for a company is the responsibility of the board of directors, but it affects all stakeholders, including employees, creditors, customers, vendors, and the community at large. The large number of corporate failures of the last decade brought the topic of corporate governance to the forefront.

The collapse of Enron, along with its independent auditor, Arthur Andersen, prompted the U.S. Congress to pass the Sarbanes-Oxley Act of 2002 (or SOX), which was intended to address weaknesses affecting U.S. capital markets. Although SOX deals primarily with issues pertaining to the relationship between publicly traded companies and the capital markets, some of its requirements have become a standard for corporate responsibility and governance affecting both public and private companies, as well as not-for-profit organizations.

SOX consists of 66 sections, including such topics as external auditing standards, auditor conflicts of interest, codes of ethics for financial officers, review of internal controls, and criminal penalties for fraud. Probably the most important provisions of SOX, from a managerial accounting standpoint, are those related to internal control systems. **Internal control systems** generally are made up of the policies and procedures that exist to ensure that company objectives are achieved with regard to (a) effectiveness and efficiency of operations, (b) reliability of financial reporting, and (c) compliance with laws and regulations.

SOX imposes the requirement that CEOs and CFOs annually review and assess the effectiveness of their company's internal controls over financial reporting, and issue a report of their assessment. Although many CEOs and CFOs have argued that the cost of SOX compliance is unjustified by the benefits to investors, the following Research Insight provides evidence that SOX is improving the quality of financial reporting. Even though SOX limits the internal control review to aspects of the system related to financial reporting, in practice there is very little that takes place in any organization that does not impact the financial statements. Therefore, if SOX is resulting in improvements in data that goes into financial reports, it is likely that data supporting managerial accounting is also enhanced by a more reliable internal control system.

Many of the models and processes that we discuss in this text have either a direct or indirect impact on a company's financial statements; hence, they are likely subject to the SOX internal control review. An overlap often exists between the systems that produce the data for the external financial statements and those that produce data for internal decision making. For example, cost data produced by the product costing system is often used for both financial reporting and managerial decision making purposes. A more detailed discussion of SOX and internal control systems can typically be found in financial accounting and auditing textbooks.

RESEARCH INSIGHT

SOX Improves Financial Reporting   A recent study of about 1,000 firms reported that companies subject to Sarbanes-Oxley internal control system reviews were significantly less likely to issue materially misstated financial statements, thereby suggesting that the SOX legislation is probably meeting its objective of improving the quality of financial reports. The study based its conclusions on the fact that smaller companies exempt from the SOX internal control reviews were 40% more likely to have material misstatements in their financial statements than companies required to conduct internal control reviews. The study did not attempt to answer the question of whether the reduction in misstatements was sufficient to justify the expense incurred as a result of SOX requirements.

Source: Albert Nagy, "Section 404 Compliance and Financial Reporting Quality," Accounting Horizons, September, 2010, Vol. 24, Issue 3, p441-454.

Corporate Social Responsibility

Closely related to the concepts of ethics and corporate governance is the topic of **corporate social responsibility**, which can simply be defined as being a good corporate citizen. It entails balancing the objective of profitability with the objective of giving proper attention to issues such as environmental sustainability and energy conservation, and avoiding actions that would lower the quality of life in the communities in which a company operates and sells its products or services. In earlier generations it would have meant giving a day's wage for a day's labor, not hiring underage children, or not dumping untreated waste into the local river.

Managerial accounting includes a variety of models that help managers determine the cost of a particular activity or product, or the benefits and costs of various decision alternatives. Although such models in their current state of development may not take into account all external social costs, accountants are more aware today than in the past of the need to consider such costs. For example, when calculating the cost of building a new capital asset that is going to last for 25 years, it is necessary to include in that calculation the present value of the cost of the ultimate disposal of the asset, including any environmental cleanup.

Being a socially responsible company does not mean abandoning the profit motive or the goal of providing an attractive return to investors. It means that while pursuing these essential objectives, a for-profit company attempts to measure the total benefits and costs of its actions and accepts the responsibility for those actions. Also, being a good competitor should not be confused with social responsibility. For example, many companies offer certain fringe benefits, such as on-site childcare, because it attracts better employees, not because they feel they have a social responsibility to provide such services. Obviously, the line between being a good competitor and being socially responsible is sometimes blurred.

RESEARCH INSIGHT

Environmental Disclosures—Silence Is Not Golden Various regulatory sources have been calling for increased disclosure regarding a firm's effect on the environment, including a report on the firm's carbon emissions. Shareholder activists have also driven increased reporting of climate-change risks to their investee firms. In 2004, only 14 percent of shareholder resolutions involved environmental initiatives, but that number had grown to 27 percent by 2009, according to a report by **EY**. The authors of a recent study note that firms with a reputation for environmental responsibility enjoy higher revenues, lower compliance costs, more motivated employees, and positive perceptions among customers and suppliers.

EY analyzed carbon emissions data from 2006 to 2008 for S&P 500 firms and found that for each additional thousand metric tons of carbon emissions produced by the firm, the firm's value (as measured by market value of equity) decreases by $212,000. The difference in value between the first and third quartiles of carbon emission levels correlates to a 1.4-billion-dollar difference in firm value. However, silence is not golden. The authors state that although all firms are penalized for their carbon emissions, those firms that do not disclose the information to the public are penalized to a larger extent by the stock market.

Source: Ella Mae Matsumura, Rachna Prakash, and Sandra Vera-Munoz, "Firm-Value Effects of Carbon Emissions and Carbon Disclosures," *The Accounting Review*, forthcoming.

CHAPTER-END REVIEW

Classify each of the following as a structural, organizational, or activity cost driver.

a. Meals served to airplane passengers aboard **Delta Airlines**.
b. **GM**'s decision to manufacture the Volt, an all-electric automobile.
c. **Zenith**'s decision to sell its computer operations and focus on the core television business.
d. Number of tax returns filed electronically by **H&R Block**.
e. Number of passenger cars in an **Amtrak** train.
f. **Coors**' decision to expand its market area east from the Rocky Mountains.
g. **Boeing**'s decision to invite airlines to assist in designing the model 777 airplane.
h. **Daimler Benz**'s decision to use cross-disciplinary teams to design a new automobile.
i. **St.Jude Hospital**'s decision to establish review committees on the appropriateness and effectiveness of medical procedures for improving patient care.
j. **Harley-Davidson**'s efforts to restructure production procedures to reduce inventories and machine setup times.

The solution is on page 28.

GUIDANCE ANSWERS . . . YOU MAKE THE CALL

You are the CEO It is important that an organization's cost structure be aligned with its strategy. If your goal is to be a cost leader (such as Wal-Mart or Costco), you will want to make sure that the structural cost drivers, such as the type of buildings acquired and the displays used, are consistent with this strategy. As the CEO of Wal-Mart you would not permit many of the costs that would be incurred in an organization such as Tiffany or Nordstrom.

KEY TERMS

activity, 14
activity cost drivers, 16
controlling, 11
corporate governance, 18
corporate social responsibility, 19
cost driver analysis, 7
cost drivers, 14
ethics, 17

financial accounting, 4
for-profit organizations, 8
goal, 8
internal control systems, 18
managerial accounting, 4
mission, 7
not-for-profit organizations, 8
organization chart, 11

organizing, 11
planning, 11
strategic cost management, 7
strategic position, 9
strategic position analysis, 7
strategy, 8
value chain analysis, 7

MULTIPLE CHOICE

1. Which of the following is not a characteristic of Managerial Accounting?
    a. No external standards
    b. Reports primarily on past decisions
    c. Provides information for internal users
    d. Information is more detailed

2. Controlling is the process of:
    a. Selecting goals and adopting strategies for achieving them
    b. Delegating authority to others to take action to implement plans
    c. Organizing employees into line and staff functions
    d. Ensuring that results agree with plans

3. Which of the following is not a cost driver?
    a. The gender of the wait staff at a restaurant
    b. The number of customers in a restaurant
    c. The size of a restaurant
    d. The policy of empowering a waitress to make the decision to give a customer a free dessert because of the delay in delivering the main entrée.

4. Which of the following is not one of the three basic types of cost drivers discussed in the text?
    a. Activity cost drivers
    b. Organizational cost drivers
    c. Direct cost drivers
    d. Structural cost drivers

5. Which of the following is not likely to be regarded as an action that has ethical implications in today's business environment?
    a. Purchasing supplies from a relative or friend rather than seeking bids
    b. Using different depreciation methods for calculating depreciation expense for the financial statements and the income tax return
    c. Failing to recognize obsolete inventory to avoid missing a profit forecast
    d. Shifting costs for one contract to another to make the profits of the contracts line up with initial forecasts

DISCUSSION QUESTIONS

Q1-1. Contrast financial and managerial accounting on the basis of user orientation, purpose of information, level of aggregation, length of time period, orientation toward past or future, conformance to external standards, and emphasis on objective data.

Q1-2. What three themes are a part of strategic cost management?

Q1-3. Distinguish between a mission and a goal.

Q1-4. Describe the three strategic positions that Porter views as leading to business success.

Q1-5. Distinguish between how managerial accounting would support the strategy of cost leadership and the strategy of product differentiation.

Q1-6. Why are the phases of planning, organizing, and controlling referred to as a *continuous cycle*?

Q1-7. Identify three advances that have fostered the move away from isolated national economic systems toward an interdependent global economy.

Q1-8. What are the three interrelated dimensions of today's competition?

Q1-9. Differentiate among structural, organizational, and activity cost drivers.

Q1-10. What is the link between performing activities and incurring costs?

Q1-11. How can top management establish an ethical tone in an organization?

Q1-12. Describe how pressures to have desirable short-run outcomes can lead to ethical dilemmas.

Assignments with the ✔ logo in the margin are available in ᵐʸBusinessCourse.
See the Preface of the book for details.

MINI EXERCISES

LO1-5 **M1-13. Management Accounting Terminology**

Match the following terms with the best descriptions. Each description is used only once.

Terms

1. Ethics	9.	Organizational cost driver
2. Mission	10.	Financial accounting
3. Controlling	11.	Activity cost driver
4. Goal	12.	Structural cost driver
5. Cost drivers	13.	Managerial accounting
6. Quality	14.	Resources
7. Balance sheet	15.	Product differentiation
8. Income statement		

Description

a. Designing components so they are easily assembled

b. Factors that influence costs

c. Prepared as of a point in time

d. Accounting for external users

e. Increase year 2014 sales by 10 percent over year 2013 sales

f. Shows the results of operations for a period of time

g. Packing an order for shipment

h. Deciding to limit market focus to a region rather than the entire nation

i. The degree to which a new e-book reader meets a buyer's expectations

j. Used internally to make decisions

k. Consumed by activities

l. The propriety of taking some action

m. Reduces customer price sensitivity

n. Basic purpose toward which activities are directed

o. Comparing the budget with the actual results

LO1 **M1-14. Financial and Managerial Accounting**

Indicate whether each phrase is more descriptive of financial accounting or managerial accounting.

a. May be subjective

b. Often used to state corporate goals

c. Typically prepared quarterly or annually

  d.   May measure time or customer satisfaction
  e.   Future oriented
  f.   Has a greater emphasis on cost-benefit analysis
  g.   Keeps records of assets and liabilities
  h.   Highly aggregated statements
  i.   Must conform to external standards
  j.   Special-purpose reports
  k.   Decision-making tool
  l.   Income statement, balance sheet, and statement of cash flows

M1-15. Missions, Goals, and Strategies   LO2
Identify each of the following as a mission, goal, or strategy.

  a.   Budget time for study, sleep, and relaxation
  b.   Provide shelter for the homeless
  c.   Provide an above-average return to investors
  d.   Protect the public
  e.   Locate fire stations so that the average response time is less than five minutes
  f.   Overlap police patrols so that there are always police cars on major thoroughfares
  g.   Achieve a 12 percent market share
  h.   Lower prices and costs
  i.   Select the most scenic route to drive between Las Vegas and Denver
  j.   Graduate from college

M1-16. Line and Staff Organization   LO2
Presented are the names of several departments often found in a merchandising organization such   ✔   TARGET
as **Target**.   (TGT)

  a.   Maintenance   d.   Payroll
  b.   Home Furnishings   e.   Human Resources
  c.   Store Manager   f.   Advertising

Required
Identify each as a line or a staff department.

M1-17. Line and Staff Organization   LO2
Presented are the names of several departments often found in a manufacturing organization such   ✔   CATERPILLAR
as **Caterpillar**.   (CAT)

  a.   Manager, Plant 2   d.   Controller
  b.   Design Engineering   e.   Property Accounting
  c.   President   f.   Sales Manager, District 1

Required
Identify each as a line or a staff department.

M1-18. Classifying Cost Drivers   LO4
Classify each of the following as structural, organizational, or activity cost drivers.   ✔

  a.   **Illinois Tool Works** reorganizes production facilities from a layout in which all similar types   ILLINOIS TOOL WORKS
       of machines are grouped together to a layout in which a set of machines is designated for the   (ITW)
       production of a particular product and that set of machines is grouped together.
  b.   A cable television company decides to start offering telephone service.
  c.   **IBM** decides to stop making personal computers.   IBM (IBM)
  d.   **Canon** decides to start making high-volume photocopy equipment to compete head-to-head   CANON (CAJ)
       with Xerox.
  e.   The number of meals a cafeteria serves.
  f.   The number of miles a taxi is driven.
  g.   A company eliminates the position of supervisor and has each work group elect a team leader.
  h.   **Toyota** empowers employees to halt production if a quality problem is identified.   TOYOTA (TM)
  i.   The number of tons of grain a ship loads.
  j.   Northbrook Mall decides to build space for 80 additional stores.

LO4   **M1-19.   Classifying Cost Drivers**

Henderson Construction managers provide design and construction management services for various commercial construction projects. Senior managers are trying to apply cost driver concepts to their firm to better understand Henderson's costs.

Required

Classify each of the following actions or decisions as structural, organizational, or activity cost drivers.

a. The decision to be a regional leader in computer-assisted design services.
b. The decision to allow staff architects to follow a specific project through to completion.
c. The daily process of inspecting the progress on various construction projects.
d. The process of conducting extensive client interviews to assess the exact needs for Henderson services.
e. The decision to expand the market area by establishing an office in another state.
f. The decision to use only Henderson staff rather than relying on subcontractors.
g. The process of receiving approval from government authorities along with appropriate permits for each project.
h. The decision to organize the workforce into project teams.
i. The decision to build a new headquarters facility with areas for design and administration as well as storage and maintenance of construction equipment.
j. The process of grading building sites and preparing forms for foundations.

EXERCISES

LO1   **E1-20.   Financial and Managerial Accounting**

KRAFT FOODS GROUP
(KRFT)

Assume Amy Fuller has just been promoted to product manager at Kraft Foods. Although she is an accomplished sales representative and well versed in market research, her accounting background is limited to reviewing her paycheck, balancing her checkbook, filing income tax returns, and reviewing the company's annual income statement and balance sheet. She commented that while the financial statements are no doubt useful to investors, she just doesn't see how accounting can help her be a good product manager.

Required

Based on her remarks, it is apparent that Amy's view of accounting is limited to financial accounting. Explain some of the important differences between financial and managerial accounting and suggest some ways managerial accounting can help Amy be a better product manager.

LO2   **E1-21.   Developing an Organization Chart**

Develop an organization chart for a three-outlet bakery chain with a central baking operation and deliveries every few hours. Assume the business is incorporated and that the president has a single staff assistant. Also assume that the delivery truck driver reports to the bakery manager.

LO2   **E1-22.   Identifying Monetary and Nonmonetary Performance Measures**

Identify possible monetary and nonmonetary performance measures for each of the following situations. One nonmonetary measure should relate to quality, and one should relate to time.

DUKE UNIVERSITY
GRADY MEMORIAL
HOSPITAL
WAL-MART STORES
(WMT)
MARRIOTT (MAR)
FEDEX (FDX)

a. Duke University wishes to evaluate the success of last year's graduating class.
b. Grady Memorial Hospital wishes to evaluate the performance of its emergency room.
c. Wal-mart wishes to evaluate the performance of its online order–filling operations.
d. Marriott Hotels wishes to evaluate the performance of registration activities at one of its hotels.
e. FedEx wishes to evaluate the success of its operations in Knoxville.

LO2   **E1-23.   Identifying Monetary and Nonmonetary Performance Measures**

Identify possible monetary and nonmonetary performance measures for each of the following situations. One nonmonetary measure should relate to quality, and one should relate to time.

AT&T (T)
COMCAST (CMCSA)
DELL COMPUTER
(DELL)

a. AT&T's evaluation of the performance of its Internet service in Boston.
b. Comcast Cable's evaluation of the performance of new customer cable installations in Springfield.

c. Dell Computer's evaluation of the performance of its logistical arrangements for delivering computers to residential customers.

d. Amazon.com's evaluation of the performance of its Web site.

e. Rice University's evaluation of the success of its freshman admissions activities.

AMAZON.COM (AMZN)
RICE UNIVERSITY

E1-24. **Identifying Information Needs of Different Managers**

LO2

Matt Parker operates a number of auto dealerships for Ford and Mitsubishi. Identify possible monetary and nonmonetary performance measures for each of the following situations. One nonmonetary measure should relate to quality, and one should relate to time.

FORD
MITSUBISHI

a. An individual sales associate.

b. The sales manager of a single dealership.

c. The general manager of a particular dealership.

d. The corporate chief financial officer.

e. The president of the corporation.

E1-25. **Activities and Cost Drivers**

LO4

For each of the following activities, select the most appropriate cost driver. Each cost driver may be used only once.

Activity	Cost Driver
1. Pay vendors	a. Number of different raw material items
2. Receive material deliveries	b. Number of classes offered
3. Inspect raw materials	c. Number of machine hours
4. Plan for purchases of raw materials	d. Number of employees
5. Packaging	e. Number of maintenance hours
6. Supervision	f. Number of units of raw materials received
7. Employee training	g. Number of new customers
8. Operating machines	h. Number of deliveries
9. Machine maintenance	i. Number of checks issued
10. Opening accounts at a bank	j. Number of customer orders

CASES AND PROJECTS

C1-26. **Goals and Strategies**

LO2

a. What is your instructor's goal for students in this course? What strategies has he or she developed to achieve this goal?

b. What is your goal in this course? What strategies will help you achieve this goal?

c. What is your goal for this semester or term? What strategies will help you achieve this goal?

d. What is your next career goal? What strategies will help you achieve this goal?

C1-27. **Product Differentiation**

LO3

You are the owner of Lobster's Unlimited. You have no trouble catching lobsters, but you have difficulty in selling all that you catch. The problem is that all lobsters from all vendors look the same. You do catch high-quality lobsters, but you need to be able to tell your customers that your lobsters are better than those sold by other vendors.

Required

a. What are some possible ways of distinguishing your lobsters from those of other vendors?

b. Explain the possible results of this differentiation.

C1-28. **Ethics and Short-Term Borrowing**

LO5

Jill, an administrative assistant, is in charge of petty cash for a local law firm. Normally, about $300 is kept in the petty cash box. When Jill is short on cash and needs some for lunch or to pay her babysitter, she sometimes takes a few dollars from the box. Since she is in charge of the box, nobody knows that she takes the money, and she always replaces it within a few days.

Required

a. Is Jill's behavior ethical?

b. Assume that Jill has recently had major problems meeting her bills. She also is in charge of purchasing supplies for the office from petty cash. Last week when she needed $50 for the babysitter, she falsified a voucher for the amount of $50. Is this behavior ethical?

LO5 **C1-29.** **Ethics and Travel Reimbursement**

Bill takes many business trips throughout the year. All of his expenses are paid by his company. Last week he traveled to Rio De Janeiro, Brazil, and stayed there on business for five days. He is allowed a maximum of $50 per day for food and $150 per day for lodging. To his surprise, the food and accommodations in Brazil were much less than he expected. Being upset about traveling last week and having to sacrifice tickets he'd purchased to a Red Sox baseball game, he decided to inflate his expenses a bit. He increased his lodging expense from $80 per day to $100 per day and his food purchased from $30 per day to $40 per day. Therefore, for the five-day trip, he overstated his expenses by $150 total. After all, the allowance was higher than the amount he spent.

Required

Assume that the company would never find out that he had actually spent less. Are Bill's actions ethical? Are they acceptable?

LO5 **C1-30.** **Ethical Issues with Supplier-Buyer Partnerships**

John Snyder was excited to learn of his appointment as Circuit Electronics Corporation's sales representative to Household Appliance, Inc. For the past four years, Circuit Electronics has supplied all of the electric switches used in Household's washers and dryers. As Circuit Electronics' sales representative, John Snyder's job involves the following tasks.

1. Working with Household engineers to design electric switches that can be manufactured to meet Household's cost and quality requirements.

2. Assisting Household in resolving any problems related to electric switches.

3. Monitoring the inventory levels of electric switches at Household and placing orders for additional switches when appropriate.

This appointment will require John to move to Stutgart, Germany, for two years. Although John has mixed feelings about the move, he is familiar with the success of the program in improving Circuit Electronics' financial performance. He is also very much aware of the fact that the two previous sales representatives received promotions at the end of their appointments.

As John toured the Household factory in Stutgart with his predecessor, Janet Smith, his excitement turned to concern. It became apparent that Circuit Electronics had not been supplying Household with the best available switches at the lowest possible costs. Although the switches were adequate, they were more likely to wear out after five or six years of use than would switches currently on the market (and being used by Household's competitors). Furthermore, taking into account the current number of switches in transit by ship from North America to Europe, it also appeared that the inventory level of electric switches would soon be more than enough to satisfy Household's needs for the next four months.

Required

If you were John, what would you do?

LO5 **C1-31.** **Expected Values of Questionable Decisions**

EXXON MOBIL (XOM)

The members of the jury had to make a decision in a lawsuit brought by the State of Alabama against Exxon Mobil. The suit revolved around natural-gas wells that Exxon drilled in state-owned waters. After signing several leases obligating Exxon to share revenues with Alabama, company officials started questioning the terms of the agreement that prohibited deducting several types of processing costs before paying the state royalties.

ROYAL DUTCH/SHELL (RDS-B)

During the course of the trial, a memo by an in-house attorney of Exxon Mobil came to light. The memo noted that Royal Dutch/Shell, which had signed a similar lease, interpreted it "in the same manner as the state." The memo then presented arguments the company might use to claim the deduction, estimated the probability of the arguments being successful (less than 50 percent), and proceeded to consider whether Exxon should obey the law using a cost-benefit analysis. According to the memo, "If we adopt anything beyond a 'safe' approach, we should anticipate a quick audit and subsequent litigation." The memo also observed that "our exposure is 12 percent interest on underpayments calculated from the due date, and the cost of litigation." Deducting the questionable costs did, indeed, result in an audit and a lawsuit. Source: *Business Week*.[9]

Required

If you were a member of the jury, what would you do? Why?

C1-32. Management Decisions Affecting Cost Drivers   LO4

An avid bicycle rider, you have decided to use an inheritance to start a new business to sell and repair bicycles. Two college friends have already accepted offers to work for you.

Required

a. What is the mission of your new business?

b. Suggest a strategic positioning goal you might strive for to compete with area hardware and discount stores that sell bicycles.

c. Identify two items that might be long-range goals.

d. Identify two items that might be goals for the coming year.

e. Mention two decisions that will be structural cost drivers.

f. Mention two decisions that will be organizational cost drivers.

g. Identify two activity cost drivers.

C1-33. Success Factors and Performance Measurement   LO2

Three years ago, Vincent Chow completed his college degree. The economy was in a depressed state at the time, and Vincent managed to get an offer of only $25,000 per year as a bookkeeper. In addition to its relatively low pay, this job had limited advancement potential. Since Vincent was an enterprising and ambitious young man, he instead started a business of his own. He was convinced that because of changing lifestyles, a drive-through coffee establishment would be profitable. He was able to obtain backing from his parents to open such an establishment close to the industrial park area in town. Vincent named his business The Cappuccino Express and decided to sell only two types of coffee: cappuccino and decaffeinated.

As Vincent had expected, The Cappuccino Express was very well received. Within three years, Vincent had added another outlet north of town. He left the day-to-day management of each site to a manager and turned his attention toward overseeing the entire enterprise. He also hired an assistant to do the record keeping and other selected chores.[10]

Required

a. Develop an organization chart for The Cappuccino Express.

b. What factors can be expected to have a major impact on the success of The Cappuccino Express?

c. What major tasks must Vincent undertake in managing The Cappuccino Express?

d. What are the major costs of operating The Cappuccino Express?

e. Vincent would like to monitor the performance of each site manager. What measure(s) of performance should he use?

f. If you suggested more than one measure, which of these should Vincent select if he could use only one?

g. Suppose that last year, the original site had yielded total revenues of $146,000, total costs of $122,000, and hence, a profit of $24,000. Vincent had judged this profit performance to be satisfactory. For the coming year, Vincent expects that due to factors such as increased name recognition and demographic changes, the total revenues will increase by 20 percent to $175,200. What amount of profit should he expect from the site? Discuss the issues involved in developing an estimate of profit.

---

[9] Mike France, "When Big Oil Gets Too Slick," *Business Week*, April 9, 2001, p. 70.

[10] Based on Chee W. Chow, "Instructional Case: Vincent's Cappuccino Express—A Teaching Case to Help Students Master Basic Cost Terms and Concepts Through Interactive Learning," *Issues in Accounting Education*, Spring 1995, pp. 173–190.

SOLUTIONS TO REVIEW PROBLEMS

<u>**Mid-Chapter Review**</u>

Solution
2, 5, 7, 8, 9, and 10

<u>**Chapter-End Review**</u>

Solution
- *a.*   Activity cost driver
- *b.*   Structural cost driver
- *c.*   Structural cost driver
- *d.*   Activity cost driver
- *e.*   Activity cost driver
- *f.*   Structural cost driver
- *g.*   Organizational cost driver
- *h.*   Organizational cost driver
- *i.*   Organizational cost driver
- *j.*   Organizational cost driver

© Getty Images

2

Cost Behavior, Activity Analysis, and Cost Estimation

The creator of Twitter, Jack Dorsey, founded Square, Inc. in 2009 to address a void in payment processing services for small, portable businesses. Square makes a postage-stamp-sized plastic card reader that attaches to smartphones, which gives businesses such as food trucks, kiosk boutiques, taxi drivers, and the like the ability to accept credit card payments. The San Francisco–based company has been so successful that it now processes $15 billion in transactions each year. Square provides the card readers to businesses free of charge, but collects either a 2.75 percent fee per transaction or a flat fee of $275 per month to compensate for its services. The company has extended the card reader technology to an iPad version for brick-and-mortar merchants called SquareStand. The Stand can integrate with the businesses' receipt printers, kitchen printers, cash drawers, and barcode scanners.

SQUARE, INC.
www.squareup.com

Another new product, Square Wallet, allows customers to pay for merchandise with a smartphone (or a barcode, or simply the customer's name) by using stored credit, debit, or gift card information. Square has enjoyed tremendous success, but it is not satisfied with its rapid growth. When PayPal expressed an interest in developing its own card reader for physical stores, Square announced a new effort to compete on PayPal's home turf by starting development of a Square-hosted website called Square Market, which would allow merchants to list their products online. Of course, Square would process the online payments, much like PayPal's core business.

With Square's hand in so many business lines coupled with the company's phenomenal growth, it's difficult for outsiders and insiders, including Square's management team, to predict future costs. This is an important task because the company's growth plans require either internally generated profit or external financing to continue on its trajectory. The cost of making the card readers is directly related to the number of new businesses adopting the technology. In other words, the hardware cost is driven by the number of new merchants in any given period. But the number of new adoptions is difficult to estimate in advance. The costs associated with processing payments are even more difficult to predict. Consider that the company remits most of the payments received from customers' credit card companies to the merchant minus Square's fee. However, what is Square's cost of processing each payment? Does the cost of processing a payment differ based on volume or seasonality? In order to predict processing costs, we must be able to predict merchant sales volume or number of transactions. If the processing costs vary proportionately with this activity, the processing costs are referred to as variable costs.

And what about the costs that do not vary with the number or type of transactions processed? The company recently moved into its new corporate headquarters in San Francisco, but it also has offices

continued on following page

continued from previous page

in New York, Atlanta, and Tokyo. Its workforce is expected to approach 1,000 employees, many of whom are salaried engineers and software developers. These costs are likely to be unrelated to the number of card readers issued, SquareStands sold, or payments processed. We call costs that do not vary with activity fixed costs. As we'll see throughout the chapter, many costs are neither variable nor fixed, but a mixture of the two.

Mixed costs present a challenge to a company in estimating future costs. Square needs the ability to accurately predict its future costs if it is to maintain the financial flexibility necessary to go up against better-financed, well-established competitors such as PayPal. This requires a thorough understanding of cost behavior, activity analysis, and cost estimation, which are the topics of this chapter.

Sources: Michal Lev-Ram, "Jack Dorsey: The Pride of St. Louis," *Fortune*, September 19, 2013; Greg Bensinger, "Square Takes on PayPal Online," *Wall Street Journal*, June 26, 2013, p. B5; Tomio Geron, "Square Launches Stand, A New Point of Sale Device," *Forbes*, May 14, 2013; Danielle Kucera, "Square Introduces Hardware to Convert iPads into Cash Registers," *Bloomberg Businessweek*, May 14, 2013; Danielle Kucera, "Square Debuts Mobile Gift Cards in Challenge to PayPal," *Bloomberg Businessweek*, December 10, 2012; and Amir Efrati and Annie Gasparro, "Starbucks Invests in Square," *Wall Street Journal*, August 8, 2012, p. B8.

CHAPTER ORGANIZATION

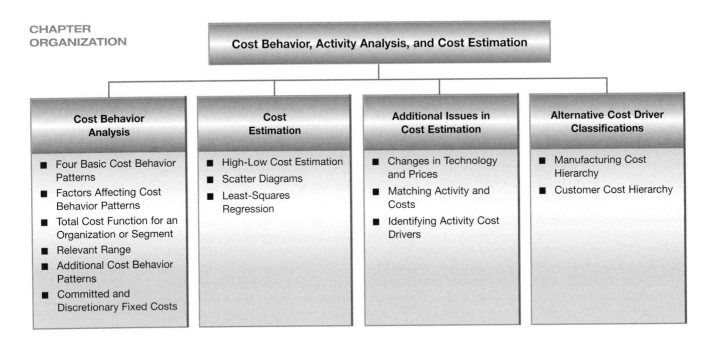

COST BEHAVIOR ANALYSIS

This chapter introduces **cost behavior**, which refers to the relationship between a given cost item and the quantity of its related cost driver. Cost behavior, therefore, explains how the total amount for various costs respond to changes in activity volume. Understanding cost behavior is essential for estimating future costs. In this chapter we examine several typical cost behavior patterns and methods for developing cost equations that are useful for predicting future costs.

Four Basic Cost Behavior Patterns

LO1 Identify basic patterns of how costs respond to changes in activity cost drivers.

Although there are an unlimited number of ways that costs can respond to changes in cost drivers, as a starting point it is useful to classify cost behavior into four categories: variable, fixed, mixed, and step. Graphs of each are presented in Exhibit 2.1. Observe that total cost (the dependent variable) is measured on the vertical axis, and total activity for the time period (the independent variable) is measured on the horizontal axis. Consider new pizza chain, Blaze Pizza, which is specializing in fast-casual artisan pizzas. Based on a customizable, healthy approach popularized at Chipotle, Blaze Pizza hopes to fuel their planned national expansion. But to manage its growth, the company must understand the behavior underlying its cost structure.

1. **Variable costs** change in total in direct proportion to changes in activity. Their total amount increases as activity increases, equaling zero dollars when activity is zero and increasing at a

| EXHIBIT 2.1 | Cost Behavior Patterns |

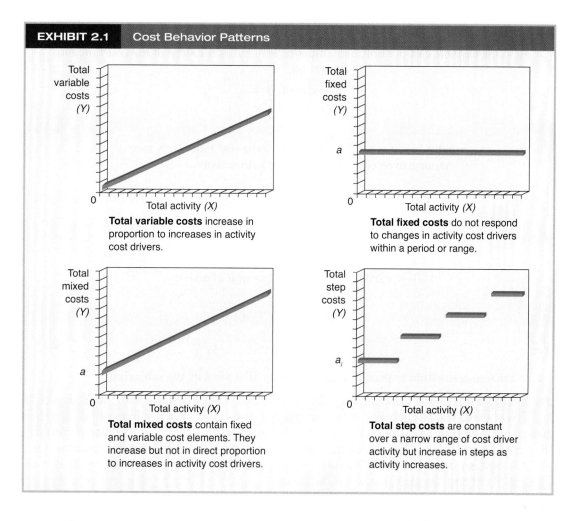

Total variable costs increase in proportion to increases in activity cost drivers.

Total fixed costs do not respond to changes in activity cost drivers within a period or range.

Total mixed costs contain fixed and variable cost elements. They increase but not in direct proportion to increases in activity cost drivers.

Total step costs are constant over a narrow range of cost driver activity but increase in steps as activity increases.

constant amount per unit of activity. The higher the variable cost per unit of activity, the steeper the slope of the line representing total cost. With the number of pizzas served as the activity cost driver for Blaze Pizza restaurants, the cost of cheese is an example of a variable cost.

2. **Fixed costs** do not change in response to a change in activity volume. Hence, a line representing total fixed costs is flat with a slope (incline) of zero. With the number of Blaze Pizza pizzas sold as the cost driver, annual depreciation, property taxes, and property insurance are examples of fixed costs. While fixed costs may respond to structural and organizational cost drivers over time, they do not respond to short-run changes in activity cost drivers.

3. **Mixed costs** (sometimes called **semivariable costs**) contain a fixed and a variable cost element. Total mixed costs are positive (like fixed costs) when activity is zero, and they increase in a linear fashion (like total variable costs) as activity increases. With the number of pizzas sold as the cost driver, the cost of electric power is an example of a mixed cost. Some electricity is required to provide basic lighting, while an increasing amount of electricity is required to prepare food as the number of pizzas served increases.

4. **Step costs** are constant within a narrow range of activity but shift to a higher level when activity exceeds the range. Total step costs increase in a steplike fashion as activity increases. With the number of pizzas served as the cost driver, employee wages is an example of a step cost. Up to a certain number of pizzas, only a small staff needs to be on duty. Beyond that number, additional employees are needed for quality service and so forth.

The relationship between total cost (Y axis) and total activity (X axis) for the four cost behavior patterns is mathematically expressed as follows:

$$\text{Variable cost: } Y = bX$$

where

b = the variable cost per unit, sometimes referred to as the slope of the cost function.

$$\text{Fixed cost: } Y = a$$

where

a = total fixed costs. The slope of the fixed cost function is zero because fixed costs do not change with activity.

$$\text{Mixed cost: } Y = a + bX$$

where

a = total fixed cost element
b = variable cost element per unit of activity.

$$\text{Step cost: } Y = a_i$$

where

a_i = the step cost within a specific range of activity, identified by the subscript i.

The total cost function of most organizations has shifted in recent years toward more fixed costs and fewer variable costs, making it increasingly important for organizations to manage their fixed costs. Some organizations have done this by outsourcing activities rather than performing the activities internally. This avoids the many fixed costs of infrastructure in exchange for a variable cost per unit of activity. The Business Insight box below considers how **FedEx** is managing its fixed costs by changing its product mix.

BUSINESS INSIGHT

Understanding Cost Behavior Is the First Step in Cutting Costs   **FedEx** wants to herd its customers away from express shipping via air and toward other modes of shipping, such as passenger plane cargo, ocean, and third-party networks, where its profit margin is 17 percent as opposed to 3.6 percent. It's accomplishing this by increasing the price of its airborne packages. However, to confidently predict how price increases are going to affect profits, the company must also understand which of its costs are variable and which are fixed.

By increasing price, laws of economic supply and demand suggest that there will be fewer units shipped by air at the higher price. Total variable costs will decrease accordingly. FedEx is also reducing its variable cost per package by replacing old planes with newer models to save on jet fuel and aircraft maintenance. Reducing fixed costs will improve profit margins regardless of price or volume changes. FedEx is decreasing fixed costs by eliminating 3,600 workers. Managers must anticipate the profit effects of their actions before taking action, and understanding cost behaviors is a critical skill in gaining that knowledge.

Souce: Kyle Stock, "FedEx Delivers Higher Prices into Economic Headwinds," *Bloomberg Businessweek*, September 18, 2013.

Factors Affecting Cost Behavior Patterns

The four cost behavior patterns presented are based on the fundamental assumption that a unit of final output is the primary cost driver. The implications of this assumption are examined later in this chapter.

Another important assumption is that the time period is too short to incorporate changes in strategic cost drivers such as the scale of operations. Although this assumption is useful for short-range planning, for the purpose of developing plans for extended time periods, it is more appropriate to consider possible variations in one or more strategic cost drivers. When this is done, many costs otherwise classified as fixed are better classified as variable.

Even the cost of depreciable assets can be viewed as variable if the time period is long enough. Assuming that the number of pizzas served is the cost driver, for a single month the depreciation on all Blaze Pizza restaurants in the world is a fixed cost. Over several years, if sales are strong, a strategic decision will be made to open additional restaurants; if sales are weak, strategic decisions will likely be made to close some restaurants. Hence, over a multiple-year period, the number of restaurants varies with sales volume, making depreciation appear as a variable cost with sales revenue as the cost driver.

Total Cost Function for an Organization or Segment

To obtain a general understanding of an organization, to compare the cost structures of different organizations, or to perform preliminary planning activities, managers are often interested in how total costs respond to a single measure of overall activity such as units sold or sales revenue. This overview can be useful, but presenting all costs as a function of a single cost driver is seldom accurate enough to support decisions concerning products, services, or activities. Doing so implies that all of an organization's costs can be manipulated by changing a single cost driver. This is seldom true.

In developing a total cost function, the independent variable usually represents some measure of the goods or services provided customers, such as total student credit hours in a university, total sales revenue in a store, total guest-days in a hotel, or total units manufactured in a factory. The resulting cost function is illustrated in Exhibit 2.2.

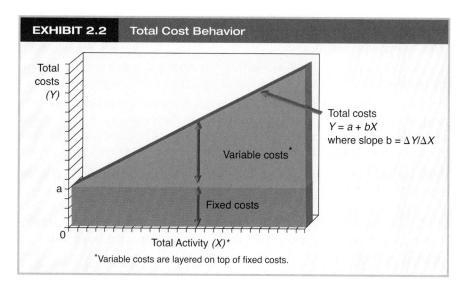

EXHIBIT 2.2   **Total Cost Behavior**

Total costs
$Y = a + bX$
where slope b = $\Delta Y/\Delta X$

Variable costs*

Fixed costs

Total costs (Y)

a

0

Total Activity (X)*

*Variable costs are layered on top of fixed costs.

The equation for total costs is:

$$Y = a + bX$$

where

        Y = total costs
        a = vertical axis intercept (an approximation of fixed costs)
        b = slope (an approximation of variable costs per unit of X)
        X = value of independent variable

In situations where the variable, fixed, and mixed costs, and the related cost functions, can be determined, a total cost equation can be useful in predicting future costs for various activity levels. However, generally, a total cost equation is useful for predicting costs in only a limited range of activity. The **relevant range** of a total cost equation is that portion of the range associated with the fixed cost of the current or expected capacity. For example, assume that a Pinkberry frozen yogurt shop's only fixed cost is the depreciation on its frozen yogurt making machines, and that it is able to produce a maximum of 50 gallons of frozen yogurt per day with a single machine. If it has four machines in operation, and if it can readily adjust its fixed capacity cost by increasing or decreasing the number of machines, the relevant range of activity for the shop's current total cost equation is 151 to 200 gallons. In the future, if the shop expects to operate at more than 200 gallons per day, the current total cost equation would not predict total cost accurately, because fixed costs would have to be increased for additional machines. Conversely, if it expects to operate at 150 gallons or less, it may reduce the number of machines in the shop, thereby reducing total fixed costs.

Relevant Range

The use of straight lines in accounting models of cost behavior assumes a linear relationship between cost and activity with each additional unit of activity accompanied by a uniform increment in total cost. This uniform increment is known as the *variable cost of one unit*.

Economic models show a nonlinear relationship between cost and activity with each incremental unit of activity being accompanied by a varying increment in total cost. Economists identify the varying increment in total cost as the **marginal cost** *of one unit*.

It is useful to relate marginal costs to the following three levels of activity:

1. *Below the activity range for which the facility was designed,* the existence of excess capacity results in relatively high marginal costs. Having extra time, employees complete assignments at a leisurely pace, increasing the time and the cost to produce each unit above what it would be if employees were more pressed to complete work. Frequent starting and stopping of equipment may also add to costs.

2. *Within the activity range for which the facility was designed,* activities take place under optimal circumstances and marginal costs are relatively low.

3. *Above the activity range for which the facility was designed,* the existence of capacity constraints again results in relatively high marginal costs. Near capacity, employees may be paid overtime wages, less-experienced employees may be used, regular equipment may operate less efficiently, and old equipment with high energy requirements may be placed in service.

Based on marginal cost concepts, the economists' short-run total cost function is illustrated in the first graph in Exhibit 2.3. The vertical axis intercept represents capacity costs. Corresponding to the high marginal costs at low levels of activity, the initial slope is quite steep. In the normal activity range, where marginal costs are relatively low, the slope becomes less steep. Then, corresponding to high marginal costs above the normal activity range, the slope of the economists' total cost function increases again.

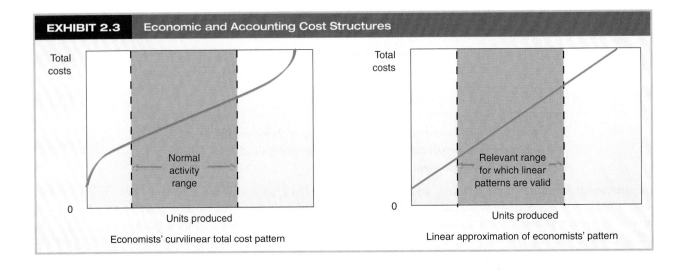

| **EXHIBIT 2.3** | **Economic and Accounting Cost Structures** |

Economists' curvilinear total cost pattern

Linear approximation of economists' pattern

BUSINESS INSIGHT

When Is a Variable Cost Fixed?   Direct labor takes on a different characteristic when we're talking about the Big 3 automakers: **GM, Ford,** and **Chrysler.** These companies have contracts with their labor unions, most of which were negotiated in the 1980s, that address not only wages but retiree health care and pensions as well. The Center for Automotive Research claims that once these contractual obligations are factored in, GM spends $78 per hour for each worker, whereas Japanese automaker **Toyota** spends only $50 per hour in its U.S. plants.

Add to that a concession made to the unions in the 1980s called the Jobs Bank, which states that the company must pay 95 percent of workers' salaries if they are laid off until they find a new job. The Jobs Bank essentially converted direct labor from a variable to a fixed cost for U.S. automakers. In the light of the automotive industry's financial woes, the United Auto Workers (UAW) union and the Detroit Three renegotiated the contracts in 2007. Now there are two-tiered pay scales with new workers earning half of what their senior coworkers make, and they were able to settle their health-care obligations through a one-time $54 billion payment into a trust fund to be managed by the UAW. Last but not least, direct labor is a variable cost again. The Jobs Bank is in the process of being phased out, and Ford and Chrysler have reported their best profits since before the recession.

Source: Drake Bennett, "GM, Ford, and Chrysler: The Detroit Three Are Back, Right?" *Bloomberg Businessweek*, April 4, 2013.

If the economists' total cost curve is valid, how can we reasonably approximate it with a straight line? The answer to this question is in the notion of a *relevant range*. A linear pattern may be a poor approximation of the economists' curvilinear pattern over the entire range of possible activity, but a linear pattern as illustrated in the right-hand graph in Exhibit 2.3 is often sufficiently accurate within the range of probable operations. The range of activity within which a linear cost function is valid is called the **relevant range**. Linear estimates of cost behavior are valid only within the relevant range. Extreme care must be exercised when making comments about cost behavior outside the relevant range.

Additional Cost Behavior Patterns

Although we have considered the most frequently used cost behavior patterns, remember that there are numerous ways that costs can respond to changes in activity. Avoid the temptation to automatically assume that the cost in question conforms to one of the patterns discussed in this chapter. As illustrated by the preceding Business Insight box, it is important to think through each situation and then select a behavior pattern that seems logical and fits the known facts.

Particular care needs to be taken with the vertical axis. So far, all graphs have placed *total* costs on the vertical axis. Miscommunication is likely if one party is thinking in terms of *total* costs while the other is thinking in terms of *variable* or *average* costs. Consider the following cost function:

$$\text{Total costs} = \$3,000 + \$5X$$

where

$$X = \text{customers served}$$

The total, variable, and average costs at various levels of activity are computed here and graphed in Exhibit 2.4 on the following page. As the number of customers served increases, total costs increase, the variable costs of each unit remain constant, and the average cost decreases because fixed costs are spread over a larger number of units.

Customers Served	Total Costs	Average Cost*	Variable Costs per Customer
100	$3,500	$35.00	$5.00
200	4,000	20.00	5.00
300	4,500	15.00	5.00
400	5,000	12.50	5.00
500	5,500	11.00	5.00

* Total costs/customers served

To predict total costs for the coming period, management will use the first graph in Exhibit 2.4. To determine the minimum price required to avoid a loss on each additional customer served, management is interested in the variable costs per customer, yet if a manager inquired as to the cost of serving a customer, a financial accountant would probably provide average cost information, as illustrated in the third graph in Exhibit 2.4. The specific average cost would likely be a function of the number of customers served during the most recent accounting period.

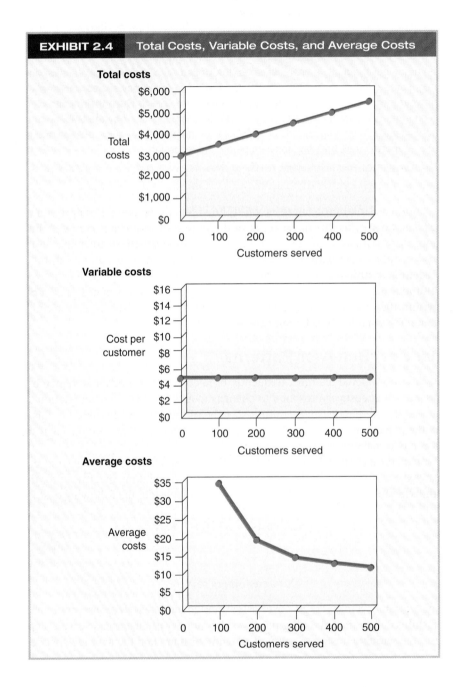

EXHIBIT 2.4   Total Costs, Variable Costs, and Average Costs

Errors can occur if last period's average costs, perhaps based on a volume of 500 customers, were used to predict total costs for a future period when the anticipated volume was some other amount, say 300 units. Using average costs, based on the 500 customers, the predicted total costs of 300 units are $3,300 ($11 × 300). In fact, using the proper total cost function, a more accurate prediction of total costs is $4,500 [$3,000 + ($5 × 300)]. The prediction error could cause a number of problems. If management budgeted $3,300 to pay bills and the bills actually totaled $4,500, the company might have to curtail activities or borrow under unfavorable terms to avoid running out of cash.

RESEARCH INSIGHT

Understanding Cost Behaviors Can Grow the Business   In a recent survey of managers of Fortune 1000 companies, Deloitte found that most managers are focused on cost containment. However, they see reducing costs as a way to gain a competitive advantage so that they can take advantage of investment opportunities as they arise. Managers also say the biggest impediment to their cost reduction is that employees don't understand the need for the reductions and/or how those reductions can help grow the business. They cite poor tracking of costs as a primary reason behind why cost objectives are not met.

Deloitte stated that managers need to ask themselves hard questions to accomplish their cost reduction targets, such as the following: Is your cost of goods sold competitive with the industry? Are your procurement and sourcing strategies aimed at minimizing the unit cost of your goods or services? Are you efficiently utilizing all of your resources and capacity? Do you have hedging plans and/or alternative strategies in place for highly volatile commodity-based inputs? Do your logistics and supply functions maximize efficiency? Are your general and administrative costs comparable to those of others in the industry? Have you exhausted the capability for resource sharing throughout the organization? Managers who can answer these questions will often find additional sources of unlocked value within the firm's operations. But first, it is important that managers understand cost behavior of variable versus fixed costs so they can accurately predict the impact of proposed changes.

Source: Deloitte, "Save to Grow: Deloitte's Third Biennial Cost Survey: Cost Improvement Practices and Trends in the Fortune 1000," March 2013.

Committed and Discretionary Fixed Costs

Fixed costs are often classified as *committed* or *discretionary,* depending on their immediate impact on the organization if management attempts to change them. **Committed fixed costs**, sometimes referred to as **capacity costs**, are the fixed costs required to maintain the current service or production capacity or to fill previous legal commitments. Examples of committed fixed costs include depreciation, property taxes, rent, and interest on bonds.

Committed fixed costs are often the result of structural decisions about the size and nature of an organization. For example, years ago the management of Santa Fe Railroad made decisions concerning what communities the railroad would serve. Track was laid on the basis of those decisions, and the Santa Fe Railroad now pays property taxes each year on the railroad's miles of track. These property taxes could be reduced by disposing of track. However, reducing track would also diminish the Santa Fe's capacity to serve.

Discretionary fixed costs, sometimes called **managed fixed costs**, are set at a fixed amount each period at the discretion of management. It is possible to reduce discretionary fixed costs without reducing production or service capacity in the short term. Typical discretionary fixed costs include advertising, maintenance, charitable contributions, employee training, and research and development.

Maintenance expenditures for discretionary fixed costs are frequently regarded as investments in the future. Research and development, for example, is undertaken to develop new or improved products that can be profitably produced and sold in future periods. During periods of financial well-being, organizations may make large expenditures on discretionary cost items. Conversely, during periods of financial stress, organizations likely reduce discretionary expenditures before reducing capacity costs. Unfortunately, fluctuations in the funding of discretionary fixed costs may reduce the effectiveness of long-range programs. A high-quality research staff may be difficult to reassemble if key personnel are laid off. Even the contemplation of layoffs may reduce the staff's effectiveness. In all periods, discretionary costs are subject to debate and are likely to be changed in the budgeting process.

MID-CHAPTER REVIEW

Identify each of the following cost behavior patterns as variable, committed fixed, discretionary fixed, mixed, or step.

a. Total cost of bakery products used at a **McDonald's** restaurant when the number of meals served is the activity cost driver.

b. Total cost of operating the **Mayo Clinic** when the number of patients served is the cost driver.

c. Total property taxes for a **Midas Muffler Shop** when the number of vehicles serviced is the cost driver.

d. Total cost of motherboards used by **Apple Computer** when the number of computers manufactured and shipped is the cost driver.

e. Total cost of secretarial services at **Indiana University** with each secretary handling the needs of ten faculty members and where part-time secretarial help is not available. The number of faculty is the cost driver.

f. Total advertising costs for **International Business Machines** (IBM).

g. Automobile rental costs at **Alamo** in Orlando, Florida, when there is no mileage charge. The cost driver is the number of miles driven.

h. Automobile rental cost at **Hertz** in Dallas, Texas, which has a base charge plus a mileage charge. The cost driver is the number of miles driven.

i. Salaries paid to personnel while conducting on-campus employment interviews for **Champion International**. Number of on-campus interviews is the cost driver.

j. The cost of contributions to educational institutions by **Microsoft Corporation**.

The solution is on pages 63–64.

COST ESTIMATION

LO2 Determine a linear cost estimating equation.

Cost estimation, the determination of the relationship between activity and cost, is an important part of cost management. In this section, we develop equations for the relationship between total costs and total activity.

To properly estimate the relationship between activity and cost, we must be familiar with basic cost behavior patterns and cost estimating techniques. Costs known to have a variable or a fixed pattern are readily estimated by interviews or by analyzing available records. Sales commission per sales dollar, a variable cost, might be determined to be 15 percent of sales. In a similar manner, annual property taxes might be determined by consulting tax documents.

Mixed (semivariable) costs, which contain fixed and variable cost elements, are more difficult to estimate. According to a basic rule of algebra, two equations are needed to determine two unknowns. Following this rule, at least two observations are needed to determine the variable and fixed elements of a mixed cost.

High-Low Cost Estimation

The most straightforward approach to determining the variable and fixed elements of mixed costs is to use the **high-low method of cost estimation**. This method utilizes data from two time periods, a *representative* high-activity period and a *representative* low-activity period, to estimate fixed and variable costs. Assuming identical fixed costs in both periods, any difference in total costs between these two periods is due entirely to variable costs. The variable costs per unit are found by dividing the difference in total costs by the difference in total activity:

$$\text{Variable costs per unit} = \frac{\text{Difference in total costs}}{\text{Difference in activity}}$$

Once variable costs are determined, fixed costs, which are identical in both periods, are computed by subtracting the total variable costs of either the high or the low activity period from the corresponding total costs.

Fixed costs = Total costs − Variable costs

Assume a retailer such as Pottery Barn wants to develop a monthly cost function for its packaging department and that the number of shipments is believed to be the primary cost driver. The following observations are available for the first four months of 2014.

		Number of Shipments	Packaging Costs
(Low-activity period)	January	6,000	$17,000
	February.	9,000	26,000
(High-activity period)	March.	12,000	32,000
	April	10,000	20,000

Equations for total costs for the packaging department in January and March (the periods of lowest and highest activity) follow:

January: $17,000 = a + b (6,000 shipments)

March: $32,000 = a + b (12,000 shipments)

where

a = fixed costs per month

b = variable costs per shipment

Solving for the estimated variable costs:

$$b = \frac{\textbf{Difference in total costs}}{\textbf{Difference in activity}}$$

$$b = \frac{\$32,000 - \$17,000}{12,000 - 6,000}$$

$$= \$2.50$$

Next, the estimated monthly fixed costs are determined by subtracting variable costs from total costs of *either* the January or March equation:

a = Total costs − Variable costs

January: a = $17,000 − ($2.50 per shipment × 6,000 shipments)

= $2,000

or

March: a = $32,000 − ($2.50 per shipment × 12,000 shipments)

= $2,000

The cost estimating equation for total packaging department costs is

Y = $2,000 + $2.50X

where

X = number of shipments

Y = total costs for the packing department

The concepts underlying the high-low method of cost estimation are illustrated in Exhibit 2.5.

Cost prediction, the forecasting of future costs, is a common purpose of cost estimation. Previously developed estimates of cost behavior are often the starting point in predicting future costs. Continuing the Pottery Barn example, if 5,000 shipments are budgeted for June 2014, the predicted June 2014 packaging department costs are $14,500 [$2,000 + ($2.50 per shipment × 5,000 shipments)].

EXHIBIT 2.5 **High-Low Cost Estimation**

$$\frac{\text{Variable costs}}{\text{per unit}} = \frac{\text{Difference in total costs}}{\text{Difference in activity}}$$

$$\text{Fixed costs} = \begin{array}{c}\text{Total costs at either}\\\text{the high or low cost}\\\text{activity level}\end{array} - \begin{array}{c}\text{Variable costs}\\\text{computed}\\\text{for that level}\end{array}$$

Scatter Diagrams

A **scatter diagram** is a graph of past activity and cost data, with individual observations represented by dots. Plotting historical cost data on a scatter diagram is a useful approach to cost estimation, especially when used in conjunction with other cost-estimating techniques. As illustrated in Exhibit 2.6, a scatter diagram helps in selecting high and low activity levels representative of normal operating conditions. The periods of highest or lowest activity may not be representative because of the cost of overtime, the use of less efficient equipment, strikes, and so forth. If the goal is to develop an equation to predict costs under normal operating conditions, then the equation should be based on observations of normal operating conditions. A scatter diagram is also useful in determining whether costs can be reasonably approximated by a straight line.

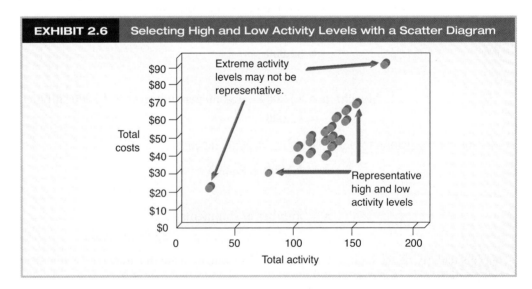

EXHIBIT 2.6 **Selecting High and Low Activity Levels with a Scatter Diagram**

Scatter diagrams are sometimes used alone as a basis of cost estimation. This requires the use of professional judgment to draw a representative straight line through the plot of historical data. Typically, the analyst tries to ensure that an equal number of observations are on either side of the line while minimizing the total vertical differences between the line and actual cost observations at each value of the independent variable. Once a line is drawn, cost estimates at any representative volume are made by studying the line. Alternatively, an equation for the line may be developed by applying the high-low method to any two points on the line.

Least-Squares Regression

Least-squares regression analysis uses a mathematical technique to fit a cost-estimating equation to the observed data. The technique mathematically accomplishes what the analyst does visually with a scatter diagram. The least-squares technique creates an equation that minimizes the sum of the vertical squared differences between the estimated and the actual costs at each observation. Each of these differences is an estimating error. Using the packaging department example, the least-squares criterion is illustrated in Exhibit 2.7. Estimated values of total monthly packaging costs are represented by the straight line, and the actual values of total monthly packaging costs are represented by the dots. For each dot, such as the one at a volume of 10,000 shipments, the line is fit to minimize the vertical squared differences.

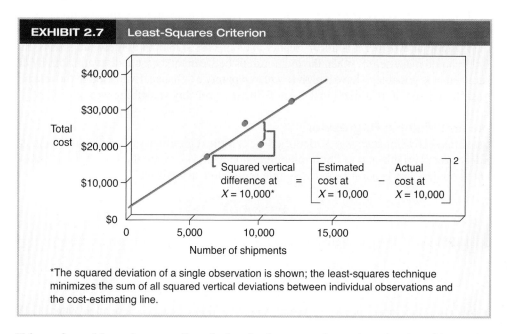

| EXHIBIT 2.7 | Least-Squares Criterion |

$$\text{Squared vertical difference at } X = 10{,}000^* = \left[\text{Estimated cost at } X = 10{,}000 - \text{Actual cost at } X = 10{,}000 \right]^2$$

*The squared deviation of a single observation is shown; the least-squares technique minimizes the sum of all squared vertical deviations between individual observations and the cost-estimating line.

Values of *a* and *b* can be manually calculated using a set of equations developed by mathematicians or by using spreadsheet software packages such as Microsoft Excel®. Many calculators also have built-in functions to compute these coefficients. The least-squares equation for monthly packaging costs is:

$$Y = \$3{,}400 + \$2.20X$$

Using the least-squares equation, the predicted June 2011 packaging department costs with 5,000 budgeted shipments are $14,400 [$3,400 + ($2.20 per shipment × 5,000 shipments)]. Recall that the high-low method predicted June 2014 costs of $14,500. Although this difference is small, we should consider which prediction is more reliable.

Advantage of Least-Squares Regression

Mathematicians regard least-squares regression analysis as superior to both the high-low and the scatter diagram methods. It uses all available data, rather than just two observations, and does not rely on subjective judgment in drawing a line. Statistical measures are also available to determine how well a least-squares equation fits the historical data. These measures are often contained in the output of spreadsheet software packages.

In addition to the vertical axis intercept and the slope, least-squares regression calculates the coefficient of determination. The **coefficient of determination** is a measure of the percent of variation in the dependent variable (such as total packaging department costs) that is explained by variations in the independent variable (such as total shipments). Statisticians often refer to the coefficient of determination as R-squared and represent it as R^2.

The coefficient of determination can have values between zero and one, with values close to zero suggesting that the equation is not very useful and values close to one indicating that the equation explains most of the variation in the dependent variable. When choosing between two cost-estimating equations, the one with the higher coefficient of determination is generally preferred. The coefficient of determination for the packaging department cost estimation equation, determined using least-squares regression analysis, is 0.68. This means that 68 percent of the variation in packaging department costs is explained by the number of shipments.

Managers, Not Models, Are Responsible

Although computers make least-squares regression easy to use, the generated output should not automatically be accepted as correct. Statistics and other mathematical techniques are tools to help managers make decisions. Managers, not mathematical models, are responsible for decisions. Judgment should always be exercised when considering the validity of the least-squares approach, the solution, and the data. If the objective is to predict future costs under normal operating conditions, observations reflecting abnormal operating conditions should be deleted. Also examine the cost behavior pattern to determine whether it is linear. Scatter diagrams assist in both of these judgments. Finally, the results should make sense. When the relationships between total cost and several activity drivers are examined, it is possible to have a high R-squared purely by chance. Even though the relationship has a high R-squared, if it "doesn't make sense" there is probably something wrong.

Simple and Multiple Regression

Least-squares regression analysis is identified as "simple regression analysis" when there is only one independent variable and as "multiple regression analysis" when there are two or more independent variables. The general form for simple regression analysis is:

$$Y = a + bX$$

The general form for multiple regression analysis is:

$$Y = a + \Sigma b_i X_i$$

In this case, the subscript i is a general representation of each independent variable. When there are several independent variables, i is set equal to 1 for the first, 2 for the second, and so forth. The total variable costs of each independent variable is computed as $b_i X_i$, with b_i representing the variable cost per unit of independent variable X_i. The Greek symbol sigma, Σ, indicates that the costs of all independent variables are summed in determining total variable costs.

As an illustration, assume that Staples' costs are expressed as a function of the unit sales of its two products: executive desks and task desks. Assume fixed costs are $18,000 per month and the variable costs are $250 per executive desk and $120 per task desk. The mathematical representation of monthly costs with two variables is:

$$Y = a + b_1 X_1 + b_2 X_2$$

where

$$a = \$18,000$$

$$b_1 = \$250$$

$$b_2 = \$120$$

$$X_1 = \text{unit sales of executive desks}$$

$$X_2 = \text{unit sales of task desks}$$

During a month if 105 executive desks and 200 task desks are sold, Staples' estimated total costs are:

$$Y = \$18,000 + \$250(105) + \$120(200)$$
$$= \$68,250$$

In addition to estimating costs, multiple regression analysis can be used to determine the effect of individual product features on the market value of a product or service. The following Research Insight reports on a low-cost approach, using a model similar to multiple regression analysis to predict future health and life expectancy.

RESEARCH INSIGHT

Is Social Data a Cost Effective and Acceptable Predictor of Health?   According to the insurance industry, the underwriting costs of issuing a life insurance policy range up to $1,000, with a significant portion spent on medical tests and exams. Using information on 60,000 insurance applicants gathered by data-assembly and mining firms, Deloitte Consulting LLP has developed a model that predicts a person's risk for diseases (and life expectancy) related to lifestyle. The information is gathered from a variety of sources including: public records, surveys, online behavior such as surfing and purchases, and social networking sites. Independent variables in the model include: activity indicators, financial indicators, purchases related to health or obesity, and television consumption. Although Deloitte estimates insurers could save an average of $125 per applicant by using the model, insurance companies are concerned that efforts to use the model for decision making will likely raise a number of privacy issues and objections from state insurance commissions.

Source: Leslie Scism and Mark Maremont, "Insurers Test Data Profiles to Identify Risky Clients," *The Wall Street Journal*, November 19, 2010, pp. A1, A16.

YOU MAKE THE CALL

You are the Purchasing Manager   Your department has been experiencing increased activity in recent periods as the company has grown, and you have observed that the average cost per purchase order processed has been declining, but not at a constant rate. You have been given an estimate by the production manager of the number of purchase orders that will be processed next period and have been asked by the accounting department to provide within one hour an estimate of the cost to process those orders. How can the scatter diagram method help you to meet this deadline? [Answer, p. 50]

ADDITIONAL ISSUES IN COST ESTIMATION

We have mentioned several items to be wary of when developing cost estimating equations:

- Data that are not based on normal operating conditions.
- Nonlinear relationships between total costs and activity.
- Obtaining a high R-squared purely by chance.

LO3 Identify and discuss problems encountered in cost estimation.

Additional items of concern include:

- Changes in technology or prices.
- Matching activity and cost within each observation.
- Identifying activity cost drivers.

Changes in Technology and Prices

Changes in technology and prices make cost estimation and prediction difficult. When telecommunications companies changed from using landlines to voice over internet protocol (VOIP) to place long-distance telephone calls, cost estimates based on the use of fiber optic cables were of little or no value in predicting future costs. Care must be taken to make sure that data used in developing cost estimates are based on the existing technology. When this is not possible, professional judgment is required to make appropriate adjustments.

Only data reflecting a single price level should be used in cost estimation and prediction. If prices have remained stable in the past but then uniformly increase by 20 percent, cost-estimating equations based on data from previous periods will not accurately predict future costs. In this case, all that is required is a 20 percent increase in the prediction. Unfortunately, adjustments for price changes are seldom this simple. The prices of various cost elements are likely to change at different rates and at different times. Furthermore, there are probably several different price levels included in the past data used to develop cost-estimating equations. If data from different price levels are used, an attempt should be made to restate them to a single price level.

Matching Activity and Costs

The development of accurate cost-estimating equations requires the matching of the activity to related costs within each observation. This accuracy is often difficult to achieve because of the time lag between an activity and the recording of the cost of resources consumed by the activity. Current activities usually consume electricity, but the electric bill won't be received and recorded until next month. Driving an automobile requires routine maintenance for items such as lubrication and oil, but the auto can be driven several weeks or even months before the maintenance is required. Consequently, daily, weekly, and perhaps even monthly observations of miles driven and maintenance costs are unlikely to match the costs of oil and lubrication with the cost-driving activity, miles driven.

In general, the shorter the time period, the higher the probability of error in matching costs and activity. The cost analyst must carefully review the database to verify that activity and cost are matched within each observation. If matching problems are found, it may be possible to adjust the data (perhaps by moving the cost of electricity from one observation to another). Under other circumstances, it may be necessary to use longer periods to match costs and activity.

Identifying Activity Cost Drivers

Identifying the appropriate activity cost driver for a particular cost requires judgment and professional experience. In general, the cost driver should have a logical, causal relationship with costs. In many cases, the identity of the most appropriate activity cost driver, such as miles driven for the cost of automobile gasoline, is apparent. In other situations, where different activity cost drivers might be used, scatter diagrams and statistical measures, such as the coefficient of determination, are helpful in selecting the activity cost driver that best explains past variations in cost. When scatter diagrams are used, the analyst can study the dispersion of observations around the cost-estimating line. In general, a small dispersion is preferred. If regression analysis is used, the analyst considers the coefficient of determination. In general, a higher coefficient of determination is preferred. The relationship between the activity cost driver and the cost must seem logical, and the activity data must be available.

ALTERNATIVE COST DRIVER CLASSIFICATIONS

LO4 Describe and develop alternative classifications for activity cost drivers.

So far we have examined cost behavior and cost estimation using only a unit-level approach, which assumes changes in costs are best explained by changes in the number of units of product or service provided customers. This approach may have worked for Carnegie Steel Company, but it is inappropriate for multidimensional organizations, such as Square. The unit-level approach becomes increasingly inaccurate for analyzing cost behavior when organizations experience the following types of changes:

■ From face-to-face customer interactions to web-based interface,

■ From stand-alone products to products with multiple layers of customer interface, such as Square's hardware versus the processing of payments executed by Square for its customers, and

■ From internet-based operations to mobile platforms, thus engaging a more geographically diverse set of customers.

Exhibit 2.8 illustrates the composition of total manufacturing costs for the past century, illustrating changes in the percentage of manufacturing costs for three major cost categories.

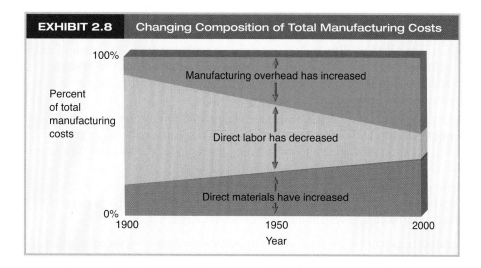

EXHIBIT 2.8 Changing Composition of Total Manufacturing Costs

1. **Direct materials**, the cost of primary raw materials converted into finished goods, have increased slightly as organizations purchase components they formerly fabricated. The word "direct" is used to indicate costs that are easily or directly traced to a finished product or service.

2. **Direct labor**, the wages earned by production employees for the time they spend converting raw materials into finished products, has decreased significantly as employees spend less time physically working on products and more time supporting automated production activities.

3. **Manufacturing overhead**, which includes all manufacturing costs other than direct materials and direct labor, has increased significantly due to automation, product diversity, and product complexity.

Changes in the composition of manufacturing costs have implications for the behavior of total costs and the responsiveness of costs to changes in cost drivers. Because direct materials and direct labor vary directly with the number of units, they are easy to measure. In the past, when manufacturing overhead was relatively small, it was possible to assume units of product or service was the primary cost driver. This is no longer true. Units of final product is no longer an adequate explanation of changes in manufacturing overhead for many organizations.

The past tendency to ignore overhead, while focusing on direct materials and direct labor, led one researcher to describe overhead-causing activities as "the hidden factory."[1] To better understand the hidden factory, several researchers have developed frameworks for categorizing cost-driving activities. The crucial feature of these frameworks is the inclusion of nonunit cost drivers. Depending on the characteristics of a particular organization, as well as management's information needs, there are an almost unlimited number of cost driver classification schemes. We consider two frequently applied cost driver classification schemes: one based on a manufacturing cost hierarchy and a second based on a customer cost hierarchy. We also illustrate variations of each.

Manufacturing Cost Hierarchy

The most well-known framework, developed by Cooper[2] and Cooper and Kaplan[3] for manufacturing situations, classifies activities into the following four categories.

1. A **unit-level activity** is performed *for each unit* of product produced. Christofle is a French manufacturer of high-end silver flatware. In the production of forks, the stamping of each fork into the prescribed shape is an example of a unit-level cost driver.

---

[1] Jeffrey G. Miller and Thomas E. Vollmann, "The Hidden Factory," *Harvard Business Review,* September-October 1985, pp. 142–150.

[2] Robin Cooper, "Cost Classification in Unit-Based and Activity-Based Manufacturing Cost Systems," *The Journal of Cost Management,* Fall 1990, pp. 4–14.

[3] Robin Cooper and Robert S. Kaplan, "Profit Priorities from Activity-Based Costing," *Harvard Business Review,* May-June 1991, pp. 130–135.

2. A **batch-level activity** is performed *for each batch* of product produced. At Christofle, a batch is a number of identical units (such as a fork of a specific design) produced at the same time. Batch-level activities include setting up the machines to stamp each fork in an identical manner, moving the entire batch between workstations (i.e., molding, stamping, and finishing), and inspecting the first unit in the batch to verify that the machines are set up correctly.

3. A **product-level activity** is performed *to support* the production of *each different type of product*. At Christofle, product-level activities for a specific pattern of fork include initially designing the fork, producing and maintaining the mold for the fork, and determining manufacturing operations for the fork.

4. A **facility-level activity** is performed *to maintain* general manufacturing capabilities. At Christofle's, facility-level activities include plant management, building maintenance, property taxes, and electricity required to sustain the building.

Several additional examples of the costs driven by activities at each level are presented in Exhibit 2.9.

EXHIBIT 2.9	**Hierarchy of Activity Costs**	
Activity Level	**Reason for Activity**	**Examples of Activity Cost**
1. Unit level	Performed for each unit of product produced or sold	• Cost of raw materials • Cost of inserting a component • Utilities cost of operating equipment • Some costs of packaging • Sales commissions
2. Batch level	Performed for each batch of product produced or sold	• Cost of processing sales order • Cost of issuing and tracking work order • Cost of equipment setup • Cost of moving batch between workstations • Cost of inspection (assuming same number of units inspected in each batch)
3. Product level	Performed to support each different product that can be produced	• Cost of product development • Cost of product marketing such as advertising • Cost of specialized equipment • Cost of maintaining specialized equipment
4. Facility level	Performed to maintain general manufacturing capabilities	• Cost of maintaining general facilities such as buildings and grounds • Cost of nonspecialized equipment • Cost of maintaining nonspecialized equipment • Cost of real property taxes • Cost of general advertising • Cost of general administration such as the plant manager's salary

When using a cost hierarchy for analyzing and estimating costs, total costs are broken down into the different cost levels in the hierarchy, and a separate cost driver is determined for each level of cost. For example, using the above hierarchy, the costs that are related to the number of units produced (such **as** direct materials or direct labor) may have direct labor hours or machines hours as the cost driver; whereas, batch costs may be driven by the number of setups of production machines or the number of times materials are move from one machine to another. Other costs may be driven by the number of different products produced. Facility-level costs are generally regarded as fixed costs and do not vary unless capacity is increased or decreased.

Customer Cost Hierarchy

The manufacturing hierarchy presented is but one of many possible ways of classifying activities and their costs. Classification schemes should be designed to fit the organization and meet user needs. A merchandising organization or the sales division of a manufacturing organization might use the following hierarchy.

1. **Unit-level activity**: performed for each unit sold.
2. **Order-level activity**: performed for each sales order.
3. **Customer-level activity**: performed to obtain or maintain each customer.
4. **Facility-level activity**: performed to maintain the general manufacturing function

This classification scheme assists in answering questions concerning the cost of individual orders or individual customers.

If an organization sells to distinct market segments (for profit, not for profit, and government), the cost hierarchy can be modified as follows:

1. Unit-level activity
2. Order-level activity
3. Customer-level activity
4. **Market-segment-level activity**: performed to obtain or maintain operations in a segment.
5. Facility-level activity

The market-segment-level activities and their related costs differ with each market segment. This classification scheme assists in answering questions concerning the profitability of each segment.

Finally, an organization that completes unique projects for different market segments (such as buildings for IBM and the U.S. Department of Defense) can use the following hierarchy to determine the profitability of each segment:

1. **Project-level activity**: performed to support the completion of each project.
2. Market-segment-level activity
3. Facility-level activity

The possibilities are endless. The important point is that both the cost hierarchy and the costs included in the hierarchy be tailored to meet the specific circumstances of an organization and the interests of management.

CHAPTER-END REVIEW

Assume a local **Subway** reported the following results for April and May:

	April	May
Unit sales	2,100	2,700
Cost of food sold	$1,575	$2,025
Wages and salaries	1,525	1,675
Rent on building	1,500	1,500
Depreciation on equipment	200	200
Utilities	710	770
Supplies	225	255
Miscellaneous	113	131
Total	$5,848	$6,556

Required

a. Identify each cost as being fixed, variable, or mixed.
b. Using the high-low method, estimate an equation for the month of April for the cost of food, wages and salaries, rent on building, and total monthly costs.
c. Predict total costs for monthly volumes of 1,000 and 2,000 units.
d. Predict the average cost per unit at monthly volumes of 1,000 and 2,000 units. Explain why the average costs differ at these two volumes.

The solution is on pages 64–65.

GUIDANCE ANSWERS . . . YOU MAKE THE CALL

You are the Purchasing Manager One of the quickest methods for gaining a general understanding of the relationship between a given cost and its cost driver is to graph the relationship using data from several recent periods. As purchasing manager you could probably quickly obtain information about the amount of the total purchasing department costs and number of purchase orders processed for each of the most recent eight or ten periods. By graphing these data with costs on the vertical axis and number of purchase orders on the horizontal axis, you should be able to visually determine if there is an obvious behavioral pattern (variable, fixed, or mixed). Since costs have been declining as volume has increased, this would suggest that there are some fixed costs, and that they have been declining on a per unit basis as they are spread over an increasing number of purchase orders. Using two representative data points in the scatter diagram, you can plot a cost curve on the graph, and then use the data for those two points to calculate the estimated fixed and variable costs using the high-low cost estimation method. Using these cost estimates, you can predict the total cost for next period. This method may not give you a precise estimate of the cost, but coupled with your subjective estimate of cost based on your experience as manager of the department, it should give you more confidence than merely making a best guess. Hopefully, you will have an opportunity before presenting your budget for the next period to conduct additional analyses using more advanced methods.

KEY RATIOS

Variable costs: $Y = bX$

Where b = the variable cost per unit, sometimes referred to as the slope of the cost function.

Fixed costs: $Y = a$

Where a = total fixed costs. The slope of the fixed cost function is zero because fixed costs do not change with activity.

Mixed costs: $Y = a + bX$

Where a = total fixed cost element and b = variable cost element per unit of activity.

Step cost: $Y = a_i$

Where a_i = the step cost within a specific range of activity, identified by the subscript i.

Total costs: $Y = a + bX$

Where Y = total costs, a = vertical axis intercept (an approximation of fixed costs), b = slope (an approximation of variable costs per unit of X) and X = value of independent variable.

$$\text{Variable costs per unit} = \frac{\text{Difference in total costs}}{\text{Difference in activity}}$$

Fixed costs = Total costs − Variable costs

General form for simple regression analysis: $Y = a + bX$

Where a = total fixed cost element and b = the variable cost per unit of independent variable X.

General form for multiple regression analysis is: $Y = a + \sum b_i X_i$

Where the subscript i is a general representation of each independent variable. When there are several independent variables, i is set equal to 1 for the first, 2 for the second, and so forth. The total variable costs of each independent variable is computed as $b_i X_i$, with b_i representing the variable cost per unit of independent variable X_i. The Greek symbol sigma, $\sum$, indicates that the costs of all independent variables are summed in determining total variable costs.

KEY TERMS

batch-level activity, 48

capacity costs, 39

coefficient of determination, 43

committed fixed costs, 39

cost behavior, 32

cost estimation, 40

cost prediction, 41

customer-level activity, 49

direct labor, 47

direct materials, 47

discretionary fixed costs, 39

facility-level activity, 48, 49

fixed costs, 33

high-low method of cost estimation, 40

least-squares regression analysis, 43

managed fixed costs, 39

manufacturing overhead, 47

marginal cost, 36

market-segment-level activity, 49

mixed costs, 33

order-level activity, 49

product-level activity, 48

project-level activity, 49

relevant range, 35, 37

scatter diagram, 42

semivariable costs, 33

step costs, 33

unit-level activity, 47, 49

variable costs, 32

MULTIPLE CHOICE

1. A graph of the total cost of ingredients used in Blaze Pizza's pizzas most closely resembles this total cost behavior pattern:
   a. Variable cost
   b. Fixed cost
   c. Mixed cost
   d. Step cost

2. At a sales volume of 50 units the average cost is $ 410 per unit and the variable cost is $ 10 per unit. Assuming a linear cost behavior pattern, if sales double to 100 units the average cost will be:
   a. $ 10
   b. $200
   c. $205
   d. $210

3. Increasing the length of the time period included in each observation of activity and cost will assist in overcoming this possible problem in cost estimation:
   a. Data not based on normal operations
   b. Nonlinear relationship between total costs and activity
   c. Changes in technology or prices
   d. Failure to match activity and costs within each observation

4. Arch manufactures a product with the following manufacturing cost hierarchy for its only current product:

	Cost
Unit.	$20/unit
Batch	$500/batch
Product	$10,000/year
Facility	$50,000/year

Next year Arch plans to manufacture 50,000 units of product in batches of 500 units. Arch's predicted manufacturing costs for next year are:
   a. $1,560,000
   b. $1,500,000
   c. $1,110,000
   d. $660,000

5.   West sells specialized products produced by electronics companies to 100 engineering firms at a selling price based on West's purchase price. West's customer cost hierarchy is as follows:

	Cost
Unit.	80 percent of selling price
Batch	$200 per sales order
Customer.	$1,000 per customer per year
Facility	$120,000 per year

Next year West plans to sell $4,000,000 of product to the 100 engineering firms they serve. They anticipate that each firm will place an average of 4 orders. West's predicted customer costs for next year are:
a. $80,000
b. $300,000
c. $3,200,000
d. $3,500,000

DISCUSSION QUESTIONS

Q2-1.   Briefly describe variable, fixed, mixed, and step costs and indicate how the total cost function of each changes as activity increases within a time period.

Q2-2.   Why is presenting all costs of an organization as a function of a single independent variable, although useful in obtaining a general understanding of cost behavior, often not accurate enough to make specific decisions concerning products, services, or activities?

Q2-3.   Explain the term "relevant range" and why it is important in estimating total costs.

Q2-4.   How are variable and fixed costs determined using the high-low method of cost estimation?

Q2-5.   Distinguish between cost estimation and cost prediction.

Q2-6.   Why is a scatter diagram helpful when used in conjunction with other methods of cost estimation?

Q2-7.   Identify two advantages of least-squares regression analysis as a cost estimation technique.

Q2-8.   Why is it important to match activity and costs within a single observation? When is this matching problem most likely to exist?

Q2-9.   During the past century, how have direct materials, direct labor, and manufacturing overhead changed as a portion of total manufacturing costs? What is the implication of the change in manufacturing overhead for cost estimation?

Q2-10.   Distinguish between the unit-, batch-, product-, and facility-level activities of a manufacturing organization.

Assignments with the ✔ logo in the margin are available in ^{my}BusinessCourse.
See the Preface of the book for details.

MINI EXERCISES

LO1   **M2-11.   Classifying Cost Behavior**

Classify the total costs of each of the following as variable, fixed, mixed, or step. Sales volume is the cost driver.

a.   Salary of the department manager
b.   Memory chips in a computer assembly plant
c.   Real estate taxes
d.   Salaries of quality inspectors when each inspector can evaluate a maximum of 1,000 units per day
e.   Wages paid to production employees for the time spent working on products
f.   Electric power in a factory
g.   Raw materials used in production

    h.   Automobiles rented on the basis of a fixed charge per day plus an additional charge per mile driven

    i.   Sales commissions

    j.   Depreciation on office equipment

M2-12. **Classifying Cost Behavior**   LO1

Classify the total costs of each of the following as variable, fixed, mixed, or step.

    a.   Straight-line depreciation on a building

    b.   Maintenance costs at a hospital

    c.   Rent on a photocopy machine charged as a fixed amount per month plus an additional charge per copy

    d.   Cost of goods sold in a bookstore

    e.   Salaries paid to temporary instructors in a college as the number of course sessions varies

    f.   Lumber used by a house construction company

    g.   The costs of operating a research department

    h.   The cost of hiring a dance band for three hours

    i.   Laser printer paper for a department printer

    j.   Electric power in a restaurant

M2-13. **Classifying Cost Behavior**   LO1

For each of the following situations, select the most appropriate cost behavior pattern (as shown in the illustrations following this problem) where the lines represent the cost behavior pattern, the vertical axis represents costs, the horizontal axis represents total volume, and the dots represent actual costs. Each pattern may be used more than once.

    a.   Variable costs per unit

    b.   Total fixed costs

    c.   Total mixed costs

    d.   Average fixed costs per unit

    e.   Total current manufacturing costs

    f.   Average variable costs

    g.   Total costs when employees are paid $15 per hour for the first 40 hours worked each week and $20 for each additional hour.

    h.   Total costs when employees are paid $15 per hour and guaranteed a minimum weekly wage of $300.

    i.   Total costs per day when a consultant is paid $200 per hour with a maximum daily fee of $1,000.

    j.   Total variable costs

    k.   Total costs for salaries of social workers where each social worker can handle a maximum of 25 cases

    l.   A water bill where a flat fee of $800 is charged for the first 100,000 gallons and additional water costs $0.005 per gallon

    m.   Total variable costs properly used to estimate step costs

    n.   Total materials costs

    o.   Rent on exhibit space at a convention

Graphs for Mini Exercise 2-13

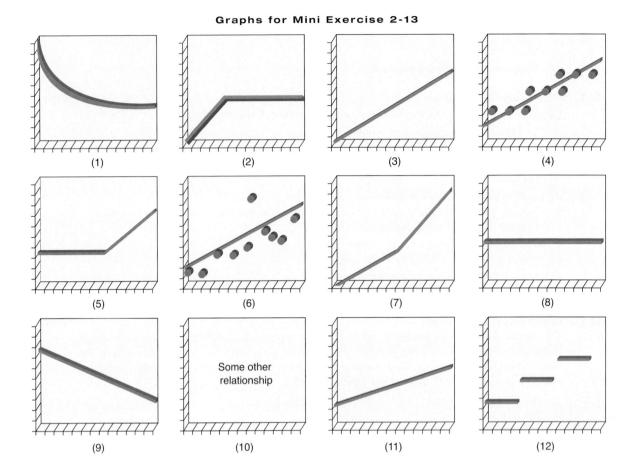

(1)	(2)	(3)	(4)
(5)	(6)	(7)	(8)
(9)	(10)	(11)	(12)

LO1 **M2-14. Classifying Cost Behavior**

For each of the graphs displayed following this problem, select the most appropriate cost behavior pattern where the lines represent the cost behavior pattern, the vertical axis represents total costs, the horizontal axis represents total volume, and the dots represent actual costs. Each pattern may be used more than once.

a. A cellular telephone bill when a flat fee is charged for the first 500 minutes of use per month and additional use costs $0.25 per minute

b. Total selling and administrative costs

c. Total labor costs when employees are paid per unit produced

d. Total overtime premium paid production employees

e. Average total cost per unit

f. Salaries of supervisors when each one can supervise a maximum of 10 employees

g. Total idle time costs when employees are paid for a minimum 40-hour week

h. Materials costs per unit

i. Total sales commissions

j. Electric power consumption in a restaurant

k. Total costs when high volumes of production require the use of overtime and obsolete equipment

l. A good linear approximation of actual costs

m. A linear cost estimation valid only within the relevant range

Graphs for Mini Exercise 2-14

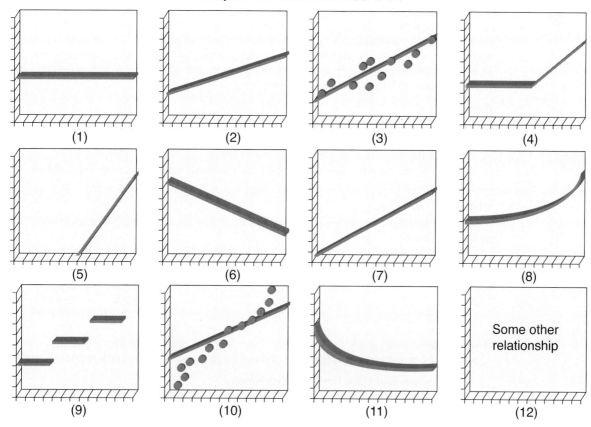

EXERCISES

E2-15. **Computing Average Unit Costs**

The total monthly operating costs of Chili To Go are:

$$\$12{,}000 + \$0.50X$$

where

$$X = \text{servings of chili}$$

Required

a. Determine the average cost per serving at each of the following monthly volumes: 100; 1,000; 5,000; and 10,000

b. Determine the monthly volume at which the average cost per serving is $0.70.

LO2

E2-16. **Automatic versus Manual Processing**

Photo Station Company operates a printing service for customers with digital cameras. The current service, which requires employees to download photos from customer cameras, has monthly operating costs of $6,000 plus $0.20 per photo printed. Management is evaluating the desirability of acquiring a machine that will allow customers to download and make prints without employee assistance. If the machine is acquired, the monthly fixed costs will increase to $10,000 and the variable costs of printing a photo will decline to $0.04 per photo.

Required

a. Determine the total costs of printing 20,000 and 50,000 photos per month:
1. With the current employee-assisted process.
2. With the proposed customer self-service process.

b. Determine the monthly volume at which the proposed process becomes preferable to the current process.

LO2

LO2 **E2-17.** **Automatic versus Manual Processing**

Mid-Town Copy Service processes 2,100,000 photocopies per month at its mid-town service center. Approximately 50 percent of the photocopies require collating. Collating is currently performed by high school and college students who are paid $8 per hour. Each student collates an average of 5,000 copies per hour. Management is contemplating the lease of an automatic collating machine that has a monthly capacity of 6,000,000 photocopies, with lease and operating costs totaling $1,550, plus $0.05 per 1,000 units collated.

Required

a. Determine the total costs of collating 500,000 and 1,500,000 per month:
1. With student help.
2. With the collating machine.

b. Determine the monthly volume at which the automatic process becomes preferable to the manual process.

LO2 **E2-18.** **High-Low Cost Estimation**

DHL (DHL)

Assume the local DHL delivery service hub has the following information available about fleet miles and operating costs:

Year	Miles	Operating Costs
2012	556,000	$182,000
2013	684,000	214,000

Required

Use the high-low method to develop a cost-estimating equation for total annual operating costs.

LO2, 3 **E2-19.** **Scatter Diagrams and High-Low Cost Estimation**

PEARLE VISION

Assume the local Pearle Vision has the following information on the number of sales orders received and order-processing costs.

Month	Sales Orders	Order-Processing Costs
1	3,000	$32,000
2	1,500	22,400
3	4,400	55,400
4	2,800	31,200
5	2,300	25,600
6	1,200	17,000
7	2,000	24,000

Required

a. Use information from the high- and low-volume months to develop a cost-estimating equation for monthly order-processing costs.

b. Plot the data on a scatter diagram. Using the information from representative high- and low-volume months, develop a cost-estimating equation for monthly production costs.

c. What factors might have caused the difference in the equations developed for requirements (*a*) and (*b*)?

LO2, 3 **E2-20.** **Scatter Diagrams and High-Low Cost Estimation**

From April 1 through October 31, Will County Highway Department hires temporary employees to mow and clean the right-of-way along county roads. The County Road Commissioner has asked you to help her in determining the variable labor cost of mowing and cleaning a mile of road. The following information is available regarding current-year operations:

Month	Miles Mowed and Cleaned	Labor Costs
April	350	$8,000
May	300	7,500
June	400	9,000
July	250	5,500
August	375	8,500
September	200	5,000
October	100	4,800

Required

a. Use the information from the high- and low-volume months to develop a cost-estimating equation for monthly labor costs.

b. Plot the data on a scatter diagram. Using the information from representative high- and low-volume months, use the high-low method to develop a cost-estimating equation for monthly labor costs.

c. What factors might have caused the difference in the equations developed for requirements (a) and (b)?

d. Adjust the equation developed in requirement (b) to incorporate the effect of an anticipated 7 percent increase in wages.

E2-21.   Cost Behavior Analysis in a Restaurant: High-Low Cost Estimation

LO2

JIMMY JOHN'S
(SANDWICHES)

Assume a Jimmy John's restaurant has the following information available regarding costs at representative levels of monthly sales:

	Monthly sales in units		
	5,000	8,000	10,000
Cost of food sold	$10,000	$16,000	$20,000
Wages and fringe benefits	4,250	4,400	4,500
Fees paid delivery help	1,250	2,000	2,500
Rent on building	1,200	1,200	1,200
Depreciation on equipment	600	600	600
Utilities	500	560	600
Supplies (soap, floor wax, etc.)	150	180	200
Administrative costs	1,300	1,300	1,300
Total	$19,250	$26,240	$30,900

Required

a. Identify each cost as being variable, fixed, or mixed.

b. Use the high-low method to develop a schedule identifying the amount of each cost that is mixed or variable per unit. Total the amounts under each category to develop an equation for total monthly costs.

c. Predict total costs for a monthly sales volume of 10,000 units.

E2-22.   Developing an Equation from Average Costs

LO2

The Desert Dog and Cat Hotel is a pet hotel located in Las Vegas. Assume that in March, when dog-days (occupancy) were at an annual low of 500, the average cost per dog-day was $22. In July, when dog-days were at a capacity level of 4,500, the average cost per dog-day was $8.

Required

a. Develop an equation for monthly operating costs.

b. Determine the average cost per dog-day at an annual volume of 24,000 dog-days.

LO2, 3   **E2-23.**   **Selecting an Independent Variable: Scatter Diagrams**

Peak Production Company produces backpacks that are sold to sporting goods stores throughout the Rocky Mountains. Presented is information on production costs and inventory changes for five recent months:

	January	February	March	April	May
Finished goods inventory in units:					
Beginning......................	30,000	40,000	50,000	30,000	60,000
Manufactured	60,000	90,000	80,000	90,000	100,000
Available.....................	90,000	130,000	130,000	120,000	160,000
Sold	(50,000)	(80,000)	(100,000)	(60,000)	(120,000)
Ending	40,000	50,000	30,000	60,000	40,000
Manufacturing costs...........	$300,000	$500,000	$450,000	$450,000	$550,000

Required

a.   With the aid of scatter diagrams, determine whether units sold or units manufactured is a better predictor of manufacturing costs.

b.   Prepare an explanation for your answer to requirement (a).

c.   Which independent variable, units sold or units manufactured, should be a better predictor of selling costs? Why?

LO2, 3   **E2-24.**   **Selecting a Basis for Predicting Shipping Expenses (Requires Computer Spreadsheet[*])**

Penn Company assembles and sells computer boards in western Pennsylvania. In an effort to improve the planning and control of shipping expenses, management is trying to determine which of three variables—units shipped, weight shipped, or sales value of units shipped—has the closest relationship with shipping expenses. The following information is available:

Month	Units Shipped	Weight Shipped (lbs.)	Sales Value of Units Shipped	Shipping Expenses
May	3,000	6,200	$100,000	$ 5,600
June.....................	5,000	8,000	110,000	7,700
July.....................	4,000	8,100	80,000	6,500
August	7,000	10,000	114,000	10,400
September................	6,000	7,000	140,000	8,600
October	4,500	8,000	160,000	8,200

Required

a.   With the aid of a spreadsheet program, determine whether units shipped, weight shipped, or sales value of units shipped has the closest relationship with shipping expenses.

b.   Using the independent variable that appears to have the closest relationship to shipping expenses, develop a cost-estimating equation for total monthly shipping expenses.

c.   Use the equation developed in requirement (b) to predict total shipping expenses in a month when 5,000 units, weighing 7,000 lbs., with a total sales value of $114,000 are shipped.

PROBLEMS

LO2, 3   **P2-25.**   **High-Low and Scatter Diagrams with Implications for Regression**

Trumpet Bagels produces and sells bagels at each of its restaurants. Presented is monthly cost and sales information for one of Trumpet's restaurants.

[*] This exercise and several subsequent assignments require the use of a computer spreadsheet such as Excel® to solve. This assignment assumes previous knowledge of computer spreadsheets.

Month	Sales (Dozens)	Total Costs
January	7,500	$28,800
February.	6,000	26,400
March.	4,000	20,400
April	1,500	19,200
May	5,000	21,600
June	5,500	23,400

Required

a. Using the high-low method, develop a cost-estimating equation for total monthly costs.

b. 1. Plot the equation developed in requirement (a).

   2. Using the same graph, develop a scatter diagram of all observations for the bagel shop. Select representative high and low values and draw a second cost-estimating equation.

c. Which is a better predictor of future costs? Why?

d. If you decided to develop a cost-estimating equation using least-squares regression analysis, should you include all the observations? Why or why not?

e. Mention two reasons that the least-squares regression is superior to the high-low and scatter diagram methods of cost estimation.

P2-26. Multiple Cost Drivers   LO4

Scottsdale Ltd. manufactures a variety of high-volume and low-volume products to customer demand. Presented is information on 2013 manufacturing overhead and activity cost drivers.

Level	Total Cost	Units of Cost Driver
Unit.	$500,000	10,000 machine hours
Batch	100,000	500 customer orders
Product	200,000	25 products

Product X1 required 2,000 machine hours to fill 10 customer orders for a total of 8,000 units.

Required

a. Assuming all manufacturing overhead is estimated and predicted on the basis of machine hours, determine the predicted total overhead costs to produce the 8,000 units of product X1.

b. Assuming manufacturing overhead is estimated and predicted using separate rates for machine hours, customer orders, and products (a multiple-level cost hierarchy), determine the predicted total overhead costs to produce the 8,000 units of product X1.

c. Calculate the error in predicting manufacturing overhead using machine hours versus using multiple cost drivers. Indicate whether the use of only machine hours results in overpredicting or underpredicting the costs to produce 8,000 units of product X1.

d. Determine the error in the prediction of X1 batch-level costs resulting from the use of only machine hours. Indicate whether the use of only machine hours results in overpredicting or underpredicting the batch-level costs of product X1.

e. Determine the error in the prediction of X1 product-level costs resulting from the use of only machine hours. Indicate whether the use of only machine hours results in overpredicting or underpredicting the product-level costs of product X1.

P2-27. Unit- and Batch-Level Cost Drivers   LO4

KC, a fast-food restaurant, serves fried chicken, fried fish, and French fries. The managers have estimated the costs of a batch of fried chicken for KC's all-you-can-eat Friday Fried Fiesta. Each batch must be 100 pieces. The chicken is precut by the chain headquarters and sent to the stores in 10-piece bags. Each bag costs $4. Preparing a batch of 100 pieces of chicken with KC's special coating takes one employee two hours. The current wage rate is $8 per hour. Another cost driver is the cost of putting fresh oil into the fryers. New oil, costing $6, is used for each batch.

Required

a. Determine the cost of preparing one batch of 100 pieces.

b. If management projects that it will sell 300 pieces of fried chicken, determine the total batch and unit costs.

c. If management estimates the sales to be 350 pieces, determine the total costs.

> *d.* How much will the batch costs increase if the government raises the minimum wage to $10 per hour?
>
> *e.* If management decided to reduce the number of pieces in a batch to 50, determine the cost of preparing 350 pieces. Assume that the batch would take half as long to prepare, and management wants to replace the oil after 50 pieces are cooked.

LO4 P2-28. Optimal Batch Size
This is a continuation of parts "c" and "e" of P2-27.

Required
Should management reduce the batch size to 50? Why or why not?

CASES AND PROJECTS

LO3 C2-29. Negative Fixed Costs
"This is crazy!" exclaimed the production supervisor as he reviewed the work of his new assistant. "You and that computer are telling me that my fixed costs are negative! Tell me, how did you get these negative fixed costs, and what am I supposed to do with them?"

Required
Explain to the supervisor the meaning of the negative "fixed costs" and what can be done with them.

LO3 C2-30. Significance of High R-Squared
Mark Adams had always been suspicious of "newfangled mathematical stuff," and the most recent suggestion of his new assistant merely confirmed his belief that schools are putting a lot of useless junk in students' heads. It seems that after an extensive analysis of historical data, the assistant suggested that the number of pounds of scrap was the best basis for predicting manufacturing overhead. In response to Mr. Adams's rage, the slightly intimidated assistant indicated that of the 35 equations he tried, pounds of scrap had the highest coefficient of determination with manufacturing overhead.

Required
Comment on Adams's reaction. Is it justified? Is it likely that the number of pounds of scrap is a good basis for predicting manufacturing overhead? Is it a feasible basis for predicting manufacturing overhead?

LO3 C2-31. Estimating Machine Repair Costs
In an attempt to determine the best basis for predicting machine repair costs, the production supervisor accumulated daily information on these costs and production over a one-month period. Applying simple regression analysis to the data, she obtained the following estimating equation:

$$Y = \$800 - \$2.60X$$

where

$$Y = \text{total daily machine repair costs}$$
$$X = \text{daily production in units}$$

Because of the negative relationship between repair costs and production, she was somewhat skeptical of the results, even though the R-squared was a respectable 0.765.

Required
a. What is the most likely explanation of the negative variable costs?
b. Suggest an alternative procedure for estimating machine repair costs that might prove more useful.

LO3 C2-32. Ethical Problem Uncovered by Cost Estimation
Mesa Management Company owns and provides management services for several shopping centers. After five years with the company, Mike Moyer was recently promoted to the position of manager of Charlestown, an 18-store mall on the outskirts of a downtown area. When he accepted the assignment, Mike was told that he would hold the position for only a couple of years because Charlestown would likely be torn down to make way for a new sports stadium. Mike was also told that if he did well in this assignment, he would be in line for heading one of the company's new 200-store operations that were currently in the planning stage.

While reviewing Charlestown's financial records for the past few years, Mike observed that last year's oil consumption was up by 8 percent, even though the number of heating degree days was down by 4 percent. Somewhat curious, Mike uncovered the following information:

- Charlestown is heated by forced-air oil heat. The furnace is five years old and has been well maintained.
- Fuel oil is kept in four 5,000-gallon underground oil tanks. The oil tanks were installed 25 years ago.
- Replacing the tanks would cost $80,000. If pollution was found, cleanup costs could go as high as $2,000,000, depending on how much oil had leaked into the ground and how far it had spread.
- Replacing the tanks would add more congestion to Charlestown's parking situation.

Required

What should Mike do? Explain.

C2-33. **Activity Cost Drivers and Cost Estimation**   LO3, 4

Cool Mountain Ice Cream Company produces ten varieties of ice cream in large vats, several thousand gallons at a time. The ice cream is distributed to several categories of customers. Some ice cream is packaged in large containers and sold to college and university food services. Some is packaged in half-gallon or small containers and sold through wholesale distributors to grocery stores. Finally, some is packaged in a variety of individual servings and sold directly to the public from trucks owned and operated by Cool Mountain. Management has always assumed that costs fluctuated with the volume of ice cream, and cost-estimating equations have been based on the following cost function:

$$\text{Estimated costs} = \text{Fixed costs} + \text{Variable costs per gallon} \times \text{Production in gallons}$$

Lately, however, this equation has not been a very accurate predictor of total costs. At the same time, management has noticed that the volumes and varieties of ice cream sold through the three distinct distribution channels have fluctuated from month to month.

Required

a. What *relevant* major assumption is inherent in the cost-estimating equation currently used by Cool Mountain?

b. Why might Cool Mountain wish to develop a cost-estimating equation that recognizes the hierarchy of activity costs? Explain.

c. Develop the general form of a more accurate cost-estimating equation for Cool Mountain. Clearly label and explain all elements of the equation, and provide specific examples of costs for each element.

C2-34. **Multiple Regression Analysis for a Special Decision (Requires Computer Spreadsheet)**   LO2, 3

For billing purposes, South Town Health Clinic classifies its services into one of four major procedures, X1 through X4. A local business has proposed that South Town provide health services to its employees and their families at the following set rates per procedure:

X1	$ 45
X2	90
X3	60
X4	105

Because these rates are significantly below the current rates charged for these services, management has asked for detailed cost information on each procedure. The following information is available for the most recent 12 months.

| Month | Total Cost | Number of Procedures | | | |
		X1	X2	X3	X4
1	$23,000	30	100	205	75
2	25,000	38	120	180	90
3	27,000	50	80	140	150
4	19,000	20	90	120	100
5	20,000	67	50	160	80
6	27,000	90	75	210	105
7	25,500	20	110	190	110
8	21,500	15	120	175	80
9	26,000	60	85	125	140
10	22,000	20	90	100	140
11	22,800	20	70	150	130
12	26,500	72	60	200	120

Required

a. Use multiple regression analysis to determine the unit cost of each procedure. How much variation in monthly cost is explained by your cost-estimating equation?

b. Evaluate the rates proposed by the local business. Assuming South Town has excess capacity and no employees of the local business currently patronize the clinic, what are your recommendations regarding the proposal?

c. Evaluate the rates proposed by the local business. Assuming South Town is operating at capacity and would have to turn current customers away if it agrees to provide health services to the local business, what are your recommendations regarding the proposal?

LO2, 3   **C2-35.**   **Cost Estimation, Interpretation, and Analysis (Requires Computer Spreadsheet)**
Newport Table Company produces two styles of tables, dining room and kitchen. Presented is monthly information on production volume and manufacturing costs:

	Total Manufacturing Costs	Total Tables Produced	Dining Room Tables Produced	Kitchen Tables Produced
June 2012	$46,650	250	50	200
July.	50,888	205	105	100
August	60,630	285	105	180
September.	39,743	210	40	170
October	42,120	175	75	100
November	52,575	210	110	100
December	53,018	245	90	155
January 2013	47,325	250	50	200
February.	47,235	220	70	150
March.	44,475	180	80	100
April	97,800	315	180	135
May	59,933	280	105	175
June	52,043	255	75	180
July.	55,380	235	110	125
August	46,223	195	85	110
September.	60,435	260	120	140
October	53,708	250	90	160
November	57,600	270	100	170
December	37,650	165	60	105

Required

a.   Use the high-low method to develop a cost-estimating equation for total manufacturing costs. Interpret the meaning of the "fixed" costs and comment on the results.

b.   Use the chart feature of a spreadsheet to develop a scatter graph of total manufacturing costs and total units produced. Use the graph to identify any unusual observations.

c.   Excluding any unusual observations, use the high-low method to develop a cost-estimating equation for total manufacturing costs. Comment on the results, comparing them with the results in requirement (a).

d.   Use simple regression analysis to develop a cost-estimating equation for total manufacturing costs. What advantages does simple regression analysis have in comparison with the high-low method of cost estimation? Why must analysts carefully evaluate the data used in simple regression analysis?

e.   A customer has offered to purchase 50 dining room tables for $220 per table. Management has asked your advice regarding the desirability of accepting the offer. What advice do you have for management? Additional analysis is required.

C2-36.   Simple and Multiple Regression (Requires Computer Spreadsheet)   LO2, 3

Dan Mullen is employed by a mail-order distributor and reconditions used desktop computers, broadband routers, and laser printers. Dan is paid $12 per hour, plus an extra $6 per hour for work in excess of 40 hours per week. The distributor just announced plans to outsource all reconditioning work. Because the distributor is pleased with the quality of Dan's work, he has been asked to enter into a long-term contract to recondition used desktop computers at a rate of $40 per computer, plus all parts. The distributor also offered to provide all necessary equipment at a rate of $200 per month. Dan has been informed that he should plan on reconditioning as many computers as he can handle, up to a maximum of 20 per week.

Dan has room in his basement to set up a work area, but he is unsure of the economics of accepting the contract, as opposed to working for a local Radio Stuff store at $11 per hour. Data related to the time spent and the number of units of each type of electronic equipment Dan has reconditioned in recent weeks is as follows:

Week	Laser Printers	Broadband Routers	Desktop Computers	Total Units	Total Hours
1	4	5	5	14	40
2	0	7	6	13	42
3	4	3	7	14	40
4	0	2	12	14	46
5	11	6	4	21	48
6	5	8	3	16	44
7	5	8	3	16	44
8	5	6	5	16	43
9	2	6	10	18	53
10	8	4	6	18	46
Total				160	446

Required

Assuming he wants to work an average of 40 hours per week, what should Dan do?

SOLUTIONS TO REVIEW PROBLEMS

Mid-Chapter Review

Solution

a.   Variable cost

b.   Mixed cost

c.   Committed fixed cost

d.   Variable cost

e.   Step cost

f.   Discretionary fixed cost

g. Fixed cost (Without knowing the purpose of renting the car, the cost cannot be classified as committed or discretionary.)

h. Mixed cost

i. Step cost

j. Discretionary fixed cost

Chapter-End Review

Solution

a. Fixed costs are easily identified. They are the same at each activity level. Variable and mixed costs are determined by dividing the total costs for an item at two activity levels by the corresponding units of activity. The quotients of the variable cost items will be identical at both activity levels. The quotients of the mixed costs will differ, being lower at the higher activity level because the fixed costs are being spread over a larger number of units.

Cost	Behavior
Cost of food sold.	Variable
Wages and salaries	Mixed
Rent on building	Fixed
Depreciation on equipment.	Fixed
Utilities	Mixed
Supplies	Mixed
Miscellaneous	Mixed

b. The cost of food sold was classified as a variable cost. Hence, the cost of food may be determined by dividing the total costs at either observation by the corresponding number of units.

$$b = \frac{\$1{,}575 \text{ total variable costs}}{2{,}100 \text{ units}}$$

$$= \$0.75X$$

Wages and salaries were previously classified as a mixed cost. Hence, the cost of wages and salaries is determined using the high-low method.

(variable cost)
$$b = \frac{\$1{,}675 - \$1{,}525}{2{,}700 - 2{,}100}$$

$$= 0.25X$$

(fixed cost)
$$a = \$1{,}525 \text{ total cost} - (\$0.25 \times 2{,}100) \text{ variable cost}$$

$$= \$1{,}000$$

Rent on building was classified as a fixed cost.

$$a = \$1{,}500$$

Total monthly costs most likely follow a mixed cost behavior pattern. Hence, they can be determined using the high-low method.

$$b = \frac{\$6{,}556 - \$5{,}848}{2{,}700 - 2{,}100}$$

$$= \$1.18X$$

$$a = \$5{,}848 - (\$1.18 \times 2{,}100)$$

$$= \$3{,}370$$

$$\text{Total costs} = \$3{,}370 + \$1.18X$$

where

$$X = \textbf{unit sales}$$

c. and *d.*

Volume	Total Costs	Average Cost per Unit
1,000.	\$3,370 + (\$1.18 × 1,000) = \$4,550	\$4,550/1,000 = \$4.550
2,000.	\$3,370 + (\$1.18 × 2,000) = \$5,730	\$5,730/2,000 = \$2.865

The average costs differ at 1,000 and 2,000 units because the fixed costs are being spread over a different number of units. The larger the number of units, the smaller the average fixed cost per unit.

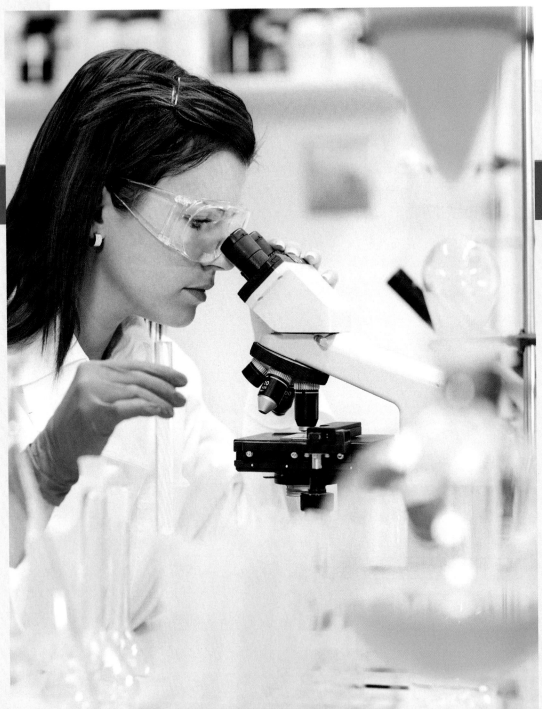

Cost-Volume-Profit Analysis and Planning

3

In 1802, **DuPont** was founded as a producer of gunpowder. Two centuries later, DuPont defines itself as a science company. DuPont's mission states that it seeks to "find sustainable, innovative, market-driving solutions to solve some of the world's biggest challenges: making lives better, safer, and healthier for people everywhere." Those are lofty aspirations that require future investment. Given DuPont's lengthy operating history, we might think the company can forecast its future profitability with precision. However, DuPont *has* a lengthy history because of its ability to adapt to the world by continuously retooling its product offerings and geographical scope. While this agility protects the company from downturns, it also complicates the process of predicting future profits.

DUPONT
www.dupont.com

DuPont's scope remains vast. It currently employs over 70,000 people across 90 countries in dozens of industries ranging from agriculture, electronics and communications, industrial biosciences, and nutrition and health to performance chemicals, performance materials, safety and protection, and pharmaceuticals. Yet the company's current growth strategy is predicated on its ability to confront three challenges: (1) feeding the world, (2) reducing its dependence on fossil fuels, and (3) keeping people and the environment safe. As evidence of that commitment, over half of DuPont's research and development costs were incurred in the agriculture sector over the past year.

If the company is to accomplish its goals, it must generate profits, meaning that its revenues must exceed its costs. With the current industry mix, the company's manufacturing processes consume a significant amount of energy and raw materials. The price of these inputs, including oil and natural gas, are extremely volatile. This volatility makes forecasts of future profitability often unreliable. Indeed, the company's desire to reduce its dependence on fossil fuels (the primary inputs for the performance chemicals sector) stems from the uncertainty these inputs have on estimations of future profitability. In order to grow and accomplish its goals, DuPont must know where the funds for future expenditures will come from (i.e., internally generated profit or external financing).

The financial reporting system will indicate where DuPont is performing well. For example, the company experienced substantial increases in 2012 revenue from its agriculture, nutrition and health, and industrial biosciences segments. However, these revenues were offset by poor performance in the performance chemicals division. Likewise, revenue increases from developing markets such as China, India, Latin America, Eastern and Central Europe, the Middle East, Africa, and Southeast Asia dominated revenues from the United States and Western Europe. But remember that profitability considers a company's costs in addition to its revenues. By decomposing DuPont's costs into its variable and fixed components, the company can perform profitability analyses to determine where to direct its

continued on following page

continued from previous page

future efforts. In fact, DuPont can utilize the tools presented in this chapter to determine how much revenue it has to generate within a division, given that division's cost structure, to achieve a desired profit.

The financial success of DuPont illustrates that the optimal cost structure varies over time, depending on competitive conditions, changing demographics, and changes in strategy. This chapter examines the relation between cost structure, volume, and profitability as a tool for planning and decision making.

Sources: E.I. DuPont de Nemours and Company 2012 Annual Report; Christina Larson, "DuPont Sees Niche in Curing China's Indigestion," *Bloomberg Businessweek*, July 24, 2013; and Ben Lefebvre, "DuPont Considers Selling Chemicals Unit," *Wall Street Journal*, July 24, 2013, p. B4.

CHAPTER ORGANIZATION

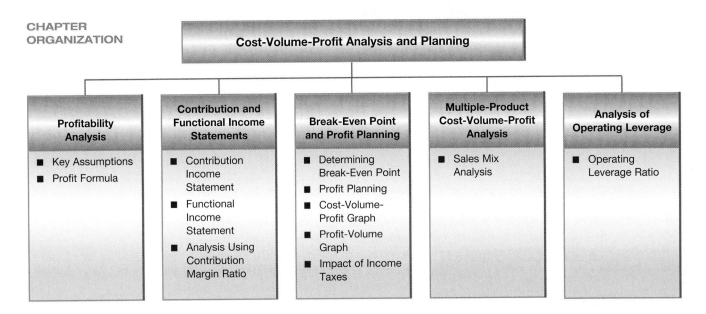

This chapter introduces basic approaches to profitability analysis and planning. We consider single-product, multiple-product, and service organizations; income taxes, sales mix, and the effects of cost structure on the relation between profit potential and the risk of loss.

PROFITABILITY ANALYSIS

LO1 Identify the uses and limitations of traditional cost-volume-profit analysis.

Profitability analysis involves examining the relationships among revenues, costs, and profits. Performing profitability analysis requires an understanding of selling prices and the behavior of activity cost drivers. Profitability analysis is widely used in the economic evaluation of existing or proposed products or services. Typically, it is performed before decisions are finalized in the operating budget for a future period.

Cost-volume-profit (CVP) analysis is a technique used to examine the relationships among the total volume of an independent variable, total costs, total revenues, and profits for a time period (typically a quarter or year). With CVP analysis, volume refers to a single activity cost driver, such as unit sales, that is assumed to correlate with changes in revenues, costs, and profits.

Cost-volume-profit analysis is useful in the early stages of planning because it provides an easily understood framework for discussing planning issues and organizing relevant data. CVP analysis is widely used by for-profit as well as not-for-profit organizations. It is equally applicable to service, merchandising, and manufacturing firms.

In for-profit organizations, CVP analysis is used to answer such questions as these: How many photocopies must the local FedEx Small Business Center produce to earn a profit of $80,000? At what dollar sales volume will Trader Joe's total revenues and total costs be equal? What profit will DuPont earn at an annual sales volume of $35 billion? What will happen to the profit of P.F. Chang's if there is a 20 percent increase in the cost of food and a 10 percent increase in the selling price of meals? The Research Insight box on the following page indicates the importance of the concepts discussed in this and other chapters to the success of new businesses.

In not-for-profit organizations, CVP analysis is used to establish service levels, plan fund-raising activities, and determine funding requirements. How many meals can the downtown Salvation Army serve with an annual budget of $600,000? How many tickets must be sold for the benefit concert to raise $20,000? Given the current cost structure, current tuition rates, and projected enrollments, how much money must Cornell University raise from other sources?

Key Assumptions

CVP analysis is subject to a number of assumptions. Although these assumptions do not negate the usefulness of CVP models, especially for a single product or service, they do suggest the need for further analysis before plans are finalized. Among the more important assumptions are:

1. *All costs are classified as fixed or variable.* This assumption is most reasonable when analyzing the profitability of a specific event (such as a concert) or the profitability of an organization that produces a single product or service on a continuous basis.

2. *The total cost function is linear within the relevant range.* This assumption is often valid within a relevant range of normal operations, but over the entire range of possible activity, changes in efficiency are likely to result in a nonlinear cost function.

3. *The total revenue function is linear within the relevant range.* Unit selling prices are assumed constant over the range of possible volumes. This implies a purely competitive market for final products or services. In some economic models in which demand responds to price changes, the revenue function is nonlinear. In these situations, the linear approximation is accurate only within a limited range of activity.

4. *The analysis is for a single product, or the sales mix of multiple products is constant.* The **sales mix** refers to the relative portion of unit or dollar sales derived from each product or service. If products have different selling prices and costs, changes in the mix affect CVP model results.

5. *There is only one cost driver: unit or sales dollar volume.* In a complex organization it is seldom possible to represent the multitude of factors that drive cost with a single cost driver.

When applied to a single product (such as pounds of potato chips), service (such as the number of pages printed), or event (such as the number of tickets sold to a banquet), it is reasonable to assume the single independent variable is the cost driver. The total costs associated with the single product, service, or event during a specific time period are often determined by this single activity cost driver.

Although cost-volume-profit analysis is often used to understand the overall operations of an organization or business segment, accuracy decreases as the scope of operations being analyzed increases.

RESEARCH INSIGHT

Three Out of Four *Is* Bad When You're Talking About Startup Failures The National Venture Capital Association estimates that 25 to 30 percent of venture-backed businesses fail. However, Shikhar Ghosh, a senior lecturer at Harvard Business School, asserts that three out of four U.S. venture-backed firms do not return investors' capital. He studied 2,000 companies over the period 2004 through 2010 and concluded that venture capitalists "bury their dead very quietly." Ghosh states that venture-backed firms tend to fail after their fourth year when venture capital injections cease, but that non-venture-capital-backed companies fail even more frequently because they lack the cash infusions during their first four years. The U.S. Bureau of Labor Statistics reports that 60 percent of startups survive until year 3, but only 35 percent survive to year 10.

Source: Deborah Gage, "The Venture Capital Secret: 3 Out of 4 Start-Ups Fail," *Wall Street Journal*, September 20, 2012.

Profit Formula

The profit associated with a product, service, or event is equal to the difference between total revenues and total costs as follows:

$$\pi = R - Y$$

where

$$\pi = \textbf{Profit}$$
$$\textbf{R} = \textbf{Total revenues}$$
$$\textbf{Y} = \textbf{Total costs}$$

The revenues are a function of the unit sales volume and the unit selling price, while total costs for a time period are a function of the fixed costs per period and the unit variable costs as follows:

$$\textbf{R} = \textbf{pX}$$
$$\textbf{Y} = \textbf{a} + \textbf{bX}$$

where

$$\textbf{p} = \textbf{Unit selling price}$$
$$\textbf{a} = \textbf{Fixed costs}$$
$$\textbf{b} = \textbf{Unit variable costs}$$
$$\textbf{X} = \textbf{Unit sales}$$

The equation for profit can then be expanded to include the above details of the total revenue and total cost equations as follows:

$$\pi = \textbf{pX} - (\textbf{a} + \textbf{bX})$$

Using information on the selling price, fixed costs per period, and variable costs per unit, this formula is used to predict profit at any specified activity level.

To illustrate, assume that DuPont's only product is a high-quality agricultural product that it manufactures and sells to wholesale distributors at $8.00 per carton. Applying inventory minimization techniques, DuPont does not maintain inventories of raw materials or finished goods. Instead, newly purchased raw materials are delivered directly to the factory, and finished goods are loaded directly onto trucks for shipment. DuPont's variable and fixed costs follow.

1. **Direct materials** refer to the cost of the primary raw materials converted into finished goods. Because the consumption of raw materials increases as the quantity of goods produced increases, *direct materials represents a variable cost*. DuPont's raw materials consist primarily of organic and chemical compounds and packing supplies such as boxes. DuPont also treats the costs of purchasing, receiving, and inspecting raw materials as part of the cost of direct materials. Assume that all together, these costs are $1.00 per carton of finished product.

2. **Direct labor** refers to wages earned by production employees for the time they spend working on the conversion of raw materials into finished goods. Based on DuPont's manufacturing procedures, *direct labor represents a variable cost*. Further assume these costs are $0.25 per carton.

3. **Variable manufacturing overhead** includes all other variable costs associated with converting raw materials into finished goods. Assume DuPont's variable manufacturing overhead costs include the costs of lubricants for cutting and packaging machines, electricity to operate these machines, and the cost to move materials between receiving and shipping docks and the mixing and packaging machines. These costs are $1.25 per carton.

4. **Variable selling and administrative costs** include all variable costs other than those directly associated with converting raw materials into finished goods. Assume at DuPont, these costs include sales commissions, transportation of finished goods to wholesale distributors, and the cost of processing the receipt and disbursement of cash. These costs are $0.50 per carton.

5. **Fixed manufacturing overhead** includes all fixed costs associated with converting raw materials into finished goods. Suppose DuPont's fixed manufacturing costs include the depreciation, property taxes, and insurance on buildings and machines used for manufacturing, the salaries of manufacturing supervisors, and the fixed portion of electricity used to light the factory. Further assume these costs are $5,000.00 per month.

6. **Fixed selling and administrative costs** include all fixed costs other than those directly associated with converting raw materials into finished goods. These costs include the salaries of DuPont's divisional manager and many other staff personnel such as accounting and marketing. Also included are depreciation, property taxes, insurance on facilities used for administrative purposes, and any related utilities costs. Assume these costs are $10,000.00 per month.

DuPont's hypothetical variable and fixed costs are summarized here.

Variable Costs per Carton			Fixed Costs per Month	
Manufacturing			Manufacturing overhead.	$ 5,000.00
Direct materials	$1.00		Selling and administrative.	10,000.00
Direct labor.	0.25		Total.	$15,000.00
Manufacturing overhead	1.25	$2.50		
Selling and administrative.		0.50		
Total.		$3.00		

The cost estimation techniques discussed in Chapter 2 can be used to determine many detailed costs. Least-squares regression, for example, might be used to determine the variable and monthly fixed amount of electricity used in manufacturing. Assume DuPont manufactures and sells a single product on a continuous basis with all sales to distributors under standing contracts. Therefore, it is reasonable to assume that in the short run, DuPont's total monthly costs respond to a single cost driver, cartons sold. Combining all this information, DuPont's profit equation is assumed to be:

$$\text{Profit} = \$8.00X - (\$15,000.00 + \$3.00X)$$

where

$$X = \text{cartons sold}$$

Using this equation, DuPont's profit at a volume of 5,400 units is $12,000.00, computed as ($8.00 × 5,400) − [$15,000.00 + ($3.00 × 5,400)].

CONTRIBUTION AND FUNCTIONAL INCOME STATEMENTS

Contribution Income Statement

To provide more detailed information on anticipated or actual financial results at a particular sales volume, a contribution income statement is often prepared. DuPont's hypothetical contribution income statement for a volume of 5,400 units is in Exhibit 3.1. In a **contribution income statement**, costs are classified according to behavior as variable or fixed, and the **contribution margin** (the difference between total revenues and total variable costs) that goes toward covering fixed costs and providing a profit is emphasized.

LO2 Prepare and contrast contribution and functional income statements.

EXHIBIT 3.1	Contribution Income Statement

DUPONT COMPANY
Contribution Income Statement
For a Monthly Volume of 5,400 Cartons

Sales (5,400 × $8.00)		$43,200
Less variable costs		
Direct materials (5,400 × $1.00)	$ 5,400	
Direct labor (5,400 × $0.25).	1,350	
Manufacturing overhead (5,400 × $1.25)	6,750	
Selling and administrative (5,400 × $0.50)	2,700	(16,200)
Contribution margin		27,000
Less fixed costs		
Manufacturing overhead.	5,000	
Selling and administrative.	10,000	(15,000)
Profit.		$12,000

Functional Income Statement

Contrast the contribution income statement in Exhibit 3.1 with DuPont's hypothetical income statement in Exhibit 3.2. This statement is called a **functional income statement** because costs are classified according to function (rather than behavior), such as manufacturing, selling, and administrative. This is the type of income statement typically included in corporate annual reports.

A problem with a functional income statement is the difficulty of relating it to the profit formula in which costs are classified according to behavior rather than function. The relationship between sales volume, costs, and profits is not readily apparent in a functional income statement. Consequently, we emphasize contribution income statements because they provide better information to internal decision makers.

EXHIBIT 3.2	Functional Income Statement		
DUPONT COMPANY **Functional Income Statement** **For a Monthly Volume of 5,400 Cartons**			
Sales (5,400 × $8.00)			$43,200
Less cost of goods sold			
Direct materials (5,400 × $1.00)		$ 5,400	
Direct labor (5,400 × $0.25).		1,350	
Variable manufacturing overhead (5,400 × $1.25).		6,750	
Fixed manufacturing overhead		5,000	(18,500)
Gross margin.			24,700
Less other expenses			
Variable selling and administrative (5,400 × $0.50)		2,700	
Fixed selling and administrative		10,000	(12,700)
Profit.			$12,000

Analysis Using Contribution Margin Ratio

While the contribution income statement (shown in Exhibit 3.1) presents information on total sales revenue, total variable costs, and so forth, it is sometimes useful to present information on a per-unit or portion of sales basis.

	Total	Per Unit	Ratio to Sales
Sales (5,400 units)	$43,200	$8	1.000
Variable costs	(16,200)	(3)	(0.375)
Contribution margin	27,000	$5	0.625
Fixed costs	(15,000)		
Profit.	$12,000		

The per-unit information assists in short-range planning. The **unit contribution margin** is the difference between the unit selling price and the unit variable costs. It is the amount, $5.00 in this case, that each unit contributes toward covering fixed costs and earning a profit.

The contribution margin is widely used in **sensitivity analysis** (the study of the responsiveness of a model to changes in one or more of its independent variables). DuPont's income statement is an economic model of the firm, and the unit contribution margin indicates how sensitive DuPont's income model is to changes in unit sales. If, for example, sales increase by 100 cartons per month, the increase in profit is readily determined by multiplying the 100-carton increase in sales by the $5 unit contribution margin as follows:

100 (carton sales increase) × $5 (unit contribution margin) = $500 (profit increase)

There is no increase in fixed costs, so the new profit level becomes $12,500 ($12,000 + $500) per month.

When expressed as a ratio to sales, the sales margin is identified as the **contribution margin ratio**. It is the portion of each dollar of sales revenue contributed toward covering fixed costs and earning a profit. In the abbreviated income statement above, the portion of each dollar of sales revenue contributed toward covering fixed costs and earning a profit is $0.625 ($27,000 ÷ $43,200). This is DuPont's assumed contribution margin ratio. If sales revenue increases by $800 per month, the increase in profits is computed as follows:

$800 (sales increase) × 0.625 (contribution margin ratio) = $500 (profit increase)

The contribution margin ratio is especially useful in situations involving several products or when unit sales information is not available.

BREAK-EVEN POINT AND PROFIT PLANNING

The **break-even point** occurs at the unit or dollar sales volume when total revenues equal total costs. The break-even point is of great interest to management. Until break-even sales are reached, the product, service, event, or business segment of interest operates at a loss. Beyond this point, increasing levels of profits are achieved. Also, management often wants to know the **margin of safety**, the amount by which actual or planned sales exceed the break-even point. Other questions of interest include the probability of exceeding the break-even sales volume and the effect of some proposed change on the break-even point.

LO3 Apply cost-volume-profit analysis to find a break-even point and for preliminary profit planning.

Determining Break-Even Point

In determining the break-even point, the equation for total revenues is set equal to the equation for total costs and then solved for the break-even unit sales volume. Using the general equations for total revenues and total costs, the following results are obtained. Setting total revenues equal to total costs:

$$\text{Total revenues} = \text{Total costs}$$
$$pX = a + bX$$

Solving for the break-even sales volume:

$$pX - bX = a$$
$$(p - b)X = a$$
$$X = a/(p - b)$$

In words:

$$\text{Break-even unit sales volume} = \frac{\text{Fixed costs}}{\text{Selling price per unit} - \text{Variable costs per unit}}$$

Because the denominator is the unit contribution margin, the break-even point is also computed by dividing fixed costs by the unit contribution margin:

$$\text{Break-even unit sales volume} = \frac{\text{Fixed costs}}{\text{Unit contribution margin}}$$

With an assumed $5 unit contribution margin and fixed costs of $15,000 per month, DuPont's break-even point is 3,000 units per month ($15,000 ÷ $5). Stated another way, at a $5 per-unit contribution margin, 3,000 units of sales are required to cover $15,000 of fixed costs. With a break-even point of 3,000 units, the monthly margin of safety and expected profit for a sales volume of 5,400 units are 2,400 units (5,400 expected unit sales − 3,000 break-even sales) and $12,000 (2,400 unit margin of safety × $5 unit contribution margin), respectively.

The break-even point concept is applicable to a wide variety of business and personal planning situations. The following Research Insight box illustrates how a personal financial planner might use break-even point concepts to assist a client making a retirement decision.

RESEARCH INSIGHT

Determining the Cash Break-Even Point for Delaying Retirement Social Security retirement benefits are a function of years worked, contributions to the Social Security System, and the age at which the recipient files for Social Security retirement benefits. Currently, persons retiring at age 67 are entitled to "full" retirement benefits, while those retiring at age 62 are eligible for only 70 percent of "full" benefits. A person contemplating retirement at age 62 might ask: (1) how large is the reduction in benefits and (2) what is the break-even age at which the benefits from delaying retirement until age 67 equals the cumulative benefits from retiring at age 62?

An individual with the analytic skills obtained from a managerial accounting course can readily determine the answers to these questions after consulting the Social Security web site www.ssa.gov. Others might consult a personal financial planner.

(1) Assume the individual's full Social Security retirement benefits at age 67 are $2,265 per month. If that person started receiving benefits at age 62 their monthly benefits are reduced by 30 percent or $679.50 ($2,265 × 0.30) to $1,585.50.

(2) With retirement at age 62, the early retiree would receive total benefits of $95,130 ($1,585.50 × 12 months × 5 years) by age 67, the normal "full" age. Treating this as a fixed amount to be recovered by the subsequent incremental monthly benefits of $679.50 from delaying the receipt of monthly benefits to age 67, the break-even age is computed as follows:

Months beyond age 67 = $95,130/$679.50 = 140 months or 11.67 years.

Hence, the break-even age is 78.67 years (67 + 11.67).

The analysis suggests that life expectancy is an important consideration in deciding when to start taking Social Security benefits.

Note that this analysis does not consider any return on the $95,130 that might be earned by investing the benefits received during early retirement. Such returns would increase the break-even age. Nor does it consider the lost wages that could have been earned between age 62 and age 67.

Source: www.ssa.gov

Profit Planning

Establishing profit objectives is an important part of planning in for-profit organizations. Profit objectives are stated in many ways. They can be set as a percentage of last year's profits, as a percentage of total assets at the start of the current year, or as a percentage of owners' equity. They might be based on a profit trend, or they might be expressed as a percentage of sales. The economic outlook for the firm's products as well as anticipated changes in products, costs, and technology are also considered in establishing profit objectives.

Before incorporating profit plans into a detailed budget, it is useful to obtain some preliminary information on the feasibility of those plans. Cost-volume-profit analysis is one way of doing this. By manipulating cost-volume-profit relationships, management can determine the sales volume corresponding to a desired profit. Management might then evaluate the feasibility of this sales volume. If the profit plans are feasible, a complete budget might be developed for this activity level. The required sales volume might be infeasible because of market conditions or because the required volume exceeds production or service capacity, in which case management must lower its profit objective or consider other ways of achieving it. Alternatively, the required sales volume might be less than management believes the firm is capable of selling, in which case management might raise its profit objective.

Assume that DuPont's management desires to know the unit sales volume required to achieve a monthly profit of $18,000. Using the profit formula, the required unit sales volume is determined by setting profits equal to $18,000 and solving for X, the unit sales volume.

$$\textbf{Profit} = \textbf{Total revenues} - \textbf{Total costs}$$

$$\$18,000 = \$8X - (\$15,000 + \$3X)$$

Solving for X

$$\$8X - \$3X = \$15,000 + \$18,000$$

$$X = (\$15,000 + \$18,000) \div \$5$$

$$= \textbf{6,600 units}$$

The total contribution must cover the desired profit as well as the fixed costs. Hence, the target sales volume required to achieve a desired profit is computed as the fixed costs plus the desired profit, all divided by the unit contribution margin.

$$\textbf{Target unit sales volume} = \frac{\textbf{Fixed costs} + \textbf{Desired profit}}{\textbf{Unit contribution margin}}$$

The Business Insight box below considers CVP analysis for Costco, a large wholesale club whose strategic position for consumer goods focuses on cost leadership.

BUSINESS INSIGHT

Cost, Volume, What Profit? Costco customers are loyal. Its competitors have lost customers to Internet retailers, but Costco's sales have grown by nearly 40 percent over the past several years. Costco's customers are happy, its employees are happy, and its management is happy. The company's workers are paid on average $20.89 per hour, which is nearly 65 percent higher than the average Wal-Mart worker. Nearly 90 percent of its employees have company-sponsored health insurance, whereas slightly over half of Wal-Mart workers do. Employees rarely leave the company—its turnover rate is only 5 percent.

But once Costco accounts for its real estate costs and wages for its employees, its merchandise barely breaks even. The company passes along its cost savings from buying its merchandise in bulk to the consumer, which ensures the company will have plenty of volume in its CVP analysis. But how has the company been in business for three decades without turning a profit on its merchandise? The company's profit is earned from its annual membership dues. Each member pays $55 per year, but clearly Costco's customers believe this is a good bargain. Ninety percent of members renew their membership year over year. By selling their products to the customer at their break-even points, Costco will always make its necessary profit. Now that's a business model.

Source: Brad Stone, "Costco CEO Craig Jelinek Leads the Cheapest, Happiest Company in the World," *Bloomberg Businessweek*, June 6, 2013.

Cost-Volume-Profit Graph

A **cost-volume-profit graph** illustrates the relationships among activity volume, total revenues, total costs, and profits. Its usefulness comes from highlighting the break-even point and depicting revenue, cost, and profit relationships over a range of activity. This representation allows management to view the relative amount of important variables at any graphed volume. DuPont's hypothetical monthly CVP graph is in Exhibit 3.3. Total revenues and total costs are measured on the vertical axis, with unit sales measured on the horizontal axis. Separate lines are drawn for total variable costs, total costs, and total revenues. The vertical distance between the total revenue and the total cost lines depicts the amount of profit or loss at a given volume. Losses occur when total revenues are less than total costs; profits occur when total revenues exceed total costs.

The total contribution margin is shown by the difference between the total revenue and the total variable cost lines. Observe that as unit sales increase, the contribution margin first goes to cover the fixed costs. Beyond the break-even point, any additional contribution margin provides a profit.

Profit-Volume Graph

In cost-volume-profit graphs, profits are represented by the difference between total revenues and total costs. When management is primarily interested in the impact of changes in sales volume on profits and less interested in the related revenues and costs, a **profit-volume graph** is sometimes used. A profit-volume graph illustrates the relationship between volume and profits; it does not show revenues and costs. Profits are read directly from a profit-volume graph, rather than being computed as the difference between total revenues and total costs. Profit-volume graphs are developed by plotting either unit sales or total revenues on the horizontal axis.

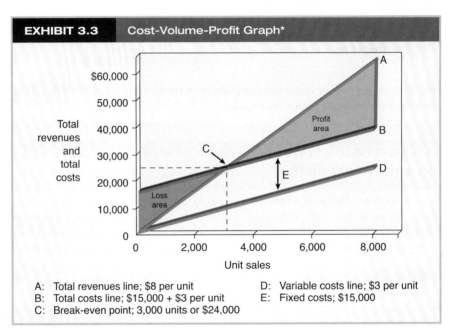

EXHIBIT 3.3 Cost-Volume-Profit Graph*

A: Total revenues line; $8 per unit
B: Total costs line; $15,000 + $3 per unit
C: Break-even point; 3,000 units or $24,000
D: Variable costs line; $3 per unit
E: Fixed costs; $15,000

* The three lines are developed as follows:

1. Total variable costs line, D, is drawn between the origin and total variable costs at an arbitrary sales volume. At 8,000 units, total variable costs are $24,000.
2. Total revenues line, A, is drawn through the origin and a point representing total revenues at some arbitrary sales volume. At 8,000 units, DuPont's hypothetical total revenues are $64,000.
3. Total cost line, B, is computed by layering fixed costs, $15,000 in this case, on top of total variable costs. This gives a vertical axis intercept of $15,000 and total costs of $39,000 at 8,000 units.

DuPont's assumed monthly profit-volume graph, is presented in Exhibit 3.4. Profit or loss is measured on the vertical axis, and volume (total revenues) is measured on the horizontal axis, which intersects the vertical axis at zero profit. A single line, representing total profit, is drawn intersecting the vertical axis at zero sales volume with a loss equal to the fixed costs. The profit line crosses the horizontal axis at the break-even sales volume. The profit or loss at any volume is depicted by the vertical difference between the profit line and the horizontal axis. The slope of the profit line is determined by the contribution margin. The greater the contribution margin ratio or the unit contribution margin, the steeper the slope of the profit line.

EXHIBIT 3.4   Profit-Volume Graph*

A: Total profit or loss line
B: Break-even point; $24,000

* The profit line is drawn by determining and plotting profit or loss at two different volumes and then drawing a straight line through the plotted values. Perhaps the easiest values to select are the loss at a volume of zero (with a loss equal to the fixed costs) and the volume at which the profit line crosses the horizontal axis (this is the break-even volume).

BUSINESS INSIGHT

Smart Managers Consider Not Only Volume, But Also Duration   Several years ago, video game developer Activision had to make a tough decision. A segment of development companies was creating products for the "casual" gamers market. Examples include Zynga Inc.'s "Words with Friends" and "Farmville." These games are largely played on mobile platforms and sell at extremely low price points, often in the $1–2 range or even free of charge.

Although Activision's managers conceded that casual game revenues were likely in the short run, they didn't think the duration of the revenue stream would be sufficient to recoup its investment. Instead, Activision plowed its profits back into established games like "Call of Duty" and "World of Warcraft," while developing a new game, "Skylanders." Consumers can augment the video game with collectible characters, each of which "comes to life" when placed on a game portal. Characters, sold separately, retail for approximately $8 each, and Activision estimates unit sales to date of over 100 million units. Some characters have fetched as much as $2,400 on eBay. Activision's experience shows that any CVP analysis should incorporate the dimension of time to provide the most reliable decision outcomes.

Source: Cliff Edwards, "Activision, the Anti-Zynga," *Bloomberg Businessweek*, October 4, 2012.

Impact of Income Taxes

Income taxes are imposed on individuals and for-profit organizations by government agencies. The amount of an individual's or organization's income tax is determined by laws that specify the calculation of taxable income (the income subject to tax) and the calculation of the amount of tax on taxable income. Income taxes are computed as a percentage of taxable income, with increases in taxable income usually subject to progressively higher tax rates. The laws governing the computation of taxable income differ in many ways from the accounting principles that guide the computation of accounting income. Consequently, taxable income and accounting income are seldom the same.

In the early stages of profit planning, income taxes are sometimes incorporated in CVP models by assuming that taxable income and accounting income are identical and that the tax rate is constant. Although these assumptions are seldom true, they are useful for assisting management in developing an early prediction of the sales volume required to earn a desired after-tax profit. Once management has developed a general plan, this early prediction should be refined with the advice of tax experts.

Assuming taxes are imposed at a constant rate per dollar of before-tax profit, income taxes are computed as before-tax profit multipled by the tax rate. After-tax profit is equal to before-tax profit minus income taxes.

$$\textbf{After-tax profit} = \textbf{Before-tax profit} - (\textbf{Before-tax profit} \times \textbf{Tax rate})$$

After-tax profit can also be expressed as before-tax profit times 1 minus the tax rate.

$$\textbf{After-tax profit} = \textbf{Before-tax profit} \times (1 - \textbf{Tax rate})$$

This formula can be rearranged to isolate before-tax profit as follows:

$$\textbf{Before-tax profit} = \frac{\textbf{After-tax profit}}{(1 - \textbf{Tax rate})}$$

Since all costs and revenues in the profit formula are expressed on a before-tax basis, the most straight-forward way of determining the unit sales volume required to earn a desired after-tax profit is to:

1. Determine the required before-tax profit.
2. Substitute the required before-tax profit into the profit formula.
3. Solve for the required unit sales volume.

To illustrate, assume that DuPont is subject to a 40 percent tax rate and that management desires to earn an after-tax profit of $18,000 for November 2013. The required before-tax profit is $30,000 [$18,000 ÷ (1 − 0.40)], and the unit sales volume required to earn this profit is 9,000 units [($15,000 + $30,000) ÷ $5].

Income taxes increase the sales volume required to earn a desired after-tax profit. A 40 percent tax rate increased the sales volume required for DuPont to earn a profit of $18,000 from 6,600 to 9,000 units. These amounts are verified in Exhibit 3.5.

Another way to remember the computation of before-tax profit is shown on the right side of Exhibit 3.5. The before-tax profit represents 100 percent of the pie, with 40 percent going to income taxes and 60 percent remaining after taxes. Working back from the remaining 60 percent ($18,000), we can determine the 100 percent (before-tax profit) by dividing after-tax profit by 0.60.

EXHIBIT 3.5	Contribution Income Statement with Income Taxes		

DUPONT COMPANY
Contribution Income Statement
Planned for the Month of November 2013

Sales (9,000 × $8.00)		$72,000	
Less variable costs			
Direct materials (9,000 × $1.00)	$ 9,000		
Direct labor (9,000 × $0.25)................................	2,250		
Manufacturing overhead (9,000 × $1.25).....................	11,250		
Selling and administrative (9,000 × $0.50)....................	4,500	(27,000)	
Contribution margin		45,000	
Less fixed costs			
Manufacturing overhead....................................	5,000		
Selling and administrative..................................	10,000	(15,000)	
Before-tax profit		30,000	100%
Income taxes ($30,000 × 0.40).............................		(12,000)	(40)%
After-tax profit..		$18,000	60%

MID-CHAPTER REVIEW

Assume **Solo Cup Company** produces 16-ounce beverage containers. Further assume Solo sells the cups for $40 per box of 50 containers. Variable and fixed costs follow:

Variable Costs per Box			Fixed Costs per Month	
Manufacturing			Manufacturing overhead..........	$15,000
Direct materials..............	$15		Selling and administrative........	10,000
Direct labor..................	3		Total.........................	$25,000
Manufacturing overhead.......	10	$28		
Selling and administrative........		2		
Total........................		$30		

Suppose in September 2013, Solo produced and sold 3,000 boxes of beverage containers.

Required

a. Prepare a contribution income statement for September 2013.
b. Prepare a cost-volume-profit graph with unit sales as the independent variable. Label the revenue line, total costs line, fixed costs line, loss area, profit area, and break-even point. The recommended scale for the horizontal axis is 0 to 5,000 units, and the recommended scale for the vertical axis is $0 to $200,000.
c. Determine Solo's unit contribution margin and contribution margin ratio.
d. Determine Solo's monthly break-even point in units.
e. Determine the monthly dollar sales required for a monthly profit of $5,000 (ignoring taxes).
f. Assuming Solo is subject to a 40 percent income tax, determine the monthly unit sales required to produce a monthly after-tax profit of $4,500.

The solution is on pages 102–103.

MULTIPLE-PRODUCT COST-VOLUME-PROFIT ANALYSIS

Unit cost information is not always available or appropriate when analyzing cost-volume-profit relationships of multiple-product firms. Assuming the sales mix is constant, the contribution margin ratio (the portion of each sales dollar contributed toward covering fixed costs and earning a profit) can be used to determine the break-even dollar sales volume or the dollar sales volume required to achieve a desired profit. Treating a dollar of sales revenue as a unit, the break-even point in dollars is computed as fixed costs divided by the contribution margin ratio (the number of cents from each dollar of revenue contributed to covering fixed costs and providing a profit).

LO4 Analyze the profitability and sales mix of a multiple-product firm.

$$\text{Dollar break-even point} = \frac{\text{Fixed costs}}{\text{Contribution margin ratio}}$$

If unit selling price and cost information were not available, DuPont's dollar break-even point could be computed as $24,000 ($15,000 ÷ 0.625).

Corresponding computations can be made to find the dollar sales volume required to achieve a desired profit as follows.

$$\text{Target dollar sales volume} = \frac{\text{Fixed costs} + \text{Desired profit}}{\text{Contribution margin ratio}}$$

To achieve a desired profit of $12,000, DuPont needs sales of $43,200 [($15,000 + $12,000) ÷ 0.625].

These relationships can be graphed by placing sales dollars, rather than unit sales, on the horizontal axis. The slope of the variable and total cost lines, identified as the **variable cost ratio**, presents variable costs as a portion of sales revenue. It indicates the number of cents from each sales dollar required to pay variable costs. The Business Insight box on the following page demonstrates how CVP information can be developed from the published financial statements of a multiple-product firm.

Sales Mix Analysis

Sales mix refers to the relative portion of unit or dollar sales that are derived from each product. One of the limiting assumptions of the basic cost-volume-profit model is that the analysis is for a single product or the sales mix is constant. When the sales mix is constant, managers of multiple-product organizations can use the average unit contribution margin, or the average contribution margin ratio, to determine the break-even point or the sales volume required for a desired profit. Often, however, management is interested in the effect of a change in the sales mix rather than a change in the sales volume at a constant mix. In this situation, it is necessary to determine either the average unit contribution margin or the average contribution margin ratio for each alternative mix.

Unit Sales Analysis

Assume the Hallmark Cards sells two kinds of greeting cards, regular and deluxe. At a 1:1 (one-to-one) unit sales mix in which Hallmark sells one box of regular cards for every box of deluxe cards, assume the following revenue and cost information is available:

	Regular Box	Deluxe Box	Average Box*
Unit selling price	$4	$12	$8
Unit variable costs.	(3)	(3)	(3)
Unit contribution margin	$1	$ 9	$5
Fixed costs per month			$15,000

* At a 1:1 sales mix, the average unit contribution margin is $5[{($1 × 1 unit) + ($9 × 1 unit)} ÷ 2 units].

At a 1:1 mix, Hallmark's assumed monthly break-even sales volume is 3,000 units ($15,000 ÷ $5), consisting of 1,500 boxes of regular cards and 1,500 boxes of deluxe cards. The top line in Exhibit 3.6 represents the current sales mix. Suppose management wants to know the break-even sales volume if the unit sales mix became 3:1; that is, on average, a sale of 4 units contains 3 regular units and 1 deluxe unit. With no changes in the selling prices or variable costs of individual products, the average contribution margin becomes $3[{($1 × 3 units) + ($9 × 1 unit)} ÷ 4 units], and the revised break-even sales volume is 5,000 units ($15,000 ÷ $3). The revised break-even sales volume includes 3,750 boxes of regular cards [5,000 × $\frac{3}{4}$] and 1,250 boxes of deluxe cards [5,000 × $\frac{1}{4}$].

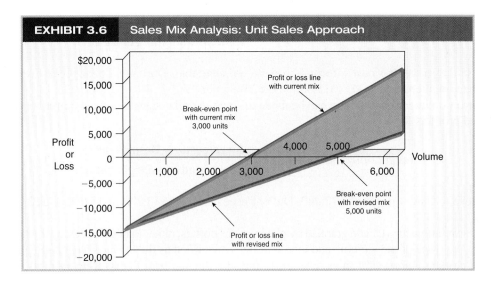

EXHIBIT 3.6   Sales Mix Analysis: Unit Sales Approach

The bottom line in Exhibit 3.6 represents the revised sales mix. Because a greater portion of the revised mix consists of lower contribution margin regular cards, the shift in the mix increases the break-even point.

BUSINESS INSIGHT

Using CVP for Financial Analysis and Prediction   Williams-Sonoma operates a chain of 581 merchandise retail stores in the U.S. and Canada. Their mission is to enhance their customers' lives at home. Condensed 2011 and 2012 income statements in millions follow.

	For the Year Ending	
	January 29, 2012	January 30, 2011
Net sales	$3,721	$3,504
Cost of sales and operating expenses.	(3,484)	(3,304)
Operating profit.	$ 237	$ 200

We can determine Williams-Sonoma's cost-volume-profit relationships and predict future profits for a given level of sales after using the high-low method to develop cost estimating equations. First determine variable costs as a percent of sales:

$$\text{Variable cost ratio} = \frac{\$3,484 - \$3,304}{\$3,721 - \$3,504} = \underline{\underline{0.8295}}$$

Next determine annual fixed costs by calculating and subtracting the variable costs of either period (revenues multiplied by the variable cost ratio) from the corresponding total costs. Using 2012 revenues and costs annual fixed costs are determined as follows:

$$\text{Annual fixed costs} = \$3,484 - (\$3,721 \times 0.8295) = \underline{\underline{\$397}} \text{ million}$$

Williams-Sonoma's annual cost estimating equation is:

$$\text{Total annual costs} = \$397 \text{ million} + (0.8295 \times \text{Net sales})$$

Using the fixed costs and the contribution margin ratio (1 minus the variable cost ratio) Williams-Sonoma's break-even point in sales dollars is computed.

$$\text{Break-even point} = \$397 \text{ million}/(1 - 0.8295) = \underline{\underline{\$2,328}} \text{ million}$$

For 2013, Williams-Sonoma's net sales and operating profits were $4,043 million and $257 million. Using the CVP relationships developed from 2011 and 2012 data, the predicted 2013 operating profits are $292 million $4,043 − [($4,043 × 0.8295) + $397]. In this case, because of Williams-Sonoma's stable cost structure, the model error is small.

Sales Dollar Analysis

The preceding analysis focused on units and the unit contribution margin. An alternative approach focuses on sales dollars and the contribution margin ratio. Following this approach, the sales mix is expressed in terms of sales dollars.

Assume Hallmark's current sales dollars are 25 percent from regular cards and 75 percent from deluxe cards. The following display indicates the contribution margin ratios at the current sales mix and monthly volume of 5,400 units.

	Regular	Deluxe	Total
Unit sales.	2,700	2,700	
Selling price.	$4.00	$12.00	
Sales	$10,800	$32,400	$43,200
Variable costs	8,100	8,100	16,200
Contribution margin	$ 2,700	$24,300	$27,000
Contribution margin ratio	0.25	0.75	0.625

If monthly fixed costs are $15,000, Hallmark's current break-even sales revenue is $24,000 ($15,000 ÷ 0.625), consisting of $6,000 from regular cards ($24,000 × 0.25) and $18,000 from Deluxe cards ($24,000 × 0.75). The top line in Exhibit 3.7 illustrates the current sales mix.

Now suppose management wants to know the break-even sales volume if the dollar sales mix became 70 percent regular and 30 percent deluxe. With no changes in the selling prices or variable costs of individual products, the total contribution margin ratio becomes 0.40 [(0.25 × 0.70) + (0.75 × 0.30)], and the revised break-even sales volume is $37,500 ($15,000 ÷ 0.40). The revised break-even sales volume includes $26,250 from regular cards ($37,500 × 0.70) and $11,250 from deluxe cards (37,500 × 0.30).

The bottom line in Exhibit 3.7 represents the revised sales mix. Because a greater portion of the revised mix consists of lower contribution ratio regular cards, the shift in the mix increases the break-even point.

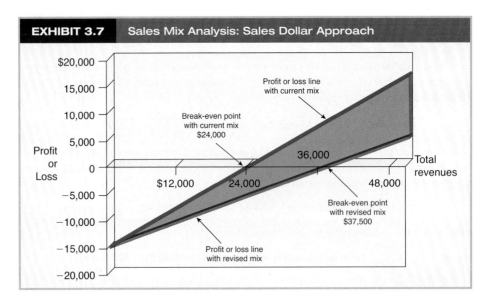

EXHIBIT 3.7 Sales Mix Analysis: Sales Dollar Approach

Sales mix analysis is important in multiple-product or service organizations. Management is just as concerned with the mix of products as with the total unit or dollar sales volume. A shift in the sales mix can have a significant impact on the bottom line. Profits may decline, even when sales increase, if the mix shifts toward products or services with lower unit margins. Conversely, profits may increase, even when sales decline, if the mix shifts toward products or services with higher unit margins. Other things being equal, managers of for-profit organizations strive to increase sales of high-margin products or services.

ANALYSIS OF OPERATING LEVERAGE

LO5 Apply operating leverage ratio to assess opportunities for profit and the risks of loss.

Operating leverage refers to the extent that an organization's costs are fixed. The **operating leverage ratio** is computed as the contribution margin divided by before-tax profit as follows.

$$\text{Operating leverage ratio} = \frac{\text{Contribution margin}}{\text{Before-tax profits}}$$

The rationale underlying this computation is that as fixed costs are substituted for variable costs, the contribution margin as a percentage of income before taxes increases. Hence, a high degree of operating leverage signals the existence of a high portion of fixed costs. As noted in Chapter 1, the shift from labor-based to automated activities has resulted in a decrease in variable costs and an increase in fixed costs, producing an increase in operating leverage.

Operating leverage is a measure of risk and opportunity. Other things being equal, the higher the degree of operating leverage, the greater the opportunity for profit with increases in sales. Conversely, a higher degree of operating leverage also magnifies the risk of large losses with a decrease in sales.

	Operating Leverage	
	High	Low
Profit opportunity with sales increase	High	Low
Risk of loss with sales decrease	High	Low

In addition to indicating the relative amount of fixed costs in the overall cost structure of a company, the operating leverage ratio can be used to measure the expected change in net income resulting from a change in sales. The operating leverage ratio multiplied times the percentage change in sales equals the percentage change in income before taxes. For example, if DuPont currently has an operating leverage ratio of 4.0, a change in sales of 12.5 percent will result in a 50 percent change in income before taxes; whereas, suppose Monsanto has an operating leverage ratio of 5.2, which will result in an increase in sales of 65%.

	Current		Projected	
	DuPont	Monsanto	DuPont	Monsanto
Unit selling price	$ 8.00	$ 8.00	$ 8.00	$ 8.00
Unit variable costs....................	(3.00)	(1.50)	(3.00)	(1.50)
Unit contribution margin	5.00	6.50	5.00	6.50
Unit sales...........................	× 4,000	× 4,000	× 4,500	× 4,500
Contribution margin	20,000	26,000	22,500	29,250
Fixed costs	(15,000)	(21,000)	(15,000)	(21,000)
Before-tax profit	$ 5,000	$ 5,000	$ 7,500	$ 8,250
Contribution margin	$20,000	$26,000		
Before-tax profit	÷ 5,000	÷ 5,000		
Operating leverage ratio	4.0	5.2		
Percent increase in sales			12.5%	12.5%
Percent increase in income before sales...			50%	65%

Although both companies have identical before-tax profits at a sales volume of 4,000 units, assume Monsanto has a higher degree of operating leverage and its profits vary more with changes in sales volume.

If sales are projected to increase by 12.5 percent, from 4,000 to 4,500 units, the percentage of increase in each firm's profits is computed as the percent change in sales multiplied by the degree of operating leverage.

	DuPont	Monsanto
Increase in sales	12.5%	12.5%
Degree of operating leverage.......................................	× 4.0	× 5.2
Increase in profits	50.0%	65.0%

As noted in the following Business Insight box, operating leverage is an important consideration when changes in demand, and consequently sales, occur.

Management is interested in measures of operating leverage to determine how sensitive profits are to changes in sales. Risk-averse managers strive to maintain a lower operating leverage, even if this results in some loss of profits. One way to reduce operating leverage is to use more direct labor and less automated equipment. Another way is to contract outside organizations to perform tasks that could be done internally. While operating leverage is a useful analytic tool, long-run success comes from keeping the overall level of costs down, while providing customers with the products or services they want at competitive prices.

BUSINESS INSIGHT

Financial Flexibility Is Imperative When Operating Below the Break-Even Point The recent economic recession has forced U.S. automakers to reduce costs by closing 18 factories, many of which were owned by **GM** and **Chrysler**. Chrysler was subsequently acquired by Italian automaker **Fiat**. However, European automakers also have experienced a downturn in demand. For example, Fiat's Mirafiori plant in Turin, Italy, used to employ tens of thousands of workers to produce 300,000 cars each year. Last year, the plant produced only 50,000 cars, while keeping 5,500 workers employed at the plant.

Half of Europe's auto factories are operating below their break-even points (break-even is generally at 75 percent capacity in the European factories). Because many of the workers are unionized, the factories are limited in the number of workers they can permanently lay off. Instead, many workers are on forced leave for years, receiving part of their pay from Fiat and part from the Italian government. Managers must think about how contractual obligations limit their financial flexibility when performing CVP analysis.

Source: Gilles Castonguay, "At Fiat, Getting Paid Not to Work," *Wall Street Journal*, August 10, 2013, pp. B1–B2.

YOU MAKE THE CALL

You are the Division Manager As manager of a division responsible for both production and sales of products and, hence, division profits, you are looking for ways to leverage the profits of your division to a higher level. You are considering changing your cost structure to include more fixed costs and less variable costs by automating some of the production activities currently performed by people. What are some of the considerations that you should keep in mind as you ponder this decision? [Answer, p. 88]

CHAPTER-END REVIEW

Suppose the Coffee Bean has a new shop in a Cambridge village shopping center that sells high-end teas and coffees. Further, suppose they have added smoothie drinks to their product line. Below are the assumed sales and cost data for the company:

	Coffee	Tea	Smoothie
Sales price per (12 oz.) serving..................	$1.35	$1.25	$1.95
Variable cost per serving	0.60	0.45	0.75
Fixed costs per month $8,000			

Suppose the company sells each month an average of 6,000 servings of coffee, 3,750 servings of tea, and 2,250 servings of smoothies.

Required

a. Calculate the current before-tax profit, contribution margin ratio, and sales mix based on sales dollars.
b. Using a sales dollar analysis, calculate the monthly break-even point assuming the sales mix does not change.
c. Calculate Coffee Bean's operating leverage ratio. If sales increase by 20 percent, by how much will before-tax income be expected to change? If sales decrease by 20 percent, by how much will before-tax income be expected to change?

The solution is on page 104.

APPENDIX 3A: Profitability Analysis with Unit and Nonunit Cost Drivers

A major limitation of cost-volume-profit analysis and the related contribution income statement is the exclusive use of unit-level activity cost drivers. Even when multiple products are considered, the CVP approach either restates volume in terms of an average unit or in terms of a dollar of sales volume. Additionally, CVP analysis does not consider other categories of cost drivers.

We now expand profitability analysis to incorporate nonunit cost drivers. While the addition of multiple levels of cost drivers makes it difficult to develop graphical relationships (illustrating the impact of cost driver changes on revenues, costs, and profits), it is possible to modify the traditional contribution income statement to incorporate a hierarchy of cost drivers. The expanded framework is not only more accurate, but it encourages management to ask important questions concerning costs and profitability.

Multi-Level Contribution Income Statement

To illustrate the use of profitability analysis with unit and nonunit cost drivers, assume Anthropologie, a multiple-product merchandising organization has the following cost hierarchy:

Unit-level activities
    Cost of goods sold . . . . $0.80 per sales dollar
Order-level activities
    Cost of processing order. . . . . $20 per order
Customer-level activities
    Mail, phone, sales visits, recordkeeping, etc. . . . . $200 per customer per year
Facility-level costs
    Depreciation, manager salaries, insurance, etc. . . . . $120,000 per year

Assume that Anthropologie is subject to a 40 percent income tax rate and has the following plans for the year 2014:

Sales $3,000,000
Number of sales orders. 3,200
Number of customers 400

While Anthropologie's plans could be summarized in a functional income statement, we have previously considered the limitations of such statements for management. Contribution income statements are preferred because they correspond to the cost classification scheme used in CVP analysis. In this case, Anthropologie's cost structure (unit level, order level, customer level, and facility level) does not correspond to the classification scheme used in traditional contribution income statements (variable and fixed). The problem occurs because traditional contribution income statements consider only unit-level cost drivers. When a larger set of unit and nonunit cost drivers is used for cost analysis, an expanded contribution income statement should be used for profitability analysis.

A hypothetical multi-level contribution income statement for Anthropologie is presented in Exhibit 3.8. Costs are separated using a cost hierarchy and there are several contribution margins, one for each level of costs that responds to a short-run change in activity. Suppose that in the case of Anthropologie, the contribution margins are at the unit level, order level, and customer level. Because the facility-level costs do not vary with short-run variations in activity, the final customer-level contribution goes to cover facility-level costs and to provide for a profit. If a company had a different activity cost hierarchy, it would use a different set of contribution margins.

EXHIBIT 3.8	Multi-Level Contribution Income Statement with Taxes

ANTHROPOLOGIE
Multi-Level Contribution Income Statement
For Year 2014

Sales	$3,000,000
Less unit-level costs	
Cost of goods sold ($3,000,000 × 0.80)	(2,400,000)
Unit-level contribution margin	600,000
Less order-level costs	
Cost of processing order (3,200 orders × $20)	(64,000)
Order-level contribution margin	536,000
Less customer-level costs	
Mail, phone, sales visits, recordkeeping, etc. (400 customers × $200)	(80,000)
Customer-level contribution margin.	456,000
Less facility-level costs	
Depreciation, manager salaries, insurance, etc.	(120,000)
Before-tax profit	336,000
Income taxes ($336,000 × 0.40).	(134,400)
After-tax profit.	$ 201,600

A number of additional questions of interest to management can be formulated and answered using the multi-level hierarchy. Consider the following examples:

■   Holding the number of sales orders and customers constant, what is the break-even dollar sales volume? The answer is found by treating all other costs as fixed and dividing the total nonunit-level costs by the contribution margin ratio. Here the contribution margin ratio indicates how many cents of each sales dollar is available for profits and costs above the unit level.

$$\begin{matrix} \text{Unit-level break-even point} \\ \text{in dollars with no changes} \\ \text{in other costs} \end{matrix} = \frac{\text{Current order-level costs} + \text{Current customer-level costs} + \text{Facility-level costs}}{\text{Contribution margin ratio}}$$

$$= (\$64{,}000 + \$80{,}000 + \$120{,}000) \div (1 - 0.80)$$

$$= \$1{,}320{,}000$$

■   What order size is required to break even on an individual order? Answering this question might help management to evaluate the desirability of establishing a minimum order size. To break even, each order must have a unit-level contribution equal to the order-level costs. Any additional contribution is used to cover customer- and facility-level costs and provide for a profit.

$$\text{Break-even order size} = \$20 \div (1 - 0.80)$$
$$= \$100$$

■   What sales volume is required to break even on an average customer? Answering this question might help management to evaluate the desirability of retaining certain customers. Based on the preceding information, an average customer places 8 orders per year (3,200 orders ÷ 400 customers). With costs of $20 per order and $200 per customer, the sales to an average customer must generate an annual contribution of $360 [($20 × 8) + $200]. Hence, the break-even level for an average customer is $1,800 [$360 ÷ (1 − 0.80)]. Management might consider discontinuing relations with customers with annual purchases of less than this amount. Alternatively, they might inquire as to whether such customers could be served in a less costly manner.

The concepts of multi-level break-even analysis and profitability analysis are finding increasing use as companies such as FedEx, Best Buy, and Bank of America strive to identify profitable and unprofitable customers. At FedEx, customers are sometimes rated as "the good, the bad, and the ugly." FedEx strives to retain the "good" profitable customers, turn the "bad" into profitable customers, and ignore the "ugly" who seem unlikely to become profitable.

Variations in Multi-Level Contribution Income Statement

Classification schemes should be designed to fit the organization and user needs. In Chapter 2, when analyzing the costs of a manufacturing company, we used a manufacturing cost hierarchy. While formatting issues can seem mundane and routine, format is important because the way information is presented encourages certain types of questions while discouraging others. Hence, management accountants must inquire as to user needs before developing management accounting reports, just as users of management accounting information should be knowledgeable enough to request appropriate information and know whether the information they are receiving is the information they need. With computers to reduce computational drudgery and to provide a wealth of available data, the most important issues involve identifying the important questions and presenting information to address those questions.

In the case of Anthropologie, we used a customer cost hierarchy with information presented in a single column. A multiple-column format is also useful for presenting and analyzing information. Assume that Anthropologie's managment believes that the differences between the in-store and internet-based markets are such that these markets could be better served with separate marketing activities. They would have two market segments, one for the in-store customers and one for internet-based customers, giving the following cost hierarchy:

1. Unit-level activities
2. Order-level activities
3. Customer-level activities
4. Market segment activities
5. Facility-level activities

One possible way of presenting Anthropologie's 2014 hypothetical multi-level income statement with two market segments is shown in Exhibit 3.9. The details underlying the development of this statement are not presented. In developing the statement, we assume the mix of units sold, their cost structure, and the costs of processing an order are unchanged. Finally, we present new market segment costs and assume that the addition of the segments allows for some reduction in previous facility-level costs.

EXHIBIT 3.9	Multi-Level Contribution Income Statement with Segments and Taxes		

ANTHROPOLOGIE
Multi-Level Contribution Income Statement
For Year 2014

	In-Store Segment	Internet Segment	Total
Sales	$1,500,000	$2,000,000	$3,500,000
Less unit-level costs			
Cost of goods sold (0.80)	(1,200,000)	(1,600,000)	(2,800,000)
Unit-level contribution margin	300,000	400,000	700,000
Less order-level costs			
Cost of processing order			
(1,000 × $20; 3,000 × $20)	(20,000)	(60,000)	(80,000)
Order-level contribution margin	280,000	340,000	620,000
Less customer-level costs			
Mail, phone, sales visits, recordkeeping, etc.			
(150 × $200, 300 × $200)	(30,000)	(60,000)	(90,000)
Customer-level contribution margin	250,000	280,000	530,000
Less market segment-level costs	(80,000)	(20,000)	(100,000)
Market segment-level contribution	$ 170,000	$ 260,000	430,000
Less facility-level costs			
Depreciation, manager salaries, insurance, etc.			(90,000)
Before-tax profit			340,000
Income taxes ($340,000 × 0.40)			(136,000)
After-tax profit			$ 204,000

The information in the total column is all that is required for a multi-level contribution income statement. The information in the two detailed columns for the government and private segments can, however, prove useful in analyzing the profitability of each. Observe that the facility-level costs, incurred for the benefit of both segments, are not assigned to specific segments. Depending on the nature of the goods sold, it may be possible to further analyze the profitability of each product (or type of product) sold in each market segment. The profitability analysis of business segments is more closely examined in Chapter 11.

GUIDANCE ANSWERS . . . YOU MAKE THE CALL

You are the Division Manager   Fixed costs represent a two-edged sword. When a company is growing its sales, fixed costs cause profits to grow faster than sales; however, if a company should experience declining sales, the rate of reduction in profits is greater than the rate of reduction in sales. When sales decline, variable costs decline proportionately, while fixed costs continue. For this reason, when a company faces serious declines that are expected to continue, one of the first steps its top management should consider is reducing capacity in order to reduce fixed costs. The automobile companies in the U.S. have been employing this technique in recent years to try to offset the effect of sales lost to importers.

KEY RATIOS

Profit = Revenues − Total costs

Revenues = Unit selling price × Unit sales volume

Total costs = Fixed costs + (Unit variable costs × Unit sales)

Profit: $\pi = pX - (a + bX)$
Where p = unit selling price, X = unit sales, a = fixed costs, b = unit variable costs.

$$\text{Break-even unit sales volume} = \frac{\text{Fixed costs}}{\text{Selling price per unit} - \text{Variable costs per unit}}$$

$$\text{Break-even unit sales volume} = \frac{\text{Fixed costs}}{\text{Unit contribution margin}}$$

$$\text{Target unit sales volume} = \frac{\text{Fixed costs} + \text{Desired profit}}{\text{Unit contribution margin}}$$

After-tax profit = Before-tax profit × (1 − Tax rate)

$$\text{Dollar break-even point} = \frac{\text{Fixed costs}}{\text{Contribution margin ratio}}$$

$$\text{Target dollar sales volume} = \frac{\text{Fixed costs} + \text{Desired profit}}{\text{Contribution margin ratio}}$$

$$\text{Operating leverage ratio} = \frac{\text{Contribution margin}}{\text{Before-tax profits}}$$

KEY TERMS

break-even point, 73
contribution income
   statement, 71
contribution margin, 71
contribution margin ratio, 73
cost-volume-profit (CVP)
   analysis, 68
cost-volume-profit graph, 75
direct labor, 70
direct materials, 70

fixed manufacturing overhead,
   70
fixed selling and administrative
   costs, 70
functional income statement, 72
margin of safety, 73
operating leverage, 82
operating leverage ratio, 82
profitability analysis, 68
profit-volume graph, 76

sales mix, 69
sensitivity analysis, 72
unit contribution margin, 72
variable cost ratio, 79
variable manufacturing
   overhead, 70
variable selling and
   administrative costs, 70

MULTIPLE CHOICE

1. With fixed costs of $20,000/month and variable costs of $3/unit, Ace reported a monthly profit of $5,000 at a volume of 12,500 units. The unit selling price was:
    a. $1.60
    b. $3.00
    c. $4.60
    d. $5.00

2. Presented is information from Wayne's contribution income statement:

Sales		$70,000
Less variable costs:		
Manufacturing	$20,000	
Selling and administrative	10,000	(30,000)
Contribution margin		40,000
Less fixed costs:		
Manufacturing	15,000	
Selling and administrative	8,000	(23,000)
Profit		$17,000

    With a functional income statement Wayne would have reported a gross margin of:
    a. $35,000
    b. $40,000
    c. $47,000
    d. $50,000

3. Based on the information in question 2, if Wayne had a $5,000 increase in sales, profits would increase by:
    a. $5,000
    b. $3,570
    c. $2,855
    d. $2,500

4. Penn Company produces a product sold for $40 per unit. Variable and fixed cost information is presented below:

Variable costs per unit		Fixed costs per month	
Manufacturing	$ 8	Manufacturing	$29,000
Selling and administrative	2	Selling and administrative	16,000
Total	$10	Total	$45,000

    The sales volume required for a monthly profit of $36,000 is:
    a. 900 units
    b. 2,050 units
    c. 2,700 units
    d. 3,600 units

5. Based on the information in question 4, with an income tax rate of 40 percent the sales volume required for a monthly after-tax profit of $36,000 is:
    a. 2,000 units
    b. 3,500 units
    c. 3,700 units
    d. 4,500 units

Superscript ᴬ denotes assignments based on Appendix 3A.

DISCUSSION QUESTIONS

Q3-1.   What is cost-volume-profit analysis and when is it particularly useful?

Q3-2.   Identify the important assumptions that underlie cost-volume-profit analysis.

Q3-3.   When is it most reasonable to use a single independent variable in cost-volume-profit analysis?

Q3-4.   Distinguish between a contribution and a functional income statement.

Q3-5.   What is the unit contribution margin? How is it used in computing the unit break-even point?

Q3-6.   What is the contribution margin ratio and when is it most useful?

Q3-7.   How is the break-even equation modified to take into account the sales required to earn a desired profit?

Q3-8.   How does a profit-volume graph differ from a cost-volume-profit graph? When is a profit-volume graph most likely to be used?

Q3-9.   What impact do income taxes have on the sales volume required to earn a desired after-tax profit?

Q3-10.   How are profit opportunities and the risk of losses affected by operating leverage?

Assignments with the ✅ logo in the margin are available in ᵐʸ BusinessCourse.
See the Preface of the book for details.

MINI EXERCISES

LO3 **M3-11.**   **Profitability Analysis**

✅

Assume a local Cost Cutters provides cuts, perms, and hairstyling services. Annual fixed costs are $120,000, and variable costs are 40 percent of sales revenue. Last year's revenues totaled $250,000.

Required

a.   Determine its break-even point in sales dollars.

b.   Determine last year's margin of safety in sales dollars.

c.   Determine the sales volume required for an annual profit of $80,000.

LO3 **M3-12.**   **Cost-Volume-Profit Graph: Identification and Sensitivity Analysis**

A typical cost-volume-profit graph is presented below.

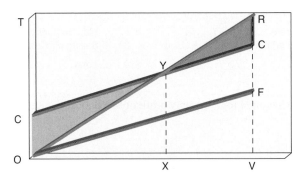

Required

a.   Identify each of the following:

1.   Line OF
2.   Line OR
3.   Line CC
4.   The difference between lines OF and OV
5.   The difference between lines CC and OF
6.   The difference between lines CC and OV
7.   The difference between lines OR and OF

8. Point X
9. Area CYO
10. Area RCY

b. Indicate the effect of each of the following independent events on lines CC, OR, and the break-even point:
1. A decrease in fixed costs
2. An increase in unit selling price
3. An increase in the variable costs per unit
4. An increase in fixed costs and a decrease in the unit selling price
5. A decrease in fixed costs and a decrease in the unit variable costs

M3-13. Profit-Volume Graph: Identification and Sensitivity Analysis   LO3
A typical profit-volume graph follows.

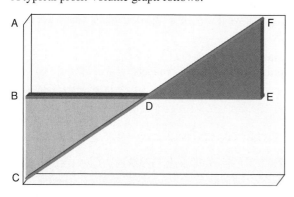

Required
a. Identify each of the following:
1. Area *BDC*
2. Area *DEF*
3. Point *D*
4. Line *AC*
5. Line *BC*
6. Line *EF*

b. Indicate the effect of each of the following on line *CF* and the break-even point:
1. An increase in the unit selling price
2. An increase in the variable costs per unit
3. A decrease in fixed costs
4. An increase in fixed costs and a decrease in the unit selling price
5. A decrease in fixed costs and an increase in the variable costs per unit

M3-14. Preparing Cost-Volume-Profit and Profit-Volume Graphs   LO3
Assume a Domino's Pizza shop has the following monthly revenue and cost functions: DOMINO'S PIZZA (DPZ)

$$\text{Total revenues} = \$10.00X$$
$$\text{Total costs} = \$16,000 + \$4.00X$$

Required
a. Prepare a graph (similar to that in Exhibit 3.3) illustrating Domino's cost-volume-profit relationships. The vertical axis should range from $0 to $72,000, in increments of $12,000. The horizontal axis should range from 0 units to 6,000 units, in increments of 2,000 units.
b. Prepare a graph (similar to that in Exhibit 3.4) illustrating Domino's profit-volume relationships. The horizontal axis should range from 0 units to 6,000 units, in increments of 2,000 units.
c. When is it most appropriate to use a profit-volume graph?

LO3   **M3-15.**   **Preparing Cost-Volume-Profit and Profit-Volume Graphs**

Hometown Dog Company is a hot dog concession business operating at five baseball stadiums. It sells hot dogs, with all the fixings, for $6.00 each. Variable costs are $4.50 per hot dog, and fixed operating costs are $750,000 per year.

Required

a.   Determine the annual break-even point in hot dogs.

b.   Prepare a cost-volume-profit graph for the company. Use a format that emphasizes the contribution margin. The vertical axis should vary between $0 and $5,000,000 in increments of $1,000,000. The horizontal axis should vary between 0 hot dogs and 1,000,000 hot dogs, in increments of 250,000 hot dogs. Label the graph in thousands.

c.   Prepare a profit-volume graph for the company. The vertical axis should vary between $(750,000) and $750,000 in increments of $150,000. The horizontal axis should vary as described in requirement (b). Label the graph in thousands.

d.   Evaluate the profit-volume graph. In what ways is it superior and in what ways is it inferior to the traditional cost-volume-profit graph?

LO4   **M3-16.**   **Multiple Product Break-Even Analysis**

Presented is information for Stafford Company's three products.

	A	B	C
Unit selling price	$6	$8	$7
Unit variable costs.	(4)	(5)	(3)
Unit contribution margin	$2	$3	$4

With monthly fixed costs of $112,500, the company sells two units of A for each unit of B and three units of B for each unit of C.

Required

Determine the unit sales of product A at the monthly break-even point.

EXERCISES

LO2, 3   **E3-17.**   **Contribution Income Statement and Cost-Volume-Profit Graph**

Jasper Company produces a product that is sold for $40 per unit. The company produced and sold 6,000 units during June 2013. There were no beginning or ending inventories. Variable and fixed costs follow.

Variable Costs per Unit			Fixed Costs per Month	
Manufacturing:			Manufacturing overhead.	$40,000
Direct materials	$10		Selling and administrative.	20,000
Direct labor.	2		Total	$60,000
Manufacturing overhead	5	$17		
Selling and administrative.		5		
Total		$22		

Required

a.   Prepare a contribution income statement for June.

b.   Prepare a cost-volume-profit graph. Label the horizontal axis in units with a maximum value of 10,000. Label the vertical axis in dollars with a maximum value of $400,000. Draw a vertical line on the graph for the current (6,000) unit sales level, and label total variable costs, total fixed costs, and total profits at 6,000 units.

LO3, 4   **E3-18.**   **Contribution Margin Concepts**

The following information is taken from the 2013 records of Cherokee Jewelry Shop.

	Fixed	Variable	Total
Sales			$750,000
Costs			
Goods sold.....................................		$337,500	
Labor	$160,000	60,000	
Supplies	2,000	5,000	
Utilities	12,000	13,000	
Rent	24,000	—	
Advertising....................................	6,000	24,500	
Miscellaneous	6,000	10,000	
Total costs	$210,000	$450,000	(660,000)
Net income....................................			$ 90,000

Required

a. Determine the annual break-even dollar sales volume.

b. Determine the current margin of safety in dollars.

c. Prepare a cost-volume-profit graph for the jewelry shop. Label both axes in dollars with maximum values of $1,000,000. Draw a vertical line on the graph for the current ($750,000) sales level, and label total variable costs, total fixed costs, and total profits at $750,000 sales.

d. What is the annual break-even dollar sales volume if management makes a decision that increases fixed costs by $35,000?

E3-19. **Multiple Product Planning with Taxes**   LO3, 4

In the year 2013, Wiggins Processing Company had the following contribution income statement:

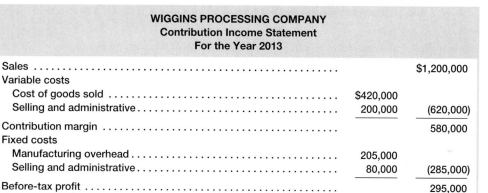

WIGGINS PROCESSING COMPANY
Contribution Income Statement
For the Year 2013

Sales		$1,200,000
Variable costs		
Cost of goods sold	$420,000	
Selling and administrative..................	200,000	(620,000)
Contribution margin		580,000
Fixed costs		
Manufacturing overhead....................	205,000	
Selling and administrative..................	80,000	(285,000)
Before-tax profit		295,000
Income taxes (36%).		(106,200)
After-tax profit............................		$ 188,800

Required

a. Determine the annual break-even point in sales dollars.

b. Determine the annual margin of safety in sales dollars.

c. What is the break-even point in sales dollars if management makes a decision that increases fixed costs by $57,000?

d. With the current cost structure, including fixed costs of $285,000, what dollar sales volume is required to provide an after-tax net income of $200,000?

e. Prepare an abbreviated contribution income statement to verify that the solution to requirement (d) will provide the desired after-tax income.

E3-20. **Not-for-Profit Applications**   LO3

Determine the solution to each of the following independent cases:

a. Hillside College has annual fixed operating costs of $13,000,000 and variable operating costs of $1,000 per student. Tuition is $8,000 per student for the coming academic year, with a projected enrollment of 1,500 students. Expected revenues from endowments and federal and state grants total $250,000. Determine the amount the college must obtain from other sources.

b. The Hillside College Student Association is planning a fall concert. Expected costs (renting a hall, hiring a band, etc.) are $30,000. Assuming 4,000 people attend the concert, determine the break-even price per ticket. How much will the association lose if this price is charged and only 2,700 tickets are sold?

c. City Hospital has a contract with the city to provide indigent health care on an outpatient basis for $30 per visit. The patient will pay $5 of this amount, with the city paying the balance ($25). Determine the amount the city will pay if the hospital has 10,000 patient visits.

d. A civic organization is engaged in a fund-raising program. On Civic Sunday, it will sell newspapers at $1.50 each. The organization will pay $0.75 for each newspaper. Costs of the necessary permits, signs, and so forth are $500. Determine the amount the organization will raise if it sells 5,000 newspapers.

e. Christmas for the Needy is a civic organization that provides Christmas presents to disadvantaged children. The annual costs of this activity are $6,000, plus $10 per present. Determine the number of presents the organization can provide with $20,000.

LO3, 5 **E3-21.** **Alternative Production Procedures and Operating Leverage**

PAPER MATE

Assume Paper Mate is planning to introduce a new executive pen that can be manufactured using either a capital-intensive method or a labor-intensive method. The predicted manufacturing costs for each method are as follows:

	Capital Intensive	Labor Intensive
Direct materials per unit	$ 5.00	$ 8.00
Direct labor per unit	$ 5.00	$12.00
Variable manufacturing overhead per unit.	$ 4.00	$ 2.00
Fixed manufacturing overhead per year	$2,440,000.00	$700,000.00

Paper Mate's market research department has recommended an introductory unit sales price of $40. The incremental selling costs are predicted to be $500,000 per year, plus $2 per unit sold.

Required

a. Determine the annual break-even point in units if Paper Mate uses the:
   1. Capital-intensive manufacturing method.
   2. Labor-intensive manufacturing method.

b. Determine the annual unit volume at which Paper Mate is indifferent between the two manufacturing methods.

c. Management wants to know more about the effect of each alternative on operating leverage.
   1. Explain operating leverage and the relationship between operating leverage and the volatility of earnings.
   2. Compute operating leverage for each alternative at a volume of 250,000 units.
   3. Which alternative has the higher operating leverage? Why?

LO3, 5 **E3-22.** **Contribution Income Statement and Operating Leverage**

Florida Berry Basket harvests early-season strawberries for shipment throughout the eastern United States in March. The strawberry farm is maintained by a permanent staff of 10 employees and seasonal workers who pick and pack the strawberries. The strawberries are sold in crates containing 100 individually packaged one-quart containers. Affixed to each one-quart container is the distinctive Florida Berry Basket logo inviting buyers to "Enjoy the berry best strawberries in the world!" The selling price is $100 per crate, variable costs are $85 per crate, and fixed costs are $275,000 per year. In the year 2013, Florida Berry Basket sold 50,000 crates.

Required

a. Prepare a contribution income statement for the year ended December 31, 2013.

b. Determine the company's 2013 operating leverage.

c. Calculate the percentage change in profits if sales decrease by 10 percent.

d. Management is considering the purchase of several berry-picking machines. This will increase annual fixed costs to $375,000 and reduce variable costs to $81.50 per crate. Calculate the effect of this acquisition on operating leverage and explain any change.

E3-23. Multiple Product Break-Even Analysis

Yuma Tax Service prepares tax returns for low- to middle-income taxpayers. Its service operates January 2 through April 15 at a counter in a local department store. All jobs are classified into one of three categories: standard, multiform, and complex. Following is information for last year. Also, last year, the fixed cost of rent, utilities, and so forth were $45,000.

	Standard	Multiform	Complex
Billing rate	$50	$125	$250
Average variable costs	(30)	(75)	(150)
Average contribution margin	$20	$ 50	$100
Number of returns prepared.	1,950	750	300

Required

a. Determine Yuma's break-even dollar sales volume.
b. Determine Yuma's margin of safety in sales dollars.
c. Prepare a profit-volume graph for Yuma's Tax Service.

E3-24. Cost-Volume-Profit Relations: Missing Data

Following are data from 4 separate companies.

	Case A	Case B	Case C	Case D
Unit sales.	1,000	800	?	?
Sales revenue	$20,000	?	?	$60,000
Variable cost per unit	$10	$1	$12	?
Contribution margin	?	$800	?	?
Fixed costs	$7,000	?	$80,000	?
Net income.	?	$500	?	?
Unit contribution margin	?	?	?	$15
Break-even point (units)	?	?	4,000	2,000
Margin of safety (units)	?	?	300	1,000

Required

Supply the missing data in each independent case.

E3-25. Cost-Volume-Profit Relations: Missing Data

Following are data from 4 separate companies.

	Case 1	Case 2	Case 3	Case 4
Sales revenue	$120,000	$80,000	?	?
Contribution margin	$60,000	?	$20,000	?
Fixed costs	$30,000	?	?	?
Net income.	?	$5,000	$10,000	?
Variable cost ratio	?	0.50	?	0.20
Contribution margin ratio	?	?	0.40	?
Break-even point (dollars).	?	?	?	$25,000
Margin of safety (dollars)	?	?	?	$20,000

Required

Supply the missing data in each independent case.

E3-26.[A] Customer-Level Planning

7-Eleven operates a number of convenience stores worldwide. Assume that an analysis of operating costs, customer sales, and customer patronage reveals the following:

Fixed costs per store	$80,000.00/year
Variable cost ratio	0.80
Average sale per customer visit	$17.00
Average customer visits per week	1.50
Customers as portion of city population	0.05

Required

Determine the city population required for a single 7-Eleven to earn an annual profit of $40,000.

E3-27.[A] **Multiple-Level Break-Even Analysis**

Jensen Associates provides marketing services for a number of small manufacturing firms. Jensen receives a commission of 10 percent of sales. Operating costs are as follows:

Unit-level costs	$0.04 per sales dollar
Sales-level costs	$300 per sales order
Customer-level costs	$900 per customer per year
Facility-level costs.	$60,000 per year

Required

a. Determine the minimum order size in sales dollars for Jensen to break even on an order.
b. Assuming an average customer places four orders per year, determine the minimum annual sales required to break even on a customer.
c. What is the average order size in (b)?
d. Assuming Jensen currently serves 100 customers, with each placing an average of four orders per year, determine the minimum annual sales required to break even.
e. What is the average order size in (d)?
f. Explain the differences in the answers to (a), (c), and (e).

PROBLEMS

LO3 P3-28. **Profit Planning with Taxes**

Chandler Manufacturing Company produces a product that it sells for $40 per unit. Last year, the company manufactured and sold 20,000 units to obtain an after-tax profit of $54,000. Variable and fixed costs follow.

Variable Costs per Unit		Fixed Costs per Year	
Manufacturing	$21	Manufacturing	$ 80,000
Selling and administrative.	9	Selling and administrative.	30,000
Total	$30	Total	$110,000

Required

a. Determine the tax rate the company paid last year.
b. What unit sales volume is required to provide an after-tax profit of $90,000?
c. If the company reduces the unit variable cost by $2.50 and increases fixed manufacturing costs by $20,000, what unit sales volume is required to provide an after-tax profit of $90,000?
d. What assumptions are made about taxable income and tax rates in requirements (a) through (c)?

LO2, 3 P3-29. **Contribution Income Statement, Cost-Volume-Profit Graph, and Taxes**

New York Tours (NYT) provides daily sightseeing tours that include transportation, admission to selected attractions, and lunch. Ticket prices are $85 each. During June 2013, NYT provided 3,000 tours.

Variable Costs per Customer		Fixed Costs per Month	
Admission fees	$30	Operations.	$25,000
Lunch	17	Selling and administration	15,000
Overhead	10		
Selling and administrative.	8		
Total	$65	Total	$40,000

NYT is subject to an income tax rate of 40 percent.

Required

a. Prepare a contribution income statement for June.

b. Determine NYT's monthly break-even point in units.

c. Determine NYT's margin of safety for June 2013.

d. Determine the unit sales required for a monthly after-tax profit of $15,000.

e. Prepare a cost-volume-profit graph. Label the horizontal axis in units with a maximum value of 4,000. Label the vertical in dollars with a maximum value of $300,000. Draw a vertical line on the graph for the current (3,000) unit level and label total variable costs, total fixed costs, and total before-tax profits at 3,000 units.

P3-30. High-Low Cost Estimation and Profit Planning   LO3, 4

Comparative 2012 and 2013 income statements for Dakota Products Inc. follow:

DAKOTA PRODUCTS INC. Comparative Income Statements For Years Ending December 31, 2012 and 2013		
	2012	**2013**
Unit sales.	6,000	9,000
Sales revenue	$78,000	$117,000
Expenses.	(70,000)	(85,000)
Profit (loss).	$ 8,000	$ 32,000

Required

a. Determine the break-even point in units.

b. Determine the unit sales volume required to earn a profit of $12,000.

P3-31. CVP Analysis and Special Decisions   LO3, 4

Sweet Grove Citrus Company buys a variety of citrus fruit from growers and then processes the fruit into a product line of fresh fruit, juices, and fruit flavorings. The most recent year's sales revenue was $4,200,000. Variable costs were 60 percent of sales and fixed costs totaled $1,300,000. Sweet Grove is evaluating two alternatives designed to enhance profitability.

*   One staff member has proposed that Sweet Grove purchase more automated processing equipment. This strategy would increase fixed costs by $300,000 but decrease variable costs to 54 percent of sales.

*   Another staff member has suggested that Sweet Grove rely more on outsourcing for fruit processing. This would reduce fixed costs by $300,000 but increase variable costs to 65 percent of sales.

Required

a. What is the current break-even point in sales dollars?

b. Assuming an income tax rate of 34 percent, what dollar sales volume is currently required to obtain an after-tax profit of $500,000?

c. In the absence of income taxes, at what sales volume will both alternatives (automation and outsourcing) provide the same profit?

d. Briefly describe one strength and one weakness of both the automation and the outsourcing alternatives.

P3-32. Break-Even Analysis in a Not-for-Profit Organization   LO3

Melford Hospital operates a general hospital but rents space to separately owned entities rendering specialized services such as pediatrics and psychiatry. Melford charges each separate entity for patients' services (meals and laundry) and for administrative services (billings and collections). Space and bed rentals are fixed charges for the year, based on bed capacity rented to each entity. Melford charged the following costs to Pediatrics for the year ended June 30, 2013:

	Patient Services (Variable)	Bed Capacity (Fixed)
Dietary	$ 600,000	
Janitorial		$ 70,000
Laundry	300,000	
Laboratory	450,000	
Pharmacy	350,000	
Repairs and maintenance		30,000
General and administrative		1,300,000
Rent		1,500,000
Billings and collections	300,000	
Total	$2,000,000	$2,900,000

In addition to these charges from Melford Hospital, Pediatrics incurred the following personnel costs:

	Annual Salaries*
Supervising nurses	$100,000
Nurses	200,000
Assistants	180,000
Total	$480,000

* These salaries are fixed within the ranges of annual patient-days considered in this problem.

During the year ended June 30, 2013, Pediatrics charged each patient $300 per day, had a capacity of 60 beds, and had revenues of $6,000,000 for 365 days. Pediatrics operated at 100 percent capacity on 90 days during this period. It is estimated that during these 90 days, the demand exceeded 80 beds. Melford has 20 additional beds available for rent for the year ending June 30, 2012. This additional rental would proportionately increase Pediatrics' annual fixed charges based on bed capacity.

Required

a. Calculate the minimum number of patient-days required for Pediatrics to break even for the year ending June 30, 2014, if the additional beds are not rented. Patient demand is unknown, but assume that revenue per patient-day, cost per patient-day, cost per bed, and salary rates for the year ending June 30, 2014, remain the same as for the year ended June 30, 2013.

b. Assume Pediatrics rents the extra 20-bed capacity from Melford. Determine the net increase or decrease in earnings by preparing a schedule of increases in revenues and costs for the year ending June 30, 2014. Assume that patient demand, revenue per patient-day, cost per patient-day, cost per bed, and salary rates remain the same as for the year ended June 30, 2013.

(CPA adapted)

LO3 **P3-33.** **CVP Analysis of Alternative Products**

Mountain Top Boot Company plans to expand its manufacturing capacity to allow up to 20,000 pairs of a new product each year. Because only one product can be produced, management is deciding between the production of the Sure Foot for backpacking and the Trail Runner for exercising. A marketing analysis indicates Mountain Top could sell between 8,000 and 14,000 pairs of either product.

The accounting department has developed the following price and cost information:

	Product	
	Sure Foot	Trail Runner
Selling price per pair	$ 80.00	$ 75.00
Variable costs per pair	50.00	50.00
Product costs	$130,000.00	$50,000.00

Facility costs for expansion, regardless of product, are $150,000. Mountain Top is subject to a 40 percent income tax rate.

Required

a.   Determine the number of pairs of Sure Foot boots Mountain Top must sell to obtain an after tax profit of $30,000.

b.   Determine the number of pairs of each product Mountain Top must sell to obtain identical before-tax profit.

c.   For the solution to requirement b, calculate Mountain Top's after-tax profit or loss.

d.   Which product should Mountain Top produce if both products were guaranteed to sell at least 13,000 pairs. Verify your solution with calculations.

e.   How much would the variable costs per pair of the product *not* selected in requirement d have to fall before both products provide the same profit at sales of 13,000 pairs? Verify your solution with calculations.

P3-34.   CVP Analysis Using Published Financial Statements

Condensed data in thousands of dollars (000) from Netflix's 2009 and 2010 income statements follow:

LO3, 4

NETFLIX
(NFLX)

	2010	2009
Revenues..	$2,162,625	$1,670,269
Total cost of revenues and operating expenses	(1,878,984)	(1,478,330)
Operating income	$ 283,641	$ 191,939

Required

a.   Develop a cost-estimation equation for Netflix's annual cost of revenues and operating expenses.

b.   Determine Netflix's annual break-even point.

c.   Predict operating profit for 2011, assuming 2011 sales of $3,204,577 thousand.

d.   Identify the assumptions required to use the equations and amounts computed above.

P3-35.[A]   Multiple-Product Profitability Analysis, Multiple-Level Profitability Analysis

College Avenue Bookstore sells new college textbooks at the publishers' suggested retail prices. It then pays the publishers an amount equal to 75 percent of the suggested retail price. The store's other variable costs average 5 percent of sales revenue and annual fixed costs amount to $360,000.

Required

a.   Determine the bookstore's annual break-even point in sales dollars.

b.   Assuming an average textbook has a suggested retail price of $120, determine the bookstore's annual break-even point in units.

c.   College Avenue Bookstore is planning to add used book sales to its operations. A typical used book costs the store 25 percent of the suggested retail price of a new book. The bookstore plans to sell used books for 75 percent of the suggested retail price of a new book. Assuming unit sales are unchanged, describe the effect on bookstore profitability of shifting sales toward more used and fewer new textbooks.

d.   College Publishing produces and sells new textbooks to college and university bookstores. Typical project-level costs total $325,000 for a new textbook. Production and distribution costs amount to 20 percent of the net amount the publisher receives from the bookstores. Textbook authors are paid a royalty of 15 percent of the net amount received from the bookstores. Determine the dollar sales volume required for College Publishing to break even on a new textbook. This is the amount the bookstore pays the publisher, not the bookstore's sales revenue.

e.   For a project with predicted sales of 8,000 new books at $120 each, determine:

1.   The bookstores' contribution.

2.   The publisher's contribution.

3.   The author's royalties.

LO3, 4   **P3-36.**   **Multiple-Product Profitability Analysis**

Hearth Manufacturing Company produces two models of wood-burning stoves, Cozy Kitchen and All-House. Presented is sales infvormation for the year 2014.

	Cozy Kitchen	All-House	Total
Units manufactured and sold	1,000	1,500	2,500
Sales revenue	$300,000	$750,000	$1,050,000
Variable costs	(200,000)	(450,000)	(650,000)
Contribution margin	$100,000	$300,000	400,000
Fixed costs			(240,000)
Before-tax profit			160,000
Income taxes (40 percent)			(64,000)
After-tax profit.			$ 96,000

Required

a.   Determine the current break-even point in sales dollars.

b.   With the current product mix and break-even point, determine the average unit contribution margin and unit sales.

c.   Sales representatives believe that the total sales will increase to 3,000 units, with the sales mix likely shifting to 80 percent Cozy Kitchen and 20 percent All-House over the next few years. Evaluate the desirability of this projection.

LO3, 4   **P3-37.**   **Multiple-Product Break-Even Analysis**

Currently, Corner Lunch Counter sells only Super Burgers for $3.00 each. During a typical month, the Counter reports a profit of $9,000 with sales of $60,000 and fixed costs of $21,000. Management is considering the introduction of a new Super Chicken Sandwich that will sell for $3.50 and have variable costs of $2.30. The addition of the Super Chicken Sandwich will require hiring additional personnel and renting additional equipment. These actions will increase monthly fixed costs by $7,760.

In the short run, management predicts that Super Chicken sales will average 10,000 sandwiches per month. However, almost all short-run sales of Super Chickens will come from regular customers who switch from Super Burgers to Super Chickens. Consequently, management predicts monthly sales of Super Burgers will decline by 10,000 units to $30,000. In the long run, management predicts that Super Chicken sales will increase to 15,000 sandwiches per month and that Super Burger sales will increase to 30,000 burgers per month.

Required

a.   Determine each of the following:

   1.   The current monthly break-even point in sales dollars.

   2.   The short-run monthly profit and break-even point in sales dollars subsequent to the introduction of Super Chickens.

   3.   The long-run monthly profit and break-even point in sales dollars subsequent to the introduction of Super Chickens.

b.   Based on your analysis, what are your recommendations?

P3-38.[A]   **Multi-Level Profitability Analysis**

AccuMeter manufactures and sells its only product (Z1) in lot sizes of 500 units. Because of this approach, lot (batch)-level costs are regarded as variable for CVP analysis. Presented is sales and cost information for the year 2014:

Sales revenue (50,000 units at $45)	$2,250,000
Direct materials (50,000 units at $12).	600,000
Processing (50,000 units at $18).	900,000
Setup (100 lots at $2,000)	200,000
Batch movement (100 lots at $400)	40,000
Order filling (100 lots at $200).	20,000
Fixed manufacturing overhead.	800,000
Fixed selling and administrative.	300,000

Required

  a. Prepare a traditional contribution income statement in good form.

  b. Prepare a multi-level contribution income statement in good form. (*Hint:* First determine the appropriate cost hierarchy.)

  c. What is the current contribution per lot (batch) of 500 units?

  d. Management is contemplating introducing a limited number of specialty products. One product would sell for $65 per unit and have direct materials costs of $17 per unit. All other costs and all production and sales procedures will remain unchanged. What lot (batch) size is required for a contribution of $700 per lot?

CASES AND PROJECTS

C3-39. Ethics and Pressure to Improve Profit Plans   LO1

Art Conroy is the assistant controller of New City Muffler, Inc., a subsidiary of New City Automotive, which manufactures tailpipes, mufflers, and catalytic converters at several plants throughout North America. Because of pressure for lower selling prices, New City Muffler has had disappointing financial performance in recent years. Indeed, Conroy is aware of rumblings from corporate headquarters threatening to close the plant.

One of Conroy's responsibilities is to present the plant's financial plans for the coming year to the corporate officers and board of directors. In preparing for the presentation, Conroy was intrigued to note that the focal point of the budget presentation was a profit-volume graph projecting an increase in profits and a reduction in the break-even point.

Curious as to how the improvement would be accomplished, Conroy ultimately spoke with Paula Mitchell, the plant manager. Mitchell indicated that a planned increase in productivity would reduce variable costs and increase the contribution margin ratio.

When asked how the productivity increase would be accomplished, Mitchell made a vague reference to increasing the speed of the assembly line. Conroy commented that speeding up the assembly line could lead to labor problems because the speed of the line was set by union contract. Mitchell responded that she was afraid that if the speedup were opened to negotiation, the union would make a big "stink" that could result in the plant being closed. She indicated that the speedup was the "only way to save the plant, our jobs, and the jobs of all plant employees." Besides, she did not believe employees would notice a 2 or 3 percent increase in speed. Mitchell concluded the meeting observing, "You need to emphasize the results we will accomplish next year, not the details of how we will accomplish those results. Top management does not want to be bored with details. If we accomplish what we propose in the budget, we will be in for a big bonus."

Required

What advice do you have for Art Conroy?

C3-40. CVP Analysis with Changing Cost Structure   LO1, 3, 5

Homestead Telephone was formed in the 1940s to bring telephone services to remote areas of the U.S. Midwest. The early equipment was quite primitive by today's standards. All calls were handled manually by operators, and all customers were on party lines. By the 1970s, however, all customers were on private lines, and mechanical switching devices handled routine local and long distance calls. Operators remained available for directory assistance, credit card calls, and emergencies. In the 1990s Homestead Telephone added local Internet connections as an optional service to its regular customers. It also established an optional cellular service, identified as the Home Ranger.

Required

  a. Using a unit-level analysis, develop a graph with two lines, representing Homestead Telephone's cost structure (1) in the 1940s and (2) in the late 1990s. Be sure to label the axes and lines.

  b. With sales revenue as the independent variable, what is the likely impact of the changed cost structure on Homestead Telephone's (1) contribution margin percent and (2) break-even point?

  c. Discuss how the change in cost structure affected Homestead's operating leverage and how this affects profitability under rising or falling sales scenarios.

LO2, 3, 4   C3-41.   Cost Estimation and CVP Analysis

Presented are the 2012 and 2013 functional income statements of Regional Distribution, Inc.:

		REGIONAL DISTRIBUTION, INC. Functional Income Statements For Years Ending December 31, 2012 and 2013			
		2012		**2013**	
Sales		$5,520,000		$5,000,000	
Expenses					
Cost of goods sold	$4,140,000		$3,750,000		
Shipping	215,400		200,000		
Sales order processing	52,500		50,000		
Customer relations	120,000		100,000		
Depreciation.	80,000		80,000		
Administrative	250,000	(4,857,900)	250,000	(4,430,000)	
Before-tax profit		662,100		570,000	
Income taxes (40%).		(264,840)		(228,000)	
After-tax profit		$ 397,260		$ 342,000	

Required

a.   Determine Regional Distribution's break-even point in sales dollars.

b.   What dollar sales volume is required to earn an after-tax profit of $480,000?

c.   Assuming budgeted 2014 sales of $6,000,000, prepare a 2014 contribution income statement.

d.   Discuss the reliability of the calculations in requirements *a-c*, including the limitations of the CVP model and how they affect the reliability of the model.

SOLUTIONS TO REVIEW PROBLEMS

Mid-Chapter Review

Solution

a.

	SOLO CUP COMPANY Contribution Income Statement For the Month of September 2014		
Sales (3,000 × $40)			$120,000
Less variable costs			
Direct materials (3,000 × $15).	$45,000		
Direct labor (3,000 × $3)	9,000		
Manufacturing overhead (3,000 × $10)	30,000		
Selling and administrative (3,000 × $2)	6,000	(90,000)	
Contribution margin		30,000	
Less fixed costs			
Manufacturing overhead	15,000		
Selling and administrative	10,000	(25,000)	
Profit.		$ 5,000	

b.

c.

Selling price..	$40 per unit
Variable costs..	(30) per unit
Contribution margin..	$10 per unit

$$\text{Contribution margin ratio} = \frac{\text{Unit contribution margin}}{\text{Unit selling price}}$$

$$= \$10 \div \$40$$

$$= 0.25$$

d.

$$\text{Break-even point} = \frac{\text{Fixed costs}}{\text{Unit contribution margin}}$$

$$= \$25{,}000 \div \$10$$

$$= 2{,}500 \text{ units}$$

e.

$$\text{Required dollar sales} = \frac{\text{Fixed costs} + \text{Desired profit}}{\text{Contribution margin ratio}}$$

$$= (\$25{,}000 + \$5{,}000) \div 0.25$$

$$= \$120{,}000$$

f.

$$\text{Required unit sales} = \frac{\text{Fixed costs} + \text{Desired before-tax profit}}{\text{Contribution margin per unit}}$$

$$\text{Desired before-tax profit} = \$4{,}500 \div (1 - 0.40) = \$7{,}500$$

$$\text{Required units sales} = (\$25{,}000 + \$7{,}500) \div \$10$$

$$= 3{,}250 \text{ units}$$

Chapter-End Review

Solution

a.

	Coffee	Tea	Smoothies	Total
Monthly unit sales	6,000	3,750	2,250	
Selling price	$1.35	$1.25	$1.95	
Sales	$8,100.00	$4,687.50	$4,387.50	$17,175.00
Variable cost	3,600.00	1,687.50	1,687.50	6,975.00
Contribution margin	$4,500.00	$3,000.00	$2,700.00	10,200.00
Fixed cost				8,000.00
Before-tax profit				$ 2,200.00
Contribution margin (CM) ratio	0.5556	0.640	0.6154	0.5939
Current sales mix (based on sales dollars) . . .	47.16%	27.29%	25.55%	

b.
$$\text{Break-even} = \text{Fixed costs/Total contribution margin ratio}$$
$$= \$8,000/0.5939$$
$$= \$13,470$$

Proof:		Sales		C/M Ratio		
Coffee:	$13,470 × 47.16% =	$ 6,352.45	× 0.5556	=	$3,529.42	
Tea:	$13,470 × 27.29% =	3,675.96	× 0.640	=	2,352.62*	
Smoothies:	$13,470 × 25.55% =	3,441.59	× 0.6154	=	2,117.96*	
		$13,470.00				
Total contribution margin					8,000.00	
Fixed costs					8,000.00	
Before-tax profit					–0–	

* Amounts adjusted to correct for minor rounding error.

c. The Coffee Bean has an operating leverage of 4.636, calculated as a contribution margin of $10,200 divided by before-tax profit of $2,200. Therefore, if sales dollars increase by 20% to $20,610, before-tax profit should increase by 4.636 times 20%, or 92.72%, to $4,240. Because of the leverage caused by fixed costs, a 20% increase in sales results in a 92.72% increase in before-tax profit. Conversely, a 20% decrease in sales would result in a 92.72% decrease in before-tax profits to $160.

Proof:	20% Sales Increase	20% Sales Decrease
Sales	$20,610	$13,740
CM %	× 0.5939	× 0.5939
Total CM	12,240	8,160
Fixed costs	8,000	8,000
Before-tax profit	$ 4,240	$ 160

Current before-tax profit of $2,200 × (1 + 0.9272) = $4,240
Current before-tax profit of $2,200 × (1 − 0.9272) = $160

1. Distinguish between relevant and irrelevant revenues and costs. (p. 108)

2. Analyze relevant costs and indicate how they differ under alternative decision scenarios. (p. 112)

3. Apply differential analysis to decision scenarios, including whether to change plans; to accept a special order; to make, buy, or outsource; and to sell or further process a product. (p. 114)

4. Allocate limited resources for purposes of maximizing short-run profit. (p. 122)

© iStock

Relevant Costs and Benefits for Decision Making

4

Every day companies, both large and small, are faced with making critical decisions that can drastically alter their likelihood of success. Some of these decisions are long term in nature, such as where a company should invest in property, plant, and equipment. Others are short-run decisions, such as whether or not to sell product or service to a new customer at a price that is below the normal market price.

UBER
www.uber.com

San Francisco startup company **Uber** got its start from pondering a common dilemma: how to get home from the club late at night. CEO Travis Kalanick explains that he and friend joked, "…let's go buy 10 Mercedes S-Classes, let's go hire 20 drivers, let's get parking garages and let's make it so we could push a button and an S-Class would roll up, for only us, in the city of San Francisco, where you cannot get a ride." Shortly thereafter, an iPhone application called Uber was launched in 2010. Uber has now expanded to 42 cities in 18 countries. Uber is the poster child for a disruptive innovator taking on the $6-billion-a-year taxi industry where a single medallion (license to operate) can sell for as much as $1 million in New York City.

Uber's intent was to act as a broker by matching riders to available drivers with a summons via smartphones. But the company first had to decide whether it should purchase cars and pay for insurance, storage, and other associated costs or whether to contract with existing drivers, either limousine companies or individual drivers. In the end, Uber decided to contract with partners (limo companies or individuals) who had their own vehicles. These partners take responsibility for licensing, vehicle cost and maintenance, gas, auto insurance, and storage. In return, Uber trains the drivers on the software platform and pays them 80 percent of the fare.

By acting as a broker instead of owning its own vehicles, Uber was able to minimize its fixed costs. This "operating leverage" results in a greater benefit from increases in customers, because the fixed costs don't need to increase to handle the higher capacity. However, the company's capacity is limited by how many drivers it has on contract. This limited resource can be maximized by minimizing the downtime of its drivers. Uber invested in engineers to build algorithms to manage its supply of drivers and demand of riders. The efficient management of this limited resource benefits both drivers (who are more likely to be engaged in fare-generating activity) and riders, who can use the software's tracking feature to see their car's progress toward the predetermined pickup destination.

Other decisions relevant to Uber include whether or not to segment its market with differing fee structures. To that end, Uber has launched a taxi-hailing service (using existing taxi companies) called UberTAXI, a low-cost limousine service called UberX that utilizes economy cars (e.g., **Honda** Civics and **Toyota** Priuses) instead of black town cars, UberSUV that dispatches **Cadillac** Escalades, and

continued on following page

continued from previous page

even UberMOTO, available in Paris, that will send a motorcycle taxi to the rider. And all fee structures are dynamic, meaning that fees increase proportionately as demand increases. On New Year's Eve, one San Francisco entrepreneur paid $75 for a ride that lasted two minutes and sixteen seconds!

Clearly, Uber's decision making is paying off. Employees (excluding drivers) have grown to over 400, revenues have been growing monthly at a rate of 18 percent, and Google recently made a $258 million investment in the company. In this chapter, we, too, will learn to incorporate the relevant revenues and costs to simplify decision making in wide variety of applications, even when operating in a complex and sometimes disruptive environment.

Sources: Jessi Hempel, "Hey, Taxi Company, You Talkin' to Me?" *Fortune*, September 23, 2013; Joshua Brustein, "From Google, Uber Gets Money and Political Muscle," *Bloomberg Businessweek*, August 26, 2013; Josh Linkner, "Uber's Borrowed Creativity," *Forbes*, August 19, 2013; and Andy Kessler, "The Transportation Trustbuster," *Wall Street Journal*, January 26, 2013, p. A13.

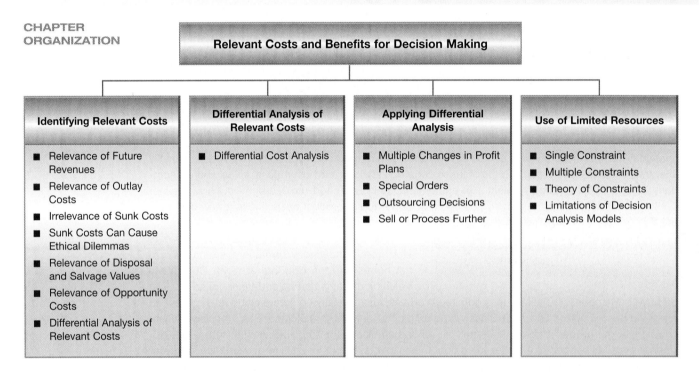

The purpose of this chapter is to examine approaches to identifying and analyzing revenue and cost information for specific decisions, such as the decision to outsource. Our emphasis is on identifying **relevant costs** (future costs that differ among competing decision alternatives) and distinguishing relevant costs from **irrelevant costs** that do not differ among competing decision alternatives. We consider a number of frequently encountered decisions: to make multiple changes in profit plans, to accept or reject a special order, to acquire a component or service internally or externally, to sell a product or process it further, and how to best use limited capacity. These decision situations are not exhaustive; they only illustrate relevant cost concepts. Once we understand these concepts, we can apply them to a variety of decision scenarios.

Although our focus in this chapter is on profit maximization, decisions should not be based solely on this criterion, especially maximizing profit in the short run. Managers must consider the implications decision alternatives have on long-run profit, as well as legal, ethical, social, and other nonquantitative factors. These factors can lead management to select a course of action other than that selected by financial information alone.

IDENTIFYING RELEVANT COSTS

LO1 Distinguish between relevant and irrelevant revenues and costs.

For a specific decision, the key to relevent cost analysis is first to identify the relevant costs (and revenues) and then to organize them in a manner that clearly indicates how they differ under each alternative. Consider the following equipment replacement decision.

Beats Electronics is a start-up company that produces Beats by Dr. Dre Studio headphones and now supplies high-quality components and equalizer software to HP for its line of personal computers. Assume that one of its components used in wireless headsets is forecasted to sell 10,000 units during the coming year at a price of $20 per unit. Further assume that each of Beats' components is manufactured with separate machines in a shared plant.

Headset Component Costs:	
Direct materials	$3.00 per unit
Conversion	5.00 per unit
Selling and distribution	1.00 per unit
Inspection and adjustment	$500 per batch (1,000 units)
Depreciation on machines	$15,000 per year
Machine maintenance	$200 per month
Advertising	$5,000 per year
Common Costs:	
Administrative salaries	$65,000 per year
Building operations	23,000 per year
Building rent	24,000 per year

The machine used in the manufacture of headset components is two years old and has a remaining useful life of four years. Its purchase price was $90,000 (new), and it has an estimated salvage value of zero dollars at the end of its useful life. Its current book value (original cost less accumulated depreciation) is $60,000, but it could be sold today for only $35,000.

Management is evaluating the desirability of replacing the machine with a new machine. The new machine costs $80,000, has a useful life of four years, and a predicted salvage value of zero dollars at the end of its useful life. Although the new machine has the same production capacity as the old machine, its predicted operating costs are lower because it consumes less electricity. Further, because of a computer control system, the new machine allows production of twice as many units between inspections and adjustments, and the cost of inspections and adjustments is lower. The new machine requires only annual, rather than monthly, overhauls. Hence, machine maintenance costs are lower. Costs for the new machine are predicted as follows:

Conversion costs	$4.00 per unit
Inspection and adjustment	$300 per batch (2,000 units)
Machine maintenance	$200 per year

All other costs and all revenues remain unchanged.

The decision alternatives are to keep the old machine or to replace it with a new machine. An analysis of how costs and revenues differ under each alternative assists management in making the best choice. The first objective of this chapter is to study the distinction between relevant and irrelevant items. After evaluating the relevance of each item, we develop an analysis of relevant costs.

Relevance of Future Revenues

Revenues, which are inflows of resources from the sale of goods and services, are relevant to a decision only if they differ between alternatives. In this example, revenues are not relevant because they are identical under each alternative. They would be relevant if the new machine had greater capacity or if management intended to change the selling price should it acquire the new machine. (The $35,000 disposal value of the old machine is an inflow. However, *revenues* refer to resources from the sale of goods and services to customers in the normal course of business. We include the sale of the old machine under disposal and salvage values.)

The hypothetical keep-or-replace decision facing Beats' management might be called a **cost reduction proposal** because it is based on the assumption that the organization is committed to an activity and that management desires to minimize the cost of activities. Here, the two alternatives are either to continue operating with the old machine or to replace it with a new machine.

Although this approach is appropriate for many activities, managers should remember that they have another alternative—discontinue operations. To simplify the analysis, managers normally do not consider the alternative to discontinue when operations appear to be profitable. However, if there is any doubt about an operation's profitability, this alternative should be considered.

Because revenues change if an operation is discontinued, revenues are relevant whenever this alternative is considered.

Relevance of Outlay Costs

Outlay costs are costs that require future expenditures of cash or other resources. Outlay costs that differ under the decision alternatives are relevant; outlay costs that do not differ are irrelevant. Assume Beats' relevant and irrelevant outlay costs for the equipment replacement decision follow.

Relevant Outlay Costs	Irrelevant Outlay Costs
Conversion Costs	Direct Materials
Inspection and Adjustment Costs	Selling and Distributon
Cost of New Machine	Advertising
Machine Maintenance	Common Outlay Costs

Irrelevance of Sunk Costs

Sunk costs result from past decisions that cannot be changed. Suppose we purchased a car for $15,000 five years ago. Today we must decide whether to purchase another car or have major maintenance performed on our current car. In making this decision, the purchase price of our current car is a sunk cost.

Although the relevance of outlay costs is determined by the decision scenario, sunk costs are never relevant. The cost of the old machine is a sunk cost, not a future cost. This cost and the related depreciation result from the past decision to acquire the old machine. Even though all the outlay costs discussed earlier would be relevant to a decision to continue or discontinue operations, the sunk cost of the old machine is not relevant even to this decision.

If management elects to keep the old machine, its book value will be depreciated over its remaining useful life of four years. However, if management elects to replace the old machine, its book value is written off when it is replaced. Even if management elects to discontinue operations, the book value of the old machine must be written off.

Sunk Costs Can Cause Ethical Dilemmas

Although the book value of the old machine has no economic significance, the accounting treatment of past costs may make it psychologically difficult for managers to regard them as irrelevant. If management replaces the old machine, a $25,000 accounting loss is recorded in the year of replacement:

Book value	$60,000
Disposal value	(35,000)
Loss on disposal	$25,000

The possibility of recording an accounting loss can create an ethical dilemma for managers. Although an action may be desirable from the long-run viewpoint of the organization, in the short run, choosing the action may result in an accounting loss. Fearing the loss will lead superiors to question her judgment, a manager might prefer to use the old machine (with lower total profits over the four-year period) as opposed to replacing it and being forced to record a loss on disposal. Although this action may avoid raising troublesome questions in the near term, the cumulative effect of many decisions of this nature is harmful to the organization's long-run economic health.

From an economic viewpoint, the analysis should focus on future costs and revenues that differ. The decision should not be influenced by sunk costs. Although there is no easy solution to this behavioral and ethical problem, managers and management accountants should be aware of its potential impact.

Relevance of Disposal and Salvage Values

Beats' assumed revenues (inflows of resources from operations) from the sale of headset components were discussed earlier. The sale of fixed assets is also a source of resources. Because the sale of fixed assets is a nonoperating item, cash inflows obtained from these sales are discussed separately.

The disposal value of the old machine is a relevant cash inflow. It is obtained only if the replacement alternative is selected. Any salvage value available at the end of the useful life of either machine is also relevant. A loss on disposal can have a favorable tax impact if the loss can be offset against taxable gains or taxable income. To simplify the analysis, we ignore any tax implications at this point. The tax effects related to capital asset transactions are discussed in Chapter 12.

Relevance of Opportunity Costs

When making a decision between alternative courses of action, accepting one alternative results in rejecting the other alternative(s). Any benefit foregone as a result of rejecting one opportunity in favor of another opportunity is described as an **opportunity cost** of the accepted alternative. For example, if you are employed at a salary of $40,000 per year and you have the opportunity to continue to work or the opportunity to go back to school full-time for two years to earn a graduate degree, the cost of getting the degree includes not only all the outlay costs for tuition, books, and so forth, it also includes the salary foregone (or opportunity cost) of $40,000 per year. So, if your tuition and other outlay costs are going to be $25,000 per year for two years, the cost of earning the degree will be $50,000 of outlay costs and $80,000 of opportunity costs, for a total cost of earning the degree of $130,000. Opportunity costs are always relevant in making decisions among competing alternatives.

The following is a summary of all the relevant and irrelevant costs discussed in this section.

Relevant Costs		Irrelevant Costs	
Future costs that differ among competing alternatives		Future costs that do not differ among competing alternatives	
Opportunity Costs	**Relevant Outlay Costs**	**Irrelevant Outlay Costs**	**Sunk Costs**
Net benefits foregone of rejected alternatives	Future costs requiring future expenditures that differ	Future costs requiring future expenditures that do not differ	Historical costs resulting from past decisions

DIFFERENTIAL ANALYSIS OF RELEVANT COSTS

LO2 Analyze relevant costs and indicate how they differ under alternative decision scenarios.

Differential cost analysis is an approach to the analysis of relevant costs that focuses on the costs that differ under alternative actions. A differential analysis of relevant costs for Beats' equipment replacement decision is in Exhibit 4.1. Replacement provides a net advantage of $17,800 over the life of both machines versus keeping the old machine.

An alternative analysis to that presented in Exhibit 4.1 is to present all revenues and costs (relevant and irrelevant) for each alternative in separate columns, such that the bottom line of the analysis is the total profit or loss for each alternative. This method is preferred if the goal is to determine the total profitability of each alternative. If the goal is to determine which of the two alternatives is most profitable, then a differential analysis is preferred.

Assuming the organization is committed to providing a particular product or service, a differential analysis of relevant costs (as shown in Exhibit 4.1) is preferred to a complete analysis of all costs and revenues for a number of reasons:

■ A differential analysis focuses on only those items that differ, providing a clearer picture of the impact of the decision. Management is less apt to be confused by this analysis than by one that combines relevant and irrelevant items.

■ A differential analysis contains fewer items, making it easier and quicker to prepare.

■ A differential analysis can help to simplify complex situations (such as those encountered by multiple-product or multiple-plant firms), when it is difficult to develop complete firmwide statements to analyze all decision alternatives.

Before preparing a differential analysis, it is always desirable to reassess the organization's commitment to a product or service. This helps avoid "throwing good money after bad." If Beats currently had large annual losses, acquiring the new machine would merely reduce total losses over the next four years by $17,800. In this case, discontinuing operations (a third alternative) should also be considered.

EXHIBIT 4.1	Differential Analysis of Relevant Costs			
		Differential Analysis of Four-Year Totals		
		(1)	**(2)**	**(1) − (2)**
				Difference
		Replace with New Machine	**Keep Old Machine**	**(effect of replacement on income)**
Conversion:				
Old Machine (10,000 units × $5 × 4 years)			$200,000	
New Machine (10,000 units × $4 × 4 years)		$160,000		($40,000)
Inspection and adjustment:				
Old Machine (10* setups × $500 × 4 years)			20,000	
New Machine (5** setups × $300 × 4 years)		6,000		(14,000)
Machine maintenance:				
Old Machine ($200 per month × 12 months × 4 years) . . .			9,600	
New Machine ($200 per month × 4 years)		800		(8,800)
Disposal of Old Machine.		(35,000)		(35,000)
Cost of New Machine		80,000		80,000
Totals		$211,800	$229,600	($17,800)
Advantage of replacement			$17,800	

* Old Machine: 10,000 units ÷ 1,000 units per batch

** New Machine: 10,000 units ÷ 2,000 units per batch

MID-CHAPTER REVIEW

TaylorMade-Adidas Golf Company (TMaG) manufactures golf clubs using "adjustable weight technology" or AWT. Suppose a European machine company has proposed to sell TaylorMade a new highly automated machine that would reduce significantly the labor cost of producing its golf clubs. The cost of the machine is $1,000,000, and would have an expected life of 5 years, at the end of which it would have a residual value of $100,000. It has an estimated operating cost of $10,000 per month. The direct labor cost savings per club from using the machine is estimated to be $5 per club. In addition, one monthly salaried manufacturing manager, whose salary is $6,000 per month would no longer be needed. Assume the Vice President of Manufacturing earns $10,000 per month. Also, the new machine would free up about 5,000 square feet of space from the displaced workers. Assume TaylorMade's building is held under a 10-year lease that has eight years remaining. The current lease cost is $1 per square foot per month. TaylorMade may be able to use the space for other purposes, and it has received an offer to rent it to a nearby related company for $3,500 per month.

Required
a. Identify all of the costs described above as either "relevant" or "irrelevant" to the decision to acquire the new machine.
b. Assuming the new machine would be used to produce an average of 5,000 clubs per month, prepare a differential analysis of the relevant costs of buying the machine and using it for the next five years, versus continuing to use hand labor.
c. In addition to the quantitative analysis in requirement b., what qualitative considerations are important for making the right decision?

The solution is on pages 142–143.

APPLYING DIFFERENTIAL ANALYSIS

LO3 Apply differential analysis to decision scenarios, including whether to change plans; to accept a special order; to make, buy, or outsource; and to sell or further process a product.

Differential analysis is used to provide information for a variety of planning and decision-making situations. This section illustrates some of the more frequently encountered applications of differential analysis. To focus on differential analysis concepts, we will use a simple example involving the production of one product on a continuous basis with all output sold to distributors. From the viewpoint of our single-product firm, all costs can be classified as either (1) costs that vary with units produced and sold or (2) costs that are fixed in the short run.

Multiple Changes in Profit Plans

Rovio Entertainment, located in Finland, develops the popular video game, Angry Birds. Assume that the entire Angry Birds suite of games is sold to distributors for €22 per unit (the Euro, represented by the symbol €, is the basic unit of currency in Finland, which is a member of the European Union). Variable costs per unit and fixed costs per month follow:

Variable Costs per Unit		Fixed Costs per Month	
Direct materials	€ 5	Manufacturing overhead.	€30,000
Direct labor	3	Selling and administrative.	15,000
Manufacturing overhead.	2	Total	€45,000
Selling	2		
Total	€12		

Assume the unit contribution margin (UCM) is €10 (€22 selling price − €12 variable costs). Rovio's hypothetical contribution income statement for April 2014 is presented in Exhibit 4.2. The April 2014 operations are typical. Monthly production and sales average 5,000 units, and monthly profits average €5,000.

Management wants to know the effect that each of the following three mutually exclusive alternatives would have on monthly profits.

1. Increasing the monthly advertising budget by €4,000, which should result in a 1,000-unit increase in monthly sales.

2. Increasing the selling price by €3, which should result in a 2,000-unit decrease in monthly sales.

3. Decreasing the selling price by €2, which should result in a 2,000-unit increase in monthly sales. However, because of capacity constraints, the last 1,000 units would be produced during overtime with the direct labor costs increasing by €1 per unit.

It is possible to develop contribution income statements for each alternative and then determine the profit impact of the proposed change by comparing the new income with the current income. A more direct approach is to use differential analysis and focus on only those items that differ under each alternative.

Alternative 1
Profit increase from increased sales (1,000 additional unit sales × €10 UCM).	€10,000
Profit decrease from increased advertising expenditures.	(4,000)
Increase in monthly profit	€ 6,000

Alternative 2
Profit decrease from reduced sales given no changes in prices or costs (2,000 lost unit sales × €10 UCM)	€(20,000)
Profit increase from increased selling price [(5,000 current unit sales − 2,000 lost unit sales) × €3 increase in unit selling price and UCM].	9,000
Decrease in monthly profit	€(11,000)

Alternative 3

Profit increase from increased sales given no changes in prices or costs (2,000 increased unit sales × €10 UCM)	€20,000
Profit decrease from reduced selling price of all units [(5,000 current unit sales + 2,000 additional unit sales) × €2 decrease in unit selling price and UCM]	(14,000)
Profit decrease from increased direct labor costs of the last 1,000 units (1,000 units × €1 increase in unit labor costs and decrease in UCM)	(1,000)
Increase in monthly profit	€ 5,000

Alternative 2 is undesirable because it would result in a decrease in monthly profit. Because Alternative 1 results in a larger increase in monthly profit, it is preferred to Alternative 3.

Special Orders

Assume an Australian distributor offered Rovio a reduced price of €12 per unit for a special, one-time order for 1,000 units. The Australian distributor will contract for a shipping company to handle all packing and transportation. Rovio has sufficient production capacity to produce the additional units without reducing sales to its regular distributors. Management desires to know the profit impact of accepting the order. The following analysis focuses on those costs and revenues that will differ if the order is accepted.

Increase in revenues (1,000 units × €12)		€12,000
Increase in costs		
Direct materials (1,000 units × €5)	€5,000	
Direct labor (1,000 units × €3)	3,000	
Variable manufacturing overhead (1,000 units × €2)	2,000	(10,000)
Increase in profits		€ 2,000

Accepting the special order will result in a profit increase of €2,000.

If management were unaware of relevant cost concepts, it might be tempted to compare the special order price to average unit cost information developed from accounting reports. Based on Rovio's hypothetical April 2014 contribution income statement in Exhibit 4.2, the average cost of all manufacturing, selling, and administrative expenses was €21 per unit as follows.

Variable costs	€ 60,000
Fixed costs	45,000
Total costs	€105,000
Unit production and sales	÷ 5,000
Average unit cost	€ 21

Comparing the special order price of €12 per unit to the average unit cost of €21, management might conclude the order would result in a loss of €9 per unit.

It is apparent that the €21 figure encompasses variable costs of €12 per unit (including irrelevant selling and administrative costs of €2 per unit) and irrelevant fixed costs of €45,000 spread over 5,000 units. But remember, management may not have detailed cost information. To obtain appropriate information for decision-making purposes, management must ask its accounting staff for the specific information needed. Different configurations of cost information are provided for different purposes. In the absence of special instructions, the accounting staff might not supply relevant cost information.

EXHIBIT 4.2 Contribution Income Statement		
ROVIO ENTERTAINMENT **Contribution Income Statement** **For the Month of April 2014**		
Sales (5,000 units × €22)		€110,000
Less variable costs		
Direct materials (5,000 units × €5).	€25,000	
Direct labor (5,000 units × €3)	15,000	
Manufacturing overhead (5,000 units × €2).	10,000	
Selling and administrative (5,000 units × €2)	10,000	(60,000)
Contribution margin		50,000
Less fixed costs		
Manufacturing overhead	30,000	
Selling and administrative	15,000	(45,000)
Profit.		€ 5,000

Importance of Time Span and Opportunity Costs

The special order is a one-time order for 1,000 units that will use current excess capacity. Because no special setups or equipment are required to produce the order, it is appropriate to consider only variable costs in computing the order's profitability.

But what if the Australian distributor wanted Rovio to sign a multiyear contract to provide 1,000 units per month at €12 each? Under these circumstances, management would be well advised to reject the contract because there is a high probability that cost increases would make the order unprofitable in later years. At the very least, management should insist that a cost escalation clause be added to the purchase agreement, specifying that the selling price would increase to cover any cost increases and detailing the cost computation.

Of more concern is the variable nature of all long-run costs. Given adequate time, management must replace fixed assets and may adjust both the number of machines as well as the size of machines used in the manufacturing process. Accordingly, *in the long run, all costs (including costs classified as fixed in a given period) are relevant*. To remain in business in the long run, Rovio must replace equipment, pay property taxes, pay administrative salaries, and so forth. Consequently, management should consider *all costs* (fixed and variable, manufacturing and nonmanufacturing) in evaluating a long-term contract.

Full costs include all costs, regardless of their behavior pattern or activity level. The average full cost per unit is sometimes used to approximate long-run variable costs. If accepting a long-term contract increases the monthly production and sales volume to 6,000 units, the average full cost per unit will be €19.5.

Direct materials	€ 5.0
Direct labor	3.0
Variable manufacturing overhead.	2.0
Variable selling and administrative	2.0
Fixed manufacturing overhead (€30,000/6,000 units).	5.0
Fixed selling and administrative (€15,000/6,000 units).	2.5
Average full cost per unit	€19.5

If the Australian distributor agrees to pay separately all variable selling and administrative expenses associated with the contract, the estimated long-run variable costs are €17.5 per unit (€19.5 − €2). Many managers would say this is the minimum acceptable selling price, especially if the order extends over a long period of time.

Because Rovio has excess productive capacity, no opportunity cost is associated with accepting the Australian distributor's one-time order. There is no alternative use of the productive capacity in the short run, so there is no opportunity cost.

But what if Rovio were operating at capacity? In that case, accepting the special order would require reducing regular sales (assume overtime production is not possible). With an alternative use of the production capacity, an opportunity cost is associated with its use to fill the special order.

Each unit sold to the Australian distributor could otherwise generate a €10 contribution from regular customers. Accepting the special order would cause Rovio to incur an opportunity cost of €10,000 for the contribution margin lost from foregoing sales to regular customers.

Lost sales to regular customers (units)	1,000
Regular unit contribution margin	× €10
Opportunity cost of accepting special order	€10,000

Because this opportunity cost exceeds the €2,000 contribution derived from the special order, management should reject the special order. Accepting the order will reduce profits by €8,000 (€2,000 contribution − €10,000 opportunity cost).

Qualitative Considerations

Although an analysis of cost and revenue information may indicate that a special order is profitable in the short run, management might still reject the order because of qualitative considerations. Any concerns regarding the order's impact on regular customers might lead management to reject the order even if there is excess capacity. If the order involves a special low price, regular customers might demand a similar price reduction and threaten to take their business elsewhere. Alternatively, management might accept the special order while operating at capacity if they believed there were long-term benefits associated with penetrating a new market. Legal factors must also be considered if the special order is from a buyer who competes with regular customers.

Outsourcing Decisions (Make or Buy)

One of the most common applications of relevant cost analysis involves the make-or-buy decision. Virtually any service, product, or component that can be produced or manufactured internally can also be acquired from an external source. The procurement of services, products or components from an external source is call **outsourcing**. For example, the management of the bookstore at your college or university is likely outsourced to Barnes and Noble or Follett, and the dining facilities may be outsourced to Compass Group North America or Aramark Corporation. Similarly, HP and more recently, Samsung, actually manufacture very few of the components of their computers. Instead the manufacture of components is outsourced to other firms such as Intel for computer chips and Seagate for storage devices. Virtually all computer manufacturers, with the exception of Apple, outsource their operating systems to Microsoft.

Any time you call a customer support call center, the representative reached is likely to be working in a different country. A growing number of companies even outsource employees from employee leasing companies. In the past 25 years, outsourcing of goods and services has expanded exponentially with the emergence of well-trained, low-cost labor forces in China and India and other parts of the world.

As the above discussion reveals, the decision to outsource rather than to produce a service or product internally involves a vast array of qualitative issues. The quantitative issues surrounding the outsourcing (or make-or-buy) decision are often less challenging. To illustrate, we continue the Rovio Entertainment example. Suppose a Canadian manufacturer offers a one-year contract to supply Rovio with an Angry Bird action figure at a cost of 2 Euros per unit. Rovio is now faced with the decision to continue to make the figure internally or outsource the component from the Canadian company. An analysis of the materials and operations required to manufacture the figure internally reveals that if Rovio accepts the offer, it will be able to reduce the following:

- Materials costs by 10 percent per unit.
- Direct labor and variable factory overhead costs by 20 percent per unit.
- Fixed manufacturing overhead by €20,000 per year.

A differential analysis of Rovio's make or buy decision is presented in Exhibit 4.3. Continuing to make the figure has a net advantage of €10,000.

EXHIBIT 4.3 Differential Analysis of Make or Buy Decision			
	(1) Cost to Make	**(2)** Cost to Buy	**(1) – (2)** Difference (income effect of buying)
Cost to buy (€2 × 60,000* units)		€120,000	€(120,000)
Cost to make			
Direct materials (€5 × 0.10 × 60,000 units)......	€ 30,000		30,000
Direct labor (€3 × 0.20 × 60,000 units)	36,000		36,000
Variable manufacturing overhead			
(€2 × 0.20 × 60,000 units)	24,000		24,000
Fixed manufacturing overhead	20,000		20,000
Total	€110,000	€120,000	€ (10,000)
Advantage of making		€10,000	

* 5,000 units per month × 12 months

But what if the space currently used to manufacture the figure can be rented to a third party for €40,000 per year? In this case, the production capacity has an alternative use, and the net cash flow from this alternative use is an opportunity cost of making the component. Treating the rent Rovio will not receive if it continues to make the component as an opportunity cost, the analysis in Exhibit 4.4 indicates that buying now has a net advantage of €30,000.

Although outsourcing has become widely accepted across virtually all industries, the results of outsourcing are not uniformly positive. Some companies that made a strong commitment to extensive outsourcing have discovered that there are many problems that can occur when they shift key processes and functions to other companies. It is usually easier to make major changes and to correct production problems related to in-house functions and processes than for those outsourced to other companies, especially if they are located offshore. The following Business Insight discusses the outsourcing experiences of Boeing, Sony, and Samsung.

EXHIBIT 4.4	Differential Analysis of Make or Buy Decision with Opportunity to Rent Facilities			
		(1) Cost to Make	(2) Cost to Buy	(1) − (2) Difference (income effect of buying)
Cost to buy (€2 × 60,000* units)			€120,000	€(120,000)
Cost to make				
Direct materials (€5 × 0.10 × 60,000 units)		€ 30,000		30,000
Direct labor (€3 × 0.20 × 60,000 units)		36,000		36,000
Variable manufacturing overhead				
(€2 × 0.20 × 60,000 units)		24,000		24,000
Fixed manufacturing overhead		20,000		20,000
Opportunity cost of lost rent income		40,000		40,000
Total		€150,000	€120,000	€ (30,000)
Advantage of buying.			€30,000	

* 5,000 units per month × 12 months

BUSINESS INSIGHT

Outsourcing at Boeing, Sony, and Samsung The Boeing Company's design and manufacture of its new generation of passenger aircraft, the Boeing 787 Dreamliner®, represents one of the most extensive examples of outsourcing ever undertaken by a major company. Not only does it represent a radically new design for commercial aircraft, with extensive utilization of carbon-fiber instead of aluminum, it is the first jet in Boeing's history designed and built largely by other companies. Boeing enlisted 43 supplier partners from many countries, including Japan, Korea, Australia, France, Sweden, Italy, and Canada, to finalize the design at 135 sites around the world. Eleven partners have built 3 million square feet of manufacturing facilities to bring this new aircraft to market. The plan was to save about $10 billion of the cost of developing the plane by having parts suppliers from around the world design and build major sections that would be assembled at Boeing's Seattle factory.

The Wall Street Journal reported in late 2007 that, "outsourcing so much responsibility [by Boeing] has turned out to be far more difficult than anticipated. The supplier problems ranged from language barriers to snafus that erupted when some contractors themselves outsourced chunks of work. . . . The missteps underscore the hazards and limits of outsourcing." Boeing had originally planned for a maiden flight for the 787 Dreamliner in August 2007, but due to the unexpected delays, the actual maiden flight was in December 2009, delaying the delivery of the first production units to September of 2011. Still, Boeing is certain that the new airliner will be profitable, and is committed to its outsourcing strategy. Despite the problems of bringing the 787 to market, Boeing and its supplier partners still, "believe that this new method of developing planes is the model for future projects. Once the production line is running smoothly, they argue, it will be more efficient and profitable than existing construction methods."

Sony and Samsung are two of the largest producers in the television market, both offering very similar product lines. With a goal of outsourcing 40% of all production, Sony has adopted a policy of increasing dependence on outside manufacturers for its products. It recently sold its largest North American TV plant to a Taiwan-based company. On the other hand, Samsung's president is committed to the company making its own products, stating that "giving up manufacturing is tantamount to abandoning your brand." With Sony selling production facilities to other companies, Samsung is now the only major TV maker that produces computer chips for its digital TVs. Interestingly, Sony outsources the production of its digital TV computer chips to Samsung.

Sources: J. Lynn Lunsford, "Jet Blues: Boeing Scrambles to Repair Problems With New Plane—Layers of Outsourcing Slow 787 Production; 'Hostage to Suppliers'," *The Wall Street Journal*, December 7, 2007, p. A1. Dominic Gates, "Boeing Still Sure Delayed 787 Will Be Profitable," *The Seattle Times*, August 28, 2009. Moon Ihlwan, "Sony and Samsung's Strategic Split," *Bloomberg Businessweek*, January 18, 2010, p. 52.

Even if outsourcing appears financially advantageous in the short run, management should not decide to outsource before considering a variety of qualitative risk factors. Is the outside supplier interested in developing a long-term relationship or merely attempting to use some temporarily idle capacity? If so, what will happen at the end of the contract period? What impact would a decision to outsource have on the morale of Rovio's employees? Will Rovio have to rehire laid-off employees after the contract expires? Will the outside supplier meet delivery schedules? Does the supplied part meet Rovio's quality standards? Will it continue to meet them? Organizations often manufacture products or provide services they can obtain elsewhere in order to control quality, to have an assured supply source, to avoid dealing with a potential competitor, or to maintain a core competency. Some of these issues are discussed in the Business Insight that follows.

BUSINESS INSIGHT

Rethinking Outsourcing Entrepreneur Farouk Shami's $1 billion dollar manufacturing company announced the decision to move all China-based production operations back to the United States. Citing "loss of control over manufacturing and distribution" as the primary reason for abandoning outsourcing, Shami said "we'll make more money this way because we'll have better quality and a better image" as a made-in-the-USA manufacturer.

Also reversing some of their offshore outsourcing decisions is General Electric, whose CEO, Jeffrey Immelt, stated that "overseas outsourcing had gone too far and that U.S. companies needed to expand domestic production." Daniel Meckstroth, with the Manufacturers Alliance, stated that "many U.S. producers got hurt when the recession hit and they were left holding large backlogs of goods ordered from overseas. Producing closer to customers—and limiting the inventory in the pipeline—is one solution."

Source: Timothy Aeppel, "Coming Home: Appliance Maker Drops China to Produce in Texas," *The Wall Street Journal*, August 24, 2009, p. B1.

The qualitative risk factors discussed above are often magnified when a company goes global, either as an outsourcing buyer or provider. Global outsourcing is often motivated by the desire to get projects completed "on time" and "within budget." However, as the study summarized in the following Research Insight showed, fewer than half of companies engaged in global outsourcing effectively manage their risks.

RESEARCH INSIGHT

Global Assessment of Outsourcing Risks A survey by ESI International of more than 600 key outsourcing decision makers in organizations in North and South America, UK/Europe, Asia/Pacific, the Middle East, and India highlighted the risks faced by companies that buy and/or provide outsourcing services and functions. The top risks identified by the survey respondents are:

Diminished product or service quality	70%
Vendor delays	63
Failure to clearly define contract scope	61
Poor vendor management	50
Loss of in-house skills/capabilities	45
Regulatory compliance failures	40
Lack of financial viability of outsourcing partner	37
Poorly trained contract managers	32

The study found that fewer than half of the participating managers felt that their organization effectively manages the associated risks. More than half expressed a need for improvement in their outsourcing capabilities. Only 11 percent stated that they excel in managing outsourcing projects, thereby providing them with a potential competitive advantage.

Source: Caroline McDonald, "Firms Going Global Often Overlook Supply Chain Risks," *National Underwriter Buyers Report*, September 6/13, 2010, pp. 21-22.

Sell or Process Further

When a product is salable at various stages of completion, management must determine the product's most advantageous selling point. As each stage is completed, management must determine whether to sell the product then or to process it further. For example, petroleum companies have to determine how much crude oil to refine as diesel fuel and how much to process further as gasoline. We consider two types of sell or process further decisions: (1) for a single product and (2) for joint products.

Single Product Decisions

Assume that Scandinavian Furniture, Inc. manufactures modular wood furniture from precut and shaped wood. Although all units are salable before they are sanded and painted, Scandinavian Furniture, Inc. sands and paints all units before they are sold. Management wishes to know if this is the optimal selling point.

A complete listing of unit costs and revenues for the alternative selling points for a low-end storage cabinet follows:

	Per Cabinet		
	Sell after Assembly	Sell after Painting	Difference (income effect of painting)
Selling price....................................	$40	$75	$35
Assembly costs.................................	(25)	(25)	
Sanding and painting costs		(12)	(12)
Contribution margin	$15	$38	$23
Advantage of painting...........................		$23	

The sanding and painting operation has an additional contribution of $23 per unit. The storage cabinets should be sold after they are painted.

The assembly costs are the same under both alternatives. This illustrates that *all costs incurred prior to the decision point are irrelevant*. Given the existence of an assembled chair, the decision alternatives are to sell it now or to process it further. A differential analysis for the decision to sell or process further should include only revenues and the incremental costs of further processing as follows.

Increase in revenues		
Sell after painting..	$75	
Sell after assembly	(40)	$35
Additional costs of sanding and painting..		(12)
Advantage of sanding and painting		$23

The identical solution is obtained if the selling price without further processing is treated as an opportunity cost as follows.

Revenues after painting		$75
Additional costs of sanding and painting..	$12	
Opportunity cost of not selling after assembly	40	(52)
Advantage of sanding and painting		$23

By processing a chair further, Scandinavian Furniture has foregone the opportunity to receive $40 from its sale. Since the chair is already assembled, and the cost of assembly is an irrelevant sunk cost, this $40 is the net cash inflow from the most desirable alternative; it is the opportunity cost of painting.

Joint Product Decisions

Two or more products simultaneously produced by a single process from a common set of inputs are called **joint products**. Joint products are often found in basic industries that process natural raw materials such as dairy, chemical, meat, petroleum, and wood products. In the petroleum industry, crude oil is refined into fuel oil, gasoline, kerosene, diesel, lubricating oil, and other products.

The point in the process where the joint products become separately identifiable is called the **split-off point**. Materials and conversion costs incurred prior to the split-off point are called **joint costs**. For external reporting purposes, a number of techniques are used to allocate joint costs among joint products. We do not discuss these techniques here (interested students should consult a cost accounting textbook), except to note that none of the methods provide information useful for determining what to do with a joint product once it is produced. Because joint costs are incurred prior to the decision point, they are sunk costs. Consequently, *joint costs are irrelevant to a decision to sell a joint product or to process it further*. The only relevant factors are the alternative costs and revenues subsequent to the split-off point.

BUSINESS INSIGHT

Dethroning the Queen of the Skies—Boeing Faces Difficult Product Mix Decisions The Boeing 747 was a symbol of glamour when it was first introduced in 1970 for Pan Am Airways. The plane was massive and promised to reduce the cost-per-seat-mile with its wide-bodied twin-aisled layout. The 747 sparked demand for air travel such that airfares dropped 30 percent. Even though the design has been in service for over four decades, its production is winding down in favor of the Boeing 777X.

The 777X, slated for 2019 deliveries, will seat 35 more passengers and fly thousands of miles farther than the first 747s. The 747s will still find a secondary market, however, because of their convenience for cargo companies. The 747 can open its nose door to load oversized equipment such as construction cranes. Product mix decisions can be solved by using the decision relevance framework outlined in this chapter.

Sources: Jon Ostrower, "Queen of the Skies Nears End of Road," *Wall Street Journal*, April 30, 2013, pp. B1–B2; and Christine Negroni, "Airbus' A380 Is a Huge Jet, But Lacks 747's Glamour," *Seattle Pi*, April 7, 2007.

USE OF LIMITED RESOURCES

LO4 Allocate limited resources for purposes of maximizing short-run profit.

All of us have experienced time as a limiting or constraining resource. With two exams the day after tomorrow and a paper due next week, our problem is how to allocate limited study time. The solution depends on our objectives, our current status (grades, knowledge, skill levels, and so forth), and available time. Given this information, we devise a work plan to best meet our objectives.

Managers must also decide how to best use limited resources to accomplish organizational goals. A supermarket may lose sales because limited shelf space prevents stocking all available brands of soft drinks. A manufacturer may lose sales because limited machine hours or labor hours prevent filling all orders. Managers of for-profit organizations will likely find the problems of capacity constraints less troublesome than the problems of excess capacity; nonetheless, these problems are real. Ultimately, the problem often boils down to a product-mix decision, in which we must decide the mix of products or services we are going to offer our customers with the limited resources available to us.

If the limited resource is not a core business activity, it may be appropriate to outsource additional units of the limited resource externally. For example, many organizations have a small legal staff to handle routine activities; if the internal staff becomes fully committed, the organization seeks outside legal counsel. The external acquisition of such resources was discussed earlier in this chapter.

The long-run solution to the problem of limited resources to perform core activities may be to expand capacity. However, this is usually not feasible in the short run. Economic models suggest that another solution is to reduce demand by increasing the price. Again, this may not be desirable. A hotel, for example, may want to maintain competitive prices. A manufacturer might want to maintain a long-run price to retain customer goodwill to avoid attracting competitors, or to prevent accusations of "price gouging."

Single Constraint

The allocation of limited resources should be made only after a careful consideration of many qualitative factors. The following rule provides a useful starting point in making short-run decisions of how to best use limited resources: *To achieve short-run profit maximization, a for-profit organization should allocate limited resources in a manner that maximizes the contribution per unit of the limited resource.* The application of this rule is illustrated in the following example.

Assume Snap Fitness offers three different personal training packages (A, B, and C) to its customers. These packages vary from a personalized nutrition and exercise training to a one-time consultation. Suppose a limitation of 120 labor hours per week prevents Snap from meeting the demand for its services. Information for the three service packages is as follows:

	A	B	C
Unit selling price	$100	$80	$50
Unit variable costs	(60)	(35)	(25)
Unit contribution margin	$ 40	$45	$25
Hours per unit	4	3	1

Package A has the highest selling price and Package B has the highest unit contribution margin. Package C is shown below to have the highest contribution per hour.

	A	B	C
Unit contribution margin	$40	$45	$25
Hours per unit	÷ 4	÷ 3	÷ 1
Contribution per hour	$10	$15	$25

Following the rule of maximizing the contribution per unit of a single constraining factor (labor hours), Snap should use its limited labor hours to sell Package C. As shown in the following analysis, any other plan would result in lower profits:

	A Highest Selling Price per Unit	B Highest Contribution per Unit	C Highest Contribution per Constraining Factor
Hours available	120	120	120
Hours per unit	÷ 4	÷ 3	÷ 1
Weekly production in units	30	40	120
Unit contribution margin	× $40	× $45	× $25
Total weekly contribution margin	$1,200	$1,800	$3,000

Despite this analysis, management may decide on a product mix that includes some units of A or B or both to satisfy the requests of some "good" customers or to offer a full product line. However, such decisions sacrifice short-run profits.

Multiple Constraints

Continuing our illustration, assume a second constraint; that is, the maximum weekly demand for C is only 90 units, although the company is capable of producing 120 units of C each week. In this case, the limited labor resource should first be used to satisfy the demand for Package C, with any remaining capacity going to produce Package B, which has the next highest contribution per unit of constraining factor. This allocation provides a total weekly contribution of $2,700 as follows.

Available hours	120
Required for C (90 units × 1 hour)	(90)
Hours available for B.	30
Labor hours per unit	÷ 3
Production of B in units	10
Unit contribution margin of B.	× $45
Contribution from B.	$ 450
Contribution from C ($25 per unit × 90 units)	2,250
Total weekly contribution margin	$2,700

When an organization has alternative uses for several limited resources, such as limited labor hours and limited space, the optimal use of those resources cannot be determined using the rule for short-run profit maximization. In these situations, techniques such as linear programming can be used to assist in determining the optimal mix of products or services.

Theory of Constraints

The **theory of constraints** states that every process has a bottleneck (constraining resource) and that production cannot take place faster than it is processed through that bottleneck. The goal of the theory of constraints is to maximize **throughput** (defined as sales revenue minus direct materials costs) in a constrained environment.[1] The theory has several implications for management.

■ Management should identify the bottleneck. This is often difficult when several different products are produced in a facility containing many different production activities. One approach is to walk around and observe where inventory is building up in front of workstations. The bottleneck will likely have the largest piles of work that have been waiting for the longest time.

■ Management should schedule production to maximize the efficient use of the bottleneck resource. Efficiently using the bottleneck resource might necessitate inspecting all units before they reach the bottleneck rather than after the units are completed. The bottleneck resource is too valuable to waste on units that may already be defective.

■ Management should schedule production to avoid a buildup of inventory. Reducing inventory lowers the cost of inventory investments and the cost of carrying inventory. It also assists in improving quality by making it easier to identify quality problems that might otherwise be hidden in large piles of inventory. Reducing inventory will require a change in the attitude of managers who like to see machines and people constantly working. To avoid a buildup of inventory in front of the bottleneck, it may be necessary for people and equipment to remain idle until the bottleneck resource calls for additional input.

■ Management should work to eliminate the bottleneck, perhaps by increasing the capacity of the bottleneck resource, redesigning products so they can be produced with less use of the bottleneck resource, rescheduling production procedures to substitute nonbottleneck resources, or outsourcing work performed by bottleneck resources.

The theory of constraints has implications for management accounting performance reports. Keeping people and equipment working on production full-time is often a goal of man-

---

[1] *The Goal,* by Eliyah M. Goldratt and Jeff Cox, presents the concepts underlying the theory of constraints in the form of a novel.

agement. To support this goal, management accounting performance reports have traditionally highlighted underutilization as an unfavorable variance (see Chapter 10). This has encouraged managers to have people and equipment producing inventory, even if the inventory is not needed or cannot be further processed because of bottlenecks. The theory of constraints suggests that it is better to have nonbottleneck resources idle than it is to have them fully utilized. To support the theory of constraints, performance reports should:

■ Measure the utilization of bottleneck resources
■ Measure factory throughput
■ Not encourage the full utilization of nonbottleneck resources
■ Discourage the buildup of excess inventory

While the theory of constraints is *similar* to our general rule for how to best use limited resources, it emphasizes throughput (selling price minus direct materials) rather than contribution (selling price minus variable costs) in allocating the limited resource. The exclusion of direct labor and variable manufacturing overhead yields larger unit margins, and it may affect resource allocations based on throughput rankings. The result will likely be a reduction in profits from those that could be achieved using our general rule for how to allocate limited resources. Although the theory of constraints has not been widely embraced by companies, many of its users are enthusiastic about its benefits.

Limitations of Decision Analysis Models

Analytical models, such as the relevant cost analysis model and applications presented in this chapter, are very useful in organizing information for purposes of determining the economics of a decision. However, it is important always to keep in mind that models do not make decisions—managers make decisions. The results of analytical models are an essential and necessary starting point in many decisions, but often there are other factors that weigh heavily on a decision that may cause the manager to go against the most economical alternative. There may be human resource, marketing, cultural, logistical, technological, or other factors that outweigh the analytics of a decision situation. It is in these situations where managers demonstrate leadership, problem-solving, and executive skill and potential, or the lack thereof.

CHAPTER-END REVIEW

Epson produces color cartridges for inkjet printers. Suppose cartridges are sold to mail-order distributors for $4.80 each and that manufacturing and other costs are as follows:

Variable Costs per Unit		Fixed Costs per Month	
Direct materials	$2.00	Factory overhead	$15,000
Direct labor	0.20	Selling and administrative.	5,000
Factory overhead	0.25	Total	$20,000
Distribution	0.05		
Total	$2.50		

The variable distribution costs are for transportation to mail-order distributors. Also assume the current monthly production and sales volume is 15,000 and monthly capacity is 20,000 units.

Required
Determine the effect of the following independent situations on monthly profits.

a. A $1.50 increase in the unit selling price should result in an 1,800 unit decrease in monthly sales.

    b. A $1.80 decrease in the unit selling price should result in a 6,000 unit increase in monthly sales. However, because of capacity constraints, the last 1,000 units would be produced during overtime, when the direct labor costs increase by 50 percent.

    c. A Russian distributor has proposed to place a special, one-time order for 4,000 units next month at a reduced price of $4.00 per unit. The distributor would pay all transportation costs. There would be additional fixed selling and administrative costs of $500.00

    d. An Austrian distributor has proposed to place a special, one-time order for 8,000 units at a special price of $4.00 per unit. The distributor would pay all transportation costs. There would be additional fixed selling and administrative costs of $500.00. Assume overtime production is not possible.

    e. A Mexican manufacturer has offered a one-year contract to supply ink for the cartridges at a cost of $1.00 per unit. If Epson accepts the offer, it will be able to reduce variable manufacturing costs by 40 percent and rent some of its factory space to another company for $1,000.00 per month.

    f. The cartridges are currently unpackaged; that is, they are sold in bulk. Individual packaging would increase costs by $0.10 per unit. However, the units could then be sold for $5.05.

The solution is on pages 143–144.

GUIDANCE ANSWERS . . . YOU MAKE THE CALL

You are the Vice President of Manufacturing This is a decision that has both economic and ethical dimensions. Economically, the cost of the old machine is a sunk cost, since the expenditure to acquire it has already been made. If it can be sold to another company to recover part of the initial cost, that amount would be relevant to the decision regarding the new technology. However, you should ignore the cost of the recently purchased machine and consider only the outlay costs that will differ between keeping the recently purchased machine and purchasing the new technology, plus any opportunity costs that may be involved with disposing of the existing machine and acquiring the new machine. From an ethical standpoint, managers are often hesitant to recommend an action that reflects poorly on their past decisions. The temptation is to try to justify the past decision. If you have evaluated all of the relevant costs and have considered all of the qualitative issues associated with upgrading the machine, these should be the basis for making your recommendation, not what it will do to your reputation with your superiors.

KEY TERMS

cost reduction proposal, 109	joint products, 122	revenues, 109
differential cost analysis, 112	opportunity cost, 111	split-off point, 122
full costs, 116	outlay costs, 110	sunk costs, 110
irrelevant costs, 108	outsourcing, 117	theory of constraints, 124
joint costs, 122	relevant costs, 108	throughput, 124

MULTIPLE CHOICE

Multiple Choice Answers
1. a 2. c 3. d 4. a 5. a

  1. Jabo, Inc. is considering a new bifro-spectra machine for its production plant to replace an old machine that originally cost $12,000 and has $9,000 of accumulated depreciation. The new machine can be purchased at a cash cost of $18,000, but the distributor of the new machine has offered to take the old machine in as a trade-in, thereby reducing the cost of the new machine to $16,000. Based only on this information, calculate the total relevant cost of acquiring the new machine.

    a. $16,000, or the net cash paid to the distributor

    b. $18,000, or the gross cost of the new machine

    c. $19,000, or the net cash paid plus the book value ($3,000) of the old machine

    d. $17,000, or the gross cost of the new machine minus the $1,000 loss on disposing of the old machine

2. Bruno Company is a Rhode Island company that sells a branded product regionally to retail customers in New England. It normally sells its product for $30 per unit; however, it has received a one-time offer from a private-brand company on the West Coast to buy 1,000 units at $19 per unit. Even though the company has excess capacity to produce the units, the President of the company immediately rejected the offer; however, the chief accountant stated that it might be a profitable opportunity for the company, even though $19 is below its unit cost of $21, calculated as follows:

Direct materials	$ 9.00
Direct labor	5.00
Variable overhead	4.00
Depreciation & other fixed overhead	3.00
Total unit cost	$21.00

Also, the special order will save $1 per unit in packaging costs since the product will be bulk packaged instead of being individually packaged. Calculate the amount of profit or loss per unit if Bruno accepts the special order.
 a. $2 loss
 b. $1 loss
 c. $2 profit
 d. $1 profit

3. Sitro, LTD had been making a component for one of its products, but is now considering outsourcing the component to a Chinese company, which has offered to sell an unlimited quantity of components for $6 per unit. If Sitro outsources, it could shut down a whole department and rent the building for $2,000 per month. The cost of making the component is $5 per unit, which includes $1.50 of fixed costs, of which only $1.00 per unit can be avoided if the department is shut down. Sitro currently produces about 1,000 units per month. What is the cost advantage or disadvantage of per unit of outsourcing the component?
 a. $1.00 disadvantage
 b. $1.50 disadvantage
 c. $1.00 advantage
 d. $0.50 advantage

4. Mitrex Company makes a simi-finished machine component for the heavy equipment industry that has a unit contribution margin of $250 to Mitrex. A major customer has been purchasing 100 units per month from Mitrex for many years, but has indicated that it would prefer to purchase them already machined to its specifications. It has offered to pay an additional $50 per unit for the finished units. To meet those specifications, Mitrex would have to rent additional equipment at a cost of $2,000 per month and incur labor and other direct costs of $15 per unit. Calculate the per-unit advantage or disadvantage of further processing.
 a. $15 advantage
 b. $35 advantage
 c. $50 advantage
 d. $15 disadvantage

5. Giko, LTD makes three products (Abba, Babba, and Cabba), all of which use a very rare ingredient called, Mecogen. Giko can purchase only 500 ounces of Mecogen per month from its East Asian source. Below are data for the three products:

	Abba	Babba	Cabba
Unit selling price	$80	$65	$100
Unit variable costs.	45	40	60
Unit contribution margin	35	25	40
Mecogen (ounces per unit)	10	15	20

How should Giko allocate the 500 ounces of Mecogen assuming it can sell unlimited quantities of all three produces?
 a. All 500 ounces should be allocated to Abba
 b. All 500 ounces should be allocated to Babba
 c. All 500 ounces should be allocated to Cabba
 d. None of the above

DISCUSSION QUESTIONS

Q4-1. Distinguish between relevant and irrelevant costs.

Q4-2. In evaluating a cost reduction proposal, what three alternatives are available to management?

Q4-3. When are outlay costs relevant and when are they irrelevant?

Q4-4. Relate the manufacturing cost hierarchy discussed in Chapter 2 to the concept of relevant costs. Under what conditions would product-level costs be relevant?

Q4-5. Why is a differential analysis of relevant items preferred to a detailed listing of all costs and revenues associated with each alternative?

Q4-6. How can cost predictions be made when the acquisition of new equipment results in a technological change?

Q4-7. When are opportunity costs relevant to the evaluation of a special order?

Q4-8. Identify some important qualitative considerations in evaluating a decision to make or buy a part.

Q4-9. In a decision to sell or to process further, of what relevance are costs incurred prior to the decision point? Explain your answer.

Q4-10. How should limited resources be used to achieve short-run profit maximization?

Q4-11. What should performance reports do in support of the theory of constraints?

Assignments with the ✅ logo in the margin are available in BusinessCourse.
See the Preface of the book for details.

MINI EXERCISES

LO1 **M4-12.** **Relevant Cost Terms: Matching**

A company that produces three products, M, N, and O, is evaluating a proposal that will result in doubling the production of N and discontinuing the production of O. The facilities currently used to produce O will be devoted to the production of N. Furthermore, additional machinery will be acquired to produce N. The production of M will not be affected. All products have a positive contribution margin.

Required

Presented below are a number of phrases related to the proposal followed by a list of cost terms. For each phrase, select the most appropriate cost term. Each term is used only once.

Phrases

1. Cost of equipment to produce O
2. Increased variable costs of N
3. Property taxes on the new machinery
4. Revenues from the sale of M
5. Increased revenue from the sale of N
6. Contribution margin of O
7. Variable costs of M
8. Company president's salary

Cost terms

a. Opportunity cost
b. Sunk cost
c. Irrelevant variable outlay cost
d. Irrelevant fixed outlay cost
e. Relevant variable outlay cost
f. Relevant fixed outlay cost
g. Relevant revenues
h. Irrelevant revenues

M4-13. Relevant Cost Terms: Matching

A company that produces and sells 4,000 units per month, with the capacity to produce 5,000 units per month, is evaluating a one-time, special order for 2,000 units from a large chain store. Accepting the order will increase variable manufacturing costs and certain fixed selling and administrative costs. It will also require the company to forego the sale of 1,000 units to regular customers.

Required

Presented below are a number of statements related to the proposal followed by a list of cost terms. For each statement, select the most appropriate cost term. Each term is used only once.

Statements

1. Increased revenues from special order
2. Lost contribution margin from foregone sales to regular customers
3. Revenues from 4,000 units sold to regular customers
4. Variable cost of 4,000 units sold to regular customers
5. Increase in fixed selling and administrative expenses
6. Cost of existing equipment used to produce special order
7. Salary paid to current supervisor who oversees manufacture of special order
8. Increased variable costs of special order

Cost terms

a. Irrelevant variable outlay cost
b. Irrelevant fixed outlay cost
c. Sunk cost
d. Relevant variable outlay cost
e. Relevant fixed outlay cost
f. Opportunity cost
g. Relevant revenues
h. Irrelevant revenues

M4-14. Identifying Relevant Costs and Revenues

The City of Ridgeland operates a power plant on a river that flows through town. The village uses some of this generated electricity to operate a water treatment plant and sells the excess electricity to a local utility. The city council is evaluating two alternative proposals:

*   *Proposal A* calls for replacing the generators used in the plant with more efficient generators that will produce more electricity and have lower operating costs. The salvage value of the old generators is higher than their removal cost.
*   *Proposal B* calls for raising the level of the dam to retain more water for generating power and increasing the force of water flowing through the dam. This will significantly increase the amount of electricity generated by the plant. Operating costs will not be affected.

Required

Presented are a number of cost and revenue items. Indicate in the appropriate columns whether each item is relevant or irrelevant to proposals A and B.

	Proposal A	Proposal B
1. Cost of new furniture for City Manager's office		
2. Cost of old generators		
3. Cost of new generators		
4. Operating cost of old generators		
5. Operating cost of new generators		
6. Police Chief's salary		
7. Depreciation on old generators		
8. Salvage value of old generators		
9. Removal cost of old generators		
10. Cost of raising dam		
11. Maintenance costs of water plant		
12. Revenues from sale of electricity		

LO1 **M4-15.** **Classifying Relevant and Irrelevant Items**

The law firm of Taylor, Taylor, and Tower has been asked to represent a local client. All legal proceedings will be held out of town in Chicago.

Required

The law firm's accountant has asked you to help determine the incremental cost of accepting this client. Classify each of the following items on the basis of their relationship to this engagement. Items may have multiple classifications.

| | Relevant costs | | Irrelevant costs | |
	Opportunity	Outlay	Outlay	Sunk

1. The case will require three attorneys to stay four nights in a Chicago hotel. The predicted hotel bill is $2,400.
2. Taylor, Taylor, and Tower's professional staff is paid $2,000 per day for out-of-town assignments.
3. Last year, depreciation on Taylor, Taylor, and Tower's office was $25,000.
4. Round-trip transportation to Chicago is expected to cost $250 per person.
5. The firm has recently accepted an engagement that will require partners to spend two weeks in Cincinnati. The predicted out-of-pocket costs of this trip are $8,500.
6. The firm has a maintenance contract on its computer equipment that will cost $2,200 next year.
7. If the firm accepts the client and sends attorneys to Chicago, it will have to decline a conflicting engagement in Miami that would have provided a net cash inflow of $15,000.
8. The firm's variable overhead is $80 per client hour.
9. The firm pays $250 per year for Mr. Tower's subscription to a law journal.
10. Last year the firm paid $3,500 to increase the insulation in its building.

LO1, 2, 3 **M4-16.** **Relevant Costs for Equipment Replacement Decision**

Health Scan, Inc., paid $50,000 for X-ray equipment four years ago. The equipment was expected to have a useful life of 10 years from the date of acquisition with annual operating costs of $35,000. Technological advances have made the machine purchased four years ago obsolete with a zero salvage value. An improved X-ray device incorporating the new technology is available at an initial cost of $55,000 and annual operating costs of $21,000. The new machine is expected to last only six years before it, too, is obsolete. Asked to analyze the financial aspects of replacing the obsolete but still functional machine, Health Scan's accountant prepared the following analysis. After looking over these numbers, the company's manager rejected the proposal.

Six-year savings [($35,000 − $21,000) × 6]	$84,000
Cost of new machine	(55,000)
Undepreciated cost of old machine	(30,000)
Advantage (disadvantage) of replacement	$ (1,000)

Required

Perform an analysis of relevant costs to determine whether the manager made the correct decision.

LO1, 2, 3 **M4-17.** **Special Order**

Shanghai Exporters, LTD produces wall mounts for flat panel television sets. The forecasted income statement for 2014 is as follows:

SHANGHAI EXPORTERS, LTD Budgeted Income Statement For the Year 2014	
Sales ($44 per unit)	$4,400,000
Cost of good sold ($32 per unit)	(3,200,000)
Gross profit	1,200,000
Selling expenses ($3 per unit)	(300,000)
Net income	$ 900,000

Additional Information

(1) Of the production costs and selling expenses, $800,000 and $100,000, respectively, are fixed.
(2) Shanghai Exporters, LTD received a special order from a hospital supply company offering to buy 12,500 wall mounts for $30. If it accepts the order, there will be no additional selling expenses, and there is currently sufficient excess capacity to fill the order. The company's sales manager argues for rejecting the order because "we are not in the business of paying $32 to make a product to sell for $30."

Required

Do you think the company should accept the special order? Should the decision be based only on the profitability of the sale, or are there other issues that Shanghai should consider? Explain.

M4-18. Sell or Process Further   LO1, 2, 3

Great Lakes Boat Company manufactures sailboat hulls at a cost of $4,200 per unit. The hulls are sold to boat- yards for $5,000. The company is evaluating the desirability of adding masts, sails, and rigging to the hulls prior to sale at an additional cost of $1,500. The completed sailboats could then be sold for $6,000 each.

Required

Determine whether the company should sell sailboat hulls or process them further into complete sailboats. Assume sales volume will not be affected.

EXERCISES

E4-19. Special Order   LO1, 2, 3

Healthy Foods Farms grows organic vegetables and sells them to local restaurants after processing. The firm's leading product is Salad-in-a-Bag, which is a mixture of organic green salad ingredients prepared and ready to serve. The company sells a large bag to restaurants for $25. It calculates the variable cost per bag at $17 (including $0.50 for local delivery), and the average total cost per bag is $20.10. Because the vegetables are perishable and Healthy Foods Farms is experiencing a large crop, the firm has extra capacity. A representative of a restaurant association in another city has offered to buy fresh salad stock from the company to augment its regular supply during an upcoming international festival. The restaurant association wants to buy 2,500 bags during the next month for $19 per bag. Delivery to restaurants in the other city will cost the company $0.75 per bag. It can meet most of the order with excess capacity but would sacrifice 400 bags of regular sales to fill this special order. Please assist Healthy Foods Farms' management by answering the following questions.

Required

a. Using differential analysis, what is the impact on profits of accepting this special order?
b. What nonquantitative issues should management consider before making a final decision?
c. How would the analysis change if the special order were for 2,500 bags per month for the next five years?

LO1, 2, 3 **E4-20.** **Special Order**

Nature's Garden, a new restaurant situated on a busy highway in Pomona, California, specializes in a chef's salad selling for $9. Daily fixed costs are $1,200, and variable costs are $5 per meal. With a capacity of 800 meals per day, the restaurant serves an average of 750 meals each day.

Required

a. Determine the current average cost per meal.

b. A busload of 30 Girl Scouts stops on its way home from the San Bernardino National Forest. The leader offers to bring them in if the scouts can all be served a meal for a total of $180. The owner refuses, saying he would lose $0.60 per meal if he accepted this offer. How do you think the owner arrived at the $0.60 figure? Comment on the owner's reasoning.

c. A local businessman on a break overhears the conversation with the leader and offers the owner a one-year contract to feed 300 of the businessman's employees one meal each day at a special price of $5.50 per meal. Should the restaurant owner accept this offer? Why or why not?

LO1, 2, 3 **E4-21.** **Special Order: High-Low Cost Estimation**

SafeRide, Inc. produces air bag systems that it sells to North American automobile manufacturers. Although the company has a capacity of 300,000 units per year, it is currently producing at an annual rate of 180,000 units. SafeRide, Inc. has received an order from a German manufacturer to purchase 60,000 units at $9.00 each. Budgeted costs for 180,000 and 240,000 units are as follows:

	180,000 Units	240,000 Units
Manufacturing costs		
Direct materials	$ 450,000	$ 600,000
Direct labor.	315,000	420,000
Factory overhead.	1,215,000	1,260,000
Total	1,980,000	2,280,000
Selling and administrative.	765,000	780,000
Total	$2,745,000	$3,060,000
Costs per unit		
Manufacturing	$11.00	$ 9.50
Selling and administrative.	4.25	3.25
Total	$15.25	$12.75

Sales to North American manufacturers are priced at $20 per unit, but the sales manager believes the company should aggressively seek the German business even if it results in a loss of $3.75 per unit. She believes obtaining this order would open up several new markets for the company's product. The general manager commented that the company cannot tighten its belt to absorb the $225,000 loss ($3.75 × 60,000) it would incur if the order is accepted.

Required

a. Determine the financial implications of accepting the order.

b. How would your analysis differ if the company were operating at capacity? Determine the advantage or disadvantage of accepting the order under full-capacity circumstances.

LO1, 2, 3 **E4-22.** **Outsourcing (Make-or-Buy) Decision**

HEWLETT-PACKARD (HPQ)

SANMINA-SCI (SANM)

Assume a division of Hewlett-Packard currently makes 10,000 circuit boards per year used in producing diagnostic electronic instruments at a cost of $34 per board, consisting of variable costs per unit of $24 and fixed costs per unit of $8. Further assume Sanmina-SCI offers to sell Hewlett-Packard the 10,000 circuit boards for $34 each. If Hewlett-Packard accepts this offer, the facilities currently used to make the boards could be rented to one of Hewlett-Packard's suppliers for $27,000 per year. In addition, $5 per unit of the fixed overhead applied to the circuit boards would be totally eliminated.

Required

Should HP outsource this component from Samina-SCI? Support your answer with relevant cost calculations.

E4-23. **Outsourcing (Make-or-Buy) Decision**

Mountain Air Limited manufactures a line of room air purifiers. Management is currently evaluating the possible production of an air purifier for automobiles. Based on an annual volume of 10,000 units, the predicted cost per unit of an auto air purifier follows.

Direct materials	$ 8.00
Direct labor	1.50
Factory overhead	7.00
Total	$16.50

These cost predictions include $50,000 in fixed factory overhead averaged over 10,000 units.

The completed air purifier units include a battery-operated electric motor, which Mountain Air assembles with parts purchased from an outside vendor for $2.00 per motor. Mini Motor Company has offered to supply an assembled battery-operated motor at a cost of $5.00 per unit, with a minimum annual order of 5,000 units. If Mountain Air accepts this offer, it will be able to reduce the variable labor and variable overhead costs of the auto air purifier by 50 percent.

Required

a. Determine whether Mountain Air should continue to make the electric motor or outsource it from Mini Motor Company. (Hint: analyze the relevant costs of making the "motors," not the entire air purifier.)

b. If it could otherwise rent the motor-assembly space for $20,000 per year, should it make or outsource this component?

c. What additional factors should it consider in deciding whether to make or outsource the electric motors?

E4-24. **Make or Buy**

Rashad Rahavy, M.D., is a general practitioner whose offices are located in the South Falls Professional Building. In the past, Dr. Rahavy has operated his practice with a nurse, a receptionist/secretary, and a part-time bookkeeper. Dr. Rahavy, like many small-town physicians, has billed his patients and their insurance companies from his own office. The part-time bookkeeper, who works 10 hours per week, is employed exclusively for this purpose.

North Falls Physician's Service Center has offered to take over all of Dr. Rahavy's billings and collections for an annual fee of $12,000. If Dr. Rahavy accepts this offer, he will no longer need the bookkeeper. The bookkeeper's wages and fringe benefits amount to $15 per hour, and the bookkeeper works 50 weeks per year. With all the billings and collections done elsewhere, Dr. Rahavy will have two additional hours available per week to see patients. He sees an average of three patients per hour at an average fee of $30 per visit. Dr. Rahavy's practice is expanding, and new patients often have to wait several weeks for an appointment. He has resisted expanding his office hours or working more than 50 weeks per year. Finally, if Dr. Rahavy signs on with the center, he will no longer need to rent a records storage facility for $100 per month.

Required

Conduct a relevant cost analysis to determine if it is profitable to outsource the bookkeeping.

E4-25. **Sell or Process Further**

Port Allen Chemical Company processes raw material D into joint products E and F. Raw material D costs $6 per liter. It costs $100 to convert 100 liters of D into 60 liters of E and 40 liters of F. Product F can be sold immediately for $6 per liter or processed further into Product G at an additional cost of $5 per liter. Product G can then be sold for $13 per liter.

Required

Determine whether Product F should be sold or processed further into Product G.

E4-26. **Limited Resources**

Toledo Manufacturing Company, Ltd., produces three products: X, Y, and Z. A limitation of 240 labor hours per week prevents the company from meeting the sales demand for these products. Product information is as follows:

	X	Y	Z
Unit selling price	$160	$100	$210
Unit variable costs	(100)	(50)	(180)
Unit contribution margin	$ 60	$ 50	$ 30
Labor hours per unit	6	4	6

Required

a. Determine the weekly contribution from each product when total labor hours are allocated to the product with the highest
   1. Unit selling price.
   2. Unit contribution margin.
   3. Contribution per labor hour.
   (*Hint:* Each situation is independent of the others.)

b. What generalization can be made regarding the allocation of limited resources to achieve short-run profit maximization?

c. Determine the opportunity cost the company will incur if management requires the weekly production of 12 units of Z.

d. Give reasons why a company may not allocate resources in the most economical way in some situations.

LO4 E4-27. Limited Resources

Maria Pajet, a regional sales representative for UniTec Systems, Inc., has been working about 80 hours per week calling on a total of 123 regular customers each month. Because of family and health considerations, she has decided to reduce her hours to a maximum of 160 per month. Unfortunately, this cutback will require Maria to turn away some of her regular customers or, at least, serve them less frequently than once a month. Maria has developed the following information to assist her in determining how to best allocate time:

	Customer Classification		
	Large Business	Small Business	Individual
Number of customers	8	35	80
Average monthly sales per customer	$2,500	$1,500	$600
Commission percentage	5%	8%	10%
Hours per customer per monthly visit	5.0	3.0	2.5

Required

a. Develop a monthly plan that indicates the number of customers Maria should call on in each classification to maximize her monthly sales commissions.

b. Determine the monthly commissions Maria will earn if she implements this plan.

c. Give one or two reasons why Maria might decide not to follow the conclusions of the above analysis entirely?

PROBLEMS

LO1, 2, 3 P4-28. Multiple Changes in Profit Plans

In an attempt to improve profit performance, Anderson Company's management is considering a number of alternative actions. An October 2014 contribution income statement for Anderson Company follows.

ANDERSON COMPANY
Contribution Income Statement
For Month of October 2014

Sales (10,000 units × $40)		$400,000
Less variable costs		
Direct materials (10,000 units × $5)	$ 50,000	
Direct labor (10,000 units × $14).	140,000	
Variable factory overhead (10,000 units × $6)	60,000	
Selling and administrative (10,000 units × $5)	50,000	(300,000)
Contribution margin (10,000 units × $10)		100,000
Less fixed costs		
Factory overhead.	50,000	
Selling and administrative	60,000	(110,000)
Net income (loss).		$ (10,000)

Required
Determine the effect of each of the following independent situations on monthly profit.
a. Purchasing automated assembly equipment, which should reduce direct labor costs by $5 per unit and increase variable overhead costs by $2 per unit and fixed factory overhead by $22,000 per month.
b. Reducing the selling price by $5 per unit. This should increase the monthly sales by 5,000 units. At this higher volume, additional equipment and salaried personnel would be required. This will increase fixed factory overhead by $2,800 per month and fixed selling and administrative costs by $2,500 per month.
c. Buying rather than manufacturing a component of Jacobson's final product. This will increase direct materials costs by $12 per unit. However, direct labor will decline $4 per unit, variable factory overhead will decline $1 per unit, and fixed factory overhead will decline $15,000 per month.
d. Increasing the unit selling price by $4 per unit. This action should result in a 1,000-unit decrease in monthly sales.
e. Combining alternatives (a) and (d).

P4-29. Multiple Changes in Profit Plans: Multiple Products　　　　　　　　　　　　　LO1, 2, 3
Information on Guadalupe Ltd.'s three products follows:

	A	B	C
Unit sales per month.	800	1,500	800
Selling price per unit	$ 5.00	$7.50	$4.00
Variable costs per unit.	(5.20)	(6.00)	(2.00)
Unit contribution margin	$(0.20)	$1.50	$2.00

Required
Determine the effect each of the following situations would have on monthly profits. Each situation should be evaluated independently of all others.
a. Product A is discontinued.
b. Product A is discontinued, and the subsequent loss of customers causes sales of Product B to decline by 100 units.
c. The selling price of A is increased to $5.50 with a sales decrease of 150 units.
d. The price of Product B is increased to $8.00 with a resulting sales decrease of 200 units. However, some of these customers shift to Product A; sales of Product A increase by 140 units.
e. Product A is discontinued, and the plant in which A was produced is used to produce D, a new product. Product D has a unit contribution margin of $0.30. Monthly sales of Product D are predicted to be 600 units.
f. The selling price of Product C is increased to $4.50, and the selling price of Product B is decreased to $7.00. Sales of C decline by 200 units, while sales of B increase by 300 units.

LO1, 2 **P4-30.** **Relevant Costs and Differential Analysis**

College Station Bank paid $60,000 for a check-sorting machine in January 2010. The machine had an estimated life of 10 years and annual operating costs of $55,000, excluding depreciation. Although management is pleased with the machine, recent technological advances have made it obsolete. Consequently, as of January 2014, the machine has a book value of $20,000, a remaining operating life of 6 years, and a salvage value of $0.

The manager of operations is evaluating a proposal to acquire a new optical scanning and sorting machine. The new machine would cost $100,000 and reduce annual operating costs to $35,000, excluding depreciation. Because of expected technological improvements, the manager believes the new machine will have an economic life of 6 years and no salvage value at the end of that life. Prior to signing the papers authorizing the acquisition of the new machine, the president of the bank prepared the following analysis:

Six-year savings [($55,000 − $35,000) × 6 years]	$120,000
Cost of new machine	(100,000)
Loss on disposal of old machine	(20,000)
Advantage (disadvantage) of replacement	$ 0

After looking at these numbers, the manager rejected the proposal and commented that he was "tired of looking at marginal projects. This bank is in business to make a profit, not to break even. If you want to break even, go work for the government."

Required

a. Evaluate the president's analysis.
b. Prepare a differential analysis of six-year totals for the old and the new machines.
c. Speculate on some limitations of the model or other issues that might be a factor in making a final decision.

LO1, 2, 3 **P4-31.** **Special Order**

Mobile Solutions Company produces a variety of electric scooters. Management follows a pricing policy of manufacturing cost plus 60 percent. In response to a request from Northern Cycles, LLC, the following price has been developed for an order of 300 scooters (the smallest scooter Mobile Solutions produces):

Manufacturing costs	
Direct materials	$12,000
Direct labor	15,000
Factory overhead	18,000
Total	45,000
Markup (60%)	27,000
Selling price	$72,000

Northern Cycles rejected this price and offered to purchase the 300 scooters at a price of $60,000. The following additional information is available:

- Mobile Solutions has sufficient excess capacity to produce the scooters.
- Factory overhead is applied on the basis of direct labor dollars.
- Budgeted factory overhead is $400,000 for the current year. Of this amount, $100,000 is fixed. Of the $18,000 of factory overhead assigned to the Northern Cycles order, only $13,500 is driven by the special order; $4,500 is a fixed cost.
- Selling and administrative expenses are budgeted as follows:

Fixed	$90,000 per year
Variable	$20 per unit manufactured and sold

Required

a. The president of Mobile Solutions wants to know if he should allow Northern Cycles to have the scooters for $60,000. Determine the effect on profits of accepting Northern Cycles' offer.

    b.   Briefly explain why certain costs should be omitted from the analysis in requirement (a).

    c.   Assume Mobile Solutions is operating at capacity and could sell the 300 scooters at its regular markup.

       1.   Determine the opportunity cost of accepting Northern Cycles' offer.

       2.   Determine the effect on profits of accepting Northern Cycles' offer.

    d.   What other factors should Mobile Solutions consider before deciding to accept the special order?

P4-32.   **Special Order**   **LO1, 2, 3**

Every Halloween, Glacier Ice Cream Shop offers a trick-or-treat package of 25 coupons for $4. The coupons are redeemable by children 12 years or under, for a single-scoop cone, with a limit of one coupon per child per visit. Coupon sales average 500 books per year. The printing costs are $50. A single-scoop cone of Glacier ice cream normally sells for $0.60. The variable costs of a single-scoop cone are $0.40.

Required

    a.   Determine the loss if all coupons are redeemed without any other effect on sales.

    b.   Assume all coupons will not be redeemed. With regular sales unaffected, determine the coupon redemption rate at which Glacier will break even on the offer.

    c.   Assuming regular sales are not affected and one additional single-scoop cone is sold at the regular price each time a coupon is redeemed, determine the coupon redemption rate at which Glacier will break even on the offer.

    d.   Determine the profit or loss incurred on the offer if the coupon redemption rate is 60 percent and:

       1.   One-fourth of the redeemed coupons have no effect on sales.

       2.   One-fourth of the redeemed coupons result in additional sales of two single-scoop cones.

       3.   One-fourth of the redeemed coupons result in additional sales of three single-scoop cones.

       4.   One-fourth of the redeemed coupons come out of regular sales of single-scoop cones.

P4-33.   **Applications of Differential Analysis**   **LO1, 2, 3**

Nantucket Optics Company manufactures high-end sunglasses that it sells to mail-order distributors for $60. Manufacturing and other costs follow:

Variable Costs per Unit		Fixed Costs per Month	
Direct materials	$13	Factory overhead	$20,000
Direct labor	12	Selling and administrative.	10,000
Factory overhead	2	Total	$30,000
Distribution	3		
Total	$30		

The variable distribution costs are for transportation to mail-order distributors. The current monthly production and sales volume is 5,000 units. Monthly capacity is 6,000 units.

Required

Determine the effect of each of the following independent situations on monthly profits.

    a.   A $2.00 increase in the unit selling price should result in a 1,200-unit decrease in monthly sales.

    b.   A 10% decrease in the unit selling price should result in a 2,000-unit increase in monthly sales. However, because of capacity constraints, the last 1,000 units would be produced during overtime with the direct labor costs increasing by 60 percent.

    c.   A British distributor has proposed to place a special, one-time order for 1,000 units at a reduced price of $55 per unit. The distributor would pay all transportation costs. There would be additional fixed selling and administrative costs of $1,000.

    d.   A Swiss distributor has proposed to place a special, one-time order for 2,500 units at a special price of $55 per unit. The distributor would pay all transportation costs. There would be additional fixed selling and administrative costs of $1,500. Assume overtime production is not possible.

e. Nantucket Optics provides a designer case for each pair of sunglasses that it manufactures. A Chinese manufacturer has offered a one-year contract to supply the cases at a cost of $4 per unit. If Nantucket Optics accepts the offer, it will be able to reduce variable manufacturing costs by 10%, reduce fixed costs by $1,500, and rent out some freed-up space for $2,000 per month.

f. The glasses also come with four different color inserts that allow the user to change the appearance of the glasses to match her or his clothing. Making the glasses in only one color without the color inserts would reduce the cost by $5, and Nantucket Optics believes the selling price would have to decrease to $55.

LO1, 2, 3 **P4-34.** **Applications of Differential Analysis**

Adventure Expeditions offers guided back-country hiking/camping trips in British Columbia. Adventure provides a guide and all necessary food and equipment at a fee of $50 per person per day. Adventure currently provides an average of 600 guide-days per month in June, July, August, and September. Based on available equipment and staff, maximum capacity is 800 guide-days per month. Monthly variable and fixed operating costs (valued in Canadian dollars) are as follows:

Variable Costs per Guide-Day		Fixed Costs per Month	
Food..........................	$ 5	Equipment rental................	$ 5,000
Guide salary....................	25	Administration..................	5,000
Supplies.......................	2	Advertising.....................	2,000
Insurance......................	8	Total..........................	$12,000
Total..........................	$40		

Required

Determine the effect of each of the following situations on monthly profits. Each situation is to be evaluated independently of all others.

a. A $12 increase in the daily fee should result in a 150-unit decrease in monthly sales.

b. A $7 decrease in the daily fee should result in a 300-unit increase in monthly sales. However, because of capacity constraints, the last 100 guide-days would be provided by subcontracting to another firm at a cost of $46 per guide-day.

c. A French tour agency has proposed to place a special, one-time order for 75 guide-days at a reduced fee of $45 per guide-day. The agency would pay all insurance costs. There would be additional fixed administrative costs of $200.

d. An Italian tour agency has proposed to place a special, one-time order for 300 guide-days next month at a special fee of $40 per guide-day. The agency would pay all insurance costs. There would be additional fixed administrative costs of $200. Assume additional capacity beyond 800 guide-days is not available.

e. An Alberta outdoor supply company has offered to supply all necessary food and camping equipment at $7.50 per guide-day. This eliminates the current food costs and reduces the monthly equipment rental costs to $1,800.

f. Clients currently must carry a backpack and assist in camp activities such as cooking. Adventure is considering the addition of mules to carry all food and equipment and the hiring of college students to perform camp activities such as cooking. This will increase variable costs by $12 per guide-day and fixed costs by $1,000 per month. However, 600 full-service guide-days per month could now be sold at $75 each.

LO1, 2 **P4-35.** **Continue or Discontinue**

Lakeland Eye Clinic primarily performs three medical procedures: cataract removal, corneal implants, and laser keratotomy. At the end of the first quarter of this year, Dr. Pathaja, president of Lakeland, expressed grave concern about the cataract sector because it had reported a loss of $50,000. He rationalized that "since the cataract market is losing $50,000, and the overall practice is making $165,000, if we eliminate the cataract market, our total profits will increase to $215,000."

Required

a. Is the president's analysis correct?

b. Will total profits increase if the cataract section is dropped?

c. Is it possible total profits will decline?

CASES AND PROJECTS

C4-36. Assessing the Impact of an Incentive Plan[2]

Overview

Ladbrecks is a major department store with fifty retail outlets. The company's stores compete with outlets run by companies such as Nordstrom, Macys, Bloomingdales, and Saks Fifth Avenue. During the early nineties the company decided that providing excellent customer service was the key ingredient for success in the retail industry. Therefore, during the mid 1990s the company implemented an incentive plan for its sales associates in twenty of its stores. Your job is to assess the financial impact of the plan and to provide a recommendation to management to continue or discontinue the plan based on your findings.

Incentives in Retail

The past decade has evidenced a concerted effort by many firms to empower and motivate employees to improve performance. A recent New York Times article reported that more and more firms are offering bonus plans to hourly workers. An Ernst and Young survey of the retail industry indicates that virtually all department stores currently offer incentive programs such as straight commissions, base salary plus commission, and quota bonus programs. Although these programs can add to payroll costs, the survey respondents indicated that they believe these plans have contributed to major improvements in customer service.

Company's Background

Ladbrecks was founded by members of the Ladbreck family in the 1880s. The first store opened under the name Ladbreck Dry Goods. Growth was fueled through acquisitions as the industry consolidated during the 1960s. Over this hundred-year period, sales associates were paid a fixed hourly wage. Raises were based on seniority. Sales associates were expected to be neat and courteous to customers. The advent of specialty stores and the stated intention of an upscale west coast retailer to begin opening stores in the Midwest concerned Ladbreck's management. Building on its history of excellence in customer service, the company initiated its performance-based incentive plan to support its stated firm-wide strategy of "customer emphasis" with "employee empowerment." Management expected it to result in further enhancement of customer service and, consequently, in an increase in sales generated at its stores.

Incentive Plan

The plan was implemented in stores sequentially as company managers intended to examine and evaluate the plan's impact on sales and profitability. Initially, the firm selected one store from a group of similar stores in the same general area to begin the implementation. By the end of 1994, ten stores had implemented the plan. In 1995, ten more stores implemented the plan, bringing the total to 20 out of a total of 50.

 The performance-based incentive plan is best described as a bonus program. At the time of the plan's implementation, sales associates received little in the form of annual merit increases, and promotions were rare. The bonus payment became the only significant reward for high performance. Each week sales associates are paid a base hourly rate times hours worked. In addition, under the plan sales associates could increase their compensation by receiving a bonus at the end of each quarter. The contract provides sales-force personnel with a cash bonus only if the actual quarterly sales generated by the employee exceed a quarterly sales goal. Individualized pre-specified sales goals were established for each employee based only on the individual's base hourly rate, hours worked and a multiplier (multiplier = 1/bonus rate). The bonus is computed as a fixed percentage of the excess sales (actual sales minus a pre-specified sales goal) by the employee in a quarter (see Exhibit 1).

$$\text{Employee's Bonus} = .08 \times (\text{Employee's actual sales for quarter} - \text{employee's targeted sales for quarter})$$

$$\text{Where employee's targeted sales for quarter} = \text{Employee's hourly wage} \times \text{Hours worked in quarter} \times 12.5$$

[2] Written to illustrate the use of relevant costs and revenues for decision making. This example is based on an actual company's experience with implementing an incentive plan. The company name and the financial numbers and key ratios have been altered.

Senior managers regarded the incentive plan as a major change for the firm and its sales force. Management expected that the new incentive scheme would motivate many changes in employee behavior that would enhance customer service. Sales associates were now expected to build a client base to generate repeat sales. Actions consistent with this approach include developing and updating customer address lists (including details of their needs and preferences), writing thank you notes and contacting customers about upcoming sales and new merchandise that matched their preferences.

Consultant's Task

Management decided to call you in to provide an independent assessment. While the company thought that sales had increased with the plan's implementation, the human resource department did not know exactly how to quantify the plan's impact on sales and expenses. It suspected that employee salaries, cost of goods sold, and inventory carrying costs, as well as sales, may have changed due to the plan's implementation. You, therefore, requested information on these financial variables.

Sales Analysis: Because each of the twenty stores implemented the plan at different dates, and store sales fluctuated greatly with the seasons and the economy, you could not simply plot store sales. Instead, for each of the twenty stores, you picked another Ladbreck store as a control and computed for 48 months the following series of monthly sales[3]:

$$\text{Percent Change in Sales} = \frac{[(\text{Plan Store Sales in Month t} \div \text{Plan Store Sales in Month t-24}) -}{(\text{Control Store Sales in Month t} \div \text{Control Store Sales in Month t-24})] \times 100}$$

The plan's implementation was denoted as month 25, so you had 24 months prior to the plan and 24 months after the plan. Averages were then taken for the twenty stores. If the control procedure worked then you expected that the first 24 months of the series would fluctuate around zero. The actual results are reported in Figure 1 below. Month 25 is denoted as the rollout month, the month the incentive plan began.

Expense Analysis: You then plotted wage expense/sales, cost of goods sold/sales, and inventory turnover for the twenty stores for the 24 months preceding the plan and the first 24 months after plan implementation. After pulling out seasonal effects these monthly series are presented in figures 2, 3 and 4. If the plan has no impact on these expenses then you would expect no dramatic change in the series around month 25.

Figure 2   plots (wage expense in month t/sales in month t)
Figure 3   plots (cost of goods sold in month t/sales in month t)
Figure 4   plots "annual" turnover computed as (12 × cost of goods sold in month t/inventory at beginning of month t)

> For example, if monthly cost of sales is $100 and the annual inventory turnover ratio is 4, it suggests a monthly turnover of 0.333 with the firm holding an average inventory of $300 throughout the year. (Note that a monthly inventory turnover of .333 implies an annual turnover of 4 (from 12 × 0.333).)

Financial Report for Store: A typical annual income statement for a pre-plan Ladbreck store before fixed charges, taxes and incidentals looks as follows.

	Total	Percent
Sales	10,000,000	100
Cost of Goods Sold	6,300,000	63
Gross Profit	3,700,000	37
Employee salaries	800,000	8
Profit before fixed charges	2,900,000	29

---

[3] For instance, assume sales for plan store were $2,200 this January and $2,000 two Januarys ago. Also assume that sales in the control store were $4,400 this January and $4,000 two Januarys ago. Percent change = 2,200/2,000 − 4,400/4,000 = 0.

A store also has substantial charges for rent, management salaries, insurance, etc. but they are fixed with respect to the incentive plan.

Required

a. Suppose the goal of the firm is to now provide superior customer service by having the sales consultant identify and sell to the specific needs of the customer. What does this goal suggest about a change in managerial accounting and control systems?

b. Provide an estimate of the impact of the incentive plan on sales.

c. Did the sales impact occur all at once, or did it occur gradually?

d. What is the impact of the incentive plan on wage expense as a percent of sales?

e. What is the impact of the incentive plan on cost of good sold as a percent of sales?

f. What is the impact of incentive plan on inventory turnover (turnover = cost of goods sold ÷ inventory)? [If sales go up then stores are selling more goods; therefore, more goods need to be on the floor or those goods on floor need to turn over faster].

g. What is the additional dollar amount of inventory that must be held?

h. Using the information on sales and expenses for a typical store, provide an analysis of the additional store profit contributed by the plan. Assume that it costs 12% a year to carry the added inventory.

i. Look at Exhibit 1 which provides a partial listing of employee pay for one small department within a store. Which "type" of employee is receiving the bonus.

j. Should the company keep the plan? Explain your estimate of the financial impact of the plan and also incorporate any nonfinancial information you feel is relevant in justifying your decision.

EXHIBIT 1

Wages by subset of employees in Ladbreck's fashion department.

Name	Years of Service	Hourly Wage Rate	Hours Worked in Quarter	Regular Pay	Actual Sales for Quarter	Bonus	Total Pay Quarter
BOB MARLEY	2	4.00	400	1,600	25,000	400	2,000
JIMI HENDRIX	16	7.50	440	3,300	41,000	0	3,300
MILLIE SMALL.	24	9.99	440	4,396	40,000	0	4,396
AL GREEN	11	6.00	400	2,400	36,000	480	2,880
BOB DYLAN.	4	5.00	400	2,000	30,000	400	2,400
JANIS JOPLIN	10	6.00	400	2,400	30,000	0	2,400
WILSON PICKETT	16	7.50	440	3,300	50,000	700	4,000
BRUCE SPRINGSTEEN.	23	9.99	440	4,396	30,000	0	4,396
MICHIGAN & SMILEY	13	7.00	400	2,800	38,000	240	3,040
RICHIE FURAY.	22	9.90	400	3,960	30,000	0	3,960
JOHN LENNON	5	5.00	400	2,000	34,000	720	2,720
JULIO IGLESIAS	4	5.00	480	2,400	46,000	1,280	3,680
TOMMY PETTY	11	6.00	400	2,400	36,000	480	2,880
JOAN BAEZ	21	9.90	400	3,960	40,000	0	3,960
BB KING.	8	6.00	400	2,400	38,000	640	3,040
GLADYS KNIGHT.	14	8.00	480	3,840	46,000	0	3,840
NEIL YOUNG	15	8.00	480	3,840	36,000	0	3,840
BO DIDDLEY	4	5.00	400	2,000	30,000	400	2,400

Figure 1
Percentage Change in Sales

Figure 3
Cost of Goods Sold as a Percent of Sales

Figure 2
Wage Expense as a Percent of Sales

Figure 4
Inventory Turnover

SOLUTIONS TO REVIEW PROBLEMS

Mid-Chapter Review

Solution

a.

Relevant costs	Irrelevant costs
Cost of machine	Building lease cost
Residual value of machine	Vice President's salary
Operating cost of machine	
Direct labor savings	
Cost of manager	
Opportunity cost of renting released space	

b.

	(1) Purchase Machine	(2) Use Labor	(1) − (2) Difference (in total cost of purchasing machine)
Cost of new machine	$1,000,000		$1,000,000
Residual value of machine	(100,000)		(100,000)
Operating cost of machine			
($10,000 × 60 months)	600,000		600,000
Cost of direct laborers			
(5,000 clubs × $5 × 60 months)		$1,500,000	(1,500,000)
Cost of one manager			
($6,000 × 60 months)		360,000	(360,000)
Rental value of freed up			
space ($3,500 × 60 months)		210,000	(210,000)
Total costs	$1,500,000	$2,070,000	$ (570,000)
Advantage of purchasing machine. . . .		$570,000	

c. Even though the new machine would save estimated costs of $570,000 over the next five years, there are several qualitative questions that should be answered, including the following:
- Will the new machine provide the same quality product as the current workers?
- How important is it to have a cost structure that includes variable labor costs versus more fixed machine costs? If a business decline should occur, variable costs are often easier to eliminate than fixed costs.
- What is the expected effect on worker morale and community image of eliminating a significant number of jobs in the plant?
- How important is it for the sales staff to be able to promote the product as primarily handmade, versus machine made?

Chapter-End Review

Solution

Unit selling price	$4.80
Unit variable costs.	(2.50)
Unit contribution margin	$2.30

a.

Profit decrease from reduced sales given no changes in prices or costs (1,800 units × $2.30)	$ (4,140)
Profit increase from increase in selling price [(15,000 units − 1,800 units) × $1.50].	19,800
Increase in monthly profit	$15,660

b.

Profit increase from increased sales given no changes in prices or costs (6,000 units × $2.30)	$13,800
Profit decrease from reduced selling price of all units [(15,000 units + 6,000 units) × $1.80].	(37,800)
Profit decrease from increased direct labor costs for the last 1,000 units [1,000 units × ($0.20 × 0.50)]	(100)
Decrease in monthly profit	$(24,100)

c.

Increase in revenues (4,000 units × $4.00)		$16,000
Increase in costs		
Direct materials (4,000 units × $2.00).	$ 8,000	
Direct labor (4,000 units × $0.20)	800	
Factory overhead (4,000 units × $0.25)	1,000	
Selling and administrative.	500	(10,300)
Increase in profits		$ 5,700

d.

Increase in revenues (8,000 units × $4.00)		$32,000
Increase in costs		
Direct materials (8,000 units × $2.00).	$16,000	
Direct labor (8,000 units × $0.20)	1,600	
Factory overhead (8,000 units × $0.25)	2,000	
Selling and administrative.	500	
Opportunity cost of lost regular sales		
[(15,000 units + 8,000 units −		
20,000 unit capacity) × $2.30].	6,900	(27,000)
Increase in profits		$ 5,000

e.

	Cost to Make	Cost to Buy	Difference (income effect of buying)
Cost to buy (15,000 units × $1.00).		$15,000	$(15,000)
Cost to make			
Direct materials			
(15,000 units × $2.00 × 0.40)	$12,000		12,000
Direct labor			
(15,000 units × $0.20 × 0.40)	1,200		1,200
Factory overhead			
(15,000 units × $0.25 × 0.40)	1,500		1,500
Opportunity cost	1,000		1,000
Totals	$15,700	$15,000	$ 700
Advantage of buying.		$700	

f.

Increase in revenues		
Package individually (15,000 units × $5.05)	$75,750	
Sell in bulk (15,000 units × $4.80)	(72,000)	$3,750
Additional packaging costs (15,000 units × $0.10).		(1,500)
Advantage of individual packaging		$2,250

1. Describe inventory requirements and measurement issues for service, merchandising, and manufacturing organizations. (p. 148)

2. Explain the framework of inventory costing for financial reporting. (p. 149)

3. Describe the production environment as it relates to product costing systems. (p. 154)

4. Explain the operation of a job costing system. (p. 155)

5. Explain the operation of a process costing system. (p. 165)

Product Costing: Job and Process Operations

5

Merchandising firms such as ModCloth have one type of inventory—the goods purchased from suppliers that will be resold to customers. However, the inventory of a manufacturing firm such as South Korea's Samsung Electronics is more complicated. Let's consider Samsung's smartphones. First, there are several components used in the manufacturing process of a smartphone, including external cases, batteries, SIM cards, circuit boards, motherboards, speaker assemblies, cameras, flash memory, controller chips, and numerous other elements. Of these components, some are purchased from outside vendors, whereas others are made internally by Samsung. In fact, one of Samsung's competitive advantages is that it makes everything from chips to screens in its own factories, thereby controlling the processing time and technological know-how that goes into its smartphones. This allows the company to bring its products to market more quickly than its competitors, especially because its competitors often buy their components from Samsung. Clearly, Samsung will satisfy its own demand for the components before selling its output to its competitors.

SAMSUNG
www.samsung.com

Given that Samsung makes many of its smartphone components internally, the company will have something called raw materials inventory. These are materials that will be transformed during the manufacturing process to become smartphone components. Examples of Samsung's raw materials include steel, glass, chemicals, wood, papers, metals, and polycarbonates. However, Samsung purchases some components from external vendors, for example, chips for the American version of its smartphones come from the San Diego–based company Qualcomm. These components are also considered raw materials inventory until they are requisitioned into the manufacturing process.

Samsung's smartphone manufacturing complex, called Gumi, is located 150 miles south of Seoul and employs more than 10,000 people. Within the factory, employees assemble smartphones at a three-sided workbench that has all the needed tools and raw materials within arm's reach. Once the raw materials are requisitioned into this part of the facility and direct labor and overhead are added to the raw materials to manufacture the smartphones, these costs are accumulated in another type of inventory called work in process inventory. When the smartphones are completed, they are transferred into a third type of inventory called finished goods, where they will await sale to a customer. This means that for manufacturing companies, the line item "inventory" on the balance sheet may be the sum of three types of inventory: raw materials inventory, work in process inventory, and finished goods inventory.

This chapter will illustrate how the costs of products and services flow through these inventory accounts and how we allocate costs to individual products or services based on those products' or services' consumption of the resources. Sometimes, this allocation is straightforward; for example, we

continued from previous page

can track the amount of raw materials or direct labor hours that go into a product or service. Other times, however, this allocation is more complicated.

Sources: Tim Worstall, "Why Samsung Beats Apple or Perhaps Vice Versa," *Forbes*, September 9, 2013; and Sam Grobart, "How Samsung Became the World's No. 1 Smartphone Maker," *Bloomberg Businessweek*, March 28, 2013.

CHAPTER ORGANIZATION

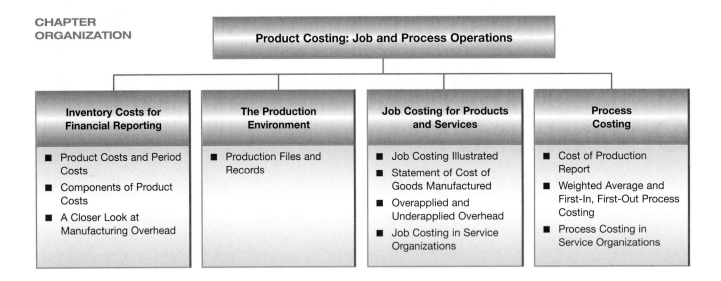

This chapter provides an overview of product costing systems and a framework for understanding costs in a production environment. It also examines aspects of the production environment that can affect product costing systems and discusses costing issues related to the production of physical products versus the production of services.

INVENTORY COSTS IN VARIOUS ORGANIZATIONS

LO1 Describe inventory requirements and measurement issues for service, merchandising, and manufacturing organizations.

Organizations can be classified as service, merchandising, or manufacturing. **Service organizations**, such as SportClips hair salons, Shriners Children's Hospitals, The Cheesecake Factory restaurants, and Delta Air Lines, perform services for others. **Merchandising organizations**, such as Wal-Mart, Urban Outfitters, and Best Buy, buy and sell goods. **Manufacturing organizations**, such as Samsung Electronics, The Boston Beer Company, and Hershey, process raw materials into finished products for sale to others.

Service organizations typically have a low percentage of their assets invested in inventory, which usually consists only of the supplies needed to facilitate their operations. In contrast, merchandising organizations usually have a high percentage of their assets invested in inventory. Their largest inventory investment is merchandise purchased for resale, but they also have supplies inventories.

Manufacturing organizations, like merchandisers, have a high percentage of their assets invested in inventories. However, rather than just one major inventory category, manufacturing organizations typically have three: raw materials, work-in-process, and finished goods. **Raw materials inventories** contain the physical ingredients and components that will be converted by machines and/or human labor into a finished product. **Work-in-process inventories** are the partially completed goods that are in the process of being converted into a finished product. **Finished goods inventories** are the completely manufactured products held for sale to customers. As of December 29, 2012, The Boston Beer Company reported the following inventories:

Raw materials	$27.9 million
Work-in-progress	8.9 million
Finished goods	9.1 million
Total	$45.9 million

Manufacturing organizations also have supplies inventories used to facilitate production and selling and administrative activities. Exhibit 5.1 illustrates the flow of inventory costs in service, merchandising, and manufacturing organizations. In all three types of organizations, the financial accounting system initially records costs of inventories as assets; when they are eventually consumed or sold, inventory costs are recorded as expenses.

EXHIBIT 5.1 Inventory Costs in Various Organizations

Most formal inventory costing systems are designed to provide information for general purpose financial statements. Before the balance sheet and income statement are prepared, the cost of ending inventory and the cost of inventory sold or used during the period must be determined.

INVENTORY COSTS FOR FINANCIAL REPORTING

In financial reporting for manufacturing organizations, an important distinction is made between the cost of *producing* products and the cost of all other activities such as selling and administration.

LO2 Explain the framework of inventory costing for financial reporting.

Product Costs and Period Costs

For financial reporting, all costs incurred in the *manufacturing* of products are called **product costs**; these costs are carried in the accounts as an asset (inventory) until the product is sold, at which time they are recognized as an expense (cost of goods sold). Product costs include the costs of raw materials, production employee salaries and wages, and all other *manufacturing* costs incurred to transform raw materials into finished products. Expired costs (other than those related to manufacturing inventory) are called **period costs** and are recognized as expenses when incurred. Period costs include the president's salary, sales commissions, advertising costs, and all other *nonmanufacturing* costs. Product and period costs are illustrated in Exhibit 5.2.

EXHIBIT 5.2 Product Costs and Period Costs

Costs such as research and development, marketing, distribution, and customer service are important for strategic analyses; however, since these costs are not incurred in the production process, they are not product costs for *financial reporting purposes*. For *internal managerial purposes*, accountants and managers often use the term *product costing* to embrace all costs incurred in connection with a product or service throughout the value chain.

To summarize, in the *product cost* versus *period cost* framework of *financial reporting*, costs are classified based on whether or not they are related to the production process. If they are related to the production process, they are product costs; otherwise, they are period costs. In this framework, costs that seem very similar may be treated quite differently. For example, note in Exhibit 5.2 that the expired cost of insurance on the *plant* is a *product cost*, but the expired cost of insurance on the *showroom* is a *period cost*. The reason is that the plant is used in production, but the showroom is not. This method of accounting for inventory that assigns all production costs to inventory is sometimes referred to as the **absorption cost** (or **full absorption cost**) method because all production costs are said to be fully absorbed into the cost of the product.

Three Components of Product Costs

The manufacture of even a simple product, such as a small wooden table, requires three basic ingredients: materials (wood), labor (the skill of a worker) and production facilities (a building to work in, a saw, and other tools). Corresponding to these three basic ingredients of any product are three basic categories of product costs: direct materials, direct labor, and manufacturing overhead.

Direct materials are the costs of the primary raw materials converted into finished goods. Examples of primary raw materials include iron ore to a steel mill, coiled aluminum to a manufacturer of aluminum siding, cow's milk to a dairy, logs to a sawmill, and lumber to a builder. The finished product of one firm may be the raw materials of another firm down the value chain. For example, rolled steel is a finished product of U.S. Steel, but it is the raw material of the Whirlpool Corporation for the manufacture of washers and dryers. **Direct labor** consists of wages earned by *production employees for the time they actually spend working on a product,* and **manufacturing overhead** includes all manufacturing costs other than direct materials and direct labor. (Manufacturing overhead is also called *factory overhead, burden, manufacturing burden,* and just *overhead.* Merchandising organizations occasionally refer to administrative costs as *overhead.*) **Conversion cost** consists of the combined costs of direct labor and manufacturing overhead incurred to convert raw materials into finished goods.

Examples of manufacturing overhead are manufacturing supplies, depreciation on manufacturing buildings and equipment, and the costs of plant taxes, insurance, maintenance, security, and utilities. Also included are production supervisors' salaries and all other manufacturing-related labor costs for employees who do not work directly on the product (such as maintenance, security, and janitorial personnel).

Just as raw materials, labor, and production facilities are combined to produce a finished product, direct materials costs, direct labor costs, and manufacturing overhead costs are accumulated to obtain the total cost of goods produced. Exhibit 5.3 illustrates that these product costs are accumulated in the general ledger in Work-in-Process Inventory (or just Work-in-Process) as production takes place and then are transferred to Finished Goods Inventory when production is completed. Product costs are finally assigned to Cost of Goods Sold when the finished goods are sold. (Account titles are capitalized to make it easier to determine when reference is being made to a physical item, such as work-in-process inventory, or to the account, Work-in-Process Inventory, in which costs assigned to the work-in-process inventory are accumulated.)

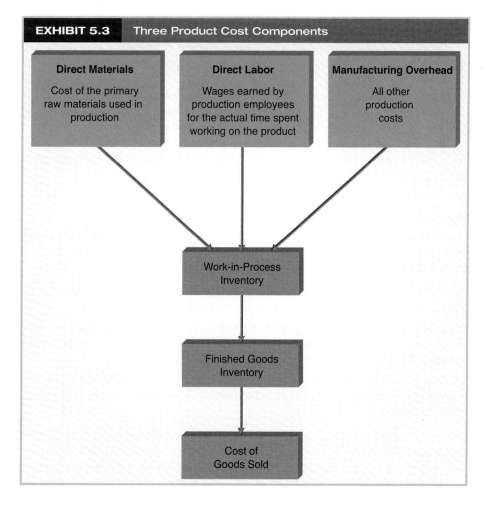

EXHIBIT 5.3   Three Product Cost Components

A Closer Look at Manufacturing Overhead

The biggest challenge in measuring the cost of a product is determining the amount of overhead incurred to produce it. Direct materials cost is driven by the number of raw materials units used; hence, its cost is simply the number of units of raw materials used multiplied by the related cost per unit. Direct labor cost is driven by the number of directly traceable labor hours worked on the product; so its cost is the number of direct labor hours used times the appropriate rate per hour. But what about manufacturing overhead? Manufacturing overhead often consists of dozens of different cost elements, potentially with many different cost drivers. Electricity cost is based on kilowatt-hours and water cost on gallons used; depreciation is usually measured in years of service and insurance in premium dollars per thousand dollars of coverage; and supervisors' salaries are a fixed amount per month.

Historically, accountants have believed that, even when possible, it is not cost effective to try to separately measure the cost incurred for each manufacturing overhead item to produce a unit of finished product. Instead of identifying separate cost drivers for each individual cost component in manufacturing overhead, all overhead costs for a department or plant are frequently placed in a cost pool and a single unit-level cost driver is used to assign (or apply) overhead to products.

If a company produced only one product, it would be simple to assign (or apply) overhead to the units produced because it would merely involve dividing total manufacturing overhead cost incurred by the number of units produced to get a cost per unit. For example, if total manufacturing overhead costs were $100,000 for a period when 20,000 units of product were produced, the overhead cost assigned to each unit would be $5.

Selecting a Basis (or Cost Driver) for Assigning Overhead

When multiple products are manufactured in the same facilities, using a simple average of manufacturing overhead cost per unit seldom provides a good estimate of the overhead costs incurred to produce each product. Units requiring extensive manufacturing activity will have too little cost assigned to them, while others requiring only a small amount of manufacturing effort will absorb too much cost. In these cases, units of production is not an appropriate cost driver for manufacturing overhead.

To solve this allocation problem, an overhead application base (or cost driver) other than number of units produced is used. The overhead application base selected is typically a unit-level activity that is common to all products and has a causal relationship with the incurrence of overhead costs. For example, *machine hours* may be used to assign manufacturing overhead costs if the *number of machine hours used* is believed to be the primary cause of manufacturing overhead cost incurred.

Using Predetermined Overhead Rates

Although some organizations assign actual manufacturing overhead to products at the end of each period (normally a month), three problems often result from measuring product cost using "actual" manufacturing overhead costs:

1. Actual manufacturing overhead cost may not be known until days or weeks after the end of the period, delaying the calculation of unit product cost.

2. Some costs that are seasonal, such as property taxes, are not incurred each period, thus making the actual cost of a product produced in one month greater than that of another, even though nonseasonal costs may have been identical for both months.

3. When there is a significant amount of fixed manufacturing overhead, the costs assigned to each unit of product will vary from period to period, depending on the overall volume of activity for the period.

To overcome these problems, most firms use a **predetermined manufacturing overhead rate** to assign manufacturing overhead costs to products. A predetermined rate is established at the start of each year by dividing the *predicted overhead costs for the year* by the *predicted volume of* *activity in the overhead base* for the year. A predetermined manufacturing overhead rate based on direct labor hours is computed as follows:

$$
\text{Predetermined manufacturing overhead rate per direct labor hour} = \frac{\text{Predicted total manufacturing overhead cost for the year}}{\text{Predicted total direct labor hours for the year}}
$$

If management believes machine hours is the major driver of manufacturing overhead, the denominator should be predicted machine hours.

Using a predetermined manufacturing overhead rate based on direct labor hours, we compute the assignment of overhead to Work-in-Process Inventory as follows:

$$
\text{Manufacturing overhead applied to Work-in-Process Inventory} = \text{Actual direct labor hours} \times \text{Predetermined manufacturing overhead rate per direct labor hour}
$$

To illustrate, assume that late in 2013, one of Samsung's plants predicted a 2014 activity level of 25,000 direct labor hours with manufacturing overhead totaling $187,500. Using this information, its 2014 predetermined overhead rate per direct labor hour was computed as follows:

$$
\text{Predetermined overhead rate} = \frac{\$187{,}500}{25{,}000 \text{ direct labor hours}}
$$
$$
= \$7.50 \text{ per direct labor hour}
$$

If 2,000 direct labor hours were used in September 2014, the applied overhead for September would be $15,000, as shown here:

$$
2{,}000 \times \$7.50 = \$15{,}000
$$

When a predetermined rate is used, monthly variations between actual and applied manufacturing overhead are expected because of the seasonality in costs and the variations in monthly activity. Hence, in some months overhead will be "overapplied" as applied overhead exceeds actual overhead; in other months overhead will be "underapplied" as actual overhead exceeds applied overhead. If the beginning-of-the-year estimates are accurate for annual overhead costs and annual activity, monthly over- and underapplied amounts during the year should offset each other by the end of the year. Later in this chapter, we consider accounting for any over- or underapplied manufacturing overhead balance that may exist at the end of the year.

Changing Cost Structures Affect the Basis of Overhead Application

By using a single overhead rate, we assume that overhead costs are primarily caused by a single cost driver. Historically, a single plantwide overhead application rate based on direct labor hours was widely used when direct labor was the predominant cost factor in production, and manufacturing overhead costs were driven by the utilization of direct labor.

Changes in manufacturing processes have produced major shifts in the composition of conversion costs, resulting in significantly less direct labor and significantly more manufacturing overhead. An example of this shift is the automobile industry where firms such as Ford and Toyota have spent billions of dollars on robotics and other technologies, thereby reducing direct labor in the production process. In many cases, direct labor hours are no longer an appropriate basis for assigning manufacturing costs to products. In others, these changes mean there is no longer a single cost driver that is appropriate for assigning manufacturing overhead to products.

Although some companies continue to use a single manufacturing overhead rate because it is convenient, many companies no longer use this approach. Instead, they have adopted multiple overhead rates based on either major departments or activities within the organization. One method for using multiple overhead rates is activity-based costing, discussed in Chapter 6.

THE PRODUCTION ENVIRONMENT

LO3 Describe the production environment as it relates to product costing systems.

Production personnel need to know the specific products to produce on specific machines on a daily or even hourly basis. The detailed scheduling of products on machines is performed by production scheduling personnel. Exactly how production is scheduled depends on whether process manufacturing or job production is used and whether production is in response to a specific customer sales order or for the company's inventory in anticipation of future sales.

In **process manufacturing**, production of identical units is on a *continuous* basis; a production facility may be devoted exclusively to one product or to a set of closely related products. Companies where you would likely find a process manufacturing environment include Exxon Mobil and Bowater Incorporated (which makes rolled paper for the printing of daily newspapers such as the Chicago Tribune). Process manufacturing is discussed later in this chapter.

In **job production**, also called **job order production**, products are manufactured in single units or in batches of identical units. Of course, the products included in different jobs may vary considerably. Examples of single-unit jobs are found at Schumacher Homes, a builder of custom-designed homes; Bechtel Corporation, the largest commercial construction company in the U.S., and Cray, Inc. which manufacturers supercomputers. Examples of multiple-unit jobs are found at True Religion Brand Jeans, a clothing manufacturer; Herman Miller, a large producer of office chairs including the ergonomic Aeron model; and Denso Global Corporation, the company that makes Toyota's navigation systems.

In a job production environment, when a customer's order is received, the marketing department forwards the order to production scheduling, where employees determine when and how the product is to be produced. Important scheduling considerations include the overall workload, raw materials availability, specific equipment or labor requirements, and the delivery date(s) of the finished product.

Important staff groups involved in production planning and control include engineering, scheduling, and accounting. Engineering is primarily concerned with determining how a product should be produced. Based on an engineering analysis and cost data, engineering personnel develop manufacturing specifications for each product. These manufacturing specifications are often summarized in two important documents: a bill of materials and an operations list. Each product's **bill of materials** specifies the kinds and quantities of raw materials required for one unit of product. The **operations list** (sometimes called an **activities list**) specifies the manufacturing operations and related times required for one unit or batch of product. The operations list should also include information on any machine setup time, movements between work areas, and other scheduled activities, such as quality inspections.

Scheduling personnel prepare a production order for each job. The **production order** contains a job's unique identification number and specifies such details as the quantity to be produced, raw materials requirements, manufacturing operations and other activities to be performed, and perhaps even the time when each manufacturing operation should be performed. In preparing a production order, scheduling personnel use the product's bill of materials and operations list to determine the materials, operations, and manufacturing times required for the job.

A **job cost sheet** is a document used to accumulate the costs for a specific job. The job cost sheet serves as the basic record for recording actual progress on the job. As production takes place, the materials, labor, and machine resources utilized are recorded on the job cost sheet along with the related costs. When a job is completed, the final cost of the job is determined by totalling the costs on the job cost sheet.

Production Files and Records

Certain files in the cost system (typically in a computer database) provide the necessary detail for amounts maintained in total in the general ledger. For example, the raw materials inventory file contains separate records for each type of raw materials, indicating increases, decreases, and the available balance for both units and costs. Every time there is a change in the Raw Materials Inventory general ledger account, there must be an equal change in one or more individual inventory records. Therefore, at any given time, the total of the balances in the raw materials inventory file for all raw materials inventory items should equal the balance in the Raw Materials Inventory general ledger account. Because of this relationship between the raw materials inventory file and Raw Materials Inventory in the general ledger, Raw Materials Inventory is called a *control account* and the raw materials file of detailed records is called a *subsidiary ledger.* Other general ledger accounts related to the product cost system that have subsidiary files are Work-in-Process, Finished Goods Inventory, and Cost of Goods Sold.

Other records required to operate a job cost system include production orders, job cost sheets, materials requisition forms, and work tickets. Production orders and job cost sheets were previously discussed. The production order serves as authorization for production supervisors to obtain materials from the storeroom and to issue work orders to production employees, and the job cost sheet accumulates the cost of the job.

A **materials requisition form** indicates the type and quantity of each raw material issued to the factory. This form is used to record the transfer of responsibility for materials and to record materials changes on raw materials and job cost sheet records. The materials requisition form has a place to record the job number; the job cost sheet has a place to record the requisition number. If a question arises regarding the issuance of materials, the requisition number and job number provide a trail for tracing the destination and the source of the materials. The materials requisition form also identifies the materials warehouse employee who issued the materials and the production employee who received them.

A **work ticket** is used to record the time a job spends in a specific manufacturing operation. Each manufacturing operation performed on a job is documented by a work ticket. The completed work tickets for a job should correspond to the operations specified on the job production order. Time information on the work tickets is used by production scheduling or expediting personnel to determine whether the job is on schedule, and to assign costs to the job.

A production operation can involve a single employee, a group of employees, a machine, or even heating, cooling, or aging processes. When the operation involves a single employee, the rate recorded on the work ticket is simply the employee's wage rate. When it involves a group of employees, the rate is composed of the wage rates of all employees in the group. When the work involves a machine operation, the rate includes a charge for machine time, as well as the time of any machine operators. Other operations, such as heating, cooling, or aging, will also have a rate for each unit of time.

JOB COSTING FOR PRODUCTS AND SERVICES

Exhibit 5.4 shows how inventory costs in a manufacturing organization flow in a logical pattern through the financial accounting system. Pay particular attention to the major inventory accounts (Raw Materials, Work-in-Process, and Finished Goods Inventory), Manufacturing Overhead, and the flow of costs through the inventory accounts. Each of the numbered items, representing a cost flow affecting an inventory account or Manufacturing Overhead, is explained here:

LO4 Explain the operation of a job costing system.

1. The costs of purchased raw materials and manufacturing supplies are recorded in Raw Materials and Manufacturing Supplies, respectively. An increase in Accounts Payable typically offsets these increases.

2. As primary raw materials are requisitioned to the factory, direct materials costs are transferred from Raw Materials to Work-in-Process.

3. Direct labor costs are assigned to Work-in-Process on the basis of the time devoted to processing raw materials. Indirect labor costs associated with production employees are initially assigned to Manufacturing Overhead.

4.–6. Other production related costs are also assigned to Manufacturing Overhead. Other Payables represents the incurrence of a variety of costs such as repairs and maintenance, utilities, and property taxes.

7. Costs assigned to Manufacturing Overhead are periodically reassigned (applied) to Work-in-Process, preferably with the use of a predetermined overhead rate such as direct labor hours, machine hours, or some other cost assignment base.

8. When products are completed, their accumulated product costs are totaled on a job cost sheet and transferred from Work-in-Process to Finished Goods Inventory.

9. When the completed products are sold, their costs are transferred from Finished Goods Inventory to Cost of Goods Sold.

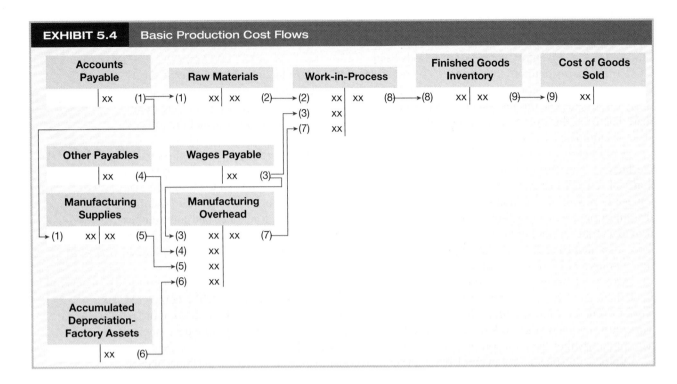

EXHIBIT 5.4 Basic Production Cost Flows

Creating a New Production Environment . . . Mass Customization Recent technological advantages have paved the way for retailers to compete on a new dimension. Customers have more product choices available to them with the availability of Internet-based retailing, and mobile application platforms allow the shopper to shop from anywhere at any time. Now shopping fits the schedule of the customer rather than vice versa. Together these factors create a perfect storm for the success of mass customization.

British fashion label Burberry lets customers develop their own custom designs of the company's classic trench coat. The Burberry "Bespoke" program allows customers to select the style, fabric, color, and options (including studs, straps, and mink or shearling trim), and the custom coat arrives at the customer's door in four to six weeks. The customization translates into nearly 12 million different combinations of coat parameters. Of course the custom coats demand a premium. Whereas stock coats retail from $700 to $6,000, the custom coats can run as high as $8,800. The strategy is clearly working. Burberry's annual revenue has grown 250 percent since 2006 and its stock price has risen 300 percent over the same time frame. Who's next to catch the mass-customization wave? Burberry's CEO, Angela Ahrendts, recently announced she is leaving Burberry for a newly created position at Apple: the Vice President of Retail and Online Stores.

Source: Paul Sonne, "Mink or Fox? The Trench Gets Complicated," *Wall Street Journal*, November 3, 2011.

Job Costing Illustrated

Even though data are almost always processed with computerized systems, data processing procedures are best illustrated within the context of a paper-based manual system. Consider the Burberry "Bespoke" trench coats featured in the Business Insight box. Because variations in styles cause differences in costs, detailed records are kept concerning the costs assigned to specific jobs. Suppose raw materials consist of outer coat fabric, liner fabric, and accessories.

Assume total inventory on August 1, 2014, included Raw Materials, $71,000; Work-in-Process, $109,900; and Finished Goods, $75,000. In addition there were manufacturing supplies of $1,600, consisting of various items such as thread, needles, sheers, and machine lubricant. The August 1 balance in Manufacturing Overhead was $0.

Raw Materials			
Description	**Quantity**	**Unit Cost**	**Total Cost**
Outer fabric	3,000 square yards	$20	$60,000
Liner	2,000 square yards	3	6,000
Accessories	1,000 units	5	5,000
Total			$71,000

Manufacturing Supplies	
Item	**Total Cost**
Various	$1,600

Work-in-Process	
Job	**Total Cost**
425	$ 58,600
426	51,300
Total	$109,900

Finished Goods Inventory	
Job	**Total Cost**
424	$75,000

To illustrate manufacturing cost flows in a job cost system, "T" accounts are presented in the margin for the cost system transactions for Burberry, for August 2014. Each cost assignment is supported by documented information that is recorded in subsidiary cost system records. The hypothetical manufacturing cost transactions for Burberry for August 2014 are discussed here. The numbered jobs combine coat orders that share the same outer and liner fabric choices.

1. Raw materials and manufacturing supplies are purchased on account. The vendor's invoice totals $31,000, including $1,000 of manufacturing supplies and $30,000 of raw materials. The cost of the raw materials must be assigned to specific raw materials inventory records:

Outer fabric	850 square yards ×	$20 =	$17,000
Liner	2,000 square yards ×	$3 =	6,000
Accessories	1,400 units ×	$5 =	7,000
Total			$30,000

Raw Materials Inventory
Beg. Bal. 71,000
(1) 30,000

Manufacturing Supplies
Beg. Bal. 1,600
(1) 1,000

Accounts Payable
31,000 (1)

2. Materials needed to complete Jobs 425 and 426 are requisitioned. Two new jobs, 427 and 428, were also started and direct materials were requisitioned for them. A total of $54,300 of raw materials was requisitioned:

	Job 425	**Job 426**	**Job 427**	**Job 428**	**Total**
Outer fabric					
975 sq. yds. × $20			$19,500		$19,500
955 sq. yds. × $20				$19,100	19,100
Liner					
500 sq. yds. × $3			1,500		1,500
1,100 sq. yds. × $3				3,300	3,300
Accessories					
960 units × $5	$4,800				4,800
720 units × $5		$3,600			3,600
500 × $5			2,500		2,500
Total	$4,800	$3,600	$23,500	$22,400	$54,300

Work-in-Process Inventory
Beg. Bal. 109,900
(2) 54,300

Raw Materials Inventory
Beg. Bal. 71,000 | 54,300 (2)
(1) 30,000

3. Assume the August payroll liability was $41,650, including $34,450 for direct labor and $7,200 for indirect labor. Direct labor was assigned to the jobs as follows:

Work-in-Process Inventory

Beg. Bal. 109,900	
(2) 54,300	
(3) 34,450	

Manufacturing Overhead

Beg. Bal. -0-	
(3) 7,200	

Wages Payable

	41,650 (3)

	Job 425	Job 426	Job 427	Job 428	Total
Labor hours	600	900	1,000	945	
Labor rate	× $10	× $10	× $10	× $10	
Total	$6,000	$9,000	$10,000	$9,450	$34,450

Note: The $7,200 of indirect labor costs is assigned to products as part of applied overhead.

4.-6. In addition to indirect labor, suppose Burberry incurred the following manufacturing overhead costs:

Manufacturing Overhead

Beg. Bal. -0-	
(3) 7,200	
(4) 950	
(5) 2,400	
(6) 3,230	

Manufacturing Supplies

Beg. Bal. 1,600	950 (4)
(1) 1,000	

Accumulated Depreciation

	2,400 (5)

Other Payables

	3,230 (6)

Manufacturing Supplies	$ 950
Accumulated Depreciation—Factory Assets	2,400
Miscellaneous (Other Payables)	3,230

7. Assume manufacturing overhead is applied to jobs using a predetermined rate of $4 per direct labor hour. Assignments to individual jobs are as follows:

Work-in-Process Inventory

Beg. Bal. 109,900	
(2) 54,300	
(3) 34,450	
(7) 13,780	

Manufacturing Overhead

Beg. Bal. -0-	13,780 (7)
(3) 7,200	
(4) 950	
(5) 2,400	
(6) 3,230	

	Job 425	Job 426	Job 427	Job 428	Total
Labor hours	600	900	1,000	945	
Overhead rate per labor hour	× $4	× $4	× $4	× $4	
Total	$2,400	$3,600	$4,000	$3,780	$13,780

8. Jobs 425, 426, and 427 are completed with the following costs:

Finished Goods Inventory

Beg. Bal. 75,000	
(8) 176,800	

Work-in-Process Inventory

Beg. Bal. 109,900	176,800 (8)
(2) 54,300	
(3) 34,450	
(7) 13,780	

	Job 425	Job 426	Job 427	Total
Beginning balance	$58,600	$51,300	$ 0	$109,900
Current costs:				
Direct materials (entry 2)	4,800	3,600	23,500	31,900
Direct labor (entry 3)	6,000	9,000	10,000	25,000
Applied overhead (entry 7)	2,400	3,600	4,000	10,000
Total	$71,800	$67,500	$37,500	$176,800

Additional analysis for the completed jobs indicates the following:

	Job 425	Job 426	Job 427
Total cost of job	$71,800	$67,500	$37,500
Units in job	÷ 1,200	÷ 900	÷ 500
Unit cost	$ 59.83	$ 75.00	$ 75.00

9. Jobs 424, 425, and 426 are delivered to customers for a sales price of $400,000. Determining the costs transferred from Finished Goods Inventory to Cost of Goods Sold requires summing the total cost of jobs sold.

Cost of Goods Sold

(9) 214,300	

Finished Goods Inventory

Beg. Bal. 75,000	214,300 (9)
(8) 176,800	

Job 424	$ 75,000
Job 425	71,800
Job 426	67,500
Total	$214,300

At this point we can determine the gross profit on the completed jobs:

Sales	$400,000
Cost of goods sold	(214,300)
Gross profit	$185,700

If inventory were produced in anticipation of future sales rather than in response to specific customer orders, it is likely that not all units in a job would be sold at the same time. In this case, the unit cost information is used to determine the amount transferred from Finished Goods Inventory to Cost of Goods Sold.

Exhibit 5.5 shows the cost system records supporting the ending balances in the major inventory accounts and Cost of Goods Sold. Note the importance of the job cost sheets for determining cost transfers affecting Work-in-Process and Finished Goods Inventory. The job cost sheets are also used in determining the ending balances of these accounts.

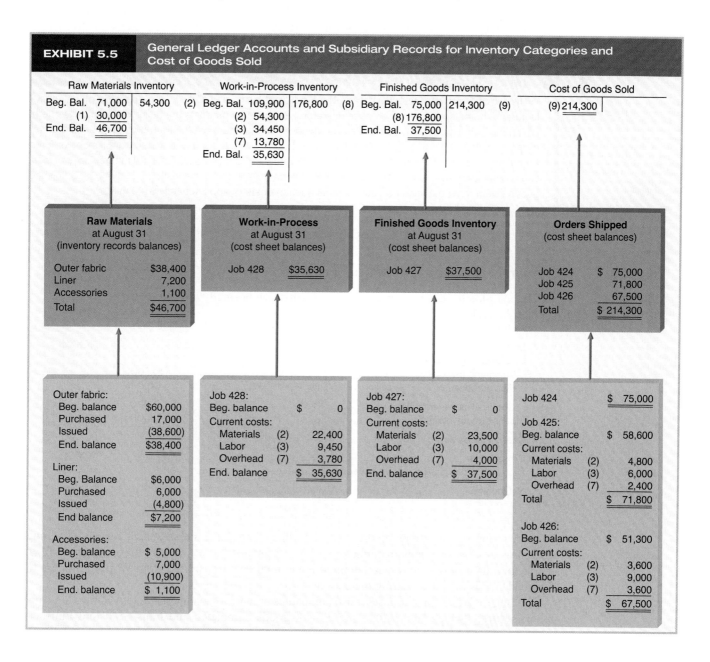

EXHIBIT 5.5 General Ledger Accounts and Subsidiary Records for Inventory Categories and Cost of Goods Sold

Burberry's product costing system is adequate for determining the cost for each job for purposes of valuing ending inventories and cost of goods sold in its external financial statements. The costing system recognizes the differences in materials costs by carefully tracking each type of material as a separate cost pool. Assuming all direct labor employees are paid the same rate, it is necessary to maintain only one labor cost pool. Although there are three distinct operations in making trench coats (cutting, sewing, and finishing), the various styles of trench coats likely require the same proportionate times on each operation. Hence, even with only one plantwide manufacturing overhead cost pool applied on the basis of direct labor hours, individual product costs are reasonably accurate.

Although the Burberry's assumed costing system may be adequate for inventory costing for financial statement purposes, the data it routinely generates will not provide management with information for many management decisions. To evaluate product or customer profitability, management needs additional information concerning marketing, distributing, selling, and customer service costs, which are not included in the product cost system. The following Business Insight illustrates the importance of distribution costs in decision making at Whirlpool.

Furthermore, the cost system does not provide information for decisions concerning individual operations, such as cutting. To answer questions regarding how best to perform operations, Burberry's accountants should perform a special cost study to obtain relevant activity-cost information.

BUSINESS INSIGHT

Whirlpool Scrubs Distribution—Its Second Largest Cost   Whirlpool is a global manufacturer of home appliances such as refrigerators. Because its products are bulky, distribution is one of Whirlpool's largest cost categories. Before Whirlpool completed a $600 million project to build a state-of-the-art distribution system, retailers had to wait up to a week or more to receive appliances ordered from Whirlpool. After building its new distribution system, product delivery times fell to three days or less. Other benefits of the new distribution system include a $250 million reduction in warehoused finished goods inventory and annual reductions in distribution costs of approximately $100 million.

Source: Joe Barrett, "Whirlpool Cleans Up Its Delivery Act, *The Wall Street Journal*, September 23, 2009, pp. B1-B2.

Statement of Cost of Goods Manufactured

The income statement for a merchandising organization normally includes a calculation of cost of goods sold as shown below:

Sales		$X,XXX
Less cost of goods sold		
Beginning inventory	$X,XXX	
Plus purchases	X,XXX	
Goods available for sale	X,XXX	
Less ending inventory	(X,XXX)	
Cost of goods sold		(X,XXX)
Gross profit		X,XXX
Less selling and administrative expenses		(X,XXX)
Net income		$X,XXX

Manufacturing organizations modify only one line of this income statement format, changing Purchases to Cost of goods manufactured. Since a manufacturer acquires finished goods from the factory, its cost of goods manufactured is the total cost transferred from Work-in-Process to Finished Goods Inventory during the period.

For internal reporting purposes, most companies prepare a separate **statement of cost of goods manufactured**, which summarizes the cost of goods completed and transferred into Finished

Goods Inventory during the period. A hypothetical statement of cost of goods manufactured and an income statement for Burberry, are presented in Exhibit 5.6 for August 2014.

EXHIBIT 5.6	Statement of Cost of Goods Manufactured and Income Statement

BURBERRY
Statement of Cost of Goods Manufactured
For Month Ending August 31, 2014

Current manufacturing costs			
Cost of materials placed in production			
Raw materials, 8/1/14	$ 71,000		
Purchases.	30,000		
Total available.	101,000		
Raw materials, 8/31/14	(46,700)	$ 54,300	
Direct labor.		34,450	
Manufacturing overhead		13,780	$102,530
Work-in-process, 8/1/14			109,900
Total costs in process			212,430
Work-in-process, 8/31/14			(35,630)
Cost of goods manufactured			$176,800

BURBERRY
Income Statement
For Month Ending August 31, 2014

Sales		$400,000
Cost of goods sold		
Finished goods inventory, 8/1/14	$ 75,000	
Cost of goods manufactured	176,800	
Total goods available for sale	251,800	
Finished goods inventory, 8/31/14	(37,500)	214,300
Gross profit		185,700
Selling and administrative expenses*.		(90,000)
Net income.		$ 95,700

* Selling and administrative expenses for Burberry are assumed to be $90,000.

Overapplied and Underapplied Overhead

In the Burberry example, assume that the predetermined manufacturing overhead rate of $4 per direct labor hour was based on predicted manufacturing overhead for the year of $100,000 and predicted direct labor hours of 25,000. Assume further that it was determined that the company actually incurred $100,000 in manufacturing overhead during the year and that actual direct labor hours for the year were 25,000, resulting in applied overhead of $100,000 (25,000 hours × $4). The activity in Manufacturing Overhead is summarized as follows:

Manufacturing Overhead	
Beginning balance.	$ 0
Actual overhead	100,000
Total	100,000
Applied overhead	(100,000)
Ending balance	$ 0

With identical amounts of actual and applied overhead, the ending balance in Manufacturing Overhead is zero. However, if either the actual overhead cost or the actual level of the production activity base differed from its predicted value, there would be a balance in Manufacturing Overhead representing overapplied or underapplied overhead.

Assume, for example, that the prediction of 25,000 direct labor hours was correct but that actual overhead cost was $105,000. In this case, Manufacturing Overhead shows a $5,000 positive balance, representing underapplied manufacturing overhead:

Manufacturing Overhead	
Beginning balance..	$ 0
Actual overhead	105,000
Total...	105,000
Applied overhead	(100,000)
Ending balance	$ 5,000*

* Underapplied; actual exceeds applied.

If actual manufacturing overhead were only $98,000, Manufacturing Overhead would be overapplied and show a $2,000 negative balance.

If the *prediction* of total manufacturing overhead cost is not accurate, there will be an underapplied or overapplied balance in Manufacturing Overhead at the end of the year. A similar result occurs when the *predicted* activity level used in computing the predetermined rate differs from the actual activity level. It is not uncommon for such differences to occur. Predictions are exactly that—predictions.

Month-to-month balances in Manufacturing Overhead are usually allowed to accumulate during the year. In the absence of evidence to the contrary, it is assumed that such differences result from seasonal variations in production or costs or both. However, any year-end balance in Manufacturing Overhead must be eliminated.

Theoretically, the disposition of any year-end balance in Manufacturing Overhead should be accomplished in a manner that adjusts every account to what its balance would have been if an actual, rather than a predetermined, overhead rate had been used. This involves adjusting the ending balances in Work-in-Process, Finished Goods Inventory, and Cost of Goods Sold. Procedures to do this are examined in cost accounting textbooks.

In most situations, the simple procedure of treating the remaining overhead as an adjustment to Cost of Goods Sold is adequate. Unless there are large ending balances in inventories and a large year-end balance in Manufacturing Overhead, this simple procedure produces acceptable results. Underapplied overhead indicates that the assigned costs are less than the actual costs, understating Cost of Goods Sold. Hence, disposing of an underapplied balance in Manufacturing Overhead increases the balance in Cost of Goods Sold.

Manufacturing Overhead		
Beginning balance..............................	$ 0	
Actual overhead	105,000	
Total...	105,000	
Applied overhead	(100,000)	
Ending balance	$ 5,000*	← Increase Cost of Goods Sold

* Underapplied; actual exceeds applied.

Conversely, overapplied overhead indicates that the assigned costs are more than the actual costs, overstating Cost of Goods Sold. Hence, disposing of an overapplied balance in Manufacturing Overhead decreases Cost of Goods Sold.

Job Costing in Service Organizations

Service costing, the assignment of costs to services performed, uses job costing concepts to determine the cost of filling customer service orders in organizations such as automobile repair shops, charter airlines, CPA firms, hospitals, and law firms. Many of these organizations bill clients on the basis of resources consumed. Consequently, they maintain detailed records for billing purposes. On the invoice sent to the client, the organization itemizes any materials consumed on the job at a selling price per unit, the labor hours worked on the job at a billing rate per hour, and the time special facilities were used at a billing rate per unit of time. Employees with different capabilities and experience often have different billing rates. In a CPA firm, for example, a partner or a senior manager has a higher billing rate than a staff accountant.

The prices and rates must be high enough to cover costs not assigned to specific jobs and to provide for a profit. To evaluate the contribution to common costs and profit from a job, a comparison must be made between the price charged the customer and the actual cost of the job. This is easily done when the actual cost of resources itemized on the customer's invoice is presented on a job cost sheet. A CPA firm, for example, should accumulate the actual hardware and software costs of an accounting system installed for a client, along with the actual wages earned by employees while working on the job and any related travel costs. Comparing the total of these costs with the price charged, the client indicates the total contribution of the job to common costs and profit.

Although service organizations may identify costs with individual jobs for management accounting purposes, there is considerable variation in the way job cost information is presented in financial statements. Some organizations report the cost of jobs completed in their income statements using an account such as Cost of Services Provided. They use procedures similar to those outlined in Exhibit 5.6; the only major change involves replacing Cost of Goods Sold with Cost of Services Provided.

BUSINESS INSIGHT

Redefining Advertising, Redefining Job Costing David Droga, founder of the advertising agency Droga5, defines the traditional television commercials as the "disruption model of uninvited guests." He has redefined advertising as an experiential form of marketing. However, when we dig deeper into his business models, he's also turned cost accounting on its head. Each marketing campaign is unique, which places the campaigns in the realm of a job cost environment.

When Jay-Z released his biography *Decoded*, Droga5 hailed the event by placing single pages of the book in locations inspired by those pages in the book. The pages were found everywhere from on top of pool tables to the bottom of the swimming pool of the Delano Hotel in Miami, Florida. Imagine the travel costs in putting that campaign together, all of which were part of the costs of the "job." Many of Droga5's clients are more traditional than Jay-Z, but their campaigns are no less imaginative. His client list includes Kraft Foods, Prudential, Microsoft, Puma, Coca-Cola, Unilever, Activision, and Hennessey. Modern-day managers need to use the flexibility inherent in traditional managerial accounting models to adapt to today's constantly changing business models.

Source: Avi Dan, "Droga5's David Droga About Redefining Advertising," *Forbes*, December 31, 2011.

More often, however, service organizations do not formally establish detailed procedures to trace the flow of service costs. Instead, service job costs are left in their original cost categories such as materials expense, salaries and wages expense, travel expense, and so forth. Because all service costs are typically regarded as expenses rather than product costs, either procedure is acceptable for financial reporting. Regardless of the formal treatment of service costs in financial accounting records and statements, the managers of a well-run service organization need information regarding job cost and contribution. The previous Business Insight considers the importance of accurate cost estimation by service contractors.

All preceding examples of service costing involve situations in which the order is filled in response to a specific customer request. Job order costing can also be used to determine the cost of making services available even when the names of specific customers are not known in advance and the service is being provided on a speculative basis. A regularly scheduled airline flight, for example, could be regarded as a job. Management is interested in knowing the cost of the job in order to determine its profitability. This is but another example of the versatility of job order costing.

YOU MAKE THE CALL

You are the Chief Financial Officer You have asked the accounting staff to provide you with cost information on each of the products manufactured by your company so you can conduct profitability analysis on each product. Accounting provided you with the costs that are used in the company's external financial statements. What additional information are you going to need before you can conduct a complete profitability analysis? [Answer p. 175]

MID-CHAPTER REVIEW

Stratasys, Ltd. is a manufacturer of 3D production systems. Assume that the company has a division that does custom prototypes for large clients. Production costs are accounted for using a job cost system. Suppose that at the beginning of June 2014, raw materials inventories totaled $7,000; manufacturing supplies amounted to $800; two jobs were in process—Job 225 with assigned costs of $13,750, and Job 226 with assigned costs of $1,800—and there were no finished goods inventories. There was no underapplied or overapplied manufacturing overhead on June 1. The following information summarized June manufacturing activities:

- Purchased raw materials costing $40,000 on account.
- Purchased manufacturing supplies costing $9,000 on account.
- Requisitioned materials needed to complete Job 226. Started two new jobs, 227 and 228, and requisitioned direct materials for them as follows:

Job 226	$ 2,600
Job 227	18,000
Job 228	14,400
Total	$35,000

- Incurred June salaries and wages as follows:

Job 225 (500 hours × $10 per hour)	$ 5,000
Job 226 (1,500 hours × $10 per hour)	15,000
Job 227 (2,050 hours × $10 per hour)	20,500
Job 228 (800 hours × $10 per hour)	8,000
Total direct labor	48,500
Indirect labor	5,000
Total	$53,500

- Used manufacturing supplies costing $5,500.
- Recognized depreciation on factory fixed assets of $5,000.
- Incurred miscellaneous manufacturing overhead cost of $10,750 on account.
- Applied manufacturing overhead at the rate of $5 per direct labor hour.
- Completed Jobs 225, 226, and 227.
- Delivered Jobs 225 and 226 to customers.

Required

a. Prepare "T" accounts showing the flow of costs through the Work-in-Process, Finished Goods, and Cost of Goods Sold accounts.

b. Show the job cost details to support the June 30, 2014, balances in Work-in-Process, Finished Goods and Cost of Goods Sold.

c. Prepare a statement of cost of goods manufactured for June 2014.

The solution is on pages 193–194.

PROCESS COSTING

A job costing system works well when products are made one at a time (building houses) or in batches of identical items (making blue jeans). However, if products are produced in a continuous manufacturing environment, where production does not have a distinct beginning and ending (refining fossil fuels such as gasoline or diesel), companies usually use a process costing system.

LO5 Explain the operation of a process costing system.

In job costing, the unit cost is the total cost of the "job" divided by the units produced in the job. Costs are accumulated for each job on a job cost sheet, and those costs remain in Work-in-Process until the job is completed, regardless of how long the job is in progress. A multiple-unit job is not considered completed until all units in the job are finished. The cost is not determined until the job is completed, which will not necessarily coincide with the end of an accounting period. Large jobs (such as construction projects) and jobs started near the end of the period frequently overlap two or more accounting periods.

In process costing, the cost of a single unit is equal to the total product costs assigned to a "process" or "department" during the accounting period (frequently a month) divided by the number of units produced. Since goods in the beginning and ending work-in-process inventory are only partially processed during the period, it is necessary to determine the total production for the period in terms of the equivalent number of completed units. For example, if 300 units were started and completed through 40 percent of the process during the period, then the equivalent of 120 fully completed units (300 units × 0.40) were produced. The average cost per unit is computed as total product costs divided by the number of equivalent units produced.

A good example of a process costing environment involving continuous production is the soft drink bottling process. At Coca-Cola's bottling facility in Atlanta, more than 2,000 twelve-ounce cans of Coca-Cola are produced per minute in a continuous process. The process adds the ingredients (concentrate syrup, water, sweetener, and the carbonation agent) at various points in the process and blends the ingredients in the can. At the end of the process, the cans are automatically wrapped in either 6-pack or 12-pack sizes. For another example, see the following Business Insight box for a discussion of the process costing environment for Coca-Cola's Simply Orange.

In a job cost system, job cost sheets are used to collect cost information for each and every job. In a process costing system, cost accumulation requires fewer records because each department's production is treated as the only job worked on during the period. In a department that has just one manufacturing process, process costing is particularly straightforward because the Work-in-Process account is, in effect, the departmental cost record. If a department has more than one manufacturing process, separate records should be maintained for each process.

BUSINESS INSIGHT

Simply Orange Juice Is Not So Simple When Assigning Costs Product costing is made complex by two key things: (1) a high proportion of indirect costs and (2) continuous production or process costing. Coca-Cola's Simply Orange is a study in both. Its production uses satellite imagery, data algorithms, and juice pipelines. Over 600 flavors and ingredients go into the Simply Orange product because these are the flavor profiles found in an actual orange. Coke starts with a batch of raw orange juice, but the taste of the juice will differ based on weather patterns such as temperature, sunshine, and moisture during the oranges' growing season. Coke augments the natural juice to achieve the optimal flavor profile based on exact measurements of acidity, sweetness, pulp content, and other undisclosed attributes. The algorithm then formulates each batch of juice to achieve the desired taste.

Through technology, Coke is able to stabilize the cost of Simply Orange per batch, even though the engineers, equipment, and software costs increase the product's indirect costs. Despite the enhanced engineering, Coke cannot completely escape the fact that main raw material and the flavorings are still commodity-based goods. As such, cost fluctuations for raw materials will be expected due to crop yields and cost pressures. However, Coke can minimize the variation in cost, and demand should be more predictable when the company is able to turn out a consistent product regardless of Mother Nature's whims.

Source: Duane Stanford, "Coke Engineers Its Orange Juice—With an Algorithm," *Bloomberg Businessweek*, January 31, 2013.

Cost of Production Report

To illustrate process costing procedures, consider Intel, which manufactures memory chips for microcomputers using sophisticated machinery. Assume each finished unit requires one unit of raw materials added at the beginning of the manufacturing process. A hypothetical production and cost data for the month of July 2014 for Intel is as follows:

July Production Data	
Units in process, beginning of period (75% converted)	4,000
Units started	36,000
Completed and transferred to finished goods.	35,000
Units in process, end of period (20% converted)	5,000

July Cost Data		
Beginning work-in-process		
Materials costs.		$ 16,000
Conversion costs		9,000
Total		$ 25,000
Current manufacturing costs		
Direct materials (36,000 × $4).		$144,000
Conversion costs		
Direct labor.	$ 62,200	
Manufacturing overhead applied	46,700	108,900
Total		$252,900

Developing a cost of production report is a useful way of organizing and accounting for costs in a process costing environment. A **cost of production report**, which summarizes unit and cost data for each department or process for each period, consists of the following sections:

■   Summary of units in process.

■   Equivalent units.

■   Total cost to be accounted for and cost per equivalent unit.

■   Accounting for total costs.

The cost of production report for Intel is shown in Exhibit 5.7, and its four sections are discussed next.

Summary of Units in Process

This section of the cost of production report provides a summary of all units in the department during the period—both from an input and an output perspective—regardless of their stage of completion. From an input perspective, total units in process during the period consisted of the following:

■   Units in process at the beginning of the period, plus

■   Units started during the period.

From an output perspective, these units in process during the period were either

■   Completed and transferred out of the department, or

■   Still on hand at the end of the period.

In the summary of units in process, all units are treated as the same, regardless of the amount of processing that took place on them during the period. The objective here is to account for all discrete units of product in process at any time during the period. In the summary of units in process in Exhibit 5.7, suppose 40,000 individual units were in process, including 4,000 partially

EXHIBIT 5.7	Cost of Production Report for Process Costing

INTEL
Cost of Production Report
For the Month Ending July 31, 2014

Summary of units in process

Beginning............	4,000
Units started	36,000
In process	40,000
Completed...........	(35,000)
Ending	5,000

Equivalent units in process	Materials	Conversion	
Units completed	35,000	35,000	
Plus equivalent units in ending inventory..........	5,000	1,000*	
Equivalent units in process.....................	40,000	36,000	

Total cost to be accounted for and cost per equivalent unit in process	Materials	Conversion	Total
Beginning work-in-process.....................	$ 16,000	$ 9,000	$ 25,000
Current cost................................	144,000	108,900**	252,900
Total cost in process.........................	$160,000	$117,900	$277,900
Equivalent units in process....................	÷ 40,000	÷ 36,000	
Cost per equivalent unit in process	$ 4.00	$ 3.275	$ 7.275
Accounting for total costs			
Transferred out (35,000 × $7.275)			$254,625
Ending work-in-process			
Materials (5,000 × $4.00).....................................		$20,000	
Conversion (1,000 × $3.275)..................................		3,275	23,275
Total cost accounted for......................................			$277,900

* 5,000 units, 20% converted

** Includes direct labor of $62,200 and applied manufacturing overhead of $46,700

completed units in the beginning inventory and 36,000 new units started during the month. During the period, 35,000 units were completed, and the remaining 5,000 were still in process at the end of the month.

Equivalent Units in Process

This section of the report translates the number of units in process during the period into equivalent completed units of production. The term **equivalent completed units** refers to the number of completed units that is equal, in terms of production effort, to a given number of partially completed units. For example, 80 units for which 50 percent of the expected total processing cost has been incurred is the equivalent of 40 completed units (80 × 0.50).

Frequently, direct materials costs are incurred largely, if not entirely, at the beginning of the process, whereas direct labor and manufacturing overhead costs are added throughout the production process. If direct labor and manufacturing costs are added to the process simultaneously, it is common to treat them jointly as conversion costs. Assume Intel adds all materials at the beginning of the process; all conversion costs are added evenly throughout the process. Therefore, separate computations are made for equivalent units of materials and equivalent units of conversion. Although the department worked on 40,000 units during the period, the total number of equivalent units in process with respect to conversion costs was only 36,000 units, consisting of 35,000 finished units plus 1,000 equivalent units in ending inventory (5,000 units 20 percent converted).

Because all materials are added at the start of the process, 40,000 equivalent units (35,000 finished and 5,000 in process) were in process with respect to materials costs.

Total Cost to Be Accounted for and Cost per Equivalent Unit in Process

This section of the report summarizes total costs in Work-in-Process during the period and calculates the cost per equivalent unit for materials, conversion, and in total. Total cost consists of the beginning Work-in-Process balance (if any) plus current costs incurred. For our Intel example, the total cost to be accounted for during July was $277,900, consisting of $25,000 in Work-in-Process at the beginning of the period plus current costs of $252,900 incurred in July. Exhibit 5.7 shows these amounts broken down between materials costs and conversion costs.

To compute cost per equivalent unit, divide total cost in process by the equivalent units in process. This is done separately for materials cost and conversion cost. The total cost per equivalent unit is the sum of the unit costs for materials and conversion. Because the number of equivalent units in process was different for materials and conversion, it is not possible to get the total cost per unit by dividing total costs of $277,900 by some equivalent unit amount.

Accounting for Total Costs

This section shows the disposition of the total costs in process during the period divided between units completed (and sent to finished goods) and units still in process at the end of the period. As noted in the previous section, total cost in process is $277,900 and each equivalent unit in process has $4.00 of materials cost and $3.275 of conversion costs for a total of $7.275.

The first step in assigning total costs is to calculate the cost of units transferred out by multiplying the units completed during the period by the total cost per unit (35,000 units × $7.275). This assigns $254,625 of the total cost to units transferred out, leaving $23,275 ($277,900 − $254,625) to be assigned to ending Work-in-Process. To verify that $23,275 is the correct amount of cost remaining in ending Work-in-Process, the materials and conversion costs in ending Work-in-Process are calculated separately. Recall that the 5,000 units in process at the end of the period are 100 percent completed with materials costs, but only 20 percent completed with conversion costs. Therefore, in ending Work-in-Process, the materials cost component is $20,000 (5,000 × 1.00 × $4.00), the conversion cost component is $3,275 (5,000 × 0.20 × $3.275), and the total cost of ending Work-in-Process is $23,275 ($20,000 + $3,275).

The cost of production report summarizes manufacturing costs assigned to Work-in-Process during the period and provides information for determining the transfer of costs from Work-in-Process to Finished Goods Inventory. The supporting documents are similar to those previously illustrated for job costing, except that the single cost of production report replaces all the job cost sheets that flow through a department or process. The flow of costs through Work-in-Process is as follows:

Work-in-Process		
Beginning balance.		$ 25,000
Current manufacturing costs		
Direct materials	$144,000	
Direct labor.	62,200	
Applied overhead.	46,700	252,900
Total		277,900
Cost of goods manufactured		(254,625)
Ending balance		$ 23,275

The reduction in Work-in-Process for the units completed during the period is determined in the cost of production report (see Exhibit 5.7). This amount is transferred to Finished Goods Inventory. The $23,275 ending balance in Work-in-Process is also determined in the cost of production report as the amount assigned to units in ending Work-in-Process.

Weighted Average and First-In, First-Out Process Costing

Because the costs of materials, labor, and overhead are constantly changing, unit costs are seldom exactly the same from period to period. Hence, if a unit is manufactured partially in one period and partially in the following period, its actual cost is seldom equal to the unit cost of units produced in either period.

In the cost of production report in Exhibit 5.7, we made no attempt to account separately for the completed units that came from beginning inventory and those that were started during the current period. The method illustrated in Exhibit 5.7 is called the **weighted average method**, and it simply spreads the combined beginning inventory cost and current manufacturing costs (for materials, labor, and overhead) over the units completed and those in ending inventory on an average basis. For example, the total cost in process for conversion ($117,900) included both beginning inventory cost and current costs; the 36,000 equivalent units in process for conversion included both units from beginning inventory and units started during the current period. Hence, the average cost per unit of $3.275 (or $117,900 ÷ 36,000) is a weighted average cost of the partially completed units in beginning inventory (prior period costs) and units started during the current period. It is not a precise cost per unit for the current period's production activity but an average cost that includes the cost of partially completed units in beginning inventory carried over from the previous period.

An alternative, more precise process costing method is the **first-in, first-out (FIFO) method**. It accounts for unit costs of beginning inventory units separately from those started during the current period. Under this method, the first costs incurred each period are assumed to have been used to complete the unfinished units carried over from the previous period. Hence, the cost of the beginning inventory is partially based on the prior period's unit costs and partially based on the current period's unit costs.

If unit costs are changing from period to period and beginning inventories are large in relation to total production for the period, the FIFO method is more accurate. However, with the current trend toward smaller inventories, the additional effort and cost of the FIFO method may not be justified. Detailed coverage of the FIFO method is included in cost accounting textbooks. Unless stated otherwise, weighted average process costing is used in chapter assignments.

Process Costing in Service Organizations

There are many applications of process costing for service organizations. Process costing in service organizations is similar to that in manufacturing organizations, the primary purpose being to assign costs to cost objects. Generally, the use of process costing techniques for service organizations is easier than for manufacturing organizations because the raw materials element is not necessary. The applications for the labor and overhead costs are similar, if not identical, to those of a manufacturing firm.

Process costing for services is similar to job costing for batches in that an average cost for similar or identical services is determined. There are important differences, though, between batch and process costing. In a batch environment, a discrete group of services is identified, but in a process environment, services are performed on a continuous basis. Batch costing accumulates the cost for a specific group of services as the batch moves through the various activities that make up the service. Process service costing measures the average cost of identical or similar services performed each period (each month) in a department. An example of batch service costing is determining the cost of registering a student at your college during the fall term registration period; an example of process service costing is determining the cost each month of processing a check by a bank. If continuously performed services involved multiple processes, the total cost of the service would be the sum of the costs for each process.

After it is determined that process costing would be appropriate for a service activity, the actual decision to use it is generally contingent on two important factors about the items being evaluated. First, is average cost per unit acceptable as an input item to the decision process? For some activities, the answer is obvious. For instance, tracking the actual cost of processing each check through a bank would probably not be as useful as determining the average cost of processing checks for a given period; therefore, average cost is acceptable. For other activities, the answer is more difficult to determine. Should the decision model include average cost per patient-day or actual cost per individual patient?

The second issue relates to the benefits versus the costs of the resulting information. Normally, it is easier to track and record the cost of an activity or process than it is to track and record the cost of each individual item in the activity. Often actual cost tracking is impossible for practical reasons (the actual cost of processing a check through a banking system, for example). Although process costing will not work in every situation, it has many applications in service organizations. As illustrated in this text, there are many possibilities for applying either job or process costing to activities in service organizations.

CHAPTER-END REVIEW

SanDisk manufactures USB flash drives that are used in computing. Since there is little product differentiation between SanDisk's products, assume it uses a process costing system to determine inventory costs. Production and manufacturing cost data for 2014 are as follows:

Production data (units)	
Units in process, beginning of period (60% converted)	3,000,000
Units started	27,000,000
Completed and transferred to finished goods.	25,000,000
Units in process, end of period (30% converted)	5,000,000

Manufacturing costs	
Work-in-Process, beginning of period (materials, $468,000; conversion, $252,000).	$ 720,000
Current manufacturing costs:	
Raw materials transferred to processing	6,132,000
Direct labor for the period.	1,550,000
Overhead applied for the period.	3,498,000

Required
Prepare a cost of production report for SanDisk for 2014.

The solution is on page 194.

APPENDIX 5A: Absorption and Variable Costing

Product costing for inventory valuation is the link between financial and managerial accounting. Product costing systems determine the cost-based valuation of the manufactured inventories used in making key financial accounting measurements (cost of goods sold and income on the income statement as well as inventory and total assets on the balance sheet). They also provide vital information to managers for setting prices, controlling costs, and evaluating management performance. The influence of financial accounting on product costing systems is apparent in the design of traditional job order and process costing systems. These systems reflect the requirement of financial accounting (i.e., generally accepted accounting principles) that all manufacturing costs be included in inventory valuations for external financial reporting purposes. In these systems, all other costs incurred, such as selling, general, and administrative costs, are treated as expenses of the period.

Basic Concepts

A debate exists over how to treat fixed manufacturing overhead costs in the valuation of inventory. The debate centers around whether fixed costs such as depreciation on manufacturing equipment should be considered an *inventoriable product cost* and treated as an asset cost until the inventory is sold, or as a *period cost* and recorded immediately as an operating expense. **Absorption costing** (also called **full costing**) treats fixed manufacturing overhead as a product cost, whereas **variable costing** (also called **direct costing**) treats it as a period cost. Therefore, fixed manufacturing overhead is recorded initially as an asset (inventory) under absorption costing but as an operating expense under variable costing.

> **Fixed manufacturing costs:**
>
> **Absorption costing** treats **fixed manufacturing costs** as **product costs**.
>
> **Variable costing** treats **fixed manufacturing costs** as **period costs**.

Since fixed product costs are eventually recorded as expenses under both variable and absorption costing by the time the inventory is sold, why does it matter whether fixed overhead is treated as a product cost or a period cost? It matters because the way it is treated affects the measurement of income for a particular period and the valuation assigned to inventory on the balance sheet at the end of the period. Because absorption costing presents fixed manufacturing overhead as a cost per unit rather than a total cost per period, management's perceptions of cost behavior, and decisions based on perceptions of cost behavior, may also be affected.

Inventory Valuations

To illustrate the difference in inventory valuations between absorption and variable costing, assume the following cost data for a single component of a Trek bicycle at a monthly volume of 4,000 units:

Direct materials	$ 5	per unit
Direct labor	2	per unit
Variable manufacturing overhead	3	per unit
Total variable cost	$ 10	per unit
Fixed manufacturing overhead	$8,000	per month

To determine the unit cost of inventory using absorption costing, an average fixed overhead cost per unit is calculated by dividing the monthly fixed manufacturing overhead by the monthly volume. Even though fixed manufacturing overhead is not a variable cost, under absorption costing it is applied to inventory on a per-unit basis, the same as variable costs. At a monthly volume of 4,000 units, Trek's total component inventory cost per unit, is $10 under variable costing, and $12 under absorption costing.

The $2 difference in total unit cost is attributed to the treatment of fixed overhead of $8,000 divided by 4,000 units. The difference in the total component inventory valuation on the balance sheet between absorption and variable costing is the number of units in ending inventory times $2. So if 1,000 units are on hand at the end of the month, they are valued at $12,000 if absorption costing is used but at only $10,000 with variable costing.

Income Under Absorption and Variable Costing

The income statement formats used for variable and absorption costing are not the same. One benefit of variable costing is that it separates costs into variable and fixed costs, making it possible to present the income statement in a contribution format. As illustrated in Chapter 3, in a contribution income statement, variable costs are subtracted from revenues to compute contribution margin; fixed costs are then subtracted from contribution margin to calculate profit, also called net income or earnings.

When absorption costing is used, the income statement is usually formatted using the functional format, which classifies costs based on cost function, such as manufacturing, selling, or administrative. The functional income statement, used for financial reporting, subtracts manufacturing costs (represented by cost of goods sold) from revenues to calculate gross profit; selling and administrative costs are then subtracted from gross profit to calculate profit or income.

The contribution format provides information for determining the contribution margin ratio, which is calculated as total contribution margin divided by total sales. It also provides the total amount of fixed costs. These are the primary items of data needed to determine the break-even point and to conduct other cost-volume-profit analysis (see Chapter 3).

Not only is the income statement format different for absorption and variable costing methods, but also as illustrated in the following hypothetical examples for Trek, the amount of income reported on the income statement might not be the same because of the difference in the treatment of fixed manufacturing overhead. The following additional information is assumed for the Trek component examples:

Selling price	$30	per unit
Variable selling and administrative expenses	$3	per unit
Fixed selling and administrative expenses	$10,000	per month

Production Equals Sales

Assume Trek has no component inventory on June 1, 2014. Production and sales for the third quarter of 2014 are:

Month	Production	Sales
June	3,200 units	3,200 units
July.	4,000 units	3,500 units
August	4,000 units	4,500 units
Third quarter	11,200 units	11,200 units

Production and sales both total 11,200 units for the third quarter. A summary of unit production, sales, and inventory levels is presented in Exhibit 5.8. Using previously presented cost and a selling price of $30 per unit, monthly contribution (variable costing) and functional (absorption costing) income statements are presented in Exhibit 5.8 parts B and C. An analysis of fixed manufacturing overhead with absorption costing is presented in part D.

In June, with 3,200 units produced and sold all $8,000 of fixed manufacturing overhead is deducted as a period cost under variable costing and expensed as part of the cost of goods sold under absorption costing. No costs were assigned to ending inventory under either method.

Production Exceeds Sales

July production of 4,000 units exceeded sales of 3,500 units by 500 units. The ending inventory under variable costing consisted of only the variable cost of production, $5,000 (500 × $10). The entire $8,000 of fixed manufacturing overhead is deducted as a period cost.

Under absorption costing, in addition to the variable cost of production, a portion of the fixed manufacturing overhead is assigned to the ending inventory. As shown in the July column of Exhibit 5.8, part D, absorption costing assigns $1,000 of the month's fixed manufacturing overhead to the July ending inventory and $7,000 to the cost of goods sold. Consequently, under absorption costing the July ending inventory is $1,000 higher, the July expenses are $1,000 lower, and the July net income is $1,000 higher than under variable costing.

Sales Exceed Production

In August just the opposite of July's situation occurred: sales of 4,500 units exceeded production of 4,000 units by 500 units. The additional units came from the July production. Under variable costing all current manufacturing costs are expensed either as the variable cost of goods sold or as part of the fixed expense. Additionally, the August variable cost of goods sold includes variable costs assigned the July ending inventory.

Under absorption costing all current manufacturing costs are expensed as part of the cost of goods sold. Additionally, the cost of goods sold includes the variable and fixed costs assigned the July ending inventory. The inclusion of the July fixed costs caused absorption costing net income to be $1,000 lower than the corresponding variable costing amount.

The above relationships between absorption and variable costing are summarized in Exhibit 5.9.

Exhibits 5.8 and 5.9 reveal several important relationships between absorption costing net income and variable costing net income, as well as the way net income responds to changes in sales and production under both methods.

For each period, the income differences between absorption and variable costing can be explained by analyzing the change in inventoried fixed manufacturing overhead under absorption costing net income. In general, the following relationship exists:

Variable costing net income	+	Increase (or minus decrease) in inventoried fixed manufacturing overhead	=	Absorption costing net income

Using Trek's July information, the equation is as follows:

$$\$41,500 + (500 \times \$2.00) = \$42,500$$

For any given time period, regardless of length, if total units produced equals total units sold, net income is the same for absorption costing and variable costing, all other things being equal. Under absorption costing, all fixed manufacturing overhead is released as a product cost through cost of goods sold when

EXHIBIT 5.8	Contribution (Variable Costing) and Functional (Absorption Costing) Income Statements with Variations in Production and Sales

	June (Production equals sales)	July (Production exceeds sales)	August (Sales exceed production)
A. Trek's Component: Summary of Unit Inventory Changes			
Beginning inventory	0	0	500
Production	3,200	4,000	4,000
Total available	3,200	4,000	4,500
Sales	(3,200)	(3,500)	(4,500)
Ending inventory	0	500	0
B. Contribution (Variable Costing) Income Statements			
Sales ($30/unit)	$96,000	$105,000	$135,000
Less variable expenses:			
Cost of goods sold ($10/unit)	$32,000	$ 35,000	$ 45,000
Selling & admin. ($3/unit).	9,600	10,500	13,500
Total	(41,600)	(45,500)	(58,500)
Contribution margin	54,400	59,500	76,500
Less fixed expenses			
Manufacturing overhead	8,000	8,000	8,000
Selling & admin.	10,000	10,000	10,000
Total	(18,000)	(18,000)	(18,000)
Net income.	$36,400	$ 41,500	$ 58,500
C. Functional (Absorption Costing) Income Statements			
Sales ($30/unit)	$96,000	$105,000	$135,000
Cost of goods sold (Part D.)	(40,000)	(42,000)	(54,000)
Gross profit	56,000	63,000	81,000
Selling & admin. expenses			
Variable ($3/unit)	9,600	10,500	13,500
Fixed.	10,000	10,000	10,000
Total	(19,600)	(20,500)	(23,500)
Net income.	$36,400	$ 42,500	$ 57,500
D. Analysis of Fixed Manufacturing Overhead under Absorption Costing			
Fixed manufacturing overhead.	$ 8,000	$ 8,000	$ 8,000
Units produced	÷ 3,200	÷ 4,000	÷ 4,000
Absorption fixed cost per unit*	$ 2.50	$ 2.00	$ 2.00
Units in ending inventory	× 0	× 500	× 0
Fixed costs in ending inv.	$ 0	$ 1,000	$ 0
Fixed cost of goods sold:			
From beginning inventory	$ 0	$ 0	$ 1,000
June (3,200 units × $2.50).	8,000		
July (3,500 units × $2.00)		7,000	
August (4,000 × $2.00)			8,000
Total fixed.	8,000	7,000	9,000
Variable cost of goods sold	32,000	35,000	45,000
Absorption cost of goods sold	$40,000	$ 42,000	$ 54,000

* To simplify the illustration, the example does not use a predetermined overhead rate. If a predetermined overhead rate were used, an increase or decrease in the balance of Manufacturing Overhead is treated as an adjustment to ending inventory.

EXHIBIT 5.9	Comparative Effects of Absorption and Variable Costing		
Relationship between period production and sales	**Effect on inventory costs**	**Effect on operating income**	**Explanation**
Production = Sales	No change in inventory costs.	Absorption costing income = Variable costing income	All current fixed manufacturing costs are expensed under both absorption and variable costing.
Production > Sales	Absorption costing ending inventory increases more than variable costing inventory.	Absorption costing income > Variable costing income	Under absorption costing some current fixed manufacturing costs are assigned to ending inventory. Under variable costing all current fixed manufacturing costs are expensed.
Sales > Production	Absorption costing ending inventory declines more than variable costing inventory.	Absorption costing income < Variable costing income	Under absorption costing fixed manufacturing costs previously assigned to ending inventory are expenses along with current fixed manufacturing costs. Under variable costing only current fixed manufacturing costs are expensed.

inventory is sold. Under variable costing, all fixed manufacturing overhead is reported as a period cost and expensed in the period incurred. Consequently, over the life of a product, the income differences within periods are offset since they occur only because of the timing of the release of fixed manufacturing overhead to the income statement.

Evaluating Alternatives to Inventory Valuation

The issue in the variable costing debate is whether or not fixed manufacturing costs add value to products. Proponents of variable costing argue that these costs do not add value to a product. They believe that fixed costs are incurred to provide the capacity to produce during a given period, and these costs expire with the passage of time regardless of whether the related capacity was used. Variable manufacturing costs, on the other hand, are incurred only if production takes place. Consequently, these costs are properly assignable to the units produced.

Proponents of variable costing also argue that inventories have value only to the extent that they avoid the necessity of incurring costs in the future. Having inventory available for sale avoids the necessity of incurring some future variable costs, but the availability of finished goods inventory does not avoid the incurrence of future fixed manufacturing costs. Proponents conclude that inventories should be valued at their variable manufacturing cost, and fixed manufacturing costs should be expensed as incurred.

Opponents of variable costing argue that fixed manufacturing costs are incurred for only one purpose, namely, to manufacture the product. Because they are incurred to manufacture the product, they should be assigned to the product. It is also argued that in the long run all costs are variable. Consequently, by omitting fixed costs, variable costing understates long-run variable costs and misleads decision makers into underestimating true production costs.

On a pragmatic level, the central arguments for variable costing center around the fact that use of variable costing facilitates the development of contribution income statements and cost-volume-profit analysis. With costs accumulated on an absorption costing basis, contribution income statements are difficult to develop, and cost-volume-profit analysis becomes very complicated unless production and sales are equal.

Proponents of activity-based costing typically do not favor variable costing because ABC is based on the assumption that, in the long run, all costs are variable and that fixed costs should be assigned to products or services to represent long-run variable costs. Hence, inventory valuation using an ABC approach will tend to be closer to absorption costing values than variable costing values.

As inventory levels have remained steady in recent years (see the following Research Insight), the significance of the debate over absorption versus variable costing has quieted. If a company has no inventories, all its costs are deducted as expenses (either as operating expenses or cost of goods sold expense) during the current period whether it uses absorption or variable costing. Hence, from an income determination standpoint, it does not matter in such cases whether fixed costs are considered a product or period cost.

RESEARCH INSIGHT

Inventory Levels Are Holding Steady Using data from 2012 financial statements from 1,000 public companies, research has found that overall U.S. inventory levels have remained flat since 2005 when compared to sales. There was a temporary spike in the inventory-to-sales ratio immediately after the recession of 2008 when companies were temporarily left with excess inventory in the face of decreased demand. The construction equipment, food manufacturing, and contract manufacturing sectors decreased their inventory holdings over the past year, whereas the spirits, electric utilities, and retail wireless services sectors saw an increase in their inventories over the same period.

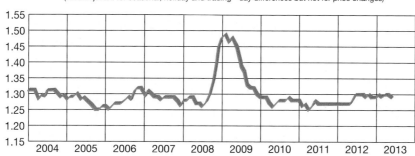

Total Business Inventories/Sales Ratios: 2004 to 2013
(Data adjusted for seasonal, holiday and trading—day differences but not for price changes)

Source: Dan Gilmore, "Supply Chain News: Inventory Performance 2013," *Supply Chain Digest*, July 26, 2013.

GUIDANCE ANSWERS . . . YOU MAKE THE CALL

You are the Chief Financial Officer Inventory costs that are provided for financial statement purposes for external stockholders and lenders are required by generally accepted accounting principles to include only the manufacturing costs of the product for direct materials, direct labor, and manufacturing overhead. To conduct a complete profitability analysis, the CFO will need to gather data for all other costs that relate to the marketing, sales, and distribution of each product, as well as any costs related to providing service to customers who buy the products.

KEY RATIOS

$$\text{Predetermined manufacturing overhead rate per direct labor hour} = \frac{\text{Predicted total manufacturing overhead cost for the year}}{\text{Predicted total direct labor hours for the year}}$$

$$\text{Manufacturing overhead applied to Work-in-Process Inventory} = \text{Actual direct labor hours} \times \text{Predetermined manufacturing overhead rate per direct labor hour}$$

$$\text{Variable costing net income} + \text{Increase (or minus decrease) in inventoried fixed manufacturing overhead} = \text{Absorption costing net income}$$

KEY TERMS

absorption cost, 150
absorption costing, 170
activities list, 154
bill of materials, 154
conversion cost, 151
cost of production report, 166
direct costing, 170
direct labor, 151
direct materials, 151
equivalent completed units, 167
finished goods inventories, 148
first-in, first-out (FIFO)
    method, 169

full absorption cost, 150
full costing, 170
job cost sheet, 154
job order production, 154
job production, 154
manufacturing organizations, 148
manufacturing overhead, 151
materials requisition form, 155
merchandising organizations, 148
operations list, 154
period costs, 150
predetermined manufacturing
    overhead rate, 152

process manufacturing, 154
product costs, 149
production order, 154
raw materials inventories, 148
service costing, 162
service organizations, 148
statement of cost of goods
    manufactured, 160
variable costing, 170
weighted average method, 169
work-in-process inventories, 148
work ticket, 155

MULTIPLE CHOICE

1. Kay Company's formula for annual manufacturing overhead is:

    $Y = \$120,000 + \$10X$, where x is direct labor dollars

    The predicted activity for 2014 is 50,000 direct labor hours and the actual activity for January of 2014 was 4,000 direct labor hours. Using a predetermined overhead rate the applied January overhead is:
    a. $40,000
    b. $49,600
    c. $160,000
    d. $169,600

2. Presented is selected information from Took's April income statement and statement of cost of goods manufactured:

Cost of goods sold	$230,000
Cost of goods manufactured	$210,000
Finished goods inventory, April 30	$ 40,000

    Took's finished goods inventory on April 1 was:
    a. $20,000
    b. $40,000
    c. $60,000
    d. $80,000

3. Presented is selected information from Fred's January statement of cost of goods manufactured.

Predetermined overhead rate	80 percent of direct labor dollars
Direct materials	$ 60,000
Cost of goods manufactured	$150,000

    Fred's January direct labor was:
    a. $40,000
    b. $50,000
    c. $75,000
    d. $90,000

4. The beginning inventory consisted of 10,000 units, 30 percent complete and the ending inventory consisted of 8,000 units, 40 percent complete. There were 22,000 units started during the period. Determine the equivalent units of conversion in process.
   - a. 17,800
   - b. 20,800
   - c. 25,200
   - d. 27,200

5. Presented is selected information from Micro Systems cost of production report:

Cost per equivalent unit in process	$ 20
Units completed	30,000
Total costs in process	$664,000
Equivalent units of materials in ending inventory	4,000
Cost per equivalent unit of materials	$ 12

   The ending inventory of work-in-process is complete as to materials. The cost of conversion in the ending inventory is:
   - a. $16,000
   - b. $32,000
   - c. $48,000
   - d. $64,000

Superscript ᴬ denotes assignments based on Appendix 5A.

DISCUSSION QUESTIONS

Q5-1. Distinguish among service, merchandising, and manufacturing organizations on the basis of the importance and complexity of inventory cost measurement.

Q5-2. Distinguish between product costing and service costing.

Q5-3. When is depreciation a product cost? When is depreciation a period cost?

Q5-4. What are the three major product cost elements?

Q5-5. How are predetermined overhead rates developed? Why are they widely used?

Q5-6. Briefly distinguish between process manufacturing and job order production. Provide examples of products typically produced under each system.

Q5-7. Briefly describe the role of engineering personnel and production scheduling personnel in the production planning process.

Q5-8. Identify the primary records involved in the operation of a job cost system.

Q5-9. Describe the flow of costs through the accounting system of a labor-intensive manufacturing organization.

Q5-10. Identify two reasons that a service organization should maintain detailed job cost information.

Q5-11. What are the four major elements of a cost of production report?

Q5-12. What are equivalent completed units?

Q5-13. Under what conditions will equivalent units in process be different for materials and conversion costs?

Assignments with the ⊘ logo in the margin are available in BusinessCourse.
See the Preface of the book for details.

MINI EXERCISES

M5-14. Classification of Product and Period Costs   LO2
   Classify the following costs incurred by a manufacturer of golf clubs as product costs or period costs. Also classify the product costs as direct materials or conversion costs.
   - a. Depreciation on computer in president's office
   - b. Salaries of legal staff

    c.   Graphite shafts
    d.   Plant security department
    e.   Electricity for the corporate office
    f.   Rubber grips
    g.   Golf club heads
    h.   Wages paid assembly line maintenance workers
    i.   Salary of corporate controller
    j.   Subsidy of plant cafeteria
    k.   Wages paid assembly line production workers
    l.   National sales meeting in Orlando
    m.   Overtime premium paid assembly line workers
    n.   Advertising on national television
    o.   Depreciation on assembly line

LO2

MILLIKEN & COMPANY

M5-15. Developing and Using a Predetermined Overhead Rate

Assume that the following predictions were made for 2014 for one of the plants of **Milliken & Company**:

Total manufacturing overhead for the year	$40,000,000
Total machine hours for the year	3,200,000

Actual results for February 2014 were as follows:

Manufacturing overhead...	$4,410,000
Machine hours...	410,000

Required

    a.   Determine the 2014 predetermined overhead rate per machine hour.
    b.   Using the predetermined overhead rate per machine hour, determine the manufacturing overhead applied to Work-in-Process during February.
    c.   As of February 1, actual overhead was underapplied by $400,000. Determine the cumulative amount of any overapplied or underapplied overhead at the end of February.

LO4, 5   **M5-16. Job Order Costing and Process Costing Applications**

For each of the following manufacturing situations, indicate whether job order or process costing is more appropriate and why.
    a.   Manufacturer of chocolate candy bars
    b.   Manufacturer of carbonated beverages
    c.   Manufacturer of high-quality men's suits
    d.   Manufacturer of subway cars
    e.   Book printing

LO4, 5   **M5-17. Job Order Costing and Process Costing Applications**

For each of the following situations, indicate whether job order or process costing is more appropriate and why.
    a.   Building contractor for residential dwellings
    b.   Manufacturer of nylon yarn that sells to fabric-making textile companies
    c.   Evening gown manufacturer that makes gowns in several different fabrics, colors, styles, and sizes
    d.   Hosiery mill that manufactures a one-size-fits-all product
    e.   Vehicle battery manufacturer that has just received an order for 400,000 identical batteries to be delivered as completed over the next 12 months

LO5   **M5-18. Process Costing**

Tempe Manufacturing Company makes a single product that is produced on a continuous basis in one department. All materials are added at the beginning of production. The total cost per equivalent unit in process in March was $5.80, consisting of $4.20 for materials and $1.60 for conversion.

During the month, 9,000 units of product were transferred to finished goods inventory; on March 31, 3,500 units were in process, 10 percent converted. The company uses weighted average costing.

Required

a. Determine the cost of goods transferred to finished goods inventory.

b. Determine the cost of the ending work-in-process inventory.

c. What was the total cost of the beginning work-in-process inventory plus the current manufacturing costs?

M5-19.[A] **Absorption and Variable Costing; Inventory Valuation**

Boxtel, Inc., has a highly automated assembly line that uses very little direct labor. Therefore, direct labor is part of variable overhead. For October, assume that it incurred the following unit costs:

Direct materials	$250
Variable overhead	220
Fixed overhead	80

The 100 units of beginning inventory for October had an absorption costing value of $45,000 and a variable costing value of $38,000. For October, assume that Boxtel, Inc. produced 500 units and sold 540 units.

Required

Compute Boxtel's October amount of ending inventory under both absorption and variable costing if the FIFO inventory method was used.

M5-20.[A] **Absorption and Variable Costing; Cost of Goods Sold**

Use data from Mini Exercise 5-19.[A]

Required

Compute Boxtel's October Cost of Goods Sold using both the variable and absorption costing methods.

EXERCISES

E5-21. **Analyzing Activity in Inventory Accounts**

LO2, 4

Selected data concerning operations of Cascade Manufacturing Company for the past fiscal year follow:

Raw materials used.	$400,000
Total manufacturing costs charged to production during the year (includes raw materials, direct labor, and manufacturing overhead applied at a rate of 60 percent of direct labor costs).	731,000
Cost of goods available for sale.	936,000
Selling and general expenses.	40,000

	Inventories	
	Beginning	**Ending**
Raw materials	$70,000	$ 80,000
Work-in-process	85,000	30,000
Finished goods	90,000	110,000

Required

Determine each of the following:

a. Cost of raw materials purchased

b. Direct labor costs charged to production

c. Cost of goods manufactured

d. Cost of goods sold

LO4   **E5-22.   Statement of Cost of Goods Manufactured and Income Statement**

Information from the records of the Valley Manufacturing Company for August 2014 follows:

Sales	$210,000
Selling and administrative expenses	85,000
Purchases of raw materials.	30,000
Direct labor	20,000
Manufacturing overhead.	37,000

	Inventories	
	August 1	**August 31**
Raw materials	$ 8,000	$ 5,000
Work-in-process	14,000	11,000
Finished goods	15,000	19,000

Required

Prepare a statement of cost of goods manufactured and an income statement for August 2014.

LO4   **E5-23.   Statement of Cost of Goods Manufactured from Percent Relationships**

✓   Information about NuWay Products Company for the year ending December 31, 2014, follows:

- Sales equal $525,000.
- Direct materials used total $72,000.
- Manufacturing overhead is 150 percent of direct labor dollars.
- The beginning inventory of finished goods is 20 percent of the cost of goods sold.
- The ending inventory of finished goods is twice the beginning inventory.
- The gross profit is 20 percent of sales.
- There is no beginning or ending work-in-process.

Required

Prepare a statement of cost of goods manufactured for 2014. (*Hint:* Prepare an analysis of changes in Finished Goods Inventory.)

LO2, 4   **E5-24.   Account Activity and Relationships**

	Case A	Case B	Case C	Case D
Sales	$90,000	?	$110,000	?
Direct materials	15,000	21,000	?	21,000
Direct labor	5,000	?	20,000	?
Total direct costs.	?	32,000	?	30,000
Conversion cost	?	26,000	?	?
Manufacturing overhead.	8,000	?	10,000	?
Current manufacturing costs	?	?	95,000	79,000
Work in process, beginning	7,000	10,000	?	21,000
Work in process, ending	5,000	?	21,000	?
Cost of goods manufactured	?	32,000	?	82,000
Finished goods inventory, beginning	9,000	8,000	7,000	12,000
Finished goods inventory, ending.	6,000	?	8,000	?
Cost of goods sold	?	35,000	?	80,000
Gross profit	?	?	18,000	15,000
Selling and administrative expenses	20,000	15,000	?	?
Net income.	?	22,000	12,000	6,000

Required

Supply the missing data in each independent case.

LO2   **E5-25.   Developing and Using a Predetermined Overhead Rate: High-Low Cost Estimation**

For years, Concord Components Company has used an actual plantwide overhead rate and based its prices on cost plus a markup of 30 percent. Recently the marketing manager, Kate Baker, and the production manager, Sue Walsh, confronted the controller with a common problem. The marketing manager expressed a concern that Concord's prices seem to vary widely throughout the year. According to Baker, "It seems irrational to charge higher prices when business is bad and lower prices when business is good. While we get a lot of business during high-volume months because we charge less than our competitors, it is a waste of time to even call on customers during low-volume months because we are raising prices while our competitors are lowering them." Walsh also believed that it was "folly to be so pushed that we have to pay overtime in some months and then lay employees off in others." She commented, "While there are natural variations in customer demand, the accounting system seems to amplify this variation."

Required

a. Evaluate the arguments presented by Baker and Walsh. What suggestions do you have for improving the accounting and pricing procedures?

b. Assume that the Concord Components Company had the following total manufacturing overhead costs and direct labor hours in 2012 and 2013:

	2012	2013
Total manufacturing overhead	$210,000	$248,000
Direct labor hours	20,000	28,000

Use the high-low method to develop a cost estimating equation for total manufacturing overhead.

c. Develop a predetermined rate for 2014, assuming 25,000 direct labor hours are budgeted for 2014.

d. Assume that the actual level of activity in 2014 was 30,000 direct labor hours and that the total 2014 manufacturing overhead was $250,000. Determine the underapplied or overapplied manufacturing overhead at the end of 2014.

e. Describe two ways of handling any underapplied or overapplied manufacturing overhead at the end of the year.

E5-26. Manufacturing Cost Flows with Machine Hours Allocation

On November 1, Robotics Manufacturing Company's beginning balances in manufacturing accounts and finished goods inventory were as follows:

Raw Materials	$11,000
Manufacturing Supplies	500
Work-in-Process	4,500
Manufacturing Overhead	0
Finished Goods	27,000

During November, Robotics Manufacturing completed the following manufacturing transactions:

1. Purchased raw materials costing $47,000 and manufacturing supplies costing $3,000 on account.
2. Requisitioned raw materials costing $40,000 to the factory.
3. Incurred direct labor costs of $27,000 and indirect labor costs of $4,800.
4. Used manufacturing supplies costing $2,500.
5. Recorded manufacturing depreciation of $15,000.
6. Miscellaneous payables for manufacturing overhead totaled $3,600.
7. Applied manufacturing overhead, based on 2,250 machine hours, at a predetermined rate of $10 per machine hour.
8. Completed jobs costing $90,000.
9. Finished goods costing $96,000 were sold.

Required

a Prepare "T" accounts showing the flow of costs through all manufacturing accounts, Finished Goods Inventory, and Cost of Goods Sold.

b. Calculate the balances at the end of November for Work-in-Process Inventory and Finished Goods Inventory.

LO4 **E5-27.** **Service Cost Flows**

Viva Marketing, Ltd., produces television advertisements for businesses that are marketing products in the western provinces of Canada. To achieve cost control, Viva Marketing uses a job cost system similar to that found in a manufacturing organization. It uses some different account titles:

Account	Replaces
Videos-in-Process	Work-in-Process
Video Supplies Inventory	Manufacturing Supplies Inventory
Cost of Videos Completed	Cost of Goods Sold
Accumulated Depreciation, Studio Assets	Accumulated Depreciation, Factory Assets
Studio Overhead	Manufacturing Overhead

Viva Marketing does not maintain Raw Materials or Finished Goods Inventory accounts. Materials, such as props needed for videos, are purchased as needed from outside sources and charged directly to Videos-in-Process and the appropriate job. Videos are delivered directly to clients upon completion. The October 1, balances were as follows:

Video Supplies.	$ 300
Videos-in-Process.	1,000
Studio Overhead	250 underapplied

During October, Viva Marketing completed the following production transactions:

1. Purchased video supplies costing $1,675 on account.
2. Purchased materials for specific jobs costing $27,000 on account.
3. Incurred direct labor costs of $65,000 and indirect labor costs of $3,100.
4. Used production supplies costing $850.
5. Recorded studio depreciation of $3,500.
6. Incurred miscellaneous payables for studio overhead of $1,800.
7. Applied studio overhead at a predetermined rate of $18 per studio hour, with 520 studio hours.
8. Completed jobs costing $95,000 and delivered them directly to clients.

Required

a. Prepare "T" accounts showing the flow of costs through all service accounts and Cost of Videos Completed.

b. Calculate the cost incurred as of the end of October for the incomplete jobs still in process.

LO5 **E5-28.** **Cost of Production Report: No Beginning Inventories**

Oregon Paper Company produces newsprint paper through a special recycling process using scrap paper products. Production and cost data for October 2014, the first month of operations for the company's new Portland plant, follow:

Units of product started in process during October	80,000 tons
Units completed and transferred to finished goods	75,000 tons
Machine hours operated.	8,000
Direct materials costs incurred.	$486,000
Direct labor costs incurred	$190,200

Raw materials are added at the beginning of the process for each unit of product produced, and labor and manufacturing overhead are added evenly throughout the manufacturing process. Manufacturing overhead is applied to Work-in-Process at the rate of $24 per machine hour. Units in process at the end of the period were 60 percent converted.

Required

Prepare a cost of production report for Oregon Paper Company for October.

E5-29. Cost of Production Report: No Beginning Inventories

Sure Grip Paving Products Company manufactures asphalt paving materials for highway construction through a one-step process in which all materials are added at the beginning of the process. During October 2014, the company accumulated the following data in its process costing system:

Production data	
Work-in-process, 10/1/14	0 tons
Raw materials transferred to processing	25,000 tons
Work-in-process, 10/31/14 (75% converted)	5,000 tons
Cost data	
Raw materials transferred to processing	$650,000
Conversion costs	
Direct labor cost incurred	$38,000
Manufacturing overhead applied	?

Manufacturing overhead is applied at the rate of $6 per equivalent unit (ton) processed.

Required

Prepare a cost of production report for October.

E5-30.[A] **Absorption and Variable Costing Comparisons: Production Equals Sales**

Assume that Smuckers manufactures and sells 15,000 cases of jelly each quarter. The following data are available for the third quarter of 2014.

Total fixed manufacturing overhead...	$45,000
Fixed selling and administrative expenses	10,000
Sales price per case	32
Direct materials per case	12
Direct labor per case..	6
Variable manufacturing overhead per case	3

Required

a. Compute the cost per case under both absorption costing and variable costing.

b. Compute net income under both absorption costing and variable costing.

c. Reconcile any differences in income. Explain.

E5-31.[A] **Absorption and Variable Costing Income Statements: Production Exceeds Sales**

Glendale Company sells its product at a unit price of $13.00. Unit manufacturing costs are direct materials, $2.50; direct labor, $3.00; and variable manufacturing overhead, $1.50. Total fixed manufacturing costs are $25,000 per year. Selling and administrative expenses are $1.00 per unit variable and $10,000 per year fixed. Though 25,000 units were produced during 2014, only 22,000 units were sold. There was no beginning inventory.

Required

a. Prepare a functional income statement using absorption costing.

b. Prepare a contribution income statement using variable costing.

E5-32.[A] **Absorption and Variable Costing Comparisons: Sales Exceed Production**

Eskew Development purchases, develops, and sells commercial building sites. As the sites are sold, they are cleared at an average cost of $3,000 per site. Storm drains and driveways are also installed at an average cost of $5,500 per site. Selling costs are 10 percent of sales price. Administrative costs are $425,000 per year. During 2013, the company bought 1,000 acres of land for $5,000,000 and divided it into 200 sites of equal size. The average selling price per site was $80,000 during 2013 when 50 sites were sold. During 2014, the company purchased and developed another 1,000 acres, divided into 200 sites. The purchase price was again $5,000.000. Sales totaled 300 sites in 2014 at an average price of $80,000.

Required

a. Prepare 2013 and 2014 functional income statements using absorption costing.

b. Prepare 2013 and 2014 contribution income statements using variable costing.

PROBLEMS

LO4   **P5-33.**   **Cost of Goods Manufactured and Income Statement**

Following is information from the records of the Toronto Company for July 2014.

Purchases	
Raw materials	$ 85,000
Manufacturing supplies	3,500
Office supplies	1,200
Sales	445,800
Administrative salaries	12,000
Direct labor	117,500
Production employees' fringe benefits*	4,000
Sales commissions	55,000
Production supervisors' salaries	7,200
Plant depreciation	14,000
Office depreciation	22,000
Plant maintenance	10,000
Plant utilities	35,000
Office utilities	8,000
Office maintenance	2,000
Production equipment rent	6,000
Office equipment rent	1,300

* Classified as manufacturing overhead

Inventories	July 1	July 31
Raw materials	$17,000	$26,000
Manufacturing supplies	1,500	3,000
Office supplies	600	1,000
Work-in-process	51,000	40,000
Finished goods	35,000	27,100

Required

Prepare a statement of cost of goods manufactured and an income statement. Actual overhead costs are assigned to products.

LO2, 4   **P5-34.**   **Cost of Goods Manufactured and Income Statement with Predetermined Overhead and Labor Cost Classifications**

CALLAWAY GOLF
COMPANY (ELY)

Assume information pertaining to Callaway Golf Company for April 2014 follows.

Sales	$200,000
Purchases	
Raw materials	37,000
Manufacturing supplies	800
Office supplies	500
Salaries (including fringe benefits)	
Administrative	6,000
Production supervisors	3,600
Sales	15,000
Depreciation	
Plant and machinery	8,000
Office and office equipment	4,000
Utilities	
Plant	5,250
Office	890

Inventories	April 1	April 30
Raw materials	$3,000	$4,000
Manufacturing supplies	1,000	1,300
Office supplies	900	600
Work-in-process	2,000	2,500
Finished goods	8,000	9,200

Additional information follows:

- Manufacturing overhead is applied to products at 85 percent of direct labor dollars.
- Employee base wages are $12 per hour.
- Employee fringe benefits amount to 40 percent of the base wage rate. They are classified as manufacturing overhead.
- During April, production employees worked 5,600 hours, including 4,800 regular hours and 200 overtime hours spent working on products. There were 600 indirect labor hours.
- Employees are paid a 50 percent overtime premium. Any overtime premium is treated as manufacturing overhead.

Required

a. Prepare a statement of cost of goods manufactured and an income statement for April.
b. Determine underapplied or overapplied overhead for April.
c. Recompute direct labor and actual manufacturing overhead assuming employee fringe benefits for direct labor hours are classified as direct labor.

P5-35. Actual and Predetermined Overhead Rates   LO2, 4

Allison's Engines, which builds high performance auto engines for race cars, started operations on January 1, 2014. During the month, the following events occurred:

- Materials costing $7,000 were purchased on account.
- Direct materials costing $3,200 were placed in process.
- A total of 390 direct labor hours was charged to individual jobs at a rate of $15 per hour.
- Overhead costs for the month of January were as follows:

Depreciation on building and equipment	$ 600
Indirect labor	1,500
Utilities	600
Property taxes on building	650
Insurance on building	550

- On January 31, only one job (A06) was in process with materials costs of $550, direct labor charges of $400 for 30 direct labor hours, and applied overhead.
- The building and equipment were purchased before operations began and the insurance was prepaid. All other costs will be paid during the following month.

Note: Predetermined overhead rates are used throughout the chapter. An alternative is to accumulate actual overhead costs for the period in Manufacturing Overhead, and apply actual costs at the close of the period to all jobs in process during the period.

Required

a. Assuming Allison's Engines assigned actual monthly overhead costs to jobs on the basis of actual monthly direct labor hours, prepare an analysis of Work-in-Process for the month of January.
b. Assuming Allison's Engines uses a predetermined overhead rate of $10.50 per direct labor hour, prepare an analysis of Work-in-Process for the month of January. Describe the appropriate treatment of any overapplied or underapplied overhead for the month of January.
c. Review the overhead items and classify each as fixed or variable in relation to direct labor hours. Next, predict the actual overhead rates for months when 200 and 1,000 direct labor hours are used. Assuming jobs similar to A06 were in process at the end of each month, determine the costs assigned to these jobs. (*Hint:* Determine a variable overhead rate.)
d. Why do you suppose predetermined overhead rates are preferred to actual overhead rates?

P5-36.   **Job Costing with Predetermined Overhead Rate**

KUBOTA CORPORATION
(KUB)

Kubota Corporation manufactures equipment in batches for inventory stock. Assume that Kubota's production costs are accounted for using a job cost system. At the beginning of April raw materials inventories totaled $8,500,000, manufacturing supplies amounted to $1,200,000 and finished goods inventories totaled $6,000,000. Two jobs were in process: Job 522 with assigned costs of $5,750,000 and Job 523 with assigned costs of $2,600,000. The following information summarizes April manufacturing activities:

- Purchased raw materials costing $25,000,000 on account.
- Purchased manufacturing supplies costing $3,000,000 on account.
- Requisitioned materials needed to complete Job 523. Started two new jobs, 524 and 525, and requisitioned direct materials for them.

Direct materials

Job 523.	$ 3,000,000
Job 524.	12,900,000
Job 525.	9,600,000
Total	$25,500,000

- Recorded April salaries and wages as follows:

Direct labor

Job 522 (300,000 hours × $20 per hour)	$ 6,000,000
Job 523 (800,000 hours × $20 per hour)	16,000,000
Job 524 (1,200,000 hours × $20 per hour)	24,000,000
Job 525 (1,000,000 hours × $20 per hour)	20,000,000
Total direct labor	66,000,000
Indirect labor	6,400,000
Total	$72,400,000

- Used manufacturing supplies costing $2,250,000.
- Recognized depreciation on factory fixed assets of $4,000,000.
- Incurred miscellaneous manufacturing overhead costs of $5,500,000 on account.
- Applied manufacturing overhead at the rate of $6 per direct labor hour.
- Completed Jobs 522, 523, and 524.

Required

Prepare a complete analysis of all activity in Work-in-Process. Be sure to show the beginning and ending balances, all increases and decreases, and label each item. Provide support information on decreases with job cost sheets.

P5-37.   **Job Costing with Predetermined Overhead Rate**

TruCut Mower Company manufactures a variety of gasoline-powered mowers for discount hardware and department stores. TruCut uses a job cost system and treats each customer's order as a separate job. The primary mower components (motors, chassis, and wheels) are purchased from three different suppliers under long-term contracts that call for the direct delivery of raw materials to the production floor as needed. When a customer's order is received, a raw materials purchase order is electronically placed with suppliers. The purchase order specifies the scheduled date that production is to begin as the delivery date for motors and chassis; the scheduled date production is to be completed is specified as the delivery date for the wheels. As a consequence, there are no raw materials inventories; raw materials are charged directly to Work-in-Process upon receipt. Upon completion, goods are shipped directly to customers rather than transferred to finished goods inventory. At the beginning of July TruCut had the following work-in-process inventories:

Job 365	$21,000
Job 366	15,400
Job 367	16,000
Job 368	8,500
Total	$60,900

During July, the following activities took place:
- Started Jobs 369, 370, and 371.
- Ordered and received the following raw materials for specified jobs:

Job	Motors	Chassis	Wheels	Total
366	$ 0	$ 0	$ 800	$ 800
367	0	0	1,200	1,200
368	0	0	1,600	1,600
369	12,000	4,000	1,000	17,000
370	9,000	3,500	900	13,400
371	8,500	3,800	0	12,300
Total	$29,500	$11,300	$5,500	$46,300

- Incurred July manufacturing payroll:

Direct labor	
Job 365	$ 500
Job 366	3,200
Job 367	3,400
Job 368	4,160
Job 369	1,300
Job 370	2,620
Job 371	2,000
Total	17,180
Indirect labor	3,436
Total	$20,616

- Incurred additional manufacturing overhead costs for July:

Manufacturing supplies purchased on account and used	$ 2,800
Depreciation on factory fixed assets	6,000
Miscellaneous payables	5,100
Total	$13,900

- Applied manufacturing overhead using a predetermined rate based on predicted annual overhead of $190,000 and predicted annual direct labor of $200,000.
- Completed and shipped Jobs 365 through 370.

Required

Prepare a complete analysis of all activity in Work-in-Process. Be sure to show the beginning and ending balances, all increases and decreases, and label each item. Provide support information on decreases with job cost sheets.

P5-38. **Weighted Average Process Costing**   LO5

Minot Processing Company manufactures one product on a continuous basis in two departments, Processing and Finishing. All materials are added at the beginning of work on the product in the Processing Department. During November 2014, the following events occurred in the Processing Department:

Units started	17,000 units
Units completed and transferred to Finishing Department	14,500 units

Costs assigned to processing

Raw materials (one unit of raw materials for each unit of product started)	$142,900
Manufacturing supplies used	18,000
Direct labor costs incurred	53,000
Supervisors' salaries	12,000
Other production labor costs	14,000
Depreciation on equipment.	6,000
Other production costs	18,000

Additional information follows:

* Minot uses weighted average costing and applies manufacturing overhead to Work-in-Process at the rate of 100 percent of direct labor cost.
* Ending inventory in the Processing Department consists of 3,000 units that are one-third converted.
* Beginning inventory contained 2,000 units, one-half converted, with a cost of $27,300 ($17,300 for materials and $10,000 for conversion).

Required

a. Prepare a cost of production report for the Processing Department for November.
b. Prepare an analysis of all changes in Work-in-Process.

LO5 P5-39. Weighted Average Process Costing

Assume that **JIF**, which is part of **J.M. Smucker Company**, processes its only product, 12-ounce jars of peanut butter, in a single process and uses weighted average process costing to account for inventory costs. All materials are added at the beginning of production. Assume the following inventory, production, and cost data are provided for September 2014:

Production data

Beginning inventory (25% converted).	220,000 units
Units started.	650,000 units
Ending inventory (50% converted)	180,000 units

Manufacturing costs

Beginning inventory in process:	
Materials cost.	$154,000
Conversion cost	88,000
Raw materials cost added at beginning of process.	739,800
Direct labor cost incurred	410,000
Manufacturing overhead applied	333,600

Required

a. Prepare a cost of production report for September.
b. Prepare a statement of cost of goods manufactured for September.

LO5 P5-40. Weighted Average Process Costing with Error Correction

Horizon Manufacturing Company began operations on December 1. On December 31 a new accounting intern was assigned the task of calculating and costing ending inventories.

The intern estimated that the ending work-in-process inventory was 40 percent complete as to both materials and conversion, resulting in 4,000 equivalent units of materials and conversion. The ending work-in-process was then valued at $80,000, including $40,000 for materials and $40,000 for conversion. A subsequent review of the intern's work revealed that although the materials portion of the ending inventory was correctly estimated to be 40 percent complete, the units in ending inventory, on average, were only 20 percent complete as to conversion.

Required

a. Determine the number of units in the ending inventory.
b. How many equivalent units of conversion were in the ending inventory?
c. What cost per unit did the intern calculate for conversion?
d. Assuming 9,000 units were completed during the month of December, determine the correct cost per equivalent unit. *Hint:* Find the total conversion costs in process.

e. Determine the corrected cost of the ending inventory.

f. By how much was the cost of goods manufactured misstated as a result of the intern's error? Indicate whether the cost of goods manufactured was overstated or understated.

P5-41.ᴬ Absorption and Variable Costing Comparisons

Never Quit Shoe Company is concerned with changing to the variable costing method of inventory valuation for making internal decisions. Functional income statements using absorption costing for January and February follow.

NEVER QUIT SHOE COMPANY Functional (Absorption Costing) Income Statements For January and February 2014		
	January	**February**
Sales (8,000 units)	$160,000	$160,000
Cost of goods sold	(96,000)	(104,000)
Gross profit	64,000	56,000
Selling and administrative expenses	(30,000)	(30,000)
Net income	$ 34,000	$ 26,000

Production data follow.

Production units	12,000	8,000
Variable costs per unit	$10	$10
Fixed overhead costs	$24,000	$24,000

The preceding selling and administrative expenses include variable costs of $1 per unit sold.

Required

a. Compute the absorption cost per unit manufactured in January and February.

b. Explain why the net income for January was higher than the net income for February when the same number of units was sold in each month.

c. Prepare contribution income statements for both months using variable costing.

d. Reconcile the absorption costing and variable costing net income figures for each month. (Start with variable costing net income.)

P5-42.ᴬ Absorption and Variable Costing Comparisons

Peachtree Company manufactures peach jam. Because of bad weather, its peach crop was small. The following data have been gathered for the summer quarter of 2014:

Beginning inventory (cases)	0
Cases produced	9,000
Cases sold	8,200
Sales price per case	$60
Direct materials per case	$8
Direct labor per case	$9
Variable manufacturing overhead per case	$3
Total fixed manufacturing overhead	$320,000
Variable selling and administrative cost per case	$2
Fixed selling and administrative cost	$48,000

Required

a. Prepare a functional income statement for the quarter using absorption costing.

b. Prepare a contribution income statement for the quarter using variable costing.

c. What is the value of ending inventory under absorption costing?

d. What is the value of ending inventory under variable costing?

e. Reconcile the difference in ending inventory under absorption costing and variable costing.

P5-43.[A]   **Variable and Absorption Costing with High-Low Cost Estimation and CVP Analysis Including Taxes**

Presented are the Patriot Company's functional income statements for January and February of 2014.

PATRIOT COMPANY Functional (Absorption Costing) Income Statements For the Months of January and February 2014		
	January	February
Production and sales	40,000	50,000
Sales Revenue.	$1,000,000	$1,250,000
Cost of goods manufactured and sold.	(525,000)	(625,000)
Gross profit	475,000	625,000
General and administrative expenses	(235,000)	(235,000)
Net income before taxes.	240,000	390,000
Income taxes at 0.35.	(84,000)	(136,500)
Net income after taxes	$ 156,000	$ 253,500

Required

a.   Using the high-low method, develop a cost estimating equation for total monthly manufacturing costs.

b.   Determine Patriot Company's monthly break-even point.

c.   Determine the unit sales required to earn a monthly after-tax income of $175,000.

d.   Prepare a January 2014 contribution income statement using variable costing.

e.   If the January 2014 net income amounts differ using absorption and variable costing, explain why. If they are identical, explain why.

CASES AND PROJECTS

LO2, 4   **C5-44.   Cost Data for Financial Reporting and Special Order Decisions**

Friendly Greeting Card Company produces a full range of greeting cards sold through pharmacies and department stores. Each card is designed by independent artists. A production master is then prepared for each design. The production master has an indefinite life. Product designs for popular cards are deemed to be valuable assets. If a card sells well, many batches of the design will be manufactured over a period of years. Hence, Friendly Greeting maintains an inventory of production masters so that cards may be periodically reissued. Cards are produced in batches that may vary by increments of 1,000 units. An average batch consists of 10,000 cards. Producing a batch requires placing the production master on the printing press, setting the press for the appropriate paper size, and making other adjustments for colors and so forth. Following are facility-, product-, batch-, and unit-level cost information:

Product design and production master per new card.	$ 2,000.00
Batch setup (typically per 10,000 cards)	200.00
Materials per 1,000 cards	100.00
Conversion per 1,000 cards	80.00
Shipping	
Per batch	25.00
Per card	0.02
Selling and administrative	
Companywide	200,000.00
Per product design marketed	500.00

Information from previous year:

Product designs and masters prepared for new cards	90
Product designs marketed	120
Batches manufactured	500
Cards manufactured and sold	5,000,000

Required

You may need to review materials in Chapter 4 to complete the requirements.

a. Describe how you would determine the cost of goods sold and the value of any ending inventory for financial reporting purposes. (No computations are required.)

b. You have just received an inquiry from Mall-Mart department stores to develop and manufacture 20 special designs for sale exclusively in Mall-Mart stores. The cards would be sold for $1.50 each, and Mall-Mart would pay Friendly Greeting $0.35 per card. The initial order is for 20,000 cards of each design. If the cards sell well, Mall-Mart plans to place additional orders for these and other designs. Because of the preestablished sales relationship, no marketing costs would be associated with the cards sold to Mall-Mart. How would you evaluate the desirability of the Mall-Mart proposal?

c. Explain any differences between the costs considered in your answer to requirement (a) and the costs considered in your answer to requirement (b).

C5-45. Continue or Discontinue: Plantwide Overhead with Labor- and Machine-Intensive Operations LO2, 4

When Dart Products started operation five years ago, its only product was a radar detector known as the Bear Detector. The production system was simple, with Bear Detectors manually assembled from purchased components. With no ending work-in-process inventories, unit costs were calculated once a month by dividing current manufacturing costs by units produced.

Last year, Dart Products began to manufacture a second product, code-named the Lion Tamer. The production of Lion Tamers involves both machine-intensive fabrication and manual assembly. The introduction of the second product necessitated a change in the firm's simple accounting system. Dart Products now separately assigns direct material and direct labor costs to each product using information contained on materials requisitions and work tickets. Manufacturing overhead is accumulated in a single cost pool and assigned on the basis of direct labor hours, which is common to both products. Following are last year's financial results by product:

	Bear Detector		Lion Tamer	
Sales				
Units		5,000		2,000
Dollars		$ 500,000		$ 300,000
Cost of goods sold				
Direct materials	$110,000		$65,000	
Direct labor	150,000		45,000	
Applied overhead	270,000		81,000	
Total		(530,000)		(191,000)
Gross profit		$ (30,000)		$ 109,000

Management is concerned about the mixed nature of last year's financial performance. It appears that the Lion Tamer is a roaring success. The only competition, the Nittney Company, has been selling a competing product for considerably more than Dart's Lion Tamer; this company is in financial difficulty and is likely to file for bankruptcy. The management of Dart Products attributes the Lion Tamer's success to excellent production management. Management is concerned, however, about the future of the Bear Detector and is likely to discontinue that product unless its profitability can be improved. You have been asked to help with this decision and have obtained the following information:

- The labor rate is $15 per hour.
- Dart has two separate production operations, fabrication and assembly. Bear Detectors undergo only assembly operations and require 2.5 assembly hours per unit. Lion Tamers undergo both fabrication and assembly and require 1.5 fabrication hour and 0.5 assembly hour per unit.

- The annual Fabricating Department overhead cost function is:

$$\$200{,}000 + \$5 \text{ (labor hours)}$$

- The annual Assembly Department overhead cost function is:

$$\$20{,}000 + \$11 \text{ (labor hours)}$$

Required

You may need to review materials in Chapter 6 to complete this case. Evaluate the profitability of Dart's two products and make any recommendations you believe appropriate.

C5-46.[A] **Absorption Costing and Performance Evaluation**

On July 2, 2014 Innovative Financial acquired 90 percent of the outstanding stock of Medioker Industries in exchange for 2,000 shares of its own stock. Innovative Financial has a reputation as a "high flier" company that commands a high price-to-earnings ratio because its management team works wonders in improving the performance of ailing companies.

At the time of the acquisition, Medioker was producing and selling at an annual rate of 100,000 units per year. This is in line with the firm's average annual activity. Fifty thousand units were produced and sold during the first half of 2014.

Immediately after the acquisition Innovative Financial installed its own management team and increased production to practical capacity. One-hundred thousand units were produced during the second half of 2014.

At the end of the year, the new management declared another dramatic turnaround and a $100,000 cash dividend when the following set of income statements were issued:

MEDIOKER INDUSTRIES Income Statement For the first and second half-years of 2014			
	First	**Second**	**Total**
Sales	$1,400,000	$1,400,000	$2,800,000
Cost of goods sold*....................	(1,200,000)	(700,000)	(1,900,000)
Gross profit	200,000	700,000	900,000
Selling and administrative expenses	(200,000)	(400,000)	(600,000)
Net income..........................	$ 0	$ 300,000	$ 300,000

* Absorption costing with any under-absorbed or over-absorbed overhead written off as an adjustment to cost of goods sold. Medioker applies manufacturing overhead using a predetermined overhead rate based on predicted annual fixed overhead of $1,000,000 and annual production of 100,000 units.

Required

As the only representative of the minority interest on the board of directors, evaluate the performance of the new management team.

SOLUTIONS TO REVIEW PROBLEMS

Mid-Chapter Review

Solution

a.

b. Job in Work-in-Process at June 30, 2014:

	Job 228
Direct materials	$14,400
Direct labor	8,000
Applied overhead (800 × $5)	4,000
Total	$26,400

Job in Finished Goods at June 30, 2014:

	Job 227
Direct materials	$18,000
Direct labor	20,500
Applied overhead (2,050 × $5)	10,250
Total	$48,750

Jobs sold in June 2014:

	Job 225	Job 226	Total
Costs assigned from prior period.	$13,750	$ 1,800	$15,550
June Costs: Direct materials	–0–	2,600	2,600
Direct labor.	5,000	15,000	20,000
Applied overhead (500 & 1,500 × $5)	2,500	7,500	10,000
Total	$21,250	$26,900	$48,150

c. Statement of cost of goods manufactured for June 2014.

STRATASYS, LTD. Statement of Cost of Goods Manufactured For Month Ending June 30, 2014			
Current manufacturing costs			
Cost of materials placed in production			
Raw materials, 6/1/14	$ 7,000		
Purchases.....................................	40,000		
Total available..................................	47,000		
Raw materials, 6/30/14	(12,000)	$35,000	
Direct labor.....................................		48,500	
Manufacturing overhead applied		24,250	$107,750
Work-in-process, 6/1/14.............................			15,550
Total costs in process...............................			123,300
Work-in-process, 6/30/14............................			(26,400)
Cost of goods manufactured			$ 96,900

Chapter-End Review

Solution

SANDISK Cost of Production Report For the Year 2014			
Summary of units in process			
Beginning..................................	3,000,000		
Units started	27,000,000		
In process	30,000,000		
Completed.................................	(25,000,000)		
Ending	5,000,000		

Equivalent units in process	**Materials**	**Conversion**	
Units completed	25,000,000	25,000,000	
Plus equivalent units in ending inventory.......	5,000,000	1,500,000	
Equivalent units in process.................	30,000,000	26,500,000	

Total costs to be accounted for and cost per equivalent unit in process	**Materials**	**Conversion**	**Total**
Work-in-Process, beginning	$ 468,000	$ 252,000	$ 720,000
Current cost...............................	6,132,000	5,048,000	11,180,000
Total cost in process.......................	$ 6,600,000	$ 5,300,000	$11,900,000
Equivalent units in process.................	÷ 30,000,000	÷26,500,000	
Cost per equivalent unit in process	$0.22	$0.20	$0.42
Accounting for total costs:			
Transferred out (25,000,000 × $0.42)			$10,500,000
Work-in-Process, ending:			
Materials (5,000,000 × $0.22)		$ 1,100,000	
Conversion (1,500,000 × $0.20)		300,000	1,400,000
Total cost accounted for....................			$11,900,000

1. Explain the changes in the modern production environment that have affected cost structures. (p. 198)

2. Understand the concept of activity-based costing (ABC) and how it is applied. (p. 199)

3. Explain the difference between traditional plantwide and departmental overhead methods and ABC. (p. 201)

4. Describe the implementation of an activity-based costing system. (p. 209)

5. Explain customer profitability analysis based on ABC. (p. 210)

6. Explain the difference between ABC and activity-based management. (p. 213)

© Getty Images

Activity-Based Costing, Customer Profitability, and Activity-Based Management

We learned in the last chapter that indirect product costs need to be allocated to units of products or services based on a cost driver, that is, a measure of activity that causes that cost to increase. However, the choice of one activity driver over another may result in widely differing costs for the same unit of the good. In this chapter, we will address which driver is the correct driver; in many instances, product costing will be improved if we incorporate multiple drivers into the computation, choosing the drivers based on the activities undertaken to produce the good or service.

UNILEVER
www.unilever.com

Consider the Anglo-Dutch company **Unilever**, which makes consumer products in the food and drink, personal care, and home care markets. The company's well-known brands include Lipton, Ben & Jerry's, Bertolli, Hellmann's, Dove Beauty Products, Axe, Vaseline, and Pond's, among others. The company is in the midst of two overarching strategic shifts: (1) increasing market share in emerging markets, and (2) sustainability. While continuing growth in established markets, Unilever is now moving into new markets such as Central Africa and Myanmar where there is increased demand for grooming products. And although Unilever has been in Indonesia for nearly a century, changing demographics require that the company rethink its packaging and distribution strategies. Women in Indonesia are drawn to skin care products but cannot afford the $10 price of a container of Pond's Skin Cream. By repackaging skin care products into single-serve containers and selling through street vendors, the product line has experienced an 80 percent growth in sales throughout the region.

Unilever's sustainability plan reaches from its sourcing of raw materials through its production facilities to the communities it serves. Unilever is the world's biggest consumer of palm oil, which is used in many of its products, including Dove soap, Magnum ice cream, and Vaseline lotion. Traditionally, rain forests in Indonesia and Malaysia have made way for palm plantations, which has destroyed the habitats of orangutans, tigers, and rhinoceroses. Unilever is in the process of building a $100 million palm-oil processing plant in an attempt to slow the rate of deforestation. The company also sources nearly half of its tea from farms certified by the Rainforest Alliance, which works to improve the living conditions of farmers by improving soil fertility and by enhancing water quality and availability. Unilever's factories have greatly diminished the amount of waste generated by their production processes by recycling and redirecting the waste products into new products such as animal bedding and wallpapers. The company is also investing its profits into community health and hygiene projects such as hand washing, sanitation, and safe drinking water campaigns in the countries where it operates.

These investments are made possible by streamlining operations and reducing manufacturing and distribution inefficiencies. Specifically, by analyzing the activities undertaken in producing and delivering its products to consumers, the company has been able to better determine the cost of each activity in its value chain, thereby eliminating waste and redundancies from costly activities. As a result, engineering

continued on following page

continued from previous page

has adopted "cookie-cutter" templates for factories, product designs, and supplier specifications to reduce inconsistencies in product quality across geographic regions. The company's 22 geographic segments have reorganized down to eight markets, vastly reducing duplicative activities. Two hundred separate information technology systems have been simplified into four global systems. This move increases the uniformity of and access to data, which means Unilever can better determine where to re-allocate its resources and effort. Distribution systems have been pushed down to mobile platforms, which allows for more efficient and effective servicing of remote and emerging markets. Even the financial reporting system has been streamlined—its previous production of 20,000 different types of financial reports has been reduced by 90 percent. Even marketing is fair game for cost reductions. Unilever is creating fewer, but more global advertising campaigns, which has substantially reduced its advertising costs.

When we break down our costs by activity and then allocate those costs based on the set of activities a product or service consumes, we provide the basis by which a company such as Unilever can make broad strategic and operational changes to its business. This chapter will demonstrate how to develop and implement costing systems based on activity consumption, which will lead to better decision making regarding product, geographic, and customer selection.

Sources: Unilever 2012 Annual Report; Paul Sonne and Simon Zekaria, "Unilever Tallies Hefty Sales Gain," *Wall Street Journal*, January 24, 2013, p. B6; Matthew Boyle, "In Emerging Markets, Unilever Finds a Passport to Profit," *Bloomberg Businessweek*, January 3, 2013; and Paul Sonne, "Unilever Takes Palm Oil in Hand," *Wall Street Journal*, April 12, 2012, p. B3.

CHAPTER ORGANIZATION

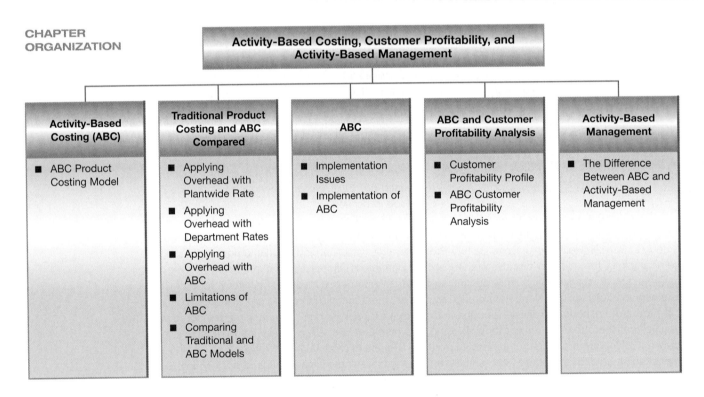

Activity-Based Costing (ABC)	Traditional Product Costing and ABC Compared	ABC	ABC and Customer Profitability Analysis	Activity-Based Management
■ ABC Product Costing Model	■ Applying Overhead with Plantwide Rate ■ Applying Overhead with Department Rates ■ Applying Overhead with ABC ■ Limitations of ABC ■ Comparing Traditional and ABC Models	■ Implementation Issues ■ Implementation of ABC	■ Customer Profitability Profile ■ ABC Customer Profitability Analysis	■ The Difference Between ABC and Activity-Based Management

CHANGING COST ENVIRONMENT

LO1 Explain the changes in the modern production environment that have affected cost structures.

As technology has advanced and competition has intensified over the last century, there has been a fundamental shift in manufacturing organizations from labor-intensive to automated assembly techniques. These changes have influenced the activities performed to meet customer needs and, consequently, the costs of producing goods and services.

At the beginning of the twentieth century, products had long life cycles, production procedures were relatively straightforward, production was labor based, and only a limited number of related products were produced in a single plant. It was said of the Model T Ford that "you could have any color you wanted, as long as it was black." The largest cost elements of most manufactured goods were the cost of raw materials and the wages paid to production employees. Manufacturing overhead was a relatively small portion of the overall cost of manufacturing products.

The twentieth century saw an accelerating shift from traditional labor-based activities to production procedures requiring large investments in automated equipment. In the past, production employees used equipment to assist them in performing their jobs. Now employees spend considerable time scheduling, setting up, maintaining, and moving materials to and from, equipment. They spend relatively little time on actual production. The equipment does the work, and the employees keep it running efficiently. Increased complexity of production procedures and an increase in the variety of products produced in a single facility have also caused a shift toward more support personnel and fewer production employees. The result is a significant increase in manufacturing overhead as a percentage of total product cost. This change in the typical production cost structure over the past century is illustrated in Exhibit 6.1.

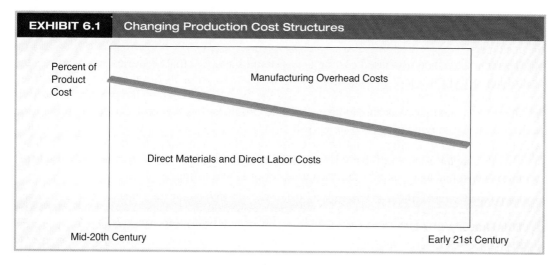

In the "low-tech," labor-intensive manufacturing environment, factors related to direct labor were often the primary drivers of manufacturing overhead costs; however, in today's "high-tech" automated environment there are many other factors that drive manufacturing overhead costs, and the specific set of cost drivers differs from organization to organization.

The previous chapter on product costing illustrated a simplified traditional system for allocating manufacturing overhead to products using a single, volume-based cost driver, such as direct labor hours. The following section introduces activity-based costing, which recognizes the multiple activities that drive manufacturing overhead costs in today's production environment.

ACTIVITY-BASED COSTING

The manufacturing overhead cost pool has been referred to as a "blob" of common costs. The constant growth of costs classified as overhead has forced us to search for increasingly detailed methods to analyze these costs. If overhead costs are low in comparison with other costs and if factories produce few products in large production runs, the use of an overhead rate based on direct labor hours or machine hours may be adequate. However, as the amount of overhead costs continues to grow, as manufacturing facilities produce a wider variety of products, and as competition intensifies, the inadequacies of a single overhead rate based on a single cost driver such as direct labor hours become evident.

LO2 Understand the concept of activity-based costing (ABC) and how it is applied.

Fortunately, advances in information technology and the declining costs of computerized information systems have facilitated the development and maintenance of increasingly detailed databases. The increased complexity of the production environment, coupled with faster and cheaper computing technology, gave rise to the emergence and development of activity-based costing during the 1980s and 1990s.

Activity-based costing involves determining the cost of activities and tracing their costs to cost objects on the basis of the cost object's utilization of units of activity.

The concepts underlying ABC can be summarized in the following two statements and illustrations:

1. Activities performed to fill customer needs consume resources that cost money.

2. The cost of resources consumed by activities should be assigned to cost objects on the basis of the units of activity consumed by the cost object.

*Based on units of activity utilized by the cost object.

The cost object is typically a product or service provided to a customer. Depending on the information needs of decision makers, as we will discuss later in this chapter, the cost object might be the customer.

To summarize, activity-based costing is a system of analysis that identifies and measures the cost of key activities, and then traces these activity costs to products or other cost objects based on the quantity of activity consumed by the cost objects. ABC is based on the premise that activities drive costs and that costs should be assigned to products (or other cost objects) in proportion to the volume of activities they consume. Although activity cost analysis is most often associated with product costing, it offers many benefits for controlling and managing costs, as we will see later in this chapter. As the following Research Insight box explains, ABC was actually used first to improve cost management before it was used for product costing.

RESEARCH INSIGHT

The History of ABC   ABC came to the forefront in the 1980s and 1990s; however, it was beginning to evolve as early as the 1960s when General Electric's (GE) finance and accounting staff attempted to improve the usefulness of accounting information in controlling ever-increasing indirect costs. The GE staff noted that indirect costs were often the result of "upstream" decisions, such as engineering design and change orders, which were made long before the costs were actually incurred. Frequently, the engineering department was not informed of the consequences their actions had on the other parts of the organization.

The second phase of the development of ABC was accomplished by business consultants, professors, and manufacturing companies during the 1970s and early 1980s. By generating more accurate cost and profitability measures for the various products offered by companies, these consultants and professors hoped to improve product cost information used in pricing and product mix decisions. ABC has since been extended to assess customer profitability.

In the late 1980s and 1990s, ABC was being promoted by many of the leading consulting firms, and it almost became a fad, much as TQM and JIT had become before it. Consequently, many companies that jumped on the ABC bandwagon early in its life, later determined that it was not for them. Most of the companies that abandoned ABC, probably adopted it initially for the wrong reasons.

Knowledge of the historical development of activity-based costing is important in order to clearly understand what ABC analysis was intended to accomplish, as well as what it was not intended to accomplish.

Source: Latshaw, Craig A. Cortese-Danile, Teresa M., "Activity-based costing: usage and pitfalls," *Review of Business*, Winter, 2002.

ABC Product Costing Model

Traditional costing considers the cost of a product to be its direct costs for materials and labor plus some allocated portion of factory overhead, using overhead rates typically based on direct labor or machine hours. Activity-based costing is based on the notion that companies incur costs because of the activities they conduct in pursuit of their goals and objectives. For example, various activities take place to produce a particular product, such as setting up, maintaining, or monitoring the machines to make the product, physically moving raw materials and work in process, and so forth. Each of these activities has a cost; therefore, the total cost of producing a product using ABC is the sum of the direct materials and direct labor costs of that product, plus the cost of other activities conducted to produce that product.

The general two-stage ABC product cost model is illustrated in Exhibit 6.2. The first stage includes the assignment of manufacturing overhead resource costs, such as indirect labor, depreciation, and utilities, to activity cost pools for the key activities identified. Typical activity cost pools in a manufacturing environment include pools for machine setup, material movement, and engineering. The second stage assigns those activity cost pools to products.

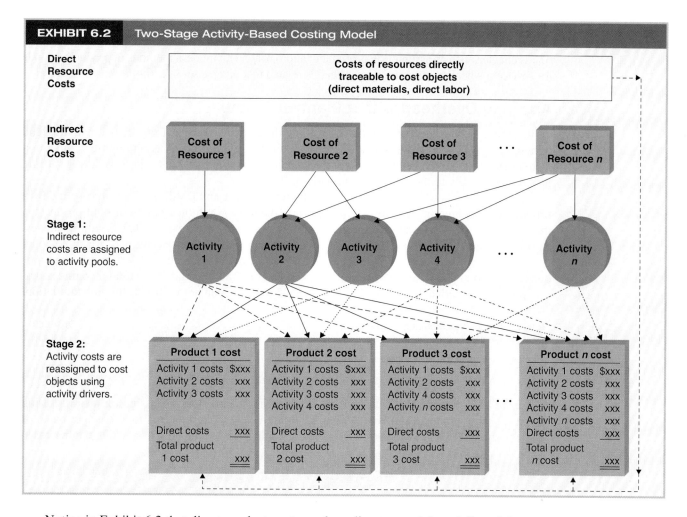

EXHIBIT 6.2 Two-Stage Activity-Based Costing Model

Notice in Exhibit 6.2 that direct product costs, such as direct materials and direct labor, are directly assigned to products and are excluded from the activity cost pools. Only indirect product costs (manufacturing overhead) are assigned to products via activity cost pools.

Probably the most critical step in ABC is identifying cost drivers. The activity cost driver for a particular cost (or cost pool) is the characteristic selected for measuring the quantity of the activity for a particular period of time. For example, if an activity cost pool is established for machine setup, it is necessary to select some basis for measuring the quantity of machine setup activity associated with the costs in the pool. The quantity of setup activity could be measured by the number of different times machines are set up to produce a different product, the amount of time used in completing machine setups, the number of staff working on setups, or some other measure. It is critical that the activity measure used has a logical causal relationship to the costs in the pool and that the quantity of the activity is highly correlated with the amount of cost in the pool. Statistical methods, such as regression analysis and correlation analysis, can be very useful in selecting activity cost drivers.

Once the total cost in the activity pool and the activity cost driver have been determined, the cost per unit of activity is calculated as the total cost divided by the total amount of activity. For example, if total costs assigned to the setup activity pool in July were $100,000 and 200 setups were completed in July, the cost per setup for the month would be $500. If during July machines were set up 10 times to make product JX2, the total setup cost that would be assigned to product JX2 would be $5,000 ($500 × 10).

TRADITIONAL PRODUCT COSTING AND ABC COMPARED

Recall that we assumed Burberry in Chapter 5 recognized manufacturing overhead using a plantwide manufacturing overhead rate of $4 per direct labor hour. It was assumed that each hour of labor

LO3 Explain the difference between traditional plantwide and departmental overhead methods and ABC.

worked on product caused $4 of manufacturing overhead to be incurred. In that case, all manufacturing costs were assumed to be driven by one factor, direct labor hours. As discussed at the beginning of this chapter, such an assumption is often not appropriate with modern methods of producing goods (or services) where manufacturing overhead is related to a diverse set of activities and cost drivers.

Applying Overhead with a Plantwide Rate

To illustrate, assume that Campbell's V8 brand produces two beverages fortified with vitamins and minerals, regular V8 and V8 Splash, a fruit based drink. V8 has been facing intense competition from other health beverage producers in the vegetable drink market, and it is considering shifting its strategy entirely to the fruit drink market.

Each product is worked on in two departments, Mixing and Bottling. Both Mixing and Bottling operations are highly automated; therefore, the most common element of both products is machine hours in Mixing and Bottling. The products are produced in large 1,000-gallon batches. Assume regular V8 requires 3 machine hours per batch and V8 Splash requires 2 machine hours per batch. Suppose for July, 232 batches of regular V8 and 400 batches of V8 Splash were produced, with total plantwide manufacturing overhead of $187,000 and 1,496 total machine hours. The plantwide overhead rate is calculated as $125 per machine hour in the following tabulation.

Total plantwide manufacturing overhead.	$187,000
Total plantwide machine hours.	÷ 1,496
Plantwide overhead rate per machine hour.	$ 125

Assigning $125 to each machine hour used is the simplest method of assigning manufacturing overhead to the products and, as the tabulation below shows, results in a total cost per batch of $610 for regular V8 and $400 for V8 Splash after adding the direct materials and direct labor costs.

	Unit Costs	
	V8	**V8 Splash**
Direct materials	$125	$120
Direct labor	110	30
Manufacturing overhead		
V8: 3 machine hours × $125.	375	
V8 Splash: 2 machine hours × $125.		250
Total unit cost	$610	$400

A plantwide overhead allocation method is often used in situations where companies produce only one product in a plant, or where multiple products are very similar in regard to the use of activities, such as machine or labor hours, that drive most of the overhead costs. If multiple products are produced that consume varying levels of activities in multiple production departments, departmental overhead allocation rates will produce a more accurate allocation of overhead costs to the various products.

Applying Overhead with Department Rates

For Campbell's to establish separate overhead allocation rates for each of the two production departments, it is necessary first to assign the $187,000 of total overhead costs for the plant to the two production departments, some of which is directly assignable to the departments. For example, the departmental supervisors' salaries could be directly assignable to the departments. Other manufacturing overhead costs, such as support costs for maintenance, payroll, and so forth, are allocated to the production departments. Assume that after these allocations, the total costs assigned to the departments were $59,100 for Mixing and $127,900 for Bottling.

The next step in the product costing process is to assign the departmental costs to the products. Assume that the manufacturing process at Campbell's V8 division is labor intensive in the Mixing Department and machine intensive in the Bottling Department, and that manufacturing overhead is applied to products as follows:

Department	Manufacturing Overhead Application Base
Mixing	Direct labor hours
Bottling	Machine hours

During the month of July, 500 direct labor hours were worked in Mixing, and Bottling used 800 machine hours. The department manufacturing overhead rates based on actual costs for July, and the total product costs using departmental overhead rates, are calculated in the following tables:

Overhead costs per unit for July	V8	V8 Splash
Total department manufacturing overhead		
(direct department costs plus allocated costs)	$59,100	$127,900
Quantity of overhead application base		
Direct labor hours	÷ 500	
Machine hours..		÷ 800
Department manufacturing overhead rates.............................	$118.20	$159.875
	Per direct labor hour	Per machine hour

	Unit Costs per Batch	
Total costs per unit for July using department rates	V8	V8 Splash
Direct materials	$125	$120
Direct labor	110	30
Manufacturing overhead		
Mixing: 1** labor hr. × $118.20..	118*	
0.67** labor hrs. × $118.20		79*
Bottling: 1** machine hr. × $159.875....................................	160*	
1.42** machine hrs. × $159.875		227*
Total costs	$513	$456

* Rounded
** Given

Allocating factory overhead costs based on department rates (rather than on a plantwide rate of $125 per machine hour) causes a shift in costs from regular V8 to V8 Splash because V8's overhead activity is incurred evenly in both Mixing and Bottling (1.00 hour each) while V8 Splash incurs more of its overhead activity in Bottling (1.42 hours versus 0.67 hour).

The per-unit costs with multiple allocations are substantially different from the per-unit costs when using plantwide rates and, in fact, show the cost of V8 to be slightly below a competitor's bid of $525 that was offered to one of V8 Splash's customers. Assume that based on the plantwide rate, the cost of $610 for V8 was higher than the competitor's price.

By creating separate manufacturing overhead cost allocation pools, allocation bases, and overhead application rates for Mixing and Bottling, it is possible to recognize overhead cost differences in various products based on differences in Mixing Department labor hours used and Bottling Department machine hours used for each product. In most multiproduct manufacturing environments, this approach represents a cost system improvement over using a single, plantwide overhead rate, and it reduces the likelihood of cost cross-subsidization, which occurs when one product is assigned too much cost as a result of another being assigned too little cost. While department overhead rates may improve product costing results for many organizations, and in fact may be satisfactory, this method does not attempt to reflect the actual activities used in producing the different product.

Applying Overhead with Activity-Based Costing

An even more precise method of measuring the cost of products than plantwide or departmental rates is the activity-based costing method. As stated earlier, activity-based costing involves determining the cost of activities associated with a particular cost object. ABC for product costing identifies and measures the cost of activities used to produce the various products and sums the cost of those activities to determine the cost of the products. The following Business Insight compares three key benefits regarding the accuracy of cost systems for ABC users and non-ABC users.

BUSINESS INSIGHT

Key Benefits of Using ABC A 2009 study of 348 manufacturing and service companies worldwide indicated that activity-based costing continues to provide strategic and operational benefits. Although the study showed that there has been a decline in ABC users since the 1990s, when it was first widely adopted, the following graphics from the study report support the conclusion that users of ABC have a higher level of confidence than non-ABC users that their cost system provides more accurate cost measurements.

Comparisons of ABC to Non-ABC Users on Three Key Benefits

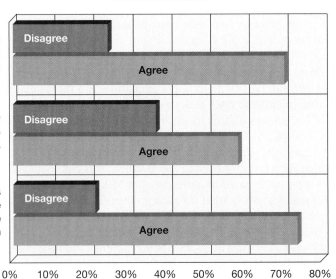

Source: William O. Stratton, Denis Desroches, Raef Lawson, and Toby Hatch, "Activity-Based Costing: Is It Still Relevant?" *Management Accounting Quarterly*, Spring 2009, Vol. 10, No. 3, pp. 31-40.

For Campbell's V8 division, assume Mixing and Bottling have overhead costs of $59,100 and $127,900, respectively. The overhead rates for each department were determined in the last section as $118.20 and $159.875, respectively, per relevant hour of use. The easiest way to assign these costs to products is by using one base and one rate for all products going through a given process (e.g., mixing). However, different products typically use different amounts of resources from a given process and using the same base and overhead rate for all may distort the cost for some or all products.

Overhead costs in the Mixing and Bottling departments consisted of two types of costs: direct department costs and allocated costs from other support departments. Direct department overhead costs are costs that are incurred directly by the department such indirect labor, indirect materials, depreciation on equipment, supervisory wages, and so forth. Allocated support costs are costs allocated from other departments (specifically, engineering, support services, and building and grounds) that provide services to both Mixing and Bottling. Campbell's accountants determined that the *direct* department overhead costs in Mixing were driven primarily by labor hours, whereas *direct* department overhead costs in Bottling were driven primarily by machine hours. It was also determined that each component of engineering, support services, and building and grounds represents a separate activity cost pool, and that these costs should be assigned to the products based on specific cost drivers rather than a single cost driver for the entire department.

The following is a detailed analysis of overhead cost data for July's operations:

Overhead Activity	Total Activity Cost	Activity Cost Driver (number of)	Quantity of Activity	Unit Activity Rates
Direct departmental overhead costs				
Mixing........................	$ 40,000	Labor hours..........	500	$ 80.00
Bottling.....................	90,000	Machine hours........	800	112.50
Common overhead costs				
Support Services				
Receiving	14,000	Purchase orders	100	140.00
Inventory control	13,000	Units produced	632	20.57*
Engineering Resources				
Production setup	12,000	Production runs.......	20	600.00
Engineering and testing........	8,000	Machine hours........	800	10.00
Building and Grounds				
Maintenance, machines........	4,000	Machine hours........	800	5.00
Depreciation, machines........	6,000	Units produced	632	9.49*
Total	$187,000			

* Rounded

Suppose the amounts of activity attributed to V8 and V8 Splash and the factory overhead cost per unit based on ABC costs are as follows:

Activity (cost per unit of driver activity)	V8 Quantity of Activity	V8 Cost of Activity	V8 Splash Quantity of Activity	V8 Splash Cost of Activity
Mixing ($80.00 per labor hour)	232	$18,560	268	$ 21,440
Bottling ($112.50 per machine hour)	174	19,575	626	70,425
Receiving ($140.00 per order)....................	40	5,600	60	8,400
Inventory control ($20.57 per unit produced)........	232	4,772*	400	8,228
Production setup ($600.00 per run)	5	3,000	15	9,000
Engineering and testing ($10.00 per machine hour) ...	174	1,740	626	6,260
Maintenance, machines ($5.00 per machine hour)	174	870	626	3,130
Depreciation, machines ($9.49 per unit produced)	232	2,202*	400	3,796
Total factory overhead product cost..............		$56,319		$130,679
Units produced		÷ 232		÷ 400
Factory overhead cost per unit of product*..........		$ 243*		$ 327*
Direct materials cost per unit of product............		125		120
Direct labor cost per unit of product		110		30
Total unit product cost using ABC		$ 478		$ 477

* Rounded

The following table summarizes the total product costs for Campbell's two products using the three different overhead cost assignment methods:

	V8	V8 Splash
Plantwide overhead rate..	$610	$400
Departmental overhead rates..	513	456
ABC..	478	477

ABC product costing reveals a dramatically different cost picture. Using either a plantwide overhead rate or departmental rates, the regular V8 drink is bearing more than its share of total overhead costs. Using either of these methods could lead the company into the very damaging strategy of abandoning the vegetable drink market. With an actual per-batch cost of $478, rather than $513 or $610, the company clearly has significant latitude to compete on price with other companies in this market and remain profitable. Obviously, the effect of adopting ABC is not always as significant as it was for Campbell's V8 division in this example. However, even with less dramatic differences among the various cost methods, inaccurate costing can affect management's assessment of product profitability and its decisions regarding which products to continue to produce and which products to discontinue. Flawed product costing information can cause management mistakenly to decide to keep products that are losing money, while deciding to discontinue products that are profitable. Using a plantwide or departmental overhead allocation method could have led Campbell's management to shift its emphasis from the vegetable to the fruit drink market, a decision that could have been devastating to the company.

BUSINESS INSIGHT

The Cost of Occupancy—A Collection of Activities Marriott International manages over 3,800 hotels throughout the world ranging from its Ritz Carlton luxury brands to its Fairfield Inn economy-based chain. A key performance metric in the lodging industry is the revenue per room night. But what does each room cost for a given day? From a cost standpoint, each property is a collection of activities surrounding several major functions: front office, housekeeping, food and beverage, and marketing. Some of these costs increase only when a room is occupied, whereas others are incurred regardless of occupancy.

For example, Marriott's front office activities include reservation-taking, check-in and check-out, and customer account management, all of which consume more labor hours for occupied rooms. Yet, some of those costs are fixed—for example, someone must be at the front desk during all hours. Housekeeping tasks can be divided into laundry, common areas, and guest rooms. In fact, Marriott has guest room cleaning down to a 66-step 30-minute science. Food and beverage includes not only food preparation and service, but also cleaning and purchasing activities. And marketing relates to promotion, in addition to customer service functions such as the concierge and tour desk. Then there are auxiliary services in some locations, such as grounds and pool maintenance, valet and bell service, and merchandising. It's clear that using simple occupancy rates as a cost driver will not be as accurate as examining each type of cost by its activities that make up the entire Marriott experience.

Source: Halah Touryalai, "Ready, Set, Clean! Secrets to Cleaning a Marriott Hotel Room," *Forbes*, July 15, 2013.

YOU MAKE THE CALL

You are the Controller You have heard about companies that have adopted ABC and experienced significant differences in product costs compared with previous cost calculations using traditional costing methods. Consequently, you were surprised when your newly implemented ABC system provided product costs that were almost identical to those from the old costing system. You are, therefore, thinking about abandoning the ABC system, since it is quite costly to maintain. Should you abandon your ABC system? [Answer, p. 215]

MID-CHAPTER REVIEW

Assume that one of **Illinois Tool Works Inc's (ITW)** divisions has the following predicted indirect costs and cost drivers for 2014 for the given activity cost pools:

	Fabrication Department	Finishing Department	Cost Driver
Maintenance	$ 20,000	$10,000	Machine hours
Materials handling.	30,000	15,000	Material moves
Machine setups.	70,000	5,000	Machine setups
Inspections	—	25,000	Inspection hours
	$120,000	$55,000	

The following activity predictions were also made for the year:

	Fabrication Department	Finishing Department
Machine hours.	10,000	5,000
Materials moves	3,000	1,500
Machine setups.	700	50
Inspection hours	—	1,000

It is assumed that the cost per unit of activity for a given activity does not vary between departments.

Suppose ITW's divisional manager is trying to evaluate the company's product mix strategy regarding two of its five product models, Cobra Latch and GrimLoc. The company has been using a plantwide overhead rate based on machine hours but is considering switching to either department rates or activity-based rates. The production manager has provided the following data for the production of a batch of 100 units for each of these models:

	Cobra Latch	GrimLoc
Direct materials cost.	$12,000	$18,000
Direct labor cost	$5,000	$4,000
Machine hours (Fabrication).	500	700
Machine hours (Finishing).	200	100
Materials moves	30	50
Machine setups.	5	9
Inspection hours	30	60

Required

a. Determine the cost of one unit each of Cobra Latch and GrimLoc, assuming a plantwide overhead rate is used based on total machine hours.

b. Determine the cost of one unit of Cobra Latch and GrimLoc, assuming department overhead rates are used. Overhead is assigned based on machine hours in both departments.

c. Determine the cost of one unit of Cobra Latch and GrimLoc, assuming activity-based overhead rates are used for maintenance, materials handling, machine setup, and inspection activities.

d. Comment on the results of these cost calculations.

The solution is on pages 232–234.

Limitations of ABC Illustration

Several limitations of the Campbell's V8 division illustration should be mentioned. For the sake of simplicity, the example was limited to manufacturing cost considerations. A complete analysis would also require considerations of nonmanufacturing costs, such as marketing, distribution, and customer service, before a final determination of product profitability could be made. Finally, in calculating the activity cost per unit of activity, it is necessary to decide how to measure the total quantity of activity. For example, for the V8 division, the receiving cost per purchase order was calculated as $140.00 based on the actual quantity of 100 purchase orders for the period. Alternatively, the receiving cost could have been calculated based on **practical capacity**, which is the maximum possible volume of activity, while allowing for normal downtime for repairs and maintenance. If the plant has a practical capacity to prepare 140 purchase orders per period, the cost per purchase order based on the practical capacity is $100 per purchase order, or $14,000 ÷ 140. Using this overhead rate in costing product, only $10,000 would have been assigned to the two products, which required only 100 purchase orders, and the remaining $4,000 for the 40 purchase orders of excess (or idle) capacity not used would be written off as an operating expense of the period as underapplied overhead. Practical capacity is generally regarded as better than actual capacity for calculating activity costs because it does not hide the cost of idle capacity within product costs, and it gives a truer cost of the activities used to produce the product.

Comparing Traditional and Activity-Based Costing

Procedurally, ABC is not a new method for assigning costs to cost objects. Traditional costing systems have used a two-stage allocation model (similar to the ABC model) to assign costs to cost pools (such as departments) and subsequently assign those cost pools to products using an allocation base. In most traditional costing systems, overhead is assigned to one or more cost pools based on departments and functional characteristics (such as labor-related, machine-related, and space-related costs) and then reassigned to products using a general allocation base such as direct labor hours or machine hours. ABC is different in that it divides the overall manufacturing processes into activities. ABC accumulates costs in cost pools for the major activities and then assigns the costs of these activities to products or other cost objects that benefit from these activities. *Conceptually,* ABC is different because of the way it views the operations of the company; *procedurally,* it uses a methodology that has been around for a long time.

The challenge in using ABC is specifying the model; that is, determining how many activity pools should be established for a given cost measurement purpose, which costs should be assigned to each activity pool, and the appropriate activity driver for each pool. Specifying the model also includes determining the resource cost drivers for assigning indirect resource costs to the various activity cost pools.

BUSINESS INSIGHT

Batch Size Matters in Brooklyn, New York   Today managers accept as conventional wisdom that manufacturing cannot be competitive in the United States, given the country's labyrinth of regulation and compliance costs. Even if a company wanted to manufacture its products domestically, it seems that the U.S. factories have all but shuttered their operations. One reason this perception persists is because small U.S. manufacturers cannot afford the resources to properly market their manufacturing capabilities to potential clients.

However, Brooklyn firm Makers Row believes that outsourcing is not saving the apparel industry money. The company argues that shipping costs and costs due to inferior production quality outweigh the benefits of overseas production for small-batch manufacturers. Companies spend significant amounts in travel and/or living expenses as their executives travel overseas to periodically supervise production, and the sporadic supervision also negatively affects quality. Makers Row believes it has found a niche market by connecting startups with domestic manufacturing companies through its maintenance of a database of 1,200 factories mostly located in Los Angeles, Chicago, and New York. Makers Row believes that startup companies that rely on small-batch production will boost profitability and quality by keeping production within arm's reach.

Source: Karsten Strauss, "Made in the USA: Bringing Industry Back Home," *Forbes*, November 12, 2012.

ABC IMPLEMENTATION ISSUES

The distortion in product costs for Campbell's V8 division from using traditional cost systems based on plantwide or departmental rates, while hypothetical, is not uncommon. Studies have shown that distortions of this type occur regularly in traditional systems in which a significant variation exists in the volume and complexity of products and services produced.[1] Traditional systems tend to overcost high-volume, low-complexity products, and they tend to undercost low-volume, high-complexity products. These studies indicate that the typical amount of overcosting is up to 200 percent for high-volume products with low complexity and that the typical undercosting can be more than 1,000 percent for low-volume, highly complex products. In companies with a large number of different products, traditional costing can show that most products are profitable. After changing to ABC, however, these companies might find that 10 to 15 percent of the products are profitable while the remainder are unprofitable. Adopting ABC often leads to increased profits merely by changing the product mix to minimize the number of unprofitable products.

LO4 Describe the implementation of an activity-based costing system.

Most companies initially do not abandon their traditional cost system and move to a system that uses ABC for management and financial reporting purposes because financial statements must withstand the scrutiny of auditors and tax authorities. This scrutiny typically implies more demands on the cost accounting system for consistency, objectivity, and uniformity than required when the system is used only for management purposes. In addition, ABC systems must be built facility by facility rather than being embedded in a software program that can be used by all facilities within the company.[2] Often companies maintain traditional costing for external reporting purposes and ABC for pricing and other internal decision-making purposes.

Once an ABC system has been developed for a production facility, including an activities list (sometimes called an activities dictionary), identification of activity cost drivers, and calculation of cost per unit of driver activity, the activity costs of a current or proposed product can be readily determined. In ABC, as illustrated for Campbell's, manufacturing a product is viewed simply as the combination of activities selected to make it; therefore, the activity cost of a product or service is the sum of the costs of those activities. This approach to viewing a product enables management to evaluate the importance of each of the activities consumed in making a product. Possibly some activities can be eliminated or a lower cost activity substituted for a more costly one without reducing the quality or performance of the product. In the 1980s, the Coca-Cola Company used ABC to determine that it was less costly—and thus, more profitable—to deliver soft drink concentrate to some fountain drink retailers (such as fast-food restaurants) in nonreturnable, disposable containers rather than in returnable stainless steel containers, which had been standard in the industry for many years.

Although an ABC system may be complex, it merely mirrors the complexity of an organization's design, manufacturing, and distribution systems. If a firm's products are diverse and its production and distribution procedures complex, the ABC system will also be complex; however, if its products are homogeneous and its production environment relatively simple, its ABC system should also be relatively simple. Even in highly complex manufacturing environments, ABC systems usually have no more than 10 to 20 cost pools. Many ABC experts in practice have observed that creating a large number of activity cost pools for a given costing application normally does not significantly improve cost accuracy above that of a smaller number of cost pools. As with any information system design, the costs of developing and maintaining the system must not exceed its benefits; hence, although adding more activity cost pools may result in some small amount of increased accuracy, it may be so small as not to be cost effective.

In addition to using ABC for product costing purposes, other important uses for ABC have also been found. One of the most useful applications for ABC discussed in the next section is in evaluating customer costs and distribution channel costs. Other applications include costing administrative functions such as processing accounts receivable or accounts payable; costing the process of hiring and training employees; and costing such menial tasks as processing a letter or copying a document.

---

[1] Gary Cokins, Alan Stratton, and Jack Helbling, *An ABC Manager's Primer* (Montvale, NJ: Institute of Management Accountants, 1993).

[2] Robert S. Kaplan and Robin Cooper, *Cost and Effect* (Boston: Harvard Business School Press, 1998), p. 105.

Any process, function, or activity performed in an organization, whether it is related to production, marketing and sales, finance and accounting, human resources, or even research and development, is a candidate for ABC analysis. In short, almost any cost object that has more than an insignificant amount of indirect costs can be more effectively measured using ABC.

RESEARCH INSIGHT

Are Supply and Consumption of Product Costs the Same Thing? A Refinement of ABC Robin Cooper and Robert Kaplan popularized activity-based costing (ABC) in the 1980s; however, Kaplan extended the model in 2004 to a "time-driven" ABC (TDABC) model. TDABC is simpler and less expensive to implement than traditional ABC systems. TDABC eliminates the need to allocate resource costs to activities before allocating the costs to cost objects.

The first step of TDABC is to develop the cost of supplying resource capacity. The authors use an order processing setting as an example. First the TDABC model calculates the cost of all order processing costs: employees, supervision, occupancy, technology, and supplies. It divides this total cost by the capacity, or the time available from employees performing the order processing work, to obtain the capacity cost rate. In the second stage, TDABC assigns the resource costs to each cost object. Once an order is processed, the time it took to process the order is multiplied by the capacity cost rate (which is denominated in hours) to assign the order processing cost to the customer's order. This model allows the time estimate to vary by order—for example, different types of orders would require different amounts of time: manual order, automated order, expedited order, international order, orders for fragile or hazardous goods, orders from new customers with no existing credit record, and so forth.

TDABC can easily integrate with enterprise resource planning (ERP) or customer relationship management software programs and can be used to budget future costs. It is adaptable to any industry and can deal with any level of complexity with respect to customers, products, distribution channels, segments, and other factors.

Sources: Ramji Balakrishnan, Eva Labro, and K. Sivaramakrishnan, "Product Costs as Decision Aids: An Analysis of Alternative Approaches (Part 1)," *Accounting Horizons*, 2013, 26(1): pp. 1–20; and Robert Kaplan and Steven Anderson, "The Innovation of Time-Driven Activity Based Costing," *Cost Management*, March/April 2007, pp. 5–15.

ABC AND CUSTOMER PROFITABILITY ANALYSIS

LO5 Explain customer profitability analysis based on ABC.

One of the most beneficial applications of activity-based costing is in the analysis of the profitability of customers. Companies that have a large number of diverse customers also usually have widely varied profits from serving those customers. Many companies never attempt to calculate the profit earned from individual customers. They merely assume that if they are selling products above their costs, and that overall the company is earning a profit, then each of the customers must be profitable. Unfortunately, the cost incurred to sell goods and services, and to provide service, to individual customers is not usually proportionate with the gross profits generated by those sales. Customers with high sales volume are not necessarily the most profitable. Profitability of individual customers depends on whether the gross profits from sales to those customers exceed the customer-specific costs of serving those customers. Some customers are simply more costly than others, and some may even be unprofitable, and the unprofitable customers are eating away at the total profits of the company. In an ideal world, only profitable customers would be retained, and unprofitable customers would be either converted to a profitable status or they would be dropped as customers.

Customer Profitability Profile

If a company knows the amount of profits (or losses) generated by each of its customers, a customer profitability profile can be prepared similar to the one illustrated in Exhibit 6.3.

This hypothetical company has 350 customers and has current total profits of $5 million, but only 200 of its customers are profitable. Cumulative profits reach $7.5 million when the 200th customer is added to the graph, but the 201st through the 350th customers cause cumulative profits to decline to $5 million because they are unprofitable. Once a company has profitability data on each of its customers (or categories of customers), only then can it proceed to try to convert them to profitability, or seek to terminate the relationship with those customers. Just as we saw that ABC provided a model for producing more accurate product cost data, ABC is also a valuable tool for generating customer profitability data.

EXHIBIT 6.3 **Customer Profitability Profile Graph**

ABC Customer Profitability Analysis Illustrated

Pure Water Company is a "green" company located in the Midwest that manufactures and sells all-natural compounds for purifying water distributed through large public water systems. The CEO and founder of Pure Water, personally developed the compounds using natural materials obtained from remote regions of the world. He knows that he has a product that is far superior to the traditional processes based on synthetic chemicals that have been used for generations to purify water. After five years in business, Pure Water has built a solid and growing customer base, but it has to invest significant time and expense servicing customers, especially those who have recently embraced its approach to water purification. Some customers require a lot of "hand-holding" with frequent visits and telephone calls, and they tend to purchase frequently in small amounts, often requiring repackaging. Other customers require little attention and support, and many of them purchase in large amounts once a year.

Although the company is making money, there is concern that profits could be higher if sales and other customer-related costs could be decreased. Pure Water's accountant has decided to conduct a customer profitability analysis using activity-based costing. As a first step, she determined that there were five primary activities related to serving customers: visits of customers by sales representatives, remote contacts (phone, email, fax), processing and shipping of customer orders, repackaging, and billing and collection. After extensive analysis, including numerous interviews and statistical analyses of activity and cost data, the accountant determined the following cost drivers and cost per unit of activity for the five customer-related activities:

Activity	Activity Cost Driver	Cost per Unit of Driver Activity
Visits to customers	Visits	$800
Remote contacts.	Number of contacts	75
Processing & shipping	Customer orders	450
Repackaging	Number of requests	250
Billing & Collection	Invoices	90

After collecting activity driver data on each of these activities for its major customers, the accounting group prepared the customer activity cost and profitability analysis presented in Exhibit 6.4 for its five largest customers (in terms of sales dollars) in the order of greatest to least profit for the most recent year.

EXHIBIT 6.4	Pure Water Company					
Customer Activity Cost and Profitability Analysis						
	Seattle Water District	Manhattan Water Authority	Great Lakes Utility	Gulf Coast Utilities	Consoli-dated Water, Inc.	Total
Customer Activity Cost Analysis:						
Activity Cost Driver Data						
Visits to customers	3	5	4	1	1	
Remote contacts	5	7	8	2	3	
Processing & shipping.	3	3	5	4	1	
Repackaging	0	2	3	0	0	
Billing & Collection.	3	3	5	4	1	
Customer Activity Cost						
Visits to customers	$ 2,400	$ 4,000	$ 3,200	$ 800	$ 800	
Remote contacts	375	525	600	150	225	
Processing & shipping.	1,350	1,350	2,250	1,800	450	
Repackaging	0	500	750	0	0	
Billing & Collection.	270	270	450	360	90	
Total Activity Cost	$ 4,395	$ 6,645	$ 7,250	$ 3,110	$ 1,565	
Customer Profitability Analysis:						
Customer sales	$17,500	$20,000	$12,000	$15,000	$16,250	$80,750
Less cost of goods sold	10,500	12,000	7,200	9,000	9,750	48,450
Gross profit on sales	7,000	8,000	4,800	6,000	6,500	32,300
Less activity costs	4,395	6,645	7,250	3,110	1,565	22,965
Customer profitability	$ 2,605	$ 1,355	$ (2,450)	$2,890	$4,935	$ 9,335
Customer profitability ratio* . . .	14.9%	6.8%	(20.4%)	19.3%	30.4%	11.6%

* Customer profitability ÷ Sales

Since Pure Water is selling only one product to all of its customers, and has the same pricing policy for all customers, there is a constant 40% gross profit ratio across all customers, and the combined net profitability of these customers is 11.6% of sales. However, all customers are not equally profitable. The high level of support required by Manhattan and Great Lakes resulted in a net customer loss from sales to Great Lakes and only a 6.8% customer profitability ratio for Manhattan.

Armed with the information in the customer activity cost and profitability analysis, Pure Water can take proactive steps to increase its overall profitability ratio. An obvious option would be to try to terminate its relationship with Great Lakes since the company is clearly losing money on that customer. If Great Lakes were terminated as a customer, and assuming that all of the activity costs associated with Great Lakes could be avoided by the termination, Pure Water's total sales would drop to $68,750 (or $80,750 minus $12,000), but its total profit would increase to $11,785 (or $9,335 plus $2,450), resulting in a profitability ratio on the remaining four customers of 17.1%.

A more proactive approach would be to work with Great Lakes and Manhattan that have high support requirements, such as repackaging, frequent visits, and phone contacts to try to lower the level of high-cost support activities without reducing sales to those customers. This could result in maintaining the current level of gross profit, but generating a significantly higher level of total net customer profitability.

Two caveats should be considered when using activity cost data to manage customer profitability. First, there may be justifiable reasons (such as having a new customer that requires a high level of early-stage support, trying to penetrate a new geographic market, or existing relationships with other more profitable customers) for keeping customers that have lower profitability, or even customers that are not profitable. If so, these customers should be managed intensely to attempt to reduce the activities devoted to their support. Another caveat is that eliminating a customer may not immediately translate into an immediate reduction of activity costs. Some activity costs may not have a variable cost behavior pattern, and eliminating customers may merely create excess capacity in the short term. Of course, as stated previously, activity-based costing views virtually all costs as variable in the longer term. As the following Business Insight illustrates, despite these limitations, activity analysis of customer profitability provides managers with valuable insights into the differences among customers that may otherwise not be apparent, and which can be used to enhance the overall performance of the organization.

> ## BUSINESS INSIGHT
>
> **Activity-Based Costing Can Facilitate Decision Making as Established Players Enter New Markets** American Express has partnered with Wal-Mart stores to serve a new demographic, the "underbanked" or "unbanked," meaning the estimated 68 million Americans who do not have traditional bank accounts or credit cards. A prepaid debit card called Bluebird is available at 4,000 Wal-Mart locations nationwide. Customers can add money to the card at Wal-Mart locations or while online and can use the card to make purchases wherever traditional American Express cards are accepted. American Express will generate revenue via swipe fees from the retailers where Bluebird is used.
>
> Bluebird adds one more product to the enterprise growth segment within American Express, which also includes the Serve program. Serve allows customers to make instant person-to-person payments via email, text message, or through a Facebook account. Both of these programs serve customers who are discouraged by traditional banks, where overdraft fees, monthly fees, minimum balance fees, and other charges are driving consumers out of the market.
>
> Additionally, both Bluebird and Serve allow American Express to expand into developing countries where consumers rely on cell phones to make payments and to transfer cash between entities. American Express can use activity-based costing to obtain more accurate costs for serving new versus existing market segments within the company so that it can make targeted investments that will reap the highest return for its shareholders.
>
> Source: Nick Summers, "American Express Wants to Be Your Banker," *Bloomberg Businessweek*, October 25, 2012.

ACTIVITY-BASED MANAGEMENT

Activity-based costing has been highly touted as a technique for improving the measurement of the cost and profitability of products, customers, and other cost objects. In the early development of ABC, it was discovered that a by-product of accurately measuring the cost using ABC is that management invariably gains a much better understanding of the processes and activities that are used to create cost objects, such as products. Although ABC could be justified on the basis of its value as a tool in helping produce more accurate cost measurements for various cost objects, its greatest potential value may be in its by-products. The access to ABC data enables managers to engage in **activity-based management (ABM),** defined as the identification and selection of activities to maximize the value of the activities while minimizing their cost from the perspective of the final consumer. In other words, ABM is concerned with how to efficiently and effectively manage activities and processes to provide value to the final consumer.

Defining processes and identifying key activities helps management better understand the business and to evaluate whether activities being performed add value to the customer. ABM focuses managerial attention on what is most important among the activities performed to create value for customers.

A helpful analogy in understanding what ABC can do for a company is to compare a company's operations with a large retail store, such as a Home Depot store. In a Home Depot store there is a clearly marked price on each of the tens of thousands of individual items that customers may decide to purchase. Similarly, every activity that takes place in any organization has a cost that can be determined and that management can use to make a judgment about the activity's value. In an ideal world, a manager could walk through the business and evaluate the cost of every activity being performed—maybe thousands of different activities—and then decide which ones are worth the cost and which ones are not adding value. Since generating ABC data has a cost, management must decide which ABC data are likely to be useful and cost beneficial. Our discussion here is only an introduction to activity-based costing and some of its applications. As the following Research Insight points out, over the past quarter of a century, ABC has matured well beyond merely accurately measuring cost of products and customers. More advanced topics such as those shown in the graphic are covered in advanced managerial accounting (or cost accounting) courses.

LO6 Explain the difference between ABC and activity-based management.

RESEARCH INSIGHT

The Maturing of Activity-Based Costing One of the leading thinkers and authors on the topic of activity-based costing over the past 25 years has been Peter B. B. Turney. He recently traced the evolution of ABC within the context of a product life cycle showing how ABC functionality has expanded since it was first introduced in the 1980s. As this graphic shows, ABC is now in its fourth generation, where it has become "an integral part of business performance management solutions, including profitability management, performance measurement, financial management, sustainability, and human capital management." In its current state of development, a single ABC model can support a number of needs, including historical cost measurement, resource planning, performance measurement, and other analyses.

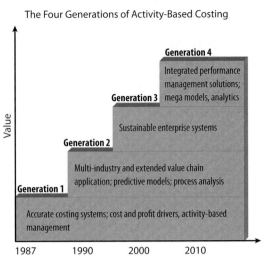

The Four Generations of Activity-Based Costing

Source: Peter B. B. Turney, "Activity-Based Costing: An Emerging Foundation for Performance Management," *Cost Management*, July/August 2010, pp. 33-42.

CHAPTER-END REVIEW

Customer Profitability Analysis

Suppose SAP is a systems design and implementation firm that serves five different types of customers. Assume SAP's design and installation projects are fairly standardized and routine; hence, the pricing is also standardized for all customers. While the company is profitable overall, the CFO thinks the net margins should be higher. She is concerned that customer support costs are eating up some of the margin and has decided to do a customer profitability analysis based on the five different types of customers to see if some of the customer groups may actually be less profitable than others. The following data for the most recent period have been collected to support the analysis.

	Support Activity		Driver	Cost per Driver Unit
A.	Minor systems maintenance		Hours on jobs	$160
B.	Visits to customer..................................		Number of visits	$300
C.	Communication		Number of calls	$ 50

Customer Group	Activity A	Activity B	Activity C	Profit Before Support Costs
1.........................	69	25	128	$80,000
2.........................	141	42	205	85,000
3.........................	74	19	99	83,000
4.........................	61	28	106	90,000
5.........................	136	39	189	78,000

Required

a. Calculate the customer profitability for each customer group taking into account the support activity required for each customer group.

b. Comment on the usefulness of this type of analysis. What reasonable actions might the company take as a result of this analysis?

The solution is on page 234.

GUIDANCE ANSWERS . . . YOU MAKE THE CALL

You are the Controller It probably is not the right decision to abandon the ABC system because there are many benefits to using ABC other than just calculating product costs. Indeed, in cases where companies produce multiple products that are fairly homogeneous in terms of the use of resources, ABC may not produce more accurate costs than traditional methods; however, there are many uses of ABC information beyond just calculating the cost of products. Having detailed information about activities and their costs can significantly improve the management of those activities. Identifying key activities and measuring their costs often causes companies to seek more efficient processes, possibly considering outsourcing activities that are currently performed internally, or even looking for ways to eliminate activities altogether. Activity cost information can also be used to identify best practices within an organization, or to benchmark internal activity costs with other organizations.

KEY TERMS

activity-based costing, 199

activity-based management (ABM), 213

practical capacity, 208

MULTIPLE CHOICE

1. Assume that Arco, Inc. has three activity pools which have the following costs: Machine Setups, $30,000; Material Moves, $45,000; and Machine Operations, $28,000. The activity cost drivers (and driver quantity) for the three pools are, respectively, number of setups (200), number of material moves (450), and number of machine hours (350). Product XJ3 used the following quantity of activity drivers to produce 100 units of final product: 25 setups, 40 material moves, and 75 machine hours. The total ABC cost and unit ABC cost assigned to Product XJ3 is:

   a. $103,000 total ABC cost and $1,030 unit ABC cost
   b. $103,000 total ABC cost and $103 unit ABC cost
   c. $13,750 total ABC cost and $137.50 unit ABC cost
   d. $3,300 total ABC cost and $330 unit ABC cost

2. Marko Company produces two products, Xeon and Zeon in a small manufacturing plant which had total manufacturing overhead of $45,000 in January and used 600 direct labor hours. The factory has two departments, Preparation, which incurred $25,000 of manufacturing overhead, and Processing which incurred $20,000 of manufacturing overhead. Preparation used 400 hours of direct labor and Processing used 160 machine hours. During January, 300 direct labor hours were used in making 100 units of Xeon, and 300 were used in making 100 units of Zeon. If Marko uses a plantwide rate based on direct labor hours to assign manufacturing costs to products, the total manufacturing overhead assigned to each unit of Xeon and Zeon in January were:

   a. $22,500 for Xeon and $22,500 for Zeon
   b. $225 for Xeon and $225 for Zeon
   c. $25,000 for Xeon and $20,000 for Zeon
   d. $107.14 for Xeon, and $42.86 for Zeon

3. Refer to the previous question. Assume that instead of using a plantwide overhead rate, Marko used departmental rates based on direct labor hours for the Preparation Department and machine hours for the Processing Department. The departmental overhead rates for the Preparation and Processing Departments were:

   a. $75 per direct labor hour for both Preparation and Processing
   b. $62.50 per direct labor hour for Preparation, and $125 per machine hour for Processing
   c. $125 per direct labor hour for Preparation, and $62.50 per machine hour for Processing
   d. $80.35 per direct labor hour for Preparation, and $80.35 per machine hour for Processing

4. Refer to the previous questions regarding Marko Company. Assume that Xeon used 175 direct labor hours and Zeon used 225 direct labor hours in the Preparation Department. Also, assume that Xeon used 100 machine hours and Zeon used 60 machine hours in the Processing Department. The overhead costs assigned to each unit of Xeon and Zeon were:
    a. $253.50 for Xeon and $196.50 for Zeon
    b. $62.50 for Xeon and $125 for Zeon
    c. $215.63 for Zeon and $215.63 for Xeon
    d. $234.38 for Xeon and $215.63 for Zeon

5. Refer to the previous questions regarding Marko Company. Assume that Marko used an ABC product costing system and that its total manufacturing overhead costs of $45,000 were assigned to the following ABC cost pools:

Material inspections & preparation ($20,000).	$20 per pound of raw materials
Material moves ($5,000)	$50 per move
Machine setups ($6,000).	$300 per setup
Machine operations ($14,000).	$87.50 per machine hour

    Xeon and Zeon used the following quantities of the four activity drivers:

	Xeon	Zeon
Pounds of raw materials	500	500
Material moves	60	40
Setups	12	8
Machine hours.	100	60

    The overhead costs assigned to each unit of Xeon and Zeon were:
    a. $253.50 for Xeon and $196.50 for Zeon
    b. $62.50 for Xeon and $125 for Zeon
    c. $215.63 for Xeon and $234.63 for Zeon
    d. $234.38 for Xeon and $215.63 for Zeon

DISCUSSION QUESTIONS

Q6-1. Summarize the concepts underlying activity-based costing in two sentences.

Q6-2. What steps are required to implement the two-stage activity-based costing model?

Q6-3. Define activity cost pool, activity cost driver, and cost per unit of activity.

Q6-4. Name two possible activity cost drivers for each of the following activities: maintenance, materials movement, machine setup, inspection, materials purchases, and customer service.

Q6-5. What is the premise of activity-based costing for product costing purposes?

Q6-6. In what ways does ABC product costing differ from traditional product cost methods?

Q6-7. Explain why ABC often reveals existing product cost cross-subsidization problems.

Q6-8. How can ABC be used to improve customer profitability analysis?

Q6-9. Explain activity-based management and how it differs from activity-based costing.

Assignments with the ✓ logo in the margin are available in BusinessCourse.
See the Preface of the book for details.

MINI EXERCISES

M6-10. Activities and Cost Drivers

LO2

For each of the following activities, select the most appropriate cost driver. Each cost driver may be used only once.

Activity		**Cost Driver**
1. Pay vendors	*a.*	Number of different kinds of raw materials
2. Evaluate vendors	*b.*	Number of classes offered
3. Inspect raw materials	*c.*	Number of tables
4. Plan for purchases of raw materials	*d.*	Number of employees
5. Packaging	*e.*	Number of operating hours
6. Supervision	*f.*	Number of units of raw materials received
7. Employee training	*g.*	Number of moves
8. Clean tables	*h.*	Number of vendors
9. Machine maintenance	*i.*	Number of checks issued
10. Move in-process product from one work	*j.*	Number of customer orders station to the next

M6-11. Developing a List of Activities for Baggage Handling at an Airport

LO2

As part of a continuous improvement program, you have been asked to determine the activities involved in the baggage-handling process of a major airline at one of the airline's hubs. Prior to conducting observations and interviews, you decide that a list of possible activities would help you to better observe key activities and ask meaningful questions.

Required

For incoming aircraft only, develop a sequential list of baggage-handling activities. Your list should contain between 8 and 10 activities.

M6-12. Stage 1 ABC at a College: Assigning Costs to Activities

LO2

An economics professor at Prince Town University devotes 55 percent of her time to teaching, 35 percent of her time to research and writing, and 10 percent of her time to service activities such as committee work and student advising. The professor teaches two semesters per year. During each semester, she teaches one section of an introductory economics course (with a maximum enrollment of 50 students) and one section of a graduate economics course (with a maximum enrollment of 30 students). Including course preparation, classroom instruction, and appointments with students, each course requires an equal amount of time. The economics professor is paid $135,000 per year.

Required

Determine the activity cost of instruction per student in both the introductory and the graduate economics courses.

M6-13. Stage 1 ABC for a Machine Shop: Assigning Costs to Activities

LO2

As the chief engineer of a small fabrication shop, Brenda Tolliver refers to herself as a "jack-of-all-trades." When an order for a new product comes in, Brenda must do the following:

1. Design the product to meet customer requirements.
2. Prepare a bill of materials (a list of materials required to produce the product).
3. Prepare an operations list (a sequential list of the steps involved in manufacturing the product).

Each time the foundry manufactures a batch of the product, Brenda must perform these activities:

1. Schedule the job.
2. Supervise the setup of machines that will work on the job.
3. Inspect the first unit produced to verify that it meets specifications.

Brenda supervises the production employees who perform the actual work on individual units of product. She is also responsible for employee training, ensuring that production facilities are in proper operating condition, and attending professional meetings. Brenda's estimates (in percent) of time spent on each of these activities last year are as follows:

Designing product.	14%
Preparing bills of materials	5
Preparing operations lists.	12
Scheduling jobs.	15
Supervising setups	5
Inspecting first units	2
Supervising production.	20
Training employees	17
Maintaining facility	6
Attending professional meetings	4
	100%

Required

Assuming Brenda Tolliver's salary is $134,000 per year, determine the dollar amount of her salary assigned to unit-, batch-, product-, and facility-level activities. (You may need to review Chapter 2 before answering this question.)

LO2 **M6-14.** **Stage 2 ABC for a Wholesale Company**

Information is presented for the activity costs of Oxford Wholesale Company:

Activity	Cost per Unit of Activity Driver
Customer relations	$100.00 per customer per month
Selling	0.06 per sales dollar
Accounting.	5.00 per order
Warehousing	0.50 per unit shipped
Packing	0.25 per unit shipped
Shipping.	0.20 per pound shipped

The following information pertains to Oxford Wholesale Company's activities in Massachusetts for the month of March 2014:

Number of orders	240
Sales revenue	$124,400
Cost of goods sold	$ 68,940
Number of customers	30
Units shipped.	4,700
Pounds shipped	70,500

Required

Determine the profitability of sales in Massachusetts for March 2014.

LO2 **M6-15.** **Stage 2 ABC for Manufacturing: Reassigning Costs to Cost Objects**

National Technology, LTD. has developed the following activity cost information for its manufacturing activities:

Activity	Activity Cost
Machine setup.	$65.00 per batch
Movement	15.00 per batch move
	0.10 per pound
Drilling	4.00 per hole
Welding	4.00 per inch
Shaping	25.00 per hour
Assembly.	17.00 per hour
Inspection	2.00 per unit

Filling an order for a batch of 50 fireplace inserts that weighed 150 pounds each required the following:

- Three batch moves
- Two sets of inspections
- Drilling five holes in each unit
- Completing 80 inches of welds on each unit
- Thirty minutes of shaping for each unit
- One hour of assembly per unit

Required
Determine the activity cost of converting the raw materials into 50 fireplace inserts.

M6-16.   Two-Stage ABC for Manufacturing   LO2

Detroit Foundry, a large manufacturer of heavy equipment components, has determined the following activity cost pools and cost driver levels for the year:

Activity Cost Pool	Activity Cost	Activity Cost Driver
Machine setup.....................................	$660,000	12,000 setup hours
Material handling..................................	100,000	2,000 tons of materials
Machine operation	450,000	10,000 machine hours

The following data are for the production of single batches of two products, C23 Cams and U2 Shafts during the month of August:

	C23 Cams	U2 Shafts
Units produced	500	300
Machine hours...	4	5
Direct labor hours	200	400
Direct labor cost	$5,000	$10,000
Direct materials cost..................................	$30,000	$20,000
Tons of materials.......................................	12.5	8
Setup hours..	3	7

Required
Determine the unit costs of C23 Cams and U2 Shafts using ABC.

M6-17.   Two-Stage ABC for Manufacturing   LO2

Assume Sherwin-Williams Company, a large paint manufacturer, has determined the following activity cost pools and cost driver levels for the latest period: SHERWIN-WILLIAMS (SHW)

Activity Cost Pool	Activity Cost	Activity Cost Driver
Machine setup..........................	$975,000	2,500 setup hours
Material handling.......................	830,000	5,000 material moves
Machine operation	180,000	20,000 machine hours

The following data are for the production of single batches of two products, Mirlite and Subdue:

	Mirlite	Subdue
Gallons produced	50,000	30,000
Direct labor hours	400	250
Machine hours...	800	250
Direct labor cost	$10,000	$7,500
Direct materials cost..................................	$350,000	$150,000
Setup hours..	15	12
Material moves	60	35

Required
Determine the batch and unit costs per gallon of Mirlite and Subdue using ABC.

LO5   **M6-18.**   **Customer Profitability Analysis**

HyStandard Services, Inc. provides residential painting services for three home building compa-nies, Alpine, Blue Ridge, and Pineola, and it uses a job costing system for determining the costs for completing each job. The job cost system does not capture any cost incurred by HyStandard for return touchups and refinishes after the homeowner occupies the home. HyStandard paints each house on a square footage contract price, which includes painting as well as all refinishes and touchups required after the homes are occupied. Each year, the company generates about one-third of its total revenues and gross profits from each of the three builders. The HyStandard owner has observed that the builders, however, require substantially different levels of support following the completion of jobs. The following data have been gathered:

Support Activity	Driver	Cost per Driver Unit
Major refinishes.	Hours on jobs	$ 75
Touchups	Number of visits	$120
Communication	Number of calls	$ 30

Builder	Major Refinishes	Touchups	Communication
Alpine.	80	150	360
Blue Ridge.	35	110	205
Pineola.	42	115	190

Required

Assuming that each of the three customers produces gross profits of $100,000, calculate the profit-ability from each builder after taking into account the support activity required for each builder.

EXERCISES

LO2   **E6-19.**   **Two-Stage ABC for Manufacturing**

Merlot Company has determined its activity cost pools and cost drivers to be the following:

Cost pools

Setup	$ 56,000
Material handling	12,800
Machine operation.	240,000
Packing.	60,000
Total indirect manufacturing costs	$368,800

Cost drivers

Setups	400
Material moves.	800
Machine hours	16,000
Packing orders.	1,000

One product made by Merlot, metal casements, used the following activities during the period to produce 500 units:

Setups	20
Material moves	80
Machine hours.	1,900
Packing orders	150

Required

a.   Calculate the cost per unit of activity for each activity cost pool for Merlot Company.

b.   Calculate the manufacturing overhead cost per metal casement manufactured during the period.

E6-20. **Calculating Manufacturing Overhead Rates**

LO3

Glassman Company, accumulated the following data for 2014:

Milling Department manufacturing overhead.............................	$362,000
Finishing Department manufacturing overhead	$130,000
Machine hours used	
Milling Department	10,000 hours
Finishing Department	2,000 hours
Labor hours used	
Milling Department	1,000 hours
Finishing Department	1,000 hours

Required

a. Calculate the plantwide manufacturing overhead rate using machine hours as the allocation base.

b. Calculate the plantwide manufacturing overhead rate using direct labor hours as the allocation base.

c. Calculate department overhead rates using machine hours in Milling and direct labor hours in Finishing as the allocation bases.

d. Calculate department overhead rates using direct labor hours in Milling and machine hours in Finishing as the allocation bases.

e. Which of these allocation systems seems to be the most appropriate? Explain.

E6-21. **Calculating Activity-Based Costing Overhead Rates**

LO2, 3, 4

Assume that manufacturing overhead for Glassman Company in the previous exercise consisted of the following activities and costs:

Setup (1,000 setup hours)...	$146,000
Production scheduling (400 batches)...................................	60,000
Production engineering (60 change orders).............................	90,000
Supervision (2,000 direct labor hours)	56,000
Machine maintenance (12,000 machine hours)	96,000
Total activity costs..	$460,000

The following additional data were provided for Job 845:

Direct materials costs	$8,000
Direct labor cost (5 Milling direct labor hours; 35 Finishing direct labor hours)...	$1,000
Setup hours..	5 hours
Production scheduling	1 batch
Machine hours used (25 Milling machine hours;	
5 Finishing machine hours)..	30 hours
Production engineering...	3 change orders

Required

a. Calculate the cost per unit of activity driver for each activity cost category.

b. Calculate the cost of Job 845 using ABC to assign the overhead costs.

c. Calculate the cost of Job 845 using the plantwide overhead rate based on machine hours calculated in the previous exercise.

d. Calculate the cost of Job 845 using a machine hour departmental overhead rate for the Milling Department and a direct labor hour overhead rate for the Finishing Department (see E6-20).

E6-22. **Activity-Based Costing and Conventional Costs Compared**

LO2, 3, 4

Hickory Grill Company manufactures two types of cooking grills: the Gas Cooker and the Charcoal Smoker. The Cooker is a premium product sold in upscale outdoor shops; the Smoker is sold in major discount stores. Following is information pertaining to the manufacturing costs for the current month.

	Gas Cooker	Charcoal Smoker
Units......................................	1,000	5,000
Number of batches	40	10
Number of batch moves	80	40
Direct materials................................	$40,000	$100,000
Direct labor	$22,000	$27,000

Manufacturing overhead follows:

Activity	Cost	Cost Driver
Materials acquisition and inspection	$30,800	Amount of direct materials cost
Materials movement	16,200	Number of batch moves
Scheduling....................................	36,000	Number of batches
	$83,000	

Required

a. Determine the total and per-unit costs of manufacturing the Gas Cooker and Charcoal Smoker for the month, assuming all manufacturing overhead is assigned on the basis of direct labor dollars.

b. Determine the total and per-unit costs of manufacturing the Gas Cooker and Charcoal Smoker for the month, assuming manufacturing overhead is assigned using activity-based costing.

LO3, 4   E6-23.   Activity-Based Costing Versus Conventional Costing
Refer to the previous exercise in E6-22 for Hickory Grill.

Required

a. Comment on the differences between the solutions to requirements (a) and (b). Which is more accurate? What errors might managers make if all manufacturing overhead costs are assigned on the basis of direct labor dollars?

b. Comment on the adequacy of the preceding data to meet management's needs.

LO2, 3, 4   E6-24.   Traditional Product Costing versus Activity-Based Costing

PANASONIC COMPANY

Assume that **Panasonic Company** has determined its estimated total manufacturing overhead cost for one of its plants to be $206,700, consisting of the following activity cost pools for the current month:

Activity Centers	Activity Costs	Cost Drivers	Activity Level
Assembly setups...............	$ 45,000	Setup hours....................	1,500
Materials handling..............	15,300	Number of moves	300
Assembly.....................	120,000	Assembly hours................	12,000
Maintenance	26,400	Maintenance hours	1,200
Total	$206,700		

Total direct labor hours used during the month were 7,950. Panasonic produces many different electronic products, including the following two products produced during the current month:

	Model X301	Model Z205
Units produced	1,000	1,000
Direct materials costs.................................	$15,000	$15,000
Direct labor costs	$12,500	$12,500
Direct labor hours	500	500
Setup hours..	50	100
Materials moves	25	50
Assembly hours.......................................	800	800
Maintenance hours	10	40

Required

a. Calculate the total per-unit cost of each model using direct labor hours to assign manufacturing overhead to products.

b. Calculate the total per-unit cost of each model using activity-based costing to assign manufacturing overhead to products.

c. Comment on the accuracy of the two methods for determining product costs.

d. Discuss some of the strategic implications of your answers to the previous requirements.

E6-25. Traditional Product Costing versus Activity-Based Costing   LO2, 3, 4

High Country Outfitters, Inc., makes backpacks for large sporting goods chains that are sold under the customers' store brand names. The Accounting Department has identified the following overhead costs and cost drivers for next year:

Overhead Item	Expected Costs	Cost Driver	Maximum Quantity
Setup costs	$ 972,000	Number of setups	7,200
Ordering costs.	270,000	Number of orders	60,000
Maintenance	1,200,000	Number of machine hours.	80,000
Power.	150,000	Number of kilowatt hours	600,000

Total predicted direct labor hours for next year is 60,000. The following data are for two recently completed jobs:

	Job 201	Job 202
Cost of direct materials.	$13,500	$15,000
Cost of direct labor	$19,125	$71,250
Number of units completed	1,125	915
Number of direct labor hours	270	330
Number of setups	18	22
Number of orders	24	45
Number of machine hours.	540	450
Number of kilowatt hours	270	360

Required

a. Determine the unit cost for each job using a traditional plantwide overhead rate based on direct labor hours.

b. Determine the unit cost for each job using ABC. (Round answers to two decimal places.)

c. As the manager of High Country, is there additional information that you would want to help you evaluate the pricing and profitability of Jobs 201 and 202?

d. Assuming the company has been using the method required in part a, how should management react to the findings in part b?

E6-26. Customer Profitability Analysis   LO5, 6

Gonalong, Inc., has 10 customers that account for all of its $4,200,000 of net income. Its activity-based costing system is able to assign all costs, except for $650,000 of general administrative costs, to key activities incurred in connection with serving its customers. A customer profitability analysis based on activity costing produced the following customer profits and losses:

Customer	#1	$306,000
	#2	624,000
	#3	(257,000)
	#4	909,000
	#5	950,000
	#6	872,000
	#7	598,000
	#8	322,000
	#9	(105,000)
	#10	631,000
Total		$4,850,000

Required

Prepare a customer profitability profile like the one in Exhibit 6.3.

LO5 **E6-27.** **Customer Profitability Analysis**
Refer to the previous exercise E6-26 for Gonalong, Inc.

Required
a. If Gonalong were to notify customers 3 and 9 that it will no longer be able to provide them services in the future, will that increase company profits by $362,000? Why or why not?
b. What is the primary benefit of preparing a customer profitability analysis?

PROBLEMS

LO2, 3, 4 **P6-28.** **Two-Stage ABC for Manufacturing with ABC Variances**
Montreat Manufacturing has developed the following activity cost pool information for its 2014 manufacturing activities:

	Budgeted Activity Cost	Activity Cost Driver at Practical Capacity
Purchasing and materials handling	$1,080,000	900,000 kilograms
Setup	700,000	1,120 setups
Machine operations	978,000	12,000 hours
First unit inspection	50,000	1,000 batches
Packaging	328,125	312,500 units

Actual 2014 production information is as follows:

	Standard Product A	Standard Product B	Specialty Products
Units	150,000	100,000	50,000
Batches	100	80	600
Setups*	300	160	900
Machine operations (hours)	6,000	3,000	2,000
Kilograms of raw materials	400,000	300,000	200,000
Direct materials costs	$900,000	$600,000	$820,000

* Some products require setups on two or more machines.

Required
a. Determine the unit cost of each product for Montreat Manufacturing.
b. Explain why the unit cost of the specialty products is so much higher than the unit cost of Standard Product A or Standard Product B.

LO2, 3, 4 **P6-29.** **ABC—A Service Application**
Grand Haven is a senior living community that offers a full range of services including independent living, assisted living, and skilled nursing care. The assisted living division provides residential space, meals, and medical services (MS) to its residents. The current costing system adds the cost of all of these services (space, meals, and MS) and divides by total resident days to get a cost per resident day for each month. Recognizing that MS tends to vary significantly among the residents, Grand Haven's accountant recommended that an ABC system be designed to calculate more accurately the cost of MS provided to residents. She decided that residents should be classified into four categories (A, B, C, D) based on the level of services received, with group A representing the lowest level of service and D representing the highest level of service. Two cost drivers being considered for measuring MS costs are number of assistance calls and number of assistant contacts. A contact is registered each time an assistance professional provides medical services or aid to a resident. The accountant has gathered the following data for the most recent annual period:

Resident Classification	Annual Resident Days	Annual Assistance Hours	Number of Assistance Contacts
A	8,800	15,000	60,000
B	6,570	18,000	52,000
C	4,240	22,500	52,000
D	2,190	31,500	52,000
	21,800	87,000	216,000

Other data:

Total cost of medical services for the period $2,250,000

Total cost of meals and residential space $1,700,400

Required (round answers to the nearest dollar):

a. Determine the ABC cost of a resident day for each category of residents using assistance hours as the cost driver.

b. Determine the ABC cost of a resident day for each category of residents using assistance contacts as the cost driver.

c. Which cost driver do you think provides the more accurate measure of the cost per day for a Grand Haven resident?

P6-30. **ABC Costing for a Service Organization** LO2, 3, 4

Fairfield Mortgage Company is a full-service residential mortgage company in the Atlanta area that operates in a very competitive market. The CEO, Richard Sissom, is concerned about operating costs associated with processing mortgage applications and has decided to install an ABC costing system to help him get a handle on costs. Although labor hours seem to be the primary driver of the cost of processing a new mortgage, the labor cost for the different activities involved in processing new loans varies widely. The Accounting Department has provided the following data for the company's five major cost pools for 2014:

Activity Cost Pools		Activity Drivers	
Taking customer applications	$ 300,000	Time—assistant managers	13,000 hours
Conducting credit investigations . .	500,000	Time—credit managers	16,500 hours
Underwriting	525,000	Time—Underwriting Department. .	9,000 hours
Preparing loan packages	250,000	Time—Processing Department. . .	8,000 hours
Closing loans.	600,000	Time—Legal Department hours . .	6,000 hours
	$2,175,000		52,500 hours

During 2014, the company processed and issued 5,000 new mortgages, two of which are summarized here with regard to activities used to process the mortgages:

	Loan 5066	Loan 5429
Application processing hours.	1.50	2.75
Credit investigating hours.	4.00	3.00
Underwriting hours	2.50	4.75
Processing hours.	3.50	3.00
Legal processing hours.	1.50	1.50
Total hours.	13.00	15.00

Required

a. Determine the cost per unit of activity for each activity cost pool.

b. Determine the cost of processing loans 5066 and 5429.

c. Determine the cost of preparing loans 5066 and 5429 assuming that an average cost per hour for all activities is used.

d. Compare and discuss your answers to requirements (*b*) and (*c*).

LO2, 3, 4, 6 **P6-31.**   **Activity-Based Costing in a Service Organization**

Red River Banking Company has ten automatic teller machines (ATMs) spread throughout the city maintained by the ATM Department. You have been assigned the task of determining the cost of operating each machine. Management will use the information you develop, along with other information pertaining to the volume and type of transactions at each machine, to evaluate the desirability of continuing to operate each machine and/or changing security arrangements for a particular machine.

The ATM Department consists of a total of six employees: a supervisor, a head cashier, two associate cashiers, and two maintenance personnel. The associate cashiers make between two and four daily trips to each machine to collect and replenish cash and to replenish supplies, deposit tickets, and so forth. Each machine contains a small computer that automatically summarizes and reports transactions to the head cashier. The head cashier reconciles the activities of the two associate cashiers to the computerized reports. The supervisor, who does not handle cash, reviews the reconciliation. When an automatic teller's computer, a customer, or a cashier reports a problem, the two maintenance employees and one cashier are dispatched immediately. The cashier removes all cash and transaction records, and the maintenance employees repair the machine.

Maintenance employees spend all of their time on maintenance-related activities. The associate cashiers spend approximately 50 percent of their time on maintenance-related activities and 50 percent on daily trips. The head cashier's time is divided, with 75 percent directly related to daily trips to each machine and 25 percent related to supervising cashiers on maintenance calls. The supervisor devotes 20 percent of the time to daily trips to each machine and 80 percent to the equal supervision of each employee. Cost information for a recent month follows:

Salaries	
Supervisor	$ 4,200
Head cashier	3,000
Other ($1,800 each)	7,200
Lease and operating costs	
Cashiers' service vehicle	1,500
Maintenance service vehicle	1,400
Office rent and utilities	2,500
Machine lease, space rent, and utilities ($1,500 each)	15,000
Total	$34,800

Related monthly activity information for this month follows:

Machine	Routine Trips	Maintenance Hours
1	30	5
2	90	17
3	60	15
4	60	30
5	120	15
6	30	10
7	90	25
8	120	5
9	60	20
10	60	18
Total	720	160

Additional information follows:

- The office is centrally located with about equal travel time to each machine.
- Maintenance hours include travel time.
- The cashiers' service vehicle is used exclusively for routine visits.
- The office space is divided equally between the supervisor and the head cashier.

Required

a. Determine the monthly operating costs of machines 7 and 8 when cost assignments are based on the number of machines.

b. Determine the activity cost of a routine trip and a maintenance hour for the month given. Round answers to the nearest cent.

c. Determine the operating costs assigned and reassigned to machines 7 and 8 when activity-based costing is used.

d. How can ABC cost information be used by Red River Banking Company to improve the overall management of monthly operating costs?

P6-32. **Product Costing: Plantwide Overhead versus Activity-Based Costing** LO3, 4

Dixon produces machine parts as a contract provider for a large manufacturing company. Dixon produces two particular parts, shafts and gears. The competition is keen among contract producers, and Dixon's top management realizes how vulnerable its market is to cost-cutting competitors. Hence, having a very accurate understanding of costs is important to Dixon's survival.

Dixon's president, Bob Hudson, has observed that the company's current cost to produce shafts is $21.35, and the current cost to produce gears is $12.36. He indicated to the controller that he suspects some problems with the cost system because Dixon is suddenly experiencing extraordinary competition on shafts, but it seems to have a virtual corner on the gears market. He is even considering dropping the shaft line and converting the company to a one-product manufacturer of gears. He asked the controller, George Coleman, to conduct a thorough cost study and to consider whether changes in the cost system are necessary. The controller collected the following data about the company's costs and various manufacturing activities for the most recent month:

	Shafts	Gears
Production units	50,000	10,500
Selling price	$31.86	$24
Overhead per unit (based on direct labor hours)	$12.82	$6.10
Materials and direct labor cost per unit	$8.53	$6.26
Number of production runs	10	20
Number of purchasing and receiving orders processed	40	100
Number of machine hours	12,750	6,000
Number of direct labor hours	25,000	2,500
Number of engineering hours	5,000	5,000
Number of material moves	50	40

The controller was able to summarize the company's total manufacturing overhead into the following pools:

Setup costs	$ 30,000
Machine costs	175,000
Purchasing and receiving costs	210,000
Engineering costs	200,000
Materials handling costs	90,000
Total	$705,000

Required

a. Calculate Dixon's current plantwide overhead rate based on direct labor hours.

b. Verify Dixon's calculation of overhead cost per unit of $12.82 for shafts and $6.10 for gears.

c. Calculate the manufacturing overhead cost per unit for shafts and gears using activity-based costing, assuming each of the five cost pools represents a separate activity pool. Use the most appropriate activity driver for assigning activity costs to the two products.

d. Comment on Dixon's current cost system and the reason the company is facing fierce competition for shafts but little competition for gears.

P6-33. **Customer Profitability Analysis** LO2, 5, 6

Roger's Aeronautics, LTD, is a British aeronautics subcontract company that designs and manufactures electronic control systems for commercial airlines. The vast majority of all commercial aircraft are manufactured by Boeing in the U.S. and Airbus in Europe; however, there is a relatively small group of companies that manufacture narrow-body commercial jets. Assume for this exercise that Roger's does contract work for the two major manufacturers plus three companies in the second tier.

Because competition is intense in the industry, Roger's has always operated on a fairly thin 20% gross profit margin; hence, it is crucial that it manage non-manufacturing overhead costs effectively in order to achieve an acceptable net profit margin. With declining profit margins in recent years, Roger's Aeronautics' CEO, Len Rogers, has become concerned that the cost of obtaining contracts and maintaining relations with its five major customers may be getting out of hand. You have been hired to conduct a customer profitability analysis.

Roger's Aeronautics' non-manufacturing overhead consists of $2.5 million of general and administrative (G&A) expense, (including, among other expenses, the CEO's salary and bonus and the cost of operating the company's corporate jet) and selling and customer support expenses of $3 million (including 5% sales commissions and $1,050,000 of additional costs).

The accounting staff determined that the $1,050,000 of additional selling and customer support expenses related to the following four activity cost pools:

Activity	Activity Cost Driver	Cost per Unit of Activity
1. Sales visits..............................	Number of visit days	$1,400
2. Product adjustments.......................	Number of adjustments	1,200
3. Phone and email contacts	Number of calls/contacts	200
4. Promotion and entertainment events..........	Number of events	1,600

Financial and activity data on the five customers follows (Sales and Gross Profit data in millions):

Customer	Sales	Gross Profit	Quantity of Sales and Support Activity			
			Activity 1	Activity 2	Activity 3	Activity 4
#1	$17	$3.4	106	23	220	82
#2	12	2.4	130	36	354	66
#3	3	0.6	52	10	180	74
#4	4	0.8	34	6	138	18
#5	3	0.6	16	5	104	10
	$39	$7.8	338	80	996	250

In addition to the above, the sales staff used the corporate jet at a cost of $800 per hour for trips to customers as follows:

Customer #1	24 hours
Customer #2	36 hours
Customer #3	5 hours
Customer #4	0 hours
Customer #5	6 hours

The total cost of operating the airplane is included in general and administrative expense; none is included in selling and customer support costs.

Required

a.   Prepare a customer profitability analysis for Roger's Aeronautics that shows the gross profits less all expenses that can reasonably be assigned to the five customers.

b.   Now assuming that the remaining general and administrative costs are assigned to the five customers based on relative sales dollars, calculate net profit for each customer.

c.   Discuss the merits of the analysis in part a. versus part b.

CASES AND PROJECTS

LO2, 5, 6   **C6-34.   Designing an ABC System for a Country Club**

The Reserve Club is a traditional private golf and country club that has three different categories of memberships: golf, tennis & swimming, and social. Golf members have access to all amenities and programs in the Club, Tennis & Swimming members have access to all amenities and programs except use of the golf course, and Social members have access to only the social activities of the club, excluding golf, tennis, and swimming. All members have clubhouse privileges, including use of the bar and restaurant, which is operated by an outside contractor. During the past year, the average membership in each category, along with the number of club visits during the year, was

	Members	Visits
Golf..	250	9,360
Tennis & Swimming..	55	1,500
Social...	125	2,160

Some members of the Club have been complaining that heavy users of the Club are not bearing their share of the costs through their membership fees. Dess Rosmond, General Manager of the Reserve Club, agrees that monthly fees paid by the various member groups should be based on the annual average amount of cost-related activities provided by the club for the three groups, and he intends to set fees on that basis for the coming year. The annual direct costs of operating the golf course, tennis courts, and swimming pool have been calculated by the Club's controller as follows:

Golf course	$1,000,000
Swimming pool	50,000
Tennis courts	25,000

The operation of the bar and restaurant and all related costs, including depreciation on the bar and restaurant facilities, are excluded from this analysis. In addition to the above costs, the Club incurs general overhead costs in the following amounts for the most recent (and typical) year:

General Ledger Overhead Accounts	Amounts
Indirect labor for the Club management staff (the general manager, assistant general manager, membership manager, and club controller)	$300,000
Utilities (other than those directly related to golf, swimming and tennis).............	24,000
Website maintenance	2,000
Postage	5,000
Computers and information systems maintenance.............................	7,500
Clubhouse maintenance & depreciation	30,000
Liability insurance	4,000
Security contract..	12,000
	$384,500

Dess believes that the best way to assign most of the overhead costs to the three membership categories is with an activity-based system that recognizes four key activities that occur regularly in the club:

Recruiting and providing orientation for new members
Maintaining the membership roster and communicating with members
Planning, scheduling and managing Club events
Maintaining the financial records and reporting for the Club

Required

a. Identify and explain which overhead costs can reasonably be assigned to one or more of the four key activities, and suggest a basis for making the assignment.

b. Identify a cost driver for each activity cost pool that would seem to be suitable for assigning the activity cost pool to the three membership categories.

c. Suggest a method for assigning any overhead costs to the three membership categories that cannot reasonably be assigned to activity pools.

d. Comment on the suitability of ABC to this cost assignment situation.

LO2, 4, 6 **C6-35.** **Product Costing: Department versus Activity-Based Costing for Overhead**

Advertising Technologies, Inc. (ATI) specializes in providing both published and online advertising services for the business marketplace. The company monitors its costs based on the cost per column inch of published space printed in print advertising media and based on the cost per minute of telephone advertising time delivered on "The AD Line," a computer-based, online advertising service. ATI has one new competitor, Tel-a-Ad, in its local teleadvertising market; and with increased competition, ATI has seen a decline in sales of online advertising in recent years. ATI's president, Robert Beard, believes that predatory pricing by Tel-a-Ad has caused the problem. The following is a recent conversation between Robert and Jane Minnear, director of marketing for ATI.

Jane: I just received a call from one of our major customers concerning our advertising rates on "The AD Line" who said that a sales rep from another firm (it had to be Tel-a-Ad) had offered the same service at $1 per minute, which is $1.50 per minute less than our price.

Robert: It's costing about $1.27 per minute to produce that product. I don't see how they can afford to sell it so cheaply. I'm not convinced that we should meet the price. Perhaps the better strategy is to emphasize producing and selling more published ads, which we're more experienced with and where our margins are high and we have virtually no competition.

Jane: You may be right. Based on a recent survey of our customers, I think we can raise the price significantly for published advertising and still not lose business.

Robert: That sounds promising; however, before we make a major recommitment to publishing, let's explore other possible explanations. I want to know how our costs compare with our competitors. Maybe we could be more efficient and find a way to earn a good return on teleadvertising.

After this meeting, Robert and Jane requested an investigation of production costs and comparative efficiency of producing published versus online advertising services. The controller, Tim Gentry, indicated that ATI's efficiency was comparable to that of its competitors and prepared the following cost data:

	Published Advertising	Online Advertising
Estimated number of production units.	200,000	10,000,000
Selling price.	$200	$2.50
Direct product costs	$21,000,000	$5,000,000
Overhead allocation*.	$10,175,000	$8,325,000
Overhead per unit	$49	$0.77
Direct costs per unit	$105	$0.50
Number of customers	180,000	25,000
Number of salesperson days	28,500	3,500
Number of art and design hours.	35,000	5,000
Number of creative services subcontract hours	100,000	25,000
Number of customer service calls	72,000	8,000

* Based on direct labor costs

Upon examining the data, Robert decided that he wanted to know more about the overhead costs since they were such a high proportion of total production costs. He was provided the following list of overhead costs and told that they were currently being assigned to products in proportion to direct labor costs.

Selling costs	$8,000,000
Visual and audio design costs	3,000,000
Creative services costs.	5,500,000
Customer service costs	2,000,000

Required

Using the data provided by the controller, prepare analyses to help Robert and Jane in making their decisions. (*Hint:* Prepare cost calculations for both product lines using ABC to see whether there is any significant difference in their unit costs.) Should ATI switch from the fast-growing, online advertising market back into the well-established published advertising market? Does the charge of predatory pricing seem valid? Why are customers likely to be willing to pay a higher price to get published services? Do traditional costing and activity-based costing lead to the same conclusions?

C6-36. **Unit-Level and Multiple-Level Cost Assignments with Decision Implications**   LO2, 3, 4, 6

CarryAll Company[3] produces briefcases from leather, fabric, and synthetic materials in a single production department. The basic product is a standard briefcase made from leather and lined with fabric. CarryAll has a good reputation in the market because the standard briefcase is a high-quality item that has been produced for many years.

Last year, the company decided to expand its product line and produce specialty briefcases for special orders. These briefcases differ from the standard in that they vary in size, contain both leather and synthetic materials, and are imprinted with the buyer's logo (the standard briefcase is simply imprinted with the CarryAll name in small letters). The decision to use some synthetic materials in the briefcase was made to hold down the materials cost. To reduce the labor costs per unit, most of the cutting and stitching on the specialty briefcases is done by automated machines, which are used to a much lesser degree in the production of the standard briefcases. Because of these changes in the design and production of the specialty briefcases, CarryAll management believed that they would cost less to produce than the standard briefcases. However, because they are specialty items, they were priced slightly higher; standards are priced at $30 and specialty briefcases at $32.

After reviewing last month's results of operations, CarryAll's president became concerned about the profitability of the two product lines because the standard briefcase showed a loss while the specialty briefcase showed a greater profit margin than expected. The president is wondering whether the company should drop the standard briefcase and focus entirely on specialty items. Units and cost data for last month's operations as reported to the president are as follows:

	Standard	Specialty
Units produced	10,000	2,500
Direct materials		
Leather (1 sq. yd. × $15.00; ½ sq. yd. × $15.00)..................	$15.00	$ 7.50
Fabric (1 sq. yd. × $5.00; 1 sq. yd. × $5.00)	5.00	5.00
Synthetic		5.00
Total materials	20.00	17.50
Direct labor (½ hr. × $12.00, ¼ hr. × $12.00).....................	6.00	3.00
Manufacturing overhead (½ hr. × $8.98; ¼ hr. × $8.98)	4.49	2.25
Cost per unit	$30.49	$22.75

Factory overhead is applied on the basis of direct labor hours. The rate of $8.98 per direct labor hour was calculated by dividing the total overhead ($50,500) by the direct labor hours (5,625). As shown in the table, the cost of a standard briefcase is $0.49 higher than its $30 sales price; the specialty briefcase has a cost of only $22.75, for a gross profit per unit of $9.25. The problem with these costs is that they do not accurately reflect the activities involved in manufacturing each product. Determining the costs using ABC should provide better product costing data to help gauge the actual profitability of each product line.

The manufacturing overhead costs must be analyzed to determine the activities driving the costs. Assume that the following costs and cost drivers have been identified:

- The Purchasing Department's cost is $6,000. The major activity driving these costs is the number of purchase orders processed. During the month, the Purchasing Department prepared the following number of purchase orders for the materials indicated:

Leather..	20
Fabric...	30
Synthetic material	50

---

[3] The CarryAll Company case, prepared by Professors Harold Roth and Imogene Posey, was originally published in the *Management Accounting Campus Report.*

- The cost of receiving and inspecting materials is $7,500. These costs are driven by the number of deliveries. During the month, the following number of deliveries were made:

Leather.	30
Fabric.	40
Synthetic material	80

- Production line setup cost is $10,000. Setup activities involve changing the machines to produce the different types of briefcases. Each setup for production of the standard briefcases requires one hour; each setup for specialty briefcases requires two hours. Standard briefcases are produced in batches of 200, and specialty briefcases are produced in batches of 25. During the last month, there were 50 setups for the standard item and 100 setups for the specialty item.
- The cost of inspecting finished goods is $8,000. All briefcases are inspected to ensure that quality standards are met. However, the final inspection of standard briefcases takes very little time because the employees identify and correct quality problems as they do the hand cutting and stitching. A survey of the personnel responsible for inspecting the final products showed that 150 hours were spent on standard briefcases and 250 hours on specialty briefcases during the month.
- Equipment-related costs are $6,000. Equipment-related costs include repairs, depreciation, and utilities. Management has determined that a logical basis for assigning these costs to products is machine hours. A standard briefcase requires 1/2 hour of machine time, and a specialty briefcase requires two hours. Thus, during the last month, 5,000 hours of machine time relate to the standard line and 5,000 hours relate to the specialty line.
- Plant-related costs are $13,000. These costs include property taxes, insurance, administration, and others. For the purpose of determining average unit costs, they are to be assigned to products using machine hours.

Required

a. Using activity-based costing concepts, what overhead costs should be assigned to the two products?

b. What is the unit cost of each product using activity-based costing concepts?

c. Reevaluate the president's concern about the profitability of the two product lines.

d. Discuss the merits of activity-based management as it relates to CarryAll's ABC cost system.

SOLUTIONS TO REVIEW PROBLEMS

<u>Mid-Chapter Review</u>

Solution

a.   **Plantwide overhead rate= Total manufacturing overhead ÷ Total machine hours**
$$= (\$120{,}000 + \$55{,}000) \div (10{,}000 + 5{,}000)$$
$$= \$175{,}000 \div 15{,}000$$
$$= \$11.67 \text{ per machine hour}$$

	Cobra Latch	GrimLoc
Product costs per unit		
Direct materials	$12,000	$18,000
Direct labor.	5,000	4,000
Manufacturing overhead		
700 machine hours × $11.67	8,169	
800 machine hours × $11.67		9,336
Total cost per batch	$25,169	$31,336
Number of units per batch	÷ 100	÷ 100
Cost per unit	$251.69	$313.36

b. **Departmental overhead rates = Total departmental overhead ÷ Dept. allocation base**
$$\text{Fabrication} = \$120,000 \div 10,000 \text{ machine hours}$$
$$= \$12 \text{ per machine hour}$$
$$\text{Finishing} = \$55,000 \div 5,000 \text{ machine hours}$$
$$= \$11 \text{ per machine hour}$$

	Cobra Latch	GrimLoc
Product costs per unit		
Direct materials	$12,000	$18,000
Direct labor...	5,000	4,000
Manufacturing overhead		
Fabrication Department		
500 machine hours × $12	6,000	
700 machine hours × $12		8,400
Finishing Department		
200 machine hours × $11	2,200	
100 machine hours × $11		1,100
Total cost per batch	$25,200	$31,500
Number of units per batch	÷ 100	÷ 100
Cost per unit	$252.00	$315.00

c. **Activity-based overhead rates = Activity cost pool ÷ Activity cost driver**
$$\text{Maintenance} = \$30,000 \div 15,000 \text{ machine hours}$$
$$= \$2 \text{ per machine hour}$$
$$\text{Materials handling} = \$45,000 \div 4,500 \text{ materials moves}$$
$$= \$10 \text{ per materials move}$$
$$\text{Machine setups} = \$75,000 \div 750 \text{ setups}$$
$$= \$100 \text{ per machine setup}$$
$$\text{Inspections} = \$25,000 \div 1,000 \text{ inspection hours}$$
$$= \$25 \text{ per inspection hour}$$

	Cobra Latch	GrimLoc
Product costs per unit		
Direct materials	$12,000	$18,000
Direct labor...	5,000	4,000
Manufacturing overhead		
Maintenance activity		
700 machine hours × $2	1,400	
800 machine hours × $2		1,600
Materials handling activity		
30 materials moves × $10	300	
50 materials moves × $10		500
Machine setups activity		
5 machine setups × $100	500	
9 machine setups × $100		900
Inspections activity		
30 inspection hours × $25.....................................	750	
60 inspection hours × $25.....................................		1,500
Total cost per batch	$19,950	$26,500
Number of units per batch	÷ 100	÷ 100
Cost per unit	$199.50	$265.00

d. Following is a summary of product costs for Cobra Latch and GrimLoc assigning overhead costs based on a plantwide rate, department rates, and activity-based rates:

	Cobra Latch	GrimLoc
Plantwide rate	$251.69	$313.36
Department rates.	$252.00	$315.00
Activity rates	$199.50	$265.00

Changing from a plantwide rate to department rates had little effect on unit costs because the department rates per machine hour are close to the plantwide rate per machine hour. Based on machine hours, both departments have similar cost structures.

When using activity rates, however, the cost of these two products drops dramatically because they use only a small portion (less than 2 percent) of the activities of setup (14 of 750) and materials moves (80 of 4,500). Neither a plantwide rate nor department rates recognize this fact, resulting in a large amount of cost cross-subsidization of other products by Cobra Latch and GrimLoc for these costs. Although this problem did not include cost analysis of the other three products, it shows that they are less profitable and that Cobra Latch and GrimLoc are much more profitable than management previously thought.

Chapter-End Review

Solution

a. Activity A—Minor systems maintenance
Activity B—Visits to customers
Activity C—Communications via phone

Activity	1	2	3	4	5
A (@ $160)	$11,040	$22,560	$11,840	$ 9,760	$21,760
B (@ $300)	7,500	12,600	5,700	8,400	11,700
C (@ $50)	6,400	10,250	4,950	5,300	9,450
Total support costs	$24,940	$45,410	$22,490	$23,460	$42,910
Profit before support Costs	80,000	85,000	83,000	90,000	78,000
Customer profits	$55,060	$39,590	$60,510	$66,540	$35,090
Ratio of support costs to profit before support costs: .	31%	53%	27%	26%	55%

b. This analysis is beneficial to SAP because it shows that Groups 2 and 5 are outliers among the five customer groups in terms of support services required. Groups 2 and 5 are significantly larger consumers of activities for all three of the support activities. Note also that Group 4 customers are relatively light users of minor systems maintenance, and Group 3 are relatively light users of phone communications. Calculating the ratio of total support costs to profit before support costs provides additional insight into the relative profitability of the customer groups. All five customer groups are profitable; however, this analysis provides useful information for improving profits by working with Groups 2 and 5 to control support activities and related costs and attempt to bring their support costs in line with the other customer groups.

1. Differentiate between product and service department costs and direct and indirect department costs. (p. 238)

2. Describe the allocation of service department costs under the direct, step, and linear algebra methods. (p. 239)

3. Understand lean production and just-in-time inventory management. (p. 245)

4. Explain how lean production and just-in-time affect performance evaluation and recordkeeping. (p. 248)

Additional Topics in Product Costing

Whole Foods is trying to shed its nickname "Whole Paycheck." The Austin, Texas, grocery company specializes in quality food offered in upscale locations with a focus on excellent customer service. However, the recent economic crisis along with intensified competition from companies like **Fresh Market** and **Sprouts Farmers Markets** has Whole Foods rethinking its premium-brand pricing strategy. Even large-scale grocers such as **Kroger Company** are encroaching on what was once Whole Foods' private domain by offering premium meats, cheeses, and health foods.

Because the bulk of Whole Foods' inventory is organic or certified on other dimensions (i.e., gluten- or allergen-free, kosher, etc.), the cost of its inventory is higher than that of mass-market grocers. Yet increased competition necessitates that the company uses accurate cost accounting methods and finds innovative ways to contain its operating costs. One way the company is doing this is by building new stores that are smaller in size and located in lower-rent locations like Detroit and New Orleans. But inside the store, Whole Foods must be careful not to cut costs in a way that curtails its competitive advantage. The company successfully utilizes a decentralized supply chain structure that highlights the geographic diversity of a store's local markets. To that point, the company employs "foragers" to seek out high-quality local products for the Whole Foods located within that region.

Moreover, a grocery operation has numerous support departments—areas that are necessary to the operation of the store, but not directly attributable to any one product or group of products. Examples of support departments include human resources, accounting, and custodial services. Whole Foods must develop a system of service cost allocation that will minimize distortions in profitability across grocery departments. The company must also operate as efficiently as possible; however, that efficiency shouldn't come at the expense of the quality that has become Whole Foods' bedrock. In fact, in the grocery industry, quality should arise from maintaining a clean, safe, and efficient work environment and by adhering to rigorous standards, the very same actions that should simultaneously improve efficiency.

The last, but perhaps most important factor for the company is its inventory management. Holding inventory is costly due to storage and insurance costs; and in the case of a grocer, perishable inventory is prone to spoilage and waste. Indeed, inventory turnover should be much more frequent for produce, meats, and bakery items than for vitamins and supplements. One common method in preventing spoilage is to discount certain goods that are getting close to their expiration date. By doing so, the company is betting that the lost revenue on the discounted goods will draw the customer in for repeat business, as opposed to a "one-shot" shopping experience. Whole Foods has recently used **Twitter** and **Facebook** to promote "flash" sales that run for a few hours at a time. The deep discounts of up to 60 percent have helped the company better manage its inventory of products with short shelf lives. This

continued on following page

continued from previous page

chapter discusses how companies such as Whole Foods assign the cost of their internal service departments to their products, and how they can benefit from adopting a lean operations philosophy in managing their inventory levels.

Sources: Julie Jargon, "The Battle for the Organic Shopper," *Wall Street Journal*, August 22, 2013, pp. B1–B2; Clair Suddath, "Whole Foods Local Forager Elly Truesdell Is a Grocery Tastemaker," *Bloomberg Businessweek*, May 2, 2013; Annie Gasparo, "Whole Foods Lifts Outlook as Sales Rise," *Wall Street Journal*, February 9, 2012, p. B4; and Katie Agin, "Lean Manufacturing 2.0," *Whole Foods Magazine*, January 2010.

CHAPTER ORGANIZATION

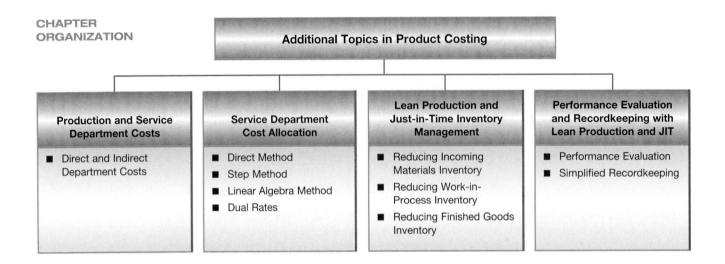

PRODUCTION AND SERVICE DEPARTMENT COSTS

LO1 Differentiate between product and service department costs and direct and indirect department costs.

In Chapter 5, we discussed two basic methods (job order costing and process costing) for accumulating, measuring and recording the costs of producing goods. In Chapter 6, we discussed both traditional and activity-based methods for assigning indirect costs to products. We now look in more detail at another aspect of assigning indirect costs.

In addition to *production* departments that actually perform work on a product, many companies have production *support* departments, such as payroll, human resources, information technology, security, and facilities, that provide support services for all of the production departments, and sometimes even for each other. These departments are typically called **service departments**. The cost of producing products, therefore, includes the costs incurred within production departments, as well as the cost of services received from service departments.

A **direct department cost** is a cost assigned directly to a department (production or service) when it is incurred. For a production department, direct department costs include both *direct* product costs (direct materials and direct labor) as well as *indirect* product costs (such as indirect labor and indirect materials) incurred directly in the department. An **indirect department cost** is a cost assigned to a department as a result of an indirect allocation, or reassignment, from another department, such as a service department.

The product costing system must include a policy for assigning to products the cost of services received from service departments. For companies that use a plantwide overhead rate, the costs of all service departments are added to the indirect product costs incurred within all of the producing departments to get total plantwide manufacturing overhead, which is then assigned to products using a single overhead rate based on a common factor such as direct labor hours. For companies that use departmental overhead rates, service department costs are allocated to the production departments that utilize their services, and the allocated service department costs are added to the indirect costs incurred within the department to arrive at total departmental overhead and allocation rates. Also, as illustrated in Chapter 6, service department costs may also be assigned to products using activity-based costing. As discussed in the following Business Insight, service department cost allocation can impact the amount of revenue received for some organizations.

SERVICE DEPARTMENT COST ALLOCATION

As discussed above, service departments (maintenance, administration, information technology, security, etc.) provide a wide range of support functions, primarily for one or more production departments. These departments, which are considered essential elements in the overall manufacturing process, do not work directly on the "product" but provide auxiliary support to the producing departments. In addition to providing support for the various producing departments, some service departments also provide services to *other service departments*. For example, the payroll and personnel departments typically provide services to all departments (producing and service), and engineering may provide services to only the producing departments. Services provided by one service department to other service departments are called **interdepartment services**.

LO2 Describe the allocation of service department costs under the direct, step, and linear algebra methods.

To illustrate service department cost allocations, suppose the Aquafina Division of PepsiCo, has two producing departments, three service departments, and two products. The service departments and their respective service functions and cost allocation bases are as follows:

Department	Service Functions	Allocation Base
Support Services	Receiving and inventory control	Total amount of department capital investment
Engineering Resources	Production setup and engineering and testing	Number of employees
Building and Grounds	Machinery maintenance and depreciation	Amount of square footage occupied

Difficulty in choosing an allocation base for service department costs is not uncommon. For example, Aquafina may have readily determined the appropriate allocation bases for the Engineering Resources and the Building and Grounds Departments but may have found the choice for Support Services to be less clear. Perhaps after conducting correlation studies, the most equitable base for allocating Support Services costs to other departments was determined to be total capital investment in the departments because they included expensive computer-tracking equipment, both manual and automated forklifts, and other material-moving equipment.

Assume direct department costs and allocation base information used to illustrate Aquafina's July service department cost allocations are summarized as follows:

	Direct Department Costs	Number of Employees		Amount of Square Footage Occupied		Total Amount of Department Capital Investment	
Service departments							
Support Services	$ 27,000	15	15%	4,000	8%	—	—
Engineering Resources . . .	20,000	—	—	2,000	4	$ 45,000	8%
Building and Grounds	10,000	5	5	—	—	50,000	9
Producing departments							
Mixing.	40,000*	24	24	11,000	22	180,000	33
Bottling.	90,000*	56	56	33,000	66	270,000	50
	$187,000	100	100%	50,000	100%	$545,000	100%

*Direct department overhead

The preceding information omitted the amount of capital investment in the Support Services Department, the number of employees in the Engineering Resources Department, and the amount of square footage used by the Building and Grounds Department. These data were omitted because a department normally does not allocate costs to itself; it allocates costs only to the departments it serves. The three methods commonly used for service department cost allocations—direct, step, and linear algebra—are discussed next.

Direct Method

The **direct method** allocates all service department costs based only on the amount of services provided to the producing departments. Exhibit 7.1 shows the flow of costs using the direct method. All arrows depicting the cost flows extend directly from service departments to producing departments; under the direct method there are no cost allocations between the service departments.

EXHIBIT 7.1   Flow of Costs—Direct Method

Exhibit 7.2 shows the service department cost allocations for the direct method. Notice the allocation base used to allocate Engineering Resources costs; only the employees in the producing

EXHIBIT 7.2   Service Department Cost Allocations—Direct Method

	Total	Mixing	Bottling
Support Services Department			
Allocation base (capital investment)............	$450,000	$180,000	$270,000
Percent of total base........................	100%	40%	60%
Cost allocations............................	$ 27,000	$ 10,800	$ 16,200
Engineering Resources Department			
Allocation base (number of employees).........	80	24	56
Percent of total base........................	100%	30%	70%
Cost allocations............................	$ 20,000	$ 6,000	$ 14,000
Building and Grounds Department			
Allocation base (square footage occupied)......	44,000	11,000	33,000
Percent of total base........................	100%	25%	75%
Cost allocations............................	$ 10,000	$ 2,500	$ 7,500

Cost Allocation Summary

	Support Services	Engineering Resources	Building and Grounds	Mixing	Bottling	Total
Department cost before allocations..............	$27,000	$20,000	$10,000	$40,000	$ 90,000	$187,000
Cost allocations						
Support Services	(27,000)			10,800	16,200	—
Engineering Resources		(20,000)		6,000	14,000	—
Building and Grounds			(10,000)	2,500	7,500	—
Department costs after allocations.............	$ 0	$ 0	$ 0	$59,300	$127,700	$187,000

departments are considered in computing the allocation percentages—24 in Mixing and 56 in Bottling, for a total of 80 employees in the allocation base. Thirty percent (24 ÷ 80) of the producing department employees work in Mixing; therefore, 30 percent of Engineering Resources costs are allocated to Mixing. Applying the same reasoning, 70 percent of Engineering Resources costs are allocated to Bottling. Similar logic is followed in computing the cost allocations for Building and Grounds and Support Services.

The cost allocation summary at the bottom of Exhibit 7.2 shows that all service department costs have been allocated, decreasing the service department costs to zero and increasing the producing department overhead balances by the amounts of the respective allocations. Also, total costs are not affected by the allocations; the total of $187,000 was merely redistributed so that all costs are reassigned to the producing departments. Total department overhead costs of the producing departments after allocation of service costs are $59,300 for Mixing and $127,700 for Bottling.

The advantage of the direct method of allocating service department costs is that it is easy and convenient to use. Its primary disadvantage is that it does not recognize the costs for interdepartment services provided by one service department to another. Instead, any costs incurred to provide services to other service departments are passed directly to the producing departments. The step method improves on the allocation procedure by redirecting some of the costs to other service departments before they are finally allocated to the production departments.

Step Method

The **step method** gives partial recognition of interdepartmental services by using a methodology that allocates the service department costs *sequentially* both to the remaining service departments and the producing departments. Any indirect costs allocated to a service department in this process are added to that service department's direct costs to determine the total costs to allocate to the remaining departments. Through this procedure, all service department costs are assigned to the production departments and ultimately to the products.

To illustrate a problem that can result from using the direct method, assume that Ramso Company has two service departments, S1 and S2, and two producing departments, P1 and P2, that provide services as follows:

	Receiver of Services			
Provider of Services	**S1**	**S2**	**P1**	**P2**
S1	0%	0%	70%	30%
S2	50%	0%	25%	25%

If the direct method is used to allocate service department costs to the producing departments, S2 total costs will be allocated equally to the producing departments because they use the same amount of S2 services (25 percent each). Is this an equitable allocation of S2 costs? S2 actually provides half of its services to the other service department (S1), which, in turn, provides the majority of its services to P1. Assume that S2 has total direct department costs of $100,000. If the direct method is used to allocate service department costs, the entire $100,000 will be divided equally between the two producing departments, each being allocated $50,000, with no allocation to S1.

	S1	S2	P1	P2
Direct allocation of S2 to P1 and P2	$0	$(100,000)	$50,000	$50,000

Consider the following alternative allocation of the $100,000 of S2 costs that takes into account interdepartment services. First, 25 percent, or $25,000, is allocated to each of the producing departments, and 50 percent, or $50,000, is allocated to S1. Next, the $50,000 allocated to S1 from S2 is reallocated to the producing departments in proportion to the amount of services provided to them by S1: 70 percent and 30 percent, respectively. In this scenario, the $100,000 of S2 costs is ultimately allocated $60,000 to P1 and $40,000 to P2 as follows:

	S1	S2	P1	P2
Step 1:				
Allocate S2 costs to S1, P1, and P2	$50,000	$(100,000)	$25,000	$25,000
Step 2:				
Reallocate S1 costs to P1 and P2	(50,000)	0	35,000	15,000
Total allocation of S2 costs via step method	$ 0	$ 0	$60,000	$40,000

This calculation shows only the ultimate allocation of S2 costs. Of course, any S1 direct department costs would also have to be allocated to P1 and P2 on a 70:30 basis. If interdepartmental services are ignored, P1 is allocated only $50,000 of S2 costs; by considering interdepartmental services, P1 is allocated $60,000. Certainly, a more accurate measure of both the direct and indirect services received by P1 from S2 is $60,000, not $50,000.

As long as all producing departments use approximately the same percentage of services of each service department, the direct method provides a reasonably accurate cost assignment. In this example, the percentages of services used by the producing departments were quite different: 70 percent and 30 percent for S1, and 50 percent and 50 percent for S2. In such situations, the direct method can result in significantly different allocations.

The step method is illustrated graphically in Exhibit 7.3 for Aquafina. Notice the sequence of the allocations: Engineering Resources, Support Services, and Building and Grounds.

EXHIBIT 7.3   Flow of Costs—Step Method

When using the step method, the sequence of allocation is typically based on the relative percentage of services provided to other service departments, with the largest provider of interdepartmental services allocated first and the smallest provider of interdepartmental services allocated last. For Aquafina, Engineering Resources is allocated first because, of the three service departments, it provides the largest percentage (20 percent) of its services to other service departments: 15 percent to Support Services and 5 percent to Building and Grounds (see previous cost allocation data). Building and Grounds is allocated last because it provides the least amount (12 percent) of its services to other service departments: 8 percent to Support Services and 4 percent to Engineering Resources. The service department cost allocations for Aquafina using the step method are shown in Exhibit 7.4.

Linear Algebra (Reciprocal) Method

The disadvantage of the step method is that it provides only partial recognition of interdepartmental services. For Aquafina, the step method recognizes Engineering Resources services provided to the other two service departments; however, no services received by Engineering Resources from

EXHIBIT 7.4	Service Department Cost Allocations—Step Method				
	Total	**Support Services**	**Building and Grounds**	**Mixing**	**Bottling**
Engineering Resources Department					
Allocation base (number of employees)	100	15	5	24	56
Percent of total base.	100%	15%	5%	24%	56%
Cost allocations.	$20,000	$3,000	$1,000	$4,800	$11,200
Support Services Department					
Allocation base (capital investment).	$500,000		$50,000	$180,000	$270,000
Percent of total base.	100%		10%	36%	54%
Cost allocations.	$30,000 ←		$3,000	$10,800	$16,200
Building and Grounds Department					
Allocation base (square footage occupied) . . .	44,000			11,000	33,000
Percent of total base.	100%			25%	75%
Cost allocations.	$14,000 ←			$3,500	$10,500

Cost Allocation Summary						
	Engineering Resources	**Support Services**	**Building and Grounds**	**Mixing**	**Bottling**	**Total**
Department costs before allocations.	$ 20,000	$ 27,000	$ 10,000	$40,000	$ 90,000	$187,000
Cost allocations						
Engineering Resources	(20,000)	3,000	1,000	4,800	11,200	—
Support Services		(30,000) ←	3,000	10,800	16,200	—
Building and Grounds			(14,000)	3,500	10,500	—
Department costs after allocations.	$ 0	$ 0	$ 0	$59,100	$127,900	$187,000

the other two departments are recognized. Similarly, services from Support Services to Building and Grounds are recognized, but not the reverse. To achieve the most mathematically accurate service department cost allocation, there should be full recognition of services between service departments as well as between service and producing departments. This requires using the linear algebra method, sometimes called the *reciprocal method*. The **linear algebra (reciprocal) method** uses a series of linear algebraic equations, which are solved simultaneously, to allocate service department costs both interdepartmentally and to the producing departments. This method is illustrated graphically in Exhibit 7.5 for a company that has two service departments and two producing departments. The cost allocation arrows run from each service department to the other service department as well as to the producing departments. Further discussion of this method can be found in cost accounting texts. Whether a company should use the direct method, step method, or linear algebra method depends on the extensiveness of interdepartmental services and how evenly services are used by the producing departments.

| EXHIBIT 7.5 | Flow of Costs—Linear Algebra Method |

YOU MAKE THE CALL

You are the Controller As the person responsible for the product costing system, you are trying to decide which method is best to use in allocating service department costs to the producing departments and to the products. Some of the service departments provide services only to producing departments; whereas, others provide services to both producing and service departments. You would like to use the method that provides reliable cost measurements, but without creating more costs than the benefits derived. Which method do you recommend? [Answer, p. 251]

Dual Rates

When allocating service department costs, it can be useful to provide separate allocations for fixed costs and variable costs. This will result in cost allocations that more accurately reflect the factors that drive costs. The capacity provided most often drives fixed costs, whereas some type of actual activity usually drives variable costs. Dual rates involve establishing separate bases for allocating fixed and variable costs. Dual rates may be used for one or all service departments, depending on the size and nature of the costs in each service department. They may also be used in conjunction with the direct, step, or linear algebra methods.

It is important to remember the relationship between capacity and cost when selecting the allocation method. Total variable costs change as activity changes. Fixed costs, however, are the same whether the activity is at or below capacity. Fixed costs should usually be allocated based on the relative capacity provided the benefiting department, while variable costs should be allocated on the basis of actual usage. The allocation methods and bases also may be different for variable and fixed costs.

Fixed costs based on capacity provided eliminates the possibility that the amount of the cost allocation to one department is affected by the level of services utilized by other departments. When fixed service department costs are allocated based on the capacity provided to the user department, managers of the user departments are charged for that capacity whether they use it or not, and their use of services has no effect on the amount of costs allocated to other departments. A benefit of this allocation system is that it reduces the temptation for managers to avoid or delay services to minimize fixed cost allocations to their departments. Dual rates are examined in more detail in most cost accounting texts.

MID-CHAPTER REVIEW

Suppose an **H&M** retail store is organized into four departments: Women's Apparel, Men's Apparel, Administrative Services, and Facilities Services. The first two departments are the primary producing departments; the last two departments provide services to the producing departments as well as to each other. Top management has decided that, for internal reporting purposes, the cost of service department operations should be allocated to the producing departments. Administrative Services costs are allocated on the basis of the number of employees, and Facilities Services costs are allocated based on the amount of square footage of floor space occupied. Hypothetical data pertaining to the cost allocations for February 2014 are as follows:

Department	Direct Department Cost	Number of Employees	Square Footage Occupied
Women's Apparel	$ 60,000	15	15,000
Men's Apparel	50,000	9	7,500
Administrative Services	18,000	3	2,500
Facilities Services	12,000	2	1,000
Total	$140,000	29	26,000

Required

a. Determine the amount of service department costs to be allocated to the producing departments under both the *direct method* and the *step method* of service department cost allocation.

b. Discuss the *linear algebra method* of service department cost allocation, explaining circumstances when it should be considered over the direct and step methods.

c. Should H&M consider using the linear algebra method?

The solution is on pages 262–263.

LEAN PRODUCTION AND JUST-IN-TIME INVENTORY MANAGEMENT

Previously, our discussions about inventories have centered around how to measure the cost of products. A related issue is how to manage the production process and physical inventory levels. Cost accounting textbooks, as well as operations management textbooks, usually discuss models that have been used for decades to determine the economic order quantities for products, given the particular level of inventory a company wants to maintain. Although these models are still relevant in many situations, managing the production process and inventory levels has changed dramatically for companies that have adopted a value chain approach to management. No longer do most managers consider only their company's strategies, goals, and objectives in deciding the characteristics and quantities of inventory that should be acquired or produced and maintained.

LO3 Understand lean production and just-in-time inventory management.

A value chain approach to inventory management requires that managers consider their suppliers' and customers' strategies, goals, and objectives as well if they hope to compete successfully in a global marketplace. Computer technology has affected the way inventories are manufactured and handled (using robotics, fully computerized manufacturing and product handling systems, bar code identification systems, etc.), and it is changing the way companies relate to other parties in the value chain. It has spawned worldwide use of alternative inventory production and management techniques and processes including just-in-time (JIT) inventory management and lean production methods.

Just-in-time (JIT) inventory management is a comprehensive inventory management philosophy that emerged in the 1970s that stresses policies, procedures, and attitudes by managers and other workers that result in the efficient production of high-quality goods while maintaining the minimum level of inventories. JIT is often described simply as an inventory model that maintains only the level of inventories required to meet current production and sales requirements, but it is, in reality, much more than that. The key elements of the JIT philosophy, which has come to be known as the "lean production" philosophy, include increased coordination throughout the value chain, reduced inventory, reduced production times, increased product quality, and increased employee involvement and empowerment.

In sum, JIT/lean production is a system aimed at reducing or eliminating waste, increasing cost efficiency, and securing a competitive advantage. Accordingly, it emphasizes a nimble production process with small lot sizes, short setup and changeover times, effective and efficient quality controls, a minimum number of bottlenecks and backups, and maximum efficiency of people.

Reducing Incoming Materials Inventory

The JIT/lean approach to reducing incoming materials includes these elements:

1. Developing long-term relationships with a limited number of vendors.

2. Selecting vendors on the basis of service and material quality, as well as price.

3. Establishing procedures for key employees to order materials for current needs directly from approved vendors.

4. Accepting vendor deliveries directly to the shop floor, and only as needed.

When fully implemented, these steps minimize or eliminate many materials inventories. Sufficient materials would be on hand to meet only immediate needs, and the materials inventories in the manufacturing setting are located on the shop floor.

To achieve this reduction, it is apparent that vendors and buyers must work as a team and that key employees must be involved in decision making. The goal of the JIT approach to purchasing is not to shift materials carrying costs to vendors. A close, long-term working relationship between purchasers and vendors should be beneficial to both. Purchasers' scheduling information is provided to vendors so that vendors also can reduce inventories and minimize costs. Vendors are therefore able to manufacture small batches frequently, rather than manufacturing large batches infrequently. Further, vendors are more confident of future sales.

BUSINESS INSIGHT

Shortage of Auxiliary Inventory Deteriorates Brand Image Luxury car producer **BMW** must believe that its customers are insensitive to price. Consider one BMW owner who is paying a car payment $770 per month for a car he can't drive. The customer is waiting for a rear fender, and BMW did not offer him a loaner while he waits. Thus, he incurs additional financial expense in paying for an alternative mode of transportation to get to work each day.

The automaker's components are housed in a central warehouse in Germany, which then dispatches the parts to its 40 distribution centers. However, the central warehouse also supplies 300 repair shops in Germany, which are closer geographically to where the components are originating. The company blames the delays on a new supply logistics management system called ATLAS (Advanced parTs Logistics in After Sales). **IBM** was the main hardware contractor, and **SAP** supplied the software for the warehouse management system. However, IBM claims it is no longer involved in setting up the program. Sophisticated inventory management systems are only as effective as the entities that manage the technology process. In the meantime, BMW may find that it has overestimated the brand loyalty of its customers.

Source: Angela Maier, "BMW Owners Vent Anger at Months-Long Wait for Spare Parts," *Bloomberg Businessweek*, August 28, 2013.

Reducing Work-in-Process Inventory

Reducing the total time required to complete a process, or the **cycle time**, is the key to reducing work-in-process inventories and is central to a lean production approach. In a manufacturing organization, cycle time is composed of the time needed for setup, processing, movement, waiting, and inspection. **Setup time** is the time required to prepare equipment to produce a specific product, or to change from producing one product to another product. **Processing time** is the time spent working on units. **Movement time** is the time units spend moving between work or inspection stations. **Waiting time** is the time units spend in temporary storage waiting to be processed, moved, or inspected. **Inspection time** is the amount of time it takes units to be inspected. Of the five elements of cycle time, only processing time adds value to the product. Efforts to reduce cycle time are appropriate for both continuous and batch production.

Devising means of reducing setup times will directly reduce the cycle time for batch production and thus reduce setup costs. Setup times can also be reduced by shifting from batch to continuous production whenever practical. Rearranging the shop floor to eliminate unnecessary movements of materials can help reduce movement time for both continuous and batch production.

Many companies have created **quality circles**, which are groups of employees involved in production who have the authority, within certain parameters, to address and resolve quality problems as they occur, without seeking management approval. Giving employees more authority and responsibility for quality, including the right to stop production whenever quality problems are noted, can reduce the need for separate inspection time.

Waiting time can be reduced by moving from a materials push to a materials pull approach to production. Under a traditional **materials push system**, employees work to reduce the pile of inventory building up at their workstations. Workers at each station remove materials from an in-process storage area, complete their operation, and place the output in another in-process storage area. Hence, they *push* the work to the next workstation. The emphasis is on production efficiency at each station.

Caught in the Strategic Pivot—How Your Customers' Supply Chains Can Affect Your Business Low-cost labor in China and throughout the rest of Southeast Asia has been a boon to United Parcel Service (UPS). It was less expensive for U.S. companies to ship their materials to China for assembly, even after factoring in the shipping cost for the goods to arrive back on U.S. soil. At the same time, inventory management software by giants like SAP were perfecting the art of lean inventory management, especially when firms could partner with shippers like UPS to get the inventory where it needed to be at a moment's notice. Finally, the rise of Internet commerce meant that sellers and customers were geographically dispersed, and UPS was only too happy to shuttle the purchased goods between the two.

But now that perfect storm is reversing direction. Rising wages in China, volatile fuel prices, and intellectual property concerns are making U.S. companies reconsider outsourcing to China. Also, companies are better managing the timing of their inventories, meaning they can use longer-term shipping, as long it is reliable and the delivery date is certain. In response, UPS may need to put the emphasis back on its ground team. Good forecasting of future revenues and costs means managers must watch for detours to their strategic plans all the way up and down the supply chain.

Source: Justin Lahart, "A Simple Twist of Freight for UPS and FedEx," *Wall Street Journal*, August 16, 2013, p. C8.

In a push system, one of the functions of work-in-process inventory is to help make workstations independent of each other. Inventories are large enough to allow for variations in processing speeds, for discarding defective units without interrupting production, and for machine downtime.

Under a **materials pull system** (often called a **Kanban system**), employees at each station work to provide inventory for the next workstation only as needed. (*Kanban*, the Japanese word for *card*, is a system created in Japan that originally used cards to indicate that a department needed additional components.) The building of excess inventories is strictly prohibited. When the number of units in inventory reaches a specified limit, work at the station stops until workers at a subsequent station pull a unit from the in-process storage area. Hence, the *pull* of inventory by a subsequent station authorizes production to continue.

A pull, or Kanban, system's low inventory levels require a team effort. To avoid idle time, processing speeds must be balanced and equipment must be kept in good repair. Quality problems are identified immediately, and the low inventory levels require immediate correction of quality problems. To make a pull system work, management must accept the notion that it is better to have employees idle than to have them building excess inventory. A pull system also requires careful planning by management and active participation in decision making by employees. A lean production process involves minimizing cycle time, eliminating waste, producing inventory only as needed, and ensuring the highest level of quality and efficiency. To achieve these results on a continuing basis, there is a strong emphasis on continuous improvement programs (see Chapter 8).

Reducing Finished Goods Inventory

Finished goods inventory can be reduced by reducing cycle time and by better predicting customer demand for finished units. Lowering cycle times reduces the need for speculative inventories. If finished goods can be replenished quickly, the need diminishes for large inventory levels to satisfy customer needs and to provide for unanticipated fluctuations in customer orders. Anticipating customers' demand for goods can be improved by adopting a value chain approach to inventory management by which the manufacturer or supplier is working as a partner with its customers to meet their inventory needs. This frequently involves having online computer access to customers' inventory levels on a real-time basis and being able to synchronize changes in production with changes in customers' inventory levels as they occur.

Sharing this type of information obviously requires an enormous amount of mutual trust between a manufacturer or supplier and its customers, but it is becoming increasingly common among world-class organizations. An example of this type of vendor-customer relationship is the relationship between Procter & Gamble, one of the world's largest consumer products companies, and its largest customer, Wal-Mart. By having access to Wal-Mart's computer inventory system, Procter & Gamble is better able to determine and fill Wal-Mart's specific needs for products, such as disposable diapers.

PERFORMANCE EVALUATION AND RECORDKEEPING WITH LEAN PRODUCTION AND JIT

LO4 Explain how lean production and just-in-time affect performance evaluation and recordkeeping.

Movement toward a JIT/lean production philosophy requires changes in performance evaluation procedures and offers opportunities for significant reductions in recordkeeping costs. These changes are discussed in this section.

Performance Evaluation

JIT regards inventory as something to be eliminated. Hence, in a manufacturing organization, inventories are kept as small as possible. Under the JIT ideal, inventories do not exist because vendors deliver raw materials in small batches directly to the shop floor. JIT also strives to minimize, or eliminate, work-in-process inventory by minimizing the non-processing elements of cycle time and by having processing times as short as possible.

Dysfunctional Effects of Traditional Performance Measures

A potential conflict exists between the goals of JIT and lean production and those of traditional performance measures applied at the level of the department or cost center. Although lean production emphasizes overall efficiency, many traditional performance measures emphasize local (departmental) cost savings and local (departmental) efficiency. Consider the following traditional performance measures for a purchasing agent and a departmental production supervisor:

- To achieve quantity discounts and favorable prices, a purchasing agent might order excess inventory, thereby increasing subsequent storage, obsolescence, and handling costs.

- To obtain a low price, a purchasing agent might order from a supplier whose goods have not been certified as meeting quality specifications, thereby causing subsequent inspection, rework, and spoilage costs, and perhaps, dissatisfied customers further down the value chain.

- To avoid having idle employees and equipment, a supervisor might refuse to halt production to determine the cause of a quality problem, thereby increasing inspection, rework, and spoilage costs.

- To obtain low fixed costs per unit under absorption costing, a supervisor might produce in excess of current needs (preferably in long production runs), thereby causing subsequent increases in storage, obsolescence, and handling costs.

Performance Measures Under Lean Production and JIT

In accordance with the goal of eliminating inventory and reducing cycle time to processing time, JIT supportive performance measures emphasize inventory turnover, cycle time, and **cycle efficiency** (the ratio of value-added to non-value-added manufacturing activities).

When applied to a specific item of raw materials or finished goods, **inventory turnover** is computed as the annual demand in units divided by the average inventory in units:

$$\text{Inventory turnover} = \frac{\textbf{Annual demand in units}}{\textbf{Average inventory in units}}$$

Progress toward the goal of reducing inventory is measured by comparing successive inventory turnover ratios. Generally, the higher the inventory turnover, the better.

When measured with inventory dollars instead of inventory units, inventory turnover can be used as a measure of the organization's overall success in reducing inventory, or in increasing sales in relation to inventories. This financial measure can be derived directly from a firm's financial statements.

$$\text{Inventory turnover} = \frac{\textbf{Cost of goods sold}}{\textbf{Average inventory (in dollars)}}$$

Another ratio often used to monitor the effectiveness of inventory levels in retail organizations, such as Whole Foods or Macy's, is gross margin return on inventory investment (GMROI), calculated as follows:

$$\text{GMROI} = \frac{\text{Gross margin (in dollars)}}{\text{Average inventory (in dollars)}}$$

Cycle time is a measure of the total time required to produce one unit of a product:

$$\begin{array}{c}\text{Cycle}\\\text{time}\end{array} = \begin{array}{c}\text{Setup}\\\text{time}\end{array} + \begin{array}{c}\text{Processing}\\\text{time}\end{array} + \begin{array}{c}\text{Movement}\\\text{time}\end{array} + \begin{array}{c}\text{Waiting}\\\text{time}\end{array} + \begin{array}{c}\text{Inspection}\\\text{time}\end{array}$$

Under ideal circumstances, cycle time would consist of only processing time, and processing time would be as low as possible. Only processing time adds value to the product; hence, the time required for all other activities should be driven toward zero. The use of flexible manufacturing systems, properly sequencing jobs, and properly placing tools will minimize setup time. If the shop floor is optimally arranged, workers pass products directly from one workstation to the next. If production is optimally scheduled, inventory will not wait in temporary storage between workstations. If raw materials are of high quality and products are manufactured so that they always conform to specifications, separate inspection activities are not needed.

Cycle efficiency is computed as the ratio of processing time to total cycle time:

$$\text{Cycle efficiency} = \frac{\text{Processing time}}{\text{Cycle time}}$$

The highest cycle efficiency possible is always sought. If all non-value-added activities are eliminated, this ratio equals one.

Simplified Recordkeeping

Lean Production and JIT enable significant reductions in the number of accounting transactions required for purchasing and production activities. This results in cost savings for bookkeeping activities and in shifting accounting resources from detailed bookkeeping to the development of more useful activity cost data.

Purchasing

In a traditional accounting system, every purchase results in the preparation of several documents. Additional documents are prepared for the issuance of raw materials to the factory. JIT, on the other hand, attempts to minimize inventory levels and stresses long-term relationships with a limited number of vendors who have demonstrated their ability to provide quality raw materials on a timely basis, as well as at a competitive price. Under a JIT inventory system, a company often has standing purchase orders for specified materials from specified vendors at specified prices. Production personnel are authorized to requisition materials directly from authorized vendors, who deliver limited quantities of materials as needed directly to the shop floor. Production personnel verify receipt of the raw materials. Periodically, each vendor sends an invoice for several shipments, which the company acknowledges and pays.

Product Costing

Another advantage of a lean production system is that it reduces the amount of detailed bookkeeping required for financial accounting purposes. If ending inventories are nonexistent, or so small that the costs assigned to them are insignificant in comparison with the costs assigned to Cost of Goods Sold, it makes little sense to track product costs through several inventory accounts. Instead of using a traditional product cost accounting system (as illustrated in Chapter 5), firms that have implemented JIT often use what is sometimes referred to as a backflush approach to accounting for product costs.

Under **backflush costing**, all costs of direct materials, direct labor, and manufacturing overhead are assigned as incurred to Cost of Goods Sold. If there are no inventories on hand at the end of the period, no additional steps are required. However, if there are inventories on hand at year-end, costs are backed out of Cost of Goods Sold and assigned to the appropriate inventory accounts. For a complete discussion of backflush costing, refer to a cost accounting text.

Also under a JIT inventory approach, many of the distinctions and arguments regarding absorption versus variable costing are moot (see Appendix 5A). If the quantity of inventory is insignificant, it matters little whether inventory cost includes only variable manufacturing costs or both variable and fixed manufacturing costs. Whether absorption or variable costing is used, the total cost assigned to inventory on the balance sheet will be small, and there is little difference in the amount of profit reported on the income statement.

As we discussed in previous chapters, traditional product costing systems go to great lengths to calculate the materials, labor, and manufacturing overhead cost per unit for each unit produced. Overhead is typically assigned to inventory using a predetermined overhead rate based on an assumed volume-based driver such as direct labor hours or machine hours. If actual production is less than budgeted production, there will be underapplied overhead, which is usually written off as an expense of the period. To avoid this expense, managers are often motivated to overproduce product in order to ensure that all overhead is allocated to product. Also, by budgeting a large amount of produced units, fixed overhead cost is spread over more units, resulting in a lower cost per unit. Such overproduction is equivalent to a cardinal sin in a lean production company.

As we will see in Chapter 10, many companies also adopt standard cost systems where they account for product cost components on both an actual and budgeted cost basis, with variances between actual cost and standard (or allowed) costs reported on the internal performance reports as increased expenses if they are unfavorable and as a reduction of expenses if they are favorable. In such cases, managers are motivated to maximize favorable variances and minimize or eliminate unfavorable variances. Such systems of reporting often lead managers to actions that are contrary to the lean production philosophy.

CHAPTER-END REVIEW

Assume **Titleist** is trying to decide which automated production line to use to produce its new Pro VI golf balls. Suppose the two best systems under consideration have the following estimated performance characteristics, based on minutes per 1,000 balls produced:

	System A	System B
Setup time	25	10
Movement time from start to finish	10	14
Waiting time.	3	16
Inspection time	5	7
Processing time.	40	30
Total time in minutes.	83	77

Required

a. Determine the cycle time per batch for each system.
b. Determine the cycle efficiency for each system.
c. Which system do you recommend and why?
d. Assuming Titleist is a "lean" manufacturer, what improvements in the selected system is it likely to pursue?

The solution is on page 264.

GUIDANCE ANSWERS . . . YOU MAKE THE CALL

You are the Controller Designing any information processing system is a matter of weighing benefits with the costs of designing and operating the system. The same is true for a cost allocation system. Also, you have to decide how the cost information will be used. If it is used only for external financial reporting purposes, a high degree of precision may not be necessary. However, if it is used to determine the most profitable product mix, it may be crucial to have the most precise cost information. For the service departments that provide only services to producing departments and that receive no services from other service departments, a direct allocation method might be adequate. For departments that provide and/or receive interdepartmental services, you should consider using either a step or linear algebra approach to assigning costs. Whether you use a direct, step or linear algebra approach, you will have to decide whether to assign the costs using a single volume-based cost driver (such as square footage or number of employees) or using multiple cost drivers that reflect the actual activities performed. In most cases, the ABC approach (discussed in Chapter 6) will give a higher level of precision, but at considerably greater cost.

KEY RATIOS

$$\text{Inventory turnover} = \frac{\text{Annual demand in units}}{\text{Average inventory in units}}$$

$$\text{Inventory turnover} = \frac{\text{Cost of goods sold}}{\text{Average inventory (in dollars)}}$$

$$\text{Gross margin return on inventory investment} = \frac{\text{Gross margin (in dollars)}}{\text{Average inventory (in dollars)}}$$

$$\frac{\text{Cycle}}{\text{time}} = \frac{\text{Setup}}{\text{time}} + \frac{\text{Processing}}{\text{time}} + \frac{\text{Movement}}{\text{time}} + \frac{\text{Waiting}}{\text{time}} + \frac{\text{Inspection}}{\text{time}}$$

$$\text{Cycle efficiency} = \frac{\text{Processing time}}{\text{Cycle time}}$$

KEY TERMS

backflush costing, 249
cycle efficiency, 248
cycle time, 246
direct department cost, 238
direct method, 240
indirect department cost, 238
inspection time, 246
interdepartment services, 239

inventory turnover, 248
just-in-time (JIT) inventory
    management, 245
Kanban system, 247
linear algebra (reciprocal)
    method, 243
materials pull system, 247
materials push system, 246

movement time, 246
processing time, 246
quality circles, 246
service departments, 238
setup time, 246
step method, 241
waiting time, 246

MULTIPLE CHOICE

1. The following budgeted information pertains to Trawbing Company:

	Service Departments		Producing Departments	
	Human Resources	Facilities	Mixing	Molding
Direct department costs.............	$75,000	$50,000	$520,000	$860,000
Direct labor hours	6,000	4,000	20,000	36,000
Square footage	2,000	3,000	24,000	36,000
# of employees	3	2	18	12

The direct department costs for Mixing and Molding represent the direct department overhead costs of those departments, not including any direct material or direct labor. Human Resource Department costs are assigned to other departments based on the number of employees, and Facilities Department costs are assigned to other departments based on square footage occupied. If the direct method is used to allocate service department costs to the producing departments, the total budgeted overhead for the Molding Department after service department costs are allocated is
   a. $920,000.00
   b. $585,000.00
   c. $584,062.50
   d. $920,937.50

2. Refer to the previous question. If the step method is used to allocate service departments to the producing departments, the total budgeted overhead for the Mixing Department after service department costs are allocated is (round all calculations to two decimal places)
   a. $920,000.00
   b. $585,000.00
   c. $584,062.50
   d. $920,937.50

3. Refer to question 1 above. Assume that the Molding Department uses a predetermined overhead rate for assigning overhead costs to products based on budgeted total overhead after service department costs are allocated using the direct allocation method. The predetermined overhead rate for the Molding Department is (round all calculations to two decimal places)
   a. $26.88 per direct labor hour
   b. $23.89 per direct labor hour
   c. $25.56 per direct labor hour
   d. $29.25 per direct labor hour

4. The key elements of JIT/lean production include which of the following?
   a. Increased coordination throughout the value chain
   b. Reduced inventories and production times
   c. Increased product quality and employee empowerment
   d. All of the above are elements of JIT/lean production

5. Topaz Company sold and produced 40,000 units of product at a cost of $1,200,000 for a sales price of $60 per unit during the most recent year. Throughout the year its average inventory was 4,000 units with an average cost of $120,000. Based on this information, which of the following cannot be determined about Topaz's inventory management performance?
   a. Topaz's inventory turnover in units was 10 times.
   b. Topaz's gross margin return on average inventory investment was 1,000%.
   c. Topaz's inventory turnover in dollars was 10 times.
   d. Topaz's production cycle efficiency was 100%.

DISCUSSION QUESTIONS

Q7-1. Distinguish between the following sets of terms:
- *a.* Direct product costs and indirect product costs.
- *b.* Direct department costs and indirect department costs.

Q7-2. Define the terms direct cost and indirect cost.

Q7-3. Differentiate between cost assignment and cost allocation.

Q7-4. Explain how a cost item can be both a direct cost and an indirect cost.

Q7-5. What is the primary advantage of separately allocating fixed and variable indirect costs?

Q7-6. Define interdepartmental services.

Q7-7. To what extent are interdepartmental services recognized under the direct, step, and linear algebra methods of service department cost allocation?

Q7-8. Is it feasible to assign interdepartmental services to production departments using ABC?

Q7-9. Explain the concept of just-in-time inventory management.

Q7-10. What are the major elements of lean production?

Q7-11. What is the relationship between JIT and the lean production concept?

Q7-12. Explain how computer technology has affected the way companies approach JIT inventory management and lean production methods.

Q7-13. What elements of the JIT approach contribute to reducing materials inventories?

Q7-14. Define and identify the elements of cycle time. Which of these elements adds value to the product?

Q7-15. Explain briefly how JIT/lean production benefits organizations that take a value-chain approach to management.

Q7-16. Explain how traditional performance evaluation systems using standard costs conflict with the lean production concept.

Assignments with the ✔ logo in the margin are available in BusinessCourse.
See the Preface of the book for details.

MINI EXERCISES

M7-17. Allocating Service Department Costs: Allocation Basis Alternatives   LO2

Boston Fabricators has two producing departments, P1 and P2, and one service department, S1. Estimated direct overhead costs per month are as follows:

P1 . . . . $150,000
P2 250,000
S1 91,000

Other data follow:

	P1	P2
Number of employees.	75	25
Production capacity (units).	50,000	30,000
Space occupied (square feet).	2,500	7,500
Five-year average percent of S1's service output used	65%	35%

Required

a. For each of the following allocation bases, determine the total estimated overhead cost for P1 and P2 after allocating S1 cost to the producing departments.
1. Number of employees
2. Production capacity in units
3. Space occupied
4. Five-year average percentage of S1 services used
5. Estimated direct overhead costs. (Round your answer to the nearest dollar.)

b.   For each of the five allocation bases, explain the circumstances (including examples) under which each allocation base might be most appropriately used to allocate service department cost in a manufacturing plant such as Boston Fabricators. Also, discuss the advantages and disadvantages that might result from using each of the allocation bases.

LO2 **M7-18. Indirect Cost Allocation: Direct Method**

Sprint Manufacturing Company has two production departments, Melting and Molding. Direct general plant management and plant security costs benefit both production departments. Sprint allocates general plant management costs on the basis of the number of production employees and plant security costs on the basis of space occupied by the production departments. In November, the following overhead costs were recorded:

Melting Department direct overhead	$175,000
Molding Department direct overhead	300,000
General plant management.	90,000
Plant security.	35,000

Other pertinent data follow:

	Melting	Molding
Number of employees.	25	45
Space occupied (square feet).	10,000	40,000
Machine hours.	10,000	2,000
Direct labor hours	4,000	20,000

Required

a.   Prepare a schedule allocating general plant management costs and plant security costs to the Melting and Molding Departments.

b.   Determine the total departmental overhead costs for the Melting and Molding Departments.

c.   Assuming the Melting Department uses machine hours and the Molding Department uses direct labor hours to apply overhead to production, calculate the overhead rate for each production department.

LO2 **M7-19. Interdepartment Services: Direct Method**

Tucson Manufacturing Company has five operating departments, two of which are producing departments (P1 and P2) and three of which are service departments (S1, S2, and S3). All costs of the service departments are allocated to the producing departments. The following table shows the distribution of services from the service departments.

	Services Provided to				
Services provided from	S1	S2	S3	P1	P2
S1.	—	5%	25%	50%	20%
S2.	10%	—	5	45	40
S3.	15	5	—	20	60

The direct operating costs of the service departments are as follows:

S1.	$49,000
S2.	93,500
S3.	18,000

Required

Using the direct method, prepare a schedule allocating the service department costs to the producing departments.

M7-20. Inventory Ratio Calculations

Delroi, Inc., provided the following data for 2013 and 2014:

LO3, 4

Inventory

December 31, 2012	$202,400
December 31, 2013	190,400
December 31, 2014	182,500

Cost of goods sold

2013	$642,000
2014	724,000

Gross margin

2013	$340,000
2014	410,000

Required

(round all calculations to two decimal places)

a. Calculate the inventory turnover ratio for 2013 and 2014.

b. Calculate the gross margin return on inventory investment for 2013 and 2014.

M7-21. Inventory Ratio Calculations

McMahan, LTD., provided the following data for 2013 and 2014:

LO3, 4

Inventory

December 31, 2012	$176,000
December 31, 2013	185,000
December 31, 2014	194,000

Cost of goods sold

2013	$586,000
2014	629,000

Gross margin

2013	$256,000
2014	287,000

Required

(round all calculations to two decimal places)

a. Calculate the inventory turnover ratio for 2013 and 2014.

b. Calculate the gross margin return on inventory investment for 2013 and 2014.

EXERCISES

E7-22. Interdepartment Services: Step Method

Refer to the data in Mini Exercise M7-19. Using the step method, prepare a schedule for Tucson Manufacturing Company allocating the service department costs to the producing departments. (Round calculations to the nearest dollar.)

LO2

E7-23. Interdepartment Services: Step Method

O'Brian's Department Stores allocates the costs of the Personnel and Payroll departments to three retail sales departments, Housewares, Clothing, and Furniture. In addition to providing services to the operating departments, Personnel and Payroll provide services to each other. O'Brian's allocates Personnel Department costs on the basis of the number of employees and Payroll Department costs on the basis of gross payroll. Cost and allocation information for June is as follows:

LO2

	Personnel	Payroll	Housewares	Clothing	Furniture
Direct department cost	$7,800	$3,200	$12,200	$20,000	$16,750
Number of employees	5	4	8	16	4
Gross payroll	$6,000	$3,300	$10,600	$17,400	$ 8,100

Required

a. Determine the percentage of total Personnel Department services that was provided to the Payroll Department.

b. Determine the percentage of total Payroll Department services that was provided to the Personnel Department.

c. Prepare a schedule showing Personnel Department and Payroll Department cost allocations to the operating departments, assuming O'Brian's uses the step method. (Round calculations to the nearest dollar.)

LO3, 4 **E7-24.** **Product Costing in a JIT/Lean Environment**

Doll Computer manufactures laptop computers under its own brand, but acquires all the components from outside vendors. No computers are assembled until the order is received online from customers, so there is no finished goods inventory. When an order is received, the bill of materials required to fill the order is prepared automatically and sent electronically to the various vendors. All components are received from vendors within three days and the completed order is shipped to the customer immediately when completed, usually on the same day the components are received from vendors. The number of units in process at the end of any day is negligible.

The following data are provided for the most recent month of operations:

Actual components costs incurred	$925,000
Actual conversion costs incurred	$203,000
Units in process, beginning of month	-0-
Units started in process during the month	5,500
Units in process, end of month	-0-

Required

a. Assuming Doll uses traditional cost accounting procedures:
   1. How much cost was charged to Work-in-Process during the month?
   2. How much cost was charged to cost of goods sold during the month?

b. Assuming Doll is a lean production company and uses backflush costing method:
   1. How much cost was charged to Work-in-Process during the month?
   2. How much cost was charged to cost of goods sold during the month?

LO4 **E7-25.** **Inventory Management Metrics**

Large retailers like Costco and Target typically use gross margin ratio (gross margin ÷ sales), inventory turnover (sometimes referred to as inventory turns), and gross margin return on investment (GMROI) to evaluate how well inventory has been managed. The goal is to maximize profits while minimizing the investment in inventory. Below are data for four scenarios, a base scenario (A) followed by three modifications (B, C, & D) to the base scenario.

	Scenario A	Scenario B	Scenario C	Scenario D
Sales	$10,000	$20,000	$12,000	$10,000
Cost of goods sold	6,000	12,000	6,000	6,000
Gross profit	$ 4,000	$ 8,000	$ 6,000	$ 4,000
Average inventory	$ 6,000	$ 6,000	$ 6,000	$ 5,000

Required

For each scenario calculate the gross margin percent, the inventory turnover, and GMROI.

LO4 **E7-26.** **Evaluating Inventory Management Metrics**

Refer to E7-25.

Required

a. For Scenarios B through D, explain what change occurred relative to Scenario A to cause GMROI to change. For example, was the change in GMROI caused by a change in inventory turns, a change in gross margin percent, or by reducing inventory levels?

b. What general conclusions can be made from the calculations and observations regarding the factors that influence GMROI?

PROBLEMS

P7-27. **Selecting Cost Allocation Bases and Direct Method Allocations**   LO2
Nevada Company has three producing departments (P1, P2, and P3) for which direct department costs are accumulated. In January, the following indirect costs of operation were incurred.

Plant manager's salary and office expense.	$15,300
Plant security.	2,400
Plant nurse's salary and office expense	3,300
Plant depreciation.	4,000
Machine maintenance.	5,400
Plant cafeteria cost subsidy	3,600
	$34,000

The following additional data have been collected for the three producing departments:

	P1	P2	P3
Number of employees.	10	15	5
Space occupied (square feet).	2,000	5,000	3,000
Direct labor hours	1,600	4,000	750
Machine hours.	4,800	8,000	3,200
Number of nurse office visits	30	35	10

Required

a.   Group the indirect cost items into cost pools based on the nature of the costs and their common basis for allocation. Identify the most appropriate allocation basis for each cost pool and determine the total January costs in the pool. (*Hint:* A cost pool may consist of one or more cost items.)

b.   Allocate the cost pools directly to the three producing departments using the allocation bases selected in requirement (*a*).

c.   How much indirect cost would be allocated to each producing department if Nevada Company were using a plantwide rate based on direct labor hours? Based on machine hours?

d.   Comment on the benefits of allocating costs in pools compared with using a plantwide rate.

P7-28. **Evaluating Allocation Bases and Direct Method Allocations**   LO2
Laramie Company has two service departments, Maintenance and Information Technology (IT), that serve two producing departments, Mixing and Packaging. The following data have been collected for these departments for the current year:

	IT	Maintenance	Mixing	Packaging
Direct department costs.	$184,000	$142,000	$465,000	$295,000
Number of employees.			50	30
Number of ethernet connections			90	70
Number of maintenance hours used			800	600
Number of maintenance orders			180	170

Required

a.   Using the direct method, allocate the service department costs under the following independent assumptions:

   1.   IT costs are allocated based on the number of employees, and Maintenance costs are allocated based on the number of maintenance hours used.

   2.   IT costs are allocated based on the number of ethernet connections served, and Maintenance costs are allocated based on the number of maintenance orders.

b.   Comment on the reasonableness of the bases used in the calculations in requirement (*a*). What considerations should determine which bases to use for allocating IT and Maintenance costs?

LO2 **P7-29.** **Cost Reimbursement and Step Allocation Method**

Samaritan's Clinic is a not-for-profit outpatient facility that provides medical services to both fee-paying patients and low-income government-supported patients. Reimbursement from the government is based on total actual costs of services provided, including both direct costs of patient services and indirect operating costs. Patient services are provided through two producing departments, Medical Services and Ancillary Services (includes X-ray, therapy, etc.). In addition to the direct costs of these departments, the clinic incurs indirect costs in two service departments, Administration and Facilities. Administration costs are allocated first based on the number of full-time employees, and Facilities costs are then allocated based on space occupied. Costs and related data for the current month are as follows:

	Administration	Facilities	Medical Services	Ancillary Services
Direct costs	$36,000	$12,000	$128,800	$39,600
Number of employees.	5	4	13	7
Amount of space occupied (square feet).	1,500	750	8,000	2,000
Number of patient visits	—	—	4,000	1,500

Required

a. Using the step method, prepare a schedule allocating the common service department costs to the producing departments.

b. Determine the amount to be reimbursed from the government for each low-income patient visit.

LO2 **P7-30.** **Budgeted Service Department Cost Allocation: Pricing a New Product**

Pro-Trim Company is adding a new diet food concentrate called Body Trim to its line of body-building and exercise products. A plant is being built for manufacturing the new product. Management has decided to price the new product based on a 100 percent markup on total manufacturing costs. A direct cost budget for the new plant projects that direct department costs of $3,250,000 will be incurred in producing an expected normal output of 700,000 pounds of finished product. In addition, indirect costs for Administration and Technical Support will be shared by Body Trim with the two exercise products divisions, Commercial Products and Retail Products. Budgeted annual data to be used in making the allocations are summarized here.

	Administration	Technical Support	Commercial Products	Retail Products	Body Trim
Number of employees.	5	5	50	30	20
Amount of technical support time (hours)	500	—	1,500	1,250	750

Direct costs are budgeted at $205,000 for the Administration Department and $280,000 for the Technical Support Department.

Required

a. Using the step method, determine the total direct and indirect costs of Body Trim.

b. Determine the selling price per pound of Body Trim. (Round calculations to the nearest cent.)

LO2 **P7-31.** **Allocation and Responsibility Accounting**

TIMBERLAND COMPANY (TBL)

Assume that Timberland Company uses a responsibility accounting system for evaluating its managers, and that abbreviated performance reports for the company's three divisions for the month of March are as follows (amounts in thousands).

	Total	East	Central	West
Income.	$206,000	$73,000	$80,000	$53,000
Less allocated costs:				
Information Technology.	(105,000)	(35,000)	(35,000)	(35,000)
Personnel.	(75,000)	(28,125)	(28,125)	(18,750)
Division income	$ 26,000	$9,875	$16,875	$ (750)

The West Division manager is very disturbed over his performance report and recent rumors that his division may be closed because of its failure to report a profit in recent periods. He believes that the reported profit figures do not fairly present operating results because his division is being unfairly burdened with service department costs. He is particularly concerned over the amount of Information Technology costs charged to his division. He believes that it is inequitable for his division to be charged with one-third of the total cost when it is using only 20 percent of the services. He believes that the Personnel Department's use of the Information Technology Department should also be considered in the cost allocations. Cost allocations were based on the following distributions of service provided:

		Services Receiver			
Services Provider	Personnel	Computer Services	East	Central	West
Information Technology	40%	—	20%	20%	20%
Personnel.	—	20%	30	30	20

Required

a. What method is the company using to allocate Personnel and Information Technology costs?

b. Recompute the cost allocations using the step method. (Round calculations to the nearest dollar.)

c. Revise the performance reports to reflect the cost allocations computed in requirement (*b*).

d. Comment on the complaint of the West Division's manager.

P7-32. Allocating Service Department Costs: Direct and Step Methods; Department and Plantwide Overhead Rates   LO2

Assume that Pennington Group, a manufacturer of fine casual outdoor furniture, allocates Human Resources Department costs to the producing departments (Cutting and Welding) based on number of employees; Facilities Department costs are allocated based on the amount of square footage occupied. Direct department costs, labor hours, and square footage data for the four departments for October are as follows: PENNINGTON GROUP

	Human Resources	Facilities	Cutting	Welding
Direct department overhead costs.	$50,000	$150,000	$900,000	$370,000
Number of employees.	5	5	40	60
Number of direct labor hours	—	—	8,000	10,000
Amount of square footage	10,000	3,000	100,000	50,000

Assume that two jobs, A1 and A2, were completed during October and that each job had direct materials costs of $1,200. Job A1 used 80 direct labor hours in the Cutting Department and 20 direct labor hours in the Welding Department. Job A2 used 20 direct labor hours in the Cutting Department and 80 direct labor hours in the Welding Department. The direct labor rate is $40 in both departments.

Required

a. Find the cost of each job using a plantwide rate based on direct labor hours.

b. Find the cost of each job using department rates with *direct* service department cost allocation.

c. Find the cost of each job using department rates with *step* service department cost allocation.

d. Explain the differences in the costs computed in requirements (*a*)–(*c*) for each job. Which costing method is best for product pricing and profitability analysis?

P7-33. JIT/Lean Production and Product Costing   LO4

Presented is information pertaining to the standard or budgeted unit cost of a product manufactured in a JIT/Lean Production environment at Towry Systems Inc.:

Direct materials	$20
Conversion.	15
Total	$35

All materials are added at the start of the production process. All raw materials purchases and conversion costs are directly assigned to Cost of Goods Sold. At the end of the period, costs are backed out and assigned to Raw Materials in Process (only for materials still in the plant) and Finished Goods Inventory (for materials and conversion costs for completed units). Costs assigned to inventories are based on the standard or budgeted cost multiplied by the number of units in inventory. Conversion costs are assigned to inventories only for fully converted units. Since inventory levels tend to be small in this JIT environment, partially completed units are assigned no conversion costs. Towry had no beginning inventories on August 1, 2014. During the month, it incurred the following manufacturing-related costs:

Purchase of raw materials on account.	$350,000
Factory wages	130,000
Factory supervision salaries	30,000
Utilities bill for month	17,000
Factory supplies purchased	15,000
Depreciation	9,500

The end-of-month inventory included raw materials in process of 750 units and finished goods of 500 units. One hundred units of raw materials were zero percent converted; the other 650 units averaged 60 percent converted.

Required

a. Calculate the total cost charged to Cost of Goods Sold during August.

b. Calculate the balances in Raw Materials in Process, Finished Goods Inventory, and Cost of Goods Sold at the end of August.

c. Assuming that August is a typical month, is it likely that using the company's shortcut backflush accounting procedures will produce misleading financial statements? Explain.

LO5 P7-34. Just-in-Time Performance Evaluation

To control operations, Rockford Company makes extensive and exclusive use of financial performance reports for each department. Although all departments have been reporting favorable cost variances in most periods, management is perplexed by the firm's low overall return on investment. You have been asked to look into the matter. Believing the purchasing department is typical of the company's operations, you obtained the following information concerning the purchases of parts for a product it started producing in 2009:

Year	Purchase Price Variance	Quantity Used (units)	Average Inventory (units)
2009	$ 1,500 F	20,000	5,000
2010	10,500 F	30,000	7,500
2011	12,000 F	35,000	10,000
2012	20,000 U	25,000	6,250
2013	8,000 F	36,000	9,000
2014	9,500 F	29,000	7,250

Required

a. Compute the inventory turnover for each year. What conclusions can be drawn from a yearly comparison of the purchase price variance and the inventory turnover?

b. Identify problems likely to be caused by evaluating purchasing only on the basis of the purchase price variance.

c. Offer whatever recommendations you believe appropriate.

LO2 P7-35. Dual Allocation Approach and Charging for Services

The Maintenance Department of Management Smart Suites Hotel has fixed costs of $500,000 a year. It also incurs $30 in out-of-pocket expenses for every hour of work. During the year the Rooms Department used 30,000 maintenance hours. The Food and Beverage (F&B) Department used 10,000 maintenance hours. When the Maintenance Department was established the Rooms and F&B departments estimated they would need 30,000 and 20,000 maintenance hours, respectively. It turns out F&B cut back on maintenance hours used to insure it would meet its budget.

Required

a. Calculate the amount of Maintenance Department costs to allocate to Rooms and F&B based entirely on actual usage.

b. Calculate the amount of Maintenance Department costs to allocate to Rooms and F&B using a dual allocation approach where fixed cost is allocated based on estimated capacity needed and variable cost is allocated based on actual usage.

c. Which of the two methods applied in parts a. and b. is more fair to the two departments?

d. Assume that the Maintenance Department allocates costs to the producing departments using a user charge. What amount would you suggest for the user charge? Is it a good idea to use a user charge for allocating costs?

CASES AND PROJECTS

C7-36. **Materials Push and Materials Pull Systems**   LO3, 4

Data Storage Inc. produces three models of external storage devices for personal computers. Each model is produced on a separate assembly line. Production consists of several operations in separate work centers. Because of a high demand for Data's products, management is most interested in high-production volume and operating efficiency. Each work center is evaluated on the basis of its operating efficiency. To avoid idle time caused by defective units, variations in machine times, and machine breakdowns, significant inventories are maintained between each workstation.

At a recent administrative committee meeting, the director of research announced that the firm's engineers have made a dramatic breakthrough in designing a low-cost, read/write optical storage device. Data Storage's president is very enthusiastic, and the vice president of marketing wishes to add an assembly line for optical storage devices as soon as possible. The equipment necessary to manufacture the new product can be purchased and installed in less than 60 days. Unfortunately, all available plant space is currently devoted to the production of conventional storage devices, and expansion is not possible at the current plant location. It appears that adding the new product will require dropping a current product, relocating the entire operation, or manufacturing the optical storage devices at a separate location.

The vice president of marketing is opposed to dropping a current product. The vice president of finance is opposed to relocating the entire operation because of financing requirements and the associated financial risks. The vice president of production is opposed to splitting up production activities because of the loss of control and the added costs for various types of overhead.

Required

Explain how switching to a materials pull (Kanban) system can help solve Data Storage's space problems while improving quality and cycle time. Describe how a materials pull system works and the changes required in management attitude toward inventory and efficiency to make it work.

C7-37. **Product Costing Using Activity-Based Costing and Just-in-Time: A Value Chain Approach**   LO3, 4

Wearwell Carpet Company is a small residential carpet manufacturer started by Don Stegall, a longtime engineer and manager in the carpet industry. Stegall began Wearwell in the early 1990s after learning about ABC, JIT, total quality management, and several other manufacturing concepts being used successfully in Japan and other parts of the world. Although it was a small company, he believed that with his many years of experience and by applying these advanced techniques, Wearwell could very quickly become a world-class competitor.

Stegall buys dyed carpet yarns for Wearwell from three different major yarn manufacturers with which he has done business for many years. He chose these companies because of their reputation for producing high-quality products and their state-of-the art research and development departments. He has arranged for two carpet manufacturing companies to produce (tuft) all of his carpets on a contractual basis. Both companies have their own brands, but they also do contract work for other companies. For each manufacturer, Stegall had to agree to use the full output of one manufacturing production line at least one day per month. Each production line was dedicated to producing only one style of carpet, but each manufacturer had production lines capable of running each type of carpet that Wearwell sold.

Stegall signed a contract with a large transport company (CTC), which specializes in carpet-related shipping, to pick up and deliver yarn from the yarn plants to the tufting mills. This company will then deliver the finished product from the tufting mills to Wearwell's ten customers, which are carpet retailers in the ten largest residential building markets in the country. These retailers pay the shipping charges to have the carpets delivered to them. Wearwell maintains a small sales staff (which also doubles as a customer service staff) to deal with the retailers and occasionally with the end customers on quality problems that arise.

Wearwell started selling only one line of carpet, a medium-grade plush, but as new carpet styles were developed, it added two additional lines, a medium-grade berber carpet and a medium-grade textured carpet. Three colors are offered in each carpet style. By selling only medium grades with limited color choices, Stegall felt that he would reach a very large segment of the carpet market without having to deal with a large number of different products. As textured (trackless) carpets have become more popular, sales of plush have diminished substantially.

Required

a.   Describe the value chain for Wearwell Carpet Company, and identify the parties who compose this value chain.

b.   Identify and discuss the cost categories that would be included in the cost of the product for financial reporting purposes.

c.   Identify and discuss the cost categories that would be included in the cost of the product for pricing and other management purposes.

d.   Discuss some of the challenges that Stegall will have trying to apply JIT to regulate the levels of control at Wearwell. Suggest changes that might be necessary to make JIT work.

e.   Does Wearwell seem to be an appropriate setting for implementing ABC? If so, what are likely to be the most important activities and related cost drivers?

SOLUTIONS TO REVIEW PROBLEMS

Mid-Chapter Review

Solution

Service Department Cost Allocation
a. Direct Method

	Total	Women's	Men's
Administrative Services Department			
Allocation base (number of employees).............	24	15	9
Percent of total base.............................	100%	62.5%	37.5%
Cost allocation...................................	$18,000	$11,250	$6,750
Facilities Services Department			
Allocation base (square footage)	22,500	15,000	7,500
Percent of total base.............................	100%	66.7%	33.3%
Cost allocation...................................	$12,000	$ 8,000	$4,000

Cost Allocation Summary

	Administrative	Facilities	Women's	Men's	Total
Departmental costs					
before allocation	$18,000	$12,000	$60,000	$50,000	$140,000
Cost allocations					
Administrative	(18,000)	—	11,250	6,750	0
Facilities................	—	(12,000)	8,000	4,000	0
Departmental costs					
after allocation............	$ 0	$ 0	$79,250	$60,750	$140,000

Step Method

Allocation Sequence

	Administrative	Facilities
Allocation base	Number of employees	Amount of square footage
Total base for other service and producing departments (a)	26	25,000
Total base for other service departments (b).	2	2,500
Percent of total services provided to other service departments (b ÷ a)	7.7%	10.0%
Order of allocation.	Second	First

Step Allocations

	Total	Administrative	Women's	Men's
Facilities Services Department				
Allocation base (square footage)	25,000	2,500	15,000	7,500
Percent of total base	100%	10%	60%	30%
Cost allocation.	$12,000	$1,200	$ 7,200	$3,600
Administrative Services Department				
Allocation base (number of employees)	24	—	15	9
Percent of total base	100%	—	62.5%	37.5%
Cost allocation ($18,000 + $1,200)	$19,200	—	$12,000	$7,200

Cost Allocation Summary

	Facilities	Administrative	Women's	Men's	Total
Departmental costs before allocation	$12,000	$18,000	$60,000	$50,000	$140,000
Cost allocations					
Facilities	(12,000)	1,200	7,200	3,600	0
Administrative	—	(19,200)	12,000	7,200	0
Departmental costs after allocations	$ 0	$ 0	$79,200	$60,800	$140,000

b. Another service department cost allocation method is the *linear algebra method*. This method simultaneously allocates service department costs both to other service departments and to the producing departments. It has an advantage over the *step method* in that it fully recognizes interdepartmental services.

c. If H&M wants the most precise allocation of service department costs to the producing departments, considering both direct services and indirect services, it must use the linear algebra method of service department allocation. As indicated in the Allocation Sequence section of the step method in (*a*), Facilities provides 10 percent of its services to Administrative, and Administrative provides 7.7 percent of its services to Facilities. The step method recognized the Facilities services provided to Administrative, but it did not recognize the Administrative services provided to Facilities.

In this case, the producing departments are using approximately the same proportion of services from each of the service departments (60.0 percent to 62.5 percent for the Women's Department and 30.0 percent to 37.5 percent for the Men's Department). Hence, using a more precise measure of cost allocation is not likely to produce significantly different results, especially since the interdepartmental services are so close (7.7 percent versus 10.0 percent). Just as the step method allocation results were quite close to the direct method results, the linear method results would likely be quite close to both the direct and step method results. Use of the linear algebra method is not recommended in this case. On the basis of simplicity and convenience, the direct method is probably the best method for H&M to use.

Chapter-End Review

Solution

a. Cycle time is the total time required to produce one batch, including both value-added and non-value-added activities: System A = 83; System B = 77

b. The cycle efficiency is the percent of total time used in value-added activities. In this case, only the processing time is adding value to the product. Cycle efficiency: System A = 40/83 = 0.48; System B = 30/77 = 0.39

c. In selecting between A and B, the system with the higher efficiency would not likely be chosen because it has the longer total cycle time. Assuming both systems produce products of equal quality and characteristics, B is appealing because it requires one-fourth less processing time than A and offers greater opportunity for continuous improvement.

d. In a lean environment, management and all employees involved will be seeking ways to reduce the cycle time while maintaining a high-quality product. For B, the most likely opportunity for significant reduction is to reduce the large amount of movement and waiting time. If these components of total cycle time can be reduced, B becomes even more attractive.

Pricing and Other Product Management Decisions

The key to a startup company's success is to have a unique product or service that customers are willing to pay for, to be able to identify what price they will pay for it, and to produce the good or service within the price constraint such that the company can generate a profit. A tall order, especially when the startup company is sailing in relatively uncharted waters. Such is the case of **Roku**, the California startup that has become the second most popular streaming video device maker behind **Apple**'s Apple TV. If a company's value chain is the set of activities that a customer is willing to pay for,

ROKU
www.roku.com

then Roku is the proverbial and literal "black box" that sits on top of the TV and allows customers to enhance their home entertainment systems. Consumers don't always understand the technology behind the functionality, but they do understand the convenience of the unit once it is installed.

Both Roku and Apple TV offer video-streaming services such as **Netflix**, **Hulu** Plus, **Vudu**, **HBO** Go (with cable or satellite subscription), photo services such as **Flickr**, and streamed sports events from the **NBA**, **MLB**, and **NHL**. However, Apple TV offers **Google**'s YouTube and its own iTunes service embedded in its unit, which no doubt accounts for its 13 million versus Roku's 5 million units sold to date. On the other hand, Roku supports over 750 channels for TV, movies, music, and game streaming and, more important, recently won exclusive access rights to **Amazon**'s On Demand and Instant video (including free programs via Amazon Prime).

Ordinarily, a company would like to set its price above the cost to produce its good or service plus some desired profit. We refer to this as cost-based pricing. Yet when a company is engaged in intense competition with a more established rival, it may not be able to capture a price that is any higher than the entrenched rival's price. In other words, the market price is established by the more powerful rival. The Apple TV sells for $99, and given its dominant market share, this price defines the market. Accordingly, Roku prices its units between $49 and $99; we refer to this as "target costing," or setting a price at what the market is willing to pay and producing within those revenue constraints.

The combination of squaring off against a powerful competitor coupled with a rapidly changing technology and regulatory environment is risky for any company, much less a new entrant. Apple has "deep pockets" and could engage a smaller player like Roku in a protracted price war. Luckily for Roku, it has attracted financing backing from media stalwarts such as **Hearst Corporation**, **News Corporation**, and Britain's **Sky Broadcasting**. However, network and cable television companies are playing defense due to lost revenue as more of their customers are dropping cable television in favor of an Internet-only streaming environment. Major players such as **CBS**, **Fox**, **Walt Disney Company**, **Comcast**, and others have recently sued **Aereo**, a company with thousands of antennas warehoused in Brooklyn, New York, that pick up signals from broadcast TV and re-transmit those signals

continued on following page

continued from previous page

to subscribers via the Internet. The courts ruled in favor of Aereo by denying a temporary injunction against its re-transmission rights. Temporarily stymied, the established cable and satellite companies are caught between the desire to protect their broadcast property rights and potentially losing out on the ground floor of this changing technology. To that end, Roku has entered into a deal with the satellite company Dish Network to stream its international content, and Time Warner Cable just became the first pay-TV company to stream its full live TV lineup through Roku.

Given the fledgling industry's vast uncertainty, we must assume that product life-cycle stages will be abbreviated either from competition or regulation. To maximize its sales and profits in the short run, a company like Roku must compete on the functionality, quality, and continuous improvement of its product. The managerial tools discussed throughout this chapter are increasingly important for managers involved in the development, production, and marketing of products and services that compete in contested environments. A company that truly understands the value chain of its production and delivery systems will remain nimble and flexible in the face of a changing regulatory and competitive landscape.

Sources: AP News, "Roku Raises $60M from Hearst, News Corp, Others," *Bloomberg Businessweek*, May 29, 2013; Kyle Stock, "Roku Sales Hit 5 Million Units, Thanks to Amazon, Netflix," *Bloomberg Businessweek*, April 11, 2013; Larry Magid, "Roku Reaches Milestone as Networks Consider Dropping Free Broadcast," *Forbes*, April 10, 2013; Larry Magid, "Review of Roku 3: Could It Kill Cable and Satellite TV?' *Forbes*, April 1, 2013; Walter Mossberg, "Roku 3: Easier Streaming and Remote Headphones," *Wall Street Journal*, March 6, 2013, pp. D1–D3; and Robert Hof, "Could TiVo and Roku Beat Apple to TV Nirvana?" *Forbes*, February 27, 2013.

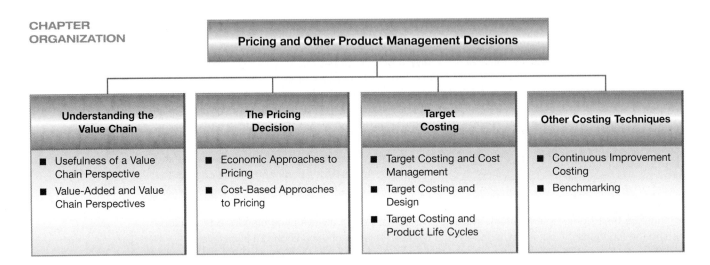

CHAPTER ORGANIZATION

Pricing and Other Product Management Decisions

Understanding the Value Chain	The Pricing Decision	Target Costing	Other Costing Techniques
■ Usefulness of a Value Chain Perspective ■ Value-Added and Value Chain Perspectives	■ Economic Approaches to Pricing ■ Cost-Based Approaches to Pricing	■ Target Costing and Cost Management ■ Target Costing and Design ■ Target Costing and Product Life Cycles	■ Continuous Improvement Costing ■ Benchmarking

Strategic cost management techniques, such as *target costing* and *continuous improvement costing*, represent important concepts for product management professionals involved in the development, manufacture, and marketing of products and services. Virtually all such techniques are grounded in the notion of managing the value chain. This chapter examines pricing, the interrelation between price and cost, and the role of benchmarking in meeting customer needs at the lowest possible price.

We begin with a discussion of the value chain, followed by an overview of the pricing model economists use to explain price equilibrium. Given the limitations of this long-run equilibrium model for determining price of a product or service, we consider the widely used cost-plus approach to identifying initial prices. We then examine how intense competition (such as that for the green car market) has inverted the cost-plus pricing model into one that starts with an acceptable market price and subtracts a desired profit to determine a target cost. We also consider *life cycle costs* from the perspectives of both the seller, who increasingly plans for all costs before production begins, and the buyer, who regards subsequent operating, maintenance, repair, and disposal costs as important as price. Finally, we consider how *benchmarking* can assist in improving competitiveness and profitability.

LO1 Explain the importance of the value chain in managing products and identify the key components of an organization's internal and external value chain.

UNDERSTANDING THE VALUE CHAIN

The **value chain** for a product or service is the set of value-producing activities that stretches from basic raw materials to the final consumer. Each product or service has a distinct value chain, and all entities along the value chain depend on the final customer's perception of the value and cost of a product or service. It is the final customer who ultimately pays all costs and provides all profits to all organizations along the entire value chain. Consequently, *the goal of every organization is to maximize the value, while minimizing the cost, of a product or service to final customers.*

The value chain provides a viewpoint that encompasses all activities performed to deliver products and services to final customers. Depending on the needs of management, value chains are developed at varying levels of detail. Analyzing a value chain from the perspective of the final consumer requires working backward from the end product or service to the basic raw materials entering into the product or service. Analyzing a value chain from the viewpoint of an organization that is in the middle of a value chain requires working forward (downstream) to the final consumer and backward (upstream) to the source of raw materials. The paper industry provides a convenient context for illustrating the value chain concept.

Exhibit 8.1 presents the value chain for the paperboard cartons used to package beverages, such as Coca-Cola, Pepsi, or Evían products. The value chain is presented at three levels, with each successive level containing additional details. The first level depicts the various business entities in the value chain:

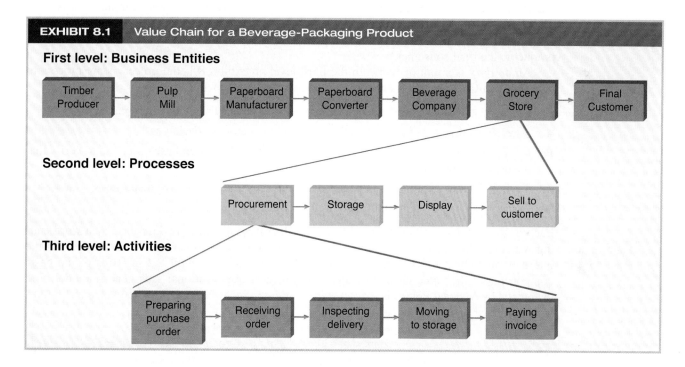

EXHIBIT 8.1 | Value Chain for a Beverage-Packaging Product

First level: Business Entities

Timber Producer → Pulp Mill → Paperboard Manufacturer → Paperboard Converter → Beverage Company → Grocery Store → Final Customer

Second level: Processes

Procurement → Storage → Display → Sell to customer

Third level: Activities

Preparing purchase order → Receiving order → Inspecting delivery → Moving to storage → Paying invoice

- Timber producers grow the pulp wood (usually pine) used as the basic input into paper products. Some large paper companies, such as Boise Cascade and Georgia Pacific, harvest much of their pulp wood from timberlands that they manage. Other companies, including International Paper, which is a leading producer of paperboard, do not manage their own timberlands, but purchase pulp for their mills on the open market through pulp intermediaries.

- Pulp mills produce the kraft (unbleached) paper used to produce the paperboard. Some of the smaller paperboard manufacturers purchase the kraft paper product from pulp mills; Graphic Packaging, however, owns its own paper mills that produce paper for its paperboard production facilities.

- Paperboard manufacturers perform a laminating process of coating paperboard material used to produce beverage packages. The paperboard consists of two layers of paper product plus three layers of coating that gives the top surface a high gloss finish that is water resistant and suitable for multicolor printing.

- The paperboard converter uses manufactured paperboard to print and produce the completed beverage packaging product, such as the cartons used to package the Diet Coca-Cola 12-pack.

■ Beverage distributors, such as Coca-Cola Enterprises and Anheuser-Busch, purchase the completed paperboard packages from Graphic Packaging to package their many different brands in various package sizes and shapes.

■ Grocery and convenience stores, such as Publix and 7-Eleven, display and sell beverages packaged in the paperboard containers.

■ The final customer purchases beverages packaged in paperboard packages and uses the packages to carry the beverages and to store them until consumed. The packages not only perform a transport and storage function but also serve as an advertising medium for the beverage company. The beverage company's advertising on the paperboard packages is intended to entice customers to purchase the beverage company's product and to help create a sense of satisfaction for the customer.

To better understand how business entities within the chain add value and incur costs, management might further refine the value chain into **processes**, collections of related activities intended to achieve a common purpose. The second level in Exhibit 8.1 represents major processes concerning the procurement and sale of Coca-Cola products by a grocery store. To simplify our illustration, we show only the processes for the grocery store related to the purchase and sale of Coca-Cola products packaged in paperboard packages. These processes include procuring Coca-Cola products from the bottling company, storing and displaying the product, and selling the product to the final consumer.

An **activity** is a unit of work. In the third level of Exhibit 8.1, the grocery store process to procure Coca-Cola products is further broken up into the following activities:

■ *Placing* a purchase order for Coca-Cola products packaged in paperboard packages.

■ *Receiving* delivery of the Coca-Cola products in paperboard packages.

■ *Inspecting* the delivery to make sure it corresponds with the purchase order and to verify that the products are in good condition.

■ *Storing* Coca-Cola products in paperboard packages until needed for display.

■ *Paying* for Coca-Cola products acquired after the invoice arrives.

Each of the activities involved in procuring product from a vendor is described by a word ending with *ing*. This suggests that most work activities involve action. One way to think about the internal value chain for a particular company is provided in Exhibit 8.2 in terms of the basic components of the value chain that are found in most organizations. This generic model, first developed by Michael Porter, is a good starting point in identifying the internal value chain links for a particular organization.

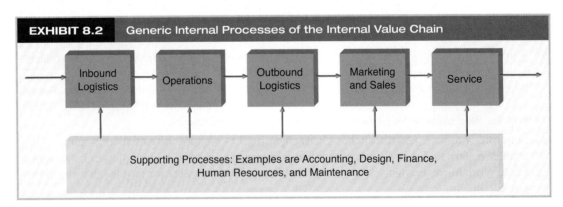

EXHIBIT 8.2 Generic Internal Processes of the Internal Value Chain

Inbound Logistics → Operations → Outbound Logistics → Marketing and Sales → Service

Supporting Processes: Examples are Accounting, Design, Finance, Human Resources, and Maintenance

Usefulness of a Value Chain Perspective

The goal of maximizing final customer value while minimizing final customer cost leads organizations to examine *internal* and *external links* in the value chain rather than the departments, processes, or activities independently. From a value chain perspective, it is total cost across the entire value chain, not the cost of individual businesses, departments, processes, or activities that is most important.

Value Chain Perspective Fosters Supplier–Buyer Partnerships

In the past, relationships between suppliers and buyers were often adversarial. Contact between suppliers and buyers was solely through the selling and purchasing departments. Suppliers attempted merely to meet purchasing contract specifications at the lowest possible cost. Buyers encouraged competition among suppliers with the primary—and often single—goal of obtaining the lowest purchase price.

As discussed in Chapter 7 with JIT and lean production, exploiting cost reduction and value-enhancing opportunities in the value chain has led many buyers and suppliers to view each other as partners rather than as adversaries. Buyers have reduced the number of suppliers they deal with, often developing long-term partnerships with a single supplier. Once they establish mutual trust, both proceed to share detailed information on internal operations and help each other solve problems. Partners work closely to examine mutual opportunities by studying their common value chain. Supplier engineers might determine that a minor relaxation in buyer specifications would significantly reduce supplier manufacturing costs with only minor increases in subsequent buyer processing costs. Working together, they determine how best to modify processes to reduce overall costs and share increased profits.

Companies such as Hewlett-Packard and Boeing involve suppliers in design, development, and manufacturing decisions. Motorola has even developed a survey asking suppliers to assess Motorola as a buyer. Among other questions, the survey asks sellers to evaluate Motorola's performance in helping suppliers to identify major cost drivers and to increase their profitability. These questions represent the concerns of a partner rather than those of an adversary. Michael Dell, at Dell Computers, stated that "rather than closely guarding our information databases, which took us years to develop, we used Internet browsers to essentially give that information to our customers and suppliers—bringing them into our business."[1] The following Business Insight box describes how Nestle assists coffee growers to make them more profitable while ensuring a supply of high-quality coffee beans.

BUSINESS INSIGHT

Nestle Trains and Supplies Thousands of Farmers Nestle CEO, Paul Bulcke, said, "We shouldn't just be the world's largest coffee buyer, we should be involved upstream . . . . We're doing it for better quality and securing our raw material." Declining coffee bean production due to aging and poorly maintained trees prompted Nestle to adopt a program to provide a new generation of plants engineered for local climates, as well as providing advice and training to thousands of farmers worldwide. Nestle projects that it will distribute 220 million plants to coffee growers over the next ten years, even though the farmers are not obligated to sell their coffee beans to Nestle. The head of one coffee cooperative in Veracruz, Mexico, stated that "price is important, but so is the attention and the commitments they [Nestle] have shown to us."

Source: Christina Passariello and Laurence Iliff, "Nestle Plans Ground Attack Over Coffee Beans," *The Wall Street Journal*, August 26, 2010, p. b1.

On a smaller scale, the grocery store in Exhibit 8.1 should examine its external links. It may be willing to pay more for Coca-Cola products if the distributors cooperate to help reduce costs such as the following:

■ Making more frequent deliveries in small lots would reduce storage costs.

■ Being responsible for maintaining and changing the product displays would relieve store workers of these tasks.

■ Streamlining ordering and payment procedures would reduce bookkeeping costs.

---

[1] *Direct from Dell*, Michael Dell with Catherine Fredman, Harper Collins Publishers, 1999. Also, see http://money.cnn.com/magazines/fortune/fortune500/2007/full_list/index.html

If partnership arrangements with upstream suppliers enable the grocery store to reduce its total costs, the store can enhance or maintain its competitive position by reducing prices charged to its consumers. Remember that competitors are also striving to reduce costs and enhance their competitive position. Hence, failing to strive for improvements will likely result in reduced sales and profits.

Value Chain Perspective Fosters Focus on Core Competencies

Using value chain concepts, relationships with suppliers often begin to represent an extended family, allowing companies to focus on core competencies; this capability provides a distinct competitive advantage. In addition, a new breed of contract manufacturers, such as Solectron Corporation and Sanmina-SCI have emerged in recent years. These organizations manufacture products for other companies, ranging from Hewlett-Packard printers to Xerox photocopy machines, with such close partnership arrangements that they behave like a single company. This allows Hewlett-Packard and Xerox to focus on marketing and product development while Solectron and SCI Systems focus on efficient, low-cost manufacturing.

Interestingly, because their facilities are available to all innovators with the necessary financing, the emergence of contract manufacturers may speed innovation. Toyota attributes much of its rapid growth and profitability to virtual integration with suppliers. **Virtual integration** is the use of information technology and partnership concepts to allow two or more entities along a value chain to act as if they were a single economic entity.

RESEARCH INSIGHT

Improving Target Costing Through the Japanese *Keiretsu*—Toyota Rejuvenates an Old Management Tool The Japanese *keiretsu* gained popularity in the 1980s and represents a close relationship between a buyer and its supplier. Traditional *keiretsus* were a network of obligational relationships based on trust and goodwill where a manufacturer would buy from suppliers that were part owners of the manufacturer. The manufacturer usually bought the inventory from the supplier at full price, meaning that inefficiencies were passed through the supply chain. In the 1990s, shareholder value became paramount to companies, and the competitive pressures of global competition dampened the importance of the *keiretsu*.

Toyota has modernized the idea of the keiretsu in four ways: (1) it sources its parts from the global market instead of its connected suppliers; (2) it uses global prices to set target prices for its suppliers; (3) it buys integrated systems from its suppliers rather than individual parts; and (4) it encourages its suppliers to get involved with the product development and planning stages to better integrate these systems into Toyota's final products. Even with its increased buying power, Toyota still promotes trust, cooperation, and educational support for its suppliers. This form of increased involvement with suppliers can facilitate the use of target costing throughout the supply chain.

Source: Katsuki Aoki, "The New, Improved *Keiretsu*," *Harvard Business Review*, September 1, 2013, pp. 109–113.

Value-Added and Value Chain Perspectives

The value chain perspective is often contrasted with a value-added perspective. Under a value-added perspective, decision makers consider only the cost of resources to their organization and the selling price of products or services to their immediate customers. Using a value-added perspective, the goal is to maximize the value added (the difference between the selling price and costs) by the organization. To do this, the value-added perspective focuses primarily on internal activities and costs. Under a value chain perspective, the goal is to maximize value and minimize cost to final customers, often by developing linkages or partnerships with suppliers and customers.

Although initial efforts to enhance competitiveness might start with a value-added perspective, it is important to expand to a value chain perspective. World-class competitors utilize both a value-added and a value chain perspective. These firms always keep the final customer in mind and recognize that the profitability of each entity in the value chain depends on the overall value and cost of the products and services delivered to final customers.

The value-added perspective is the foundation of the make or buy (outsourcing) decision considered in Chapter 4. The key differences between the partnering decisions considered here and the make or buy decision in Chapter 4 concern time frame, perspective, and attitude. The make or buy decision is a stand-alone decision, often in the short run, that does not view vendors and customers as partners. In contrast, characteristics of the value chain perspective are as follows:

- Comprehensive.
- Focused on the final customers.
- Strategic.
- Basis for partnerships between vendors and customers.

Enhancing or maintaining a competitive position requires an understanding of the entire system used to develop and deliver value to final customers, including interactions among organizations along the value chain. All organizations in the value chain are in business together and should work together as partners rather than as adversaries.

THE PRICING DECISION

Pricing products and services is one of the most important and complex decisions facing management. Pricing decisions directly affect the salability of individual products or services, as well as the profitability, and even the survival, of the organization. Many economists have spent their entire careers examining the foundations of pricing. To respond to the needs of pricing hundreds or thousands of individual items, managers have developed pricing guidelines that are typically based on costs. More recently, global competition has turned cost-based approaches upside down. Managers of world-class organizations increasingly start with a price that customers are willing to pay and then determine allowable costs.

LO2 Distinguish between economic and cost-based approaches to pricing.

Economic Approaches to Pricing

In economic models, the firm has a profit-maximizing goal and known cost and revenue functions. Typically, increases in sales quantity require reductions in selling prices, causing **marginal revenue** (the varying increment in total revenue derived from the sale of an additional unit) to decline as sales increase. Increases in production cause an increase in **marginal cost** (the varying increment in total cost required to produce and sell an additional unit of product). In economic models, profits are maximized at the sales volume at which marginal revenues equal marginal costs. Firms continue to produce as long as the marginal revenue derived from the sale of each additional unit exceeds the marginal cost of producing that unit.

Economic models provide a useful framework for considering pricing decisions. The ideal price is the one that will lead customers to purchase all units a firm can provide up to the point at which the last unit has a marginal cost exactly equal to its marginal revenue.

Despite their conceptual merit, economic models are seldom used for day-to-day pricing decisions. Perfect information and an indefinite time period are required to achieve equilibrium prices at which marginal revenues equal marginal costs. In the short run, most for-profit organizations attempt to achieve a target profit rather than a maximum profit. One reason for this is an inability to determine the single set of actions that will lead to profit maximization. Furthermore, managers are more apt to strive to satisfy a number of goals (such as profits for investors, job security for themselves and their employees, and being a "good" corporate citizen) than to strive for the maximization of a single profit goal. In any case, to maximize profits, a company's management would have to know the cost and revenue functions of every product the firm sells. For most firms, this information cannot be developed at a reasonable cost.

Cost-Based Approaches to Pricing

Although cost is not the only consideration in pricing, it has traditionally been the most important for several reasons.

- *Cost data are available.* When hundreds or thousands of different prices must be set in a short time, cost could be the only feasible basis for product pricing.

■ *Cost-based prices are defensible.* Managers threatened by legal action or public scrutiny feel secure using cost-based prices. They can argue that prices are set in a manner that provides a "fair" profit.

■ *Revenues must exceed costs if the firm is to remain in business.* In the long run, the selling price must exceed the full cost of each unit.

Cost-based pricing is illustrated in Exhibit 8.3. The process begins with market research to determine customer wants. If the product requires components to be designed and produced by vendors, the process of obtaining prices can be time consuming. When some costs, such as those fixed costs at the facility level, are not assigned to specific products, a markup is added to cover these costs. An additional markup is added to achieve a desired profit. The selling price is then set as the sum of the assigned costs, the markup to cover unassigned costs, and the markup to achieve the desired profit.

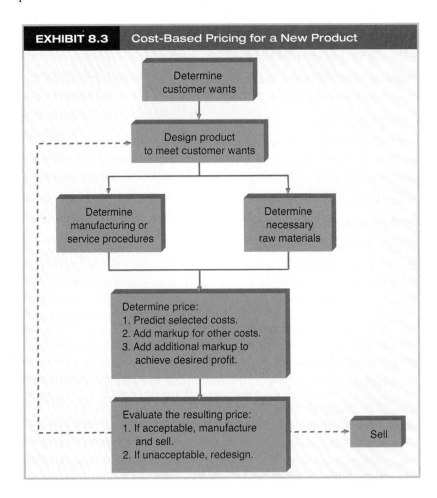

EXHIBIT 8.3 **Cost-Based Pricing for a New Product**

The proposed selling price should be evaluated with regard to competitive information and what customers are willing to pay. If the price is acceptable, the product or service is produced. If the price is too high, the product might be redesigned, manufacturing procedures might be changed, and different types of materials might be considered until either an acceptable price is achieved or it is determined that the product cannot be produced at an acceptable price. On the other hand, as the Business Insight below shows, the price can sometimes be a major driver of a company's growth.

Cost-Based Pricing in Single-Product Companies

Implementing cost-based pricing in a single-product company is straightforward if everything is known but the selling price. In this case, all known data are entered into the profit formula, which is then solved for the variable price. Assume that a ServiceMaster location's annual fixed

Advertisements Go Native Social networking sites have traditionally used display advertisements, and an advertiser measures its ads' effectiveness by capturing the number of "click-throughs" to the advertiser's home website. However, BuzzFeed is changing the definition of web advertising by using what is referred to as native advertisements. Native ads incorporate the content of a post and are incorporated seamlessly into the website's environment. With native ads, the advertiser is hoping for a "viral lift" instead of a click-through.

BuzzFeed is a website that aggregates upward-trending articles from publishing partners across the Internet, including Facebook, Google Plus, Twitter, and StumbleUpon. The more times content is flagged with a "Like" or some other kind of positive reader opinion or is shared with others by the original reader, the more likely the content will appear on BuzzFeed's site. The number of times content is shared defines its viral lift.

BuzzFeed is able to charge a premium price for native ads. On average, BuzzFeed charges $92,300 per native ad campaign. The company does this by convincing advertisers that BuzzFeed's branded content is a different animal than the oversaturated display ad market. With branded content, corporations create story-like advertisements by matching the underlying tone and technology of the host site. The company's advertising clients include General Electric, Kraft Foods, Dell, and McDonald's. One way managers can change the price the market will bear is by creating a whole new market. Such is the case with BuzzFeed and its native ads.

Sources: Benjy Boxer, "What BuzzFeed's Data Tells About the Pricing of Native Advertisements," *Forbes*, September 10, 2013; and Felix Gillette, "BuzzFeed, the Ad Model for the Facebook Era?" *Bloomberg Businessweek*, March 22, 2012.

facility-level costs are $200,000 and the unit cost of cleaning a rug is $10. Suppose management desires to achieve an annual profit of $30,000 at an annual volume of 10,000 rugs. To simplify the example, assume that management charges the same price regardless of the type, size, or shape of the rug. Using the profit formula, the cost-based price is determined to be $33:

$$\textbf{Profit} = \textbf{Total revenues} - \textbf{Total costs}$$

$$\textbf{\$30,000} = \textbf{(Price} \times \textbf{10,000 rugs)} - \textbf{(\$200,000} + \textbf{[\$10} \times \textbf{10,000 rugs])}$$

Solving for the price:

$$\textbf{(Price} \times \textbf{10,000)} = \textbf{\$300,000} + \textbf{\$30,000}$$

$$\textbf{Price} = \textbf{\$330,000} \div \textbf{10,000}$$

$$= \textbf{\$33}$$

A price of $33 to clean a rug will allow ServiceMaster to achieve its desired profit. However, before setting the price at $33, management should also evaluate the competitive situation and consider what customers are willing to pay for this service.

Cost-Based Pricing in Multiple-Product Companies

In multiple-product companies, desired profits are determined for the entire company, and standard procedures are established for determining the initial selling price of each product. These procedures typically specify the initial selling price as the costs assigned to products or services plus a markup to cover unassigned costs and provide for the desired profit. Depending on the sophistication of the organization's accounting system, possible cost bases in a manufacturing organization include markups based on a *combination of cost behavior and function*. The possible cost bases include:

■ Direct materials costs.

■ Variable manufacturing costs.

■ Total variable costs (manufacturing, selling, and administrative).

■ Full manufacturing costs.

Regardless of the cost base, the general approach to developing a markup is to recognize that the markup must be large enough to provide for costs not included in the base plus the desired profit.

$$\text{Markup on cost base} = \frac{\text{Costs not included in the base} + \text{Desired profit}}{\text{Costs included in the base}}$$

First we illustrate a pricing decision with variable costs as the cost base; full manufacturing costs is the cost base in the second illustration.

1. When the markup is based on variable costs, it must be large enough to cover all fixed costs and the desired profit. Assume that the predicted annual variable and fixed costs for one of Roku's divisions are are as follows:

Variable		Fixed	
Manufacturing	$600,000	Manufacturing	$300,000
Selling and administrative	200,000	Selling and administrative	100,000
Total	$800,000	Total	$400,000

Furthermore, assume that Roku's division has total assets of $1,250,000; management believes that an annual return of 16 percent on total assets is appropriate in Roku's industry. A 16 percent return translates into a desired annual profit of $200,000 ($1,250,000 × 0.16). Assuming all cost predictions are correct, obtaining a profit of $200,000 requires a 75 percent markup on variable costs:

$$\text{Markup on variable costs} = \frac{\$400,000 + \$200,000}{\$800,000}$$
$$= 0.75$$

If the predicted variable costs for Product A1 are $12 per unit, the initial selling price for Product A1 is $21:

$$\text{Initial selling price} = \$12 + (\$12 \times 0.75)$$
$$= \$21$$

2. When the markup is based on full manufacturing costs, it must be large enough to cover selling and administrative expenses and to provide for the desired profit. Again, it is necessary to determine the desired profit and predict all costs for the pricing period. The initial prices of individual products are then determined as their unit manufacturing costs plus the markup. For Roku, the markup on manufacturing costs would be 55.6 percent:

$$\text{Markup on manufacturing costs} = \frac{\$300,000 + \$200,000}{\$900,000}$$
$$= 0.556$$

If the predicted manufacturing costs for Product B1 are $10, the initial selling price for Product B1 is $15.56:

$$\text{Initial selling price} = \$10 + (\$10 \times 0.556)$$
$$= \$15.56$$

Cost-Based Pricing for Special Orders

Many organizations use cost-based pricing to bid on unique projects. If the project requires dedicated assets, the acquisition of new fixed assets, or an investment in employee training, the desired profit on the special order or project should allow for an adequate return on the dedicated assets or additional investment.

Critique of Cost-Based Pricing

Cost-based pricing has four major drawbacks:

1. Cost-based pricing requires accurate cost assignments. If costs are not accurately assigned, some products could be priced too high, losing market share to competitors; other products could be priced too low, gaining market share but being less profitable than anticipated.

2. The higher the portion of unassigned costs, the greater is the likelihood of over- or under-pricing individual products.

3. Cost-based pricing assumes that goods or services are relatively scarce and, generally, customers who want a product or service are willing to pay the price.

4. In a competitive environment, cost-based approaches increase the time and cost of bringing new products to market.

Cost-based pricing became the dominant approach to pricing during an era when products were relatively long-lived and there was relatively little competition. Also, these systems tend to focus on organizational units such as departments, plants, or divisions and not on activities or cost drivers. While easy to implement, reflecting the need to recover costs and earn a return on investment, and easily justified, cost-based prices might not be competitive. Competition puts intense downward pressure on prices and removes slack from pricing formulas. There is little margin for error in pricing. In a highly competitive market, small variations in pricing make significant differences in success.

MID-CHAPTER REVIEW

Assume that Penn, the tennis ball manufacturer's 2014 contribution income statement is as follows:

PENN
Contribution Income Statement
For Year Ended December 31, 2014

Sales (100,000 units at $12 per unit)		$1,200,000
Less variable costs		
Manufacturing	$300,000	
Selling and administrative	150,000	(450,000)
Contribution margin		750,000
Less fixed costs		
Manufacturing	400,000	
Selling and administrative	200,000	(600,000)
Net income		$ 150,000

Assume Penn has total assets of $2,000,000, and management desires an annual return of 10 percent on total assets.

Required

a. Determine the dollar amount by which Penn exceeded or fell short of the desired annual rate of return in 2014.

b. Given the current sales volume and cost structure, determine the unit selling price required to achieve an annual profit of $250,000.

c. Assume that management wants to state the selling price as a percentage of variable manufacturing costs. Given your answer to requirement (b) and the current sales volume and cost structure, determine the selling price as a percentage of variable manufacturing costs.

d. Restate your answer to requirement (c), dividing into two separate markup percentages:
   1. The markup on variable manufacturing costs required to cover unassigned costs.
   2. The additional markup on variable manufacturing costs required to achieve an annual profit of $250,000.

The solution is on page 294.

TARGET COSTING

LO3 Explain target costing and its acceptance in highly competitive industries.

Economists argue that cost-based prices are not realistic, because in the real world prices are determined by the confluence of supply and demand. However, when a new product is introduced into the market for which there is no previously existing supply or demand, there has to be a starting point. As discussed above, cost has often been the baseline for determining initial selling prices. All too often, however, companies introduce new products into the market based on what the designers and engineers "think" the market wants (or based on inadequate market research), only to find out later that either the market does not want the product, or it is not willing to buy the new product at a price sufficient to cover its cost plus an acceptable profit to the producer. This often leads to costly redesign, or in many cases, complete abandonment of the product, typically resulting in substantial financial losses.

Toyota, which has pioneered many innovations in manufacturing systems, turned the notion of cost-based pricing around and came up with the idea of price-based costing, referred to as target costing. Toyota determined that before a new product is introduced into the market, it must be able to be produced at a cost that will make it profitable when sold at a price acceptable to customers. The acceptable selling price to the marketplace determines the acceptable cost of producing the product.

Target Costing Is Proactive for Cost Management

Target costing starts with determining what customers are willing to pay for a product or service and then subtracts a desired profit on sales to determine the allowable, or target, cost of the product or service. This target cost is then communicated to a cross-functional team of employees representing such diverse areas as marketing, product design, manufacturing, and management accounting. Reflecting value chain concepts and the notion of partnerships up and down the value chain, suppliers of raw materials and components are often included in the teams. The target costing team is assigned the task of designing a product that meets customer price, function, and quality requirements while providing a desired profit. Its job is not completed until the target cost is met, or a determination is made that the product or service cannot be profitably introduced under the current circumstances. See Exhibit 8.4 for an overview of target costing.

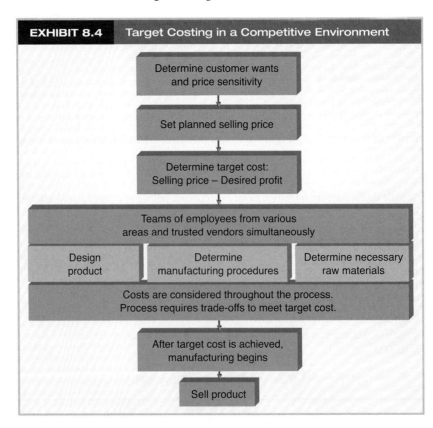

EXHIBIT 8.4 Target Costing in a Competitive Environment

Determine customer wants and price sensitivity

Set planned selling price

Determine target cost: Selling price – Desired profit

Teams of employees from various areas and trusted vendors simultaneously

Design product | Determine manufacturing procedures | Determine necessary raw materials

Costs are considered throughout the process. Process requires trade-offs to meet target cost.

After target cost is achieved, manufacturing begins

Sell product

Although a formula can be used to determine a markup on cost, it is not possible to develop a formula indicating how to achieve a target cost. Hence, target costing is not a technique. It is more a philosophy or an approach to pricing and cost management. It takes a proactive approach to cost management, reflecting the belief that costs are best managed by decisions made during product development. This contrasts with the more passive cost-plus belief that costs result from design, procurement, and manufacture. Like the value chain, target costing helps orient employees toward the final customer and reinforces the notion that all departments within the organization and all organizations along the value chain must work together. Target costing also empowers employees who will be assigned the responsibility for carrying out activities necessary to deliver a product or service with the authority to determine what activities will be selected. Like process mapping, it helps employees to better understand their role in serving the customer. The following Research Insight discusses how target costing can improve margins for companies engaged in global sourcing.

RESEARCH INSIGHT

Hitting a Moving Target in the Global Trade Economy Global sourcing raises complex new commercial and operational challenges by exposing firms to an entirely new set of variables, resulting in sourcing initiatives that often do not meet targeted costs or profits. A report by a leading trade services company attributes this to the failure to understand, track, and manage "the risks and costs of longer, more complex cross-border supply chains." The report cites target costing as an opportunity for improving global trading, stating that "dynamically tracking actual costs against previously set targets quickly uncovers targets that are unrealistic or inaccurate. Early visibility into the delta between targets and actual allows shippers to quickly adjust targets and modify plans for downstream product pricing and marketing campaigns. By reducing the lag in discovering unrealistic targets from months to weeks or even days, companies can save millions in lost profits."

Source: Patrick Burnson, "Improving Import/Export Operations: How to Hit a Moving Target," *Logistics Management*, April 1, 2010, p. 40.

Target Costing Encourages Design for Production

In the absence of a target costing approach, design engineers are apt to focus on incorporating leading-edge technology and the maximum number of features in a product. Target costing keeps the customer's function, quality, and price requirements in the forefront at all times. If customers do not want leading-edge technology (which could be expensive and untested) and several product features, they will resist paying for them. Focusing on achieving a target cost keeps design engineers tuned in to the final customer.

Left on their own, design engineers might believe that their job ends when they design a product that meets the customer's functional requirements. The tendency is to simply pass on the design to manufacturing and let manufacturing determine how best to produce the product. Further down the line, if the product needs servicing, it becomes the service department's responsibility to determine how best to service the product. A target costing approach forces design engineers to explicitly consider the costs of manufacturing and servicing a product while it is being designed. This is known as **design for manufacture**.

Minor changes in design that do not affect the product's functioning can often produce dramatic savings in manufacturing and servicing costs. Examples of design for manufacture include the following:

■ Using molded plastic parts to avoid assembling several small parts.

■ Designing two parts that must be fit together so that joining them in the correct manner is obvious to assembly workers.

■ Placing an access panel in the side of an appliance so service personnel can make repairs quickly.

■ Using standard-size parts to reduce inventory requirements, to reduce the possibility of assembly personnel inserting the incorrect part, and to simplify the job of service personnel.

■ Ensuring that tolerance requirements for parts that must fit together can be met with available equipment.

■ Using manufacturing procedures that are common to other products.

The successful implementation of target costing requires employees from all involved disciplines to be familiar with costing concepts and the notions of value-added and non-value-added activities. When considering the manufacturing process, team members should minimize non-value-added activities such as movement, storage, inspection, and setup. They should also select the lowest-cost value-added activities that do the job properly.

Target Costing Reduces Time to Introduce Products

By designing a product to meet a target cost (rather than evaluating the marketability of a product at a cost-plus price and having to recycle the design through several departments), target costing reduces the time required to introduce new products. Involving vendors in target costing design teams makes the vendors aware of the necessity of meeting a target cost. This facilitates the concurrent engineering of components to be produced outside the organization and reduces the time required to obtain components.

Target Costing Requires Cost Information

Implementing target costing requires detailed information on the cost of alternative activities. This information allows decision makers to select design and manufacturing alternatives that best meet function and price requirements. Tables that contain detailed databases of cost information for various manufacturing variables are occasionally used in designing products and selecting processes to meet target costs.

Target Costing Requires Coordination

Limitations of target costing are employee and supplier attitudes and the many meetings required to coordinate product design and to select manufacturing processes. All people involved must have a basic understanding of the overall processes required to bring a product to market and an appreciation of the cost consequences of alternative actions. They must also respect, cooperate, and communicate with other team members and be willing to engage in a negotiation process involving trade-offs. Finally, they must understand that although the total time required to bring a new product to market can be reduced, the countless coordinating meetings could be quite intrusive on the individuals' otherwise orderly schedule. See Exhibit 8.5 for an evaluation of target costing.

EXHIBIT 8.5   Pros and Cons of Target Costing
Pros
• Takes proactive approach to cost management.
• Orients organization toward customer.
• Breaks down barriers between departments.
• Enhances employee awareness and empowerment.
• Fosters partnerships with suppliers.
• Minimizes non-value-added activities.
• Encourages selection of lowest-cost value-added activities.
• Reduces time to market.
Cons
• To be effective, requires the development of detailed cost data.
• Requires willingness to cooperate.
• Requires many meetings for coordination.

This aspect of the process is even more difficult when suppliers must be brought in as part of the coordination process. This concept is frequently referred to as **chained target costing** because the supply chain's support is critical for the product to be both competitively priced and delivered to the final customer in a timely manner. When multiple suppliers are required, the organization must obtain everyone's support or the process will probably not be successful due to gaps in the reliability of delivery, quality, and cost control. Each organization and unit must understand that if the product is not brought to market within the defined constraints, all will lose. They must make firm commitments for the project undertaken and to have faith that each participant will carry out whatever part of the supply chain it has promised to fulfill. Coordination across the supply chain is vital in the overall process of continuous improvement as discussed later in this chapter.

Target Costing is Key for Products with Short Life Cycles

From a traditional marketing perspective, products with a relatively long life go through four distinct stages during their life cycle:

1. *Start-up.* Sales are low when a product is first introduced. Traditionally, initial selling prices are set high, and customers tend to be relatively affluent trendsetters.

2. *Growth.* Sales increase as the product gains acceptance. Traditionally, prices have remained high during this stage because of customer loyalty and the absence of competitive products.

3. *Maturity.* Sales level off as the product matures. Because of increased competition, pressure on prices is increasing; some price reductions could be necessary.

4. *Decline.* Sales decline as the product becomes obsolete. Significant price cuts could be required to sell remaining inventories.

Target costing is more important for products with a relatively short market life cycle. Products with a long life cycle present many opportunities to continuously improve design and manufacturing procedures that are not available when a product has a short life cycle. Hence, extra care must go into the initial planning for short-lived products. This is especially true when short product life cycles are combined with increased worldwide competition. It is important to introduce a product first and at a price that ensures rapid market penetration.

BUSINESS INSIGHT

Pricing Must Consider Your Customers' Purchasing Power New York–based Ralph Lauren is an upscale retailer of not only its signature brand, but also of Polo, Club Monaco, and Rugby, all of which are very popular with international consumers. To that end, the company has recently expanded its online shopping capability to European and Asian shoppers. It's a move that is paying off in German, British, and Scandinavian markets.

But the Japanese prime minister is ruining Ralph Lauren's party with his country's stimulus program. Japanese consumers are suffering from a reduction in buying power, such that U.S. goods are suddenly 15 percent higher in price than they were one year ago. This will significantly impact Ralph Lauren's operating results because 12 percent of the company's revenues are generated in Japan. If the company raises prices in Japan to counteract the slump in unit sales, it will only exacerbate the problem. This situation illustrates the importance of considering foreign currency exchange rate disparities when setting prices on goods targeted for export sales.

Source: Kyle Stock, "Why Ralph Lauren Is Worried About a Weakened Yen," *Bloomberg Businessweek*, June 5, 2013.

Target Costing Helps Manage Life Cycle Costs

An awareness of the impact of today's actions on tomorrow's costs underlies the notion of **life cycle costs,** which include all costs associated with a product or service ranging from those incurred with the initial conception through design, pre-production, production, and after-production support.

The lower line in Exhibit 8.6 illustrates the cumulative expenditure of funds over the life of a product. For low-technology products with relatively long product lives, decisions committing the organization to spend money are made at approximately the same time the money is spent. However, for high-technology products with relatively short product lives, most of the critical decisions affecting cost, such as product design and the selection of manufacturing procedures, are made before production begins. The top line in Exhibit 8.6 represents decisions committing the organization to expenditures for a product. It has been estimated that as much as 70 percent of the cost of the typical automobile, and 95 percent of the cost of high-technology products, is committed during the design stage.

| EXHIBIT 8.6 | Commitment and Expenditure for High-Technology Products with Relatively Short Product Lives |

* Production extends over the entire marketing life of a product: start-up, growth, maturity, and decline.

Reflecting significant changes in vehicle production since the time of Henry Ford and the Model T, General Motors estimates that 70 percent of the cost of manufacturing truck transmissions is determined during design. Others estimate that up to 95 percent of the total costs associated with high-technology products are committed before the first unit is produced.

Life cycle cost concepts have also been usefully applied to low-technology issues, such as repair versus replace decisions. The New York State Throughway Authority uses life cycle concepts to determine the point at which it is more expensive to repair than to replace bridges.

YOU MAKE THE CALL

You are the Vice President of Product Development As head of new product development for your electronics company, you are concerned that so many of the ideas for new products coming from your research and development group are not succeeding in the market. Many recent attempts to take new products to market have failed, not because of technological deficiencies in the products, but because the market would not support the high prices for new products that were necessary to produce a satisfactory profit. What should you do to try to reverse this trend of new product failures? [Answer, p. 285]

CONTINUOUS IMPROVEMENT COSTING

LO4 Describe the relation between target costing and continuous improvement costing.

Continuous improvement (Kaizen) costing calls for establishing cost reduction targets for products or services that an organization is currently providing to customers. Developed in Japan, this approach to cost management is often referred to as *Kaizen costing*. *Kaizen* means "continuous improvement" in Japanese. Continuous improvement costing begins where target costing ends. Target costing takes a proactive approach to cost management during the conception, design, and preproduction stages of a product's life; continuous improvement costing takes a proactive approach to cost management during the production stage of a product's life:

Time

Conception	Design	Preproduction	Production
	Target costing		Continuous improvement costing

Continuous improvement costing adds a specific target to be achieved during a time period to the target costing concept previously discussed. Basically, the mathematics of the concept is quite simple, but its implementation is difficult. Assume that **Publix** grocery stores wanted to reduce the cost of merchandise handling in each of its stores, and management set a target reduction of 2 percent a year. If a given store had current annual materials handling costs of $100,000 and expected an increase the next year due to 10 percent growth, the budget for the next year would be $107,800 [($100,000 × 1.10) × 0.98]. The budget for next year based on growth is $110,000 less the continuous improvement factor of 0.02.

Like target costing, Kaizen costing should be viewed as a serious attempt to make processes more efficient, while maintaining or improving quality, thereby making the company more competitive and profitable. In Kaizen costing, cost reductions can be achieved both internally and externally through continuous redesign and improved internal processes, and by working with vendors to improve their designs and processes. Kaizen is a team effort involving everyone who has an influence on costs. Kaizen is typically found in companies that have adopted a lean production philosophy. The following Business Insight discusses **Toshiba Corp.**'s use of Kaizen in its procurement processes.

Successful companies use continuous improvement costing to avoid complacency. Competitors are constantly striving to win market share through better quality or lower prices. **Hewlett-Packard** studied **Epson** to determine its strengths and weaknesses. To fend off competition, prices and costs must be continuously reduced. To maintain its competitive position, Hewlett-Packard has reduced the list price of the basic inkjet printer from nearly $400 when first introduced to less than $50 today. This could not have been done without continuous reductions in costs.

BUSINESS INSIGHT

Kaizen for Procurement at Toshiba   While **Toshiba Corp.**'s television business generated profits for the past three years, its primary rivals, **Sony** and **Panasonic**, were mired in red ink. Its success against makers of low-priced electronics is attributed largely to the use of Kaizen, or continuous improvement, in its procurement processes. This has led to several key changes in how it deals with suppliers. First, recognizing that the cost of making televisions is directly tied to the cost of acquiring the LCD panels, Toshiba made a first-in-the-industry decision to integrate the procurement of LCD panels for its television and personal computer divisions. Vice President of Procurement, Hisao Tanaka, said that "by combining procurement of the two products, our purchasing power is one of the strongest among global electronics makers." Toshiba also plans to cut costs by about 1 trillion yen (about $12 billion) over the next three years by expanding its business with original design manufacturers (ODMs), which are contract companies that manufacture products for many of the electronics firms, including Apple and HP. Other cost cutting measures at Toshiba include adopting design for improvement, where procurement staff is involved from the product planning and design stage, and assigning technology and procurement experts to factories to carry out Kaizen to enhance product quality and reduce costs.

Source: Masamichi Hoshi, "Kaizen Can Be Applied to Procurement, Toshiba Finds," *Nikkei Weekly*, November 15, 2010.

The "Toyota Way" describes **Toyota's** method to set Kaizen cost reduction targets for each cost element, including purchased parts per car, direct materials per car, labor hours per car, and office utilities. Performance reports developed at the end of each month compare targeted and actual cost reductions. If actual cost reductions are more than the targeted cost reductions, the results are favorable; if the actual cost reductions are less than the targeted cost reductions, the results are unfavorable.

Because cost reduction targets are set before it is known how they will be achieved, continuous improvement costing can be stressful to employees. A critical element in motivating employee cooperation and teamwork in aggressive cost management techniques, such as target and continuous improvement costing, is to avoid using performance reports to place blame for failure. The proper response to an unfavorable performance report must be an offer of assistance to correct the failure.

BENCHMARKING

LO5 Explain how benchmarking enhances quality management, continuous improvement, and process reengineering.

When Hewlett-Packard studies Epson to identify Epson's strengths and weaknesses, each company is engaging in *benchmarking*, a practice that has been around for centuries. In recent years, however, as globalization and increased competitiveness have forced businesses to more aggressively compete on the bases of cost, quality, and service, benchmarking has become more formalized and open. No longer regarded as spying, **benchmarking** is now a systematic approach to identifying the best practices to help an organization take action to improve performance.

The formalization of benchmarking is largely attributed to a book written in the 1980s by Robert Camp of Xerox. Since then, many managers have come to believe that benchmarking is a requirement for success. Although benchmarking can focus on anything of interest, it typically deals with target costs for a product, service, or operation, customer satisfaction, quality, inventory levels, inventory turnover, cycle time, and productivity. Benchmarking initially focused on studying competitors, but benchmarking efforts have changed dramatically in recent years to include competitors, as well as companies in very different industries. For example, an electronics company like Samsung may benchmark its order fulfillment processes against Amazon, or a grocery company like the Kroger Company may benchmark its inventory management processes against an apparel company like Gap.

In considering how to go about benchmarking, an organization must be careful because it must consider nonfinancial limitations. No single numerical measurement can completely describe the performance of a complex device such as a microprocessor or a television camera, but benchmarks can be useful tools for comparing different products, components, and systems. The only totally accurate way to measure the performance of a given product is to test it against other products while performing the exact same activity. The following Business Insight box describes how Intel Corporation makes benchmarks available with some information on how to use them.

BUSINESS INSIGHT

Intel Benchmarks Performance Intel Corporation divides its benchmarks into two types, component and system. *Component benchmarks* measure the performance of specific parts of a computer system, such as a microprocessor or hard disk drive. *System benchmarks* typically measure the performance of the entire computer system. The performance obtained will almost certainly vary from benchmark performance for a number of reasons. First, individual components must usually be tested in a complete computer system, and it is not always possible to eliminate the considerable effects that differences in system design and configuration have on benchmark results. For instance, vendors sell systems with a wide variety of disk capabilities and speeds, system memory, and video and graphics capabilities, all of which influence how the system components perform in actual use. Differences in software, including operating systems and compilers, also affect component and system performance. Finally, benchmark tests are typically written to be exemplary for only a certain type of computer application, which might or might not be similar to what is being compared.

A benchmark is, at most, only one type of information that an organization might use during the purchasing or manufacturing process. To get a true picture of the performance of a component or system being considered, the organization should consult industry sources, publicly available research reports, and even government publications of related information.

Source: As described on the Intel website at http://www.intel.com/performance/resources/benchmark_limitations.htm

Benchmarking provides measurements that are useful in setting goals. It can lead to dramatic innovations, and it can help overcome resistance to change. When presented with a major cost reduction target, employees often believe they are being asked to do the impossible. Benchmarking can be a psychological tool that helps overcome resistance to change by showing how others have already met the target.

Although each organization has its own approach to benchmarking, the following six steps are typical:

1. Decide what to benchmark.
2. Plan the benchmark project.
3. Understand your own performance.
4. Study others.
5. Learn from the data.
6. Take action.

In recent years, professional organizations, such as the Institute of Management Accountants, have set up clearinghouses for benchmark information or have performed benchmarking studies of interest to members as have certain corporations such as Intel.

CHAPTER-END REVIEW

Honda has been conducting early-stage research on hydrogen powered automobiles and is nearing the point where product development will soon begin. In order to determine the feasibility of the product, assume Honda has conducted marketing research that indicates that the price target for the product must be no more than $35,000 if it is to appeal to a large enough market segment to sell a minimum of 150,000 automobiles in the first year of production. The CFO has indicated that the new product must meet a 15% minimum profit margin requirement.

Required
a. Calculate the target cost per unit to produce the hydrogen powered automobile.
b. How would Honda go about determining whether the target cost can be achieved?
c. What should Honda do if the estimated cost to produce the product exceeds the target cost?

The solution is on page 295.

GUIDANCE ANSWERS . . . YOU MAKE THE CALL

You are the Vice President of Product Development You should consider adopting target costing methods for new product development. Great product research ideas are successful only when they translate into products that can be produced and sold for an acceptable profit. Creating and producing new products before determining what the customer wants and is willing to pay often leads to failure. Target costing methods reverse this process by applying value chain concepts to bring customers and suppliers along the value chain together to produce a product only if it has features and a selling price that are acceptable to potential customers, and if its production costs allow the seller to make an acceptable profit.

KEY RATIOS

$$\text{Markup on cost base} = \frac{\text{Costs not included in the base} + \text{Desired profit}}{\text{Costs included in the base}}$$

KEY TERMS

activity 270	design for manufacture 279	processes 270
benchmarking 284	life cycle costs 281	target costing 278
chained target costing 281	marginal cost 273	value chain 268
continuous improvement (Kaizen) costing 282	marginal revenue 273	virtual integration 272

MULTIPLE CHOICE

1. In a value chain analysis:
   - *a.* The links of the chain are the various entities beginning with the producers of raw materials and ending with the final customer
   - *b.* Processes are collections of related activities intended to achieve a common purpose, such as procurement or production
   - *c.* Activities are the units of work that take place within the various processes, such as moving products from one work station to another
   - *d.* All of the above

2. In a cost-based pricing model, the markup percentage is determined by an equation that:
   - *a.* Has the cost base in the denominator and any remaining costs plus the desired profit in the numerator.
   - *b.* Has variable costs plus fixed costs in the denominator and total profit in the numerator
   - *c.* Always has only variable costs in the numerator
   - *d.* Always has desired profit as part of the denominator

3. Brown manufacturing makes profits with varying pricing structures, but it wants to determine the minimum markup percentage for all products based on manufacturing costs that will ensure that it does not fall below break-even point. It has estimated the following costs for the coming year for its planned production of all products.

Variable manufacturing costs	$600,000
Fixed manufacturing costs	200,000
Selling expenses	100,000
Administrative expenses.	150,000

   The markup percentage required for Brown Company to break even is:
   - *a.* 320%
   - *b.* 31.25%
   - *c.* 75%
   - *d.* Cannot be determined unless desired profit is known

4. Electronics, Inc. is considering producing a new MP3 player that will offer several new features, including wireless earphones and wireless download of music and videos from any computer to the device. After much market research, it has determined that the appropriate target price for the new product is $90. To achieve its normal minimum profit margin of 20 percent, Electronics must be able to produce the product at a maximum total cost of:
   - *a.* $108
   - *b.* $70
   - *c.* $72
   - *d.* $18

5. Orange, Inc. produces electronic devices such as computers and cell phones. It has recently introduced a digital reader, called the e-pad, but realizes that to compete effectively in the future, it must be able to lower the cost of production and the selling price. The current cost per unit for producing the e-pad is $138, and Orange is estimating inflation on e-pad components and supplies purchased externally to be 1.5 percent in the coming year. In the most recent period, these items had a cost of $74. Despite these cost increases, Orange has adopted a Kaizen cost improvement model that targets a 5 percent cost decrease. Orange's Kaizen cost target (rounded to two decimal places) for the e-pad is:
   - *a.* $131.11
   - *b.* $132.15
   - *c.* $133.07
   - *d.* $130.05

DISCUSSION QUESTIONS

Q8-1. What are the relationships among an organization's value chain, processes, and activities?

Q8-2. What should be the goal of every organization along the value chain?

Q8-3. Distinguish between the value-added perspective and the value chain perspective.

Q8-4. Why are economic models seldom used for day-to-day pricing decisions?

Q8-5. Identify three reasons that cost-based approaches to pricing have traditionally been important.

Q8-6. Identify four drawbacks to cost-based pricing.

Q8-7. How does target costing differ from cost-based pricing?

Q8-8. Why is cost-based pricing more a technique, and target costing is more a philosophy? Which approach takes a more proactive approach to cost management?

Q8-9. Distinguish between the marketing life cycles of products incorporating advanced technology (such as household electronic equipment) and those using more traditional technology (such as household paper products). Why would life cycle costing be more important to a manufacturer of household electronic equipment than to a manufacturer of household paper products?

Q8-10. What is the relationship between target costing and continuous improvement (Kaizen) costing?

Q8-11. Distinguish between the seller's and the buyer's perspective of life cycle costs.

Q8-12. What advantage is derived from benchmarking against firms other than competitors?

Assignments with the ✅ logo in the margin are available in *my*BusinessCourse.
See the Preface of the book for details.

MINI EXERCISES

M8-13. Developing a Value Chain from the Perspective of the Final Customer   **LO1**
Prepare a value chain for bottled orange juice that was purchased for personal consumption at an on-campus cafeteria.

M8-14. Developing a Value Chain: Upstream and Downstream Entities   **LO1**
Prepare a value chain for a firm that produces gasoline fuel. Clearly identify upstream and downstream entities in the value chain.

M8-15. Classifying Activities Using the Generic Internal Value Chain: Aluminum Cable Manufacturer   **LO1**
Using the generic internal value chain shown in Exhibit 8.2, classify each of the following activities of an aluminum cable manufacturer as inbound logistics, operations, outbound logistics, marketing and sales, service, or support.
a.   Advertising in a construction magazine
b.   Inspecting incoming aluminum ingots
c.   Placing bar codes on coils of finished products
d.   Borrowing money to finance a buildup of inventory
e.   Hiring new employees
f.   Heating aluminum ingots
g.   Drawing wire from aluminum ingots
h.   Coiling wire
i.   Visiting a customer to determine the cause of cable breakage
j.   Filing tax returns

LO1 **M8-16. Classifying Activities Using the Generic Internal Value Chain: Cable TV Company**

Using the generic internal value chain shown in Exhibit 8.2, classify each of the following activities of a cable television company as inbound logistics, operations, outbound logistics, marketing and sales, service, or support.

 a. Installing coaxial cable in the apartment of a new customer
 b. Repairing coaxial cable after a windstorm
 c. Mailing brochures to prospective customers
 d. Discussing a rate increase with members of a regulatory agency
 e. Selling shares of stock in the company
 f. Monitoring the quality of reception at the company's satellite downlink
 g. Preparing financial statements
 h. Visiting a customer to determine the cause of poor-quality television reception
 i. Traveling to a conference to learn about technological changes affecting the industry
 j. Replacing old routers with updated technology

LO2 **M8-17. Product Pricing: Single Product**

SUE BEE HONEY

Sue Bee Honey is one of the largest processors of its product for the retail market. Assume that one of its plants has annual fixed costs totalling $8,000,000, of which $3,000,000 is for administrative and selling efforts. Sales are anticipated to be 800,000 cases a year. Variable costs for processing are $20 per case, and variable selling expenses are 25 percent of selling price. There are no variable administrative expenses.

Required

If the company desires a profit of $5,000,000, what is the selling price per case?

LO2 **M8-18. Product Pricing: Single Product**

Assume that you plan to open a soft ice cream franchise in a resort community during the summer months. Fixed operating costs for the three-month period are projected to be $5,650. Variable costs per serving include the cost of the ice cream and cone, $0.50, and a franchise fee payable to Austrian Ice, AG, $0.15. A market analysis prepared by Austrian Ice indicates that summer sales in the resort community should total 24,000 units.

Required

Determine the price you should charge for each ice cream cone to achieve a $20,000 profit for the three-month period.

LO3 **M8-19. Target Pricing**

A few years ago, Marriott International, the large hotel chain, announced that because occupancy rates had declined during the previous quarter, it was raising room rates to cover the cost of its increase in vacant rooms. Although not referring to accounting or economics, several business journalists during the week following the announcement questioned the basis for the rate increases. One stated that "Marriott increases rates of vacant rooms."

Required

 a. Did the journalist mean that vacant rooms would be more expensive? Explain.
 b. Do you think Marriott's action to raise room rates was based on economics, accounting, or both?

LO5 **M8-20. Benchmarking**

Your company is developing a new product for the computer printer industry. You have talked to several material vendors about being able to supply quality components for the new product. The product designers are satisfied with the company's ability to make the product in the current facilities. Numerous potential customers also have been surveyed, and most have indicated a willingness to buy the product if the price is competitive.

Required

What are some means of benchmarking the development and production of your new product?

EXERCISES

E8-21. Product Pricing: Single Product

Presented is the 2014 contribution income statement of Colgate Products.

COLGATE PRODUCTS Contribution Income Statement For Year Ended December 31, 2014		
Sales (13,000 units).....................................		$1,560,000
Less variable costs		
Cost of goods sold	$520,000	
Selling and administrative..................................	143,000	(663,000)
Contribution margin		897,000
Less fixed costs		
Manufacturing overhead...................................	520,000	
Selling and administrative..................................	210,000	(730,000)
Net income..		$ 167,000

During the coming year, Colgate expects an increase in variable manufacturing costs of $8 per unit and in fixed manufacturing costs of $35,000.

Required

a. If sales for 2015 remain at 13,000 units, what price should Colgate charge to obtain the same profit as last year?

b. Management believes that sales can be increased to 16,000 units if the selling price is lowered to $107. Is this action desirable?

c. After considering the expected increases in costs, what sales volume is needed to earn a profit of $167,000 with a unit selling price of $107?

E8-22. Cost-Based Pricing and Markups with Variable Costs

Compu Services provides computerized inventory consulting. The office and computer expenses are $625,000 annually and are not assigned to specific jobs. The consulting hours available for the year total 20,000, and the average consulting hour has $30 of variable costs.

Required

a. If the company desires a profit of $100,000, what should it charge per hour?

b. What is the markup on variable costs if the desired profit is $150,000?

c. If the desired profit is $60,000, what is the markup on variable costs to cover (1) unassigned costs and (2) desired profit?

E8-23. Computing Markups

The predicted 2014 costs for Osaka Motors are as follows:

Manufacturing Costs		Selling and Administrative Costs	
Variable	$100,000	Variable	$300,000
Fixed	220,000	Fixed	200,000

Average total assets for 2014 are predicted to be $5,000,000.

Required

a. If management desires a 12 percent rate of return on total assets, what are the markup percentages based on total variable costs and based on total manufacturing costs?

b. If the company desires a 10 percent rate of return on total assets, what is the markup percentage on total manufacturing costs for (1) unassigned costs and (2) desired profit?

E8-24. Product Pricing: Two Products

Quality Data manufactures two products, CDs and DVDs, both on the same assembly lines and packaged 10 disks per pack. The predicted sales are 400,000 packs of CDs and 500,000 packs of DVDs. The predicted costs for the year 2014 are as follows:

	Variable Costs	Fixed Costs
Materials	$200,000	$500,000
Other	250,000	800,000

Each product uses 50 percent of the materials costs. Based on manufacturing time, 40 percent of the other costs are assigned to the CDs, and 60 percent of the other costs are assigned to the DVDs. The management of Quality Data desires an annual profit of $100,000.

Required

a. What price should Quality Data charge for each disk pack if management believes the DVDs sell for 20 percent more than the CDs?

b. What is the total profit per product using the selling prices determined in part *a*?

LO2 **E8-25.** **Product Pricing: Two Products**

Refer to the previous exercise, E8-24. Based on your calculations of the selling price and profit for CDs and DVDs, how should Quality Data evaluate the status of these two products? Should either CDs or DVDs be discontinued? What additional information does the management of Quality Data need in order to make an appropriate judgment on the future status of these two products?

LO3 **E8-26.** **Target Costing**

Oregon Equipment Company wants to develop a new log-splitting machine for rural homeowners. Market research has determined that the company could sell 6,000 log-splitting machines per year at a retail price of $700 each. An independent catalog company would handle sales for an annual fee of $2,000 plus $50 per unit sold. The cost of the raw materials required to produce the log-splitting machines amounts to $80 per unit.

Required

If company management desires a return equal to 10 percent of the final selling price, what is the target unit cost?

PROBLEMS

LO2 **P8-27.** **Product Pricing: Two Products**

MACQUARIUM INTELLIGENT COMMUNICATIONS

Macquarium Intelligent Communications provides computer-related services to its clients. Its two primary services are are Web page design (WPD), and Internet consulting services (ICS). Assume that Macquarium's management expects to earn a 20 percent annual return on the assets invested. Macquarium has invested $8 million since its opening. The annual costs for the coming year are expected to be as follows:

	Variable Costs	Fixed Costs
Consulting support	$500,000	$1,050,000
Sales and administration	100,000	850,000

The two services expend about equal costs per hour, and the predicted hours for the coming year are 40,000 for WPD and 20,000 for ICS.

Required

a. If markup is based on variable costs, how much revenue must each service generate to provide the profit expected by corporate headquarters? What is the anticipated revenue per hour for each service?

b. If the markup is based on total costs, how much revenue must each service generate to provide the expected profit?

c. Explain why answers in requirements (*a*) and (*b*) are either the same or different.

d. Comment on the advantages and disadvantages of using a cost-based pricing model.

LO3 **P8-28.** **Target Costing**

REDBACK NETWORKS, INC.

Redback Networks, Inc., a subsidiary of Ericsson, provides networking services and related systems for 75 percent of the world's largest telephone companies. Assume that it is developing a new networking system for smaller, private telephone companies. To attract small companies, Redback must keep the price low without giving up too many of the features of larger networking systems. A marketing research study conducted on the company's behalf found that the price range must be $50,000 to $75,000. Management has determined a target price to be $60,000. The company's minimum profit percentage of sales is normally 25 percent, but the company is willing to reduce it to 18 percent to get the new product on the market. The fixed costs for the first year are anticipated to be $8,000,000. If sales reach 500 installed networks, the company needs to know how much it can spend on variable costs, which are primarily related to installation.

Required

a. What is the amount of total cost allowed if the 18 percent profit target is allowed and the sales target is met? Show the amount for fixed and for variable costs.

b. What is the amount of total costs allowed if the 25 percent normal profit target is desired at the 500 sales target? Show the amount for fixed and for variable costs.

c. Discuss the advantages of using a target costing model versus using cost-based pricing.

P8-29. Continuous Improvement (Kaizen) Costing   LO4

Patel Company does contract manufacturing of compact video cameras. At its Pacific plant, cost control has become a concern of management. The actual costs per unit for the years 2013 and 2014 were as follows:

	2013		2014	
Direct materials				
Plastic case	$ 4.50		$ 4.40	
Lens set	17.00		17.20	
Electrical component set.	6.60		5.70	
Film track	11.00		10.00	
Direct labor	32.00	(1.6 hours)	30.00	(1.5 hours)
Indirect manufacturing costs				
Variable.	7.50		7.10	
Fixed.	3.00	(100,000 unit base)	2.85	(120,000 unit base)

The company manufactures all of the camera components except the lens sets, which it purchases from several vendors. The company has used target costing in the past but has not been able to meet the very competitive global pricing. Beginning in 2014, the company implemented a continuous improvement program that requires cost reduction targets.

Required

a. If continuous improvement (Kaizen) costing sets a first-year target of a 5 percent reduction of the 2013 base, how successful was the company in meeting 2014 per unit cost reduction targets? Support your answer with appropriate computations.

b. Evaluate and discuss Patel's use of Kaizen costing.

P8-30. Continuous Improvement (Kaizen) Costing   LO4

Assume that GE Capital, a division of **General Electric**, has been displeased with the costs of ser-   GENERAL ELECTRIC
vicing its consumer loans. Assume that it has decided to implement a Kaizen-based cost improve-
ment program. For 2014, GE Capital incurred the following costs:

Loan processing	$15,500,000
Customer relations	3,000,000
Printing, mailing, and postage	700,000

For the next two years, GE Capital expects an increase in consumer loans of 4 percent annually with related increases in costs.

Required

a. If the company has a continuous improvement goal of 2 percent each year, develop a budget for the next two years for the consumer loan department.

b. Identify some possible ways that GE Capital can achieve the Kaizen costing goal.

c. Discuss the potential benefits and limitations of GE's Kaizen costing model.

P8-31. **Price Setting: Multiple Products**

Comtel Electronics Company's predicted 2014 variable and fixed costs are as follows:

	Variable Costs	Fixed Costs
Manufacturing	$400,000	$260,000
Selling and administrative.	180,000	50,400
Total	$580,000	$310,400

Comtel Electronics, Inc., is a small company producing a wide variety of computer interface devices. Per-unit manufacturing cost information about one of these products, a high-capacity flash drive, is as follows:

Direct materials	$ 8
Direct labor	7
Manufacturing overhead.	
Variable.	5
Fixed.	7
Total manufacturing costs.	$27

Variable selling and administrative costs for the flash drive is $4 per unit. Management has set a 2014 target profit of $200,000 on the sale of the flash drive.

Required

a. Determine the markup percentage on variable costs required to earn the desired profit.

b. Use variable cost markup to determine a suggested selling price for the flash drive.

c. For the flash drive, break the markup on variable costs into separate parts for fixed costs and profit. Explain the significance of each part.

d. Determine the markup percentage on manufacturing costs required to earn the desired profit.

e. Use the manufacturing costs markup to determine a suggested selling price for the flash drive.

f. Evaluate the variable and the manufacturing cost approaches to determine the markup percentage.

P8-32. **Price Setting: Multiple Products**

Augusta Golf, Inc. produces a wide variety of golfing equipment. In the past, product managers set prices using their professional judgment. Jack Woods, the new controller, believes this practice has led to the significant underpricing of some products (with lost profits) and the significant overpricing of other products (with lost sales volume). You have been asked to assist Woods in developing a corporate approach to pricing. The output of your work should be a cost-based formula that can be used to develop initial selling prices for each product. Although product managers are allowed to adjust these prices to meet competition and to take advantage of market opportunities, they must explain such deviations in writing. The following 2014 cost information from the accounting records is available:

	Manufacturing Costs	Selling and Administrative Costs
Variable	$350,000	$ 75,000
Fixed	100,000	200,000

In 2014, Augusta Golf reported earnings of $120,000. However, the controller believes that proper pricing should produce earnings of at least $150,000 on the same sales mix and unit volume. Accordingly, you are to use the preceding cost information and a target profit of $150,000 in developing a cost-based pricing formula. Selling and administrative expenses are not currently associated with individual products. However, you have obtained the following unit production cost information for the Tiger Irons:

Variable manufacturing costs	$150
Fixed manufacturing costs	50
Total	$200

Required

a. Determine the standard markup percentage for each of the following cost bases. Round answers to two decimal places.

1. Full costs, including fixed and variable manufacturing costs, and fixed and variable selling and administrative costs.
2. Manufacturing costs plus variable selling and administrative costs.
3. Manufacturing costs.
4. Variable costs.
5. Variable manufacturing costs.

b. Explain why the markup percentages become progressively larger from requirement (*a*), parts (1) through (5).

c. Determine the initial price of a set of Tiger Irons using the manufacturing cost markup and the variable manufacturing cost markup.

d. Do you believe the controller's approach to product pricing is reasonable? Why or why not?

CASES AND PROJECTS

C8-33. **Telephone Pole Rental Rates**

LO2, 3

Most utility poles carry electric and telephone lines. In areas served by cable television, they also carry television cables. However, cable television companies rarely own any utility poles. Instead, they pay utility companies a rental fee for the use of each pole on a yearly basis. The determination of the rental fee is a source of frequent disagreement between the pole owners and the cable television companies. In one situation, pole owners were arguing for a $10 annual rental fee per pole; this was the standard rate the electric and telephone companies charged each other for the use of poles.

"We object to that," stated the representative of the cable television company. "With two users, the $10 fee represents a rental fee for one-half the pole. This fee is too high because we only use about six inches of each 40-foot pole."

"You are forgetting federal safety regulations," responded a representative of the electric company. "They specify certain distances between different types of lines on a utility pole. Television cables must be a minimum of 40 inches below power lines and 12 inches above telephone lines. If your cable is added to the pole, the total capacity is reduced because this space cannot be used for anything else. Besides, we have an investment in the poles; you don't. We should be entitled to a fair return on this investment. Furthermore, speaking of fair, your company should pay the same rental fee that the telephone company pays us and we pay them. We do not intend to change this fee."

In response, the cable television company representative made two points. First, any fee represents incremental income to the pole owners because the cable company would pay all costs of moving existing lines. Second, because the electric and telephone companies both strive to own the same number of poles in a service area, their pole rental fees cancel themselves. Hence, the fee they charge each other is not relevant.

Required

Evaluate the arguments presented by the cable television and electric company representatives. What factors should be considered in determining a pole rental fee?

C8-34. **Target Costing**

LO3

The president of Houston Electronics was pleased with the company's newest product, the HE Versatile CVD. The product is portable and can be attached to a computer to play or record computer programs or sound, attached to an amplifier to play or record music, or attached to a television to play or record TV programs. It can even be attached to a camcorder to record videos directly on compact disks rather than on tape. It also can be used with a headset to play or record sound. The proud president announced that this unique and innovative product would be an important factor in reestablishing the North American consumer electronics industry.

Based on development costs and predictions of sales volume, manufacturing costs, and distribution costs, the cost-based price of the HE Versatile CVD was determined to be $425. Following a market-skimming strategy, management set the initial selling price at $525. The marketing plan was to reduce the selling price by $50 during each of the first two years of the product's life to obtain the highest contribution possible from each market segment.

The initial sales of the HE Versatile CVD were strong, and Houston Electronics found itself adding second and third production shifts. Although these shifts were expensive, at a selling price of $525, the product had ample contribution margin to remain highly profitable. The president was talking with the company's major investors about the desirability of obtaining financing for a major plant expansion when the bad news arrived. A foreign company had announced that it would shortly introduce a similar product that would incorporate new design features and sell for only $350. The president was shocked. "Why," she remarked, "it costs us $375 to put a complete unit in the hands of customers."

Required

How could the foreign competitor profitably sell a similar product for less than the manufacturing costs to Houston Electronics? What advice do you have for the president concerning the HE Versatile CVD? What advice would you have to help the company avoid similar problems in the future?

SOLUTIONS TO REVIEW PROBLEMS

Mid-Chapter Review

Solution

a.

Desired annual profit ($2,000,000 × 0.10)		$200,000
Actual profit		(150,000)
Amount actual profit fell short of achieving the desired return		$ 50,000

b.

Predicted costs		
Variable	$450,000	
Fixed	600,000	$1,050,000
Desired profit		250,000
Required revenue		$1,300,000
Unit sales		÷ 100,000
Required unit selling price		$ 13

c.

Variable manufacturing costs per unit ($300,000/100,000 unit)	= $3
Selling price as a percent of variable manufacturing costs	= $13/3
	= $433\tfrac{1}{3}$%
Markup as a percent of variable manufacturing costs ($10/$3)	= $333\tfrac{1}{3}$%

d. Detail of markup on variable manufacturing costs:

1.	Unassigned costs		
	Variable selling and administrative	$150,000	
	Fixed costs	600,000	$750,000
	Variable manufacturing costs		÷300,000
	Markup on variable manufacturing costs to cover unassigned costs		250%
2.	Desired profit		$250,000
	Variable manufacturing costs		÷300,000
	Additional markup on variable manufacturing costs to achieve desired profit ($250,000)		83\tfrac{1}{3}%

Chapter-End Review

Solution

a.

Total revenue (150,000 × $35,000)	$5,250,000,000
Required profit margin (15%)	−787,500,000
Total cost	$4,462,500,000
Number of units.	÷ 150,000
Target cost per unit	$ 29,750

b. A new product such as an automobile is an extremely complex product with hundreds, if not thousands, of different components, involving many different vendors. Once Honda has determined what product features potential customers want, its engineers must determine how best to provide those features, working with vendors and potential vendors. The idea is to determine how best to provide the final product that the customers want at a cost that will provide a reasonable profit to Honda and its vendors.

c. Teams of engineers, accountants, designers, etc. from Honda and its vendors should work together to try to achieve the target cost. If initial cost estimates are too high, they should explore every possibility, including redesign of the product, using components from existing products, developing new production systems, etc. to meet the target cost. If it is finally determined that the target cannot be reached, then management has to decide if it is willing to go forward with the product with a lower than desired initial profit margin. In some cases, managers will proceed with the idea that additional cost savings will be found (using Kaizen costing methods) after the product is in production.

Operational Budgeting and Profit Planning

Every experienced executive knows that budgeting is the lifeblood of a business enterprise. It is the mechanism by which we plan the entity's operations for the upcoming year, or even decade. It's the way we quantitatively communicate those plans and coordinate the employees' efforts throughout the organization. The budget is unambiguous and unassailable; you either make your numbers or you don't, which makes the budget a valuable feedback loop by which to evaluate past operations. More important, preparing a budget alerts management ahead of time to the risks faced by the entity in the coming periods, whether those risks are a shortage of cash, too few or too many employees, or idle versus excess capacity.

PINTEREST
www.pinterest.com

Each period, businesses prepare what is called a "master budget." The master budget covers every aspect of the financial (and often nonfinancial) operations. The first step in the master budget is to budget or forecast sales revenue. But how do you prepare a budget for a company that generates zero revenue? Pinterest has, at last count, 54 million users and has been valued at $2.5 billion. Pinterest is the third-most-popular social networking site behind Facebook and Twitter, but the company has sales revenue of zero! However, its revenue will not be zero for long. The company is working with businesses to understand how Pinterest traffic can generate sales revenue for those businesses by advertising on Pinterest. The advertising fees paid by those companies will eventually lead to a positive revenue stream for Pinterest. The way Pinterest generates traffic on its site is by allowing members use the site as a virtual scrapbook, "pinning" places that they'd eventually like to travel to, recipes that they'd eventually like to prepare, and items that they'd eventually like to buy. These members are highly dedicated, spending an average of 89 minutes on the site per month compared to 21 minutes per month for the average Twitter user.

Pinterest recently introduced corporate memberships that allow companies to use their corporate name on their pinboards. J. Crew is offering its Pinterest followers a sneak peak of the company's fall lineup before the items hit the store shelves. And with good reason—21 percent of Pinterest users eventually buy the items they pin on their boards. Nordstrom is using Pinterest in the opposite way by tagging items in brick-and-mortar Nordstrom stores that have been most popular on Pinterest. Nordstrom is also leveraging Pinterest data to aid in its inventory management. Nordstrom has developed an application that tracks the products with the most pins to make sure it has an adequate supply in the stores and online to avoid stockouts of those popular products.

Even though the benefit to potential advertisers is clear cut, Pinterest wants to make sure its future advertising revenue is sustainable. The company is in the process of running test ads, free of charge to advertisers, while it gathers feedback on members' responses to the format, frequency, and placement of the test ads. From a budgeting perspective, the company may need to prepare its sales budget using several what-if scenarios to help it determine the proper pricing for its future advertisements. In

continued on following page

continued from previous page

the meantime, Pinterest will need to develop expense budgets for everything from labor to selling to general and administrative expenses. In the last year, the company has gone from 20 employees to expected employment of over 200 in the next year, including new hires from Facebook, Google, and Amazon. It has moved from a small office in Palo Alto, California, to a sprawling 58,000-square-foot space in San Francisco. It has invested in major information technology systems to extend its applications to mobile platforms. Further, it is developing advanced data-analytic tools to better assist its future advertisers with tracking how members are interacting with their content.

Clearly, Pinterest is an evolving, dynamic company, but it will have to pay close attention to its budgeting (even without generating revenue) to manage its cash flow and capital investments. More important, if it wants to continue to raise funds from external sources, those investors and creditors will want to analyze the company's forecasted financial statements to estimate the expected rate of return on their investment in Pinterest. The budgeting techniques discussed in this chapter will aid the manager in planning and managing the organization's revenues, costs, and other quantitative variables in the face of constantly changing business conditions.

Sources: Robert Hof, "Pinterest: Here Come the Ads (But They'll Be Tasteful)," *Forbes*, September 19, 2013; Lydia Dishman, "J. Crew's Smart Pinterest Play: Move Beyond Inspiration to Make a Sale," *Forbes*, August 20 2013; Kyle Stock, "Nordstrom Racks Now Powered by Pinterest," *Bloomberg Businessweek*, July 2, 2013; Jessi Hempel, "CEO Outlines the Future of Pinterest," *Fortune*, May 30, 2013; Eric Spitznagel, "Dude! The Battle to Become the Male Pinterest!" *Bloomberg Businessweek*, April 10, 2013; and Pui-Wing Tam and Spencer Ante, "As Pinterest Grows, Startup Seeks $2.5 Billion Valuation," *Wall Street Journal*, February 6, 2013, pp. B1–B2.

CHAPTER ORGANIZATION

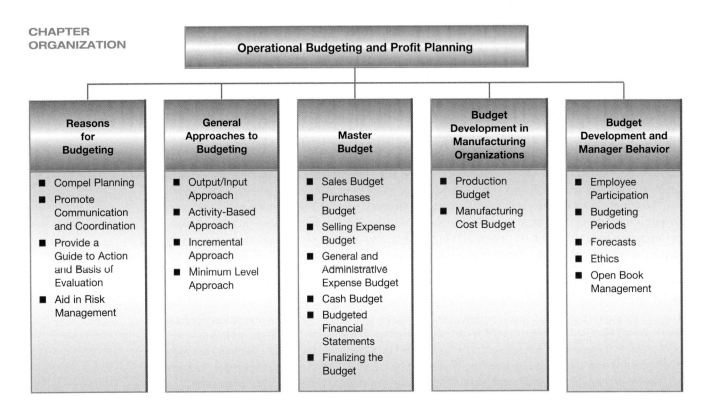

A **budget** is a formal plan of action expressed in monetary terms. The purpose of this chapter is to examine the concepts, relationships, and procedures used in budgeting. Our emphasis is on **operating budgets**, which concern the development of detailed plans to guide operations throughout the budget period. We consider the reasons that organizations budget and alternative approaches to budget development. We also examine budget assembly and consider issues related to manager behavior and the budgeting process.

REASONS FOR BUDGETING

LO1 Discuss the importance of budgets.

Operating managers frequently regard budgeting as a time-consuming task that diverts attention from current problems. Indeed, the development of an effective budget is a difficult job. It is also a necessary one. Organizations that do not plan are likely to wander aimlessly and ultimately succumb to the swirl of current events. The formal development of a budget helps to ensure both success and survival. As discussed below, budgeting compels planning; it improves communications and coordination among organizational elements; it provides a guide to action; and it provides a basis of performance evaluation. Budget models are also used to analyze and prepare for various business risks.

Compel Planning

Formal budgeting procedures require people to think about the future. Without the discipline of formal planning procedures, busy operating managers would not find time to plan. Immediate needs would consume all available time. Formal budgeting procedures, with specified deadlines, force managers to plan for the future by making the completion of the budget another immediate need. Budgeting moves an organization from an informal "reactive" style to a formal "proactive" style of management. As a result, management and other employees spend less time solving unanticipated problems and more time on positive measures and preventative actions.

Promote Communication and Coordination

When operating responsibilities are divided, it is difficult to synchronize activities. Production must know what marketing intends to sell. Purchasing and personnel must know the factory's material and labor requirements. The treasurer must plan to ensure the availability of the cash to support receivables, inventories, and capital expenditures. Budgeting forces the managers of these diverse functions to communicate their plans and coordinate their activities. It helps ensure that plans are feasible (Can purchasing obtain adequate inventories to support projected sales?) and that they are synchronized (Will inventory be available in advance of an advertising campaign?). The final version of the budget emerges after an extensive (often lengthy) process of communication and coordination.

Provide a Guide to Action and Basis of Evaluation

Once the budget has been finalized, the various operating managers know what is expected of them, and they can set about doing it. If employees do not have a guide to action, their efforts could be wasted on unproductive or even counterproductive activities.

After employees accept the budget as a guide to action, they can be held responsible for their portion of the budget. When results do not agree with plans, managers attempt to determine the cause of the divergence. This information is then used to adjust operations or to modify plans. More generally, budgeting is an important part of **management by exception**, whereby management directs attention only to those activities not proceeding according to plan. Without the budget, management might spend an inordinate amount of time seeking explanation of past activities and not enough time planning future activities.

Aid in Risk Management

The models used for budgeting are also used in managing risk. **Risk** is the danger that things will not go according to plan. Although some risk results from anticipated events having a positive impact, such as an increase in sales volume or selling prices, risk is more typically associated with events that have a negative impact, like a work stoppage at a key supplier, a fire, or hackers shutting down a retail website for an extended period of time.

Risk management (also called **enterprise risk management**) is the process of identifying, evaluating, and planning possible responses to risks that could impede an organization from achieving its plans. It also involves monitoring the sources of risk. An organization's budget model can be used to evaluate the financial impact of a risk and to determine, from a financial perspective, the best response to a risk. The Research Insight on the following page summarizes a proposed approach to risk management. The performance evaluation procedures considered in Chapter 10, if completed on a timely basis, assist in monitoring risk.

The lead responsibility for risk management is often part of the finance function. In the State of Washington, for example, the Risk Management Division is included in the Office of Financial

Management. Washington's Risk Management Division defines risk as "anything that poses a potential barrier to an agency achieving, on time, its mandated and strategic objectives/goals." Examples include: financial/budget risk, reputation risk, operational risk, safety/security risk, legal risk, regulatory/compliance risk, and document/management risk.[1]

GENERAL APPROACHES TO BUDGETING

LO2 Describe basic approaches to budgeting.

Before an organization can develop operating budgets, management must decide which approaches to budget planning will be used for the various revenue and expenditure activities and organizational units. Widely used planning approaches to budgeting include the output/input, activity-based, incremental, and minimum level approaches.

Output/Input Approach

The **output/input approach** budgets physical inputs and costs as a function of planned unit-level activities. This approach is often used for service, merchandising, manufacturing, and distribution activities that have defined relationships between effort and accomplishment. If each unit produced requires 2 pounds of direct materials that cost $5 each, and the planned production volume is 25 units, the budgeted inputs and costs for direct materials are 50 pounds (25 units × 2 pounds per unit) and $250 (50 pounds × $5 per pound).

The budgeted inputs are a function of the planned outputs. The output/input approach starts with the planned outputs and works backward to budget the inputs. It is difficult to use this approach for costs that do not respond to changes in unit-level cost drivers.

RESEARCH INSIGHT

A Systematic Approach to Risk Management

Risk Identification

Identify possible risks and their implications.

Risk Assessment and Quantification

Predict each risk's probability and impact, including financial impacts. Classify risks by importance to the organization.

Risk Response

Select a response to each risk:
- Avoid risk, e.g. do not accept project
- Transfer risk, e.g. purchase insurance
- Mitigate risk, e.g. contingency plans
- Accept risk, e.g. risk low, risk will not have a significant impact, or risk unavoidable.

Risk Monitoring

Develop procedures to continuously monitor important risks with the goal of facilitating a timely response.

Source: Alan J. Chilcott, "Risk Management—A Developing Field of Study and Application," *Cost Engineering*, September 9, 2010, pp. 21-26; Neville Turbit, "Basics of Managing Risk," The Project Perfect White Paper Collection, www.projectperfect.com.au.

---

[1] "Guide for Section 13.1—Risk Management and Self-Insurance Premiums 2011-2013 Budget," Risk Management Division, Office of Financial Management, State of Washington.

Activity-Based Approach

The **activity-based approach** is a type of output/input method, but it reduces the distortions in the transformation through emphasis on the expected cost of the planned activities that will be consumed for a process, department, service, product, or other budget objective. Overhead costs are budgeted on the basis of the cost objective's anticipated consumption of activities, not based only on some broad-based cost driver such as direct labor hours or machine hours.

The amount of each activity cost driver used by each budget objective (for example, product or service) is determined and multiplied by the cost per unit of the activity cost driver. The result is an estimate of the costs of each product or service based on cost drivers such as assembly-line setup or inspections, as well as the traditional volume-based drivers such as direct labor hours or units of direct materials consumed. Activity-based budgeting predicts costs of budget objectives by adding all costs of the activity cost drivers that each product or service is budgeted to consume. In evaluating the proposed budget, management would focus their attention on identifying the optimal set of activities rather than just the output/input relationships.

Incremental Approach

The **incremental approach** budgets costs for a coming period as a dollar or percentage change from the amount budgeted for (or spent during) some previous period. This approach is often used when the relationships between inputs and outputs are weak or nonexistent. For example, it is difficult to establish a clear relationship between sales volume and advertising expenditures. Consequently, the budgeted amount of advertising for a future period is often based on the budgeted or actual advertising expenditures in a previous period. If budgeted advertising expenditures for 2013 were $200,000, the budgeted expenditures for 2014 would be some increment, say 5 percent, above $200,000. In evaluating the proposed 2014 budget, management would accept the $200,000 base and focus attention on justifying the increment.

The incremental approach is widely used in government and not-for-profit organizations. In seeking a budget appropriation, a manager using the incremental approach need only justify proposed expenditures in excess of the previous budget. The primary advantage of the incremental approach is that it simplifies the budget process by considering only the increments in the various budget items. A major disadvantage is that existing waste and inefficiencies could escalate year after year.

Minimum Level Approach

Using the **minimum level approach**, an organization establishes a base amount for budget items and requires explanation or justification for any budgeted amount above the minimum (base). This base is usually significantly less than the base used in the incremental approach. It likely is the minimum amount necessary to keep a program or organizational unit viable. For example, the corporate director of product development would need some basic amount to avoid canceling ongoing projects. Additional increments might also be included, first to support the current level of product development and second to undertake desirable new projects.

Some organizations, especially units of government, employ a variation of the minimum level approach, identified as zero-based budgeting. Under **zero-based budgeting** every dollar of expenditure must be justified. The essence of zero-based budgeting is breaking an organizational unit's total budget into program packages with related costs. Management then ranks all program packages on the basis of the perceived benefits in relationship to their costs. Program packages are then funded for the budget period using this ranking. High-ranking packages are most likely to be funded and low-ranking packages are least likely to be funded.

Budgeting for objectives is a variation on the minimum level approach that combines elements of activity-based and zero-based budgeting with a need to live within fixed financial constraints. The minimum level approach improves on the incremental approach by questioning the necessity for costs included in the base of the incremental approach, but it is very time consuming. All three approaches are often used within the same organization. A pharmaceutical company might use the output/input or the activity-based approach to budget distribution expenditures, the incremental approach to budget administrative salaries, and the minimum level approach to budget research and development.

BUSINESS INSIGHT

Operational Budgeting Is Critical for a Company Rife with Uncertainty Few industries are as rife with uncertainty as that of oil exploration. Yet operational budgeting is critical in uncertain environments, especially where large investments of capital are needed, and even more important, when the company is the world's largest publicly traded oil company. If **Exxon** gets it wrong, the entire energy industry feels the repercussions. Exxon is in the midst of an oil and gas shortage and in response is developing innovative exploration processes and traveling to the farthest corners of the globe.

Exxon is drilling in deep-water wells off the coast of Angola (the Kizomba project) and will be exporting fuel to the Asian markets from its Banyu Urip project in Indonesia and a new project under way in Papua New Guinea, which is experiencing cost overruns of 21 percent. The overruns are due to work stoppages and foreign currency exchange losses, both of which are difficult to predict when preparing an operating budget in advance.

Another project in Alberta, Canada, is the Kearl oil-sands fields. These fields contain Canadian crude oil, but the sands must be extracted by large mechanical shovels and then transported to an $11 billion oil-sands-processing facility. Exxon is counting on this project to provide 37 percent of its growth through the year 2014. Yet once processed, the oil will be largely sold in Canadian markets due to limited pipeline capacity in bringing the oil to the United States. Not only must Exxon budget for uncertainty and high capital costs, but it also has to consider its lack of transferrable revenue streams as it builds its master budget.

Source: Tom Fowler, "Exxon Has an Oil Shortage," *Wall Street Journal*, November 29, 2012, pp. B1–B2.

MID-CHAPTER REVIEW

To illustrate the various approaches to budgeting discussed above, assume that **Pfizer** manufactures two products in institutional quantities, Centrum vitamins and Advil pain reliever. Suppose last period, Pfizer produced 18,000 units of Centrum and 45,000 units of Advil at a total unit cost of $38 for Centrum and $32 for Advil. Also suppose the current period, overall costs are expected to rise about 3.5 percent over the last period. Assume estimated overhead costs of $408,500 for the next period include the cost of assembly-line setups, engineering and maintenance, and inspections. Total estimated assembly hours is 50,000 hours; therefore, the estimated overhead cost per assembly hour is $8.17. Other predicted data for the next period follow:

	Centrum	Advil
Direct materials (per unit)	$20.00	$14.50
Direct labor hours of assembly time (per unit)	0.5	0.8
Assembly labor cost (per hour)	$18	$18
Total estimated production (in units)	20,000	50,000
Total setup hours	1,000	1,500
Total engineering and maintenance hours	500	600
Total inspections	650	580
Setup cost (per setup hour)	$25	$25
Engineering and maintenance (per hour)	$35	$35
Inspection cost (per inspection)	$250	$250

Required

a. Calculate Pfizer's budgeted cost per unit to produce Centrum and Advil during the next period, assuming it uses an output/input approach and budgets overhead cost based only on assembly hours.
b. Repeat a., assuming Pfizer uses an activity-based approach and budgets overhead cost based on budgeted activity costs.
c. Repeat a., assuming Pfizer uses an incremental approach for budgeting overhead cost.
d. Explain how the minimum level approach differs from the above methods.

The solution is on page 335.

MASTER BUDGET

The culmination of the budgeting process is the preparation of a master budget for the entire organization that considers all interrelationships among organization units. The master budget groups together all budgets and supporting schedules and coordinates all financial and operational activities, placing them into an organization-wide set of budgets for a given time period.

Because it explicitly considers organizational interrelationships, the master budget is more complex than budgets developed for products, services, organization units, or specific processes. The elements of the master budget depend on the nature of the business, its products or services, processes and organization, and management needs.

A major goal of developing a master budget is to ensure the smooth functioning of a business throughout the budget period and the organization's operating cycle. As shown in Exhibit 9.1, the operating cycle involves the conversion of cash into other assets, which are intended to produce revenues in excess of their costs. The cycle generally follows a path from cash, to inventories, to receivables (via sales or services), and back to cash. There are, of course, intermediate processes such as the purchase or manufacture of inventories, payments of accounts payable, and the collection of receivables. The master budget is merely a detailed model of the firm's operating cycle that includes all internal processes.

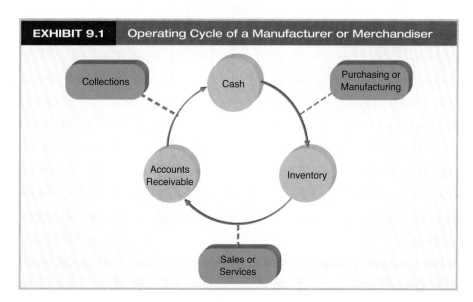

EXHIBIT 9.1 Operating Cycle of a Manufacturer or Merchandiser

Most for-profit organizations begin the budgeting process with the development of the sales budget and conclude with the development of budgeted financial statements. Exhibit 9.2 depicts the annual budget assembly process in a retail merchandising organization. Most of the budget data flow from sales toward cash and then toward the budgeted financial statements.

To illustrate the procedures involved in budget assembly, a hypothetical monthly budget for the second quarter of 2014 is developed for Orvis, a retail organization specializing in outdoor clothing and equipment. The assembly sequence follows the overview illustrated in Exhibit 9.2. Each element of the budget process in Exhibit 9.2 is illustrated in a separate exhibit. Because of the numerous elements in the budget process illustrated for Orvis, you will find it useful to refer to Exhibit 9.2 often.

The activities of a business can be summarized under three broad categories: operating activities, financing activities, and investing activities. To simplify the illustration, assume that Orvis engaged in no investing activities during the budget period and that the only anticipated financing activity is short-term borrowing. Normal profit-related activities performed in conducting the daily affairs of an organization are called **operating activities**. Assume the operating activities of Orvis include the following:

1. Purchasing inventory intended for sale.
2. Selling goods or services.

3. Purchasing and using goods and services classified as selling expenses.

4. Purchasing and using goods and services classified as general and administrative expenses.

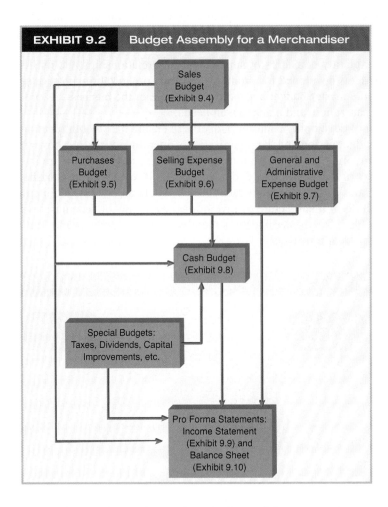

In addition to preparing the budget for each operating activity, companies prepare a cash budget for cash receipts and disbursements related to their operating activities as well as for financing and investing activities. The importance of cash planning makes this budget a vital part of the total budget process. Management must, for example, be aware in advance of the need to borrow and have some idea when borrowed funds can be repaid.

The hypothetical balance sheet for April 1, 2014, the start of the second quarter, is presented in Exhibit 9.3. It contains information used as a starting point in preparing the various budgets. To reduce complexity, we use the output/input approach to budget variable costs and assume that the budgets for other costs were previously developed using the incremental approach. Budgets to be prepared include those for sales, purchases, selling expense, general and administrative expense, and cash.

Sales Budget

The **sales budget** includes a forecast of sales revenue, and it can also contain a forecast of unit sales and sales collections. Because sales drive almost all other activities in a for-profit organization, developing a sales budget is the starting point in the budgeting process. Managers use the best available information to accurately forecast future market conditions. These forecasts, when considered along with merchandise available, promotion and advertising plans, and expected pricing policies, should lead to the most dependable sales budget. Assume the sales budget of Orvis is in Exhibit 9.4.

EXHIBIT 9.3	Initial Balance Sheet

ORVIS
Balance Sheet
April 1, 2014

Assets
Current assets

Cash	$ 15,000	
Accounts receivable, net.	59,200	
Merchandise Inventory	157,000	$231,200

Fixed assets

Buildings and equipment.	$460,000		
Less accumulated depreciation	(124,800)	335,200	
Land		60,000	395,200
Total assets			$626,400

Liabilities and Stockholders' Equity
Current liabilities

Accounts payable	$ 84,000	
Taxes payable*.	35,000	$119,000

Stockholders' equity

Capital stock	350,000	
Retained earnings	157,400	507,400
Total liabilities and stockholders' equity		$626,400

*Quarterly income taxes are paid within 30 days of the end of each quarter.

EXHIBIT 9.4	Sales Budget

ORVIS
Sales Budget
For the Second Quarter Ending June 30, 2014

	April	May	June	Quarter Total	July
Sales	$190,000	$228,000	$250,000	$668,000	$309,000

The information in the sales budget along with predictions of the expected portion of cash sales and the timing of collections from credit sales are used to calculate cash receipts. In the event of a projected cash shortfall, management could consider ways to increase cash sales or to accelerate the collection of receipts from credit sales.

Purchases Budget

The **purchases budget** indicates the merchandise that must be acquired to meet sales needs and ending inventory requirements. It can be referred to as a merchandise budget if it contains only purchases of merchandise for sale. However, for a manufacturer it would include purchase of raw materials. The purchases budget, shown in Exhibit 9.5, includes only purchases of merchandise.

In reviewing Orvis' purchases budget, note the following:

■ Because Orvis sells a wide variety of items, the purchases budget is expressed in terms of sales dollars, with the assumed cost of merchandise averaging 60 percent of the selling price. Management also keeps detailed records for budgeting the number of units of items carried. An organization that only sold a small number of items might present the sales budget in units as well as dollars.

■ Suppose management desires to have 50 percent of the inventory needed to fill the following month's sales in stock at the end of the previous month.

■ To provide for a possible delay in the receipt of inventory and to meet variations in customer demand, assume Orvis maintains an additional base inventory of $100,000.

| EXHIBIT 9.5 | Purchases Budget | | | | |

ORVIS
Purchases Budget
For the Second Quarter Ending June 30, 2014

	April	May	June	Quarter Total	July
Budgeted sales (Exhibit 9.4)	$190,000	$228,000	$250,000	$668,000	$309,000
Current cost of goods sold*	$114,000	$136,800	$150,000	$400,800	
Desired ending inventory**	168,400	175,000	192,700	192,700	
Total needs	282,400	311,800	342,700	593,500	
Less beginning inventory***	(157,000)	(168,400)	(175,000)	(157,000)	
Purchases	$125,400	$143,400	$167,700	$436,500	

*Cost of goods sold is 60 percent of selling price

**Fifty percent of inventory required for next month's budgeted sales plus base inventory of $100,000.
  April: ($228,000 May sales x 0.60 cost x 0.50 desired ending inventory) + $100,000
  May: ($250,000 June sales x 0.60 cost x 0.50 desired ending inventory) + $100,000
  June :($309,000 July sales x 0.60 cost x 0.50 desired ending inventory) + $100,000

***Fifty percent of current month sales plus base inventory of $100,000. Note monthly beginning inventory.
  Same as previous month's ending inventory.

- ■ The total inventory needs equal current sales plus desired ending inventory, including the base inventory.
- ■ Budgeted purchases are computed as total inventory needs less the beginning inventory.

The information in the purchases budget and the information on expected timing of payments for purchases are used to budget cash disbursements for purchases. In the event of a projected cash shortfall, management can consider ways to delay the purchase of inventory or the payment for inventory purchases.

Selling Expense Budget

The **selling expense budget** presents the expenses the organization plans to incur in connection with sales and distribution. In the selling expense budget, Exhibit 9.6, the budgeted variable selling expenses are determined as a percentage of budgeted sales dollars. The budgeted fixed selling expenses are based on amounts obtained from the manager of the sales department. To simplify the presentation of the cash budget, assume Orvis pays its selling expenses in the month they are incurred.

| EXHIBIT 9.6 | Selling Expense Budget | | | |

ORVIS
Selling Expense Budget
For the Second Quarter Ending June 30, 2014

	April	May	June	Quarter Total
Budgeted sales (Exhibit 9.4)	$190,000	$228,000	$250,000	$668,000
Variable selling expenses				
Setup/Display (1% sales)	$ 1,900	$ 2,280	$ 2,500	$ 6,680
Commissions (2% sales)	3,800	4,560	5,000	13,360
Miscellaneous (1% sales)	1,900	2,280	2,500	6,680
Total	7,600	9,120	10,000	26,720
Fixed selling expenses				
Advertising	2,250	2,250	2,250	6,750
Office	1,250	1,250	1,250	3,750
Miscellaneous	1,000	1,000	1,000	3,000
Total	4,500	4,500	4,500	13,500
Total selling expenses.	$ 12,100	$ 13,620	$ 14,500	$ 40,220

General and Administrative Expense Budget

The **general and administrative expense budget** presents the expenses the organization plans to incur in connection with the general administration of the organization. Included are expenses for the accounting department, the computer center, and the president's office, for example. Orvis' assumed general and administrative expense budget is presented in Exhibit 9.7.

The depreciation of $2,000 per month is a noncash item and is not carried forward to the cash budget. No variable general and administrative costs are included because most expenditures categorized as general and administrative are related to top-management operations that do not vary with unit-level cost drivers. To simplify the presentation of the cash budget, assume that general and administrative expenses, except depreciation, are paid in the month they are incurred.

EXHIBIT 9.7	General and Administrative Expense Budget			
ORVIS **General and Administrative Expense Budget** **For the Second Quarter Ending June 30, 2014**				
	April	**May**	**June**	**Quarter Total**
General and administrative expenses				
Compensation	$25,000	$25,000	$25,000	$75,000
Insurance	2,000	2,000	2,000	6,000
Depreciation.	2,000	2,000	2,000	6,000
Utilities	3,000	3,000	3,000	9,000
Miscellaneous	1,000	1,000	1,000	3,000
Total general and administrative expenses	$33,000	$33,000	$33,000	$99,000

Cash Budget

The **cash budget** summarizes all cash receipts and disbursements expected to occur during the budget period. Cash is critical to survival. Income is like food and cash is like water. Food is necessary to survive and prosper over time, but you can get along without food for a short period of time. You cannot survive very long without water. Hence, cash budgeting is very important, especially in a small business where cash receipts from sales lag purchases of inventory. As pointed out in the following Business Insight, cash budgets are also critical in large organizations undergoing restructuring.

BUSINESS INSIGHT

Budgeting Within an Entertainment Behemoth Massive, diversified businesses face hard choices in allocating their capital across divisions, especially when seasonality drives the business. Normally we think of retailers or agriculture when we think of seasonality; however, Walt Disney Co. also has major seasonal fluctuations. All major holidays are peak times for Disney theme parks and movie releases, not to mention toy, software, and merchandise sales. Disney's television group includes the ABC broadcast network and cable networks including ABC Family and the Disney Channel. Disney also holds the majority ownership is the ESPN sports network. In addition, it owns a cruise line in which it recently launched two new cruise ships at a price tag of $1 billion … each.

On top of all that, Disney just purchased Lucasfilm and is developing another Star Wars trilogy. Likewise, it bought Marvel Entertainment in 2009. Of course, Disney is at its best when it cross-sells across its product lines—for example, developing a movie franchise, Pirates of the Caribbean, out of one of its theme park rides; or transforming one of its animated films, The Lion King, into a long-running Broadway show. The company's new video game, Disney Infinity, includes numerous Disney characters in a world that players build themselves. Indeed, with a continual cash outflow on major acquisitions, capital projects, and development, Disney must carefully manage its cash budget, both to smooth out the effects of seasonality and to continually fund the new projects that fuel its growth.

Sources: Ben Fritz, "After Spree, Walt Disney to Boost Buybacks," *Wall Street Journal*, September 13, 2013, p. B4; Ben Fritz, "Setback for Disney's Interactive Division," *Wall Street Journal*, March 14, 2013, p. B7; and Devin Leonard, "How Disney Bought Lucasfilm—and Its Plans for 'Star Wars,'" *Bloomberg Businessweek*, March 7, 2013.

After it makes sales predictions, an organization uses information regarding credit terms, collections policy, and prior collection experience to develop a cash collections budget. Collections on sales normally include receipts from the current period's sales and collections from sales of prior periods. An allowance for bad debts, which reduces each period's collections, is also predicted. Other items often included are cash sales, sales discounts, allowances for volume discounts, and seasonal changes of sales prices and collections. Orvis' assumed cash budget is in Exhibit 9.8. Note the following important points:

■ Management estimates that one-half of all sales are for cash and the other half are on the company's credit card. (When sales are on bank credit cards, the collection is immediate, less any bank user fee; however, assume charges using Orvis' credit card are collected by the company from the customer.) Twenty-five percent of the credit card sales are collected in the month of sale, and 74 percent are collected in the following month. Bad debts are budgeted at 1 percent of credit sales. This resource flow is graphically illustrated as follows:

■ Assume payments for purchases are made 20 percent in the month purchased and 80 percent in the next month.

■ Information on cash expenditures for selling expenses and for general and administrative expenses is based on budgets for these items. The monthly cash expenditures for general and administrative expenses are $31,000 rather than $33,000. The $2,000 difference relates to depreciation, which does not require use of cash.

■ Assume Orvis' income taxes are determined on the basis of predicted taxable income following IRS rules. Estimated tax payments are made during the month following the end of each quarter. Hence, the taxes payable on April 1 are paid during April.

■ The cash budget shows cash operating deficiencies and surpluses expected to occur at the end of each month; this is used to plan for borrowing and loan payment.

■ Suppose the cash maintenance policy for Orvis specifies that a minimum balance of $15,000 is to be maintained.

■ Assume Orvis has a line of credit with a bank, with any interest on borrowed funds computed at the simple interest rate of 12.0 percent per year, or 1.0 percent per month. All necessary borrowing is assumed to occur at the start of each month in increments of $1,000. Repayments are assumed to occur at the end of the month. Interest is paid when loans are repaid.

■ The cash budget indicates Orvis needs to borrow $10,000 in April. The $10,000 plus interest is repaid in May.

If Orvis had any cash disbursements for dividends or capital expenditures they would be included in the cash budget. These items, along with information on income taxes, would be shown in special budgets.

Budgeted Financial Statements

The preparation of the master budget culminates in the preparation of budgeted financial statements. **Budgeted financial statements** are pro forma statements that reflect the "as-if" effects of the budgeted activities on the actual financial position of the organization. That is, the statements reflect the results of operations assuming all budget predictions are correct. Spreadsheets

EXHIBIT 9.8	Cash Budget

ORVIS
Cash Budget
For the Second Quarter Ending June 30, 2014

	April	May	June	Quarter Total
Budgeted sales (Exhibit 9.4)	$190,000	$228,000	$250,000	$668,000
Cash balance, beginning	$ 15,000	$ 15,770	$ 44,850	$ 15,000
Collections on sales				
Cash sales (50% sales)	95,000	114,000	125,000	
Credit sales				
Current month (25% credit sales)	23,750	28,500	31,250	
Prior month (74% credit sales)	59,200*	70,300	84,360	
Total	177,950	212,800	240,610	631,360
Cash available for operations	192,950	228,570	285,460	646,360
Disbursements				
Purchases (Exhibit 9.5)				
Current month (20% purchases)	25,080	28,680	33,540	
Prior month (80% purchases)	84,000**	100,320	114,720	
Total	109,080	129.000	148,260	386,340
Selling expenses (Exhibit 9.6)	12,100	13,620	14,500	40,220
General & Administrative Expenses				
(Exhibit 9.7, excluding depreciation)	31,000	31,000	31,000	93,000
Taxes (Exhibit 9.3)	35,000			35,000
Total	(187,180)	(173,620)	(193,760)	(554,560)
Excess (deficiency) cash available over disbursements	5,770	54,950	91,700	91,800
Short-term financing***				
New loans.	10,000			10,000
Repayments.		(10,000)		(10,000)
Interest	—	(100)	—	(100)
Net cash from financing	10,000	(10,100)	—	(100)
Cash balance, ending	$ 15,770	$ 44,850	$ 91,700	$ 91,700

*April 1 accounts receivable.

**April 1 accounts payable.

***Loans are obtained in $1,000 increments at the start of the month to maintain a minimum balance of $15,000 at all times. Repayments are made at the end of the month, as soon as adequate cash is available. Assume interest of 12 percent per year (1 percent per month) is paid when the loan is repaid.

that permit the user to immediately determine the impact of any assumed changes facilitate developing budgeted financial statements. The budgeted income statement can follow the functional format traditionally used for financial accounting or the contribution format introduced in Chapter 3. In either case, the balance sheet amounts reflect the corresponding budgeted entries.

Exhibit 9.9 presents the budgeted income statement for the quarter ending June 30, 2014. If all predictions made in the operating budget are correct, Orvis will produce a net income of $51,540 for the quarter. Almost every item on the budgeted income statement comes from one of the budget schedules.

The budgeted balance sheet, presented in Exhibit 9.10 shows Orvis' financial position as of June 30, 2014, assuming that all budget predictions are correct. Sources of the budgeted balance sheet data are included as part of the exhibit.

EXHIBIT 9.9   Budgeted Income Statement

ORVIS
Budgeted Income Statement
For the Second Quarter Ending June 30, 2014

Sales (Exhibit 9.4)		$668,000
Cost of goods sold:*		
Beginning inventory (Exhibit 9.3)......................................	$157,000	
Purchases (Exhibit 9.5)	436,500	
Cost of merchandise available	593,500	
Ending inventory (Exhibit 9.5)	(192,700)	(400,800)
Gross profit		267,200
Other expenses:		
Bad debt (1% of credit sales)**.......................................	3,340	
Selling (Exhibit 9.6)	40,220	
General and administrative (Exhibit 9.7)...............................	99,000	(142,560)
Income from operations		124,640
Interest expense (Exhibit 9.8).......................................		(100)
Net income from operations...		124,540
Allowance for income taxes***		(73,000)
Net income..		$ 51,540

*Also computed at sales x 0.6

**$668,000 x 0.5 credit sales x 0.01 bad debts

***Provided by accounting

EXHIBIT 9.10   Budgeted Balance Sheet

ORVIS
Balance Sheet
June 30, 2014

Assets:			
Current assets			
Cash (Exhibit 9.8)		$ 91,700	
Accounts receivable, net*		92,500	
Merchandise inventory (Exhibit 9.5 and 9.9)................		192,700	$376,900
Fixed assets			
Buildings and equipment (Exhibit 9.3)	$460,000		
Less accumulated depreciation			
(Exhibit 9.3 plus depreciation Exhibit 9.7)	(130,800)	329,200	
Land (Exhibit 9.3).......................................		60,000	389,200
Total assets			$766,100
Liabilities and Stockholders' Equity			
Current liabilities			
Accounts payable**		$134,160	
Taxes payable (Exhibit 9.9)		73,000	$207,160
Stockholders' equity			
Capital stock (Exhibit 9.3)		350,000	
Retained earnings (Exhibit 9.3 plus net income Exhibit 9.9)		208,940	558,940
Total liabilities and stockholders' equity			$766,100

*June credit sales collected in July, $250,000 x 0.50 x 0.74.

**June purchases paid in July, $167,700 x 0.80.

Finalizing the Budget

After studying the Orvis example, you might conclude that developing the master budget is a mechanical process. That is not the case. Understanding the basics of budget assembly is not the end;

it is a tool to assist in efficient and effective budgeting. Before finalizing the budget, the following two questions must be addressed:

- Is the proposed budget feasible?
- Is the proposed budget acceptable?

To be feasible, the organization must be able to actually implement the proposed budget. Without the assumed line of credit, Orvis' budget is not feasible because the company would run out of cash sometime in April. Knowing this, management can take timely corrective action. Possible actions include obtaining equity financing, issuing long-term debt, reducing the amount of inventory on hand at the end of each quarter, or obtaining a line of credit. Other constraints that would make the budget infeasible include the availability of merchandise and, in the case of a manufacturing organization, production capacity.

Once management determines that the budget is feasible, they still need to determine if it is acceptable. To evaluate acceptability, management might consider various financial ratios, such as return on assets. They might compare the return provided by the proposed budget with past returns, industry averages, or some organizational goal.

BUDGET DEVELOPMENT IN MANUFACTURING ORGANIZATIONS

The importance of inventory in various organizations was introduced in Chapter 5 where Exhibit 5.1 (page 149) summarized inventory and related expense accounts for service, merchandising, and manufacturing organizations. Recall that service organizations usually have a low percentage of their assets invested in inventory, usually consisting of the supplies needed to facilitate operations. In contrast, merchandising organizations usually have a high percentage of their total assets invested in inventory, with the largest inventory investment in merchandise purchased for resale. The preceding illustration of the development of a master budget was for a merchandising organization.

LO4 Explain and develop a basic manufacturing cost budget.

Production Budget

Because manufacturing organizations convert raw materials into finished goods that are sold to customers, there are additional steps in developing their master budget. Contrast the assembly of a budget for a merchandiser in Exhibit 9.2 with the assembly of a budget for a manufacturer in Exhibit 9.11. The management of a manufacturing organization must determine the production volume required to support sales and finished goods ending inventory requirements (production budget). Then, based on available inventories or raw materials and the raw materials required for production, management develops a purchases budget.

Manufacturing Cost Budget

In addition to a selling expense budget and a general and administrative expense budget, management needs also to develop a manufacturing cost budget, which is similar in design to a statement of cost of goods manufactured (see Exhibit 5.6, page 161) except that it is prepared in advance of production rather than after production. Reflecting these additional steps, the cash budget includes payments for direct labor and manufacturing overhead, based on information in the manufacturing cost budget, and payments for purchases of raw materials based on the purchases budget. Note cash disbursements are for materials purchased rather than materials used in production.

Continuing our Orvis example, assume that management is considering the option of manufacturing a high-quality backpack, tentatively named the "Trekpack" as an alternative to purchasing a similar item from an outside vendor. Unit variable and monthly fixed cost estimates associated with the manufacture of Trekpacks follow:

EXHIBIT 9.11   Budget Assembly for a Manufacturer

Unit costs:
    Direct materials:
        Fabric: 2 square yards at $10 per yard $20
        Hardware kits (buckles, straps, etc.). . . . .   5 $ 25

Direct labor 0.5 hours at $30 per hour   15
Variable overhead, per unit.   8

    Total variable costs per unit . . . . $ 48

Fixed costs per month (rent, utilities, supervision) $6,000

Because management anticipates an average monthly production volume of 500 Trekpacks, the average fixed cost per unit, a predetermined overhead rate, is $12 ($6,000/500).

For budgeting purposes, management uses a standard cost, a budget per unit of product, for valuing inventories and forecasting the cost of goods sold. The standard cost of a Trekpack is $60:

Direct materials $25
Direct labor   15
Variable overhead   8
Fixed overhead   12

Standard cost $60

Management, planning to introduce this new product in May, developed the sales budget shown in Exhibit 9.12. In this case, because unit information is necessary to determine production requirements, the sales budget is expressed in units as well as dollars.

Introducing Trekpacks in May requires some April production. To meet the initial sales requirement for the start of each month, management desires end-of-month inventories equal to 40 percent of the following month's budgeted sales. The sales budget and ending inventory plans, along with information on beginning inventories, is used to develop the production budget in Exhibit 9.13.

EXHIBIT 9.12 Sales Budget

ORVIS
Sales Budget (Trekpacks)
For the Second Quarter Ending June 30, 2014

	April	May	June	Quarter Total	July
Sales—Units	0	400	500	900	600
Sales—Dollars ($100 each)	0	$40,000	$50,000	$90,000	$60,000

EXHIBIT 9.13 Production Budget

ORVIS
Production Budget (Trekpacks)
For the Second Quarter Ending June 30, 2014

	April	May	June	Quarter Total
Budgeted Sales	0	400	500	900
Desired ending inventory				
40% following month sales	160	200	240	240
Total requirements	160	600	740	1,140
Less beginning inventory	0	(160)	(200)	0
Budgeted production	160	440	540	1,140

The production budget, along with information on beginning inventories of raw materials and planned ending inventory levels (500 square yards of fabric and 200 kits) is then used to budget the purchases in Exhibit 9.14 for raw materials in units and dollars. The production budget, along with standard variable and predicted fixed cost information is also used to develop the manufacturing cost budget in Exhibit 9.15.

EXHIBIT 9.14 Purchase Budget

ORVIS
Purchases Budget
For the Second Quarter Ending June 30, 2014

	April	May	June	Quarter Total
Fabric:				
Current needs (2 yards per unit)	320	880	1,080	2,280
Desired ending inventory (500 yards)	500	500	500	500
Total requirements.	820	1,380	1,580	2,780
Less beginning inventory	(0)	(500)	(500)	(0)
Fabric purchases in yards.	820	880	1,080	2,780
Assembly kits:				
Current needs (1 per unit)	160	440	540	1,140
Desired ending inventory (200 kits).	200	200	200	200
Total requirements.	360	640	740	1,340
Less beginning inventory	(0)	(200)	(200)	(0)
Kit purchases in units	360	440	540	1,340
Purchases (Dollars)				
Fabric at $10 per yard	$ 8,200	$ 8,800	$10,800	$27,800
Kits at $5 each	1,800	2,200	2,700	6,700
Total purchases in dollars.	$10,000	$11,000	$13,500	$34,500

EXHIBIT 9.15	Manufacturing Cost Budget

ORVIS
Manufacturing Cost Budget
For the Second Quarter Ending June 30, 2014

	April	May	June	Quarter Total
Direct materials				
Fabric used in production (production × 2 yards × $10) ..	$ 3,200	$ 8,800	$10,800	$22,800
Kits used in production (production × 1 kit × $5)	800	2,200	2,700	5,700
Total	4,000	11,000	13,500	28,500
Direct labor (production × 1/2 hour × $30)	2,400	6,600	8,100	17,100
Manufacturing overhead				
Variable ($8 per unit)	1,280	3,520	4,320	9,120
Fixed.	6,000	6,000	6,000	18,000
Total	7,280	9,520	10,320	27,120
Total manufacturing costs	$13,680	$27,120	$31,920	$72,720

Because it does not require the introduction of new concepts, the cash budget and the pro-forma financial statements for Orvis with the manufacturing of Trekpacks are not presented. Keep in mind that the cash budget will include disbursements for purchases shown in Exhibit 9.14 and for direct labor, variable overhead, and fixed overhead shown in Exhibit 9.15. A pro-forma functional income statement using absorption costing will include the predicted cost of goods sold for Trekpacks at a $60 standard cost per unit. A contribution income statement using variable costing would include the cost of goods sold for Trekpacks at a $48 standard cost per unit with all fixed manufacturing costs expensed in the period incurred. Finally, the pro-forma balance sheet will include standard costs of any June raw materials (500 square yards at $10 per yard and 200 kits at $5 each), work in process (none), and finished goods. Any unpaid liabilities for purchases of raw materials, direct labor, and manufacturing overhead would also be shown under current liabilities. Note that completing the cash budget and the pro-forma statements requires information on the timing of payments for the purchases of raw materials, direct labor, and manufacturing overhead.

BUDGET DEVELOPMENT AND MANAGER BEHAVIOR

LO5 Describe the relationship between budget development and manager behavior.

Organizations are composed of individuals who perform a wide variety of activities in pursuit of the organization's goals. To accomplish these goals, management must recognize the effects that budgeting and performance evaluation methods have on the behavior of the organization's employees.

Employee Participation

Budgeting should be used to promote productive employee behavior directed toward meeting the organization's goals. While no two organizations use exactly the same budgeting procedures, two approaches to employee involvement in budgeting represent possible end points on a continuum. These approaches are sometimes referred to as top-down and bottom-up methods.

With a **top-down** or **imposed budget**, top management identifies the primary goals and objectives for the organization and communicates them to lower management levels. Because relatively few people are involved in top-down budgeting, an imposed budget saves time. It also minimizes the slack that managers at lower organizational levels are sometimes prone to build into their budgets. However, this nonparticipative approach to budgeting can have undesirable motivational consequences. Personnel who do not participate in budget preparation might lack a commitment to achieve their part of the budget.

With a **bottom-up** or **participative budget**, managers at all levels—and in some cases, even nonmanagers—are involved in budget preparation. Budget proposals originate at the lowest level of management possible and are then integrated into the proposals for the next level, and so on, until the proposals reach the top level of management, which completes the budget.

Participation helps ensure that important issues are considered and that employees understand the importance of their roles in meeting the organization's goals. It also provides opportunities for problem solving and fosters employee commitment to agreed-upon goals. Hence, budget predictions are likely to be more accurate, and the people responsible for the budget are more likely to strive to accomplish its objectives. These self-imposed budgets reinforce the concept of participative management and should strengthen the overall budgeting process.

Participative approaches to budgeting have a few disadvantages. Because they require the involvement of many people, the preparation period is longer than that for an imposed budget. Another disadvantage is the tendency of some managers to intentionally understate revenues or overstate expenses to provide **budgetary slack**. A manager might do this to reduce his or her concern regarding unfavorable performance reviews or to make it easier to obtain favorable performance reviews. If a department consistently produces favorable variances (actual results versus budget) with little apparent effort, this might be a symptom of budgetary slack.

YOU MAKE THE CALL

You are the Chief Financial Officer As the CFO of a relatively new and fast-growing entrepreneurial enterprise, you and the other top managers have previously emphasized technical and marketing innovation and creativity over planning and budgeting. But now with growing competition and the maturing of the company's products, you recognized that a culture of better financial planning must be established if the company is to succeed in the long run. You feel that the financial staff has the best expertise and understanding of the business to prepare effective budgets, but you are concerned about the motivational effects of excluding the lower-level managers from the process and are seeking advice. [Answer, p. 319.]

Budgeting Periods

Although most organizations use a one-year budget period, some organizations budget for shorter or longer periods. In addition to fixed-length budget periods, two other types of budget periods commonly used are life cycle budgeting and continuous budgeting.

When a fixed time period is not particularly relevant to planning, an organization can use **life cycle budgeting**, which involves developing a budget for a project's entire life. An ice cream vendor at the beach might develop a budget for the season. A general contractor might budget costs for the entire (multiple-year) time required to construct a building.

Under **continuous budgeting**, the budget (sometimes called a **rolling budget**) is based on a moving time frame. For example, an organization on a continuous four-quarter budget system adds a quarter to the budget at the end of each quarter of operations, thereby always maintaining a budget for four quarters into the future. Under this system, plans for a full year into the future are always available, whereas under a fixed annual budget, operating plans for a full year ahead are available only at the beginning of the budget year. Because managers are constantly involved in this type of budgeting, the budget process becomes an active and integral part of the management process. Managers are forced to be future oriented throughout the year rather than just once each year.

Forecasts

Budget preparation requires the development of a variety of forecasts. The sales forecast is based on a variety of interrelated factors such as historical trends, product innovation, general economic conditions, industry conditions, and the organization's strategic position for competing on the basis of price, product differentiation, or market niche. Many organizations first determine the industry forecast for a given product or service and then extract from it their sales estimations.

Although the sales forecast is primary to most organizations, there are many other forecasts of varying importance that must be made, including (a) the collection period for sales on account, (b) percent of uncollectable sales on account, (c) cost of materials, supplies, utilities, and so forth, (d) employee turnover, (e) time required to perform activities, (f) interest rates, and (g) development time for new products or services.

BUSINESS INSIGHT

Managers Are Found to Cut Their Subordinates (Some) Slack   Participative budgeting occurs when managers solicit feedback from lower-level managers when preparing the upcoming year's operating budget. The lower-level managers are closer to the company's operations; therefore, they possess more information about future estimates than do higher-level managers. However, there may be an incentive for lower-level managers to intentionally misstate expected performance (thereby creating budgetary slack) in order to garner more resources, reduce effort, or provide a cushion against uncertainty in future operations.

But do the higher-level managers anticipate their subordinates' propensity to build slack into the budget? In an experimental setting, researchers have found that subordinates do build slack into their estimates, but they also find that higher-level managers, on average, reduce the costs that are reported by the subordinates when formulating the final operational budget, consistent with their recognition of the incentives for slack creation.

Source: Joseph Fisher, Timothy Mitchell, Sean Peffer, and Alan Webb, "Detecting Misreporting in Subordinates' Budgets," 2013, ssrn.com.

Ethics

Because most wrongful activities related to budgeting are unethical, rather than illegal, organizations often have difficulty dealing with them. However, when managers' actions cross the gray area between ethical and fraudulent behavior, organizations are not reluctant to dismiss employees or even pursue legal actions against them.

Although most managers have a natural inclination to be conservative in developing their budgets, at some level the blatant padding or building slack into the budget becomes unethical. In an extreme case, it might even be considered theft if an inordinate level of budgetary slack creates favorable performance variances that lead to significant bonuses or other financial gain for the manager. Another form of falsifying budgets occurs when managers include expense categories in their budgets that are not needed in their operations and subsequently use the funds to pad other budget categories. The deliberate falsification of budgets is unethical behavior and is grounds for dismissal in most organizations.

Ethical issues might also arise in the reporting of performance results, which usually compares actual data with budgeted data. Examples of unethical reporting of actual performance data include misclassification of expenses, overstating revenues or understating expenses, postponing or accelerating the recording of activities at the end of the accounting period, or creating fictitious activities.

Open Book Management

If an organization is to obtain the full benefit of budgeting, support for the budget must be obtained from employees at all levels. Many organizations, especially smaller ones, have used open book management to obtain employee support for the budget. **Open book management** involves sharing financial and related information with employees, teaching employees to understand financial numbers, encouraging employees to use the information in their work, and sharing financial results with employees, perhaps through a bonus program. The following Research Insight examines the success of open book management in small companies.

Properly used, an operating budget is an effective mechanism for motivating employees to higher levels of performance and productivity. Improperly developed and administered, budgets can foster feelings of animosity toward management and the budget process. Behavioral research has generally concluded that when employees participate in the preparation of budgets and believe that the budgets represent fair standards for evaluating their performance, they receive personal satisfaction from accomplishing the goals set in the budgets.

RESEARCH INSIGHT

Open Book Management Opens the Door to Profits Research performed by Dr. Jody Heymann and others at the McGill University Institute for Health and Social Policy shows that "sharing financial information with low-skilled workers helps build efficiency and profits." This is especially true at smaller companies with profit sharing plans. Examples cited by Dr. Heymann include Great Little Box, a Canadian packaging company with 213 employees, and Dancing Deer Baking, a gourmet bakery with 63 employees in Boston.

At Great Little Box, fifteen percent of the profits are split equally among all employees, and the firm's finances, production, and sales performance are discussed at monthly meetings attended by employees ranging from machine operators to senior managers. "As a result, even the lowest-level employees act like managers, looking for ways to reduce costs and improve productivity."

At Dancing Deer Baking, employees are offered "options" that are sold back to the company when workers leave or retire. When discussing finances and operations, production workers noted that fifteen percent of the brownies were scrapped because the shape of the pans required edges to be cut after baking. To alleviate this problem the company purchased new pans costing $35,000. The investment was recouped in three months.

Source: Jody Heymann, "Bootstrapping Profits by Opening the Books," *Bloomberg Businessweek*, September 27, 2010, p. 62; Jody Heymann with Magda Barrera, "Profit at the Bottom of the Ladder," *Harvard Business School Press*, 2010.

CHAPTER-END REVIEW 1: BUDGET FOR A MERCHANDISING ORGANIZATION

Cowgirl Creamery is a wholesale distributor of artisan cheese and ice cream. Suppose the following information is available for April 2014.

Estimated sales
Cheese . . . . 160,000 hoops at $10 each
Ice cream . . . . 240,000 gallons at $5 each

Estimated costs
Cheese . . . . $8 per hoop
Ice cream . . . . $2 per gallon

	Beginning	Ending
Desired inventories		
Cheese	10,000	12,000
Ice cream	4,000	5,000

Assumed financial information follows:

- Beginning cash balance is $400,000.

- Purchases of merchandise are paid 60 percent in the current month and 40 percent in the following month. Purchases totaled $1,800,000 in March and are estimated to be $2,000,000 in May.

- Employee wages and salaries are paid for in the current month. Employee expenses for April totaled $156,000.

- Overhead expenses are paid in the next month. The accounts payable amount for these expenses from March is $80,000 and for May will be $90,000. April's overhead expenses total $80,000.

- Sales are on credit and are collected 70 percent in the current period and the remainder in the next period. March's sales were $3,000,000, and May's sales are estimated to be $3,200,000. Bad debts average 1 percent of sales.
- Selling and administrative expenses are paid monthly and total $450,000, including $40,000 of depreciation.
- All unit costs for April are the same as they were in March.

Required

Prepare the following for April:
a. Sales budget in dollars.
b. Purchases budget.
c. Cash budget.
d. Budgeted income statement.

The solution is on pages 336–337.

CHAPTER-END REVIEW 2: BUDGET FOR A MANUFACTURER

Assume Stanley Tool Company manufactures and sells two industrial products in a single plant. Suppose a new manager wants to have quarterly budgets and has prepared the following information for the first quarter of 2014:

Budgeted sales

Drills		60,000 at $100 each
Saws		40,000 at $125 each

Budgeted inventories

	Beginning	Ending
Drills, finished	20,000 units	25,000 units
Saws, finished	8,000 units	10,000 units
Metal, direct materials	32,000 pounds	36,000 pounds
Plastic, direct materials	29,000 pounds	32,000 pounds
Handles, direct materials	6,000 each	7,000 each

Standard variable costs per unit

	Drills		Saws	
Direct materials				
Metal	5 pounds × $8.00	$40.00	4 pounds × $8.00	$32.00
Plastic	3 pounds × $5.00	15.00	3 pounds × $5.00	15.00
Handles	1 handle × $3.00	3.00		
Total		58.00		47.00
Direct labor	2 labor hours × $12.00	24.00	3 labor hours × $16.00	48.00
Variable manufacturing				
Overhead	2 hours × $1.50	3.00	3 hours × $1.50	4.50
Total		$85.00		$99.50

Assume fixed manufacturing overhead is $214,000 per quarter (including noncash expenditures of $156,000) and is allocated on total units produced. Financial information follows:

- Beginning cash balance is $1,800,000.
- Sales are on credit and are collected 50 percent in the current period and the remainder in the next period. Last quarter's sales were $8,400,000. There are no bad debts.
- Purchases of direct materials and labor costs are paid for in the quarter acquired.
- Manufacturing overhead expenses are paid in the quarter incurred.
- Selling and administrative expenses are all fixed and are paid in the quarter incurred. They are budgeted at $340,000 per quarter, including $90,000 of depreciation.

Required

For the first quarter of 2014, prepare the following:

a. Sales budget in dollars.

b. Production budget in units.

c. Purchases budget.

d. Manufacturing cost budget.

e. Cash budget.

f. Budgeted contribution income statement. (*Hint:* See Chapter 3.)

The solution is on pages 337–340.

GUIDANCE ANSWERS . . . YOU MAKE THE CALL

You are the Chief Financial Officer   You seem to be leaning toward using a top-down approach to budgeting. While this method may produce an effective set of benchmarks for planning and evaluation, it does not maximize the benefits of budgeting. A key element in any effective budgeting system is that it must be embraced by the managers whose performance will be evaluated by it. If the budget is imposed from the top down, it is far less likely to be embraced by managers than if they have participated from the beginning of the budget development process. The most effective budgeting systems are those that are strongly embraced by managers at all levels, which is most readily achieved through a participative (bottom-up) approach.

KEY TERMS

activity-based approach, 301

bottom-up, 315

budget, 298

budgetary slack, 315

budgeted financial
  statements, 308

cash budget, 307

continuous budgeting, 315

enterprise risk management, 299

general and administrative
  expense budget, 307

imposed budget, 314

incremental approach, 301

life cycle budgeting, 315

management by exception, 299

master budget, 303

minimum level approach, 301

open book management, 316

operating activities, 303

operating budgets, 298

output/input approach, 300

participative budget, 315

purchases budget, 305

risk, 299

risk management, 299

rolling budget, 315

sales budget, 304

selling expense budget, 306

top-down, 314

zero-based budgeting, 301

MULTIPLE CHOICE

1. Budgeted sales of the East End Burger Joint for the first quarter of the year are as follows:

January	$50,000
February	60,000
March	68,000

The cost of sales averages 40 percent of sales revenue and management desires ending inventories equal to 25 percent of the following month's sales. Assuming the January 1 inventory is $5,000, the January purchases budget is:

a. $19,000

b. $21,000

c. $31,000

d. $69,000

Multiple Choice Answers
1. b 2. c 3. b 4. b 5. c

2. Syracuse Distribution's sales budget for the second quarter follows:

January	$250,000
February	300,000
March	290,000

All sales are on account (credit) with 50 percent collected in the month of sale, 30 percent collected in the month after sale, and 20 percent collected in the second month after sale. There are no uncollectable accounts. The March cash receipts are:

a. $140,000

b. $235,000

c. $285,000

d. None of the above

3. Refer to question 2 and determine the accounts receivable at the end of March:

a. $147,000

b. $205,000

c. $235,000

d. $285,000

4. Presented is selected second quarter budget data for the Arnold Company

	Sales
April	20,000 units
May	30,000 units
June	36,000 units

Additional information:
- Each unit of finished product requires three pounds of raw materials.
- Arnold maintains ending finished goods inventories equal to 20 percent of the following month's budgeted sales.
- Arnold maintains raw materials inventories equal to 25 percent of the following month's budgeted production.
- April 1 inventories are in line with Arnold's inventory policy.

Arnold's budgeted purchases (in pounds) for April is:
a. 66,000 pounds
b. 72,900 pounds.
c. 89,400 pounds
d. None of the above

5. Presented is additional information for the Arnold Company (refer to question 4):
- Price per pound of raw materials $20
- Direct labor per unit of finished product   0.40 hours at $25 per hour
- Total monthly factory overhead $200,000 + $10 per direct labor hour

Arnold's total manufacturing cost budget for April is:
a. $880,000
b. $1,680,000
c. $1,828,000
d. $1,966,000

DISCUSSION QUESTIONS

Q9-1. What are the primary phases in the planning and control cycle?

Q9-2. Does budgeting require formal or informal planning? What are some advantages of this style of management?

Q9-3. Identify the advantages and disadvantages of the incremental approach to budgeting.

Q9-4. Explain the minimum level approach to budgeting.

Q9-5. How does activity-based budgeting predict a cost objective's budget?

Q9-6. Explain the continuous improvement concept of budgeting.

Q9-7. Which budget brings together all other budgets? How is this accomplished?

Q9-8. What budgets are normally used to support the cash budget? What is the net result of cash budget preparations?

Q9-9. Define *budgeted financial statements*.

Q9-10. Identify the two budgets that are part of the master budget of a manufacturing organization but not part of the master budget of a merchandising organization.

Q9-11. Contrast the top-down and bottom-up approaches to budget preparation.

Q9-12. Is budgetary slack a desirable feature? Can it be prevented? Why or why not?

Q9-13. Why are annual budgets not always desirable? What are some alternative budget periods?

Q9-14. Explain how continuous budgeting works.

Q9-15. In addition to the sales forecast, what forecasts are used in budgeting?

Q9-16. Why should motivational considerations be a part of budget planning and utilization? List several ways to motivate employees with budgets.

Assignments with the ✅ logo in the margin are available in BusinessCourse.
See the Preface of the book for details.

MINI EXERCISES

M9-17. Output/Input Budget   LO2

Fifth Street Health Center has the following resource input information available for a routine physical examination.

- Each exam normally requires 1.25 hours of examining room time, including:
  - 45 minutes of nursing services,
  - 30 minutes of physician services
- Each exam also utilizes one package of examination supplies costing $20 each.
- Including benefits, physicians earn $60/hour and nurses earn $25/hour.
- Variable overhead is budgeted at $25 per examining room hour and fixed overhead is budgeted at $5,000 per month.

Required
Prepare an output/input budget for October when 500 routine examinations are planned.

M9-18. Incremental Budget   LO2

Smith County uses an incremental approach to budgeting. The 2013 cash budget for the Smith County Department of Motor Vehicles is presented below:

Supplies	$10,000
Temporary and seasonal wages	18,000
Wages of full-time employees	180,000
Supervisor salaries	42,000
Rent	34,000
Insurance	16,000
Utilities	18,000
Miscellaneous	6,000
Contingencies and equipment	30,000
Total	$354,000

Required

Prepare an incremental cash budget for 2014, assuming the planned total budget increase is 2.5 percent. Budget details include a budget increment for salaries and wages of 4 percent, no change in rent, and 2 percent increases in the budget for supplies and miscellaneous. Utility companies have received approvals for rate increases amounting to 4 percent and insurance companies have announced an increase in premiums of 6 percent.

LO3   **M9-19.** **Purchases Budget in Units and Dollars**

Budgeted sales of The Music Shop for the first six months of 2014 are as follows:

Month	Unit Sales	Month	Unit Sales
January	130,000	April	215,000
February..................	160,000	May	180,000
March....................	200,000	June	240,000

Beginning inventory for 2014 is 30,000 units. The budgeted inventory at the end of a month is 40 percent of units to be sold the following month. Purchase price per unit is $5.

Required

Prepare a purchases budget in units and dollars for each month, January through May.

LO3   **M9-20.** **Cash Budget**

Wilson's Retail Company is planning a cash budget for the next three months. Estimated sales revenue is as follows:

Month	Sales Revenue	Month	Sales Revenue
January	$300,000	March.................	$200,000
February..............	250,000	April	150,000

All sales are on credit; 60 percent is collected during the month of sale, and 40 percent is collected during the next month. Cost of goods sold is 80 percent of sales. Payments for merchandise sold are made in the month following the month of sale. Operating expenses total $42,000 per month and are paid during the month incurred. The cash balance on February 1 is estimated to be $30,000.

Required

Prepare monthly cash budgets for February, March, and April.

LO4   **M9-21.** **Production and Purchases Budgets in Units**

At the end of business on June 30, 2014, the Wooly Rug Company had 100,000 square yards of rugs and 400,000 pounds of raw materials on hand. Budgeted sales for the third quarter of 2014 are:

Month	Sales
July..	210,000 sq. yards
August	180,000 sq. yards
September...	140,000 sq. yards
October	160,000 sq. yards

The Wooly Rug Company wants to have sufficient square yards of finished product on hand at the end of each month to meet 40 percent of the following month's budgeted sales and sufficient pounds of raw materials to meet 30 percent of the following month's production requirements. Five pounds of raw materials are required to produce one square yard of carpeting.

Required

Prepare a production budget for the months of July, August, and September and a purchases budget in units for the months of July and August.

LO4   **M9-22.** **Manufacturing Cost Budget**

Henrietta Products produces a product with the following standard costs:

Unit costs:
Direct materials:

Wood: 11 square feet at $5	$55		
Hardware kits (screws, etc)	5	$	60
Direct labor 0.5 hours at $26 per hour			13
Variable overhead, per unit			5
Total variable costs per unit		$	78
Fixed costs per month (rent, utilities, supervision)			$50,000

Management plans to produce 7,000 units in April 2014.

Required

Prepare a manufacturing cost budget for April 2014.

EXERCISES

E9-23.   Activity-Based Budget   LO2

Macon Industries has the following budget information available for February:

Units manufactured	20,000
Factory administration	$45,000
Assembly	½ hour per unit × $8
Direct materials	2 pounds per unit × $3
Inspection	$200 per batch of 1,000 units
Manufacturing overhead	$3 per unit
Product development	$15,000
Setup cost	$10 per batch of 1,000 units

Required

Use activity based costing to prepare a manufacturing cost budget for February. Clearly distinguish between unit, batch, and facility-level costs.

E9-24.   Product and Department Budgets Using Activity-Based Approach   LO2

The following data are from the general records of the Loading Department of Bowman Freight
Company for November.

- Cleaning incoming trucks, 20 minutes.
- Obtaining and reviewing shipping documents for loading truck and instructing loaders, 30 minutes.
- Loading truck, 1 hour and 30 minutes.
- Cleaning shipping dock and storage area after each loading, 10 minutes.
- Employees perform both cleaning and loading tasks and are currently averaging $18 per hour
  in wages and benefits.
- The supervisor spends 10 percent of her time overseeing the cleaning activities; 60 percent
  overseeing various loading activities; and the remainder of her time making general plans and
  managing the department. Her current salary is $4,500 per month.
- Other overhead of the department amounts to $9,000 per month, 20 percent for cleaning and
  80 percent for loading.

Required

Prepare an activities budget for cleaning and loading in the Loading Department for November,
assuming 20 working days and the loading of an average of 14 trucks per day.

E9-25.   Activity-Based Budgeting   LO2

St. Mary's Hospital is preparing its budget for the coming year. It uses an activity-based approach
for all costs except physician care. Its emergency room has three activity areas with cost drivers
as follows:

1. *Reception*—paperwork of incoming patients. Cost driver is the number of forms completed.
2. *Treatment*—initial diagnosis and treatment of patients. Cost driver is the number of diagnoses treated.
3. *Cleaning*—general cleaning plus preparing treatment facilities for next patient. Cost driver is the number of people visiting emergency room (patients plus person(s) accompanying them).

Activity Area	Cost Driver Rates	Budgeted Amount of Cost Driver	
		Outpatients	Admitted Patients
Reception......................	$40	7,400 forms	5,500 forms
Treatment.....................	80	7,000 diagnoses	4,400 diagnoses
Cleaning......................	14	6,400 people	2,400 people

Required

a. Prepare the total budgeted cost for each activity.
b. How might you adjust the budget approach if you found that outpatients were kept in the emergency room for one hour on average while admitted patients remained for two hours?
c. What advantage does an activity-based approach have over the hospital's former budgeting method of basing the next year's budget on the last year's actual amount plus a percentage increase?

LO3 **E9-26.** **Sales Budget**

Summer Fun T-Shirt Shop has very seasonal sales. For 2014, management is trying to decide whether to establish a sales budget based on average sales or on sales estimated by quarter. The unit sales for 2014 are expected to be 10 percent higher than 2013 sales. Unit shirt sales by quarter for 2013 were as follows:

	Children's	Women's	Men's	Total
Winter quarter	200	200	100	500
Spring quarter	200	250	200	650
Summer quarter..............................	400	300	200	900
Fall quarter.................................	200	250	100	550
Total	1,000	1,000	600	2,600

Children's T shirts sell for $6 each, women's sell for $10, and men's sell for $11.

Required

Assuming a 10 percent increase in sales, prepare a sales budget for each quarter of 2014 using the following:

a. Average quarterly sales. (*Hint:* Winter quarter children's shirts are 275 [1,000 × 1.10 ÷ 4].)
b. Actual quarterly sales. (*Hint:* Winter quarter children's shirts are 220 [200 × 1.10].)
c. Suggest advantages of each method.

LO3 **E9-27.** **Cash Budget & Short-Term Financing**

Presented are partial October, November, and December cash budgets for Seasonal Parties:

SEASONAL PARTIES Partial Cash Budgets For the Months of October, November, and December				
	October	November	December	Total
Cash balance, beginning	$13,000	$?	$?	$?
Collections on sales	25,000	30,000	70,000	?
Cash available for operations....................	?	?	?	?
Disbursements for operations	(40,000)	(50,000)	(30,000)	?
Ending cash before borrowings or replacements	?	?	?	?
Short-term finance:............................	?	?	?	?
New loans....................................	?	?	?	?
Repayments..................................	?	?	?	?
Interest	?	?	?	?
Cash balance, ending	$?	$?	$?	$?

Loans are obtained in increments of $1,000 at the start of each month to maintain a minimum end-of-month balance of $10,000. Interest is one percent simple interest (no compounding) per month, payable when the loan is repaid. Repayments are made as soon as possible, subject to the minimum end-of-month balance.

Required

Complete the short-term financing section of the cash budget.

E9-28. **Purchases and Cash Budgets**

On July 1, Five Corners Wholesalers had a cash balance of $155,000 and accounts payable of $79,000. Actual sales for May and June, and budgeted sales for July, August, September, and October are:

Month	Sales	Month	Sales
May	$130,000	September....................	$ 80,000
June......................	140,000	October	100,000
July........................	70,000		
August	60,000		

LO3

All sales are on credit with 75 percent collected during the month of sale, 20 percent collected during the next month, and 5 percent collected during the second month following the month of sale. Cost of goods sold averages 70 percent of sales revenue. Ending inventory is one-half of the next month's predicted cost of sales. The other half of the merchandise is acquired during the month of sale. All purchases are paid for in the month after purchase. Operating costs are estimated at $18,000 each month and are paid during the month incurred.

Required

Prepare purchases and cash budgets for July, August, and September.

E9-29. **Cash Receipts**

The sales budget for Perrier Inc. is forecasted as follows:

Month	Sales Revenue
May	$120,000
June..	160,000
July...	180,000
August	120,000

LO3

✔

To prepare a cash budget, the company must determine the budgeted cash collections from sales. Historically, the following trend has been established regarding cash collection of sales:

- 50 percent in the month of sale.
- 25 percent in the month following sale.
- 20 percent in the second month following sale.
- 5 percent uncollectible.

The company gives a 2 percent cash discount for payments made by customers during the month of sale. The accounts receivable balance on April 30 is $24,000, of which $7,000 represents uncollected March sales and $17,000 represents uncollected April sales.

Required

Prepare a schedule of budgeted cash collections from sales for May, June, and July. Include a three-month summary of estimated cash collections.

E9-30. **Cash Disbursements**

Montana Timber Company is in the process of preparing its budget for next year. Cost of goods sold has been estimated at 70 percent of sales. Lumber purchases and payments are to be made during the month preceding the month of sale. Wages are estimated at 15 percent of sales and are paid during the month of sale. Other operating costs amounting to 10 percent of sales are to be paid in the month following the month of sale. Additionally, a monthly lease payment of $11,000 is paid to BMI for computer services. Sales revenue is forecast as follows:

LO3

Month	Sales Revenue
February.	$120,000
March.	160,000
April	170,000
May	210,000
June	190,000
July.	230,000

Required

Prepare a schedule of cash disbursements for April, May, and June.

LO3 **E9-31.** **Cash Disbursements**

Assume that Waycross Manufacturing manages its cash flow from its home office. Waycross controls cash disbursements by category and month. In setting its budget for the next six months, beginning in July, it used the following managerial guidelines:

Category	Guidelines
Purchases	Pay half in current and half in following month.
Payroll	Pay 70 percent in current month and 30 percent in following month.
Loan payments	Pay total amount due each month.

Predicted activity for selected months follow:

Category	May	June	July	August
Purchases	$ 30,000	$ 44,000	$ 49,000	$ 55,000
Payroll	100,000	110,000	120,000	100,000
Loan payments	10,000	10,000	15,000	15,000

Required

Prepare a schedule showing cash disbursements by account for July and August.

LO3 **E9-32.** **Budgeted Income Statement**

Pendleton Company, a merchandising company, is developing its master budget for 2015. The income statement for 2014 is as follows:

PENDLETON COMPANY Income Statement For Year Ending December 31, 2014	
Gross sales	$750,000
Less estimated uncollectible accounts	(7,500)
Net sales	742,500
Cost of goods sold	(430,000)
Gross profit	312,500
Operating expenses (including $25,000 depreciation)	(200,500)
Net income.	$112,000

The following are management's goals and forecasts for 2015:

1. Selling prices will increase by 6 percent, and sales volume will increase by 4 percent.
2. The cost of merchandise will increase by 3 percent.
3. All operating expenses are fixed and are paid in the month incurred. Price increases for operating expenses will be 10 percent. The company uses straight-line depreciation.
4. The estimated uncollectibles are 2 percent of budgeted sales.

Required

Prepare a budgeted functional income statement for 2015.

E9-33. Budgeted Income Statement with CVP　　　　　　　　　　　　　　LO3

Wisconsin Booksellers is planning a budget for 2015. The estimate of sales revenue is $1,400,000 and of cost of goods sold is 70 percent of sales revenue. Depreciation on the office building and fixtures is budgeted at $50,000. Salaries and wages are budgeted at $90,000. Advertising has been budgeted at $80,000, and utilities should amount to $60,000. Income tax is estimated at 40 percent of operating income.

Required

a.　Prepare a budgeted income statement for 2015.

b.　Assuming management desired an after-tax income of $100,000, determine the necessary sales volume.

E9-34. Production and Purchases Budgets　　　　　　　　　　　　　　　LO4

At the beginning of October, Company Cushion had 1,600 cushions and 7,740 pounds of raw materials on hand. Budgeted sales for the next three months are:

Month	Sales
October	7,000 cushions
November	9,000 cushions
December	12,000 cushions

Company Cushion wants to have sufficient raw materials on hand at the end of each month to meet 25 percent of the following month's production requirements and sufficient cushions on hand at the end of each month to meet 20 percent of the following month's budgeted sales. Three pounds of raw materials, at a standard cost of $0.80 per pound, are required to produce each cushion.

Required

a.　Prepare a production budget for October and November.

b.　Prepare a purchases budget in units and dollars for October.

E9-35. Production and Purchases Budgets　　　　　　　　　　　　　　　LO4

Rocky Mountain Culvert produces small culverts for water drainage under two-lane dirt roads. Budgeted unit sales for the next several months are:

Month	Sales
September	2,000
October	1,500
November	800
December	500

At the beginning of September, 200 units of finished goods were in inventory. During the final third of the year, as road construction declines, plans are to have an inventory of finished goods equal to 25 percent of the following month's sales. Each unit of finished goods requires 500 pounds of raw materials at a cost of $5 per pound. Management wishes to maintain month-end inventories of raw materials equal to 50 percent of the following month's needs. Five hundred thousand pounds of raw materials were on hand at the start of September.

Required

a.　Prepare a production budget for September, October, and November.

b.　Prepare a purchases budget in units and dollars for September and October.

PROBLEMS

P9-36. Cash Budget　　　　　　　　　　　　　　　　　　　　　　　　　LO3

Cash budgeting for Carolina Apple, a merchandising firm, is performed on a quarterly basis. The company is planning its cash needs for the third quarter of 2014, and the following information is available to assist in preparing a cash budget. Budgeted income statements for July through October 2014 are as follows:

	July	August	September	October
Sales	$18,000	$24,000	$28,000	$36,000
Cost of goods sold	(10,000)	(14,000)	(16,000)	(20,000)
Gross profit	8,000	10,000	12,000	16,000
Less other expenses				
Selling........................	2,300	3,000	3,400	4,200
Administrative	2,600	3,000	3,200	3,600
Total	(4,900)	(6,000)	(6,600)	(7,800)
Net income......................	$ 3,100	$ 4,000	$ 5,400	$ 8,200

Additional information follows:

1. Other expenses, which are paid monthly, include $1,000 of depreciation per month.
2. Sales are 40 percent for cash and 60 percent on credit.
3. Credit sales are collected 25 percent in the month of sale, 65 percent one month after sale, and 10 percent two months after sale. May sales were $15,000, and June sales were $16,000.
4. Merchandise is paid for 50 percent in the month of purchase; the remaining 50 percent is paid in the following month. Accounts payable for merchandise at June 30 totaled $6,000.
5. The company maintains its ending inventory levels at 20 percent of the cost of goods to be sold in the following month. The inventory at June 30 is $2,500.
6. An equipment note of $5,000 per month is being paid through August.
7. The company must maintain a cash balance of at least $5,000 at the end of each month. The cash balance on June 30 is $5,100.
8. The company can borrow from its bank as needed. Borrowings and repayments must be in multiples of $100. All borrowings take place at the beginning of a month, and all repayments are made at the end of a month. When the principal is repaid, interest on the repayment is also paid. The interest rate is 12 percent per year.

Required

a. Prepare a monthly schedule of budgeted operating cash receipts for July, August, and September.
b. Prepare a monthly purchases budget and a schedule of budgeted cash payments for purchases for July, August, and September.
c. Prepare a monthly cash budget for July, August, and September. Show borrowings from the company's bank and repayments to the bank as needed to maintain the minimum cash balance.

LO3 **P9-37.** **Cash Budget**

The Peoria Supply Company sells for $30 one product that it purchases for $20. Budgeted sales in total dollars for next year are $720,000. The sales information needed for preparing the July budget follows:

Month	Sales Revenue
May	$30,000
June...	42,000
July...	51,000
August	54,000

Account balances at July 1 include these:

Cash..	$20,000
Merchandise inventory	18,000
Accounts receivable (sales)	23,000
Accounts payable (purchases)	12,000

The company pays for one-half of its purchases in the month of purchase and the remainder in the following month. End-of-month inventory must be 50 percent of the budgeted sales in units for the next month. A 2 percent cash discount on sales is allowed if payment is made during the month of sale. Experience indicates that 50 percent of the billings will be collected during the month of sale, 40 percent in the following month, 8 percent in the second following month, and 2 percent will be uncollectible. Total budgeted selling and administrative expenses (excluding bad debts) for the fiscal year are estimated at $180,000, of which one-half is fixed expense (inclusive of a $18,000 annual depreciation charge). Fixed expenses are incurred evenly during the year. The other selling and administrative expenses vary with sales. Expenses are paid during the month incurred.

Required

a. Prepare a schedule of estimated cash collections for July.

b. Prepare a schedule of estimated July cash payments for purchases.

c. Prepare schedules of July selling and administrative expenses, separately identifying those requiring cash disbursements.

d. Prepare a cash budget in summary form for July.

P9-38. Budgeting Purchases, Revenues, Expenses, and Cash in a Service Organization   **LO3**

Round Lake Medical Center is located in a summer resort community. During the summer months the center operates an outpatient clinic for the treatment of minor injuries and illnesses. The clinic is administered as a separate department within the hospital. It has its own staff and maintains its own financial records. All patients requiring extensive or intensive care are referred to other hospital departments.

An analysis of past operating data for the out-patient clinic reveals the following:

- Staff: Seven full-time employees with total monthly salaries of $42,000. On a monthly basis, one additional staff member is hired for every 500 budgeted patient visits in excess of 3,000, at a cost of $4,000 per month.
- Facilities: Monthly facility costs, including depreciation of $2,000, total $8,000.
- Supplies: The supplies expense averages $10 per patient visit. The center maintains an end-of-month supplies inventory equal to ten percent of the predicted needs of the following month, with a minimum ending inventory of $3,000, which is also the desired inventory at the end of August.
- Additional variable patient costs, such as medications, are charged directly to the patient by the hospital pharmacy.
- Payments: All staff and maintenance expenses are paid in the month the cost is incurrent. Supplies are purchased at cost directly from the hospital with an immediate transfer of cash from the clinic cash account to the hospital cash account.
- Collections: The average bill for services rendered is $60. Of the total bills, 40 percent are paid in cash at the time the service is rendered, 10 percent are never paid, and the remaining 50 percent are covered by insurance. In the past, insurance companies have disallowed 20 percent of the claims filed and paid the balance two months after services are rendered.
- May 30 status: At the end of May, the clinic had $12,000 in cash and supplies costing $3,000.

Budgeted patient visits for next summer are as follows:

Month	Patient visits
June	2,500
July	3,500
August	4,000

Required

For the Round Lake Outpatient Clinic:

a. Prepare a supplies purchases budget for June, July, and August, with a total column.

b. Prepare a revenue and expense budget for June, July, and August with a total column.

c. Prepare a cash budget for June, July and August with a total column. Hint: See requirement d.

d. Explain why you were unable to develop a feasible cash budget and make any appropriate recommendations for management's consideration.

P9-39. Developing a Master Budget for a Merchandising Organization   **LO3**

Peyton Department Store prepares budgets quarterly. The following information is available for use in planning the second quarter budgets for 2014.

PEYTON DEPARTMENT STORE
Balance Sheet
March 31, 2014

Assets		Liabilities and Stockholders' Equity	
Cash.........................	$ 3,000	Accounts payable	$26,000
Accounts receivable	25,000	Dividends payable................	17,000
Inventory	30,000	Rent payable	2,000
Prepaid insurance	2,000	Stockholders' equity..............	40,000
Fixtures	25,000		
Total assets	$85,000	Total liabilities and equity	$85,000

Actual and forecasted sales for selected months in 2014 are as follows:

Month	Sales Revenue
January	$60,000
February..	50,000
March..	40,000
April	50,000
May	60,000
June...	70,000
July..	90,000
August	80,000

Monthly operating expenses are as follows:

Wages and salaries...	$25,000
Depreciation	100
Utilities...	1,000
Rent	2,000

Cash dividends of $17,000 are declared during the third month of each quarter and are paid during the first month of the following quarter. Operating expenses, except insurance, rent, and depreciation are paid as incurred. Rent is paid during the following month. The prepaid insurance is for five more months. Cost of goods sold is equal to 50 percent of sales. Ending inventories are sufficient for 120 percent of the next month's sales. Purchases during any given month are paid in full during the following month. All sales are on account, with 50 percent collected during the month of sale, 40 percent during the next month, and 10 percent during the month thereafter. Money can be borrowed and repaid in multiples of $1,000 at an interest rate of 12 percent per year. The company desires a minimum cash balance of $3,000 on the first of each month. At the time the principal is repaid, interest is paid on the portion of principal that is repaid. All borrowing is at the beginning of the month, and all repayment is at the end of the month. Money is never repaid at the end of the month it is borrowed.

Required

a. Prepare a purchases budget for each month of the second quarter ending June 30, 2014.
b. Prepare a cash receipts schedule for each month of the second quarter ending June 30, 2014. Do not include borrowings.
c. Prepare a cash disbursements schedule for each month of the second quarter ending June 30, 2014. Do not include repayments of borrowings.
d. Prepare a cash budget for each month of the second quarter ending June 30, 2014. Include budgeted borrowings and repayments.
e. Prepare an income statement for each month of the second quarter ending June 30, 2014.
f. Prepare a budgeted balance sheet as of June 30, 2014.

P9-40. Developing a Master Budget for a Manufacturing Organization

Jacobs Incorporated manufactures a product with a selling price of $50 per unit. Units and monthly cost data follow:

Variable:

Selling and administrative.............................	$ 4 per unit sold
Direct materials	10 per unit manufactured
Direct labor...	10 per unit manufactured
Variable manufacturing overhead......................	5 per unit manufactured

Fixed:

Selling and administrative............................	$15,000 per month
Manufacturing (including depreciation of $10,000)	30,000 per month

Jacobs pays all bills in the month incurred. All sales are on account with 50 percent collected the month of sale and the balance collected the following month. There are no sales discounts or bad debts.

Jacobs desires to maintain an ending finished goods inventory equal to 20 percent of the following month's sales and a raw materials inventory equal to 10 percent of the following month's production. January 1, 2014, inventories are in line with these policies.

Actual unit sales for December and budgeted unit sales for January, February, and March of 2014 are as follows:

JACOBS INCORPORATED Sales Budget For the Months of January, February, and March 2014				
Month	December	January	February	March
Sales—Units	6,250	5,000	10,000	8,000
Sales—Dollars..................	$312,500	$250,000	$500,000	$400,000

Additional information:
- The January 1 beginning cash is projected as $5,000.
- For the purpose of operational budgeting, units in the January 1 inventory of finished goods are valued at variable manufacturing cost.
- Each unit of finished product requires one unit of raw materials.
- Jacobs intends to pay a cash dividend of $10,000 in January

Required
a.   A production budget for January and February.
b.   A purchases budget in units for January.
c.   A manufacturing cost budget for January.
d.   A cash budget for January.
e.   A budgeted contribution income statement for January.

P9-41. Risk Management in a Manufacturing Organization

Required
Continuing problem P9-40, management is concerned that their supplier of raw materials will have a strike. Determine the budget implications if management plans to increase the January-end raw materials inventory to 100 percent of February's production needs. Offer any recommendations you believe appropriate.

P9-42. Developing a Master Budget for a Manufacturing Organization: Challenge Problem

Banana Computer Accessories assembles a computer networking device from kits of imported components. You have been asked to develop a quarterly and annual operating budget and pro-forma income statements for 2014. You have obtained the following information:

Beginning-of-year balances
Cash	$40,000.00
Accounts receivable (previous quarter's sales)	$15,000.00
Raw materials	300 kits
Finished goods	400 units
Accounts payable	$40,000.00
Borrowed funds	$10,000.00

Desired end-of-year inventory balances
Raw materials	500 kits
Finished goods	200 units

Desired end-of-quarter balances
Cash	$10,000.00
Raw materials as a portion of the following quarter's production	0.2
Finished goods as a portion of the following quarter's sales	0.15

Manufacturing costs

Standard cost per unit	Units	Unit price	Total
Raw materials.	1 kit	$40.00	$40.00
Direct labor hours at rate.	0.8 hour	$20.00	16.00
Variable overhead/labor hour	0.8 hour	$10.00	8.00
Total standard variable cost			$64.00

Fixed cost per quarter
Cash	$40,000.00
Depreciation	10,000.00
Total	$50,000.00

Selling and administrative costs
Variable cost per unit.	$6.00

Fixed costs per quarter
Cash	$20,000.00
Depreciation	5,000.00
Total	$25,000.00

Interest rate per quarter	0.04

Portion of sales collected
Quarter of sale	0.75
Subsequent quarter.	0.24
Bad debts.	0.01

Portion of purchases paid
Quarter of purchase.	0.70
Subsequent quarter.	0.30
Unit selling price	$115.00

Sales forecast

Quarter	First	Second	Third	Fourth
Unit sales	2,400	1,500	2,000	3,100

Additional information

- All cash payments except purchases are made quarterly as incurred.
- All borrowings occur at the start of the quarter.
- All repayments on borrowings occur at the end of the quarter.
- All interest on borrowed funds is paid at the end of each quarter.
- Borrowings and repayments may be made in any amount.

Required

a. A sales budget for each quarter and the year. Hint: Use of spreadsheet software strongly recommended for this problem.
b. A production budget for each quarter and the year.
c. A purchases budget for each quarter and the year.
d. A manufacturing cost budget for each quarter and the year.

e. A selling and administrative expense budget for each quarter and the year.

f. A cash budget for each quarter and the year.

g. A pro-forma contribution income statement for each quarter and the year.

CASES AND PROJECTS

C9-43. Behavioral Implications of Budgeting

LO5

Cindy Jones, controller of Systematic Designs, believes that effective budgeting greatly assists in meeting the organization's goals and objectives. She argues that the budget serves as a blueprint for the operating activities during each reporting period, making it an important control device. She believes that sound management evaluations can be based on the comparisons of performance and budgetary schedules and that employees respond more favorably when they participate in the budgetary process. Kevin Dobbs, treasurer of Systematic Designs, agrees that budgeting is essential for overall organization success, but he argues that human resources are too valuable to spend much time planning and preparing the budgetary process. He thinks that the roles people play in budgetary preparation are not important in the final analysis of a budget's effectiveness.

Required

Contrast the participative versus imposed budgeting concepts and indicate how the ideas of Jones and Dobbs fit the two categories.

C9-44. Behavioral Considerations and Budgeting

LO5

Anthony Wagner, the controller in the Division of Transportation for the state, recognizes the importance of the budgetary process for planning, control, and motivation purposes. He believes that a properly implemented participative budgeting process for planning purposes and a management by exception reporting procedure based on that budget will motivate his subordinates to improve productivity within their particular departments. Based on this philosophy, Wagner has implemented the following budget procedures.

- An appropriation target figure is given to each department manager. This amount is the maximum funding that each department can expect to receive in the next fiscal year.
- Department managers develop their individual budgets within the following spending constraints as directed by the controller's staff.
  1. Expenditure requests cannot exceed the appropriation target.
  2. All fixed expenditures should be included in the budget; these should include items such as contracts and salaries at current levels.
  3. All government projects directed by higher authority should be included in the budget in their entirety.
- The controller consolidates the departmental budget requests from the various departments into one budget that is to be submitted for the entire division.
- Upon final budget approval by the legislature, the controller's staff allocates the appropriation to the various departments on instructions from the division manager. However, a specified percentage of each department's appropriation is held back in anticipation of potential budget cuts and special funding needs. The amount and use of this contingency fund are left to the discretion of the division manager.
- Each department is allowed to adjust its budget when necessary to operate within the reduced appropriation level. However, as stated in the original directive, specific projects authorized by higher authority must remain intact.
- The final budget is used as the basis of control for a management by exception form of reporting. Excessive expenditures by account for each department are highlighted on a monthly basis. Department managers are expected to account for all expenditures over budget. Fiscal responsibility is an important factor in the overall performance evaluation of department managers.

Wagner believes that his policy of allowing the department managers to participate in the budget process and then holding them accountable for their performance is essential, especially during these times of limited resources. He also believes that department managers will be positively motivated to increase the efficiency and effectiveness of their departments because they have provided input into the initial budgetary process and are required to justify any unfavorable performances.

Required

a. Explain the operational and behavioral benefits that generally are attributed to a participative budgeting process.

b. Identify deficiencies in Wagner's participative budgetary policy for planning and performance evaluation purposes. For each deficiency identified, recommend how the deficiency can be corrected.

(CMA Adapted)

LO5 **C9-45.** **Budgetary Slack with Ethical Considerations**

Karen Bailey was promoted to department manager of a production unit in Parkway Industries three years ago. She enjoys her job except for the evaluation measures that are based on the department's budget. After three years of consistently poor annual evaluations based on a set annual budget, she has decided to improve the evaluation situation. At a recent budget meeting of junior-level managers, the topic of budgetary slack was discussed as a means to maintain some consistency in budgeting matters. As a result of this meeting, Bailey decided to take the following steps in preparing the upcoming year's budget:

1. Use the top quartile for all wage and salary categories.
2. Select the optimistic values for the estimated production ranges for the coming year. These are provided by the marketing department.
3. Use the average of the three months in the current year with poorest production efficiency as benchmarks of success for the coming year.
4. Base equipment charges (primarily depreciation) on replacement values furnished by the purchasing department.
5. Base other fixed costs on current cost plus an inflation rate estimated for the coming year.
6. Use the average of the ten newly hired employees' performance as a basis of labor efficiency for the coming year.

Required

a. For each item on Bailey's list, explain whether it will create budgetary slack. Use numerical examples as necessary to illustrate.

b. Given the company's use of static budgets as one of the performance evaluation measures of its managers, can the managers justify the use of built-in budgetary slack?

c. What would you recommend as a means for Bailey to improve the budgeting situation in the company? Provide some specific examples of how the budgeting process might be improved.

LO5 **C9-46.** **Budgetary Slack with Ethical Considerations**

Norton Company, a manufacturer of infant furniture and carriages, is in the initial stages of preparing the annual budget for next year. Scott Ford recently joined Norton's accounting staff and is interested to learn as much as possible about the company's budgeting process. During a recent lunch with Marge Atkins, sales manager, and Pete Granger, production manager, Ford initiated the following conversation:

Ford: Since I'm new around here and am going to be involved with the preparation of the annual budget, I'd be interested to learn how the two of you estimate sales and production numbers.

Atkins: We start out very methodically by looking at recent history, discussing what we know about current accounts, potential customers, and the general state of consumer spending. Then we add that usual dose of intuition to come up with the best forecast we can.

Granger: I usually take the sales projections as the basis for my projections. Of course, we have to make an estimate of what this year's closing inventories will be, which is sometimes difficult.

Ford: Why does that present a problem? There must have been an estimate of closing inventories in the budget for the current year.

Granger: Those numbers aren't always reliable since Marge makes some adjustments to the sales numbers before passing them on to me.

Ford: What kind of adjustments?

Atkins: Well, we don't want to fall short of the sales projections, so we generally give ourselves a little breathing room by lowering the initial sales projection anywhere from 5 to 10 percent.

Granger: So, you can see why this year's budget is not a very reliable starting point. We always have to adjust the projected production rates as the year progresses; of course, this changes the ending inventory estimates. By the way, we make similar adjustments to expenses by adding at least 10 percent to the estimates; I think everyone around here does the same thing.

Required

a. Marge Atkins and Pete Granger have described the use of budgetary slack.
   1. Explain why Atkins and Granger behave in this manner, and describe the benefits they expect to realize from the use of budgetary slack.
   2. Explain how the use of budgetary slack can adversely affect Atkins and Granger.

b. As a management accountant, Scott Ford believes that the behavior described by Marge Atkins and Pete Granger could be unethical and that he might have an obligation not to support this behavior. Explain why the use of budgetary slack could be unethical.

(CMA Adapted)

SOLUTIONS TO REVIEW PROBLEMS

<u>Mid-Chapter Review</u>

Solution

a. Under the output/input approach, the output of units dictates the expected cost inputs. Here budgeted overhead costs are based on the number of budgeted assembly hours.

	Centrum	Advil
Direct materials (20,000 × $20)	$400,000	
(50,000 × $14.50)		$ 725,000
Direct assembly labor (20,000 × 0.5 × $18)	180,000	
(50,000 × 0.8 × $18)		720,000
Overhead (20,000 × 0.5 × $8.17)	81,700	
(50,000 × 0.8 × $8.17)		326,800
Total budgeted cost	$661,700	$1,771,800
Unit Cost	$33.085	$35.436

b. Under the activity-based approach, budgeted overhead costs are based on expected activities to produce the products, not only on assembly hours.

Direct materials (20,000 × $20)	$400,000	
(50,000 × $14.50)		$ 725,000
Direct assembly labor (20,000 × 0.5 × $18)	180,000	
(50,000 × 0.8 × $18)		720,000
Setup (1,000 hours × $25)	25,000	
(1,500 hours × $25)		37,500
Engineering and Maintenance (500 hours × $35)	17,500	
(600 hours × $35)		21,000
Inspections (650 inspections × $250)	162,500	
(580 inspections × $250)		145,000
Total budgeted cost	$785,000	$1,648,500
Unit cost	$39.25	$32.97

c. Under the incremental approach to budgeting, the cost per unit would be budgeted at last period's cost, plus an increment for expected additional costs in the current period. Based on last period's actual cost of $38 for Centrum and $32 for Advil, and using the 3.5 percent overall expected increase in costs, the current period's budgeted cost would be $39.33 for Centrum and $33.12 for Advil.

d. Under the minimum level approach, the company begins with either a zero or very low cost estimate, and then requires all additional costs beyond this minimum to be justified by the production managers. This approach forces managers to evaluate thoroughly all elements of cost each period.

<u>Chapter-End Review 1</u>

Solution

a.

COWGIRL CREAMERY
Sales Budget
For Month of April 2014

	Units	Price	Sales
Cheese...	160,000	$10	$1,600,000
Ice cream..	240,000	5	1,200,000
Total..			$2,800,000

b.

COWGIRL CREAMERY
Purchases Budget
For Month of April 2014

	Cheese	Ice Cream	Total
Units			
Sales needs	160,000	240,000	
Desired ending inventory	12,000	5,000	
Total	172,000	245,000	
Less beginning inventory	(10,000)	(4,000)	
Purchases	162,000	241,000	
Dollars			
Sales needs	$1,280,000	$480,000	
Desired ending inventory	96,000	10,000	
Total	1,376,000	490,000	
Less beginning inventory	(80,000)	(8,000)	
Purchases needed.......................	$1,296,000	$482,000	$1,778,000

c.

COWGIRL CREAMERY
Cash Budget
For Month of April 2014

Cash balance, beginning		$ 400,000
Collections on sales		
Current month's sales ($2,800,000 × 0.70)...................	$1,960,000	
Previous month's sales ($3,000,000 × 0.29).................	870,000	2,830,000
Cash available from operations		3,230,000
Less budgeted disbursements		
March purchases ($1,800,000 × 0.40)	720,000	
April purchases ($1,778,000 × 0.60)........................	1,066,800	
Wages and salaries	156,000	
Overhead (March)	80,000	
Selling and administrative ($450,000 − $40,000 depreciation)	410,000	(2,432,800)
Cash balance, ending		$ 797,200

d.

COWGIRL CREAMERY
Budgeted Income Statement
For Month of April 2014

Sales (sales budget)			$2,800,000
Allowance for bad debts			(28,000)
Net sales			2,772,000
Costs of merchandise sold			
Cheese (160,000 × $8)	$1,280,000		
Ice cream (240,000 × $2)	480,000	$1,760,000	
Wages and salaries	156,000		
Overhead	80,000		
Selling and administrative	450,000	686,000	(2,446,000)
Net income			$ 326,000

Chapter-End Review 2:

Solution

a.

STANLEY TOOL COMPANY
Sales Budget
For First Quarter of 2014

	Units	Price	Sales
Drills	60,000	$100	$ 6,000,000
Saws	40,000	125	5,000,000
Total			$11,000,000

b.

STANLEY TOOL COMPANY
Production Budget
For First Quarter of 2014

	Drills	Saws
Budget sales	60,000	40,000
Plus desired ending inventory	25,000	10,000
Total inventory requirements	85,000	50,000
Less beginning inventory	(20,000)	(8,000)
Budgeted production	65,000	42,000

c.

	STANLEY TOOL COMPANY Purchases Budget For First Quarter of 2014		
	Drills	**Saws**	**Total**
Metal purchases			
Production units (production budget)...........	65,000	42,000	
Metal (pounds)...........................	× 5	× 4	
Production needs (pounds).................	325,000	168,000	493,000
Desired ending inventory (pounds).............................			36,000
Total metal needs (pounds).....................................			529,000
Less beginning inventory (pounds).............................			(32,000)
Purchases needed (pounds).....................................			497,000
Cost per pound..			× $8
Total metal purchases...			$3,976,000
Plastic purchases			
Production units (production budget)...........	65,000	42,000	107,000
Plastic (pounds)..			× 3
Production needs (pounds).....................................			321,000
Desired ending inventory (pounds).............................			32,000
Total plastic needs (pounds)...................................			353,000
Less beginning inventory (pounds).............................			(29,000)
Purchases needed (pounds).....................................			324,000
Cost per pound..			× $5
Total plastic purchases.......................................			$1,620,000
Handle purchases			
Production units (production budget)...........	65,000		65,000
Handles..			× 1
Production needs..			65,000
Desired ending inventory.................................			7,000
Total handle needs......................................			72,000
Less beginning inventory.................................			(6,000)
Purchases needed..			66,000
Cost per handle..			× $3
Total handle purchases....................................			$198,000
Total purchases			
Metal..			$3,976,000
Plastic...			1,620,000
Handles..			198,000
Total purchases..			$5,794,000

d.

STANLEY TOOL COMPANY Manufacturing Cost Budget For First Quarter of 2014			
	Drills	**Saws**	**Total**
Direct materials			
Metal			
Production units (production budget).........	65,000	42,000	
Metal per unit of product (pounds)	× 5	× 4	
Production needs for metal (pounds)	325,000	168,000	
Unit cost.................................	× $8	× $8	
Cost of metal issued to production	$2,600,000	$1,344,000	$3,944,000
Plastic			
Production units (production budget)..........	65,000	42,000	
Plastic (pounds)............................	× 3	× 3	
Production needs for plastic (pounds)	195,000	126,000	
Unit cost..................................	× $5	× $5	
Cost of plastic issued to production	$ 975,000	$ 630,000	1,605,000
Handles			
Production units (production budget)..........	65,000		
Handles	× 1		
Production needs for handles................	65,000		
Unit cost..................................	× $3		
Cost of handles issued to production	$ 195,000		195,000
Total.......................................			5,744,000
Direct labor			
Budgeted production.......................	65,000	42,000	
Direct labor hours per unit...................	× 2	× 3	
Total direct labor hours.....................	130,000	126,000	
Labor rate.................................	× $12	× $16	
Labor expenditures..........................	$1,560,000	$2,016,000	3,576,000
Variable manufacturing overhead			
Direct labor hours	130,000	126,000	
Variable manufacturing overhead rate	× $1.50	× $1.50	
Total variable overhead.......................	$ 195,000	$ 189,000	384,000
Fixed manufacturing overhead.................			214,000
Total.......................................			$9,918,000

e.

STANLEY TOOL COMPANY		
Cash Budget		
For First Quarter of 2014		
Cash balance, beginning		$ 1,800,000
Collections on sales		
Current quarter's sales ($11,000,000 × 0.50)..............	$5,500,000	
Previous quarter's sales ($8,400,000 × 0.50)..............	4,200,000	9,700,000
Cash available from operations		11,500,000
Less budgeted disbursements		
Materials (purchases budget)	5,794,000	
Labor (manufacturing cost budget)	3,576,000	
Manufacturing overhead (manufacturing cost budget)		
([$384,000 + 214,000] − 156,000 noncash)	442,000	
Selling and administrative		
($340,000 − $90,000 depreciation)......................	250,000	(10,062,000)
Cash balance, ending		$ 1,438,000

f.

STANLEY TOOL COMPANY		
Contribution Income Statement		
For First Quarter of 2014		
Sales (sales budget)		$11,000,000
Less variable costs of goods sold		
Drills (60,000 × $85.00)	$5,100,000	
Saws (40,000 × $99.50).................................	3,980,000	(9,080,000)
Gross profit		1,920,000
Less fixed costs		
Manufacturing overhead	214,000	
Selling and administrative expenses	340,000	(554,000)
Net income...		$ 1,366,000

1. Explain responsibility accounting. (p. 344)

2. Differentiate between static and flexible budgets for performance reporting. (p. 348)

3. Determine and interpret direct materials, direct labor, and overhead cost variances. (p. 351)

4. Calculate revenue variances and prepare a performance report for a revenue center. (p. 359)

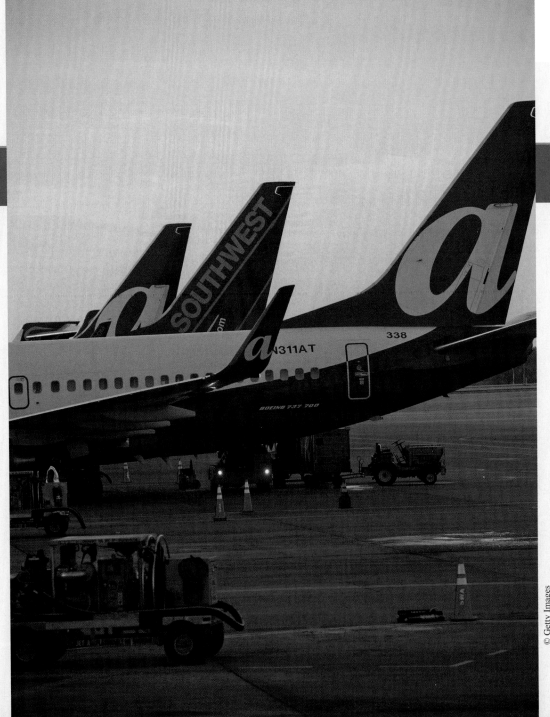

Standard Costs and Performance Reports

In the last chapter, we discussed how budgeting was critical to planning within a business. But planning is only half of the story; at the end of the period, the operating results are compared to the budget. By evaluating the differences between the budgeted and the actual results, a manager can identify areas of the business that need attention. We call these differences *budget variances*, and a thorough analysis of these variances aids the manager in controlling the human and physical resources of the business.

SOUTHWEST AIRLINES
www.southwest.com

To effectively control the business through variance analysis, it is important that the lines of responsibility are clearly defined among the managers. Managers (and the people that evaluate their results) need to understand who is responsible for revenues, costs, profits, capital investments, or some combination of those elements. This assignment of responsibility prevents managers from "passing the buck" when something goes wrong. Consider the case of Southwest Airlines, the Dallas, Texas–based airline, which recently completed a merger with Air Tran. When a structural shift such as a merger takes place, the lines of responsibility may be temporarily blurred. This can impede not only variance analysis, but also the integration of the merged entities.

While other airlines have bolstered revenue by charging fees for baggage, additional legroom, Wi-Fi, and changed flights, Southwest's strategy has been to offer passengers inexpensive and flexible flight arrangements with no hidden fees for baggage or other basic services. Inconsistencies between Southwest and Air Tran are prevalent in the merged business even three years after the fact. Southwest permits customers to buy early boarding privileges, but Air Tran does not. Bags fly free on Southwest, but not on Air Tran. There is no business class on Southwest, whereas Air Tran passengers frequently receive complementary upgrades to business class. The two reservation systems cannot easily rebook passengers across the two airlines, and their frequent flier miles are not transferrable between the two airlines.

Even once the integration of Southwest and Air Tran is complete, there are still likely to be issues between expected and actual operating results. Some of the variances may relate to usage or efficiency, whereas others may relate to the dollar amount spent on a resource. For example, the airline could use more or less fuel than is expected and the price paid per gallon of fuel could differ from expectations. Flight personnel may work more or fewer hours than expected and scheduling issues may result in paying higher- or lower-than-average wages than expected for the number of hours worked. Variance analysis can be extended to issues such as bag handling, overbooking, and number of passenger complaints. Indeed, both Southwest and Air Tran have had significant increases in mishandled baggage since the merger took place. Another important metric for airlines is adherence to the flight schedule. Airlines have "gamed" this variance by building extra minutes into flight schedules to boost on-time performance.

continued on following page

continued from previous page

Even though mergers can decrease the level of competition within an industry, customers still have some choice of airlines available to them. Managers prefer timely notification of potential variances so they still have time to "right the ship" before the end of the reporting period. Recently, airlines have utilized customer surveys to uncover potential customer service problems. For example, Southwest sends questionnaires to customers the day following their flight and scores are sent to each airport manager on a weekly basis. Yet surveys are only as valuable as the managers' responses to any problems. At least in some cases, Southwest's response has been impressive. A passenger describes the recent experience of a missed connection due to weather. He was envisioning a long wait at the customer service counter or a call to an 800 number only to be put on indefinite hold. Imagine his surprise when a Southwest agent was waiting for him at this arrival gate with a new boarding pass on his rebooked flight. By using variance analysis as a diagnostic tool and by displaying anticipatory customer service, Southwest should be able to put its brand back on top, merger and all.

Sources: Micah Solomon, "Customer Service: What Southwest Knows and You Don't (Hint: Being Nice Isn't Enough)," *Forbes*, September 22, 2013; Alanna Petroff, "Airlines Rake in $27 Billion in Customer Fees," *CNN Money*, September 19, 2013; Scott McCartney, "Airlines Mergers and Aggravations," *Wall Street Journal*, July 18, 2013, pp. D1–D3; Scott McCartney, "Dear Airline, Here's the Problem ...," *Wall Street Journal*, April 4, 2013, pp. D1–D4; and Scott McCartney, "Reality Check: Why Airlines Are Shrinking Flight Times," *Wall Street Journal*, June 14, 2012, pp. D1–D2.

CHAPTER ORGANIZATION

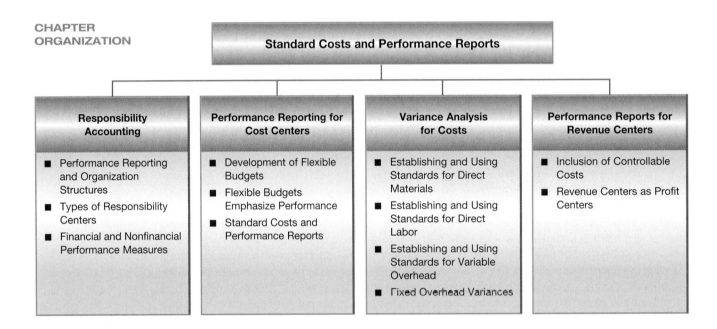

Management accounting tools aid in the assessment of the performance of the firm as a whole and all of its various components. Feedback in the form of performance reports is essential if the benefits of budgeting and other types of planning are to be fully realized. To control current operations and to improve future operations, managers must know how actual results compare with the current budget. These performance reports should be prepared in accordance with the concept of **responsibility accounting**, which is the structuring of performance reports addressed to individual (or group) members of an organization to emphasize the factors they control.

This chapter focuses on responsibility accounting and performance assessment. We examine responsibility accounting and identify various types of responsibility centers. We then take a close look at performance assessment for cost centers and conclude by considering performance reports for revenue centers. Responsibility accounting for major business segments is considered in Chapter 11.

RESPONSIBILITY ACCOUNTING

LO1 Explain responsibility accounting.

Performance reports that include comparisons of actual results with plans or budgets serve as assessment tools and attention-directors to help managers control activities. According to the concept of *management by exception*, the absence of significant differences indicates that activities are proceeding as planned whereas the presence of significant differences indicates a need to either take corrective action or revise plans. These evaluations and actions are made within the framework of an organization's overall mission, goals, and strategies.

Responsibility accounting reports are customized to emphasize the activities of specific organizational units. For example, a performance report addressed to the head of a production department contains manufacturing costs controllable by the department head; it should not contain costs (such as advertising, sales commissions, or the president's salary) that the head of the production department cannot control. Including noncontrollable costs in the report distracts the manager's attention from the controllable costs, thereby diluting a manager's efforts to deal with controllable items.

If too much pressure is placed on managers to meet performance targets, they may take actions that are not in the best interest of the organization. The Business Insight that follows presents classic examples of such actions involving a vice president of Bausch & Lomb and the CEO of Sunbeam who forced sales into one year to the detriment of the companies' sales the following year. The designers of an organization's responsibility accounting system need to be aware of the potential pressures that such a system can place on managers. The decision-making model of the organization should be such that managers are not influenced to make undesirable decisions just to receive bonuses or promotions.

BUSINESS INSIGHT

Ethics and Responsibility Accounting A few years ago, the contact lens division of Bausch & Lomb, Inc., was experiencing lower-than-anticipated sales levels. The head of the division called a meeting of its independent distributors and told them that the company had changed its sales strategy. Effective immediately, each distributor would have to boost its inventory of contact lenses if it wanted to remain a distributor of Bausch & Lomb products. The strategy was for distributors to buy only in very large quantities (some as much as a two-year supply) with prices increased by amounts up to 50 percent. Also, the distributors had to place these large orders by year-end. As one distributor stated, "When your No. 1 vendor says you'd better take it or else, what're you going to do?" All but two of Bausch & Lomb's distributors complied with the new sales strategy demands; and those two were subsequently dropped as customers.

Initially the strategy paid off; the sales in the last few days of the year totaled about $25 million and amounted to one-half of the division's profit for the entire year. The division manager was delighted. However, the long-term results were not favorable. By the following mid-year, the company announced that the high inventories of its distributors would severely reduce sales and profits for that year. The profit decline was approximately 37 percent. After the announcement, the company's stock fell from $50 to $32. The manager was forced to step down, and stockholders filed a class-action lawsuit accusing the company of falsely inflating sales and earnings.

History repeated itself when the CEO of Sunbeam followed the Bausch & Lomb plan to force sales to show how well his management style (firing employees and closing plants) was working. Sunbeam instituted a "bill and hold" plan that called for products to be produced in large quantities and sold to customers for delivery at a later date. While this made the financial report for that first year very favorable, it had a detrimental effect on the next year's report. In late March of that following year, Sunbeam acknowledged that first-quarter income would be below expectations, and in fact, a loss. Stockholders quickly filed lawsuits charging deception, and the CEO was fired.

Source: "Numbers Game at Bausch & Lomb?" *Business Week,* December 19, 1994, pp. 108–10; and "How Al Dunlap Self-Destructed," *Business Week,* July 6, 1998, pp. 58–61, 64.

Performance Reporting and Organization Structures

Before implementing a responsibility accounting system, all areas of authority and responsibility within an organization must be clearly defined. Organization charts and other documents should be examined to determine an organization's authority and responsibility structure. **Organization structure** is the arrangement of lines of authority and responsibility within an organization. These structures vary widely. Some companies have functional-based structures along the lines of marketing, production, research, and so forth; others use products, services, customers, or geography as the basis of organization. When an attempt is made to implement a responsibility accounting system, management could find instances of overlapping duties, authority not commensurate with responsibility, and expenditures for which no one appears responsible. The identification and resolution of these problems can be a major benefit of implementing a responsibility accounting system.

Although performance reports can be developed for areas of responsibility as narrow as a single worker, the basic responsibility unit in most organizations begins with the department and progresses to division and corporate levels. In manufacturing plants, separate performance reports may be prepared for each production and service department, and then summarized into a performance report for all manufacturing activities. In large universities, reports may be prepared for individual departments such as history, philosophy, and English, and then summarized into a performance report of a college, such as Liberal Arts.

Types of Responsibility Centers

Based on the nature of their responsibility, responsibility centers can be classified as cost centers, revenue centers, profit centers, or investment centers.

Cost Center

A **cost center** manager is only responsible for costs; there is no revenue responsibility. A cost center can be as small as a segment of a department or large enough to include a major aspect of the organization, such as all manufacturing activities. Typical examples of cost centers include the following:

Organization	Cost Center
Manufacturing plant	Tooling department Assembly activities
Retail store	Inventory control function Maintenance department
Hospital	Radiology Emergency room
College	History department Registrar's office
City government	Public safety (police and fire) Road maintenance

Revenue Center

A **revenue center** manager is responsible for the generation of sales revenues. Even though the basic performance report of a revenue center emphasizes sales, revenue centers are likely to be assigned responsibility for the controllable costs they incur in generating revenues. If revenues and costs are evaluated separately, the center has dual responsibility as a revenue center and as a cost center. If controllable costs are deducted from revenues to obtain some bottom-line contribution, the center is, in fact, being treated more like a profit center than a revenue center.

Profit Center

A **profit center** manager is responsible for revenues, costs, and the resulting profits. A profit center could be an entire organization, but it is more frequently a segment of an organization such as a product line, marketing territory, or store. In the context of performance evaluation, the word "profit" does not necessarily refer to the bottom line of an income statement; instead, it likely refers to the profit center's contribution to common corporate costs and profit. Profit is computed as the center's revenues less all costs directly associated with operating the center. Having limited authority regarding the size of total assets, the profit center manager is not held responsible for the relationship between profits and assets. In recent years many hospitals have been treating critical care and clinical service departments as profit centers to encourage physician chiefs to manage their departments as small businesses. The following Research Insight examines some of the issues associated with this movement.

Investment Center

An **investment center** manager is responsible for the relationship between its profits and the total assets invested in the center. Investment center managers have a high degree of organization autonomy. In general, the management of an investment center is expected to earn a target profit per dollar invested. Investment center managers are evaluated on the basis of how well they use the total resources entrusted to their care to earn a profit. An investment center is the broadest and most inclusive type of responsibility center. Managers of these centers have more authority and responsibility than other managers and are primarily responsible for planning, organizing, and controlling firm activities. Because of their authority regarding the size of corporate assets, they are held responsible for the relationship between profits and assets. Investment centers are discussed further in Chapter 11.

RESEARCH INSIGHT

Hospital Researcher Questions Use of Profit Centers As hospitals attempt to improve fiscal management, many have designated critical care departments such as cardiovascular surgery, orthopedics, and pediatrics as profit centers. After examining this movement, Professor David Young concludes that hospitals and patients would be better served by treating critical care departments as standard expense (cost) centers. Problems Young identified with designating critical care departments as profit centers include:

■ Bad feelings between departments that are inherently more lucrative such as cardiovascular surgery and departments that are normally poor financial performers such as pediatrics. According to Young, the intensity of feeling is illustrated by a cardiovascular surgeon at a large medical center who blurted out "I'm tired of subsidizing those lazy pediatricians."

■ Problems determining the proper relationships between critical care (line) departments such as orthopedics and clinical service departments such as radiology. Should a critical care department such as orthopedics be allowed to obtain radiology services outside the hospital? How much should orthopedics pay for radiology services obtained inside the hospital, and who should determine the amount they pay? (See transfer pricing discussed in Chapter 11.)

■ Many hospitals are now shifting their strategy toward service lines such as women's health that require historically independent critical care and clinical service departments to work seamlessly together toward a common goal. Treating individual departments as profit centers may be incompatible with such a strategy.

■ Critical care departments, seeking an operating profit, may try to avoid treating low-income or poorly insured patients even when treating such patients is part of the hospital's mission.

Professor Young concludes that the physician managers of standard expense (cost) centers should focus their attention on striving to provide quality medical care while meeting a flexible budget, thereby avoiding the additional decisions and conflicts associated with efforts to obtain a department operating surplus.

Source: David W. Young, "Profit Centers in Clinical Care Departments An Idea Whose Time Has Gone," *Healthcare Financial Management*, March 2008, pp. 66–71.

Financial and Nonfinancial Performance Measures

This chapter's emphasis is on financial performance reports. Dollar-based financial reports have several advantages over other financial measures. Their "bottom line" impact is readily apparent. If actual fixed costs exceed budgeted fixed costs by $10,000, the before-tax income of an organization is $10,000 less than it would be without the extra fixed costs. Additionally, because dollars are additive and applicable to all organizational units, financial measures are easily summarized and reported up the organization chart.

It is important to keep in mind that although financial measures may indicate results are not in accordance with the budget, they do not indicate the root cause of financial deviations. The identification and analysis of the root cause of financial variances requires asking questions and, frequently, the use of nonfinancial data. Managers and employees at lower levels of the organization are often better served by performance reports focusing on data directly related to their job, such as units processed or customers served per hour. Although financial performance is still critical to Southwest Airline's top management and still used to evaluate managers, aircraft and routes, the focus for the evaluation should include customer satisfaction. Other examples of nonfinancial performance measures include: defects per thousand units in a manufacturing plant, average and longest waiting time in a restaurant, nursing staff hours per patient day in a hospital, response time for a fire department, and customer satisfaction at a retail store or bank.

When organizations seek to improve financial performance beyond what is possible with current products, procedures, or services, the initial focus is most often on nonfinancial measures. Kroger grocery stores might benchmark the length of their cash-register waiting times against SuperValu's.

PERFORMANCE REPORTING FOR COST CENTERS

LO2 Differentiate between static and flexible budgets for performance reporting.

Financial performance reports for cost centers include a comparison of actual and budgeted (or allowed) costs and identify the difference as a **variance**. *Allowed costs* in performance reports are the flexible budget amounts for the actual level of activity. The variance is favorable if actual costs are less than budgeted (or allowed) costs and unfavorable if actual costs are more than budgeted (or allowed) costs. These comparisons are made in total and individually for each type of controllable cost assigned to the cost center.

Development of Flexible Budgets

A budget that is based on a prediction of sales and production is called a **static budget**. The operating budget explained in Chapter 9 is a static budget. Budgets can also be set for a series of possible production and sales volumes, or budgets can be adjusted to a particular level of production after the fact. These budgets, based on cost-volume relationships, are called **flexible budgets**; they are used to determine what costs should be for a level of activity. For example, if the college cafeteria budgets $15,000 for food during April for 5,000 meals but provides 6,000 meals, the budget needs to be adjusted by the original food budget rate of $3 ($15,000/5,000 meals). If $17,500 was spent on food during the month, the analysis might appear as follows:

Budget Item	Actual	Budget	Difference
Static analysis			
Food......................	$17,500	5,000 meals × $3 = $15,000	$2,500 over budget
Flexible analysis			
Food......................	$17,500	6,000 meals × $3 = $18,000	$500 under budget

The cafeteria manager is better evaluated based on what actually happened with the flexible budget than with the static budget, especially if the manager had no control over how many student meals were requested.

For a complete example of a flexible budget, assume that Coach, which produces high-quality handbags and accessories, has three departments: production, sales, and administration. Focusing on the production department, the flexible budget cost-estimating equations for total monthly production costs of cases are based on the production standards for variable and fixed costs. The standards follow:

Variable costs
   Direct materials—2 pounds per unit at $5 per pound, or $10 per unit
   Direct labor—0.25 hour per unit at $24 per hour, or $6 per unit
   Variable overhead—2 pounds per unit at $4 per pound, or $8 per unit
Fixed costs—$52,000

If management plans to produce 10,000 handbags in July, the budgeted manufacturing costs are $292,000:

COACH
Manufacturing Cost Budget
For Month of July

Manufacturing costs	
Variable costs	
Direct materials (10,000 units × 2 pounds × $5)	$100,000
Direct labor (10,000 units × 0.25 hours × $24).	60,000
Variable overhead (10,000 units × 2 pounds × $4)	80,000
Fixed costs.	52,000
Total.	$292,000

Flexible Budgets Emphasize Performance

If actual production happened to equal budgeted production, the production department is evaluated by comparing the actual and budgeted costs. If production needs change, perhaps due to an unexpected increase or decrease in sales volume, the production department should attempt to make appropriate changes. When the actual production volume is anything other than the originally budgeted amount, the production department's financial responsibility for costs should be based on the actual level of production.

For the purpose of evaluating the financial performance of cost centers, a flexible budget is tailored, after the fact, to the actual level of activity. A **flexible budget variance** is computed for each cost as the difference between the actual cost and the flexible budget cost. Assume actual production for July totaled 11,000 units rather than 10,000 units. Examples of a performance report for July manufacturing costs based on static and flexible budgets are presented in Exhibit 10.1. When the production department's financial performance is evaluated using the static budget, the actual cost of producing 11,000 units is compared to the budgeted cost of producing 10,000 units. The result is a series of unfavorable static budget variances totaling $20,000.

EXHIBIT 10.1	Flexible Budgets and Performance Evaluation

COACH
Production Department Performance Report
For Month of July

	Based on Static Budget			Based on Flexible Budget		
	Actual	Original Budget	Static Budget Variance	Actual	Flexible Budget*	Flexible Budget Variance
Volume.	11,000	10,000		11,000	11,000	
Variable costs						
Direct materials	$108,000	$100,000	$ 8,000 U	$108,000	$110,000	$2,000 F
Direct labor.	70,000	60,000	10,000 U	70,000	66,000	4,000 U
Variable overhead . . .	81,000	80,000	1,000 U	81,000	88,000	7,000 F
Fixed costs	53,000	52,000	1,000 U	53,000	52,000	1,000 U
Totals	$312,000	$292,000	$20,000 U	$312,000	$316,000	$4,000 F

*Flexible budget manufacturing costs: (Actual level × Budgeted unit cost)
Direct materials (11,000 units × 2 pounds × $5)
Direct labor (11,000 units × 0.25 labor hour × $24)
Variable overhead (11,000 units × 2 pounds × $4)

When the production department's financial performance is evaluated by comparing actual costs with costs allowed in a flexible budget drawn up for the actual production volume, the results are mixed. Direct materials have a $2,000 favorable variance. Direct labor has a $4,000 unfavorable variance. The variable overhead variance is $7,000 favorable. The fixed overhead variance remains $1,000 unfavorable since the static and flexible fixed budgets stay the same. The net flexible budget variance is $4,000 favorable, a substantial change from the static variance of $20,000 unfavorable.

Flexible budget variances provide a much better indicator of performance than static budget variances that do not consider the increased level of production (11,000 units rather than 10,000 units). When production exceeds the planned level, the static budget variances are usually unfavorable. Likewise, when actual production is substantially below the planned level of activity, the static variances are usually favorable. While it is important to isolate and determine the cause of any variation between planned and actual production, the financial-based performance report is not the appropriate place to mix volume-created variances with those related to the actual production levels.

MID-CHAPTER REVIEW

Suppose you receive the following performance report from the accounting department for your first month as plant manager for a new company. Your supervisor, the vice president of manufacturing, has concerns that the report does not provide an accurate picture of your performance in the area of cost control.

	Actual	Budgeted	Variance
Units..	10,000	12,000	2,000 U
Costs			
Direct materials..	$ 299,000	$ 360,000	$ 61,000 F
Direct labor	345,500	432,000	86,500 F
Variable factory overhead................................	180,000	216,000	36,000 F
Fixed factory overhead	375,000	360,000	15,000 U
Total costs	$1,199,500	$1,368,000	$168,500 F

Required
Prepare a revised budget that better reflects your performance.

The solution is on pages 381–382.

Standard Costs and Performance Reports

A **standard cost** indicates what it should cost to provide an activity or produce one batch or unit of product under planned and efficient operating conditions. In a standard costing environment, the flexible budget is based on standard unit costs. Traditionally, standard costs have been developed from an engineering analysis or from an analysis of historical data adjusted for expected changes in the product, production technology, or costs. When standards are developed using historical data, management must be careful to ensure that past inefficiencies are excluded from current standards.

To obtain the full benefit of standard costs, the standards must be based on realistic expectations. Suppose the standard cost for direct labor for Coach is $6.00 per unit, (computed as 0.25 direct labor hours × $24 per hour). Some organizations intentionally set "tight" standards to motivate employees toward higher levels of production. The management of Coach might set their standards for direct labor at 0.22 hours per unit rather than at the expected 0.25 hours per unit, hoping that employees will strive toward the lower time and, consequently, the lower cost of $5.28 ($24 × 0.22). The use of tight standards often causes planning and behavioral problems. Management expects them to result in unfavorable variances. Accordingly, tight standards should not be used to budget input requirements and cash flows because management expects to incur more labor costs than the standards allow. The use of tight standards can have undesirable behavioral effects if employees find that a second set of standards is used in the "real" budget or if they are constantly subject to unfavorable performance reports. These employees could come to distrust the entire budgeting and performance evaluation system, or they may quit trying to achieve any of the organization's standards.

Tight standards are more likely to occur in an imposed budget than in a participation budget. In a participation budget, the problem may be to avoid overstating the costs required to produce a product. Loose standards may fail to properly motivate employees and can make the company uncompetitive due to costs that are higher than competitors'.

VARIANCE ANALYSIS FOR COSTS

To use and interpret standard cost variances properly, managers must understand the processes and activities that drive costs. Cost variances are merely signals. They do not explain why costs differ from expectations. Underlying causes of variances must be investigated before final judgment is passed on the effectiveness and efficiency of an operation or activity.

LO3 Determine and interpret direct materials, direct labor, and overhead cost variances.

Standard cost variance analysis is a systematic approach to examining flexible budget variances. Actual costs are determined from the organization's financial transactions. Flexible budget costs are determined by multiplying standard quantities allowed for the output times the standard price per unit. For a company using activity-based costing, each manufacturing activity could have its own standard costs that focus on underlying concepts and cost drivers, and companies even develop their own set of variances.

Standard cost variance analysis identifies the general causes of the total flexible budget variance by breaking it into separate price and quantity variances for each production component. Two possible reasons that actual cost could differ from flexible budget cost for a given amount of output produced are (1) a difference between actual and standard prices paid for the production components—the price variance—and (2) a difference between the actual quantity and the standard quantity allowed for the production components—the quantity variance. Variances have different names for different cost categories as follows:

Cost Component	Price Variance Name	Quantity Variance Name
Direct materials	Materials price variance	Materials quantity variance
Direct labor	Labor rate variance	Labor efficiency variance
Variable overhead	Variable overhead spending variance	Variable overhead efficiency variance

Fixed overhead is excluded from the unit standard costs because, within the relevant range of normal activity, it does not vary with the volume of production. To facilitate product costing, however, many organizations develop a standard fixed overhead cost per unit.

In the following sections, we analyze the flexible budget cost variances for materials, labor and variable overhead. Our illustration is based on the following hypothetical July activity and costs of Coach's production department.

COACH Actual Manufacturing Costs For Month of July	
Actual units completed	11,000
Manufacturing costs	
Unit level costs	
Direct materials (24,000 pounds × $4.50)	$108,000
Direct labor (2,800 hours × $25.00)	70,000
Variable overhead	81,000
Fixed overhead costs	53,000
Total	$312,000

RESEARCH INSIGHT

Can Standard Cost Variances Detect Fraud?   Manufacturers lose on average $300,000 per reported incident of fraud, and nearly 40 percent of fraud cases are detected through tips from employees, customers, and suppliers. However, analyzing cost variances does more than inform managers of operating strengths and weaknesses—it can help detect fraud. Both materials and labor variances can flag activity that would give management cause for concern.

Persistent, yet small, unfavorable materials price variances could be a sign that purchasing agents are receiving vendor kickbacks, especially if the variances arise after a switch in vendors. Unfavorable materials usage variances could be symptomatic of collusion between the purchasing and receiving departments. For example, excess materials may be diverted to an unauthorized location to be sold for the employees' own gain.

There should be controls to prevent employees from changing wage rates in the payroll system. However, for a company that lacks these controls, unfavorable rate variances may be due to the employee earning a higher rate than is specified. Unfavorable labor efficiency variances, on the other hand, could be due to employees padding their time sheets or due to the presence of fictitious employees on the payroll. Variable overhead variances could arise from employees reporting overtime that they didn't actually work.

Fraudulent behavior can be prevented by a strong system of internal controls, including segregation of duties between recordkeeping, custody of assets, and handling of cash. In addition, computing and investigating variances from the standard cost system provide another level of security over the company's assets and records.

Source: Cecily Raiborn, Janet Butler, and Lucian Zelazny, "Standard Costing Variances: Potential Red Flags of Fraud?" *Cost Management*, May/June 2013, pp. 16–27.

Note that detailed information on actual pounds and an actual rate is not provided for variable overhead. That is because variable overhead represents a pool of related costs driven by a number of factors rather than a single cost with a single driver. Although the basis used in budgeting variable overhead may, and should, have a high correlation with actual variable overhead, it is a surrogate for the multiple cost elements that comprise variable overhead. Issues related to variable overhead are discussed in greater detail later in this chapter.

Establishing and Using Standards for Direct Materials

The two basic elements contained in the standards for direct materials are the *standard price* and the *standard quantity*. Materials standards indicate how much an organization should pay for each input unit of direct materials and the quantity of direct materials it should use to produce one unit of output. The standard price per unit of direct materials should include all reasonable costs necessary to acquire the materials. These costs include the invoice price of materials, less planned discounts plus freight, insurance, special handling, and any other costs related to the acquisition of the materials. The standard quantity represents the number of units of raw materials allowed for the production of one unit of finished product. This amount should include the amount dictated by the physical characteristics of the process and the product, plus a reasonable allowance for normal spoilage, waste, and other inefficiencies. The quantity standard can be determined by engineering analysis, professional judgment, or by averaging the actual amount used for several periods. An average of actual past materials usage may not be a good standard because it could include excessive wastes and inefficiencies in the standard quantity.

Direct Materials Variances

The **materials price variance** is the difference between the actual materials cost and the standard cost of actual materials inputs. The **materials quantity variance** is the difference between the standard cost of actual materials inputs and the flexible budget cost for materials. The direct materials variances for Coach follow.

*11,000 units × 2 pounds per unit

Coach had a favorable materials price variance of $12,000 because the actual cost of materials used ($108,000) was less than the standard cost of actual materials used ($120,000). The price variance can also be computed using a formula approach as the actual quantity (*AQ*) used times the difference between the actual price (*AP*) and the standard price (*SP*). Coach paid $0.50 per pound below the standard price for 24,000 pounds for a total savings of $12,000:

$$\textbf{Materials price variance} = \textbf{AQ(AP} - \textbf{SP)}$$

$$= \textbf{24,000(\$4.50} - \textbf{\$5.00)}$$

$$= \textbf{24,000} \times \textbf{\$0.50}$$

$$= \textbf{\$12,000 F}$$

The unfavorable quantity variance of $10,000 occurred because the standard cost of actual materials used, $120,000 (24,000 × $5), was higher than the cost of materials allowed by the flexible budget, $110,000 (22,000 × $5). A total of 22,000 pounds of materials is allowed to produce 11,000 units of finished outputs. This is computed as 11,000 finished units times 2.0 pounds of direct materials per unit. The materials quantity variance can also be computed using a formula approach as the standard price (*SP*) per pound times the difference between the number of pounds actually used (*AQ*) and the number of pounds allowed (*SQ*):

$$\textbf{Materials quantity variance} = \textbf{SP(AQ} - \textbf{SQ)}$$

$$= \textbf{\$5(24,000} - \textbf{22,000)}$$

$$= \textbf{\$5} \times \textbf{2,000}$$

$$= \textbf{\$10,000 U}$$

Interpreting Materials Variances

As highlighted in the following Business Insight, after computing variances, managers must understand how to use them in making decisions relevant to the items being evaluated. A *favorable materials price variance* indicates that the employee responsible for materials purchases paid less per unit than the price allowed by the standards. This could result from receiving discounts for purchasing more than the normal quantities, effective bargaining by the employee, purchasing substandard-quality materials, purchasing from a distress seller, or other factors. Ordinarily, when a favorable price variance is reported, the employee's performance is interpreted as favorable. However, if the favorable price variance results from the purchase of materials of lower than standard quality or from a purchase in more than desirable quantities, the employee's performance would be questionable. All large variances, including favorable variances, should be thoroughly investigated for causes and corrections.

BUSINESS INSIGHT

It's All in the Questions   Writing for local governments officials, Jon Johnson and Chris Fabian, senior management advisors with the International City/County Management Association (ICMA), stress the need for such officials to work closely with their finance officer and ask questions to better understand "not only the positive signs of the organization's fiscal health, but also the root causes of the fiscal 'dis-ease' impacting long-term fiscal sustainability."

One of their key questions is "Do we understand our variances – especially budget versus actual?" According to the authors, answering this question helps:

■ Determine reasons variances have occurred and adjust the budget or eliminate the source of variances where appropriate.

■ Identify areas where resources have been over-allocated with an eye toward reassigning those resources to other needs.

■ Reduce budget contingencies included in multiple department budgets by consolidation into a unified contingency budget.

■ Improve the accuracy to budgets by better identifying emerging trends.

Source: Jon Johnson and Chris Fabian, "It's All in the Questions: The Manager's Role in Achieving Fiscal Health," *Public Management*, September 2009, pp. 22-15, 33.

An *unfavorable materials price variance* means that the purchasing employee paid more per unit for materials than the price allowed by the standards. This could be caused by failure to buy in sufficient quantities to receive normal discounts; purchase of higher-quality materials than called for in the product specifications; failure to place materials orders on a timely basis; failure to bargain for the best available prices; or other factors. An unfavorable variance does not always mean that the employee performed unfavorably. Many noncontrollable factors surround the purchasing function, including unanticipated price increases, the need to increase production to meet unanticipated sales, and supply chain problems such as a work stoppage at a vendor.

A *favorable materials quantity variance* means that the actual quantity of raw materials used was less than the quantity allowed for the units produced. This could result from factors such as less materials waste than allowed by the standards, better than expected machine efficiency, direct materials of higher quality than required by the standards, and more efficient use of direct materials by employees. An *unfavorable materials quantity variance* occurs when the quantity of raw materials used exceeds the quantity allowed for the units produced. This could result from incurring more waste than provided for in the standards, poorly maintained machinery requiring larger amounts of raw materials, raw materials of lower quality than required by the standards, or poorly trained employees who were unable to use the materials at the level of efficiency required by the standards.

BUSINESS INSIGHT

Is Your Business Suffering from Unfavorable Price Variances? Blame It on McDonald's   An unfavorable price variance arises when a company has paid a higher price for a given quantity of materials than the standard specifies. But variance analysis is only powerful if management investigates the reasons behind the variances with the goal of preventing an unfavorable variance from recurring in the future. Sometimes price variances arise from circumstances beyond the company's control.

McDonald's is a case in point. When McDonald's added apples to its menu, it instantly became one of the nation's largest consumers of apples. Cucumbers are the next item that should see a spike in price, as McDonald's expects to purchase 6 million pounds of the vegetable this year for its new McWrap. Even the cost of boneless chicken breasts has increased by 24 percent since McDonald's introduced the McWrap. Chicken wings are one of McDonald's best sellers, but the company cannot put them permanently on the menu because its own demand causes shortages in the market and drives the price up beyond what McDonald's is willing to pay. During a six-week promotion, the company sold 250 million wings and drove the wholesale price up to $2 per pound from 90 cents per pound. If your company is experiencing unfavorable price variances, look for the Golden Arches . . . they may be the culprit.

Source: Venessa Wong, "Why Is Chicken More Expensive? Ask McDonald's," *Bloomberg Businessweek*, August 28, 2013.

Establishing and Using Standards for Direct Labor

To evaluate management performance in controlling labor costs, it is necessary to determine the *standard labor rate* for each hour allowed and the *standard time allowed* to produce a unit. Setting labor rate standards can be quite simple or extremely complex. If all employees have the same wage rate, determining the standard cost is relatively easy: Simply adopt the normal wage rate as the standard labor rate. If there are variations in employee wage rates, the standard labor rate should be based on the expected mix of employee wage rates.

The standard labor time per unit can be determined by an engineering approach or an empirical observation approach. When using an engineering approach, industrial engineers ascertain the amount of time required to produce a unit of finished product by applying time and motion methods or other available techniques. Normal operating conditions are assumed in arriving at the labor standard. Therefore, allowances must be made for normal machine downtime, employee personal breaks, and so forth. Under the empirical approach, the average time required to produce a unit under normal operating conditions is used as a basis for the standard.

Direct Labor Variances

Using the general variance model that was used for materials, we can compute the labor rate and efficiency variances. The **labor rate variance** is the difference between the actual cost and the standard cost of actual labor inputs. The **labor efficiency variance** is the difference between the standard cost of actual inputs and the flexible budget cost for labor.

Coach's labor standards provide for 0.25 hour of labor per unit produced at $24 per hour. During July, 2,800 hours were used at a cost of $25 per hour. Using these data, the labor rate (price) variance and labor efficiency (quantity) variance can be computed as shown in the following illustration.

*11,000 units × 0.25 hours per unit

The labor rate variance can also be computed in formula form as the actual number of hours used times the difference between the actual rate and the standard rate.

$$\text{Labor rate variance} = \text{AH}(\text{AR} - \text{SR})$$

$$= 2{,}800(\$25 - \$24)$$

$$= 2{,}800 \times \$1$$

$$= \$2{,}800 \text{ U}$$

This computation of the labor rate variance shows that the company paid $1 more than the standard rate for each of the 2,800 hours worked.

Since 11,000 units of product were finished during the period and 0.25 hour of labor was allowed for each unit, the total number of standard hours allowed was 2,750 (11,000 units × 0.25 hours). The labor efficiency variance can also be computed as the standard rate times the difference between the actual labor hours and the standard hours allowed:

$$\textbf{Labor efficiency variance} = \textbf{SR(AH} - \textbf{SH)}$$

$$= \$24(2{,}800 - 2{,}750)$$

$$= \$24 \times 50$$

$$= \$1{,}200 \ \textbf{U}$$

Coach's labor efficiency variance indicates that the company used 50 more labor hours than allowed. By itself, this inefficiency caused an unfavorable variance of $1,200.

Interpreting Labor Variances

The possible explanations for labor rate variances are rather limited. An *unfavorable labor rate variance* can be caused by the use of higher paid laborers than the standards provided. An increase in wage rates not reflected in the standards can also cause an unfavorable labor rate variance. A *favorable labor rate variance* occurs if lower paid workers were used or if actual wage rates declined.

Unfavorable labor efficiency variances occur when the actual labor hours exceed the number of hours allowed for the actual output. This could be caused by using poorly trained workers or poorly maintained machinery or by the use of low-quality materials. Low employee morale and generally poor working conditions could also adversely affect the efficiency.

Favorable labor efficiency variances occur when the actual labor hours are less than the number of hours allowed for the actual output. This above-normal efficiency can be caused by the company's use of higher-skilled (and higher-paid) workers, better machinery, or higher-quality raw materials than the standards require. High employee morale, improved job satisfaction, or generally improved working conditions could also account for the above-normal efficiency of the workers.

Establishing and Using Standards for Variable Overhead

The traditional unit-level approach to cost estimation, budgeting, and variance analysis separates overhead costs into fixed and variable elements. This separation is necessary because fixed costs are primarily driven by factors related to capacity and variable costs are primarily driven by factors related to volume.

Because it includes many heterogeneous costs, manufacturing overhead poses a unique problem in establishing standards for the standard quantity and the standard price of inputs. Direct materials have a natural physical measure of quantity such as tons, barrels, pounds, and liters. Similarly, labor or assembly is measurable in hours. However, no single quantity measure is common to all overhead items. Overhead is a cost group that can simultaneously include costs measurable in hours, pounds, liters and kilowatts.

The most frequent approach to dealing with the problem of multiple quantity measures in variable manufacturing overhead is to use a single surrogate (or substitute) measure to represent the quantity of all items in a given group. Typical substitute measures include machine hours, units of finished product, direct labor hours, and direct labor dollars. The variable overhead standard is then stated in terms of this surrogate measure.

Variable Overhead Variances

The **variable overhead spending variance** is the difference between the actual variable overhead cost and the standard variable overhead cost for the actual inputs of the surrogate measure. The **variable overhead efficiency variance** is the difference between the standard variable overhead cost for the actual inputs of the surrogate measure and the flexible budget cost allowed for variable overhead based on outputs.

Assume for Coach, the actual variable overhead in July was $81,000. This represents the actual cost of overhead items such as indirect materials and indirect labor. Pounds of materials is Coach's surrogate measure for quantity for variable overhead allowed and used. This means that the standard costs allowed for variable overhead varies with the pounds of direct materials allowed. Hence the standard cost of actual inputs is calculated as actual pounds of direct materials (AQ) times the standard variable overhead rate per pound (SR):

$$\textbf{Standard cost of actual inputs} = \textbf{(AQ} \times \textbf{SR)}$$

$$= \textbf{24,000} \times \textbf{\$4}$$

$$= \textbf{\$96,000}$$

The flexible budget cost for variable overhead allowed for the actual outputs is based on the 22,000 pounds of direct materials allowed (SQ) for the units produced during the period (11,000 units × 2 pounds). The allowed quantities are multiplied by the standard variable overhead rate (SR). The resulting variable overhead flexible budget cost is $88,000:

$$\textbf{Flexible budget cost} = \textbf{(SQ} \times \textbf{SR)}$$

$$= \textbf{22,000} \times \textbf{\$4}$$

$$= \textbf{\$88,000}$$

Using these data, the variable overhead spending (price) variance and the variable overhead efficiency (quantity) variance follow.

Standard Cost Variance Analysis

Input component: Variable overhead   **Output: 11,000 cases**

Actual Cost	Standard Cost of Actual Inputs		Flexible Budget Cost	
$81,000	Actual pounds (AQ)	24,000	Pounds allowed (SQ).	22,000*
	Standard rate (SR).	× $4	Standard rate (SR).	× $4
	Total	$96,000	Total	$88,000

Variable overhead spending variance $15,000 F   Variable overhead efficiency variance $8,000 U

Total flexible budget variable overhead variance $7,000 F

*11,000 × 2 lbs.

An alternative to the computation of the variable overhead effectiveness variance follows:

$$\textbf{Variable overhead efficiency variance} = \textbf{SR(AQ} - \textbf{SQ)}$$

$$= \textbf{\$4(24,000} - \textbf{22,000)}$$

$$= \textbf{\$8,000 U}$$

This approach emphasizes that the 2,000 extra pounds used should have increased variable overhead by $8,000 at the standard rate of $4 per pound.

Interpreting Variable Overhead Variances

A *favorable spending variance* encompasses all factors that cause actual expenditures to be less than the amount expected for the actual inputs of the measurement base, including consumption and payment. Conversely, an *unfavorable spending variance* results when the actual expenditures are more than expected for the inputs of the measurement base. This is caused by consuming more overhead items than expected, or by paying more than the expected amount for overhead items consumed, or by both. Thus, the term *spending variance* is used instead of *price variance*.

The key to understanding the variable overhead spending variance is recognizing that the amount of variable overhead cost allowed is determined by the level of the surrogate measurement base used. Any deviation from this spending budget causes a spending variance to occur.

The variable overhead efficiency variance measures the difference between the standard variable overhead cost for the actual quantity of the surrogate measurement base and the standard variable overhead cost for the allowed quantity of the surrogate measurement base. This variance measures the amount of variable overhead that should have been saved (or incurred) because of the efficient (or inefficient) use of the surrogate measurement base. It provides no information about the degree of efficiency in using variable overhead items such as indirect materials and indirect labor. This information is reflected in the spending variance.

YOU MAKE THE CALL

You Are the Vice President of Manufacturing Your company has had a practice for many years of budgeting variable overhead costs based on direct labor hours. The managerial accountants have argued that if direct labor hours are controlled, variable overhead costs will take care of themselves since direct labor hours drive variable overhead costs. You (and your plant managers) have become very skeptical of this policy because in recent years variable overhead variances have been very erratic—sometimes being large favorable amounts and other times being large unfavorable amounts. You are beginning to plan for the coming budget year. How do you think you should budget variable overhead and evaluate managers who control these costs? [Answer, p. 366]

Fixed Overhead Variances

By definition, the quantity of goods and services purchased by fixed expenditures is not expected to change in proportion to short-run changes in the level of production. For example, in the short run, the production level does not affect the amount of depreciation on buildings, the number of fixed salaried employees, or the amount of real property subject to property taxes. Whether the organization produces 10,000 or 15,000 cases, the same quantity of fixed overhead is expected to be incurred, as long as the production level is within the relevant range of activity provided by the current fixed overhead items. Therefore, an efficiency variance is not computed for fixed overhead costs.

Even though the components of fixed overhead are not expected to be affected by the production activity level in the short run, the actual amount spent for fixed overhead items can differ from the amount budgeted. For example, higher than budgeted supervisors' salaries could be paid, there may be unanticipated increases in property taxes or insurance premiums, and the cost of leased facilities may increase. Fixed overhead costs in excess of the amount budgeted are reflected in the fixed overhead budget variance. The **fixed overhead budget variance** is, simply, the difference between budgeted and actual fixed overhead. Using the assumed fixed costs of Coach as an example:

$$\text{Fixed overhead budget variance} = \text{Actual fixed overhead} - \text{Budgeted fixed overhead}$$

$$= \$53,000 - \$52,000$$

$$= \$1,000 \text{ U}$$

The fixed overhead budget variance is always the same as the total fixed overhead flexible budget variance. Because budgeted fixed overhead is the same for all outputs within the relevant range, the budget variance explains the total flexible budget variance between actual and allowed fixed overhead. Similar to variable overhead, fixed overhead variances can be caused by a combination of price and quantity factors. Fixed overhead variances are examined further in Appendix 10A.

BUSINESS INSIGHT

Guiding the Health Care Sector Toward Efficiency Gains General Electric (GE) Healthcare has developed a new product called Life Care Solutions that is part of GE's "healthymagination" initiative. The integrated system tracks vital signs, anesthesia systems, ventilators, incubators, and diagnostics, all while reducing costs and improving patients' access to health care. For example, GE is working with Mount Sinai Medical Center to improve its efficiency by using the GE equipment to streamline the patient admittance process. The company's diagnostic tools handle room assignment and provide a real-time estimate of bed capacity. The industry average capacity is 85 percent, but with the GE equipment, the hospital has been able to achieve 95 percent capacity.

GE is investing $2 billion in software systems to integrate this information with electronic medical records. This vast source of data will help health care workers in other parts of the globe better diagnose illnesses, even with skilled medical workers in short supply. In rural Africa, caregivers use manual hand ventilation during surgeries to keep patients alive, but GE's new systems can provide mechanical ventilation on a six-hour battery life at a cost low enough that clinics around the world can afford it.

By better managing health care efficiency through automated diagnostics and care, companies should be able to better predict their usage of space and materials. Companies like GE are having a real effect on what used to constitute significant variances in the health care industry.

Sources: Skoll World Forum, "How GE Healthcare Is Solving the World's Most Complex Rural Health Challenges," *Forbes*, August 9, 2013; and Ashlee Vance, "GE Tries to Make Its Machines Cool and Connected," *Bloomberg Businessweek*, December 6, 2012.

PERFORMANCE REPORTS FOR REVENUE CENTERS

The financial performance reports for revenue centers include a comparison of actual and budgeted revenues. Controllable costs can be deducted from revenues to obtain some bottom-line contribution margin. If the center is then evaluated on the basis of this contribution, it is being treated as a profit center.

LO4 Calculate revenue variances and prepare a performance report for a revenue center.

If the organization is to meet its budgeted profit goal for a period, with its budgeted fixed and variable costs, the organization's revenue centers must meet their original revenue budgets. Consequently, the original budget (a static budget) rather than a flexible budget is used to evaluate the financial performance of revenue centers.

Assume that Coach's July sales budget called for the sale of 10,000 units at $40.00 each. If Coach actually sold 11,000 units at $38.50 each, the total revenue variance is $23,500 favorable:

Actual revenues (11,000 × $38.50)	$423,500
Budgeted revenues (10,000 × $40)	(400,000)
Revenue variance	$ 23,500 F

The **revenue variance** is the difference between the budgeted sales volume at the budgeted selling price and the actual sales volume at the actual selling price. Because Coach's actual revenues exceeded budgeted revenues, the revenue variance is favorable. It can be presented as follows:

Revenue variance = (Actual volume × Actual price) − (Budgeted volume × Budgeted price)

The separate impact of changing prices and volume on revenue is analyzed with the sales price and sales volume variances. The **sales price variance** is computed as the change in selling price times the actual sales volume:

Sales price variance = (Actual selling price − Budgeted selling price) × Actual sales volume

For Coach, the sales price variance for July follows:

$$\text{Sales price variance} = (\$38.50 - \$40.00) \times 11,000 \text{ units}$$

$$= \$16,500 \text{ U}$$

The **sales volume variance** indicates the impact of the change in sales volume on revenues, assuming there was no change in selling price. The sales volume variance is computed as the difference between the actual and the budgeted sales volumes times the budgeted selling price:

Sales volume variance = (Actual sales volume − Budgeted sales volume) × Budgeted selling price

For Coach, the sales volume variance for July follows:

$$\text{Sales volume variance} = (11,000 \text{ units} - 10,000 \text{ units}) \times \$40$$

$$= \$40,000 \text{ F}$$

The net of the sales price and the sales volume variances is equal to the revenue variance:

Sales price variance	$16,500 U
Sales volume variance	40,000 F
Revenue variance	$23,500 F

Interpretation of these variances is subjective. In this case, we could say that if the increase in sales volume had not been accompanied by a decline in selling price, revenues would have increased $40,000 instead of $23,500. The $1.50 per unit decline in selling price cost the company $16,500 in revenues. Alternatively, we might note that a $1.50 reduction in the unit selling price was more than offset by an increase in sales volume. An economic analysis could explain the relationship as volume being sensitive to price (price elasticity).

In any case, variances are merely signals that actual results are not proceeding according to plan. They help managers identify potential problems and opportunities. An investigation into their cause(s) could even indicate that a manager who received a favorable variance was doing a poor job, whereas a manager who received an unfavorable variance was doing an outstanding job. Consider Coach's favorable revenue variance. This occurred because actual sales exceeded budgeted sales by 1,000 units (10 percent), which on the surface indicates good performance. But what if the total market for the company's products exceeded the company's forecast by 15 percent? In this hypothetical case, Coach's sales volume falls below its expected percentage share of the market; the favorable variance could occur (despite a poor marketing effort) because of strong customer demand that competitors could not fill.

Inclusion of Controllable Costs

Controllable costs should also be considered when evaluating the overall performance of revenue centers. A failure to consider costs could encourage uneconomic selling practices, such as excessive advertising and entertaining, and spending too much time on small accounts. The controllable costs of revenue centers include variable and fixed selling costs. These costs are sometimes further classified into order-getting and order-filling costs. **Order-getting costs** are incurred to obtain customers' orders (for example, advertising, salespersons' salaries and commissions, travel, telephone, and entertainment). **Order-filling costs** are distribution costs incurred to place finished goods in the hands of purchasers (for example, storing, packaging, and transportation).

The performance of a revenue center in controlling costs can be evaluated with the aid of a flexible budget drawn up for the actual level of activity. Assume that Coach's July budget for the sales department calls for fixed costs of $10,000 and variable costs of $5 per unit sold. If the actual fixed and variable selling expenses for July are $9,500 and $65,000, respectively, the total cost variances assigned to the sales department, detailed in Exhibit 10.2, are $9,500 unfavorable. In evaluating the sales department's performance as both a cost center and a revenue center, management should consider these cost variances as well as the revenue variances.

Although the revenue variances are based on the original budget, the cost variances are based on the flexible budget.

EXHIBIT 10.2	Sales Department Performance Report for Controllable Costs		

COACH
Sales Department Performance Report for Controllable Costs
For Month of July

		Based on Flexible Budget	
	Actual	**Flexible Budget***	**Flexible Budget Variance**
Units......................................	11,000	11,000	
Selling expenses			
Variable...............................	$65,000	$55,000	$10,000 U
Fixed.................................	9,500	10,000	500 F
Total.....................................	$74,500	$65,000	$ 9,500 U

* Flexible budget formulas:
  Variable selling expenses ($5 per unit)
  Fixed selling expenses($10,000 per month)

Revenue Centers as Profit Centers

Even though we have computed revenue and cost variances for Coach's sales department, we are still left with an incomplete picture of this revenue center's performance. Is the sales department's performance best represented by the $23,500 favorable revenue variance, by the $9,500 unfavorable cost variance, or by the net favorable variance of $14,000 ($23,500 F − $9,500 U)? Actually, it is inappropriate to attempt to obtain an overall measure of the sales department's performance by combining these separate revenue and selling cost variances. The combination of revenue and cost variances is appropriate only for a profit center; so far, we have left out one important cost that must be assigned to the sales department before it can be treated as a profit center. That cost is the *standard variable cost of goods sold.*

As a profit center, the sales department acquires units from the production department and sells them outside the firm. Its total responsibilities include revenues, the standard variable cost of goods sold, and actual selling expenses. The sales department is assigned the *standard,* rather than the *actual, variable cost of goods sold.* Because the sales department does not control production activities, it should not be assigned actual production costs. Doing so results in passing the production department's variances on to the sales department. Fixed manufacturing costs are not assigned to the sales department because short-run variations in sales volume do not normally affect the total amount of these costs.

To evaluate the sales department as a profit center, the net sales volume variance must be computed. The **net sales volume variance** indicates the impact of a change in sales volume on the contribution margin given the budgeted selling price *and* the standard variable costs. It is computed as the difference between the actual and the budgeted sales volumes times the budgeted unit contribution margin.

Net sales volume variance = (Actual volume − Budgeted volume) × Budgeted contribution margin

Using the $40 budgeted selling price, the standard variable manufacturing costs, and the standard variable selling expenses, the budgeted contribution margin is $11.00:

Sales		$40.00
Direct materials..	$10.00	
Direct labor	6.00	
Variable manufacturing overhead...	8.00	
Selling	5.00	(29.00)
Contribution margin		$11.00

The net sales volume variance is computed as follows:

$$\textbf{Net sales volume variance} = (11{,}000 - 10{,}000) \times \$11.00$$

$$= \$11{,}000 \text{ F}$$

As a profit center, the sales department has responsibility for the sales price variance, the net sales volume variance, and any cost variances associated with its operations. As shown in Exhibit 10.3, the sales department variances, as a profit center, net to $15,000 unfavorable:

EXHIBIT 10.3   Sales Department Profit Center Performance Report

COACH
Sales Department Profit Center Performance Report
For Month of July

Sales price variance	$16,500 U
Net sales volume variance	11,000 F
Selling expense variance	9,500 U
Sales Department variances, net	$15,000 U

In an attempt to improve their overall performance, managers often commit themselves to unfavorable variances in some areas, believing that these variances will be more than offset by favorable variances in other areas. When the sales department is evaluated as a revenue center, the favorable sales volume variance more than offsets the price reductions and the higher selling expenses. The more complete evaluation of the sales department as a profit center (with a $15,000 unfavorable variance) gives a very different impression than the evaluation of the sales department as a pure revenue center (with a $23,500 favorable variance) or as a revenue center responsible only for its own direct costs with net favorable variances of $14,000, computed as $23,500 F minus $9,500 U. The performance reports of all the organization's responsibility centers are summarized to reconcile budgeted and actual income in Appendix 10B.

CHAPTER-END REVIEW

Suppose the flexible budget performance report for **REI**'s camping chair product for March follows.

	Actual Costs	Flexible Budget Cost	Flexible Budget Variances
Output units.	5,000	5,000	
Direct materials.	$104,125	$100,000	$ 4,125 U
Direct labor	82,400	75,000	7,400 U
Variable manufacturing overhead			
Category 1	31,000	30,000	1,000 U
Category 2	18,000	20,000	2,000 F
Fixed manufacturing overhead.	42,000	40,000	2,000 U
Total.	$277,525	$265,000	$12,525 U

The standard unit cost for folding chairs follows:

Direct materials (4 pounds × $5.00 per pound)...	$20
Direct labor (1.25 hours × $12.00 per hour)...	15
Variable overhead, Category 1 (1.25 hours × $4.80).......................................	6
Variable overhead, Category 2 ($4 per finished unit).......................................	4
Total standard variable cost per unit..	$45

Actual cost of materials is based on 21,250 pounds of direct materials purchased and used at $4.90 per pound; actual cost of assembly is based on 7,000 labor hours. Variable overhead is applied on labor hours for Category 1 and finished units for Category 2.

Required

a. Calculate all standard cost variances for direct materials and direct labor.
b. Calculate all standard cost variances for variable manufacturing overhead.

The solution is on pages 382–383.

APPENDIX 10A: Fixed Overhead Variances

By definition, the quantity of goods and services purchased by fixed expenditures is not expected to change in proportion to short-run changes in the level of production. For example, in the short run, the production level does not affect the amount of depreciation on buildings, the number of fixed salaried employees, or the amount of real property subject to property taxes.

Even though the components of fixed overhead are not expected to be affected by the production activity level in the short run, the actual amount spent for fixed overhead items can differ from the amount budgeted. For example, higher than budgeted supervisors' salaries could be paid, insurance premiums may increase unexpectedly, and price increases could cause the amounts paid for equipment to be higher than expected. Fixed overhead costs in excess of the amount budgeted are reflected in the fixed overhead budget variance. Coach's fixed overhead budget variance was previously determined as:

$$\textbf{Fixed overhead budget variance} = \textbf{Actual fixed overhead} - \textbf{Budgeted fixed overhead}$$

$$= \$53,000 - \$52,000$$

$$= \$1,000 \text{ U}$$

The fixed overhead budget variance is always the same as the total fixed overhead flexible budget variance. Because budgeted fixed overhead is the same for all outputs within the relevant range, the budget variance explains the total flexible budget variance between actual and allowed fixed overhead.

Recall that predetermined overhead rates are computed by dividing the predicted overhead costs for the period by the predicted activity of the period. The motivation for using a standard fixed overhead rate is the same as the motivation for using a predetermined overhead rate; namely, quicker product costing and assigning identical fixed costs to identical products, regardless of when they are produced during the year.

When a standard fixed overhead rate is used, total fixed overhead costs assigned to production behave as variable costs. As production increases, the total fixed overhead assigned to production increases. Because total budgeted fixed overhead does not vary, differences arise between budgeted and assigned fixed overhead, and managers often inquire about the cause of the differences.

The standard fixed overhead rate is computed as the budgeted fixed costs divided by some budgeted standard level of activity. Assume Coach applies fixed manufacturing overhead on the basis of machine hours and that 0.40 machine hours are allowed to produce one carrying case. Further assume that the budgeted production is 10,000 carrying cases per month, a level that allows 4,000 (10,000 × 0.40) machine hours. The standard fixed overhead rate per machine hour is $13.

$$\textbf{Standard fixed overhead rate} = \textbf{Budgeted total fixed overhead} \div \textbf{Budgeted activity level}$$

$$= \$52,000 \div 4,000 \text{ hours}$$

$$= \$13 \text{ per machine hour}$$

The total fixed overhead assigned to production is computed as the standard rate of $13 multiplied by the standard hours allowed for the units produced. Note that assigned fixed overhead cost equals budgeted fixed overhead only if the allowed activity equals the budgeted activity of 4,000 hours. If less than 4,000 hours are allowed the fixed overhead assigned to production is less than the $52,000 budgeted; if more than 4,000 hours are allowed the fixed overhead assigned to production is more than the amount budgeted.

Even though budgeted fixed overhead is not affected by production below or above 4,000 hours, the fixed overhead assigned to production increases at the rate of $13 per allowed machine hour. The difference between budgeted fixed overhead and fixed overhead assigned to production is called the **fixed overhead volume variance**. This variance is sometimes referred to as the **capacity variance**, a term that emphasizes the maximum output of an operation. The fixed overhead volume variance indicates neither good nor poor performance. Instead, it indicates the difference between the activity allowed for the actual output and the budget level used as the denominator in computing the standard fixed overhead rate.

To explain the difference between actual fixed overhead and fixed overhead assigned to production, two fixed overhead variances are computed: the fixed overhead budget variance and the fixed overhead volume variance. As previously explained, the fixed overhead budget variance represents the difference between actual fixed overhead and budgeted fixed overhead. The fixed overhead budget variance is caused by a combination of price and quantity factors related to the use of fixed overhead goods and services (e.g., depreciation, insurance, supervisors' salaries). The $1,000 unfavorable budget variance for Coach was caused either by using higher quantities of fixed overhead goods and services, or by paying higher prices than expected for those items, or both.

The fixed overhead volume variance represents the difference between budgeted and assigned fixed overhead and is caused by a difference between the activity level allowed for the actual output and the budgeted activity used in computing the fixed overhead rate. Suppose for Coach, actual July output of 11,000 units resulted in 4,400 allowed machine hours and applied fixed overhead of $57,200 (11,000 units $\times$ 0.40 hours $\times$ $13). The $5,200 favorable fixed overhead volume variance (budgeted costs of $52,000 minus applied costs of $57,200) indicates that the activity level allowed for the actual output was more than the budgeted activity level. As previously stated, this variance ordinarily cannot be used to control costs. If the budgeted activity is based on production capacity, an unfavorable variance alerts management that facilities are underutilized, and a favorable variance alerts management that facilities are utilized above their expectations. A summary standard cost variance analysis for fixed costs is shown below.

†11,000 units $\times$ 0.40
‡ Also computed as: (4,400 allowed hours − 4,000 budget hours) $\times$ $13 standard rate per hour

APPENDIX 10B: Reconciling Budgeted and Actual Income

Using a contribution format, it is possible to reconcile the difference between budgeted and actual net income for an entire organization. This is done by assigning all costs and revenues to responsibility centers and summarizing the financial performance of each responsibility center. Coach's budgeted and actual income statements, in a contribution format, for July are presented in Exhibit 10.4.

EXHIBIT 10.4	Budgeted and Actual Income Statements: Contribution Format

COACH
Budgeted Income Statement
For Month of July

Sales (10,000 units × $40)			$400,000
Less variable costs			
Variable cost of goods sold			
Direct materials (10,000 units × $10)	$100,000		
Direct labor (10,000 units × $6)	60,000		
Manufacturing overhead (10,000 × $8)	80,000	$240,000	
Selling (10,000 units × $5)		50,000	(290,000)
Contribution margin			110,000
Less fixed costs			
Manufacturing overhead		52,000	
Selling		10,000	
Administrative		4,000	(66,000)
Budgeted net income			$ 44,000

Actual Income Statement
For the Month of July

Sales (11,000 units × $38.50)			$423,500
Less variable costs			
Variable cost of goods sold			
Direct materials	$108,000		
Direct labor	70,000		
Manufacturing overhead	81,000	$259,000	
Selling		65,000	(324,000)
Contribution margin			99,500
Less fixed costs			
Manufacturing overhead		53,000	
Selling		9,500	
Administrative		3,800	(66,300)
Net income			$ 33,200

We've assumed Coach contains three responsibility centers: a production department, a sales department, and an administration department. The sales department variances in Exhibit 10.3 net to $15,000 U. The production department's variances in Exhibit 10.1 net to $4,000 F. The only variance for the administration department is the $200 difference between actual and budgeted fixed administrative costs ($3,800 actual − $4,000 budget). Because the administration department is a discretionary cost center, this variance is best identified as being underbudget. For consistency in the performance reports, however, it is labeled favorable. By assigning all variances to these three responsibility centers, the reconciliation of budgeted and actual income is as shown in Exhibit 10.5.

EXHIBIT 10.5	Reconciliation of Budgeted and Actual Income

COACH
Reconciliation of Budgeted and Actual Income
For Month of July

Budgeted net income	$44,000
Sales department variances (Exhibit 10.3)	15,000 U
Production department variances (Exhibit 10.1)	4,000 F
Administration department variances ($3,800 actual − $4,000 budgeted)	200 F
Actual net income	$33,200

GUIDANCE ANSWERS . . . YOU MAKE THE CALL

You Are the Vice President of Manufacturing   It appears that direct labor hours may no longer be a reliable basis for budgeting variable overhead in your company. If actual variable overhead costs do not appear to correlate closely with direct labor hours, this could be an indication that the components of variable overhead have changed since direct labor hours was selected as the cost driver. Your cost accountants should consider other unit-level cost drivers for budgeting variable overhead costs. However, an activity-based costing method using multiple overhead cost pools with separate cost drivers might provide a more reliable basis for budgeting and controlling variable overhead costs.

KEY RATIOS

Materials price variance = Actual quantity (Actual price − Standard price)

Materials quantity variance = Standard price (Actual quantity − Standard Quantity)

Labor rate variance = Actual hours (Actual rate − Standard rate)

Labor efficiency variance = Standard rate (Actual hours − Standard hours)

Standard variable overhead cost of actual inputs = (Actual quantity × Standard variable overhead rate)

Flexible variable overhead budget cost = (Standard quantity × Standard variable overhead rate)

Variable overhead efficiency variance = Standard rate (Actual quantity − Standard quantity)

Fixed overhead budget variance = Actual fixed overhead − Budgeted fixed overhead

Revenue variance = (Actual volume × Actual price) − (Budgeted volume × Budgeted price)

Sales price variance = (Actual selling price − Budgeted selling price) × Actual sales volume

Sales volume variance = (Actual sales volume − Budgeted sales volume) × Budgeted selling price

Net sales volume variance = (Actual volume − Budgeted volume) × Budgeted contribution margin

KEY TERMS

MULTIPLE CHOICE

1. Presented is an abbreviated performance report for the month of July:

	Actual	Budget	Variance
Units..	5,500	5,000	
Costs:			
Direct materials	$ 45,500	$ 40,000	$ 5,500 U
Direct labor...	181,500	150,000	31,500 U
Variable factory overhead	208,000	160,000	48,000 U
Fixed factory overhead	125,000	120,000	5,000 U
Total costs..	$560,000	$470,000	$90,000 U

   The total flexible budget variance is:
   a. $55,000 Unfavorable
   b. $90,000 Unfavorable
   c. $50,000 Favorable
   d. $55,000 Favorable

2. The following additional information is available for the materials costs in question 1:
   • Standard cost per unit produced: 2 liters @ $4.00 per liter
   • Actual use of raw materials 13,000 liters @ $3.50 per liter

   The materials price and materials quantify variances are:
   a. $5,500 F materials price variance and $8,000 U materials quantify variance
   b. $6,500 F materials price variance and $8,000 U materials quantify variance
   c. $6,500 F materials price variance and $12,000 U materials quantify variance
   d. None of the above

3. The following additional information is available for the labor costs in question 1.
   • Standard cost per unit of product 1.5 direct labor hours @ $20 per labor hour
   • Actual use of direct labor is 8,250 hours @ $22 per hour

   The labor rate and the labor efficiency variances are:
   a. $16,500 U labor rate variance and $0 labor efficiency variance
   b. $16,500 F labor rate variance and $0 labor efficiency variance
   c. $16,500 U labor rate variance and $15,000 U labor efficiency variance
   d. None of the above

4. The following additional information is available for the variable overhead costs in question 1:
   • Standard cost per unit of product 2 liters of raw materials @ $16 per liter
   • Actual use of raw materials was 13,000 liters and actual variable overhead was $208,000

   The variable overhead spending and variable overhead efficiency variances are:
   a. $32,000 U spending and $0 efficiency
   b. $32,000 U spending and $16,000 U efficiency
   c. $16,000 U spending and $32,000U efficiency
   d. $0 spending and $32,000 U efficiency

5. Budgeted June sales of the Tack Shop include 100 western saddles at $650 each. Actual sales were 90 saddles at $725 each. The June sales price and sales volume variances for western saddles are:
   a. $250 F sales price variance and $10 U sales volume variance
   b. $6,750 F sales price variance and $6,500 U sales volume variance
   c. $7,500 F sales price variance and $6,500 U sales volume variance
   d. None of the above

Superscript ^{A(B)} denotes assignments based on Appendix 10A (10B).

DISCUSSION QUESTIONS

Q10-1. What is responsibility accounting? Why should noncontrollable costs be excluded from performance reports prepared in accordance with responsibility accounting?

Q10-2. How can responsibility accounting lead to unethical practices?

Q10-3. Responsibility accounting reports must be expanded to include what nonfinancial areas? Give some examples of nonfinancial measures.

Q10-4. What is a cost center? Give some examples.

Q10-5. How is a cost center different from either an investment or a profit center?

Q10-6. What problems can result from the use of tight standards?

Q10-7. What is a standard cost variance, and what is the objective of variance analysis?

Q10-8. Standard cost variances can usually be broken down into two basic types of variances. Identify and describe these two types of variances.

Q10-9. Identify possible causes for (1) a favorable materials price variance; (2) an unfavorable materials price variance; (3) a favorable materials quantity variance; and (4) an unfavorable materials quantity variance.

Q10-10. How is standard labor time determined? Explain the two ways.

Q10-11. In the standard cost system, what is the appropriate treatment of a change in wage rates (per new labor union contract) that dominate the cost of labor?

Q10-12. Explain the difference between the revenue variance and the sales price variance.

Q10-13. Explain the net sales volume variance and list its components.

Q10-14. Explain the difference between how the *actual costs* and the *standard cost of actual inputs* are computed in variable overhead analysis.

Q10-15. Explain what the net sales volume variance measures.

Assignments with the ✔ logo in the margin are available in BusinessCourse.
See the Preface of the book for details.

MINI EXERCISES

LO2 **M10-16.** **Flexible Budgets and Performance Evaluation**
Presented is the January performance report for the Production Department of Newport Company.

NEWPORT COMPANY
Production Department Performance Report
For Month of January

	Actual	Budget	Variance
Volume	30,000	28,000	
Manufacturing costs			
Direct materials	$ 90,000	$ 84,000	$ 6,000 U
Direct labor	165,000	140,000	25,000 U
Variable overhead	62,000	56,000	6,000 U
Fixed overhead	27,000	28,000	1,000 F
Total	$344,000	$308,000	$36,000 U

Required

a. Evaluate the performance report.

b. Prepare a more appropriate performance report.

M10-17. **Materials Variances**

LO3

North Wind manufactures decorative weather vanes that have a standard materials cost of two pounds of raw materials at $1.50 per pound. During September 5,000 pounds of raw materials costing $1.75 per pound were used in making 2,400 weather vanes.

Required

Determine the materials price and quantity variance.

M10-18. **Materials Variances**

LO3

PEARLE VISION

Assume that Pearle Vision uses standard costs to control the materials in its made-to-order sunglasses. The standards call for 2 ounces of material for each pair of lenses. The standard cost per ounce of material is $14. During July, the Santa Clara location produced 4,800 pairs of sunglasses and used 9,000 ounces of materials. The cost of the materials during July was $14.50 per ounce, and there were no beginning or ending inventories.

Required

a. Determine the flexible budget materials cost for the completion of the 4,800 pairs of glasses.

b. Determine the actual materials cost incurred for the completion of the 4,800 pairs of glasses and compute the total materials variance.

c. How much of the total variance was related to the price paid to purchase the materials?

d. How much of the difference between the answers to requirements (a) and (b) was related to the quantity of materials used?

M10-19. **Direct Labor Variances**

LO3

NORTEL (NT)

Assume that Nortel manufactures specialty electronic circuitry through a unique photoelectronic process. One of the primary products, Model ZX40, has a standard labor time of 0.5 hour and a standard labor rate of $13.00 per hour. During February, the following activities pertaining to direct labor for ZX40 were recorded:

Direct labor hours used.	2,180
Direct labor cost	$32,000
Units of ZX40 manufactured.	4,600

Required

a. Determine the labor rate variance.

b. Determine the labor efficiency variance.

c. Determine the total flexible budget labor cost variance.

M10-20. **Significance of Direct Labor Variances**

LO3

The Morgan Company's April budget called for labor costs of $125,000. Because the actual labor costs were exactly $125,000, management concluded there were no labor variances.

Required

Comment on management's conclusion.

M10-21. **Variable Overhead Variances**

LO3

SONY (SNE)

Assume that the best cost driver that Sony has for variable factory overhead in the assembly department is machine hours. During April, the company budgeted 480,000 machine hours and $4,000,000 for its Texas plant's assembly department. The actual variable overhead incurred was $4,180,000, which was related to 500,000 machine hours.

Required

a. Determine the variable overhead spending variance.

b. Determine the variable overhead effectiveness variance.

M10-22. **Sales Variances**

LO4

Presented is information pertaining to an item sold by Winding Creek General Store:

	Actual	Budget
Unit sales	150	125
Unit selling price	$26	$25
Unit standard variable costs	(20)	(20)
Unit contribution margin	$ 6	$ 5
Revenues	$3,900	$3,125
Standard variable costs	(3,000)	(2,500)
Contribution margin at standard costs	$ 900	$ 625

Required
Compute the revenue, sales price, and the sales volume variances.

LO3   **M10-23.**[A] **Fixed Overhead Variances**

MARATHON OIL (MRO)

Assume that Marathon Oil uses a standard cost system for each of its refineries. For the Texas City refinery, the monthly fixed overhead budget is $6,000,000 for a planned output of 2,000,000 barrels. For September, the actual fixed cost was $6,250,000 for 2,100,000 barrels.

Required
a.   Determine the fixed overhead budget variance.
b.   If fixed overhead is applied on a per-barrel basis, determine the volume variance.

M10-24.[B] **Reconciling Budgeted and Actual Income**

Midstate Supply Company has three responsibility centers: sales, production, and administration. The following information pertains to the November activities of Midstate Supply:

Budgeted contribution income	$18,000
Actual contribution income	27,000
Sales price variance	24,000 F
Sales volume variance	40,000 F
Net sales price variance	6,000 F
Sales department variable expense variance	18,000 U
Sales department fixed expense variance	1,500 U
Administration department variances	500 F
Production department variances	2,000 U

Required
Prepare a reconciliation of budgeted and actual contribution income.

EXERCISES

LO2   **E10-25.**   **Elements of a Flexible Budget**
Presented are partial flexible cost budgets for various levels of output.

	Rate per unit	Units		
		5,000	7,500	10,000
Direct materials	a.	$100,000	b.	c.
Direct labor	d.	e.	30,000	f.
Variable overhead	$5	g.	h.	i.
Fixed overhead		j.	k.	l.
Total		m.	n.	$400,000

Required

Solve for items "a" though "n."

E10-26. **Elements of Labor and Variable Overhead Variances**

Charlotte Fabricating applies variable overhead to products on the basis of standard direct labor hours. Presented is selected information for last month when 10,000 units were produced.

	Direct labor	Variable overhead
Actual.	a.	f.
Standard hours/unit	b.	b.
Actual hours (total)	2,100	2,100
Standard rate/hour	$12.00	$8.00
Actual rate	$12.60	
Flexible budget	$24,000	$16,000
Labor rate or variable overhead spending variance	c.	g.
Efficiency variances	d.	h.
Total flexible budget variance	e.	$1,000 F

Required

Solve for items "a" through" h."

E10-27. **Causes of Standard Cost Variances (Comprehensive)**

Following are ten unrelated situations that would ordinarily be expected to affect one or more standard cost variances:

1. A salaried production supervisor is given a raise, but no adjustment is made in the labor cost standards.
2. The materials purchasing manager gets a special reduced price on raw materials by purchasing a train carload. A warehouse had to be rented to accommodate the unusually large amount of raw materials. The rental fee was charged to Rent Expense, a fixed overhead item.
3. An unusually hot August caused the company to use 25,000 kilowatts more electricity than provided for in the variable overhead standards.
4. The local electric utility company raised the charge per kilowatt-hour. No adjustment was made in the variable overhead standards.
5. The plant manager traded in his leased company car for a new one in July, increasing the monthly lease payment by $150.
6. A machine malfunction on the assembly line (caused by using cheap and inferior raw materials) resulted in decreased output by the machine operator and higher than normal machine repair costs. Repairs are treated as variable overhead costs.
7. The production maintenance supervisor decreased routine maintenance checks, resulting in lower maintenance costs and lower machine production output per hour. Maintenance costs are treated as fixed costs.
8. An announcement that vacation benefits had been increased resulted in improved employee morale. Consequently, raw materials pilferage and waste declined, and production efficiency increased.
9. The plant manager reclassified her secretary to administrative assistant and gave him an increase in salary.
10. A union contract agreement calling for an immediate 5 percent increase in production worker wages was signed. No changes were made in the standards.

Required

For each of these situations, indicate by letter which of the following standard cost variances would be affected. More than one variance will be affected in some cases.

a. Materials price variance.
b. Materials quantity variance.
c. Labor rate variance.
d. Labor efficiency variance.
e. Variable overhead spending variance.
f. Variable overhead efficiency variance.
g. Fixed overhead budget variance.

LO4 **E10-28.** **Sales Variances**

Assume that **Casio Computer Company, LTD.** sells handheld communication devices for $100 during August as a back-to-school special. The normal selling price is $150. The standard variable cost for each device is $70. Sales for August had been budgeted for 400,000 units nationwide; however, due to the slowdown in the economy, sales were only 375,000.

Required

Compute the revenue, sales price, sales volume variance, and net sales volume variance.

LO3 **E10-29.**[A] **Fixed Overhead Variances**

Auburn Company uses standard costs for cost control and internal reporting. Fixed costs are budgeted at $18,000 per month at a normal operating level of 10,000 units of production output. During October, actual fixed costs were $20,000, and actual production output was 12,000 units.

Required

a. Determine the fixed overhead budget variance.

b. Assume that the company applied fixed overhead to production on a per-unit basis. Determine the fixed overhead volume variance.

c. Was the fixed overhead budget variance from requirement (a) affected because the company operated above the normal activity level of 10,000 units? Explain.

d. Explain the possible causes for the volume variance computed in requirement (b). How is reporting of the volume variance useful to management?

PROBLEMS

LO2 **P10-30.** **Multiple Product Performance Report**

Storage Products manufactures two models of DVD storage cases: regular and deluxe. Presented is standard cost information for each model:

Cost Components	Regular		Deluxe	
Direct materials				
Lumber............	2 board feet × $4 =	$ 8.00	3 board feet × $4 =	$12.00
Assembly kit........	=	2.00	=	2.00
Direct labor	1 hour × $4 =	4.00	1.25 hours × $4 =	5.00
Variable overhead	1 labor hr. × $2 =	2.00	1.25 labor hrs. × $2 =	2.50
Total		$16.00		$21.50

Budgeted fixed manufacturing overhead is $12,000 per month. During July, the company produced 5,000 regular and 3,000 deluxe storage cases while incurring the following manufacturing costs:

Direct materials	$ 99,000
Direct labor	36,000
Variable overhead	14,000
Fixed overhead	15,500
Total	$164,500

Required

Prepare a flexible budget performance report for the July manufacturing activities.

LO3 **P10-31.** **Computation of Variable Cost Variances**

The following information pertains to the standard costs and actual activity for Tyler Company for September:

Standard cost per unit

Direct materials . . . . 4 units of material A × $3.00 per unit

1 unit of material B × $4.00 per unit

Direct labor. . . . . 3 hours × $9.00 per hour

Activity for September

Materials purchased

Material A . . . . 4,500 units × $3.10 per unit

Material B . . . . 1,100 units × $4.15 per unit

Materials used

Material A . . . . 4,150 units

Material B . . . . 1,005 units

Direct labor used . . . . 2,950 hours × $9.40 per hour

Production output . . . . 1,000 units

There were no beginning direct materials inventories.

Required

a. Determine the materials price and quantity variances.

b. Determine the labor rate and efficiency variances.

P10-32. Variance Computations and Explanations

LO3

Outdoor Company manufactures camping tents from a lightweight synthetic fabric. Each tent has a standard materials cost of $21, consisting of 4 yards of fabric at $5.25 per yard. The standards call for 2 hours of assembly at $10 per hour. The following data were recorded for October, the first month of operations:

Fabric purchased . . . . 9,000 yards × $5.00 per yard

Fabric used in production of 1,700 tents . . . . 7,000 yards

Direct labor used . . . . 3,600 hours × $10.75 per hour

Required

a. Compute all standard cost variances for materials and labor.

b. Give one possible reason for each of the preceding variances.

c. Determine the standard variable cost of the 1,700 tents produced, separated into direct materials and labor.

P10-33. Determining Unit Costs, Variance Analysis, and Interpretation

LO2, 3

Big Dog Company, a manufacturer of dog food, produces its product in 1,000-bag batches. The standard cost of each batch consists of 8,000 pounds of direct materials at $0.40 per pound, 48 direct labor hours at $8.75 per hour, and variable overhead cost (based on machine hours) at the rate of $10 per hour with 16 machine hours per batch. The following variable costs were incurred for the last 1,000-bag batch produced:

Direct materials . . . . 8,300 pounds costing $3,154 were purchased and used

Direct labor . . . . 45 hours costing $450

Variable overhead $225

Machine hours used . . . . 18 hours

Required

a. Determine the actual and standard variable costs per bag of dog food produced, separated into direct materials, direct labor, and variable overhead.

b. For the last 1,000-bag batch, determine the standard cost variances for direct materials, direct labor, and variable overhead.

c. Explain the possible causes for each of the variances determined in requirement (b).

P10-34. Computation of Variances and Other Missing Data

LO3

The following data for O'Keefe Company pertain to the production of 500 units of Product X during December. Selected data items are omitted.

Direct materials (all materials purchased were used during period)

Standard cost per unit: (a) pounds at $2.88 per pound

Total actual cost: (b) pounds costing $5,673

Standard cost allowed for units produced: $5,760

Materials price variance: (c)

Materials quantity variance: $144 U

Direct labor

Standard cost: 2 hours at $7.00

Actual cost per hour: $7.25

Total actual cost: (d)

Labor rate variance: (e)

Labor efficiency variance: $140 U

Variable overhead

Standard costs: (f) hours at $4.00 per direct labor hour

Actual cost: $3,700

Variable overhead spending variance: (g)

Variable overhead efficiency variance: (h)

Required

Complete the missing amounts lettered (a) through (h).

LO3 **P10-35.** **Flexible Budgets and Performance Evaluation**

Anna Van Degna, supervisor of housecleaning for Hotel Dell, was surprised by her summary performance report for March given below.

HOTEL DELL Housekeeping Performance Report For the Month of March			
Actual	**Budget**	**Variance**	**%Variance**
$169,744	$159,200	$10,544 U	6.623% U

Anna was disappointed. She thought she had done a good job controlling housekeeping labor and towel usage, but her performance report revealed an unfavorable variance of $10,544. She had been hoping for a bonus for her good work, but now expected a series of questions from her manager.

The cost budget for housekeeping is based on standard costs. At the beginning of a month, Anna receives a report from Hotel Dell's Sales Department outlining the planned room activity for the month. Anna then schedules labor and purchases using this information. The budget for the housekeeping was based on 8,000 room nights. Each room night is budgeted based on the following standards for various materials, labor, and overhead:

Shower supplies . . . . 3 bottles @ $0.30 each
Towels* . . . . 1 @ $2.00
Laundry . . . . 10 lbs. @ $0.30 a lb.
Labor . . . . ½ hour @ $12.00 an hour
VOH . . . . $6.00 per labor hour
FOH . . . . $5 a room night (based on 8,000 room nights)

*Replacements for towels evaluated by housekeeping as inappropriate for cleaning and reuse.

With 8,900 room nights sold, actual costs and usage for housekeeping during April were:

$8,190 for 26,500 bottles of shower supplies.
$15,563 for 7,900 towels.
$27,339 for 88,500 lbs. of laundry.
$51,591 for 4,350 labor hours.
$25,839 in total VOH.
$41,222 in FOH.

Required

a. Develop a complete budget column for the above performance report presented to Anna. Break it down by expense category. The following format, with additional lines for expense categories, is suggested:

Account	Actual	Budget	Variance
Shower Supplies	$ 8,190	?	?
Total	$169,744	$159,200	$10,544 U

b. Evaluate the usefulness of the cost center performance report presented to Anna.

c. Prepare a more logical performance report where standard allowed is based on actual output. Also, split each variance into its price/rate/spending and quantity/efficiency components (except fixed of course). The following format, with additional lines for expense categories, is suggested:

Account	Actual	Flexible Budget	Total Variance	Price/Rate/ Spending Variance	Quantity/ Efficiency Variance
Shower Supplies	$ 8,190	?	?	?	?
Total	$169,744	?	?		

d. Explain to Anna's boss what your report suggests about Anna's department performance.

e. Identify additional nonfinancial performance measures management might consider when evaluating the performance of the housekeeping department and Anna as a manager.

P10-36. Flexible Budget Performance Evaluation with Process Costing   LO3

The Davis Company produces a single product on a continuous basis. On July 1, 400 units, 75 percent complete as to materials and 50 percent complete as to conversion, were in process. During January, 1,000 units were started and 1,200 units were completed. The July 31 ending work-in-process inventory contained 200 units, 50 percent complete as to materials and 25 percent complete as to conversion.

Davis uses standard costs for planning and control. The following standard costs are based on a monthly volume of 800 equivalent units with fixed budgeted at $6,500 per month.

Direct materials [(2 square meters per unit × $8.00 per meter) × 800]	$12,800
Direct labor [(1.5 hours per unit × $20 per hour) × 800]	24,000
Variable overhead [(1.5 labor hours per unit × $5.00 per hour) × 800]	6,000
Fixed manufacturing overhead	6,500

Actual July production costs were:

Direct materials	$20,000
Direct labor	31,400
Manufacturing overhead	11,750

Required

a. Determine the equivalent units of materials and conversion manufactured during July.

b. Based on the July equivalent units of materials and conversion, prepare a July performance report for the Davis Company.

c. Explain the treatment of overhead in the July performance report.

LO3   P10-37.   Measuring the Effects of Decisions on Standard Cost Variances (Comprehensive)

The following five unrelated situations affect one or more standard cost variances for materials, labor (assembly), and overhead:

1. Lois Jones, a production worker, announced her intent to resign to accept another job paying $1.50 more per hour. To keep Lois, the production manager agreed to raise her salary from $7.00 to $8.75 per hour. Lois works an average of 175 regular hours per month.

2. At the beginning of the month, a supplier of a component used in our product notified us that, because of a minor design improvement, the price will be increased by 15 percent above the current standard price of $100 per unit. As a result of the improved design, we expect the number of defective components to decrease by 80 units per month. On average, 1,200 units of the component are purchased each month. Defective units are identified prior to use and are not returnable.

3. In an effort to meet a deadline on a rush order in Department A, the plant manager reassigned several higher-skilled workers from Department B, for a total of 300 labor hours. The average salary of the Department B workers was $2.05 more than the standard $7.25 per hour rate of the Department A workers. Since they were not accustomed to the work, the average Department B worker was able to produce only 36 units per hour instead of the standard 48 units per hour. (Consider only the effect on Department A labor variances.)

4. Rob Celiba is an inspector who earns a base salary of $700 per month plus a piece rate of 20 cents per bundle inspected. His company accounts for inspection costs as manufacturing overhead. Because of a payroll department error in June, Rob was paid $500 plus a piece rate of 30 cents per bundle. He received gross wages totaling $1,100.

5. The materials purchasing manager purchased 5,000 units of component K2X from a new source at a price $14 below the standard unit price of $200. These components turned out to be of extremely poor quality with defects occurring at three times the standard rate of 5 percent. The higher rate of defects reduced the output of workers (who earn $9 per hour) from 20 units per hour to 15 units per hour on the units containing the discount components. Each finished unit contains one K2X component. To appease the workers (who were irate at having to work with inferior components), the production manager agreed to pay the workers an additional $0.30 for each of the components (good and bad) in the discount batch. Variable manufacturing overhead is applied at the rate of $3 per direct labor hour. The defective units also caused a 20-hour increase in total machine hours. The actual cost of electricity to run the machines is $2 per hour.

Required

For each of the preceding situations, determine which standard cost variance(s) will be affected, and compute the amount of the effect for one month on each variance. Indicate whether the effect is favorable or unfavorable. Assume that the standards are not changed in response to these situations. (Round calculations to two decimal places.)

P10-38.ᴬ   Fixed Overhead Budget and Volume Variance

Lucky Seven Company assigns fixed overhead costs to inventory for external reporting purposes by using a predetermined standard overhead rate based on direct labor hours. The standard rate is based on a normal activity level of 10,000 standard allowed direct labor hours per year. There are five standard allowed hours for each unit of output. Budgeted fixed overhead costs are $220,000 per year. During 2014, the company produced 2,200 units of output, and actual fixed costs were $230,000.

Required

a. Determine the standard fixed overhead rate used to assign fixed costs to inventory.

b. Determine the amount of fixed overhead assigned to inventory in 2014.

c. Determine the fixed overhead budget variance.

P10-39.[B] **Profit Center Performance Report**

Bach-by-Net is a classical music retailer specializing in the Internet sale of MP3 albums of the works of J. S. Bach. Although prices vary with album popularity and file sizes, the albums sell for an average of $7.75 each and Bach-by-Net pays a fixed royalty of $4.25 per MP3 album. With the exception of royalty fees, the operating costs of Bach-by-Net are fixed. Presented are budgeted and actual income statements for the month of September.

BACH-BY-NET Budgeted and Actual Contribution Statements For Month of September		
	Actual	**Budget**
Unit sales	4,400	4,200
Unit selling price	$7.25	$7.75
Sales revenue	$31,900	$32,550
Cost of goods sold	(17,850)	(17,000)
Gross profit	14,050	15,550
Operating costs	(5,000)	(6,000)
Contribution to corporate costs and profits	$ 9,050	$ 9,550

Required

Compute variances to assist in evaluating the performance of Bach-by-Net as a profit center. What was the likely cause of the shortfall in profits?

P10-40.[B] **Profit Center Performance Report**

Chili Town operates fast food restaurants in the food courts of shopping malls. It's main product is a serving of chili that requires beans (direct material) and food preparation (direct labor). The April budget for Chili Town's Riverside Mall restaurant was:

- Sales 21,000 servings at $1.50 each
- Standard food cost of $0.25 per serving (1/3 pound @ $0.75 per pound)
- Standard direct labor of $0.30 per serving (1/30th hour @ $9.00 per hour)
- Fixed occupancy expenses (equip and rent) of $7,000

Actual April performance of the Riverside Mall restaurant was:

- Sales 18,000 servings at $1.60 each
- Food cost of $4,096 for 5,600 pounds
- Direct labor cost of $6,720 for 800 hours
- Fixed occupancy expenses of $7,200

In early May, the manager received the following financial performance report:

CHILI TOWN— RIVERSIDE MALL Performance Report For the Month of April			
	Actual	**Budgeted**	**Variance**
Revenues	$28,800	$31,500	$2,700 U
Food Cost	(4,096)	(5,250)	1,154 F
Labor Cost	(6,720)	(6,300)	420 U
Occupancy	(7,200)	(7,000)	200 U
Profit	$10,784	$12,950	$2,166 U

Required

a. Partition variance into variances for 1) selling price and net sales volume, 2) food variances for price and quantity, and 3) labor variances for rate and efficiency.

b. Using the results of your analysis, prepare an alternative reconciliation of budgeted and actual profit. Be sure to include the occupancy variance.

c. Explain why the total variances for sales, food, and labor in your reconciliation differ from those originally presented to the restaurant manager.

P10-41.[B] **Comprehensive Performance Report**

Laptop Computing is a contract manufacturer of laptop computers sold under brand named companies. Presented are Laptop's budgeted and actual contribution income statements for October. The company has three responsibility centers: Production, Selling and Distribution, and Administration. Production and Administration are cost centers while Selling and Distribution is a profit center.

LAPTOP COMPUTING
Budgeted Contribution Income Statement
For Month of October

Sales (900 × $250)			$225,000
Less variable costs			
Variable cost of goods sold			
Direct materials (900 × $50)	$45,000		
Direct labor (900 × $20)	18,000		
Manufacturing overhead (900 × $15)	13,500	$ 76,500	
Selling and Distribution (900 × $60)		54,000	(130,500)
Contribution margin			94,500
Less fixed costs			
Manufacturing overhead		40,000	
Selling and Distribution		30,000	
Administrative		10,500	(80,500)
Net income			$ 14,000

LAPTOP COMPUTING
Actual Contribution Income Statement
For Month of October

Sales (1,000 × $275)			$275,000
Less variable costs			
Cost of goods sold			
Direct materials	$50,000		
Direct labor	25,000		
Manufacturing overhead	20,000	$95,000	
Selling and Distribution		88,000	(183,000)
Contribution margin			92,000
Less fixed costs			
Manufacturing overhead		38,000	
Selling and Distribution		40,000	
Administrative		22,000	(100,000)
Net income (loss)			$ (8,000)

Required

a. Prepare a performance report for Production that compares actual and allowed costs.

b. Prepare a performance report for Selling and Distribution that compares actual and allowed costs.

c. Determine the sales price and the net sales volume variances.

d. Prepare a report that summarizes the performance of Selling and Distribution.

e. Determine the amount by which Administration was over or under budget.

f. Prepare a report reconciling budgeted and actual net income. Your report should focus on the performance of each responsibility center.

CASES AND PROJECTS

C10-42. **Discretionary Cost Center Performance Reports** LO1

TruckMax had been extremely profitable, but the company has been hurt in recent years by competition and a failure to introduce new consumer products. In 2010, Tom Lopez became head of Consumer Products Research (CPR) and began a number of product development projects. Under his leadership the group had good ideas that led to the introduction of several promising products. Nevertheless, when 2011 financial results were reviewed, CPR's report revealed large unfavorable variances leading management to criticize Lopez for poor cost control. Management was quite concerned about cost control because profits were low, and the company's cash budget indicated that additional borrowing would be required throughout 2010 to cover out-of-pocket costs. Because of his inability to exert proper cost control, Lopez was relieved of his responsibilities in 2012, and Gabriella Garcia became head of Consumer Products Research. Garcia vowed to improve the performance of CPR and scaled back CPR's development activities to obtain favorable financial performance reports.

By the end of 2013, the company had improved its market position, profitability, and cash position. At this time, the board of directors promoted Garcia to president, congratulating her for the contribution CPR made to the revitalization of the company, as well as her success in improving the financial performance of CPR. Garcia assured the board that the company's financial performance would improve even more in the future as she applied the same cost-reducing measures that had worked so well in CPR to the company as a whole.

Required

a. For the purpose of evaluating financial performance, what responsibility center classification should be given to the Consumer Products Research Department? What unique problems are associated with evaluating the financial performance of this type of responsibility center?

b. Compare the performances of Lopez and Garcia in the role as head of Consumer Products Research. Did Garcia do a much better job, thereby making her deserving of the promotion? Why or why not?

C10-43. **Developing Cost Standards for Materials and Labor** LO2

After several years of operating without a formal system of cost control, DeWalt Company, a tools manufacturer, has decided to implement a standard cost system. The system will first be established for the department that makes lug wrenches for automobile mechanics. The standard production batch size is 100 wrenches. The actual materials and labor required for eight randomly selected batches from last year's production are as follows:

Batch	Materials Used (in pounds)	Labor Used (in hours)
1	504.0	10.00
2	508.0	9.00
3	506.0	9.00
4	521.0	5.00
5	516.0	8.00
6	518.0	7.00
7	520.0	6.00
8	515.0	8.00
Average	513.5	7.75

Management has obtained the following recommendations concerning what the materials and labor quantity standards should be:

- The manufacturer of the equipment used in making the wrenches advertises in the toolmakers' trade journal that the machine the company uses can produce 100 wrenches with 500 pounds of direct materials and 5 labor hours. Company engineers believe the standards should be based on these facts.

- The accounting department believes more realistic standards would be 505 pounds and 5 hours.
- The production supervisor believes the standards should be 512 pounds and 7.75 hours.
- The production workers argue for standards of 522 pounds and 8 hours.

Required

a. State the arguments for and against each of the recommendations, as well as the probable effects of each recommendation on the quantity variance for materials and labor.

b. Which recommendation provides the best combination of cost control and motivation to the production workers? Explain.

LO1, 2, 3 **C10-44.** **Behavioral Effect of Standard Costs**

Merit Inc. has used a standard cost system for evaluating the performance of its responsibility center managers for three years. Top management believes that standard costing has not produced the cost savings or increases in productivity and profits promised by the accounting department. Large unfavorable variances are consistently reported for most cost categories, and employee morale has fallen since the system was installed. To help pinpoint the problem with the system, top management asked for separate evaluations of the system by the plant manager, the controller, and the human resources director. Their responses are summarized here.

Plant Manager—The standards are unrealistic. They assume an ideal work environment that does not allow materials defects or errors by the workers or machines. Consequently, morale has gone down and productivity has declined. Standards should be based on expected actual prices and recent past averages for efficiency. Thus, if we improve over the past, we receive a favorable variance.

Controller—The goal of accounting reports is to measure performance against an absolute standard and the best approximation of that standard is ideal conditions. Cost standards should be comparable to "par" on a golf course. Just as the game of golf uses a handicap system to allow for differences in individual players' skills and scores, it could be necessary for management to interpret variances based on the circumstances that produced the variances. Accordingly, in one case, a given unfavorable variance could represent poor performance; in another case, it could represent good performance. The managers are just going to have to recognize these subtleties in standard cost systems and depend on upper management to be fair.

Human Resources Director—The key to employee productivity is employee satisfaction and a sense of accomplishment. A set of standards that can never be met denies managers of this vital motivator. The current standards would be appropriate in a laboratory with a controlled environment but not in the factory with its many variables. If we are to recapture our old "team spirit," we must give the managers a goal that they can achieve through hard work.

Required

Discuss the behavioral issues involved in Merit Inc.'s standard cost dilemma. Evaluate each of the three responses (pros and cons) and recommend a course of action.

C10-45.[B] **Evaluating a Companywide Performance Report**

Mr. Chandler, the production supervisor, bursts into your office, carrying the company's 2014 performance report and thundering, "There is villainy here, sir! And I shall get to the bottom of it. I will not stop searching until I have found the answer! Why is Mr. Richards so down on my department? I thought we did a good job last year. But Richards claims my production people and I cost the company $31,500! I plead with you, sir, explain this performance report to me." Trying to calm Chandler, you take the report from him and ask to be left alone for 15 minutes. The report is as follows:

DICKENS COMPANY, LIMITED
Performance Report
For Year 2014

	Actual	Budget	Variance
Unit sales.....................................	7,500	5,000	
Sales	$262,500	$225,000	$37,500 F
Less manufacturing costs			
Direct materials	55,500	47,500	8,000 U
Direct labor..................................	48,000	32,500	15,500 U
Manufacturing overhead	40,000	32,000*	8,000 U
Total..	(143,500)	(112,000)	(31,500) U
Gross profit	119,000	113,000	6,000 F
Less selling and administrative expenses			
Selling (all fixed).............................	57,800	40,000	17,800 U
Administrative (all fixed)	55,000	50,000	5,000 U
Total..	(112,800)	(90,000)	(22,800)
Net income...................................	$ 6,200	$ 23,000	$16,800 U
Performance summary			
Budgeted net income			$23,000
Sales department variances			
Sales revenue...............................	$ 37,500 F		
Selling expenses	17,800 U	$19,700 F	
Administration department variances		5,000 U	
Production department variances		31,500 U	16,800 U
Actual net income			$ 6,200

*Includes fixed manufacturing overhead of $22,000.

Required

a. Evaluate the performance report. Is Mr. Richards correct, or is there "villainy here"?

b. Assume that the Sales Department is a profit center and that the Production and Administration Departments are cost centers. Determine the responsibility of each for cost, revenue, and income variances, and prepare a report reconciling budgeted and actual net income. Your report should focus on the performance of each responsibility center.

SOLUTIONS TO REVIEW PROBLEMS

<u>Mid-Chapter Review</u>

Solution

The performance report prepared by the accounting department was based on a "static" budget. A better basis for evaluating your performance is to compare actual performance with a flexible budget. By dividing the budgeted variable costs amounts by 12,000 units, the budgeted unit variable costs amounts can be determined as follows:

Direct materials cost............................	$360,000 ÷ 12,000 units = $30 per unit
Direct labor	$432,000 ÷ 12,000 units = $36 per unit
Variable factory overhead.......................	$216,000 ÷ 12,000 units = $18 per unit

Using these budgeted unit values, a flexible budget can be prepared as follows:

	Actual	Flexible Budget	Variance
Units..	10,000	10,000	
Costs			
Direct materials..................................	$ 299,000	$ 300,000	$ 1,000 F
Direct labor.....................................	345,500	360,000	14,500 F
Variable factory overhead........................	180,000	180,000	
Fixed factory overhead...........................	375,000	360,000	15,000 U
Total plant costs...............................	$1,199,500	$1,200,000	$ 500 F

The plant did not produce the number of units originally budgeted. Therefore, from a cost control standpoint, a flexible budget is a better basis for evaluating performance because it compares the actual cost of producing 10,000 units with a budget also based on 10,000 units. Based on the flexible budget, your performance is still quite good; however, it is much less favorable than it appeared using a static budget.

Chapter-End Review

Solution

a.

*5,000 units × 4 pounds per unit produced

*5,000 units × 1.25 hours per unit

b.

Standard Cost Variance Analysis

Input component: Variable overhead   **Output: 5,000 units**

Actual Costs	Standard Cost of Actual Inputs	Flexible Budget Cost
Category 1 . . . $31,000	Actual labor hours 7,000	Standard hours allowed 6,250
Category 2 . . . 18,000	Standard rate . . . . × $4.80	Standard rate . . . . × $4.80
Total $49,000	Driver total $33,600	Driver total $30,000
	Finished units 5,000	Finished units 5,000
	Standard rate . . . . × $4.00	Standard rate . . . . × $4.00
	Driver total $20,000	Driver total $20,000
	Total $53,600	Total $50,000

Variable overhead
spending variance
$4,600 F

Variable overhead
efficiency variance
$3,600 U

Total flexible budget variable overhead variance $1,000 F

1. Define a strategic business segment, and prepare and use segment reports. (p. 386)

2. Explain transfer pricing and assess alternative transfer-pricing methods. (p. 391)

3. Determine and contrast return on investment and residual income. (p. 396)

4. Describe the balanced scorecard as a comprehensive performance measurement system. (p. 403)

Segment Reporting, Transfer Pricing, and Balanced Scorecard

On the shores of the Mittelland Canal, in the shadow of Wolfsburg Castle, stands the 73-million-square-foot factory of **Volkswagen** (VW). Along with employing 50,000 workers, VW's presence is felt throughout the region from the Volkswagen Arena to the VW-owned Ritz Carlton to Autostadt, VW's sprawling theme park housing the most popular car museum in the world, the ZeitHaus. But VW's products go beyond its flagship brand to include Audi, Porsche, Lamborghini, Bentley, Bugatti, Ducati, SEAT, Skoda, MAN, Scania, and Volkswagen Commercial Vehicles, encompassing a total of 280 different vehicle models. Likewise, VW's reach extends far beyond Germany. VW also has manufacturing or assembly plants in Mexico, Slovakia, China, India, Indonesia, Russia, Brazil, Argentina, Portugal, Spain, Poland, Czech Republic, Bosnia and Herzegovina, South Africa, and the United States. The worldwide presence is important for VW's future because automobile sales in Europe and the United States are leveling off, and Brazil, India, and China are expected to account for nearly half of all global auto sales by the year 2018.

VOLKSWAGEN
www.vw.com

Given the company's diversity by product line and geographic region, preparing the VW's financial and operating reports by segment assists VW managers in determining where the company should expand or contract its operations. However, the sheer complexity and volume of the company's business make the allocation of common costs across segments a difficult proposition. If managers' performance evaluations are tied to these segmented results, conflicts will undoubtedly arise regarding which allocated costs are within each manager's control.

One of VW's newest initiatives to manage the business across product and geographic lines is the introduction of modular tool-kit assemblies. This system will allow the company to build all of its vehicles using four basic setups: a different tool kit for small, midsize, sports, or large/SUV vehicles. Doing this allows VW to standardize its engineering platforms and reduce inventory costs by using shared components wherever possible. With standardization comes an increase in transfers of components across product line and geographic divisions. However, what is the correct "price" to charge between internal divisions? The "selling" division would like to maximize its divisional performance by charging the highest price possible on the transfer, while the "buying" division would prefer to minimize its costs by paying the lowest price possible to the selling division. And each country in which VW manufactures and assembles its vehicles resides in a different tax jurisdiction such that the choice of a transfer price has real economic consequences for the overall corporate entity.

Another complicating factor in VW's diversity of operations stems from evaluating the performance of the company's divisions. The company will want to compare its return on investment—that is, the income generated for each dollar of investment—across divisions to determine which managers and

continued on following page

continued from previous page

markets are delivering the best results. But the age of the capital investments, along with financial accounting rules govern-ing depreciation and research and development costs, can distort these performance metrics. In this chapter, we will discuss performance measures that overcome the weaknesses of traditional performance ratios by taking into account leverage, taxa-tion, level of investment, and the cost of accessing financial capital to make those investments. Further, we will examine per-formance evaluation models that are future oriented and emphasize nonfinancial measures such as innovation and learning, internal processes, and customer satisfaction in addition to financial performance. By utilizing the best performance analysis tools available, VW will continue to make decisions to grow the right products in the right geographical areas in order to maxi-mize its return to its employees, managers, and shareholders.

Sources: Kenneth Rapoza, "Volkswagen Stakes Out Greater Turf in China," *Forbes*, May 14, 2013; Joann Muller, "How Volkswagen Will Rule the World," *Forbes*, April 17, 2013; and Vanessa Fuhrmans and Friedrich Geiger, "A Weaker Outlook in Europe Slams Volkswagen's Stock," *Wall Street Journal*, February 23, 2013, p. B3.

CHAPTER ORGANIZATION

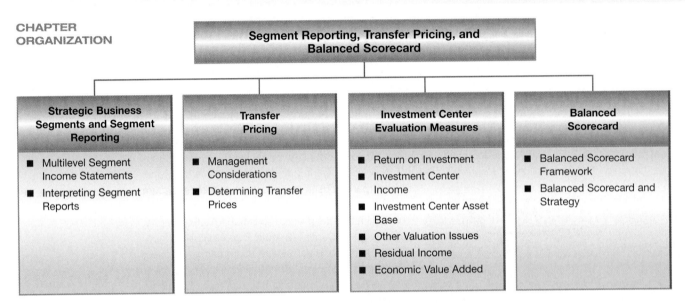

Organizations that maintain multiple product lines or that operate in several industries or in multiple markets often adopt a decentralized organization structure in which managers of major business units or strategic segments enjoy a high degree of autonomy. Examples of strategic business segments in-clude the Porsche division of Volkswagen and the Asia Pacific Group of The Coca-Cola Company. Sometimes companies establish segments within segments such as at Coca-Cola, whose Asia Pacific Group has separate business units for individual countries (Japan, Korea, etc.). In organizations such as Volkswagen and Coca-Cola, upper management typically sets specific performance and profit-ability objectives for each segment and allows the manager of the segment the decision-making freedom to achieve those objectives.

This chapter explains the ways that an organization evaluates strategic business segments. It also considers transfer pricing and some of the problems that occur when one segment provides goods or services to another segment in the same organization.

STRATEGIC BUSINESS SEGMENTS AND SEGMENT REPORTING

LO1 Define a strategic business segment, and prepare and use segment reports.

A **strategic business segment** has its own mission and set of goals. Its mission influences the decisions that top managers make in both short-run and long-run situations. The organization structure dictates to a large extent the type of financial segment reporting and other measures used to evaluate the segment and its managers. In decentralized organizations, for example, the reporting units (typically called *divisions*) normally are quasi-independent companies, often having their own computer system, cost accounting system, and administrative and marketing staffs. With this type structure, top management monitors the segments to ensure that these in-dependent units are functioning for the benefit of the entire organization.

Although segment reports are normally produced to coincide with managerial lines of responsibility, some companies also produce segment reports for smaller slices of the business that do not represent separate responsibility centers. These parts of the business are not significant enough to be identified as "strategic" business units as defined, but management could want information about them on a continuing basis.

For example, AT&T has several strategic business units, including wireless, wireline, and advertising solutions. Financial reports are prepared for each of these units. Within the wireline segment, AT&T can also prepare segment reports on a more detailed basis to determine the profitability of its smaller segments, such as phone-only and data service customers. Most public companies are required to provide some segment information in their annual reports.

The point is that segment reporting is not constrained by lines of responsibility. A segment report can be prepared for any part of the business for which management believes more detailed information is useful in managing that portion of the business.

BUSINESS INSIGHT

Segment Organization Focuses Management's Attention on Growth Areas Like Volkswagen, more companies are reorganizing their operations to take advantage of facility and information sharing. 3M has installed a new global software system to improve its business planning. The result has been a decision to decrease its number of operating segments down to five from six. The surviving segments are the consumer, industrial and transportation, health care, safety and graphics, and electronics and energy divisions.

The health care segment has experienced a surge in demand and is driving the expansion of factories in Asia and Latin America. Likewise, the industrial and transportation segment has benefited in these geographic regions due to increases in infrastructure spending on 3M products such as industrial abrasives, adhesives and tapes, highway reflective signage, telecom copper splicing, and similar items. On the other hand, the safety and graphics business, which makes passport readers and electronic devices used by libraries to track books, has been negatively impacted by reduced government spending, particularly in the U.S. markets.

Sources: Trefis Team, "3M Eyes Big Growth in Emerging Markets Consumers," *Forbes*, May 31, 2013; James Hagerty, "3M Cuts Outlook as Demand Sputters," *Wall Street Journal*, April 26, 2013, p. B4; and Associated Press, "3M Reorganizes Business Divisions," *Bloomberg Businessweek*, October 3, 2012.

Segment reports are income statements for portions or segments of a business. Segment reporting is used primarily for internal purposes, although generally accepted accounting principles also require some disclosure of segment information for public corporations. Even though there are many different types of segment reports, at least three steps are basic to the preparation of all segment reports:

1. Identify the segments.
2. Assign direct costs to segments.
3. Allocate indirect costs to segments.

The format of segment income statements varies depending on the approach adopted by a company for reporting income statements internally. The income statement formats illustrated earlier in this text, including the functional format and the contribution format, can be used for segment reporting. Data availability can, however, dictate the format used. Regardless of the format adopted, it is essential that costs be separable into those directly traceable to the segments and those not directly traceable to segments.

Determining the segment reporting structure is often a more difficult decision than choosing the format for the segment income statements. Companies must decide whether to structure segment reporting along the lines of responsibility reporting, and whether segment reports will be prepared only on one level or on several levels.

For example, assume Cisco has two market divisions, three products, and two geographic territories. Suppose Cisco's two divisions include the National Division (serving large national accounts) and the Regional Division (serving smaller regional and local accounts). Further assume Cisco's three main product lines are switching, routing, and wireless. The company is organized into two geographic territories, United States and International. If Cisco were using only a single-level segment reporting approach for all three groupings, one report would show the total company income statement broken down into the two divisions, a second report would show the total company income statement broken down into the three products, and a third report would show the total company income statement broken down into the two geographic territories.

Multilevel Segment Income Statements

If top management of Cisco wants to know how much a particular product is contributing to the income of one of the two divisions or how much income a particular product in one of its two geographic territories contributes, it is necessary to prepare multilevel segment income statements. Since Cisco sells three products and operates through two divisions in two territories, many combinations of divisions, products, and territories could be used in structuring the company's multilevel segment reporting. The goal is not to slice and dice the revenue and cost data in as many ways as possible but to provide useful and meaningful information to management. Therefore, deciding what type of reporting structure is most useful in managing the company is important.

This decision will be constrained to a great extent by data availability and cost. If there were no data constraints, Cisco could look at the company's net income for every possible combination of division, product, and territory. The more data required to support a reporting system, however, the more costly it is to maintain the system, so management must determine the value and the cost of the additional information and make an appropriate cost-benefit judgment.

Panel A of Exhibit 11.1 illustrates hypothetical multilevel segment reporting for Cisco in which the first level shows the total company income statement segmented into the two market divisions, National Accounts and Regional Accounts. Panel B of Exhibit 11.1 shows a second-level report for Cisco in which the National Division's segment income statement is broken down into its three product lines, switching, routing, and wireless. Panel C then provides a third-level income statement for the National Division's fiber optic sales in each of the company's two geographic territories, the U.S. and International territories. The example in Exhibit 11.1 shows only part of the segment reports for Cisco. The complete three-level set of segment reports would also break down the Regional Accounts Division into its product lines and all product lines for both divisions into geographic territories.

In the Cisco example in Exhibit 11.1, the first reporting level is the company's divisions, its second reporting level is product lines, and the third is geographic territories. Another approach could be to structure the segment reports with product lines as the first level, geographic territories as the second level, and divisions as the third level. Still another approach would be to make product lines the first level, divisions the second level, and geographic territories the third level.

Regardless of how many different ways the company segments the income statements, at least one set of segment reports follows the company's responsibility reporting system; therefore, one of the segment reports has the operating divisions as the first level. If each division has a product manager for each product, the division segment reports are broken down by products. Finally, if each product within each division has a territory manager, the product segment reports are broken down by territories.

Interpreting Segment Reports

Exhibit 11.1 reports costs in four categories: variable costs, direct fixed costs, allocated common costs, and unallocated common costs. Variable costs vary in proportion to the level of sales and are subtracted from sales in calculating contribution margin. **Direct segment fixed costs** are nonvariable costs directly traceable to the segments incurred for the specific benefit of the respective segments. **Segment margin** equals the contribution margin minus the direct segment fixed costs. For Cisco, segment margins are referred to as *division margins, product margins,* and *territory margins.* Segment margins represent the amount that a segment contributes directly to the company's profitability in the short run.

Common segment costs are incurred for the common benefit of all related segments shown on a segment income statement. In some cases, allocating some common costs is reasonable even though they cannot be directly traced to the various segments based on benefits received. For

EXHIBIT 11.1	Multilevel Segment Reports

Panel A: First-Level Segment Report of Cisco—For Divisions (in thousands)

	Segments (Divisions)		
	National Accounts	Regional Accounts	Company Total
Sales	$100,000	$ 200,000	$300,000
Less variable costs	(55,000)	(95,000)	(150,000)
Contribution margin	45,000	105,000	150,000
Less direct fixed costs	(20,000)	(60,000)	(80,000)
Division margin	25,000	45,000	70,000
Less allocated segment costs	(10,000)	(25,000)	(35,000)
Division income...	$ 15,000	$ 20,000	35,000
Less unallocated common costs			(12,000)
Net income..			$ 23,000

Panel B: Second-Level Segment Report of the National Division—For Products (in thousands)

	Segments (Products)			National Accounts Total
	Switching	Routing	Wireless	
Sales	$30,000	$40,000	$30,000	$100,000
Less variable costs	(15,000)	(19,000)	(21,000)	(55,000)
Contribution margin	15,000	21,000	9,000	45,000
Less direct fixed costs	(9,000)	(4,000)	(2,000)	(15,000)
Product margin	6,000	17,000	7,000	30,000
Less allocated segment costs	(5,000)	(4,000)	(1,000)	(10,000)
Product income...............................	$ 1,000	$13,000	$ 6,000	20,000
Less unallocated common costs				(5,000)
National Division income				$ 15,000

Panel C: Third-Level Segment Report of the Switching Product Line in the National Division—For Geographic Territories (in thousands)

	Segments (Territories)		Switching Total
	U.S.	International	
Sales	$20,000	$10,000	$30,000
Less variable costs	(11,000)	(4,000)	(15,000)
Contribution margin	9,000	6,000	15,000
Less direct fixed costs	(3,000)	(4,000)	(7,000)
Territory margin..	6,000	2,000	8,000
Less allocated segment costs	(2,000)	(3,000)	(5,000)
Territory income..	$ 4,000	$(1,000)	3,000
Less unallocated common costs			(2,000)
Switching income			$ 1,000

example, if segments share common space, allocating all space-related costs to the segments based on building space occupied could be appropriate. If there is no reasonable basis for allocating common costs, they should not be allocated to the segments. In Panel C of Exhibit 11.1, if advertising costs to promote the company's switching products on national television could not be reasonably allocated to the two geographic territories, they would be charged to the switching product line as an unallocated common cost, not to the individual territories.

If some portion of common costs can be reasonably allocated to the segments, those allocated costs are subtracted from the segment margins to determine segment income. Hence, **segment income** represents all revenues of the segment minus all costs directly or indirectly charged to it.

To properly interpret segment income, we should ask whether segment income represents the amount by which net income of the company will change if that segment is discontinued. For example, if Cisco discontinues the wireless product line in the National Division, does this mean that Cisco's net income will decrease by $6 million? Also, does it mean that if the National Division stops selling switching products in the International territory, Cisco's net income will increase by $1 million?

The answer to these questions depends on whether the costs allocated to the segments are avoidable. **Avoidable common costs** are allocated common costs that eventually can be avoided (that is, can be eliminated) if a segment is discontinued. If all allocated common costs are avoidable, the effect of discontinuing the segment on corporate profitability equals the amount of segment income. In most cases, the short-term impact of discontinuing a segment equals the segment margin because allocated costs are capacity costs that cannot be adjusted in the short run. Over time, the company should be able to adjust capacity and eliminate some, or possibly all, of the allocated common costs or find productive uses for that capacity in other segments of the business. The unallocated common costs cannot be changed readily in the short term or the long term without causing major disruptions to the company and its strategy. Therefore, over the long term, the impact of discontinuing a segment should be, approximately, it's segment income.

If Cisco discontinues selling switching products in the International territory (see Exhibit 11.1, Panel C) the short-term effect on the company's profits will probably be a $2 million reduction of profits, which equals the International territory's margin. The revenues and costs that make up the International territory margin would all be lost if switching sales were discontinued in the International territory, but the $3 million of common costs allocated to the International territory would continue, at least in the short term. Over the long term, however, after adjusting the capacity for selling this product in the International territory and eliminating the $3 million of allocated common costs, the effect of discontinuing switching products in the International territory on profits should be an increase of about $1 million, which is the amount of the segment loss for switching products in the International territory.

To summarize, generally, segment margin is relevant for measuring the short-term effects of decisions to continue or discontinue a segment; however, segment income is relevant for measuring the long-term effects of decisions to continue or discontinue.

MID-CHAPTER REVIEW

Refer to the Cisco example in Exhibit 11.1, Panel B. The following additional information is provided for the wireless product line in the National Division:

Sales—U.S. territory	$12,000
Sales—International territory	18,000
Direct fixed cost—U.S. territory	500
Direct fixed cost—International territory	800
Allocated segment costs—U.S. territory	200
Allocated segment costs—International territory	600

Required

a. Prepare a geographic territory segment report of the wireless product line in the National division. Assume variable costs are always the same percent of sales for wireless products.

b. Explain why the total of the Territory Margins for geographic segments of the wireless product line does not equal the product margin of the wireless product segment in Panel B of Exhibit 11.1.

The solution is on page 424.

TRANSFER PRICING

To determine whether each division is achieving its organizational objectives, managers must be accountable for the goods and services they acquire, both externally and internally. When goods or services are exchanged internally between segments of a decentralized organization, the way that the transferor and the transferee will report the transfer must be determined, either by negotiations between the two segments or by corporate policy. A **transfer price** is the internal value assigned a product or service that one division provides to another. The transfer price is recognized as revenue by the division providing goods or services and as expense (or cost) by the division receiving them. Transfer-pricing transactions normally occur between profit or investment centers rather than between cost centers of an organization; however, managers often consider cost allocations between cost centers as a type of transfer price. The focus in this chapter is on transfers between responsibility centers that are evaluated based on profits.

LO2 Explain transfer pricing and assess alternative transfer-pricing methods.

Management Considerations

The desire of the selling and buying divisions of the same company to maximize their individual performance measures often creates transfer-pricing conflicts within an organization. Acting as independent units, divisions could take actions that are not in the best interest(s) of the organization as a whole. The three examples that follow illustrate the need for organizations to maintain a *corporate* profit-maximizing viewpoint while attempting to allow *divisional* autonomy and responsibility.

Suppose Samsung Electronics has five divisions, some of which transfer products and product components to other Samsung divisions. Suppose the LCD Division manufactures two products, Alpha and Beta. It sells Alpha externally for $50 per unit and transfers Beta to the Television Division for $60 per unit. The costs associated with the two products follow:

LCD Division	Product	
	Alpha	**Beta**
Variable costs		
Direct materials	$15	$14
Direct labor.	5	10
Variable manufacturing overhead	5	16
Selling.	4	0
Fixed Costs		
Fixed manufacturing overhead	6	15
Total	$35	$55

An external company has just proposed to supply a Beta substitute product to the Television Division at a price of $52. From the company's viewpoint, this is merely a make or buy decision. The relevant costs are the differential outlay costs of the alternative actions. Assuming that the fixed manufacturing costs of the LCD Division are unavoidable, the relevant costs of this proposal from the company's perspective are as follows:

Buy.		$52
Make		
Direct materials	$14	
Direct labor.	10	
Variable manufacturing overhead	16	(40)
Difference.		$12

From the corporate viewpoint, the best decision is for the product to be transferred since the relevant cost is $40 rather than to buy it from an external source for $52. The decision for the Television Division management is basically one of cost minimization: Buy from the source that charges the lowest price. If LCD is not willing to transfer Beta at a price of $52 or less, the Television management could go to the external supplier to maximize the division's profits. (Although Television's managers are concerned about the cost of Beta, they are also concerned about the quality of the goods. If the $52 product does not meet its quality standards, Television could decide to buy from LCD at the higher price. For this discussion, assume that the internal and external products are identical; therefore, acting in its best interest, Television purchases Beta for $52 from the external source unless LCD can match the price.)

Prior to Television's receipt of the external offer, LCD had been transferring Beta to Television for $60. LCD must decide whether to reduce the contribution margin on its transfers of Beta to Television and, therefore, lower divisional profits or to try to find an alternative use for its resources. Of course, corporate management could intervene and require the internal transfer even though it would hurt LCD's profits.

As the second example, assume that the LCD Division has the option to sell an equivalent amount of Beta externally for $60 per unit if the Television Division discontinues its transfers from LCD. Now the decision for LCD's management is simple: Sell to the buyer willing to pay the most. From the corporate viewpoint, it is best for LCD to sell to the external buyer for $60 and for Television to purchase from the external provider for $52.

To examine a slightly different transfer-pricing conflict, assume that the LCD Division can sell all the Alpha that it can produce (it is operating at capacity). Also assume that there is no external market for Beta, but there is a one-to-one trade-off between the production of Alpha and Beta, which use equal amounts of the LCD Division's limited capacity.

The corporation still regards this as a make or buy decision, but the costs of producing Beta have changed. The cost of Beta now includes an outlay cost and an opportunity cost. The outlay cost of Beta is its variable cost of $40 ($14 + $10 + $16), as previously computed. Beta's opportunity cost is the net benefit foregone if the LCD Division's limited capacity is used to produce Beta rather than Alpha:

Selling price of Alpha		$50
Outlay costs of Alpha		
Direct materials	$15	
Direct labor	5	
Variable manufacturing overhead	5	
Variable selling	4	(29)
Opportunity cost of making Beta		$21

Accordingly, the relevant costs in the make or buy decision follow.

Make		
Outlay cost of Beta	$40	
Opportunity cost of Beta	21	$61
Buy		$52

From the corporate viewpoint, Television should purchase Beta from the outside supplier for $52 because in this case it costs $61 to make the product. If there were no outside suppliers, the corporation's relevant cost of manufacturing Beta would be $61. This is another way of saying that the Television Division should not acquire Beta internally unless its revenues cover all outlay costs (including the $40 in the LCD Division) and provide a contribution of at least $21 ($61 − $40). From the corporate viewpoint, the relevant costs in make or buy decisions are the external price, the outlay costs to manufacture, and the opportunity cost to manufacture. The opportunity cost is zero if there is excess capacity.

The transfer of goods and services between divisions of a company located in different countries that have unequal tax structures often attracts the attention of the taxing authorities. Companies are sometimes accused of trying to minimize their total tax costs by setting transfer prices that shift profits from the division in the higher-tax-rate country to the division in the lower-tax-rate country. For example, assume that IBM has a division in Denmark that produces software that it sells to its systems division in the U.S. Denmark's corporate tax rate is about 50 percent; whereas, the U.S. rate is about 35 percent. By setting a transfer price at the lowest possible level, the profits of the Danish division will be less, and those of the American division will be higher, resulting in lower overall taxes for the company. The taxing authorities in the high-tax-rate country always insist that the transfer price for goods and services sold to divisions in other countries be at least as high as fair market value of the goods or services transferred out. The following Business Insight discusses a recent attempt by the IRS to collect taxes of more than $500 million from Guidant Corp. related to improper transfer prices.

BUSINESS INSIGHT

International Transfer Pricing at Guidant Corp.   Boston Scientific Corp. reported that the IRS ruled that its Guidant Corp. division owes $521.1 million in taxes plus interest as a result of an audit of Guidant's prior years' tax returns. The company said "the IRS is assessing additional taxes related to transfer prices on technology license agreements between some of Guidant's U.S. and foreign businesses." Boston Scientific said it disagrees with the methodology the IRS used in determining the additional taxes and will fight the ruling through the legal process. The methodology used by the IRS was not disclosed.

Source: "Boston Scientific owes half billion in taxes, IRS says ; Company vows to fight ruling on Guidant division," *Boston Globe*, December 22, 2010, p. B9

Determining Transfer Prices

As illustrated, the transfer price of goods or services can be subject to much controversy. The most widely used and discussed transfer prices are covered in this section. Although a price must be agreed upon for each item or service transferred between divisions, the selection of the pricing method depends on many factors. The conditions surrounding the transfer determine which of the alternative methods discussed subsequently is selected.

Although no method is likely to be ideal, one must be selected if the profit or investment center concept is used. In considering each method, observe that each transfer results in a revenue entry on the supplier's books and a cost entry on the receiver's books. Transfers can be considered as sales by the supplier and as purchases by the receiver.

Market Price

When there is an existing market with established prices for an intermediate product and the transfer actions of the company will not affect prices, market prices are ideal transfer prices. If divisions are free to buy and sell outside the firm, the use of market prices preserves divisional autonomy and leads divisions to act in a manner that maximizes corporate goal congruence. Unfortunately, not all product transfers have equivalent external markets. Furthermore, the divisions should carefully evaluate whether the market price is competitive or controlled by one or two large companies. When substantial selling expenses are associated with outside sales, many firms specify the transfer price as market price less selling expenses. The internal sale may not require the incurrence of costs to get and fill the order.

To illustrate using the hypothetical Samsung example, assume that product Alpha of the LCD Division can be sold competitively at $50 per unit or transferred to a third division, the Display Division, for additional processing. Under most situations, the LCD Division will never sell Alpha for less than $50, and the Display Division will likewise never pay more than $50 for it. However, if any variable expenses related to marketing and shipping can be eliminated by divisional transfers, these costs are generally subtracted from the competitive market price. In our illustration in which variable selling expenses are $4 for Alpha, the transfer price could be reduced to $46 ($50 − $4). A price between $46 and $50 would probably be better than either extreme price. To the extent that these transfer prices represent a nearly competitive situation, the profitability of each division can then be fairly evaluated.

Variable Costs

If excess capacity exists in the supplying division, establishing a transfer price equal to variable costs leads the purchasing division to act in a manner that is optimal from the corporation's viewpoint. The buying division has the corporation's variable cost as its own variable cost as it enters the external market. Unfortunately, establishing the transfer price at variable cost causes the supplying division to report zero profits or a loss equal to any fixed costs. If excess capacity does not exist, establishing a transfer price at variable cost would not lead to optimal action because the supplying division would have to forego external sales that include a markup for fixed costs and profits. If Beta could be sold externally for $60, the LCD Division would not want to transfer Beta to the Television Division for a $40 transfer price based on the following variable costs:

Direct materials	$14
Direct labor	10
Variable manufacturing overhead	16
Total variable costs	$40

The LCD Division would much rather sell outside the company for $60, which covers variable costs and provides a profit contribution margin of $20:

Selling price of Beta	$60
Variable costs	(40)
Contribution margin	$20

Variable Costs Plus Opportunity Costs

From the organization's viewpoint, this is the optimal transfer price. Because all relevant costs are included in the transfer price, the purchasing division is led to act in a manner optimal for the overall company, whether or not excess capacity exists.

With excess capacity in the supplying division, the transfer price is the variable cost per unit. Without excess capacity, the transfer price is the sum of the variable and opportunity costs. Following this rule in the previous example, if the LCD Division had excess capacity, the transfer price of Beta would be set at Beta's variable costs of $40 per unit. At this transfer price, the Television Division would buy Beta internally, rather than externally at $52 per unit. If the LCD Division cannot sell Beta externally but can sell all the Alpha it can produce and is operating at capacity, the transfer price per unit would be set at $61, the sum of Beta's variable and opportunity costs ($40 + $21). (Refer back two pages.) At this transfer price, the Television Division would buy Beta externally for $52. In both situations, the management of the Television Division has acted in accordance with the organization's profit-maximizing goal.

There are two problems with this method. First, when the supplying division has excess capacity, establishing the transfer price at variable cost causes the supplying division to report zero profits or a loss equal to any fixed costs. Second, determining opportunity costs when the supplying division produces several products is difficult. If the problems with the previously mentioned transfer-pricing methods are too great, three other methods can be used: absorption cost plus markup, negotiated prices, and dual prices.

Absorption Cost Plus Markup

According to absorption costing, all variable and fixed manufacturing costs are product costs. Pricing internal transfers at absorption cost eliminates the supplying division's reported loss on each product that can occur using a variable cost transfer price. Absorption cost plus markup provides the supplying division a contribution toward unallocated costs. In "cost-plus" transfer pricing, "cost" should be defined as standard cost rather than as actual cost. This prevents the supplying division from passing on the cost of inefficient operations to other divisions, and it allows the buying division to know its cost in advance of purchase. Even though cost-plus transfer prices may not maximize company profits, they are widely used. Their popularity stems from several factors, including ease of implementation, justifiability, and perceived fairness. Once everyone agrees on absorption cost plus markup pricing rules, internal disputes are minimized.

Negotiated Prices

Negotiated transfer prices are used when the supplying and buying divisions independently agree on a price. As with market-based transfer prices, negotiated transfer prices are believed to preserve divisional autonomy. Negotiated transfer prices can lead to some suboptimal decisions, but this is regarded as a small price to pay for other benefits of decentralization. When they use negotiated transfer prices, some corporations establish arbitration procedures to help settle disputes between divisions. However, the existence of an arbitrator with any real or perceived authority reduces divisional autonomy.

Negotiated prices should have market prices as their ceiling and variable costs as their floor. Although frequently used when an external market for the product or component exists, the most common use of negotiated prices occurs when no identical-product external market exists. Negotiations could start with a floor price plus add-ons such as overhead and profit markups or with a ceiling price less adjustments for selling and administrative expenses and allowances for quantity discounts. When no identical-product external market exists, the market price for a similar completed product can be used, less the estimated cost of completing the product from the transfer stage to the completed stage.

Dual Prices

Dual prices exist when a company allows a difference in the supplier's and receiver's transfer prices for the same product. This method should minimize internal squabbles of division managers and problems of conflicting divisional and corporate goals. The supplier's transfer price normally approximates market price, which allows the selling division to show a "normal" profit on items that it transfers internally. The receiver's price is usually the internal cost of the product or service, calculated as variable cost plus opportunity cost. This ensures that the buying division will make an internal transfer when it is in the best interest of the company to do so.

In most cases, a market-based transfer price achieves the optimal outcome for both the divisions and the company as a whole. As discussed earlier, an exception occurs when a division is operating below full capacity and has no alternative use for its excess capacity. In this case, it is best for the company to have an internal transfer; therefore, to ensure that the receiving division makes an internal transfer, the company must require the internal transfer as long as its price does not exceed the established market rate. The only time an external price is more attractive when excess capacity exists is when the external price is below the variable cost of the providing internal division, and that scenario is highly unlikely.

A potential transfer-pricing problem exists when divisions exchange goods or services for which no established market exists. For example, suppose that a company is operating its information technology (IT) service department as a profit center that transfers services to other profit center departments using a cost-plus transfer price. If the departments using IT services can choose to use those services or to replicate them inside their departments, users might not make a decision that is best for the company. It could be best for the company to have all IT services come from the IT department, but other profit centers could believe that they can provide those services for themselves at lower cost. In this case, the company must decide how important it is to maintain the independence of its profit center. In the interest of maintaining a strong profit center philosophy, top management can decide that it is acceptable to suboptimize by allowing profit centers to provide IT services for themselves.

The ideal transfer-pricing arrangement is seldom the same for both the providing and receiving divisions for every situation. In these cases, what is good for one division is likely not to be good for the other division resulting in no transfer, even though a transfer could achieve corporate goals. These conflicts are sometimes overcome by having a higher-ranking manager impose a transfer price and insist that a transfer be made. Managers in organizations that have a policy of decentralization, however, often regard these orders as undermining their autonomy. Therefore, the imposition of a price could solve the corporate profit optimization problem but create other problems regarding the company's organization strategy. Transfer pricing thus becomes a problem with no ideal solutions.

The previous discussion has focused on the challenges of establishing transfer prices that motivate managers to make decisions that are beneficial to their divisions as well as the overall company. However, research, discussed in the following Research Insight box, concluded that there are often price benefits when dealing with outside vendors, if the company has the option of acquiring the goods or services internally.

RESEARCH INSIGHT

Transfer Pricing and External Competition Researchers found that a firm can glean benefits from discussing transfer-pricing problems with external suppliers. Though transfer prices above marginal cost introduce interdivision coordination problems, they also reduce a firm's willingness to pay outside suppliers. Knowing that costly internal transfers will eat into demand, the supplier is more willing to set lower prices. Such supplier discounts can make decentralization worthwhile for the firm. The benefit of decentralization is shown to be robust in both downstream and upstream competition.

Source: "Anil Arya and Brian Mittendorf, "Interacting Supply Chain Distortions: The Pricing of Internal Transfers and External Procurement," *The Accounting Review*, May 2007.

INVESTMENT CENTER EVALUATION MEASURES

LO3 Determine and contrast return on investment and residual income.

Two of the most common measures of investment center performance, return on investment and residual income, are discussed in the following sections. Several supporting components of these measures that help clarify the applications are also presented. (Earlier in the book, we explained the advantages of separating operating and nonoperating items to compute sales, assets, income, and so forth. We can similarly separate operating and nonoperating items for performance measurement. In this case, all measures would be adjusted to yield operating sales, operating assets, operating income, and so forth. Then, the following analysis would apply to those operating metrics and would reflect the operating performance of each center.)

Return on Investment

Return on investment (ROI) is a measure of the earnings per dollar of investment. This assumes that financing decisions are made at the corporate level rather than the division level. Hence, the corporation's investment in the division equals the division's asset base. The return on investment of an investment center is computed by dividing the income of the center by its asset base (usually total assets):

$$\text{ROI} = \frac{\text{Investment center income}}{\text{Investment center asset base}}$$

ROI can be disaggregated into investment turnover times the return-on-sales ratio:

$$\text{ROI} = \text{Investment turnover} \times \text{Return-on-sales}$$

where

$$\text{Investment turnover} = \frac{\text{Sales}}{\text{Investment center asset base}}$$

and

$$\text{Return-on-sales} = \frac{\text{Investment center income}}{\text{Sales}}$$

When investment turnover is multiplied by return-on-sales, the product is the same as investment center income divided by investment center asset base:

$$\text{ROI} = \frac{\text{Sales}}{\text{Investment center base}} \times \frac{\text{Investment center income}}{\text{Sales}} = \frac{\text{Investment center income}}{\text{Investment center asset base}}$$

Once ROI has been computed, it is compared to some previously identified performance criteria. These include the investment center's previous ROI, overall company ROI, the ROI of similar divisions, or the ROI of nonaffiliated companies that operate in similar markets. The breakdown of ROI into investment turnover and return-on-sales is useful in determining the source of variance in overall performance.

To illustrate the computation and use of ROI, suppose the following information is available concerning the 2014 operations of Yum! Brands, Inc. (in thousands):

Division	Asset Base	Sales	Divisional Income
East	$8,000,000	$12,000,000	$1,440,000
South	4,000,000	8,000,000	960,000
Midwest...........................	7,500,000	5,000,000	1,650,000
West..............................	3,800,000	5,700,000	1,026,000

Using this information and the preceding equations, a set of performance measures are shown in Exhibit 11.2. To illustrate, East Division earned a return on its investment base of 18 percent ($1,440,000 ÷ $8,000,000), consisting of an investment turnover of 1.50 ($12,000,000 ÷ $8,000,000) and a return-on-sales of 0.12 ($1,440,000 ÷ $12,000,000). Using such an analysis, the company has three measurement criteria with which to evaluate the performance of East Division: (1) ROI, (2) investment turnover, and (3) return-on-sales.

For 2014, Yum! Brands chose to evaluate its divisions based on company ROI and its interrelated components of investment turnover and return-on-sales. Because each division is different in size, the company evaluation standard is not a simple average of the divisions but is based on desired relationships between assets, sales, and income.

Based on ROI, the West Division had the best performance, the South Division excelled in investment turnover, and the Midwest Division had the highest return-on-sales. From Exhibit 11.2, the West Division had the best year because it was the only division that exceeded each of the company's performance criteria. For 2014, each division equaled or exceeded the minimum ROI established by the company even though the component criteria of ROI were not always achieved.

EXHIBIT 11.2	**Performance Evaluation Data**

YUM! BRANDS, INC.
Performance Measures
For Year Ending June 30, 2014

	Performance Measures		
	Investment Turnover	× Return-on-Sales	= ROI
Operating unit			
East.......................................	1.50	0.12	0.18
South	2.00	0.12	0.24
Midwest	0.67	0.33	0.22
West.......................................	1.50	0.18	0.27
Company performance criteria			
Projected minimums	1.20	0.15	0.18

To properly evaluate each division, the company should study the underlying components of ROI. For the East Division, management would want to know why the minimum investment turnover was exceeded while the return-on-sales minimum was not. The East Division could have incurred unfavorable cost variances by producing inefficiently. As a result of inefficient production, the return-on-sales declined to a point below the minimum desired level. Evaluating a large operating division based on one financial indicator is difficult. Management should select several key indicators of performance when conducting periodic reviews of its operating segments.

A similar analysis of ROI and its components is useful for planning. In developing plans for 2015, management wants to know the possible effect of changes in the major elements of ROI for the East Division. Sensitivity analysis can be used to predict the impact of changes in sales, the investment center asset base, or the investment center income.

Assuming the investment asset base is unchanged, a projected ROI can be determined for the East Division for a sales goal of $16,000,000 and an income goal of $1,600,000:

$$\text{ROI} = \frac{\textbf{Sales}}{\textbf{Investment center asset base}} \times \frac{\textbf{Investment center income}}{\textbf{Sales}}$$

$$= \frac{\$16,000,000}{\$8,000,000} \times \frac{\$1,600,000}{\$16,000,000}$$

$$= 2.0 \times 0.10$$

$$= 0.20, \text{ or 20 percent.}$$

ROI increased from 18 to 20 percent, even though the return-on-sales decreased from 12 to 10 percent. The change in turnover from 1.5 to 2.0 more than offset the reduced return-on-sales.

Sensitivity analysis can involve changing only one factor or a combination of factors in the ROI model. When more than one factor is changed, it is important to analyze exactly how much change is caused by each factor.

Statistics such as ROI, investment turnover, and return-on-sales mean little by themselves. They take on meaning only when compared with an objective, a trend, another division, a competitor, or an industry average. Many businesses establish minimum ROIs for each of their divisions, expecting them to attain or exceed this minimum return. The salaries, bonuses, and promotions of division managers can be tied directly to their division's ROI. Without other evaluation techniques, managers often strive for ROI maximization, sometimes to the long-run detriment of the entire organization.

RESEARCH INSIGHT

Nonprofit Donations Decrease When Donors Believe Managers Are Overpaid   Over 1.4 million nonprofit organizations across the United States received more than $260 billion in donations during the year 2009. Yet with the weakening economy, contributors to nonprofit organizations are less willing to tolerate inflated salaries of the charity's executives. Specifically, donors decrease their contributions to the organization when the media reports an increase in executive compensation. On average, organizations that draw media coverage over executive compensation increases grow 15 percent less over the two years surrounding the media mention than their peer organizations. However, when this increase is reported on Form 990 for the Internal Revenue Service (IRS), only sophisticated donors reduce their contributions. Small donors may not know where to seek the compensation information out on their own, and larger donors have a greater stake in the stewardship of their donated funds. Among these larger donors, the study reports that contributions decrease by 3 percent for every $100,000 increase in executive compensation.

Source: Steven Balsam and Erica Harris, "The Impact of CEO Compensation on Nonprofit Donations," *The Accounting Review*, forthcoming.

Investment Center Income

Despite the relevance and conceptual simplicity of ROI, a division's ROI cannot be determined until management decides how to measure divisional income and investment. Divisional income equals divisional revenues less divisional operating expenses. Determining divisional revenues is usually a relatively easy task since revenues are typically generated and recorded at the division level, but determining total operating expenses for divisions is more complicated. Because many expenses are incurred at the corporate level for the common benefit of the various operating divisions and to support corporate headquarters operations, the cost assignment issues discussed early in this chapter affect investment center income.

Direct division expenses are always included in division operating expenses, but there are conflicting viewpoints about how to deal with common corporate expenses. As stated earlier in this chapter, in corporate annual reports, many companies are required to provide segment revenues and expenses segmented by product lines, geographic territories, customer markets, and so on. Companies also show operating income for their various segments in their annual reports, but they include a category called *corporate* or *unallocated* for company expenses that cannot be reasonably allocated to the various segments. ("Unallocated" typically includes costs for corporate staffs, certain goodwill writeoffs, and nonoperational gains and losses.) For example, the Ericsson, Inc., annual report for a recent year includes the following breakdown of its operating income by segments (stated in millions of Swedish kronas):

Networks	6,879 SEK
Professional services	6,990
Multi-media	655
Sony Ericsson	(10,820)
ST-Ericsson	(2,615)
Unallocated	(855)
Inter-segment eliminations	5,684
Total operating income	5,918 SEK

For internal segment reporting, some companies do not allocate corporate costs that cannot be associated closely with individual segments. Other companies insist on allocating all common corporate costs to the operating divisions to emphasize that the company does not earn a profit until revenues have covered all costs. Some top managers believe that since only operating divisions produce revenues, they should also bear all costs, including corporate costs. These managers want to ensure that the sum of the division income for the various segments equals the total income for the company.

Division managers do not control corporate costs; therefore, these costs are seldom relevant in evaluating a division manager's performance. To deal with this conflict, some companies allocate some, or possibly all, common corporate costs in reporting segment operating income, but for ROI calculation purposes exclude allocated corporate costs that are not closely associated with the divisions. These companies include in the ROI calculation costs that represent an identifiable benefit to the divisions but not general corporate costs that provide no identifiable benefits to the divisions. In practice, the treatment of corporate costs for division performance evaluation varies widely.

Investment Center Asset Base

Because the primary purpose for computing ROI is to evaluate the effectiveness of a division's operating management in using the assets entrusted to them, most organizations define *investment* as the average total assets of a division during the evaluation period. For most companies, the *investment base* is defined as each division's operating assets. These normally include those assets held for productive use, such as accounts receivable, inventory, and plant and equipment. Nonproductive assets, such as land for a future plant site, are not included in the investment base of a division but in the investment base for the company.

General corporate assets allocated to divisions should not be included in their bases. Although the divisions might need additional administrative facilities if they were truly independent, they have no control over the headquarters' facilities. The joint nature and use of corporate facility-level expenses make any allocation arbitrary.

Other Valuation Issues

Once divisional investment and income have been operationally defined and ROI computations have been made, the significance of the resulting ratios can still be questioned. Return on investment can be overstated in terms of constant dollars because inflation as well as arbitrary inventory and depreciation procedures cause an undervaluation of the inventory and fixed assets included in the investment center asset base. Asset measurement is particularly troublesome if inventories are valued at last-in, first-out (LIFO) cost and fixed assets were acquired many years ago. A division manager could hesitate to replace an old, inefficient asset with a new, efficient one because the replacement could lower income and ROI through an increased investment base and increased depreciation.

To improve the comparability between divisions with old and new assets when computing ROI, some firms value assets at original cost rather than at net book value (cost less accumulated depreciation). This procedure does not reflect inflation, however. An old asset that cost $120,000 ten years ago is still being compared with an asset that costs $200,000 today. A better solution could be to value old assets at their replacement cost, although replacement costs are often difficult to determine.

YOU MAKE THE CALL

You are the Division Vice President   Division managers in your company are evaluated primarily based on division return on investment, and you recently received financial reports for your division for the most recent period and discovered that the ROI for your division was 14.5%; whereas, the target ROI for your division set by the CFO and the CEO was 15%. What action can you take to try to avoid missing your performance target for the next period? [Answer, p. 407]

Residual Income

Residual income is an often-mentioned alternative to ROI for measuring investment center performance. **Residual income** is the excess of investment center income over the minimum rate or dollar of return. The *minimum rate of return* represents the rate that can be earned on alternative investments of similar risks, which is the opportunity cost of the investment. The *minimum dollar return* is computed as a percentage of the investment center's asset base. When residual income is the primary basis of evaluation, the management of each investment center is encouraged to maximize residual income rather than ROI. (We can again measure assets, sales, income, and so forth, as excluding all nonoperating components; similarly, the investment base can be measured as operating assets less operating liabilities).

To illustrate the computation, assume that a company requires a minimum return of 12 percent on each division's investment base. The residual income of a division with an annual net operating income of $2,000,000 and an investment base of $15,000,000 is $200,000 as computed here:

Division income	$2,000,000
Minimum return ($15,000,000 × 0.12)	(1,800,000)
Residual income	$ 200,000

Economic Value Added

A variation of residual income, referred to as **economic value added** or **EVA®**, is also often used as a basis for evaluating investment center performance. (The term EVA is a registered trademark of the financial consulting firm of Stern Stewart and Company.) EVA is equal to income after taxes less the cost of capital employed. The three significant changes from the residual income computation in applying EVA are the use of an organization's weighted average cost of capital as the minimum return, *net assets* as the evaluation base, and after-tax income. **Weighted average cost of capital** is an average of the after-tax cost of all long-term borrowing and the cost of equity[1]; **net assets** are total

[1] Weighted average cost of capital computations are covered in introductory corporate finance textbooks.

assets less current liabilities. Economic value is added only if a division's taxable income exceeds its net cost of investing. (We can again measure assets, sales, income, and so forth, as excluding all nonoperating components; similarly, the net asset base can be measured as operating assets less operating liabilities.)

Using the preceding situation, assume that the company has a cost of capital of 10 percent, $1,800,000 in current liabilities, and a 30 percent tax rate. The economic value-added is $80,000, computed as follows:

Division income after taxes ($2,000,000 × 0.70)	$1,400,000
Cost of capital employed [($15,000,000 − $1,800,000) × 0.10]	(1,320,000)
Economic value added	$ 80,000

Another differentiating characteristic of the EVA model is that it usually corrects for potential distortions in economic net income caused by generally accepted accounting principles (GAAP). In calculating EVA, the user can abandon any accounting principles that are viewed as distorting the measurement of wealth creation. In practice, EVA consultants have identified up to 150 different adjustments to GAAP income and equity that must be made to restore equity and income to their true economic values. Most companies use no more than about five adjustments (such as the capitalization of research and development cost and the elimination of goodwill write-offs).

Proponents of EVA argue that it is the best measure of managerial performance from the standpoint of maximizing the market value added to a firm through managerial decisions. They maintain that **market value added (MVA)**, which is the increase in market value of the firm for the period, is the definitive measure of wealth creation and that MVA is maximized by maximizing EVA. By maximizing the excess of economic net income over the cost of all outside capital invested in the firm, the firm should maximize its MVA in the long run.

One might ask why we should use EVA to estimate managerial contribution to the maximization of MVA, when we could simply measure how much market value has been added to the firm by considering changes in stock prices. In practice this does not work well because of short-run changes in market prices caused by overall market factors, not just firm-specific factors, and the inability of market prices to reflect divisional wealth creation that is not transparent. Also, many firms are not publicly traded, which makes determining market value changes problematic. Finally, companies want to measure managerial performance over specific segments of a firm, as well as the firm as a whole, but market values for individual segments are seldom available.

EVA provides a good operational metric for assessing managers' performance in terms of maximizing MVA over time. It is a model that can be used to guide managerial action. Companies that use EVA for evaluating performance use it in making a broad range of decisions such as evaluating capital expenditure proposals, adding or dropping a product line, or acquiring another company. Only alternatives that provide economic value are accepted. The following Businesss Insight box discusses the impact of adopting an EVA financial management system at Ryder Systems.

BUSINESS INSIGHT

Ryder System Touts Its EVA Performance   At a recent investment conference sponsored by the financial services firm of Robert W. Baird & Co., the CEO of Ryder Systems, Greg Swienton, stated that "we have not only maintained, but we have increased our economic value added per unit sold even during the downturn." When asked why the EVA is up, Swienton attributed it to managerial discipline of only investing in assets with a high EVA, but also to the sales force. He stated that "they earn more money when they sell higher EVA.... So I think the fact [is] that they will look to try to get every additional dollar they can, sell additional add-on services, [and] get more EVA per unit, because that's how they earn a better living, not just moving units or selling revenue." These statements reflect a deep commitment to the EVA model at Ryder and to having the model deeply imbedded in the managerial performance evaluation and compensation system throughout the company.

Source: Ryder System, Inc. at Baird Industrial Conference," *CQ Transcriptions*, November 9, 2010.

Which Measure Is Best?

Many executives view residual income or EVA as a better measure of managers' performance than ROI. They believe that residual income and EVA encourages managers to make profitable investments that managers might reject if being measured exclusively by ROI.

To illustrate, assume that three divisions of DuPont have an opportunity to make an investment of $100,000 that requires $10,000 of additional current liabilities and that will generate a return of 20 percent. The manager of the Chemical Division is evaluated using ROI, the manager of the Agriculture Division is evaluated using residual income, and the manager of the Nutrition Division is evaluated using economic value added. The current ROI of each division is 24 percent. Each division has a current income of $120,000, a minimum return of 18 percent on invested capital, and a cost of capital of 14 percent. If each division has a current investment base of $500,000, current liabilities of $40,000, and a tax rate of 30 percent, the effect of the proposed investment on each division's performance is as follows:

	Current	+	Proposed	=	Total
Chemical Division					
Investment center income	$120,000		$ 20,000		$140,000
Asset base	$500,000		$100,000		$600,000
ROI	24%		20%		23.3%
Agriculture Division					
Asset base	$500,000		$100,000		$600,000
Investment center income	$120,000		$ 20,000		$140,000
Minimum return (0.18 × base)	(90,000)		(18,000)		(108,000)
Residual income	$ 30,000		$ 2,000		$ 32,000
Nutrition Division					
Assets	$500,000		$100,000		$600,000
Current liabilities	(40,000)		(10,000)		(50,000)
Evaluation base	$460,000		$ 90,000		$550,000
Investment center income	$120,000		$ 20,000		$140,000
Income taxes (30%)	(36,000)		(6,000)		(42,000)
Income after taxes	84,000		14,000		98,000
Cost of capital (0.14 × base)	(64,400)		(12,600)		(77,000)
Economic value added	$ 19,600		$ 1,400		$ 21,000

The Chemical Division manager will not want to make the new investment because it reduces the current ROI from 24 percent to 23.3 percent. This is true, even though the company's minimum return is only 18 percent. Not wanting to explain a decline in the division's ROI, the manager will probably reject the opportunity even though it could have benefited the company as a whole.

The Agriculture Division manager will probably be happy to accept the new project because it increases residual income by $2,000. Any investment that provides a return more than the required minimum of 18 percent will be acceptable to the Agriculture Division manager. Given a profit maximization goal for the organization, the residual income method is preferred over ROI evaluations because it encourages division managers to accept all projects with returns above the 18 percent cutoff. The same is true for the Nutrition Division manager, although the EVA increase is not as high as that of the residual income because it has a different base.

The primary disadvantage of the residual income and EVA methods as comparative evaluation tools is that they measure performance in absolute dollars rather than percentages. Although they can be used to compare period-to-period results of the same division or with similar-size divisions, they cannot be used effectively to compare the performance of divisions of substantially different sizes. For example, the residual income of a multimillion dollar sales division should be higher than that of a half-million-dollar sales division. Because most performance evaluations and comparisons are made between units or alternative investments of different sizes, ROI continues to be extensively used. The following Business Insight box discusses the use of multiple evaluation models for assessing IT projects.

BUSINESS INSIGHT

Methods used to Evaluate IT Projects at Harrah's   A recent article in *Computer World* discusses the methods used to evaluate IT project proposals by IT managers and corporate executives. The article outlines the differences between "operational projects" aimed at saving money, and "strategic projects" aimed at making money. Harrah's Entertainment was one of several companies cited in the article. Harrah's Entertainment uses three metrics to prioritize IT projects: net present value, internal rate of return, and economic value added. "Increased sales is usually the key benefit to be measured, but the business sponsor of a project works with IT to measure softer benefits such as increased guest visits at Harrah's hotels and casinos, customer satisfaction, and even employee satisfaction." Using more than one metric has pros and cons, says Harrah's CIO Tim Stanley. "Using multiple criteria to assess a project provides a robust framework for decisions," he says. "Each tool takes into consideration the investment and the expected business value or return, and we are not limited to a single point of view." But, he adds, "the prospect of sophisticated financial analyses can inhibit some people from submitting ideas for consideration."

Source: Gary Anthes, "What's Your Project Worth? Figuring it out isn't easy. But you can't manage what you don't measure," *Computer World*, March 10, 2008.

BALANCED SCORECARD

Although financial measures have been emphasized throughout this text, several sections stress that other measures, specifically qualitative measures, are important in evaluating managerial performance. This section examines one popular method of performance evaluation using *both* financial and nonfinancial information.

We might ask: why not use just financial measures? First, no single financial measure captures all performance aspects of an organization. More than one measure must be used. Second, financial measures have reporting time lags that could hinder timely decision making. Third, financial measures might not accurately capture the information needed for current decision making because of the delay that sometimes occurs between making financial investments and receiving their results. For example, building a new nuclear power plant can take several years with the investment in total assets increasing the entire time without generating any revenues.

LO4 Describe the balanced scorecard as a comprehensive performance measurement system.

Balanced Scorecard Framework

Comprehensive performance measurement systems are one suggested solution. The basic premise is to establish a set of diverse key performance indicators to monitor performance. The **balanced scorecard** is a performance measurement system that includes financial and operational measures related to a firm's goals and strategies. The balanced scorecard comprises several categories of measurements, the most common of which include the following:

- Financial
- Customer satisfaction
- Internal processes
- Innovation and learning

A balanced scorecard is usually a set of reports required of all common operating units in an organization. To facilitate the periodic evaluation of performance, a cover sheet (or sheets for a large operation) can be used to summarize the performance of each area using the established criteria for each category.

For example, Einstein Brothers might have a balanced scorecard that looks something like the one in Exhibit 11.3. This balanced scorecard uses four categories for evaluation and includes financial and nonfinancial information. Each category being monitored has information from the previous period and the standard related to the category. The report should always include the current period, at least one previous period, and some standard. Each store manager should attach documentation and an appropriate explanation as to the change in the measurements during the reporting period.

EXHIBIT 11.3 Balanced Scorecard Illustration	Standard	Prior Period	Current Period
Key financial indicators			
Cash flow	$ 25,000	$ 28,000	$ 21,000
Return on investment (ROI)	0.18	0.22	0.19
Sales.	$4,400,000	$4,494,000	$4,342,000
Key customer indicators			
Average customers per hour.	75	80	71
Number of customer complaints per period	22	21	17
Number of sales returns per period	10	8	5
Key operating indicators			
Bagels sold/produced per day ratio	0.96	0.93	0.91
Daily units lost (burned, dropped, etc.)	25	32	34
Employee turnover per period	0.10	0.07	0.00
Key growth and innovation indicators			
New products introduced during period.	1	1	0
Products discontinued during period	1	1	1
Number of sales promotions.	3	3	2
Special offers, discounts, etc..	4	5	3

In making assessments with the evaluation categories, it is important to consider both trailing and leading performance measures. *Trailing measures* look backward at historical data while *leading measures* provide some idea of what to expect currently or in the near future. For example, in the financial category, ROI is a trailing indicator while a budget of production units and costs for the next period is a leading indicator. In the customer category, the number of sales invoices per store might tell us whether each store is maintaining its customer base (a trailing indicator) while the number of product complaints per 1000 invoices might be a leading indicator of customer satisfaction, quality control problems, and future sales.

The use of balanced scorecard systems to monitor and assess managerial and organizational performance is increasing worldwide. The following Business Insight discusses characteristics of a successful balanced scorecard implementation.

BUSINESS INSIGHT

Understanding Your Company's Strategy—The First Step in Designing a Balanced Scorecard After eight consecutive years of losses at the Brazil Volkswagen plant, a new management team was hired to turn the company around. The company determined that the division had lost sight of its strategy, so mapping out the company's core business strategies was the first order of business. The team member's affixed the division's strategy map to walls around the plant and developed games to help the employees remember the strategic mission and keep it in the forefront of their minds. They also invented a VW Beetle–shaped robot called Giga that traveled around the plant talking to the employees about strategy initiatives.

Employees were engaged by the actions—the 22,000 factory workers offered 13,000 suggestions in a suggestion box, covering everything from car design to working with suppliers and dealers. Revenue surged by 50 percent in the division, and the company went from number three to number one in market share within two years of starting the new course of action. Re-orienting employees toward the company's strategy is the first step in developing a balanced scorecard system.

Source: Robert Kaplan and Ricardo Reisen de Pinho, "Volkswagen do Brasil: Driving Strategy with the Balanced Scorecard," Harvard Business School Case 111-049, October 2010.

A balanced scorecard gives management a perspective of the organization's performance on a recurring set of criteria. Since each reporting unit knows what reports are expected, no one is surprised by changing monthly requests for data. Because the multiple perspectives provide management a broad analysis of the organization's performance, it allows them to determine how and where the goals and objectives are either being achieved or not achieved.

For most management teams, the balanced scorecard highlights trade-offs between measures. For example, a substantial increase in customer satisfaction can result in a short-run decrease in ROI because the extra effort to please customers is expensive, thereby reducing ROI. A balanced scorecard can be filtered down the organization with successively lower-level operating units having their own scorecards that mimic those of the higher-level units. This provides all levels of management an opportunity to evaluate operations from more than just a financial perspective.

As with all management tools and techniques, the use of the balanced scorecard must be incorporated with the other information sources within the organization. Just as the accounting information system cannot stand alone in managing a business, neither can the balanced scorecard. Some areas could need extensive accounting information in great detail to make the best possible decision while other areas need great detail in production or service integration to be at the right place at the right time. By using a multi-faceted approach to managing, the organization should be able to better establish an operating strategy that coincides with its overall goals and objectives.

RESEARCH INSIGHT

A Picture May Be Worth a Higher Stock Price In his book *The Winter of Our Discontent*, John Steinbeck wrote, "For the most part people are not curious except about themselves." Psychologists define narcissism as a sense of self-importance, uniqueness, entitlement, self-absorption, arrogance, and vanity. However, some of these same traits are correlated with leadership qualities. In a recent study, researchers investigate the link between CEO narcissism and financial performance, specifically, earnings per share (EPS) and stock price.

They measure CEO narcissism by examining the size and composition of the CEO's photograph in the annual report and components of the CEO's compensation package. They find that narcissistic managers are more likely to take actions that increase sales and production levels, such as extending lenient credit terms, offering sales discounts, and overproducing. There is no evidence that these same managers attempt to manage earnings through accrual-related actions.

Source: Kari Olsen, Kelsey Dworkis, and Mark Young, "CEO Narcissism and Accounting: A Picture of Profits," *Journal of Management Accounting Research*, forthcoming.

Balanced Scorecard and Strategy

When a balanced scorecard system is fully utilized to monitor and evaluate an organization's progress, it becomes a system for operationalizing the organization's strategy. Having a goal to maximize shareholder value or generate a certain income does not constitute a strategy. Maximizing shareholder value can be an overarching corporate goal, but it will not likely be realized without a well-developed strategy that identifies and establishes a balanced set of goals on various dimensions of performance.

A balanced scorecard can be the primary vehicle for translating strategy into action and establishing accountability for performance. The balanced scorecard identifies the areas of managerial action that are believed to be the drivers of corporate achievement. If the corporate goal is to increase ROI or residual income, the balanced scorecard should include key performance indicators that drive these measures.

An interesting parallel to the successful management of a company can be drawn by considering the key performance indicators the manager of a professional baseball team uses in setting goals and evaluating progress. The manager of the New York Yankees does not just tell his players and managers at the beginning of the baseball season that the team's goal is to win the World Series or even a certain number of ball games. The win-loss record is only one metric used to set goals and evaluate performance for a baseball team. The manager looks at many different drivers of success related to hitting, pitching, and fielding, including the earned-run averages of the pitchers, the batting and on-base averages of hitters, the number of errors per game by fielders, and the number of bases stolen by base runners. At the end of the season, the manager measures success not just by whether the Yankees won the World Series, but also by the batting average, number of home runs, and number of bases stolen by individual players, and whether or not a team member won a Golden Glove award or the Cy Young award. These are all measures by which to evaluate achievement and strategic accomplishment. By achieving the goals for each of these areas of the game, the win-loss ratio will take care of itself. If the win-loss results are not acceptable, then the manager adjusts his strategic goals with respect to the key performance indicators (or the manager is dismissed).

Like a baseball team, a company can use a balanced scorecard to develop performance metrics for managers from the top of the company to the lowest-level department. The scorecard becomes a vehicle for communicating the factors that are key to the success of managers, factors that upper management will monitor in evaluating the success of lower managers in carrying out the corporate strategy. To make balanced scorecards more user friendly, several companies use performance monitoring **dashboards**, which are computer generated graphics that present scorecard results using graphics, some of which mimic the instrument displays on an automobile dashboard.

The following Business Insight provides an illustration of dashboard graphics.

BUSINESS INSIGHT

Balanced Scorecard Dashboard Balanced scorecard dashboards provide information about an organization in an "at-a-glance" format. Many software companies now provide utilities for generating dashboards from SAP, Excel, QuickBooks, and other databases. The following is an example of a dashboard for Sonatica, a fictional company, designed by Dundas Dashboard for executive assessment of financial performance. The shaded tabs present financial information graphics for Sales and Support. Additional screens would provide performance data on other scorecard dimensions such as internal processes, customers, and innovation and growth.

Source: *http://media1.dundas.com/DashboardDemo/Viewer.aspx?view=Sonatica Performance Dashboards*

CHAPTER-END REVIEW

KBR, Inc., a decentralized engineering and construction organization, has three divisions, Engineering, Construction, and Military. Assume corporate management desires a minimum return of 15 percent on its investments and has a 20 percent tax rate. Suppose the divisions' 2014 results follow (in thousands):

Division	Income	Investment
Engineering	$30,000	$200,000
Construction	50,000	250,000
Military	22,000	100,000

The company is planning an expansion project in 2015 that will cost $50,000,000 and return $9,000,000 per year.

Required

a. Compute the ROI for each division for 2014.
b. Compute the residual income for each division for 2014.
c. Rank the divisions according to their ROI and residual income.
d. Assume that other income and investments will remain unchanged. Determine the effect of the project by itself. What is the effect on ROI and residual income, if the new project is added to each division?

The solution is on pages 424–425.

GUIDANCE ANSWERS . . . YOU MAKE THE CALL

You are the Division Vice President ROI is primarily a measure of the profitability of a division's assets, which is in turn a measure of how effectively the investment in assets was used to generate sales, and how profitable those sales were. ROI is driven by investment (or asset) turnover (which is division sales divided by assets) and return on sales (which is division net income divided division sales). Therefore, increasing ROI is similar to a simultaneous balancing act involving controlling sales, expenses, and asset investment. You can increase ROI by increasing sales more than expenses, while holding asset investment constant, or by other combinations of these three variables that ultimately increase ROI. If you adjust one of these variables, at the same time you must keep your eye on the other two variables or you may not achieve your goal of increasing ROI.

KEY RATIOS

$$\text{Return on investment} = \frac{\text{Investment center income}}{\text{Investment center asset base}}$$

$$\text{Return on investment} = \text{Investment turnover} \times \text{Return-on-sales}$$

$$\text{Investment turnover} = \frac{\text{Sales}}{\text{Investment center asset base}}$$

$$\text{Return-on-sales} = \frac{\text{Investment center income}}{\text{Sales}}$$

$$\text{Return on investment} = \frac{\text{Sales}}{\text{Investment center base}} \times \frac{\text{Investment center income}}{\text{Sales}} = \frac{\text{Investment center income}}{\text{Investment center asset base}}$$

KEY TERMS

avoidable common costs, 390

balanced scorecard, 403

common segment costs, 388

dashboards, 406

direct segment fixed costs, 388

economic value added or
   EVA®, 400

market value added (MVA), 401

net assets, 400

residual income, 400

return on investment (ROI), 396

segment income, 390

segment margin, 388

segment reports, 387

strategic business segment, 386

transfer price, 391

weighted average cost of
   capital, 400

MULTIPLE CHOICE

1. Northern Communications, Inc. has two divisions (Individual and Business) and has the following information available for the current year:

Sales revenue—Individual.	$3,000,000
Sales revenue—Business	5,000,000
Variable costs—Individual.	1,200,000
Variable costs—Business	2,250,000
Direct fixed costs, Individual	400,000
Direct fixed costs, Business	550,000
Allocated fixed costs—Individual.	250,000
Allocated fixed costs—Business	350,000
Unallocated common fixed costs.	150,000

   Northern Cell's Business segment income is
   a. $2,400,000
   b. $2,200,000
   c. $1,850,000
   d. $1,765,250

2. Refer to the previous question. The following information is available for the Individual Division, which has two product lines (Land and Mobile):

Sales revenue—Land	$1,200,000
Sales revenue—Mobile	1,800,000
Variable costs—Land	680,000
Variable costs—Mobile	520,000
Direct fixed costs—Land.	150,000
Direct fixed costs—Mobile	125,000
Allocated fixed costs—Land	100,000
Allocated fixed costs—Mobile	150,000
Unallocated common fixed costs.	125,000

   The product margin for Land is
   a. $270,000
   b. $170,000
   c. $520,000
   d. $370,000

3. Varcore, Inc. is currently acquiring a key component from it's sister company, Farcore, Inc. at a transfer price of $10 per unit. Farcore's variable cost of purchasing the unit is $4, and it's fixed cost per unit is $3 per unit. Farcore does not have any excess capacity and can sell all it makes to external customers at $10 per unit. Varcore has been offered a price of $9 per unit for the component from another vendor and is insisting that Farcore reduce its price to $9. Which of the following statements below is false regarding this scenario?
   a. Varcore should not accept the outside offer because the variable cost of purchasing it inside is only $4 per unit.

b. Varcore should purchase the unit externally because the internal cost of purchasing the unit internally is a variable cost of $4 per unit plus an opportunity cost of $6 per unit, or $10.

c. The company will be better off if Farcore rejects Varcore's demand and instead sells the units that Varcore would buy to outside customers.

d. Since Farcore is operating at full capacity and has other external customers ready to purchase additional units, the best transfer price is its regular market price.

4. Shealy's Lawn and Garden Supply Company has recently acquired a lawn sod company that grows turf grasses for lawns. Previously, Shealy's was purchasing sod from other suppliers at 50 cents per square foot. The new sod division, which has substantial excess capacity, is able to produce grass sod at a cost of 35 cents per square foot, including direct materials and direct labor cost of 25 cents, variable overhead of 5 cents, and fixed overhead of 5 cents per square foot. The supply division manager argues that the transfer price should be no more than 35 cents per square foot. What transfer price between the sod and the supply divisions will lead the manger of the supply division to act in a manner that will maximize company profits?

a. 50 cents
b. 25 cents
c. 30 cents
d. 35 cents

5. SGA, Inc., which is a division of AGS, Inc., had sales of $4,000,000, total assets of $2,000,000, and net income of $400,000. Senior management of AGS, Inc. has set a target minimum rate of return for SGA, Inc. of 18%. Calculate SGA's residual income.

a. $40,000
b. $36,000
c. $72,000
d. None of the above

DISCUSSION QUESTIONS

Q11-1. What is the relationship between segment reports and product reports?

Q11-2. What is a reporting objective? How is it determined?

Q11-3. Can a company have more than one type of first-level statement in segment reporting?

Q11-4. Explain the relationships between any two levels of statements in segment reporting.

Q11-5. Distinguish between direct and indirect segment costs.

Q11-6. What types of information are needed before management should decide to drop a segment?

Q11-7. In what types of organizations and for what purpose are transfer prices used?

Q11-8. What problems arise when transfer pricing is used?

Q11-9. When do transfer prices lead to suboptimization? How can suboptimization be minimized? Can it be eliminated? Why or why not?

Q11-10. For what purpose do organizations use return on investment? Why is this measure preferred to net income?

Q11-11. What advantages do residual income and EVA have over ROI for segment evaluations?

Q11-12. Contrast the difference between residual income and EVA.

Q11-13. Explain how a balanced scorecard helps with the evaluation process of internal operations.

Q11-14. How can a balanced scorecard be used as a strategy implementation tool?

Assignments with the ✓ logo in the margin are available in BusinessCourse.
See the Preface of the book for details.

MINI EXERCISES

M11-15. Multiple Levels of Segment Reporting LO1

Sisco, Inc., manufactures four different lines of computer devices: modems, routers, servers, and drives. Each of the product lines is produced in all of the company's three plants: Abbeyville,

Bakersville, and Charlottesville. Marketing efforts of the company are divided into five regions: East, West, South, North, and Central.

Required

a. Develop a reporting schematic that illustrates how the company might prepare single-level reports segmented on three different bases.

b. Develop a segment reporting schematic that has three different levels. Be sure to identify each segment's level. Briefly explain why you chose the primary-level segment.

LO1 **M11-16. Income Statements Segmented by Territory**

Script, Inc., has two product lines. The September income statements of each product line and the company are as follows:

SCRIPT, INC. Product Line and Company Income Statements For Month of September			
	Pens	**Pencils**	**Total**
Sales	$30,000	$30,000	$60,000
Less variable expenses	(12,000)	(12,000)	(24,000)
Contribution margin	18,000	18,000	36,000
Less direct fixed expenses	(9,000)	(7,000)	(16,000)
Product margin	$ 9,000	$11,000	20,000
Less common fixed expenses			(6,000)
Net income			$14,000

Pens and pencils are sold in two territories, Florida and Alabama, as follows:

	Florida	**Alabama**
Pen sales	$18,000	$12,000
Pencil sales	9,000	21,000
Total sales	$27,000	$33,000

The common fixed expenses are traceable to each territory as follows:

Florida fixed expenses	$2,000
Alabama fixed expenses	3,000
Home office administration fixed expenses	1,000
Total common fixed expenses	$6,000

The direct fixed expenses of pens, $9,000, and of pencils, $7,000, cannot be identified with either territory. The company's accountants were unable to allocate any of the common fixed expenses to the various segments.

Required

Prepare income statements segmented by territory for September, including a column for the entire firm.

LO1 **M11-17. Income Statements Segmented by Products**

Clay Consulting Firm provides three types of client services in three health-care-related industries. The income statement for July is as follows:

CLAY CONSULTING FIRM Income Statement For Month of July		
Sales		$900,000
Less variable costs		(650,000)
Contribution margin		250,000
Less fixed expenses		
Service	$70,000	
Selling and administrative	65,000	(135,000)
Net income		$115,000

The sales, contribution margin ratios, and direct fixed expenses for the three types of services are as follows:

	Hospitals	Physicians	Nursing Care
Sales	$350,000	$250,000	$300,000
Contribution margin ratio	25%	35%	25%
Direct fixed expenses of services	$ 20,000	$ 18,000	$ 16,000
Allocated common fixed services expense	$ 1,000	$ 1,000	$ 1,500

Required
Prepare income statements segmented by client categories. Include a column for the entire firm in the statement.

M11-18. Internal or External Acquisitions: No Opportunity Costs

LO2

The Van Division of MotoCar Corporation has offered to purchase 180,000 wheels from the Wheel Division for $38 per wheel. At a normal volume of 500,000 wheels per year, production costs per wheel for the Wheel Division are as follows:

Direct materials	$13
Direct labor	10
Variable overhead	6
Fixed overhead	15
Total	$44

The Wheel Division has been selling 500,000 wheels per year to outside buyers at $53 each. Capacity is 700,000 wheels per year. The Van Division has been buying wheels from outside suppliers at $50 per wheel.

Required
a. Should the Wheel Division manager accept the offer? Show computations.
b. From the standpoint of the company, will the internal sale be beneficial?

M11-19. Transfer Prices at Full Cost with Excess Capacity: Divisional Viewpoint

LO2

Koji Cameras, Inc., has a Disposables Division that produces a camera that sells for $9 per unit in the open market. The cost of the product is $5 (variable manufacturing of $3, plus fixed manufacturing of $2). Total fixed manufacturing costs are $140,000 at the normal annual production volume of 70,000 units. The Overseas Division has offered to buy 15,000 units at the full cost of $5. The Disposables Division has excess capacity, and the 15,000 units can be produced without interfering with the current outside sales of 70,000 units. The total fixed cost of the Disposables Division will not change.

Required
Explain whether the Disposables Division should accept or reject the offer. Show calculations.

M11-20. Transfer Pricing with Excess Capacity: Divisional and Corporate Viewpoints

LO2

Eclectic Art Company has a Print Division that is currently producing 100,000 prints per year but has a capacity of 150,000 prints. The variable costs of each print are $32, and the annual fixed costs are $1,350,000. The prints sell for $48 in the open market. The company's Retail Division wants to buy 50,000 prints at $27 each. The Print Division manager refuses the order because the price is below variable cost. The Retail Division manager argues that the order should be accepted because it will lower the fixed cost per print from $9 to $6.

Required

a.   Should the Retail Division order be accepted? Why or why not?

b.   From the viewpoints of the Print Division and the company, should the order be accepted if the manager of the Retail Division intends to sell each print in the outside market for $44 after incurring additional costs of $10 per print?

c.   What action should the company take, assuming it believes in divisional autonomy?

LO3 **M11-21.**   **ROI and Residual Income: Impact of a New Investment**

The Mustang Division of Detroit Motors had an operating income of $900,000 and net assets of $5,000,000. Detroit Motors has a target rate of return of 16 percent.

Required

a.   Compute the return on investment.

b.   Compute the residual income.

c.   The Mustang Division has an opportunity to increase operating income by $200,000 with an $850,000 investment in assets.

   1.   Compute the Mustang Division's return on investment if the project is undertaken. (Round your answer to three decimal places.)

   2.   Compute the Mustang Division's residual income if the project is undertaken.

LO3 **M11-22.**   **ROI: Fill in the Unknowns**

Provide the missing data in the following situations:

	North American Division	Asian Division	European Division
Sales	?	$5,000,000	?
Net operating income	$120,000	$ 250,000	$144,000
Operating assets.............................	?	?	$800,000
Return on investment	16%	10%	?
Return on sales	0.04	?	0.12
Investment turnover	?	?	1.5

LO4 **M11-23.**   **Selection of Balanced Scorecard Items**
The International Accountants' Association is a professional association. Its current membership totals 97,600 worldwide. The association operates from a central headquarters in New Zealand but has local membership units throughout the world. The local units hold monthly meetings to discuss recent developments in accounting and to hear professional speakers on topics of interest. The association's journal, *International Accountant,* is published monthly with feature articles and topical interest areas. The association publishes books and reports and sponsors continuing education courses. A statement of revenues and expenses follows:

INTERNATIONAL ACCOUNTANTS' ASSOCIATION		
Statement of Revenues and Expenses		
For Year Ending November 30, 2014		
Revenues...		$26,700,000
Expenses		
Salaries...	$14,000,000	
Other personnel costs...................................	3,400,000	
Occupancy costs......................................	2,000,000	
Reimbursement to local units	800,000	
Other membership services	500,000	
Printing and paper......................................	320,000	
Postage and shipping	114,000	
General and administrative...............................	538,000	(21,672,000)
Excess of revenues over expenses		$ 5,028,000

Additional information follows:

- Membership dues are $200 per year, of which $50 is considered to cover a one-year subscription to the association's journal. Other benefits include membership in the association and unit affiliation.
- One-year subscriptions to *International Accountant* are sold to nonmembers for $80 each. A total of 2,500 of these subscriptions were sold. In addition to subscriptions, the journal generated $200,000 in advertising revenue. The cost per magazine was $20.
- A total of 30,000 technical reports were sold by the Books and Reports Department at an average unit selling price of $45. Average costs per publication were $12.
- The association offers a variety of continuing education courses to both members and nonmembers. During 2014, the one-day course, which cost participants an average of $250 each, was attended by 31,300 people. A total of 1,985 people took two-day courses at a cost of $400 per person.
- General and administrative expenses include all other costs incurred by the corporate staff to operate the association.
- The organization has net capital assets of $44,000,000 and had an actual cost of capital of 11 percent.

Required

a. Give some examples of key financial performance indicators (no computations needed) that could be part of a balanced scorecard for the IAA.

b. Give some examples of key customer and operating performance indicators (no computations needed) that could be part of a balanced scorecard for IAA.

EXERCISES

E11-24. Appropriate Transfer Prices: Opportunity Costs LO2

Plains Peanut Butter Company recently acquired a peanut-processing company that has a normal annual capacity of 4,000,000 pounds and that sold 2,800,000 pounds last year at a price of $2.50 per pound. The purpose of the acquisition is to furnish peanuts for the peanut butter plant, which needs 1,600,000 pounds of peanuts per year. It has been purchasing peanuts from suppliers at the market price. Production costs per pound of the peanut-processing company are as follows:

Direct materials	$0.80
Direct labor	0.42
Variable overhead	0.12
Fixed overhead at normal capacity	0.20
Total	$1.54

Management is trying to decide what transfer price to use for sales from the newly acquired Peanut Division to the Peanut Butter Division. The manager of the Peanut Division argues that $2.50, the market price, is appropriate. The manager of the Peanut Butter Division argues that the cost price of $1.54 (or perhaps even less) should be used since fixed overhead costs should be recomputed. Any output of the Peanut Division up to 2,800,000 pounds that is not sold to the Peanut Butter Division could be sold to regular customers at $2.50 per pound.

Required

a. Compute the annual gross profit for the Peanut Division using a transfer price of $2.50.

b. Compute the annual gross profit for the Peanut Division using a transfer price of $1.54.

c. What transfer price(s) will lead the manager of the Peanut Butter Division to act in a manner that will maximize company profits?

E11-25. Negotiating a Transfer Price with Excess Capacity LO2

The Foundry Division of Augusta Pumps, Inc., produces metal parts that are sold to the company's Assembly Division and to outside customers. Operating data for the Foundry Division for 2014 are as follows:

	To the Assembly Division	To Outside Customers	Total
Sales			
400,000 parts × $5.50	$2,200,000		
300,000 parts × $6.00		$1,800,000	$4,000,000
Variable expenses at $2.25	(900,000)	(675,000)	(1,575,000)
Contribution margin	1,300,000	1,125,000	2,425,000
Fixed expenses*	(700,000)	(525,000)	1,225,000
Net income.	$ 600,000	$ 600,000	$1,200,000

*Allocated on the basis of unit sales.

The Assembly Division has just received an offer from an outside supplier to supply parts at $3.50 each. The Foundry Division manager is not willing to meet the $3.50 price. She argues that it costs her $4.00 per part to produce and sell to the Assembly Division, so she would show no profit on the Assembly Division sales. Sales to outside customers are at a maximum, 300,000 parts.

Required

a. Verify the Foundry Division's $4.00 unit cost figure.

b. Should the Foundry Division meet the outside price of $3.50 for Assembly Division sales? Explain.

c. Could the Foundry Division meet the $3.50 price and still show a net profit for sales to the Assembly Division? Show computations.

LO2 E11-26. **Dual Transfer Pricing**

The Greek Company has two divisions, Beta and Gamma. Gamma Division produces a product at a variable cost of $6 per unit, and sells 150,000 units to outside customers at $11 per unit and 40,000 units to Beta Division at variable cost plus 40 percent. Under the dual transfer price system, Beta Division pays only the variable cost per unit. Gamma Division's fixed costs are $250,000 per year. Beta Division sells its finished product to outside customers at $24 per unit. Beta has variable costs of $5 per unit, in addition to the costs from Gamma Division. Beta Division's annual fixed costs are $170,000. There are no beginning or ending inventories.

Required

a. Prepare the income statements for the two divisions and the company as a whole.

b. Why is the income for the company less than the sum of the profit figures shown on the income statements for the two divisions? Explain.

LO3 E11-27. **ROI and Residual Income: Basic Computations**

Watkins Associated Industries is a highly diversified company with three divisions: Trucking, Seafood, and Construction. Assume that the company uses return on investment and residual income as two of the evaluation tools for division managers. The company has a minimum desired rate of return on investment of 10 percent with a 30 percent tax rate. Selected operating data for three divisions of the company follow.

	Trucking Division	Seafood Division	Construction Division
Sales	$1,200,000	$750,000	$900,000
Operating assets	600,000	250,000	350,000
Net operating income	116,000	66,000	63,000

Required

a. Compute the return on investment for each division. (Round answers to three decimal places.)

b. Compute the residual income for each division.

LO3 E11-28. **ROI and Residual Income: Assessing Performance**

Refer to the computations in the previous exercise E11-27. Assess the performance of the division managers, basing your conclusions on ROI. Assess the performance of the division managers, basing your conclusions on Residual Income. Which manager is doing the best job?

E11-29.   **ROI, Residual Income, and EVA with Different Bases**   LO3

Paradyme Company has a target return on capital of 12 percent. The following financial information is available for October ($ thousands):

	Software Division (Value Base)		Consulting Division (Value Base)		Venture Capital Division (Value Base)	
	Book	Current	Book	Current	Book	Current
Sales	$100,000	$100,000	$200,000	$200,000	$800,000	$800,000
Income.........	11,000	10,000	15,000	17,000	50,000	52,000
Assets	60,000	80,000	90,000	100,000	600,000	580,000
Liabilities	10,000	10,000	14,000	14,000	40,000	40,000

Required

a.   Compute the return on investment using both book and current values for each division.
(Round answers to three decimal places.)

b.   Compute the residual income for both book and current values for each division.

c.   Compute the economic value added income for both book and current values for each division if the tax rate is 30 percent and the weighted average cost of capital is 10 percent.

d.   Does book value or current value provide a better basis for performance evaluation? Which
division do you consider the most successful?

E11-30.   **Balanced Scorecard Preparation**   LO4

The following information is in addition to that presented in Mini Exercise 11-23 for the International Accountants' Association. For the year ended November 30, 2014, the organization had set
a membership goal of 100,000 members with the following anticipated results:

International Accountants' Association Planned Revenues and Expenses For Year Ending November 30, 2014		
Revenues..		$27,900,000
Expenses		
Salaries...	$13,950,000	
Other personnel costs.....................................	3,450,000	
Occupancy costs..	1,900,000	
Reimbursement to local units	780,000	
Other membership services	525,000	
Printing and paper...	300,000	
Postage and shipping	110,000	
General and administrative...............................	545,000	(21,560,000)
Excess of revenues over expenses		$ 6,340,000

Additional information follows:

• Membership dues were increased from $180 to $200 at the beginning of the year.
• One-year subscriptions to *International Accountant* were anticipated to be 2,400 units.
• Advertising revenue was budgeted at $220,000. Each magazine was budgeted at $18.
• A total of 28,000 technical reports were anticipated at an average price of $40 with average
costs
of $11.
• The budgeted one-day courses had an anticipated attendance of 32,000 with an average fee
of $225. The two-day courses had an anticipated attendance of 3,000 with an average fee
of $385 per person.
• The organization began the year with net capital assets of $40,000,000 with a planned cost
of capital of 11 percent.

Required

a.   Prepare a balanced scorecard for IAA for November 2014 with calculated key performance
indicators presented in two columns for planned performance and actual performance—include key financial, customer, and operating performance indicators.

b.   Which of the evaluation areas you selected indicated success and which indicated failure?

    c.   Give some explanations of the successes and failures.

LO4 **E11-31.** **Balanced Scorecard**

The following alphabetically ordered list of financial and nonfinancial performance metrics is provided for Midwest, Inc.

Average call wait	New product acceptance rate
Average customer survey rating	New product revenue
Employee turnover ratio	New product ROI
Expense as a % of revenue	Net profit
Expense variance %	Net profit margin
Fulfillment %	Number of complaints
Headcount growth	Number of defects reported
Industry quality rating	Service error rate
Job offer acceptance rate	Time to market on new products
Market share	Unique repeat customer count
New customer count	Year over year revenue growth
New customer sales value	

Required

a.   Assign the above metrics to the four balanced scorecard categories of (1) Financial Success, (2) Customer Satisfaction and Brand Improvement, (3) Business Process Improvement, (4) Learning and Growth of Motivated Workforce.

b.   Comment on the use of balanced scorecard versus a single financial measure such as ROI or EVA.

PROBLEMS

LO1 **P11-32.** **Multiple Segment Reports**

International Enterprises, Incorporated, sells telecommunication products throughout the world in three sales territories: Europe, Asia, and the Americas. For July, all $500,000 of administrative expense is traceable to the territories, except $100,000, which is common to all units and cannot be traced or allocated to the sales territories. The percentage of product line sales made in each of the sales territories and the assignment of traceable fixed expenses follow:

	Sales Territory			
	Europe	**Asia**	**The Americas**	**Total**
Handset sales	50%	30%	20%	100%
Switchboard sales..............	40	40	20	100
Automated switches sales	10	30	60	100
Fixed administrative expense......	$150,000	$150,000	$100,000	$ 400,000
Fixed selling expense	$300,000	$600,000	$600,000	$1,500,000

The manufacturing takes place in one large facility with three distinct manufacturing operations. Selected product-line cost data follow.

	Handset	**Switchboard**	**Automated Switches**	**Total**
Variable costs	$ 18	$ 790	$ 1,975	
Depreciation and supervision.......	150,000	150,000	120,000	$ 450,000*
Other mfg. overhead (common)				100,000
Fixed administrative expense (common)................................				500,000
Fixed selling expense (common)				1,500,000

*Includes common costs of $30,000

The unit sales and selling prices for each product follow.

	Unit Sales	Selling Price
Handset	10,000	$ 50
Switchboard.	2,000	1,500
Automated	1,500	3,200

Required

a. Prepare an income statement for July segmented by product line. Include a column for the entire firm.

b. Prepare an income statement for July segmented by sales territory. Include a column for the entire firm.

c. Prepare an income statement for July by product line for The Americas sales territory. Include a column for the territory as a whole.

d. Discuss the value of multilevel segment reporting as a managerial tool. Compare and contrast the benefits of the reports generated in parts *a*, *b*, and *c*.

P11-33. Segment Reporting and Analysis   LO1

Minnesota Bread Company bakes three products: donuts, bread, and pasteries. It sells them in the cities of Minneapolis and St. Paul. For March, its first month of operation, the following income statement was prepared:

MINNESOTA BREAD COMPANY
Territory and Company Income Statements
For Month of March

	Minneapolis	St. Paul	Total
Sales	$2,100	$500	$2,600
Cost of goods sold	(1,500)	(300)	(1,800)
Gross profit	600	200	800
Selling and administrative expenses	(400)	(225)	(625)
Net income.	$ 200	$ (25)	$ 175

Sales and selected variable expense data are as follows:

	Products		
	Donuts	Bread	Pastries
Fixed baking expenses	$200	$140	$100
Variable baking expenses as a percentage of sales	50%	50%	60%
Variable selling expenses as a percentage of sales	4%	4%	6%
City of Minneapolis, sales.	$850	$900	$350
City of St. Paul, sales	$200	$150	$150

The fixed selling expenses were $385 for March, of which $160 was a direct expense of the Minneapolis market and $225 was a direct expense of the St. Paul market. Fixed administrative expenses were $130, which management has decided not to allocate when using the contribution approach.

Required

a. Prepare a segment income statement showing the territory margin for each sales territory for March. Include a column for the entire firm.

b. Prepare segment income statements showing the product margin for each product. Include a column for the entire firm.

c. If the pastries line is dropped and fixed baking expenses do not change, what is the product margin for donuts and bread?

d. What other type of segmentation might be useful to Minnesota Bread. Explain.

LO1   **P11-34.**   **Segment Reporting and Analysis**

University Publishers, Inc., has prepared income statements segmented by divisions, but management is still uncertain about actual performance. Financial information for May is given as follows:

	Textbook Division	Professional Division	Company Total
Sales	$200,000	$410,000	$610,000
Less variable expenses			
Manufacturing	32,000	205,000	237,000
Selling and administrative................	4,400	24,600	29,000
Total	(36,400)	(229,600)	(266,000)
Contribution margin	163,600	180,400	344,000
Less direct fixed expenses................	(20,000)	(200,000)	(220,000)
Net income.............................	$143,600	$(19,600)	$ 124,000

Management is concerned about the Professional Division and requests additional analysis. Additional information regarding May operations of the Professional Division is as follows:

	Professional Division		
	Accounting Books Segment	Executive Books Segment	Management Books Segment
Sales	$140,000	$140,000	$130,000
Variable manufacturing expenses			
as a percentage of sales	60%	40%	50%
Other variable expenses			
as a percentage of sales	6%	6%	6%
Direct fixed expenses	$ 50,000	$ 73,500	$ 50,000
Allocated common fixed expenses ..	$ 4,000	$ 2,000	$ 6,000

The professional accounting books are sold to auditors and controllers. The current information on these markets is as follows:

	Accounting Books Segment		
	Auditors Market	Controllers Market	Total
Sales	$30,000	$110,000	$140,000
Variable manufacturing expenses			
as a percentage of sales	60%	60%	—
Other variable expenses			
as a percentage of sales	6%	6%	—
Direct fixed expenses	$15,000	$ 30,000	$ 45,000
Allocated common fixed expenses	$ 1,500	$ 2,000	$ 3,500

Required

a.   Prepare an income statement segmented by product for the Professional Division. Include a column for the division as a whole.

b.   Prepare an income statement segmented by market for the Accounting Books Segment of the Professional Division.

c.   Evaluate which Accounting Books Segment the Professional Division should keep or discontinue in the short run.

d.   What is the correct long-run decision? Explain fully, including any possible risks associated with your recommendation.

LO1   **P11-35.**   **Segment Reports and Cost Allocations**

Great Lakes, Inc., has three sales divisions. One of the key evaluation inputs for each division manager is the performance of his or her division based on division income. The division statements for August are as follows:

	Superior	Ontario	Michigan	Total
Sales	$400,000	$500,000	$450,000	$1,350,000
Cost of sales	200,000	240,000	230,000	670,000
Division overhead	100,000	110,000	110,000	320,000
Division expenses..................	(300,000)	(350,000)	(340,000)	(990,000)
Division contribution	100,000	150,000	110,000	360,000
Corporate overhead	(70,000)	(90,000)	(80,000)	(240,000)
Division income....................	$ 30,000	$ 60,000	$ 30,000	$ 120,000

The Michigan manager is unhappy that his profitability is the same as that of the Superior Division and one-half that of the Ontario Division when his sales are halfway between these two divisions. The manager knows that his division must carry more product lines because of customer demands, and many of these additional product lines are not very profitable. He has not dropped these marginal product lines because of idle capacity; all of the products cover their own variable costs. After analyzing the product lines with the lowest profit margins, the divisional controller for Michigan provided the following to the manager:

Sales of marginal products...	$90,000	
Cost of sales	$50,000	
Avoidable fixed costs	22,000	(72,000)
Product margin		18,000
Proportion of corporate overhead		(16,000)
Product income..		$ 2,000

Although these products were 20 percent of Michigan's total sales, they contributed only about 7 percent of the division's profits. The controller also noted that the corporate overhead allocation was based on a formula of sales and divisional contribution margin.

Required

a. Prepare a set of segment statements for August assuming that all facts remain the same except that Michigan's weak product lines are dropped and corporate overhead is allocated as follows: Superior, $80,000; Ontario, $95,000; and Michigan, $65,000. Does the Michigan Division appear better after this action? What will be the responses of the other two division managers?

b. Suggest improvements for Great Lakes' reporting process that will better reflect the actual operations of the divisions. Keep in mind the utilization of the reporting process to assist in the evaluation of the managers. What other changes could be made to improve the manager evaluation process?

P11-36. ROI, Residual Income, and EVA: Impact of a New Investment LO3

RCI Inc. is a decentralized organization with four autonomous divisions. The divisions are evaluated on the basis of the change in their return on invested assets. Operating results in the Commercial Division for 2014 follow:

RCI INC.—COMMERCIAL DIVISION Income Statement For Year Ending December 31, 2014	
Sales	$3,125,000
Less variable expenses...	(1,600,000)
Contribution margin	1,525,000
Less fixed expenses	(1,000,000)
Net operating income	$ 525,000

Operating assets for the Commercial Division currently average $2,000,000. The Commercial Division can add a new product line for an investment of $250,000. Relevant data for the new product line are as follows:

Sales	$750,000
Variable expenses (% of sales)	0.60
Fixed expenses	$250,000
Increase in current liabilities	$ 20,000

Required

a. Determine the effect on ROI of accepting the new product line. (Round calculations to three decimal places.)

b. If a return of 6 percent is the minimum that any division should earn and residual income is used to evaluate managers, would this encourage the division to accept the new product line? Explain and show computations.

c. If EVA is used to evaluate managers, should the new product line be accepted if the weighted average cost of capital is 8 percent and the income tax rate is 40 percent?

LO3 P11-37.

SIX FLAGS THEME
PARKS, INC. (SIX)

Valuing Investment Center Assets

Six Flags Theme Parks, Inc., operates theme parks in the United States, Mexico, and Europe. One of its first theme parks, Six Flags over Georgia, was built in the 1960s in Atlanta on a large tract of land that has appreciated enormously over the years. Although most of the rides and other attractions have a fairly short life, some of the major buildings that are still in use on the property have been fully depreciated since they were built. Assume that Six Flags over Georgia operates as an investment center with total assets that have a book value of $160 million and current liabilities of $20 million. Assume also that in 2014, this particular theme park had sales of $120 million and pretax division income of $40 million. The replacement cost of all the assets in this park is estimated to be $250 million. The company has a 35 percent tax rate and a target return of 10% and a cost of capital of 8%.

Required

a. Calculate the ROI, residual income, and EVA for Six Flags over Georgia using book value as the valuation basis for the investment center asset base.

b. Repeat requirement (a) using replacement cost as the investment center asset value.

c. Which valuation, accounting book value or replacement cost do you think the company uses to evaluate the managers of its various theme parks? Discuss.

LO2 P11-38.

Transfer Pricing with and without Capacity Constraints

Elite Carpets, Inc., has just acquired a new backing division that produces a rubber backing, which it sells for $2.20 per square yard. Sales are about 1,200,000 square yards per year. Since the Backing Division has a capacity of 2,000,000 square yards per year, top management is thinking that it might be wise for the company's Tufting Division to start purchasing from the newly acquired Backing Division. The Tufting Division now purchases 600,000 square yards per year from an outside supplier at a price of $2.00 per square yard. The current price is lower than the competitive $2.20 price as a result of the large quantity discounts. The Backing Division's cost per square yard follows.

Direct materials	$1.20
Direct labor	0.30
Variable overhead	0.25
Fixed overhead (1,200,000 level)	0.10
Total cost	$1.85

Required

a. If both divisions are to be treated as investment centers and their performance evaluated by the ROI formula, what transfer price would you recommend? Why?

b. Determine the effect on corporate profits of making the backing.

c. Based on your transfer price, would you expect the ROI in the Backing Division to increase, decrease, or remain unchanged? Explain.

d. What would be the effect on the ROI of the Tufting Division using your transfer price? Explain.

e.   Assume that the Backing Division is now selling 2,000,000 square yards per year to retail outlets. What transfer price would you recommend? What will be the effect on corporate profits?

f.   If the Backing Division is at capacity and decides to sell to the Tufting Division for $2.00 per square yard, what will be the effect on the company's profits?

P11-39.   Transfer Pricing and Special Orders   LO2

Silicone Valley Products has several manufacturing divisions. The Palo Alto Division produces a component part that is used in the manufacture of electronic equipment. The cost per part for July is as follows:

Variable cost	$ 80
Fixed cost (at 2,000 units per month capacity)	60
Total cost per part	$140

Some of Palo Alto Division's output is sold to outside manufacturers, and some is sold internally to the Berkeley Division. The price per part is $200. The Berkeley Division's cost and revenue structure follow.

Selling price per unit		$1,000
Less variable costs per unit		
Cost of parts from the Palo Alto Division	$200	
Other variable costs.	400	(600)
Contribution margin per unit.		400
Less fixed costs per unit (at 200 units per month).		(100)
Net income per unit.		$ 300

The Berkeley Division received a one-time order for 10 units. The buyer wants to pay only $485 per unit.

Required

a.   From the perspective of the Berkeley Division, should the $485 price be accepted? Explain.

b.   If both divisions have excess capacity, would the Berkeley Division's action benefit the company as a whole? Explain.

c.   If the Berkeley Division has excess capacity but the Palo Alto Division does not and can sell all of its parts to outside manufacturers, what would be the advantage or disadvantage of accepting the ten-unit order at the $485 price to the Berkeley Division?

d.   To make a decision that is in the best interest of the company, what transfer-pricing information does the Berkeley Division need?

P11-40.   Balanced Scorecard   LO4

The Summersworth Community Bank recently decided to adopt a balanced scorecard system of performance evaluation. Below is a list of primary performance goals for four major performance categories that have been identified by corporate management and the board of directors.

1.   Financial Perspective–Maintain and grow the bank financially
   a.   Increase customer deposits
   b.   Manage financial risk
   c.   Provide profits for the stockholders

2.   Customer Perspective – Maintain and grow the customer base
   a.   Increase customer satisfaction
   b.   Increase number of depositors & customer retention
   c.   Increase quality of deposits

3.   Internal Perspective – Improve internal processes
   a.   Achieve best practices for processing transactions
   b.   Improve employee satisfaction
   c.   Improve employee promotion opportunities

4. Learning and Innovation – Improve market differentiation
    a. Beat competitors in introducing new products
    b. Become first mover in establishing customer benefit for customers
    c. Become recognized as an innovator in the industry

Required

a. For each of the 12 goals above suggest at least one measure of performance to measure the achievement of the goal.

b. At what level of the organization should the balanced scorecard be implemented as a means of evaluating performance? Explain.

CASES AND PROJECTS

LO2   **C11-41.**   **Transfer Price Decisions**

IBM CORPORATION
(IBM)

The Consulting Division of **IBM Corporation** is often involved in assignments for which IBM computer equipment is sold as part of a systems installation. The Computer Equipment Division is frequently a vendor of the Consulting Division in cases for which the Consulting Division purchases the equipment from the Computer Equipment Division. The Consulting Division does not view itself as a sales arm of the Computer Equipment Division but as a strong competitor to the major consulting firms of information systems. The Consulting Division's goal is to maximize its profit contribution to the company, not necessarily to see how much IBM equipment it can sell. If the Consulting Division is truly an autonomous investment center, it has the freedom to purchase equipment from competing vendors if the consultants believe that a competitor's products serve the needs of a client better than the comparable IBM product in a particular situation.

Required

a. In this situation, should corporate management be concerned about whether the Consulting Division sells IBM products or those of other computer companies? Should the Consulting Division be required to sell only IBM products?

b. Discuss the transfer-pricing issues that both the Computer Equipment Division manager and the Consulting Division manager should consider. If top management does not have a policy on pricing transfers between these two divisions, what alternative transfer prices should the division managers consider?

c. What is your recommendation regarding how the managers of the Consulting and Computer Equipment Divisions can work together in a way that will benefit each of them individually and the company as a whole?

LO2   **C11-42.**   **Transfer Pricing at Absorption Cost**

The Injection Molding Division of Universal Sign Company produces molded parts that are sold to the Sign Division. This division uses the parts in constructing signs that are sold to various businesses. The Molding Division contains two operations, injection and finishing. The unit variable cost of materials and labor used in the injection operation is $100. The fixed injection overhead is $800,000 per year. Current production (20,000 units) is at full capacity. The variable cost of labor used in the finishing operation is $16 per part. The fixed overhead in this operation is $340,000 per year. The company uses an absorption-cost transfer price. The price data for each operation presented to the Sign Division by the Molding Division follow.

Injection		
Variable cost per unit.	$100	
Fixed overhead cost per unit ($800,000 ÷ 20,000 units)	40	$140
Finishing		
Labor cost per unit	16	
Fixed overhead cost per unit ($340,000 ÷ 20,000 units)	17	33
Total cost per unit		$173

An outside company has offered to lease machinery to the Sign Division that would perform the finishing portion of the parts manufacturing for $200,000 per year. With the new machinery, the labor cost per part would remain at $16. If the Molding Division transfers the units for $140, the following analysis can be made:

Current process		
Finishing process costs (20,000 × $33)		$660,000
New process		
Machine rental cost per year.	$200,000	
Labor cost ($16 × 20,000 units)	320,000	(520,000)
Savings		$140,000

The manager of the Sign Division wants approval to acquire the new machinery.

Required

a. How would you advise the company concerning the proposed lease?

b. How could the transfer-pricing system be modified or the transfer-pricing problem eliminated?

C11-43. **Transfer Pricing Dispute**   LO2

MBR Inc. consists of three divisions that were formerly three independent manufacturing companies. Bader Corporation and Roper Company merged in 2013, and the merged corporation acquired Mitchell Company in 2014. The name of the corporation was subsequently changed to MBR Inc., and each company became a separate division retaining the name of its former company.

The three divisions have operated as if they were still independent companies. Each division has its own sales force and production facilities. Each division management is responsible for sales, cost of operations, acquisition and financing of divisional assets, and working capital management. The corporate management of MBR evaluates the performance of the divisions and division management on the basis of return on investment.

Mitchell Division has just been awarded a contract for a product that uses a component manufactured by the Roper Division and also by outside suppliers. Mitchell used a cost figure of $3.80 for the component manufactured by Roper in preparing its bid for the new product. Roper supplied this cost figure in response to Mitchell's request for the average variable cost of the component; it represents the standard variable manufacturing cost and variable selling and distribution expenses.

Roper has an active sales force that is continually soliciting new prospects. Roper's regular selling price for the component Mitchell needs for the new product is $6.50. Sales of this component are expected to increase. The Roper management has indicated, however, that it could supply Mitchell the required quantities of the component at the regular selling price less variable selling and distribution expenses. Mitchell's management has responded by offering to pay standard variable manufacturing cost plus 20 percent.

The two divisions have been unable to agree on a transfer price. Corporate management has never established a transfer-pricing policy because interdivisional transactions have never occurred. As a compromise, the corporate vice president of finance suggested a price equal to the standard full manufacturing cost (i.e., no selling and distribution expenses) plus a 15 percent markup. The two division managers have also rejected this price because each considered it grossly unfair.

The unit cost structure for the Roper component and the three suggested prices follow.

Standard variable manufacturing cost.	$3.20
Standard fixed manufacturing cost	1.20
Variable selling and distribution expenses.	0.60
	$5.00
Regular selling price less variable selling and distribution expenses ($6.50 − $0.60)	$5.90
Standard full manufacturing cost plus 15% ($4.40 × 1.15).	$5.06
Variable manufacturing plus 20% ($3.20 × 1.20).	$3.84

Required

a. What should be the attitude of the Roper Division's management toward the three proposed prices?

    b. Is the negotiation of a price between the Mitchell and Roper Divisions a satisfactory method of solving the transfer-pricing problem? Explain your answer.

    c. Should the corporate management of MBR Inc. become involved in this transfer-price controversy? Explain your answer.

(CMA Adapted)

SOLUTIONS TO REVIEW PROBLEMS

Mid-Chapter Review

Solution

a.

	Segments (Territories)		
	U.S.	**International**	**Wireless Total**
Sales	$12,000	$18,000	$30,000
Less variable costs	(8,400)	(12,600)	(21,000)
Contribution margin	3,600	5,400	9,000
Less direct fixed costs	(500)	(800)	(1,300)
Territory margin	3,100	4,600	7,700
Less allocated segment costs	(200)	(600)	(800)
Territory income....................................	$ 2,900	$ 4,000	6,900
Less unallocated common costs			(900)
Fiber optic income			$ 6,000

b. The Product Margin for the wireless product line in Panel B was $7,000 and reflected $2,000 of direct fixed costs that were attributable to that product line in the National Division. However, when the wireless product segment income statement is further segmented into geographic segments, only $1,300 of the $2,000 could be directly traced to the two geographic territories. Therefore, $700 of costs that were direct costs at the product segment level became common costs (either allocated or unallocated) at the territory segment level. This reflects the general notion that as segmentation is extended down to lower and lower levels, the total amount of common costs increase and direct costs decrease. Hence, segmentation rarely is extended to more than three levels.

Chapter-End Review

Solution

a.

$$\text{Return on investment} = \frac{\text{Investment center income}}{\text{Investment center asset base}}$$

$$\text{Engineering Division} = \$30,000 \div \$200,000$$
$$= 0.15, \text{ or } 15 \text{ percent}$$

$$\text{Construction Division} = \$50,000 \div \$250,000$$
$$= 0.20, \text{ or } 20 \text{ percent}$$

$$\text{Military Division} = \$22,000 \div \$100,000$$
$$= 0.22, \text{ or } 22 \text{ percent}$$

b. Residual income = Investment center income − (Investment center asset base × Minimum return)

$$\text{Engineering Division} = \$30,000 - (0.15 \times \$200,000)$$
$$= \$0.00$$

$$\text{Construction Division} = \$50,000 - (0.15 \times \$250,000)$$

$$= \$12,500$$
$$\textbf{Military Division} = \$22,000 - (0.15 \times \$100,000)$$
$$= \$7,000$$

c. ROI ranks the Military Division first, the Construction Division second, and the Engineering Division third. Residual income ranks the Construction Division first, the Military Division second, and the Engineering Division third. Because the investments for each division are different, it is somewhat misleading to rank the divisions according to residual income. The Construction Division had the highest residual income, but it also had the largest investment. The Military Division's residual income was 56 percent of the Construction Division's income but only 40 percent of the investment of the Construction Division. This fact, along with the best ROI ranking, probably justifies the Military Division being evaluated as the best division of KBR.

d. Return on investment:

$$\textbf{Investment} = \$9,000 \div \$50,000$$
$$= 0.18, \text{ or } 18 \text{ percent}$$
$$\textbf{Engineering Division} = (\$30,000 + \$9,000) \div (\$200,000 + \$50,000)$$
$$= 0.156, \text{ or } 15.6 \text{ percent}$$
$$\textbf{Construction Division} = (\$50,000 + \$9,000) \div (\$250,000 + \$50,000)$$
$$= 0.1967, \text{ or } 19.67 \text{ percent}$$
$$\textbf{Military Division} = (\$22,000 + \$9,000) \div (\$100,000 + \$50,000)$$
$$= 0.2067, \text{ or } 20.67 \text{ percent}$$

ROI will increase for the Engineering Division but decrease for the Construction and Military Divisions, even though the project's ROI of 18 percent exceeds the company's minimum return of 15 percent. Residual income:

$$\textbf{Engineering Division} = (\$30,000 + \$9,000) - [0.15 \times (\$200,000 + \$50,000)]$$
$$= \$1,500$$
$$\textbf{Construction Division} = (\$50,000 + \$9,000) - [0.15 \times (\$250,000 + \$50,000)]$$
$$= \$14,000$$
$$\textbf{Military Division} = (\$22,000 + \$9,000) - [0.15 \times (\$100,000 + \$50,000)]$$
$$= \$8,500$$

Because the project's ROI exceeds the company's minimum return, the residual income of all divisions will increase.

1. Explain the role of capital budgeting in long-range planning. (p. 429)

2. Apply capital budgeting models, such as net present value and internal rate of return, that consider the time value of money. (p. 432)

3. Apply capital budgeting models, such as payback period and accounting rate of return, that do not consider the time value of money. (p. 436)

4. Evaluate the strengths and weaknesses of alternative capital budgeting models. (p. 439)

5. Discuss the importance of judgment, attitudes toward risk, and relevant cash flow information for capital budgeting decisions. (p. 441)

6. Determine the net present value of investment proposals with consideration of taxes. (p. 445)

12

Capital Budgeting Decisions

Seattle-based Amazon.com Inc. started out as an online bookseller in 1995 and quickly expanded its product offerings to DVDs, electronics, jewelry, apparel, and now a full spectrum of consumer goods. Amazon sells more goods online than the next 12 largest Internet retailers combined, includ-

AMAZON
www.amazon.com

ing Staples, Apple, Wal-Mart, and Best Buy. Amazon's meteoric rise was no doubt fueled by well-chosen capital investments, including its website infrastructure that highlighted customer-centric features such as the first shopping carts, one-click buying, email purchase confirmations, and post-

shipping follow-ups. Over the years Amazon has kept its prices low by leveraging its purchasing volume, thereby staving off its competition. To maintain its position, Amazon has foregone profits in favor of continual improvement of its business model. In an effort to gain more control over its fulfillment process, Amazon has invested billions of dollars in warehouses and inventory management information systems. As a result, Amazon has been able to offer expedited shipping on its orders since 2005. This program, called Amazon Prime, offers customers two-day shipping for an annual fee of $79.

Amazon could never be accused of complacency. In fact, Amazon Prime is no longer fast enough; competitors like eBay are beginning to offer same-day delivery in select cities. Increased competition helps explain why, since 2010, Amazon has invested $13.9 billion in 50 new warehouses, doubling both the dollar investment and number of warehouse facilities built since the company's inception. In order to serve a larger segment of the population, the company is building its warehouses closer to urban areas, and this means those investments have become more expensive. Amazon's capital investments don't stop at just warehouses. Software systems that sort items by delivery date and optimize storage space have allowed Amazon to double the number of items it can ship per facility. Amazon's management will need to tread carefully in evaluating these new investments. Amazon's managers should be asking themselves these questions: How will these investments be financed, and at what cost can we raise the needed funds? What tax deductions or incentives might defray some of the costs of this investment? How long before the investment has been recouped through increased revenues? Does this estimate consider increases in operating costs?

In other words, Amazon needs to determine which capital investments will have a positive effect on operating results. The company will have to look beyond the cost of the buildings. Inventory storage costs, insurance on both the buildings and the increased volume of goods stored inside of them, and shipping and delivery costs all have increased over 40 percent from 2010 to 2012, resulting in a $39 million operating loss in the most recent set of financial statements. The company is also adding 7,000 new warehouse and customer service jobs, which increases the company's total employee base to over 27,000 people. In addition, Amazon has its eye turned toward a whole new market segment, its

continued

continued from prior page

online grocery business, AmazonFresh. Growing this segment will require significant future investment in refrigeration storage and delivery vehicles.

While Amazon has a vast customer base and has established itself as one of the most-recognized brands in online retailing, its competitors are not standing on the sidelines. Best Buy and Overstock.com have recently announced they would match or beat Amazon's prices. Furthermore, recent regulatory changes will require that Amazon and other online retailers collect sales tax on sales in several states, including California, Texas, Florida, and New Jersey, further eroding their competitive edge over traditional brick-and-mortar competitors. This chapter will detail important tools that Amazon and other managers can use to increase the probability that their capital investments will be sound.

Sources: Peter Cohan, "How You Can Use The Three Big Ideas Behind Amazon's Success," *Forbes*, September 4, 2013; Tim Worstall, "Fascinating Number: Amazon Is Larger Than the Next Dozen Internet Retailers Combined," *Forbes*, September 1, 2013; Danielle Kucera, "Why Amazon Is on a Warehouse Building Spree," *Bloomberg Businessweek*, August 29, 2013; Tom Gara, "Amazon Losing Its Price Edge," *Wall Street Journal*, August 20, 2013, p. B2.

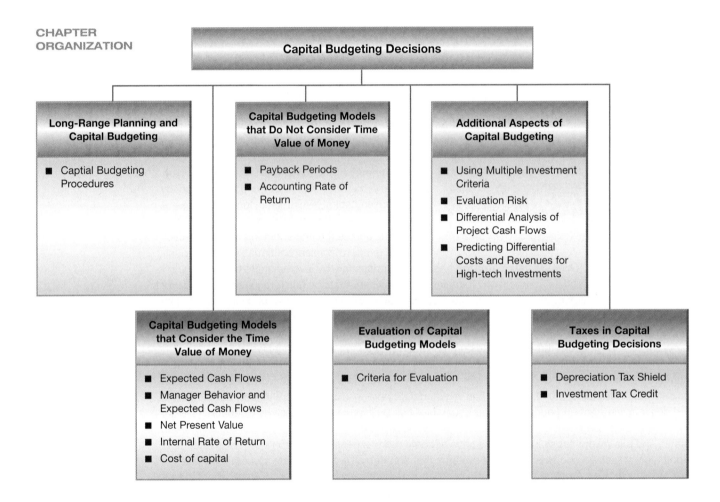

CHAPTER ORGANIZATION

Capital expenditures are investments of financial resources in projects to develop or introduce new products or services, to expand current production or service capacity, or to change current production or service facilities. Capital expenditures are made with the expectation that the new product, process, or service will generate future financial inflows that exceed the initial costs. Capital expenditure decisions affect structural cost drivers. They are made infrequently but once made are difficult to change. They commit the organization to the use of certain facilities and activities to satisfy customer needs. In making large capital expenditure decisions, such as for Amazon's warehouse facilities, management is risking the future existence of the company.

Although capital expenditure decisions are fraught with risk, management accounting provides the concepts and tools needed to organize information and evaluate the alternatives. This systematic organization and analysis is the essence of capital budgeting. This Chapter introduces important capital budgeting concepts and models, and it explains the proper use of accounting data in these models.

Capital budgeting is a process that involves identifying potentially desirable projects for capital expenditures, evaluating capital expenditure proposals, and selecting proposals that meet minimum criteria. A number of quantitative models are available to assist managers in evaluating capital expenditure proposals.

The best capital budgeting models are conceptually similar to the short-range planning models used in Chapters 3 and 4. They all emphasize cash flows and focus on future costs (and revenues) that differ among decision alternatives. The major difference is that capital budgeting models involve cash flows over several years, whereas short-range planning models involve cash flows for a year or less. When the cash flows associated with a proposed activity extend over several years, an adjustment is necessary to make the cash flows comparable when they are expected to occur at different points in time.

The *time value of money concept* explains why monies received or paid at different points in time must be adjusted to comparable values. The time value of money is introduced in Appendix 12A at the end of this chapter.

LONG-RANGE PLANNING AND CAPITAL BUDGETING

Most organizations plan not only for operations in the current period but also for the longer term, perhaps 5, 10, or even 20 years in the future. Most planning beyond the next budget year is called *long-range planning*.

Increased uncertainty and business alternatives add to the difficulty of planning as the horizon lengthens. Even though long-range planning is difficult and involves uncertainties, management must make long-range planning and capital expenditure decisions. Capital expenditure decisions will be made. The question is: How will they be made? Will they be made on the basis of the best information available? Will care be taken to ensure that capital expenditure decisions are in line with the organization's long-range goals? Will the potential consequences, both positive and negative, of capital expenditures be considered? Will important alternative uses of the organization's limited financial resources be considered in a systematic manner? Will managers be held accountable for the capital expenditure programs they initiate? The alternative to a systematic approach to capital budgeting is the haphazard expenditure of resources on the basis of a hunch, immediate need, or persuasion—without accountability by the person(s) making the decisions.

The steps of an effective capital budgeting process are outlined in Exhibit 12.1. A basic requirement for a systematic approach to capital budgeting is a defined mission, a set of long-range goals, and a business strategy. These elements provide focus and boundaries that reduce the types of capital expenditure decisions management considers. If, for example, KFC's goal is to become the largest fast-food restaurant chain in North America, its management should not consider a proposal to purchase and operate a bus line.

A well-defined business strategy will likewise guide capital expenditure decisions. If Cisco Systems is following a strategy to obtain technological leadership, it might seriously consider a proposal to meet customer needs by investing in innovative production facilities but would not consider a proposal to purchase and refurbish used (but seemingly cost-efficient) equipment. In the following Business Insight Heineken identified reducing energy consumption as a strategic goal, thereby drawing attention to an aspect of business that might otherwise go unnoticed.

Management should also develop procedures for the review, evaluation, approval, and post-audit of capital expenditure proposals. In a large organization, a capital budgeting committee that provides guidance to managers in the formulation of capital expenditure proposals is key to these procedures. This committee also reviews, analyzes, and approves or rejects major capital expenditure proposals. Major projects often require the approval of top management and even the board of directors. The capital budgeting committee should include persons knowledgeable in capital budgeting models; financing alternatives and costs; operating procedures; cost estimation and prediction methods; research and development efforts; the organization's goals and basic strategy; and the expectations of the organization's stockholders or owners. A management

LO1 Explain the role of capital budgeting in long-range planning.

accountant who is generally expert in data collection, retrieval, and analysis is normally part of the capital budgeting committee.

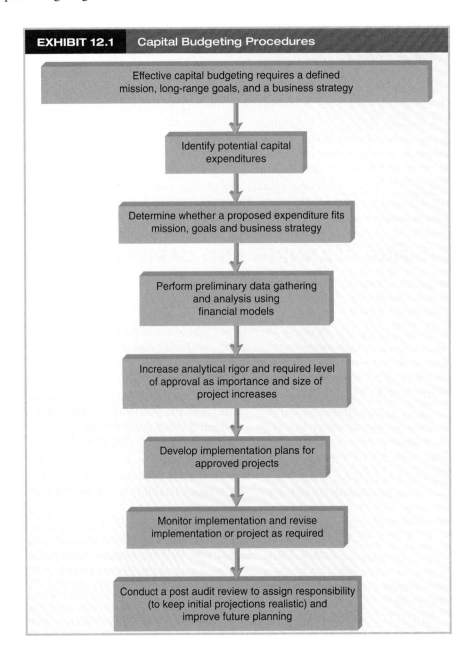

EXHIBIT 12.1 Capital Budgeting Procedures

Effective capital budgeting requires a defined mission, long-range goals, and a business strategy

Identify potential capital expenditures

Determine whether a proposed expenditure fits mission, goals and business strategy

Perform preliminary data gathering and analysis using financial models

Increase analytical rigor and required level of approval as importance and size of project increases

Develop implementation plans for approved projects

Monitor implementation and revise implementation or project as required

Conduct a post audit review to assign responsibility (to keep initial projections realistic) and improve future planning

Not all capital expenditure proposals require committee approval or are subject to formal evaluation. With the approval of top management, the committee might provide guidelines indicating the type and dollar amount of capital expenditures that managers at each level of the organization can make without formal evaluation or committee approval, or both. The guidelines might state that expenditures of less than $20,000 do not require committee approval and that only expenditures of more than $100,000 must be evaluated using capital budgeting models.

Typically, managers at higher levels have greater discretion in making capital expenditures. In a college or university, a department chairperson could have authority to purchase office and instructional equipment with a maximum limit of $10,000 per year. A dean may have authority to renovate offices or classrooms with a maximum limit of $50,000 per year, but the conversion of the power plant from one fuel source to another at a cost of $400,000 could require the formal review of a capital budgeting committee and final approval of the board of trustees.

BUSINESS INSIGHT

Energy Reduction as a Corporate Goal Fosters Green Investments With the manufacturing sector accounting for more than one-third of global energy use and energy prices soaring, there are countless opportunities for green investments that reduce energy consumption and costs. Yet, according to energy-expert Paul Waide of the International Energy Agency, corporate structure can be an obstacle. No one person is in charge of minimizing energy use. "The purchasing department might be looking for the cheapest motor to install in terms of upfront costs . . . The energy bill gets paid out of some other budget, so unless the company as a whole focuses on the issue, nothing gets done."

Netherlands-based Heineken, Europe's largest beer maker, overcame this obstacle by establishing corporate goals for reducing energy consumption. The company plans to use 15 percent less energy in 2010 than it used in 2002. This direction from the top has been important in focusing attention on projects that reduce energy consumption, according to Jasko Bakker, who leads environmental initiatives for Heineken.

HSBC Holdings, an international bank, has committed $90 million to become more energy efficient, with a seven percent targeted reduction in power consumption. HSBC investments to support this goal include software that automatically turns off desktop computers if employees leave them on at night and replacing computer monitors with more efficient models.

Source: Leila Abboud and John Biers, "Business Goes on an Energy Diet," *The Wall Street Journal*, August 27, 2007, pp. R1, R4.

The post-audit of approved capital expenditure proposals is an important part of a well-formulated approach to capital budgeting. A *post-audit* involves the development of project performance reports comparing planned and actual results. Project performance reports should be provided to the manager who initiated the capital expenditure proposal, the manager assigned responsibility for the project (if a different person), the project manager's supervisor, and the capital budgeting committee. These reports help keep the project on target (especially during the initial investment phase), identify the need to reevaluate the project if the initial analysis was in error or significant environmental changes occur, and improve the quality of investment proposals. When managers know they will be held accountable for the results of projects they initiate, they are likely to put more care into the development of capital expenditure proposals and take a greater interest in approved projects. Problems can occur when decision makers are rewarded for undertaking major projects but are not held responsible for the consequences that occur several years later.

A post-audit review of approved projects also helps the capital budgeting committee do a better job in evaluating new proposals. The committee might learn how to adjust proposals for the biases of individual managers, learn of new factors that should be considered in evaluating proposals, and avoid the routine approval of projects that appear desirable by themselves but are related to larger projects that are not meeting management's expectations. As summarized in the following Research Insight, capital budgeting models play an important role in strategic decision making.

BUSINESS INSIGHT

When There May Be a Threat from a Substitute Product, a Smart Strategy May Be to Acquire the Substitute Israeli company SodaStream makes a countertop appliance that turns tap water into flavored soda. SodaStream has gained in popularity because of the variety of flavor cartridges available to consumers and also because of its reusable containers and cartridges, which significantly reduce the environmental impact of the homemade soda compared with that of plastic containers containing store-bought brands. The company has gained access to Wal-Mart's 15,000 U.S. locations, but it could gain additional market share by partnering with an established beverage company. Both Coca-Cola and PepsiCo have the distribution network and cash reserves available to take SodaStream to the next level.

Either Coke or Pepsi could use net present value capital budgeting models to evaluate the attractiveness of the potential acquisition. Starbucks passed on the opportunity to partner with Keurig, which analysts view as a missed opportunity. It will be interesting to see if hindsight provides the same commentary about SodaStream.

Source: Kyle Stock, "Two Reasons for Pepsi to Think Twice About SodaStream," *Bloomberg Businessweek*, June 6, 2013.

CAPITAL BUDGETING MODELS THAT CONSIDER TIME VALUE OF MONEY

LO2 Apply capital budgeting models, such as net present value and internal rate of return, that consider the time value of money.

The capital budgeting models in this chapter have gained wide acceptance by for-profit and not-for-profit organizations. Our primary focus is on the *net present value* and the *internal rate of return models*, which are superior because they consider the time value of money. Later discussions will consider more traditional capital budgeting models, such as the payback period and the accounting rate of return that, while useful under certain circumstances, do not consider the time value of money. Although we briefly consider the cost of financing capital expenditures, we leave a detailed treatment of this topic, as well as a detailed examination of the sources of funds for financing investments, to books on financial management.

Expected Cash Flows

The focus of capital budgeting models that consider the time value of money is on future cash receipts and future cash disbursements that differ under decision alternatives. It is often convenient to distinguish between the following three phases of a project's cash flows:

- Initial investment
- Operation
- Disinvestment

All cash expenditures necessary to begin operations are classified as part of the project's *initial investment phase*. Expenditures to acquire property, plant, and equipment are part of the initial investment. Less obvious, but equally important, are expenditures to acquire working capital to purchase inventories and recruit and train employees. Although the initial investment phase often extends over many years, in our examples, we assume that the initial investment takes place at a single point in time.

Cash receipts from sales of goods or services, as well as normal cash expenditures for materials, labor, and other operating expenses, occur during the operation phase. The *operation phase* is typically broken down into one-year periods; for each period, operating cash expenditures are subtracted from operating cash receipts to determine the net operating cash inflow or outflow for the period.

The *disinvestment phase* occurs at the end of the project's life when assets are disposed of for their salvage value and any initial investment of working capital is recovered. Also included are any expenditures to dismantle facilities and dispose of waste. Although this phase might extend over many years, in our examples, we assume disinvestment takes place at a single point in time.

To illustrate the analysis of a project's cash flows, assume the management of Mobile Yogurt Shoppe is considering a capital expenditure proposal to operate a new shop in a resort community. Each Mobile Yogurt Shoppe is located in a specially constructed motor vehicle that moves on a regular schedule throughout the community it serves. The predicted cash flows associated with the project, which has an expected life of five years, are presented in Exhibit 12.2.

Manager Behavior and Expected Cash Flows

Accurately predicting the cash flows associated with a capital expenditure proposal is critical to properly evaluating the proposal. Managers might be overly optimistic with their predictions, and they are sometimes tempted to modify predictions to justify capital expenditures. Perhaps they are

EXHIBIT 12.2	Analysis of a Project's Predicted Cash Flows		

Initial investment (at time 0)

Vehicle and equipment			$ (90,554)
Inventories and other working capital			(4,000)
Total investment cash outflow			$ (94,554)

Operation (per year for 5 years)

Sales.			$ 175,000
Cash expenditures			
Food	$47,000		
Labor.	65,000		
Supplies	9,000		
Fuel and utilities.	8,000		
Advertising	4,000		
Miscellaneous.	12,000	(145,000)	
Net annual cash inflow			$ 30,000

Disinvestment (at the end of 5 years)

Sale of vehicle and equipment		$ 8,000	
Recovery of investment in inventories and other working capital		4,000	
Total disinvestment cash inflow		$ 12,000	

interested in personal rewards. They might also want to avoid a loss of prestige or employment for themselves or to keep a local facility operating for the benefit of current employees and the local economy. Unfortunately, if a major expenditure does not work out, not only the local plant but also the entire company could be forced out of business. For example, under pressure to increase current sales, automobile leasing companies could be tempted to overstate cash receipts during the disinvestment phase of a lease.

Net Present Value

A project's **net present value**, usually computed as of the time of the initial investment, is the present value of the project's net cash inflows from operations and disinvestment less the amount of the initial investment. Chapter Appendix 12A contains an introduction to the time value of money, including net present value fundamentals. In computing a project's net present value, the cash flows occurring at different points in time are adjusted for the time value of money using a **discount rate** that is the minimum rate of return required for the project to be acceptable. Projects with positive net present values (or values at least equal to zero) are acceptable, and projects with negative net present values are unacceptable. Two methods to compute net present value follow.

Table Approach

Assuming that management uses a 12 percent discount rate, the net present value of the proposed investment in a Mobile Yogurt Shoppe is shown in Exhibit 12.3 (a) to be $20,400. Since the net present value is more than zero, the investment in the Mobile Yogurt Shoppe is expected to be profitable, even when adjusted for the time value of money.

We can verify the amounts and computations in Exhibit 12.3. Start by tracing the cash flows back to Exhibit 12.2. Next, verify the 12 percent present value factors in Tables 12A.1 and 12A.2 in Chapter Appendix 12A. The initial investment is assumed to occur at a single point in time (identified as time 0), the start of the project. In net present value computations, all cash flows are restated in terms of their value at time 0. Hence, time 0 cash flows have a present value factor of 1. To simplify computations, all other cash flows are assumed to occur at the end of years 1 through 5, even if they occurred during the year. Although further refinements could be made to adjust for cash flows occuring throughout each year, such adjustments are seldom necessary. Observe that net operating cash inflows are treated as an *annuity*, whereas cash flows for the initial investment and disinvestment are treated as *lump-sum amounts*. If net operating cash flows varied from year to year, we would treat each year's cash flow as a separate amount.

Spreadsheet Approach

Spreadsheet software contains functions that compute the present value of a series of cash flows. With this software, simply enter a column or row containing the net cash flows for each period and the appropriate formula. The discount rate of 0.12 is entered as part of the formula. Sample spreadsheet input to determine the net present value of the proposed investment in a Mobile Yogurt Shoppe is shown on the left in Exhibit 12.3 (b). The spreadsheet output is shown on the right, in Exhibit 12.3 (b).

Two cautionary notes follow:

1. The spreadsheet formula for the net present value assumes that the first cash flow occurs at time "1," rather than at time "0." Hence, we cannot include the initial investment in the data set analyzed by the spreadsheet formula when computing the net present value. Instead, the initial investment is subtracted from the present value of future cash flows.

2. Arrange the cash flows subsequent to the initial investment from *top* to bottom in a column, or *left* to right in a row.

EXHIBIT 12.3	Net Present Value of a Project's Predicted Cash Flows

(a) Table approach:

	Predicted Cash Inflows (outflows) (A)	Year(s) of Cash Flows (B)	12% Present Value Factor (C)	Present Value of Cash Flows (A) × (C)
Initial investment	$(94,554)	0	1.000	$ (94,554)
Operation	30,000	1–5	3.605	108,150
Disinvestment	12,000	5	0.567	6,804
Net present value of all cash flows				$ 20,400

(b) Spreadsheet approach:

Input:

	A	B
1	Year of cash flow	Cash flow
2	1	$30,000
3	2	30,000
4	3	30,000
5	4	30,000
6	5	42,000
7	Present value	=NPV(0.12,B2:B6)
8	Initial investment at time 0	(94,554)
9	Net present value	=B7+B8

Output:

	A	B
1	Year of cash flow	Cash flow
2	1	$ 30,000
3	2	30,000
4	3	30,000
5	4	30,000
6	5	42,000
7	Present value	$114,952.41
8	Initial investment at time 0	(94,554.00)
9	Net present value	$ 20,398.41

Internal Rate of Return

The **internal rate of return (IRR)**, often called the **time-adjusted rate of return**, is the discount rate that equates the present value of a project's cash inflows with the present value of the project's cash outflows. Other ways to describe IRR include: (1) The minimum rate that could be paid for the money invested in a project without losing money, and (2) The discount rate that results in a project's net present value equaling zero.

All practical applications of the IRR model use a calculator or spreadsheet. Thus, we illustrate determining an IRR with a spreadsheet. A table approach to determining a project's internal rate of return is illustrated in Appendix 12B of this chapter.

With spreadsheet software, simply enter a column or row containing the net cash flows for each period and the appropriate formula. Spreadsheet input for Mobile Yogurt Shoppe's investment proposal is shown in Exhibit 12.4. The spreadsheet formula for the IRR assumes that the first cash flow occurs at time "0."

The spreadsheet approach requires an initial prediction or guess of the project's internal rate of return. Although the closeness of the prediction to the final solution affects computational speed, for textbook examples almost any number can be used. We use an initial estimate of 0.08 in all illustrations. Because the IRR formula assumes that the first cash flow occurs at time 0, the initial investment is included in the data analyzed by the IRR formula. Again, we must order the cash flows from top to bottom in a column or left to right in a row. As shown on the right column in Exhibit 12.4, the spreadsheet software computes the IRR as 20 percent.

Although a project's IRR should be compared to the discount rate established by management, such a discount rate is often unknown. In these situations, computing the IRR still provides insights into a project's profitability.

EXHIBIT 12.4	Spreadsheet Approach to Determining Internal Rate of Return

Input:

	A	B
1	Year of cash flow	Cash flow
2	0	$(94,554)
3	1	30,000
4	2	30,000
5	3	30,000
6	4	30,000
7	5	42,000
8	IRR	=IRR(B2:B7,0.08)*

Output:

	A	B
1	Year of cash flow	Cash flow
2	0	$(94,554)
3	1	30,000
4	2	30,000
5	3	30,000
6	4	30,000
7	5	42,000
8	IRR	0.20

*The formula is "=IRR(Input data range, guess)." The guess, which is any likely rate of return, is used as an initial starting point in determining the solution. We use 0.08 in all illustrations.

The calculated internal rate of return is compared to the discount rate established by management to evaluate investment proposals. If the proposal's IRR is greater than or equal to the discount rate, the project is acceptable; if it is less than the discount rate, the project is unacceptable. Because Mobile Yogurt Shoppes has a 12 percent discount rate, the project is acceptable using the IRR model.

Although a computer and appropriate software quickly and accurately perform tedious computations, computational ease increases the opportunity for inappropriate use. The ability to plug numbers into a computer or calculator and obtain an output labeled NPV or IRR could mislead the unwary into believing that capital budgeting models are easy to use. This is not true. Training and professional judgment are required to identify relevant costs, to implement procedures to obtain relevant cost information, and to make a good decision once results are available. Capital budgeting models are merely decision aids. Managers, not models, make the decisions. To better illustrate underlying concepts, all subsequent textbook illustrations use a table approach.

Cost of Capital

When discounting models are used to evaluate capital expenditure proposals, management must determine the discount rate (1) used to compute a proposal's net present value or (2) used as the standard for evaluating a proposal's IRR. An organization's cost of capital is often used as this discount rate.

The **cost of capital** is the average cost an organization pays to obtain the resources necessary to make investments. This average rate considers items such as the:

■ Effective interest rate on debt (notes or bonds).

■ Effective dividend rate on preferred stock.

■ Discount rate that equates the present value of all dividends expected on common stock over the life of the organization to the current market value of the organization's common stock.

The cost of capital for a company that has no debt or preferred stock equals the cost of equity capital, computed as follows:

$$\text{Cost of equity capital} = \frac{\text{Current annual dividend per common share}}{\text{Current market price per common share}} + \text{Expected dividend growth rate}$$

Procedures for determining the cost of capital for more complex capital structures are covered in finance books. Investing in a project that has an internal rate of return equal to the cost of capital should not affect the market value of the firm's securities. Investing in a project that has a return higher than the cost of capital should increase the market value of a firm's securities. If, however, a firm invests in a project that has a return less than the cost of capital, the market value of the firm's securities should fall.

The cost of capital is the minimum return acceptable for investment purposes. Any investment proposal not expected to yield this minimum rate should normally be rejected. Because of difficulties encountered in determining the cost of capital, many organizations adopt a discount rate or a target rate of return without complicated mathematical analysis.

MID-CHAPTER REVIEW

Consider the following investment proposal:

Initial investment	
Depreciable assets	$27,740
Working capital	3,000
Operations (per year for 4 years)	
Cash receipts.	25,000
Cash expenditures.	15,000
Disinvestment	
Salvage value of plant and equipment	2,000
Recovery of working capital	3,000

Required
Determine each of the following:

a. Net present value at a 10 percent discount rate.
b. Internal rate of return. (Refer to Appendix 12B if using the table approach.)

The solution is on pages 469–470.

CAPITAL BUDGETING MODELS THAT DO NOT CONSIDER TIME VALUE OF MONEY

LO3 Apply capital budgeting models, such as payback period and accounting rate of return, that do not consider the time value of money.

Years ago, capital budgeting models that do not consider the time value of money were more widely used than discounting models. Although most large organizations use net present value or internal rate of return as their primary evaluation tool, they often use nondiscounting models as an initial screening device. Further, as discussed in the following Research Insight, nondiscounting models remain entrenched in small businesses. We consider two nondiscounting models, the *payback period* and the *accounting rate of return*.

Payback Period

The **payback period** is the time required to recover the initial investment in a project from operations. The payback decision rule states that acceptable projects must have less than some maximum payback period designated by management. Payback emphasizes management's concern with liquidity and the need to minimize risk through a rapid recovery of the initial investment. It is frequently used for small expenditures having such obvious benefits that the use of more sophisticated capital budgeting models is not required or justified.

When a project is expected to have equal annual operating cash inflows, its payback period is computed as follows:

$$\text{Payback period} = \frac{\text{Initial investment}}{\text{Annual operating cash inflows}}$$

For Mobile Yogurt Shoppe's investment proposal, outlined in Exhibit 12.2, the payback period is 3.15 years:

$$\text{Payback period} = \frac{\$94,554}{\$30,000}$$
$$= 3.15$$

RESEARCH INSIGHT

Size and Education Matter in Capital Budgeting Danielson and Scott, after surveying the owners of small businesses, concluded that small businesses (an average of ten employees) use much less sophisticated methods in making capital expenditure decisions than recommended by theory. In their survey the most frequently used approach to making capital expenditure decisions was "gut feel" followed by payback period and the accounting rate of return, with few firms using discounted cash flow methods. Commenting on their results, Danielson and Scott observed that:

- Many small business owners have limited formal education and limited staff support. What's more, the investments made by small business are often not discretionary. The firm either makes the investment, say in a new delivery truck, or goes out of business.

- The use of payback appears to increase with the formal education of the business owner as well as the use of basic budgeting techniques such as forecasting cash flows.

- The use of the accounting rate of return increases with the growth or expansion plans of small firms, especially if the firm is required to provide banks with periodic financial information.

- Small businesses with owners having advanced degrees are most likely to use discounted cash flow approaches. They are also most likely to have written business plans and most likely to consider the tax implications of decisions.

Graham and Harvey surveyed chief financial officers (CFOs) of Fortune 500 firms as well as CFOs of smaller firms belonging to the Financial Executives Institute (FEI). CFO's and members of the FEI are likely to have formal education in capital budgeting and they are likely to network with finance professionals through organizations such as the FEI.

Of the CFOs responding to the survey, 46 percent were at firms with sales of more than $1 billion. The majority of respondents to the Graham-Harvey survey used multiple capital budgeting models:

- 75.7 percent used internal rate of return.
- 74.9 percent used net present value.
- More than 50 percent used payback.
- Approximately 20 percent used the accounting rate of return.

Even though the firms included in the Graham-Harvey study were much larger than those in the Danielson-Scott study, Graham and Harvey also noted that "small firms" (firms with sales of less than $100 million) are less likely to use net present value than large firms.

Sources: Morris G. Danielson and Jonathan A. Scott, "The Capital Budgeting Decisions of Small Businesses." *Journal of Applied Finance*, Fall/Winter 2006, pp. 45-56. John R. Graham and Campbell R. Harvey, "The Theory and Practice of Corporate Finance: Evidence from the Field," *Journal of Financial Economics*, May-June, 2001, pp: 187-243.

Determining the payback period for a project having unequal cash flows is slightly more complicated. Assume that Amazon is evaluating a capital expenditure proposal that requires an initial investment of $50,000,000 and has the following expected net cash inflows:

Year	Net Cash Inflow
1	$15,000,000
2	25,000,000
3	40,000,000
4	20,000,000
5	10,000,000

To compute the payback period, we must determine the net unrecovered amount at the end of each year. In the year of full recovery, the net cash inflows are assumed to occur evenly and are prorated based on the unrecovered investment at the start of the year. Full recovery of Amazon's investment proposal is expected to occur in Year 3:

Year	Net Cash Inflow	Unrecovered Investment
0	$ 0	$50,000,000
1	15,000,000	35,000,000
2	25,000,000	10,000,000
3	40,000,000	0

Therefore, $10,000,000 of $40,000,000 is needed in Year 3 to complete the recovery of the initial investment. This provides a proportion of 0.25 ($10,000,000 ÷ $40,000,000) and a payback period of 2.25 years (2 years plus 0.25 of Year 3). This project is acceptable if management specified a maximum payback period of three years. Because they occur after the payback period, the net cash inflows of Years 4 and 5 are ignored.

Accounting Rate of Return

The **accounting rate of return** is the average annual increase in net income that results from the acceptance of a capital expenditure proposal divided by either the initial investment or the average investment in the project. This method differs from other capital budgeting models in that it focuses on accounting income rather than on cash flow. In most capital budgeting applications, accounting net income is approximated as net cash inflow from operations minus expenses not requiring the use of cash, such as depreciation.

Consider Mobile Yogurt Shoppe's capital expenditure proposal whose cash flows were outlined in Exhibit 12.2. The vehicle and equipment costs are $90,554 and have a disposal value of $8,000 at the end of five years, resulting in an average annual increase in net income of $13,489:

Annual net cash inflow from operations.	$30,000
Less average annual depreciation [($90,554 − $8,000) ÷ 5].	(16,511)
Average annual increase in net income.	$13,489

Considering the investment in inventories and other working capital, the initial investment is $94,554 ($90,554 + $4,000), and the *accounting rate of return on initial investment* is 14.27 percent:

$$\text{Accounting rate of return on initial investment} = \frac{\text{Average annual increase in net income}}{\text{Initial investment}} = \frac{\$13,489}{\$94,554} = 0.1427$$

The average investment, computed as the initial investment plus the expected value of any disinvestment, all divided by 2, is $53,277 [($94,554 + $12,000) ÷ 2]. The *accounting rate of return on average investment* is 25.32 percent:

$$\frac{\text{Accounting rate of return}}{\text{on average investment}} = \frac{\text{Average annual increase in net income}}{\text{Average investment}} = \frac{\$13,489}{\$53,277} = 0.2532$$

When using the accounting rate of return, management specifies either the initial investment or average investment plus some minimum acceptable rate. Management rejects capital expenditure proposals with a lower accounting rate of return but accepts proposals with an accounting rate of return higher than or equal to the minimum.

EVALUATION OF CAPITAL BUDGETING MODELS

As a single criterion for evaluating capital expenditure proposals, capital budgeting models that consider the time value of money are superior to models that do not consider it. The payback model concerns merely how long it takes to recover the initial investment from a project, yet investments are not made with the objective of merely getting the money back. Indeed, not investing has a payback period of 0. Investments are made to earn a profit. Hence, what happens after the payback period is more important than is the payback period itself. The payback period model, when used as the sole investment criterion, has a fatal flaw in that it fails to consider cash flows after the payback period. Despite this flaw, payback is a rough-and-ready approach to getting a handle on investment proposals. Sometimes a project is so attractive using payback that, when its life is considered, no further analysis is necessary.

LO4 Evaluate the strengths and weaknesses of alternative capital budgeting models.

BUSINESS INSIGHT

Investing in the Not-Quite 800-Lb. Gorilla Glass Corning invented Gorilla Glass in the 1960s, when the company planned to use it in automobile windshields and prison windows. However, cost pressures placed on auto manufacturers of the day prevented the glass from coming to market, as they sought out cheaper laminated glass. But Corning prides itself on "patient capital," with patient being the key word. Gorilla Glass finally found its market in 2007 when Steve Jobs selected an ultrathin layer of Gorilla Glass to shield the iPhone. Sales of the glass went from zero to $1 billion in the five years since the iPhone was introduced. That's a lengthy but lucrative payback period!

New formulations of Gorilla Glass contain an antireflective coating to permit the screen to be used in direct sunlight. And plans are on track to make the next version of the glass with an antimicrobial coating. Ironically, Gorilla Glass may finally find a place in its intended market: Modern-day automakers are finding that the glass lowers a car's center of gravity, which increases its fuel efficiency, an attribute that is valued at a premium in today's more environmentally conscious market.

Source: Connie Guglielmo, "Working with Innovators from Thomas Edison to Steve Jobs, Corning Finds a Glass Fix," *Forbes*, September 23, 2013.

For total life evaluations, the accounting rate of return is superior to the payback period because it does consider a capital expenditure proposal's profitability. Using the accounting rate of return, a project that merely returns the initial investment will have an average annual increase in net income of 0 and an accounting rate of return of 0. The problem with the accounting rate of return is that it fails to consider the timing of cash flows. It treats all cash flows within the life of an investment proposal equally despite the fact that cash flows occurring early in a project's life are more valuable than cash flows occurring late in a project's life. Early period cash flows can earn additional profits by being invested elsewhere. Consider the two investment proposals summarized in Exhibit 12.5. Both have an accounting rate of return of 5 percent, but Proposal A is superior to Proposal B because most of its cash flows occur in the first two years. Because of the timing of the cash flows when discounted at an annual rate of 10 percent, Proposal A has a net present value of $1,140 while Proposal B has a negative net present value of $(10,940).

The net present value and the internal rate of return models both consider the time value of money and project profitability. They almost always provide the same evaluation of individual

EXHIBIT 12.5	Evaluating Capital Budgeting Models with Differences in Cash Flow Timing

Accounting rate of return analysis of Projects A and B

	Project A	Project B
Predicted net cash inflow from operations		
Year 1	$ 50,000	$ 10,000
Year 2	50,000	10,000
Year 3	10,000	50,000
Year 4	10,000	50,000
Total	120,000	120,000
Total depreciation	(100,000)	(100,000)
Total net income	$ 20,000	$ 20,000
Project life	÷ 4 years	÷ 4 years
Average annual increase in net income	$ 5,000	$ 5,000
Initial investment	÷ 100,000	÷ 100,000
Accounting rate of return on initial investment	0.05	0.05

Net present value analysis of Project A

	Predicted Cash Inflows (outflows)	Year(s) of Cash Flows	10% Present Value Factor	Present Value of Cash Flows
Initial investment	$(100,000)	0	1.000	$(100,000)
Operation	50,000	1–2	1.736	86,800
Operation	10,000	3–4	3.170−1.736	14,340
Net present value of all cash flows				$ 1,140

Net present value analysis of Project B

	Predicted Cash Inflows (outflows)	Year(s) of Cash Flows	10% Present Value Factor	Present Value of Cash Flows
Initial investment	$(100,000)	0	1.000	$(100,000)
Operation	10,000	1–2	1.736	17,360
Operation	50,000	3–4	3.170−1.736	71,700
Net present value of all cash flows				$ (10,940)

projects whose acceptance or rejection will not affect other projects. An exception can occur when periods of net cash outflows are mixed with periods of net cash inflows. Under these circumstances, an investment proposal could have multiple internal rates of return. The net present value and the internal rate of return models, however, have two basic differences that often lead to differences in the evaluation of competing investment proposals:

1. The net present value model gives explicit consideration to investment size. The internal rate of return model does not.

2. The net present value model assumes that all net cash inflows are reinvested at the discount rate; the internal rate of return model assumes that all net cash inflows are reinvested at the project's internal rate of return.

When there is a difference in the size of competing investment proposals and funds not invested in the accepted proposal can only be invested at the cost of capital, the net present value method is superior.

ADDITIONAL ASPECTS OF CAPITAL BUDGETING

The capital budgeting models discussed do not make investment decisions. Rather, they help managers separate capital expenditure proposals that meet certain criteria from those that do not. Managers then focus on those proposals that pass the initial screening.

LO5 Discuss the importance of judgment, attitudes toward risk, and relevant cash flow information for capital budgeting decisions.

Using Multiple Investment Criteria

In performing this initial screening, management can use a single capital budgeting model or multiple models, including some we have not discussed. Management might specify that proposals must be in line with the organization's long-range goals and business strategy, have a maximum payback period of three years, have a positive net present value when discounted at 14 percent, and have an initial investment of less than $500,000. The maximum payback period might be intended to reduce risk, the present value criterion might be to ensure an adequate return to investors, and the maximum investment size might reflect the resources available for investment.

Nonquantitative factors such as market position, operational performance improvement, and strategy implementation often play a decisive role in management's final decision to accept or reject a capital expenditure proposal that has passed the initial screening. Also important at this point are top management's attitudes toward risk and financing alternatives, their confidence in the professional judgment of other managers making investment proposals, their beliefs about the future direction of the economy, and their evaluation of alternative investments. In the following sections, we will focus on evaluating risk, differential analysis of project cash flows, predicting differential costs and revenues for high-tech investments, and evaluating mutually exclusive investments.

Evaluating Risk

All capital expenditure proposals involve risk, including risk related to

- Cost of the initial investment.
- Time required to complete the initial investment and begin operations.
- Whether the new facilities will operate as planned.
- Life of the facilities.
- Customers' demand for the product or service.
- Final selling price.
- Operating costs.
- Disposal values.

Projected cash flows (such as those summarized for the Mobile Yogurt Shoppe proposal in Exhibit 12.2) are based on management's best predictions. Although these predictions are likely to reflect the professional judgment of economists, marketing personnel, engineers, and accountants, they are far from certain.

Many techniques have been developed to assist in the analysis of the risks inherent in capital budgeting. Suggested approaches include the following:

- *To adjust the discount rate for individual projects based on management's perception of the risks associated with a project.* A project perceived as being almost risk free might be evaluated using a discount rate of 12 percent; a project perceived as having moderate risk may be evaluated using a discount rate of 16 percent; and a project perceived as having high risk might be evaluated using a discount rate of 20 percent.

- *To compute several internal rates of return and/or net present values for a project.* For example, a project's net present value might be computed three times: first assuming the most optimistic projections of cash flows; second assuming the most likely projections of cash flows; and third assuming the most pessimistic projections of cash flows. The final decision is then based on management's attitudes toward risk. A project whose most likely outcome is highly profitable would probably be rejected if its pessimistic outcome might lead to bankruptcy.

■ *To subject a capital expenditure proposal to sensitivity analysis*, a study of the responsiveness of a model's dependent variable(s) to changes in one or more of its independent variables. Management might want to know, for example, the minimum annual net cash inflows that will provide an internal rate of return of 12 percent with other cost and revenue projections being as expected.

RESEARCH INSIGHT

Emerging Markets: The South-South Route While Capital Spending Wanes in the United States and Europe As the United States and Western Europe were dealing with their respective financial crises, capital investment diverted to a new "south-south" route. Sovereign funds, investors, and companies hunting for acquisitions have turned to high-growth emerging markets. The so-called "south-south" route between Brazil and China has been heating up. One Brazilian billionaire is using money from Abu Dhabi's sovereign-wealth fund to build a megaport to ship Brazilian natural resources to China. Indeed, merger and acquisition activity among the BRIC nations (Brazil, Russia, India, and China) has grown from $600 million per year to over $11 billion annually in the past five years.

Meanwhile, Standard & Poor's estimates that U.S. businesses decreased their capital investments by over $175 billion during the period from 2009 to 2011. Companies that do invest, choose to invest in their own capital. Share repurchases exceeded share issuances by $274 billion in the past year. Delaying research and development, product innovation, and investments in manufacturing efficiency and technology will put these companies at a profound disadvantage relative to their global peers. Increasing cash reserves in these same companies (estimated at over $1.26 trillion) suggests that the companies had resources to fuel growth but chose not to invest.

Moreover, capital investment is equally waning in Western Europe. Lack of current and forecasted sales growth among European companies is causing capital expenditures to sink to near-historic lows when measured against gross domestic product (GDP). Companies cite high energy prices, increasing tax rates, and regulatory uncertainty as the primary cause of their pull-back. A recent survey of German companies such as BMW, Siemens, Henkel, and Adidas said they will target their future investment toward emerging markets, where stronger sales growth is expected, along with lower production costs.

Sources: Francesco Guerrera, "A Capital Shift for Emerging Markets," *Wall Street Journal*, May 8, 2012, p. C1; Tom Gara, "U.S. Companies Underinvest by Billions," *Wall Street Journal*, December 12, 2012, p. B6; Dennis Berman, "China Believes in America, so Why Doesn't America?" *Wall Street Journal*, December 19, 2012, p. B1; Nina Adam, "Germany's Largest Companies Turn Away from Home," *Wall Street Journal*, October 17, 2013, p. B1.

Differential Analysis of Project Cash Flows

All previous examples assume that capital expenditure proposals produce additional net cash inflows, but this is not always the case. Units of government and not-for-profit organizations might provide services that do not produce any cash inflows. For-profit organizations might be required to make capital expenditures to maintain product quality or to bring facilities up to environmental or safety standards. In these situations, it is impossible to compute a project's payback period, accounting rate of return, or internal rate of return. It is possible, however, to compute the present value of all life cycle costs associated with alternative ways of providing the service or meeting the environmental or safety standard. Here, the alternative with the smallest negative net present value is preferred.

Capital expenditure proposals to reduce operating costs by upgrading facilities might not provide any incremental cash inflows. Again, we can use a total cost approach and calculate the present value of the costs associated with each alternative, with the low-cost alternative being preferred. Alternatively, we can perform a differential analysis of cash flows and, treating any reduced operating costs as if they were cash inflows, compute the net present value or the internal rate of return of the cost reduction proposal. Recall from Chapter 4 that a relevant cost analysis focuses on the costs that differ under alternative actions. Once the differential amounts have been determined, they can be adjusted for the time value of money. To illustrate the differential approach, we consider an example introduced in Chapter 4.

Assume Beats Electronics produces a variety of electronic components, including 10,000 units per year of a component used in wireless headsets. Further assume the machine currently used in manufacturing the headset components is two years old and has a remaining useful life of four years. It cost $90,000 and has an estimated salvage value of zero dollars at the end of its useful life. Its current book value (original cost less accumulated depreciation) is $60,000, but its current disposal value is only $35,000.

Management is evaluating the desirability of replacing the machine with a new machine. The new machine costs $80,000, has a useful life of four years, and a predicted salvage value of zero dollars at the end of its useful life. Although the new machine has the same productive capacity as the old machine, its predicted operating costs are lower because it requires less electricity. Furthermore, because of a computer control system, the new machine will require less frequent and less expensive inspections and adjustments. Finally, the new machine requires less maintenance.

An analysis of the cash flows associated with this cost reduction proposal, separated into the three phases of the project's life, are presented in Exhibit 12.6. Because the proposal does not have a disposal value, this portion of the analysis could have been omitted. (A detailed explanation of the relevant costs included in this analysis is in Exhibit 4.1 and the accompanying Chapter 4 discussion of relevant costs.) Assuming that Beats has a discount rate of 12 percent, the proposal's net present value (computed in Exhibit 12.7) is $2,681, and the proposal is acceptable.

EXHIBIT 12.6	Differential Analysis of Predicted Cash Flows		
	Differential Analysis of Predicted Cash Flows		
	Keep Old Machine (A)	Replace with New Machine (B)	Difference (income effect of replacement) (A) − (B)
Initial investment			
Cost of new machine.		$80,000	$(80,000)
Disposal value of old machine		(35,000)	35,000
Net initial investment. . . .			$(45,000)
Annual operating cash savings			
Conversion			
Old machine (10,000 units × $5)	$50,000		
New machine (10,000 units × $4)		$40,000	$10,000
Inspection and adjustment			
Old machine (10 setups × $500 per setup)	5,000		
New machine (5 setups × $300 per setup). . . .		1,500	3,500
Machine maintenance			
Old machine ($200 per month × 12 months)	2,400		
New machine ($200 per year)		200	2,200
Net annual cost savings			$15,700
Disinvestment at end of life			
Old machine. . . .	$ 0		
New machine		$ 0	

EXHIBIT 12.7	Differential Analysis of Predicted Cash Flows			
	Predicted Cash Inflows (outflows) (A)	Year(s) of Cash Flows (B)	12% Present Value Factor (C)	Present Value of Cash Flows (A) × (C)
Initial investment	$(45,000)	0	1.000	$(45,000)
Operation. . . .	15,700	1–4	3.037	47,681
Disinvestment	0	4	0.636	0
Net present value of all cash flows. . . .				$ 2,681

Predicting Differential Costs and Revenues for High-Tech Investments

Care must be taken when evaluating proposals for investments in technological innovations such as flexible manufacturing systems and computer integrated manufacturing. The three types of errors to consider are: (1) investing in unnecessary or overly complex equipment, (2) overestimating cost saving, and (3) underestimating incremental sales.

Investing in Unnecessary or Overly Complex Equipment

A common error is to simply compare the cost associated with the current inefficient way of doing things with the predicted cost of performing the identical operations with more modern equipment. Although capital budgeting models might suggest that such investments are justifiable, the result could be the costly and rapid completion of non-value-added activities. Consider the following examples.

■ A company invests in an automated system to speed the movement of work in process between workstations without first evaluating the plant layout. The firm is still unable to compete with other companies having better organized plants that allow lower cycle times, lower work-in-process inventories, and lower manufacturing costs. Management should have evaluated the plant layout before investing in new equipment. They may have found that rearranging the factory floor would have reduced materials movement and eliminated the need for the investment.

■ A company invests in an automated warehouse to permit the rapid storage and retrieval of goods while competitors work to eliminate excess inventory. The firm is left with large inventories and a large investment in the automated warehouse while competitors, not having to earn a return on similar investments, are able to charge lower prices. Management should have evaluated the need for current inventory levels and perhaps shifted to a just-in-time approach to inventory management before considering the investment in an automated warehouse.

■ A company hires staff to perform quality inspections while competitors implement total quality management and seek to eliminate the need for quality inspections. While defective products or services are now identified before they affect customers, they still exist. Furthermore, the company has higher expenditures than competitors, resulting in a less competitive cost structure. The inspections might not have been needed if management had shifted from inspecting for conformance to an emphasis on "doing it right the first time."

■ A company invests in automated welding equipment to more efficiently produce printer casings while competitors simplify the product design and shift from welded to molded plastic casings. Although the cost of producing the welded casings might be lower, the company's cost structure is still not competitive.

All of these examples illustrate the limitations of capital budgeting models and the need for good judgment. *In the final analysis, managers, not models, make decisions.* Management must carefully evaluate the situations and determine whether they have considered the proper alternatives and all important cash flows.

Overestimating Cost Savings

When a number of activities drive manufacturing overhead costs, estimates of overhead cost savings based on a single activity cost driver can significantly overestimate cost savings. Assume, for example, that a company containing both machine-intensive and labor-intensive operations develops a cost-estimating equation for overhead with labor as the only independent variable. Because of this, all overhead costs are associated with labor. The predicted cost savings can be computed as the sum of predicted reductions in labor plus predicted reductions in overhead; the predicted reductions in overhead are computed as the overhead per direct labor dollar or labor hour multiplied by the predicted reduction in direct labor dollars or labor hours. Because a major portion of the overhead is driven by factors other than direct labor, reducing direct labor will not provide the predicted savings. Capital budgeting models might suggest that the investment is acceptable, but the models are based on inaccurate cost data.

Management should beware of overly simplistic computations of cost savings. This is an area in which management needs the assistance of well-trained management accountants and engineers.

Underestimating Incremental Sales or Cost Savings

In evaluating proposals for investments in new equipment, management often assumes that the baseline for comparison is the current sales level, but this might not be the case. If competitors are investing in equipment to better meet customer needs and to reduce costs, a failure to make similar investments might result in uncompetitive prices and declining, rather than steady, sales. Hence, the baseline for sales without the investment is overstated, and the incremental sales of the investment is understated. Not considering the likely decline in sales understates the incremental sales associated with the investment and biases the results against the proposed investment.

Investments in manufacturing technologies, such as flexible manufacturing systems (FMS) and computer integrated manufacturing (CIM), do more than simply allow the efficient production of current products. Such investments also make possible the rapid, low-cost switching to new products. The result is expanded sales opportunities.

Such investments might also produce cost savings further down the value chain, either within or outside the company. Beats' decision to acquire a new machine might have the unanticipated consequence of reducing customer warranty claims or increasing sales because customers are attracted to a higher-quality product.

Unfortunately, because such opportunities are difficult to quantify, they are often ignored in the evaluation of capital expenditure proposals. The solution to this dilemma involves the application of management's professional judgment, a willingness to take risks based on this professional judgment, and recognition that certain investments transcend capital budgeting models in that they involve strategic as well as long-range planning. At this level of planning, qualitative decisions concerning the nature of the organization are at least as important as quantified factors.

TAXES IN CAPITAL BUDGETING DECISIONS

To focus on capital budgeting concepts, we deferred consideration of the impact of taxes. Because income taxes affect cash flows and income, their consideration is important in evaluating investment proposals in for-profit organizations.

LO6 Determine the net present value of investment proposals with consideration of taxes.

The cost of investments in plant and equipment is not deducted from taxable revenues in determining taxable income and income taxes at the time of the initial investment. Instead, the amount of the initial investment is deducted as depreciation over the operating life of an asset. To illustrate the impact of taxes on cash flows, assume:

■ Revenues and operating cash receipts are the same each year.

■ Depreciation is the only noncash expense of an organization.

Depreciation Tax Shield

Depreciation does not require the use of cash (the funds were spent at the initial investment), but depreciation is said to provide a "tax shield" because it reduces cash payments for income taxes. The **depreciation tax shield** (the reduction in taxes due to the deductibility of depreciation from taxable revenues) is computed as follows:

$$\text{Depreciation tax shield} = \text{Depreciation} \times \text{Tax rate}$$

The value of the depreciation tax shield is illustrated using Mobile Yogurt Shoppe's capital expenditure proposal summarized in Exhibit 12.2. Mobile Yogurt Shoppe's annual straight line depreciation of $16,511 is computed as the initial investment of $90,554 minus the predicted disposal value of $8,000, all divided by the predicted five year life $16,511 [($90,554 − $8,000)/5]. With an assumed tax rate of 34 percent, the annual depreciation tax shield is $5,614 ($16,511 depreciation × 0.34 tax rate). The increase in annual cash flows provided by the depreciation tax shield is illustrated in Exhibit 12.8. Examine this exhibit, paying particular attention to the lines for depreciation, income taxes, and net annual cash flow.

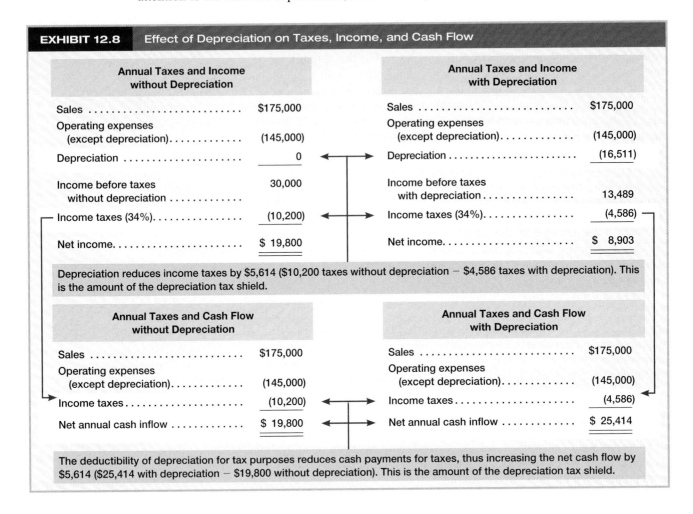

EXHIBIT 12.8	Effect of Depreciation on Taxes, Income, and Cash Flow

Annual Taxes and Income without Depreciation

Sales	$175,000
Operating expenses (except depreciation)	(145,000)
Depreciation	0
Income before taxes without depreciation	30,000
Income taxes (34%)	(10,200)
Net income	$ 19,800

Annual Taxes and Income with Depreciation

Sales	$175,000
Operating expenses (except depreciation)	(145,000)
Depreciation	(16,511)
Income before taxes with depreciation	13,489
Income taxes (34%)	(4,586)
Net income	$ 8,903

Depreciation reduces income taxes by $5,614 ($10,200 taxes without depreciation − $4,586 taxes with depreciation). This is the amount of the depreciation tax shield.

Annual Taxes and Cash Flow without Depreciation

Sales	$175,000
Operating expenses (except depreciation)	(145,000)
Income taxes	(10,200)
Net annual cash inflow	$ 19,800

Annual Taxes and Cash Flow with Depreciation

Sales	$175,000
Operating expenses (except depreciation)	(145,000)
Income taxes	(4,586)
Net annual cash inflow	$ 25,414

The deductibility of depreciation for tax purposes reduces cash payments for taxes, thus increasing the net cash flow by $5,614 ($25,414 with depreciation − $19,800 without depreciation). This is the amount of the depreciation tax shield.

The U.S. Tax Code contains guidelines concerning the depreciation of various types of assets. (Analysis of these guidelines is beyond the scope of this text.) Tax guidelines allow organizations a choice in tax depreciation procedures between straight-line depreciation and an accelerated depreciation method detailed in the Tax Code. Because of the time value of money, profitable businesses should usually select the tax depreciation procedure that provides the earliest depreciation. To illustrate the effect of accelerated depreciation on taxes and capital budgeting, we use double-declining balance depreciation rather than the accelerated method detailed in the Code. When making capital expenditure decisions, managers should, of course, refer to the most current version of the Tax Code to determine the specific depreciation guidelines in effect at that time.

Exhibits 12.9 and 12.10 illustrate the effect of two alternative depreciation procedures, straight-line and double-declining balance, on the net present value of Mobile Yogurt Shoppe's proposed investment. The cash flows for this investment were presented in Exhibit 12.2, and the effect of taxes on the investment's annual cash flows were examined in Exhibit 12.8. Ignoring taxes, the investment was shown (in Exhibit 12.3) to have a positive net present value of $20,400 at a discount rate of 12 percent. With taxes, the investment has a positive net present value of $3,867 using straight-line depreciation and $6,084 using double-declining balance depreciation. Although taxes and cash flows are identical over the entire life of the project, the use of double-declining balance depreciation for taxes results in a higher net present value because it results in lower cash expenditures for taxes in the earlier years of an asset's life.

EXHIBIT 12.9 Analysis of Capital Expenditures Including Tax Effects: Straight-Line Depreciation

	Predicted Cash Inflows (outflows) (A)	Year(s) of Cash Flows (B)	12% Present Value Factor (C)	Present Value of Cash Flows (A) × (C)
Initial investment				
Vehicle and equipment	$(90,554)	0	1.000	$ (90,554)
Inventory and other working capital.	(4,000)	0	1.000	(4,000)
Operations				
Annual taxable income without depreciation.	30,000	1–5	3.605	108,150
Taxes on income ($30,000 × 0.34)	(10,200)	1–5	3.605	(36,771)
Depreciation tax shield*	5,614	1–5	3.605	20,238
Disinvestment				
Sale of vehicle and equipment	8,000	5	0.567	4,536
Inventory and other working capital.	4,000	5	0.567	2,268
Net present value of all cash flows				$ 3,867

*Computation of depreciation tax shield:

Annual straight-line depreciation	$16,511
Tax rate	× 0.34
Depreciation tax shield	$ 5,614

EXHIBIT 12.10 Analysis of Capital Expenditures Including Tax Effects: DDB Depreciation

	Predicted Cash Inflows (outflows) (A)	Year(s) of Cash Flows (B)	12% Present Value Factor (C)	Present Value of Cash Flows (A) × (C)
Initial investment				
Vehicle and equipment	$(90,554)	0	1.000	$ (90,554)
Inventory and other working capital	4,000	0	1.000	(4,000)
Operations				
Annual taxable income without depreciation.	30,000	1–5	3.605	108,150
Taxes on income ($30,000 × 0.34)	(10,200)	1–5	3.605	(36,771)
Depreciation tax shield*				
Year 1	12,315	1	0.893	10,997
Year 2	7,389	2	0.797	5,889
Year 3	4,434	3	0.712	3,157
Year 4	2,660	4	0.636	1,692
Year 5	1,270	5	0.567	720
Disinvestment				
Sale of vehicle and equipment	8,000	5	0.567	4,536
Inventory and other working capital.	4,000	5	0.567	2,268
Net present value of all cash flows.				$ 6,084

*Computation of depreciation tax shield:

Year	Depreciation Base[†] (A)	Annual Rate (B)	Annual Depreciation (C) = (A) × (B)	Tax Rate (D)	Tax Shield (E) = (C) × (D)
1 . . .	$90,554	2/5	$36,222	0.34	$12,315
2 . . .	54,332	2/5	21,733	0.34	7,389
3 . . .	32,599	2/5	13,040	0.34	4,434
4 . . .	19,559	2/5	7,824	0.34	2,660
5 . . .	11,735	balance	3,735	0.34	1,270

[†]The depreciation base is reduced by the amount of all previous depreciation. The annual rate is twice the straight-line rate. For simplicity, we depreciated the remaining balance in the fifth year and did not switch to straight-line depreciation when the straight-line amount exceeds the double-declining balance amount. This would happen in the fourth year, when $19,559 ÷ 2 = $9,780. Although the depreciable base excludes the predicted disposal value of $8,000, under double declining balance depreciation, an asset is only depreciated down to its disposal value. Hence, year 8 depreciation is computed as the $11,735 depreciable base minus the $8,000 disposal value.

Investment Tax Credit

From time to time, for the purpose of stimulating investment and economic growth, the U.S. federal government has implemented an investment tax credit. An **investment tax credit** reduces taxes in the year a new asset is placed in service by some stated percentage of the cost of the asset. In recent years tax credits, such as the credits for purchasing hybrid automobiles, have been used to stimulate investments that reduce the emission of greenhouses gases. Typically, this is done without reducing the depreciation base of the asset for tax purposes. An investment tax credit reduces cash payments for taxes and, hence, is treated as a cash inflow for capital budgeting purposes. This additional cash inflow increases the probability that a new asset will meet a taxpayer's capital expenditure criteria.

CHAPTER-END REVIEW

Consider the following investment proposal:

Initial investment	
Depreciable assets	$27,740
Working capital	3,000
Operations (per year for 4 years)	
Cash receipts...	25,000
Cash expenditures...	15,000
Disinvestment	
Salvage value of plant and equipment...........................	2,000
Recovery of working capital	3,000

Required
Determine each of the following:
a. Payback period.
b. Accounting rate of return on initial investment and on average investment.

The solution is on page 470.

APPENDIX 12A: Time Value of Money

When asked to choose between $500 today or an IOU for $500 to be paid one year later, rational decision makers choose the $500 today. Two reasons for this involve the time *value of money* and the *risk*. A dollar today is worth more than a dollar tomorrow or at some future time. Having a dollar provides flexibility. It can be spent, buried, or invested in a number of projects. If invested in a savings account, it will amount to more than one dollar at some future time because of the effect of interest. The interest paid by a bank (or borrower) for the use of money is analogous to the rent paid for the use of land, buildings, or equipment. Furthermore, we live in an uncertain world, and, for a variety of reasons, the possibility exists that an IOU might not be paid.

Future Value

Future value is the amount that a current sum of money earning a stated rate of interest will accumulate to at the end of a future period. Suppose we deposit $500 in a savings account at a financial institution that pays interest at the rate of 10 percent per year. At the end of the first year, the original deposit of $500 will total $550 ($500 × 1.10). If we leave the $550 for another year, the amount will increase to $605 ($550 × 1.10). It can be stated that $500 today has a future value in one year of $550, or conversely, that $550 one year from today has a present value of $500. Interest of $55 ($605 − $550) was earned in the second year, whereas interest of only $50 was earned in the first year. This happened because interest during the second year was earned on the principal plus interest from the first year ($550). When periodic interest is computed on principal plus prior periods' accumulated interest, the interest is said to be *compounded*. Compound interest is used throughout this text.

To determine future values at the end of one period (usually a year), multiply the beginning amount (present value) by 1 plus the interest rate. When multiple periods are involved, the future value is determined by repeatedly multiplying the beginning amount by 1 plus the interest rate for each period. When $500 is invested for two years at an interest rate of 10 percent per year, its future value is computed as $500 $\times$ 1.10 $\times$ 1.10. The following equation is used to figure future value:

$$fv = pv(1 + i)^n$$

where:

fv = future value amount
pv = present value amount
i = interest rate per period
n = number of periods

For our $500 deposit, the equation becomes:

$$fv \text{ of } \$500 = pv(1 + i)^n$$
$$= \$500(1 + 0.10)^2$$
$$= \$605$$

In a similar manner, once the interest rate and number of periods are known, the future value amount of any present value amount is easily determined.

Present Value

Present value is the current worth of a specified amount of money to be received at some future date at some interest rate. Solving for pv in the future value equation, the new present value equation is determined as follows:

$$pv = \frac{fv}{(1 + i)^n}$$

Using this equation, the present value of $8,800 to be received in one year, discounted at 10 percent, is computed as follows:

$$pv \text{ of } \$8,800 = \frac{\$8,800}{(1 + 0.10)^1}$$
$$= \frac{\$8,800}{(1.10)}$$
$$= \$8,000$$

Thus, when the discount rate is 10 percent, the present value of $8,800 to be received in one year is $8,000. The present value equation is often expressed as the future value amount times the present value of $1:

$$pv = fv \times \frac{\$1}{(1 + i)^n}$$

Using the equation for the present value of $1, the present value of $8,800 to be received in one year, discounted at 10 percent, is computed as follows:

$$pv \text{ of } \$8,800 = \$8,800 \times \frac{\$1}{(1 + 0.10)^1}$$
$$= \$8,800 \times 0.909$$
$$= \$8,000$$

The present value of $8,800 two periods from now is $7,273, computed as [$8,800 $\div$ $(1.10)^2$] or [$8,800 $\times$ $1 $\div$ $(1.10)^2$].

If a calculator or computer with spreadsheet software is not available, present value computations can be done by hand. Tables, such as Table 12A.1 for the present value of $1 at various interest rates and time periods, can be used to simplify hand computations. Using the factors in Table 12A.1, the present value of any future amount can be determined. For example, with an interest rate of 10 percent, the present value of the following future amounts to be received in one period are as follows:

Future Value Amount		Present Value Factor of $1		Present Value
$ 100	×	0.909	=	$ 90.90
628	×	0.909	=	570.85
4,285	×	0.909	=	3,895.07
9,900	×	0.909	=	8,999.10

To further illustrate the use of Table 12A.1, consider the following application. Suppose Beats Electronics wants to invest its surplus cash at 12 percent to have $10,000 to pay off a long-term note due at the end of five years. Table 12A.1 shows that the present value factor of $1, discounted at 12 percent per year for five years, is 0.567. Multiplying $10,000 by 0.567, the present value is determined to be $5,670:

$$\text{pv of } \$10,000 = \$10,000 \times \textbf{Present value factor for } \$1$$
$$= \$10,000 \times 0.567$$
$$= \$5,670$$

Therefore, if Beats invests $5,670 today, it will have $10,000 available to pay off its note in five years.

Managers also use present value tables to make investment decisions. Assume that Monroe Company can make an investment that will provide a cash flow of $12,000 at the end of eight years. If the company demands a rate of return of 14 percent per year, what is the most it will be willing to pay for this investment? From Table 12A.1, we find that the present value factor for $1, discounted at 14 percent per year for eight years, is 0.351:

$$\text{pv of } \$12,000 = \$12,000 \times \textbf{Present value factor for } \$1$$
$$= \$12,000 \times 0.351$$
$$= \$4,212$$

If the company demands an annual return of 14 percent, the most it would be willing to invest today is $4,212.

Annuities

Not all investments provide a single sum of money. Many investments provide periodic cash flows called *annuities*. An **annuity** is a series of equal cash flows received or paid over equal intervals of time. Suppose that $100 will be received at the end of each of the next three years. If the discount rate is 10 percent, the present value of this annuity can be determined by summing the present value of each receipt:

$$\textbf{Year 1 } \$100 \times \$1 \div (1 + 0.10)^1 = \$ \ 90.90$$
$$\textbf{Year 2 } \$100 \times \$1 \div (1 + 0.10)^2 = \ \ 82.65$$
$$\textbf{Year 3 } \$100 \times \$1 \div (1 + 0.10)^3 = \ \ \underline{75.13}$$
$$\textbf{Total.} \dots \dots \dots \dots \dots \dots \underline{\$248.68}$$

Alternatively, the following equation can be used to compute the present value of an annuity with cash flows at the end of each period:

$$\text{pva} = \frac{a}{i} \times \left[1 - \frac{1}{(1 + i)^n} \right]$$

where:

pva = present value of an annuity (also called the annuity factor)
i = prevailing rate per period
n = number of periods
a = annuity amount

This equation was used to compute the factors presented in Table 12A.2 for an annuity amount of $1. The present value of an annuity of $1 per period for three periods discounted at 10 percent per period is as follows:

$$\text{pva of } \$1 = \frac{1}{0.10} \times \left[1 - \frac{1}{(1 + 0.10)^3} \right]$$
$$= 2.4868$$

TABLE 12A.1   Present Value of $1

$$\text{Present value of } \$1 = \frac{1}{(1 + r)^n}$$

Discount rate (r)

Periods (n)	6%	8%	10%	12%	14%	16%	18%	20%	22%	24%	26%	28%	30%
1	0.943	0.926	0.909	0.893	0.877	0.862	0.847	0.833	0.820	0.806	0.794	0.781	0.769
2	0.890	0.857	0.826	0.797	0.769	0.743	0.718	0.694	0.672	0.650	0.630	0.610	0.592
3	0.840	0.794	0.751	0.712	0.675	0.641	0.609	0.579	0.551	0.524	0.500	0.477	0.455
4	0.792	0.735	0.683	0.636	0.592	0.552	0.516	0.482	0.451	0.423	0.397	0.373	0.350
5	0.747	0.681	0.621	0.567	0.519	0.476	0.437	0.402	0.370	0.341	0.315	0.291	0.269
6	0.705	0.630	0.564	0.507	0.456	0.410	0.370	0.335	0.303	0.275	0.250	0.227	0.207
7	0.665	0.583	0.513	0.452	0.400	0.354	0.314	0.279	0.249	0.222	0.198	0.178	0.159
8	0.627	0.540	0.467	0.404	0.351	0.305	0.266	0.233	0.204	0.179	0.157	0.139	0.123
9	0.592	0.500	0.424	0.361	0.308	0.263	0.225	0.194	0.167	0.144	0.125	0.108	0.094
10	0.558	0.463	0.386	0.322	0.270	0.227	0.191	0.162	0.137	0.116	0.099	0.085	0.073
11	0.527	0.429	0.350	0.287	0.237	0.195	0.162	0.135	0.112	0.094	0.079	0.066	0.056
12	0.497	0.397	0.319	0.257	0.208	0.168	0.137	0.112	0.092	0.076	0.062	0.052	0.043
13	0.469	0.368	0.290	0.229	0.182	0.145	0.116	0.093	0.075	0.061	0.050	0.040	0.033
14	0.442	0.340	0.263	0.205	0.160	0.125	0.099	0.078	0.062	0.049	0.039	0.032	0.025
15	0.417	0.315	0.239	0.183	0.140	0.108	0.084	0.065	0.051	0.040	0.031	0.025	0.020
16	0.394	0.292	0.218	0.163	0.123	0.093	0.071	0.054	0.042	0.032	0.025	0.019	0.015
17	0.371	0.270	0.198	0.146	0.108	0.080	0.060	0.045	0.034	0.026	0.020	0.015	0.012
18	0.350	0.250	0.180	0.130	0.095	0.069	0.051	0.038	0.028	0.021	0.016	0.012	0.009
19	0.331	0.232	0.164	0.116	0.083	0.060	0.043	0.031	0.023	0.017	0.012	0.009	0.007
20	0.312	0.215	0.149	0.104	0.073	0.051	0.037	0.026	0.019	0.014	0.010	0.007	0.005

TABLE 12A.2   Present Value of an Annuity of $1

$$\text{Present value of an annuity of } \$1 = \frac{1}{r} \times \left[1 - \frac{1}{(1 + r)^n} \right]$$

Discount rate (r)

Periods (n)	6%	8%	10%	12%	14%	16%	18%	20%	22%	24%	25%	26%	28%	30%
1	0.943	0.926	0.909	0.893	0.877	0.862	0.847	0.833	0.820	0.806	0.800	0.794	0.781	0.769
2	1.833	1.783	1.736	1.690	1.647	1.605	1.566	1.528	1.492	1.457	1.440	1.424	1.392	1.361
3	2.673	2.577	2.487	2.402	2.322	2.246	2.174	2.106	2.042	1.981	1.952	1.923	1.868	1.816
4	3.465	3.312	3.170	3.037	2.914	2.798	2.690	2.589	2.494	2.404	2.362	2.320	2.241	2.166
5	4.212	3.993	3.791	3.605	3.433	3.274	3.127	2.991	2.864	2.745	2.689	2.635	2.532	2.436
6	4.917	4.623	4.355	4.111	3.889	3.685	3.498	3.326	3.167	3.020	2.951	2.885	2.759	2.643
7	5.582	5.206	4.868	4.564	4.288	4.039	3.812	3.605	3.416	3.242	3.161	3.083	2.937	2.802
8	6.210	5.747	5.335	4.968	4.639	4.344	4.078	3.837	3.619	3.421	3.329	3.241	3.076	2.925
9	6.802	6.247	5.759	5.328	4.946	4.607	4.303	4.031	3.786	3.566	3.463	3.366	3.184	3.019
10	7.360	6.710	6.145	5.650	5.216	4.833	4.494	4.192	3.923	3.682	3.571	3.465	3.269	3.092
11	7.887	7.139	6.495	5.938	5.453	5.029	4.656	4.327	4.035	3.776	3.656	3.544	3.335	3.147
12	8.384	7.536	6.814	6.194	5.660	5.197	4.793	4.439	4.127	3.851	3.725	3.606	3.387	3.190
13	8.853	7.904	7.103	6.424	5.842	5.342	4.910	4.533	4.203	3.912	3.780	3.656	3.427	3.223
14	9.295	8.244	7.367	6.628	6.002	5.468	5.008	4.611	4.265	3.962	3.824	3.695	3.459	3.249
15	9.712	8.559	7.606	6.811	6.142	5.575	5.092	4.675	4.315	4.001	3.859	3.726	3.483	3.268
16	10.106	8.851	7.824	6.974	6.265	5.669	5.162	4.730	4.357	4.033	3.887	3.751	3.503	3.283
17	10.477	9.122	8.022	7.120	6.373	5.749	5.222	4.775	4.391	4.059	3.910	3.771	3.518	3.295
18	10.828	9.372	8.201	7.250	6.467	5.818	5.273	4.812	4.419	4.080	3.928	3.786	3.529	3.304
19	11.158	9.604	8.365	7.366	6.550	5.877	5.316	4.844	4.442	4.097	3.942	3.799	3.539	3.311
20	11.470	9.818	8.514	7.469	6.623	5.929	5.353	4.870	4.460	4.110	3.954	3.808	3.546	3.316

Using this factor, the present value of a $100 annuity can be computed as $100 × 2.4868, which yields $248.68. To determine the present value of an annuity of any amount, the annuity factor for $1 can be multiplied by the annuity amount.

To further illustrate the use of Table 12A.2, assume that Red Kite Company is considering an investment in a piece of equipment that will produce net cash inflows of $2,000 at the end of each year for five years. If the company's desired rate of return is 12 percent, an investment of $7,210 will provide such a return:

$$\text{pva of } \$2,000 = \$2,000 \times \begin{array}{l}\textbf{Present value for an annuity of \$1}\\ \textbf{for five periods discounted at 12\%}\end{array}$$

$$= \$2,000 \times 3.605$$

$$= \$7,210$$

Here, the $2,000 annuity is multiplied by 3.605, the factor for an annuity of $1 for five periods found in Table 12A.2, discounted at 12 percent per period.

Another use of Table 12A.2 is to determine the amount that must be received annually to provide a desired rate of return on an investment. Assume that **Corning** invests $33,550 in a piece of machinery and desires a return of the investment plus interest of 8 percent in equal year-end payments for ten years. The minimum amount that must be received each year is determined by solving the equation for the present value of an annuity:

$$\text{pva} = a \times (\text{pva of } \$1)$$

$$a = \frac{\text{pva}}{\text{pva of } \$1}$$

From Table 12A.2, we see that the 8 percent factor for ten periods is 6.710. Dividing the $33,550 investment by 6.710, the required annuity is computed to be $5,000:

$$a = \frac{\$33,550}{6.710}$$

$$= \$5,000$$

Unequal Cash Flows

Many investment situations do not produce equal periodic cash flows. When this occurs, the present value for each cash flow must be determined independently because the annuity table can be used only for equal periodic cash flows. Table 12A.1 is used to determine the present value of each future amount separately. To illustrate, assume that the **Atlanta Braves** wish to acquire the contract of a popular baseball player who is known to attract large crowds. Management believes this player will return incremental cash flows to the team at the end of each of the next three years in the amounts of $2,500,000, $4,000,000, and $1,500,000. After three years, the player anticipates retiring. If the team's owners require a minimum return of 14 percent on their investment, how much would they be willing to pay for the player's contract?

To solve this problem, it is necessary to determine the present value of the expected future cash flows. Here we use Table 12A.1 to find the $1 present value factors at 14 percent for Periods 1, 2, and 3. The cash flows are then multiplied by these factors:

Year	Annual Cash Flow		Present Value of $1 at 14 Percent		Present Value Amount
1	$2,500,000	×	0.877	=	$2,192,500
2	4,000,000	×	0.769	=	3,076,000
3	1,500,000	×	0.675	=	1,012,500
Total					$6,281,000

The total present value of the cash flows for the three years, $6,281,000, represents the maximum amount the team would be willing to pay for the player's contract.

Deferred Returns

Many times, organizations make investments for which they receive no cash until several periods have passed. The present value of an investment discounted at 12 percent per year, which has a $2,000 return only at the end of Years 4, 5, and 6, can be determined as follows:

Year	Amount		Present Value of $1 at 12 Percent		Present Value Amount
1...	$ 0	×	0.893	=	$ 0
2...	0	×	0.797	=	0
3...	0	×	0.712	=	0
4...	2,000	×	0.636	=	1,272
5...	2,000	×	0.567	=	1,134
6...	2,000	×	0.507	=	1,014
Total..					$3,420

Computation of the present value of the deferred annuity can also be performed using the annuity tables if the cash flow amounts are equal for each period. The present value of an annuity for six years minus the present value of an annuity for three years yields the present value of an annuity for Years 4 through 6.

Present value of an annuity for 6 years at 12 percent: $2,000 × 4.111 = ... $8,222
Present value of an annuity for 3 years at 12 percent: 2,000 × 2.402 = ... (4,804)

Present value of the deferred annuity $3,418*

*The difference between the $3,420 above and the $3,418 here is due to rounding.

APPENDIX 12B: Table Approach to Determining Internal Rate of Return

We consider the use of present value tables to determine the internal rate of return of a series of cash flows with (1) equal net cash flows after the initial investment and (2) unequal net cash flows after the initial investment.

Equal Cash Inflows

An investment proposal's internal rate of return is easily determined when a single investment is followed by a series of equal annual net cash flows. The general relationship between the initial investment and the equal annual cash inflows is expressed as follows:

$$\text{Initial investment} = \text{Present value factor for an annuity of \$1} \times \text{Annual net cash inflow}$$

Solve for the appropriate present value factor as follows:

$$\text{Present value factor for an annuity of \$1} = \frac{\text{Initial investment}}{\text{Annual net cash inflows}}$$

Once the present value factor is calculated, use Table 12A.2 and go across the row corresponding to the expected life of the project until a table factor equal to or closest to the project's computed present value factor is found. The corresponding percentage for the present value factor is the proposal's internal rate of return. If a table factor does not exactly equal the proposal's present value factor, a more accurate answer can be obtained by interpolation (which is not discussed in this text).

To illustrate, assume that Mobile Yogurt Shoppe's proposed investment has a zero disinvestment value. Using all information in Exhibit 12.2 (except that for disinvestment), the proposal's present value factor is 3.152:

$$\text{Present value factor for an annuity of \$1} = \frac{\text{Initial investment}}{\text{Annual net cash inflows}}$$

$$= \frac{\$94,554}{\$30,000}$$

$$= 3.152$$

Using Table 12A.2, go across the row for five periods; the closest table factor is 3.127, which corresponds to an internal rate of return of 18 percent.

Unequal Cash Inflows

If periodic cash flows subsequent to the initial investment are unequal, the simple procedure of determining a present value factor and looking up the closest corresponding factor in Table 12A.2 cannot be used. Instead, a trial-and-error approach must be used to determine the internal rate of return.

The first step is to select a discount rate estimated to be close to the proposal's IRR and to compute the proposal's net present value. If the resulting net present value is zero, the selected discount rate is the actual rate of return. However, it is unlikely that the first rate selected will be the proposal's IRR. If the computation results in a positive net present value, the actual IRR is higher than the initially selected rate. In this case, the next step is to compute the proposal's net present value using a higher rate. If the second computation produces a negative net present value, the actual IRR is less than the selected rate. Therefore, the actual IRR is between the first and the second rates. This trial-and-error approach continues until a discount rate is found that equates the proposal's cash inflows and outflows. For Mobile Yogurt Shoppe's investment proposal outlined in Exhibit 12.2, the details of the trial-and-error approach are presented in Exhibit 12B.1.

In Exhibit 12B.1 the first rate produced a negative net present value, indicating that the proposal's IRR is less than 24 percent. To produce a positive net present value, a smaller rate was selected for the second trial. Since the second rate produced a positive net present value, the proposal's true IRR must be between 16 and 24 percent. The 20 percent rate selected for the third trial produced a net present value of zero, indicating that this is the proposal's IRR.

EXHIBIT 12B.1	**Internal Rate of Return with Unequal Cash Flows**				

First trial with a 24 percent discount rate

	Predicted Cash Inflows (outflows) (A)	Year(s) of Cash Flows (B)	24% Present Value Factor (C)	Present Value of Cash Flows (A) × (C)
Initial investment	$(94,554)	0	1.000	$(94,554)
Operation.	30,000	1–5	2.745	82,350
Disinvestment	12,000	5	0.341	4,092
Net present value of all cash flows.				$ (8,112)

Second trial with a 16 percent discount rate

	Predicted Cash Inflows (outflows) (A)	Year(s) of Cash Flows (B)	16% Present Value Factor (C)	Present Value of Cash Flows (A) × (C)
Initial investment	$(94,554)	0	1.000	$(94,554)
Operation.	30,000	1–5	3.274	98,220
Disinvestment	12,000	5	0.476	5,712
Net present value of all cash flows.				$ 9,378

Third trial with a 20 percent discount rate

	Predicted Cash Inflows (outflows) (A)	Year(s) of Cash Flows (B)	20% Present Value Factor (C)	Present Value of Cash Flows (A) × (C)
Initial investment	$(94,554)	0	1.000	$(94,554)
Operation.	30,000	1–5	2.991	89,730
Disinvestment	12,000	5	0.402	4,824
Net present value of all cash flows.				$ 0

GUIDANCE ANSWERS . . . YOU MAKE THE CALL

You Are the Vice President of Finance There is no single correct response to this question. It is useful to start by learning how other companies in similar circumstances handle capital expenditure decisions. This might be done through personal contacts or through professional organizations, such as the Financial Executives Institute. Another starting point might be the formation of a small capital budgeting committee, which could be expanded as necessary once formal procedures were in place. Early tasks of the committee might include developing guidelines for the size of expenditures at various organizational levels subject to committee review and developing guidelines for the criteria used in formal reviews. You would want to ensure that the CEO is in agreement with these proposals. If the company has a board of directors, you would also want some mutual understanding of the board's role in the approval of capital expenditures. Finally, you would want to make clear the importance of a post-audit review.

KEY RATIOS

$$\text{Cost of equity capital} = \frac{\text{Current annual dividend per common share}}{\text{Current market price per common share}} + \text{Expected dividend growth rate}$$

$$\text{Payback period} = \frac{\text{Initial investment}}{\text{Annual operating cash inflows}}$$

$$\text{Accounting rate of return on initial investment} = \frac{\text{Average annual increase in net income}}{\text{Initial investment}}$$

$$\text{Accounting rate of return on average investment} = \frac{\text{Average annual increase in net income}}{\text{Average investment}}$$

$$\text{Depreciation tax shield} = \text{Depreciation} \times \text{Tax rate}$$

$$fv = pv(1 + i)^n$$
Where: fv = future value amount, pv = present value amount, i = interest rate per period, n = number of periods.

$$pv = \frac{fv}{(1 + i)^n}$$
Where: fv = future value amount, pv = present value amount, i = interest rate per period, n = number of periods.

$$pva = \frac{a}{i} \times \left[1 - \frac{1}{(1 + i)^n} \right]$$
Where: pva = present value of an annuity, i = prevailing rate per period, n = number of periods, a = annuity amount.

$$\text{Present value factor for an annuity of \$1} = \frac{\text{Initial investment}}{\text{Annual net cash flows}}$$

KEY TERMS

MULTIPLE CHOICE

The following table is presented for use with questions 1, 2, and 3.

Periods	Present value of $1			Present value of an annuity of $1		
	8%	10%	12%	8%	10%	12%
1	0.926	0.909	0.893	0.926	0.909	0.893
2	0.857	0.826	0.797	1.783	1.736	1.690
3	0.794	0.751	0.712	2.577	2.487	2.402
4	0.735	0.683	0.636	3.312	3.170	3.037

1. Max is considering an investment proposal that requires an initial investment of $91,100, has predicted cash inflows of $30,000 per year for four years and no salvage value. At a discount rate of 10 percent the projects net present value is:
   a. $4,000
   b. $20,490
   c. $24,490
   d. $95,100

2. The internal rate of return of the investment proposal presented in question 1 is:
   a. 8 percent
   b. 10 percent
   c. 12 percent
   d. Less than 8 percent

3. The Pepper Shop is evaluating a capital expenditure proposal with the following predicted cash flows:

Initial investment	$(40,000)
Operations, each year for four years	15,000
Salvage	5,000

   At a discount rate of 12 percent, the project's net present value is:
   a. $2,375
   b. $5,555
   c. $8,735
   d. $20,740

4. The payback period of the investment proposal presented in question 3 is:
   a. 0.37 years
   b. 0.50 years
   c. 2.00 years
   d. 2.67 years

5. The accounting rate of return on the initial investment presented in question 3 is:
   a. 0.125
   b. 0.156
   c. 0.219
   d. 0.375

Superscript [A] denotes assignments based on Appendix 12A.

DISCUSSION QUESTIONS

Q12-1. What is the relationship between long-range planning and capital budgeting?

Q12-2. What tasks are often assigned to the capital budgeting committee?

Q12-3. What purposes are served by a post-audit of approved capital expenditure proposals?

Q12-4. Into what three phases are a project's cash flows organized?

Q12-5. State three alternative definitions or descriptions of the internal rate of return.

Q12-6. Why is the cost of capital an important concept when discounting models are used for capital budgeting?

Q12-7. What weakness is inherent in the payback period when it is used as the sole investment criterion?

Q12-8. What weakness is inherent in the accounting rate of return when it is used as an investment criterion?

Q12-9. Why are the net present value and the internal rate of return models superior to the payback period and the accounting rate of return models?

Q12-10. State two basic differences between the net present value and the internal rate of return models that often lead to differences in the evaluation of competing investment proposals.

Q12-11. Identify several nonquantitative factors that are apt to play a decisive role in the final selection of projects for capital expenditures.

Q12-12. In what way does depreciation affect the analysis of cash flows for a proposed capital expenditure?

Assignments with the ✓ logo in the margin are available in BusinessCourse.
See the Preface of the book for details.

MINI EXERCISES

M12-13.^{A} **Time Value of Money: Basics** LO2

Using the equations and tables in Appendix 12A of this chapter, determine the answers to each of the following independent situations:

a. The future value in two years of $2,000 deposited today in a savings account with interest compounded annually at 6 percent.

b. The present value of $8,000 to be received in four years, discounted at 12 percent.

c. The present value of an annuity of $2,000 per year for five years discounted at 14 percent.

d. An initial investment of $32,010 is to be returned in eight equal annual payments. Determine the amount of each payment if the interest rate is 12 percent.

e. A proposed investment will provide cash flows of $20,000, $8,000, and $6,000 at the end of Years 1, 2, and 3, respectively. Using a discount rate of 20 percent, determine the present value of these cash flows.

f. Find the present value of an investment that will pay $5,000 at the end of Years 10, 11, and 12. Use a discount rate of 14 percent.

M12-14.^{A} **Time Value of Money: Basics** LO2

Using the equations and tables in Appendix 12A of this chapter, determine the answers to each of the following independent situations:

a. The future value in two years of $5,000 invested today in a certificate of deposit with interest compounded annually at 10 percent.

b. The present value of $6,000 to be received in five years, discounted at 8 percent.

c. The present value of an annuity of $15,000 per year for four years discounted at 12 percent.

d. An initial investment of $29,480 is to be returned in six equal annual payments. Determine the amount of each payment if the interest rate is 16 percent.

e. A proposed investment will provide cash flows of $6,000, $8,000, and $20,000 at the end of Years 1, 2, and 3, respectively. Using a discount rate of 16 percent, determine the present value of these cash flows.

f. Find the present value of an investment that will pay $6,000 at the end of Years 8, 9, and 10. Use a discount rate of 12 percent.

M12-15. **NPV and IRR: Equal Annual Net Cash Inflows** LO2

Apache Junction Company is evaluating a capital expenditure proposal that requires an initial investment of $9,350, has predicted cash inflows of $2,000 per year for 15 years, and has no salvage value.

Required

a. Using a discount rate of 14 percent, determine the net present value of the investment proposal.

b. Determine the proposal's internal rate of return. (Refer to Appendix 12B if you use the table approach.)

c. What discount rate would produce a net present value of zero?

LO2 **M12-16. NPV and IRR: Equal Annual Net Cash Inflows**

Snow Devil Company is evaluating a capital expenditure proposal that requires an initial investment of $32,312, has predicted cash inflows of $8,000 per year for seven years, and has no salvage value.

Required

a. Using a discount rate of 10 percent, determine the net present value of the investment proposal.

b. Determine the proposal's internal rate of return. (Refer to Appendix 12B if you use the table approach.)

c. What discount rate would produce a net present value of zero?

LO3 **M12-17. Payback Period and Accounting Rate of Return: Equal Annual Operating Cash Flows without Disinvestment**

Amanda is considering an investment proposal with the following cash flows:

Initial investment—depreciable assets	$80,000
Net cash inflows from operations (per year for 5 years)	20,000
Disinvestment	0

Required

a. Determine the payback period

b. Determine the accounting rate of return on initial investment

c. Determine the accounting rate of return on average investment

LO3 **M12-18. Payback Period and Accounting Rate of Return: Equal Annual Operating Cash Flows with Disinvestment**

Hoi is considering an investment proposal with the following cash flows:

Initial investment—depreciable assets	$150,000
Net cash inflows from operations (per year for 5 years)	30,000
Disinvestment—depreciable assets.	20,000

Required

a. Determine the payback period

b. Determine the accounting rate of return on initial investment

c. Determine the accounting rate of return on average investment

LO3 **M12-19. Payback Period and Accounting Rate of Return: Equal Annual Operating Cash Flows with Disinvestment**

Khazanchi is considering an investment proposal with the following cash flows:

Initial investment—depreciable assets	$90,000
Initial investment—working capital.	12,500
Net cash inflows from operations (per year for 8 years)	25,000
Disinvestment—depreciable assets.	10,000
Disinvestment—working capital.	12,500

Required

a. Determine the payback period

b. Determine the accounting rate of return on initial investment

c. Determine the accounting rate of return on average investment

EXERCISES

E12-20. **NPV and IRR: Unequal Annual Net Cash Inflows**

LO2

GOODRICH
PETROLEUM
CORPORATION
(GDP)

Assume that Goodrich Petroleum Corporation is evaluating a capital expenditure proposal that has the following predicted cash flows:

Initial investment	$(82,850)
Operation	
Year 1	30,000
Year 2	50,000
Year 3	40,000
Salvage	0

Required

a. Using a discount rate of 12 percent, determine the net present value of the investment proposal.

b. Determine the proposal's internal rate of return. (Refer to Appendix 12B if you use the table approach.)

E12-21. **NPV and IRR: Unequal Annual Net Cash Inflows**

LO2

Salt River Company is evaluating a capital expenditure proposal that has the following predicted cash flows:

Initial investment	$(42,070)
Operation	
Year 1	20,000
Year 2	30,000
Year 3	10,000
Salvage	0

Required

a. Using a discount rate of 14 percent, determine the net present value of the investment proposal.

b. Determine the proposal's internal rate of return. (Refer to Appendix 12B if you use the table approach.)

E12-22. **Payback Period, IRR, and Minimum Cash Flows**

LO2, 3

The management of Mesquite Limited is currently evaluating the following investment proposal:

	Time 0	Year 1	Year 2	Year 3	Year 4
Initial investment	$250,000	—	—	—	—
Net operating cash inflows	—	$100,000	$100,000	$100,000	$100,000

Required

a. Determine the proposal's payback period.

b. Determine the proposal's internal rate of return. (Refer to Appendix 12B if you use the table approach.)

c. Given the amount of the initial investment, determine the minimum annual net cash inflows required to obtain an internal rate of return of 16 percent. Round the answer to the nearest dollar.

E12-23. **Time-Adjusted Cost-Volume-Profit Analysis**

LO2, 3

Boardwalk Treat Shop is considering the desirability of producing a new chocolate candy called Pleasure Bombs. Before purchasing the new equipment required to manufacture Pleasure Bombs, Marty Dey, the shop's proprietor performed the following analysis:

Unit selling price	$1.45
Variable manufacturing and selling costs	(1.15)
Unit contribution margin	$0.30

Annual fixed costs

Depreciation (straight-line for 4 years)	$15,000
Other (all cash)	30,000
Total	$45,000

Annual break-even sales volume = $45,000 ÷ $0.30 = 150,000 units

Because the expected annual sales volume is 160,000 units, Dey decided to undertake the production of Pleasure Bombs. This required an immediate investment of $60,000 in equipment that has a life of four years and no salvage value. After four years, the production of Pleasure Bombs will be discontinued.

Required

a. Evaluate the analysis performed by Dey.

b. If Boardwalk Treat Shop has a time value of money of 12 percent, should it make the investment with projected annual sales of 160,000 units?

c. Considering the time value of money, what annual unit sales volume is required to break even?

LO6 E12-24. Time-Adjusted Cost-Volume-Profit Analysis with Income Taxes

Assume the same facts as given in Exercise E12-23 for the Boardwalk Treat Shop.

Required

With a 40 percent tax rate and a 12 percent time value of money, determine the annual unit sales required to break even on a time-adjusted basis. Assume straight-line depreciation is used to determine tax payments.

LO2, 3 E12-25. Payback Period and IRR of a Cost Reduction Proposal—Differential Analysis

A light-emitting diode (LED) is a semiconductor diode that emits narrow-spectrum light. Although relatively expensive when compared to incandescent bulbs, they use significantly less energy and last six to ten times longer, with a slow decline in performance rather than an abrupt failure.

New York City currently has 80,000 incandescent bulbs in traffic lights at approximately 12,000 intersections. It is estimated that replacing all the incandescent bulbs with LED will cost $28 million. However, the investment is also estimated to save the City $6.3 million per year in energy costs.[1]

Required

a. Determine the payback period of converting New York City traffic lights to LEDs.

b. If the average life of an incandescent streetlight is one year and the average life of an LED street-light is seven years, should the City finance the investment in LED's at an interest rate of five percent per year? Justify your answer.

LO2, 3 E12-26. Payback Period and NPV of a Cost Reduction Proposal—Differential Analysis

Mary Zimmerman decided to purchase a new automobile. Being concerned about environmental issues, she is leaning toward the hybrid rather than the gasoline only model. Nevertheless, as a new business school graduate, she wants to determine if there is an economic justification for purchasing the hybrid, which costs $1,400 more than the regular model. She has determined that city/highway combined gas mileage of the hybrid and regular models are 27 and 23 miles per gallon respectively. Mary anticipates she will travel an average of 12,000 miles per year for the next several years.

Required

a. Determine the payback period of the incremental investment if gasoline costs $3.60 per gallon.

---

[1] Based on "Mayors Take the Lead," *Newsweek*, April 16, 2007, pp. 68-73.

b. Assuming that Mary plans to keep the car five years and does not believe there will be a trade-in premium associated with the hybrid model, determine the net present value of the incremental investment at an eight percent time value of money.

c. Determine the cost of gasoline required for a payback period of three years.

d. At $4.15 per gallon, determine the gas mileage required for a payback period of three years.

E12-27. Payback Period and NPV of Alternative Automobile Purchase   LO2, 3

Bob Wu decided to purchase a new Honda Civic. Being concerned about environmental issues he is leaning toward a Honda Civic Hybrid rather than the completely gasoline-powered LX model. Nevertheless, he wants to determine if there is an economic justification for purchasing the Hybrid, which costs $6,000 more than the LX. Based on a mix of city and highway driving he predicts that the average gas mileage of each car is 40 MPG for the Hybrid and 30 MPG for the LX. Bob also anticipates he will drive an average of 12,000 miles per year and that gasoline will cost an average of $3.75 per gallon over the next five years. He also plans to replace whichever car he purchases at the end of five years when the resale values of the Hybrid and the LX are predicted to be $11,000 and $8,500 respectively.[2]

Required

a. Determine the payback period of the incremental investment associated with purchasing the Hybrid.

b. Determine the net present value of the incremental investment associated with purchasing the Hybrid at an eight percent time value of money.

c. Determine the cost of gasoline required for a payback period of three years on the incremental investment.

d. Identify other factors Bob should consider before making his decision.

PROBLEMS

P12-28. Ranking Investment Proposals: Payback Period, Accounting Rate of Return, and Net Present Value   LO2, 3, 4

Presented is information pertaining to the cash flows of three mutually exclusive investment proposals:

	Proposal A	Proposal B	Proposal C
Initial investment	$45,000	$45,000	$45,000
Cash flow from operations			
Year 1	40,000	22,500	45,000
Year 2	5,000	22,500	
Year 3	22,500	22,500	
Disinvestment	0	0	0
Life (years)	3 years	3 years	1 year

Required

a. Rank these investment proposals using the payback period, the accounting rate of return on initial investment, and the net present value criteria. Assume that the organization's cost of capital is 12 percent. Round calculations to four decimal places.

b. Explain the difference in rankings. Which investment would you recommend?

P12-29. Cost Reduction Proposal: IRR, NPV, and Payback Period   LO2, 3

JB Chemical currently discharges liquid waste into Calgary's municipal sewer system. However, the Calgary municipal government has informed JB that a surcharge of $4 per thousand cubic liters will soon be imposed for the discharge of this waste. This has prompted management to evaluate the desirability of treating its own liquid waste.

A proposed system consists of three elements. The first is a retention basin, which would permit unusual discharges to be held and treated before entering the downstream system. The second is

---

[2] Based on Robert L. Barker, Ronald Clouse, Thomas G. Stout, and Gary R. Stout, "The Economics of Buying a More Fuel Efficient Automobile: An Interactive Analysis," *Journal of Financial Planning*, June 2009, pp.62-71.

a continuous self-cleaning rotary filter required where solids are removed. The third is an automated neutralization process required where materials are added to control the alkalinity-acidity range.

The system is designed to process 500,000 liters a day. However, management anticipates that only about 200,000 liters of liquid waste would be processed in a normal workday. The company operates 300 days per year. The initial investment in the system would be $450,000, and annual operating costs are predicted to be $142,000. The system has a predicted useful life of ten years and a salvage value of $50,000.

Required

a. Determine the project's net present value at a discount rate of 16 percent.
b. Determine the project's approximate internal rate of return. (Refer to Appendix 12B if you use the table approach.)
c. Determine the project's payback period.

LO2, 6 P12-30. NPV with Income Taxes: Straight-Line versus Accelerated Depreciation

John Paul Jones Inc. is a conservatively managed boat company whose motto is, "The old ways are the good ways." Management has always used straight-line depreciation for tax and external reporting purposes. Although they are reluctant to change, they are aware of the impact of taxes on a project's profitability.

Required

For a typical $120,000 investment in equipment with a five-year life and no salvage value, determine the present value of the advantage resulting from the use of double-declining balance depreciation as opposed to straight-line depreciation. Assume an income tax rate of 35 percent and a discount rate of 16 percent. Also assume that there will be a switch from double-declining balance to straight-line depreciation in the fourth year.

LO2, 3, 6 P12-31. Payback Period and NPV: Taxes and Straight-Line Depreciation

UNITED
TECHNOLOGIES
CORPORATION
(UTX)

Assume that United Technologies Corporation is evaluating a proposal to change the company's manual design system to a computer-aided design (CAD) system. The proposed system is expected to save 9,000 design hours per year; an operating cost savings of $45 per hour. The annual cash expenditures of operating the CAD system are estimated to be $200,000. The CAD system requires an initial investment of $550,000. The estimated life of this system is five years with no salvage value. The tax rate is 35 percent, and United Technologies uses straight-line depreciation for tax purposes. United Technologies has a cost of capital of 14 percent.

Required

a. Compute the annual after-tax cash flows related to the CAD project.
b. Compute each of the following for the project:
   1. Payback period.
   2. Net present value.

LO6 P12-32. NPV: Taxes and Accelerated Depreciation

Assume the same facts as given in P12-31, except that management intends to use double-declining balance depreciation with a switch to straight-line depreciation (applied to any undepreciated balance) starting in Year 4.

Required

Determine the project's net present value.

LO2 P12-33. NPV Total and Differential Analysis of Replacement Decision

Gusher Petro is evaluating a proposal to purchase a new processor that would cost $120,000 and have a salvage value of $12,000 in five years. Gusher's cost of capital is 14 percent. It would provide annual operating cash savings of $15,000, as follows:

	Old Processor	New Processor
Salaries	$34,000	$44,000
Supplies	6,000	5,000
Utilities	13,000	6,000
Cleaning and maintenance	22,000	5,000
Total cash expenditures	$75,000	$60,000

If the new processor is purchased, Gusher will sell the old processor for its current salvage value of $35,000. If the new processor is not purchased, the old processor will be disposed of in five years at a predicted scrap value of $3,000. The old processor's present book value is $50,000. If kept, the old processor will require repairs predicted to cost $40,000 in one year.

Required

a. Use the total cost approach to evaluate the alternatives of keeping the old processor and purchasing the new processor. Indicate which alternative is preferred.

b. Use the differential cost approach to evaluate the desirability of purchasing the new processor.

P12-34. NPV Total and Differential Analysis of Replacement Decision   LO2

White Snow Automatic Laundry must either have a complete overhaul of its current dry-cleaning system or purchase a new one. Its cost of capital is 18 percent. White Snow's accountant has developed the following cost projections:

	Present System	New System
Purchase cost (new)	$40,000	$50,000
Remaining book value...........................	15,000	
Overhaul needed................................	20,000	
Annual cash operating costs	35,000	20,000
Current salvage value	10,000	
Salvage value in 5 years	3,000	11,000

If White Snow keeps the old system, it will have to be overhauled immediately. With the overhaul, the old system will have a useful life of five more years.

Required

a. Use the total cost approach to evaluate the alternatives of keeping the old system and purchasing the new system. Indicate which alternative is preferred.

b. Use the differential cost approach to evaluate the desirability of purchasing the new system.

P12-35. NPV Differential Analysis of Replacement Decision   LO2, 5

The management of Essen Manufacturing Company is currently evaluating a proposal to purchase a new, innovative drill press as a replacement for a less efficient piece of similar equipment, which would then be sold. The cost of the equipment, including delivery and installation, is $180,000. If the equipment is purchased, Essen will incur a $5,000 cost in removing the present equipment and revamping service facilities. The present equipment has a book value of $100,000 and a remaining useful life of ten years. Because of new technical improvements that have made the present equipment obsolete, it now has a disposal value of only $40,000. Management has provided the following comparison of manufacturing costs:

	Present Equipment	New Equipment
Annual production (units)	400,000	400,000
Annual costs		
Direct labor (per unit).......................	$0.075	$0.05
Overhead		
Depreciation (10% of asset's book value)	$10,000	$18,000
Other.....................................	$48,000	$20,000

Additional information follows:

- Management believes that if the current equipment is not replaced now, it will have to wait ten years before replacement is justifiable.
- Both pieces of equipment are expected to have a negligible salvage value at the end of ten years.
- Management expects to sell the entire annual production of 400,000 units.
- Essen's cost of capital is 12 percent.

Required

Evaluate the desirability of purchasing the new equipment

CASES AND PROJECTS

MORGAN STANLEY
(MS)

LO2, 3, 5   **C12-36.**   **Payback, ARR, and IRR: Evaluating the Sale of Government Assets (Requires Spreadsheet)**

In 2008 the City of Chicago agreed to lease 35,000 parking meters to a **Morgan Stanley**-led partnership for a one-time sum of $1.15 billion. The lease has been criticized as an example of "one-shot" deals arrived at behind closed doors to balance a current budget at the expense of future generations. Some have observed that deals such as this are akin to individuals using their retirement savings to meet current needs, instead of planning for the future. "These deals are rarely done under the light of public scrutiny," says Richard G. Little, director of the Keston Institute for Public Finance at the University of Southern California. "Often the facts come out long after the deal is done."

Since the lease was signed, helped by parking-fee hikes, the partnership has earned a profit before taxes and depreciation of $0.80 per dollar of revenue. Projected revenues over the 75-year life of the lease are now projected at $11.6 billion.

Defending the city's action, Gene Saffold, Chicago's chief financial officer, stated that "The concession agreement was absolutely the best deal for Chicagoans. ... The net present value of $11.6 billion in revenue over the life of the 75-year agreement is consistent with $1.15 billion.[3]

Required

Evaluate the 75-year lease and determine if the projected revenues are consistent with the initial investment. To simplify your analysis assume equal revenues and operating costs in all periods, no investment required in working capital, and no salvage value at the end of the lease. Suggested elements of your solution include:

a.   Determine the payback period in the absence of taxes.
b.   Determine the accounting rate of return on the initial investment in the absence of taxes.
c.   Determine the accounting rate of return on the initial investment with a tax rate of 0.34.
d.   Determine the internal rate of return in the absence of taxes.
e.   Determine the internal rate of return with a tax rate of 0.34.
f.   Summary of analysis and conclusions.

LO2, 5   **C12-37.**   **Determining Terms of Automobile Leases (Requires Spreadsheet)**

Avant-Garde Motor Company has asked you to develop lease terms for the firm's popular Avant-Garde Challenger, which has an average selling price (new) of $26,000. You know that leasing is attractive because it assists consumers in obtaining new vehicles with a small down payment and "reasonable" monthly payments. Market analysts have told you that to attract the widest number of young professionals, the Challenger must have an initial down payment of no more than $1,000, monthly payments of no more than $470, and lease terms of no more than three years. When the lease expires, Avant-Garde will sell the used Challengers at the automobile's resale market price at that time. It is difficult to predict the future price of the increasingly popular Challenger, but you have obtained the following information on the average resale prices of used Challengers:

Age	Resale Price
1 year	$21,000
2 years	19,500
3 years	17,000
4 years	14,500
5 years	13,500

Avant-Garde's cost of capital is 18 percent per year, or 1.5 percent per month.

Required

a.   With the aid of spreadsheet software, develop a competitive and profitable lease payment program. Assume the down payment and the first lease payment are made immediately and that all subsequent lease payments are made at the start of the month. [Hint: Most software

---

[3] "Windfall for Investors, A Loss for the Windy City," *Bloomberg Businessweek*, August 29, 2010, pp. 44-45; Ianthe Jeanne Dugan, "Facing Budget Gaps, Cities Sell Parking, Airports, Zoo," *The Wall Street Journal*, August 23, 2010, pp. A1, A12.

packages include a function such as the following: PMT (rate,nper,pv,fv,type), where rate = the time value of money; nper = the number of periods; pv = the present value; fv = the future value; and type = 0 (when the payment is at the end of the period) or 1 (when the payment is at the beginning of the period). For monthly payments, rate should be set at the annual rate divided by 12, and npr should be set at the number of months in the lease. Here, fv is the residual value. Consider the residual value as a future value and enter it as a negative number, indicating the lessor has not paid the full cost of the car.]

b.   Reevaluate the lease program assuming a down payment of $2,000.

c.   Reevaluate the lease program assuming a down payment of $1,000 and a $2,000 increase in residual values.

d.   Reevaluate the lease program assuming a down payment of $2,000 and a $2,000 increase in residual values.

e.   What is your final recommendation? What risks are associated with your recommendation? Are there any other actions to consider?

C12-38.   **Evaluating Data and Using Payback Period for an Investment Proposal**   **LO3, 5**
To determine the desirability of investing in a 21-inch monitor (as opposed to the typical 17-inch monitor that comes with a new personal computer), researchers developed an experiment testing the time required to perform a set of tasks. The tasks included the following:

- Setting up a meeting using electronic mail.
- Reviewing meeting requests.
- Checking an on-line schedule.
- Embedding a video file into a document.
- Searching a customer database to find a specific set of contracts.
- Copying a database into a spreadsheet.
- Modifying a slide presentation.

The researchers assumed this was a typical set of tasks performed by a manager. They determined that there was a 9 percent productivity gain using the 21-inch monitor. One test manager commented that the largest productivity gain came from being able to have multiple applications open at the same time and from being able to view several files at once.

Required
Accepting the 9 percent productivity gain as accurate, what additional information is needed to determine the payback period of an investment in one 21-inch monitor that is to be used by a manager? Make any necessary assumptions and obtain whatever data you can (perhaps from computer component advertisements) to determine the payback period for the proposed investment.

C12-39.   **IRR and NPV with Performance Evaluation Conflict**   **LO2, 4, 5**
Pepperoni Pizza Company owns and operates fast-service pizza parlors throughout North America. The firm operates on a regional basis and provides almost complete autonomy to the manager of each region. Regional managers are responsible for long-range planning, capital expenditures, personnel policies, pricing, and so forth. Each year the performance of regional managers is evaluated by determining the accounting return on fixed assets in their regions; a return of 14 percent is expected. To determine this return, regional net income is divided by the book value of fixed assets at the start of the year. Managers of regions earning a return of more than 16 percent are identified for possible promotion, and managers of regions with a return of less than 12 percent are subject to replacement.

Mr. Light, with a degree in hotel and restaurant management, is the manager of the Northeast region. He is regarded as a "rising star" and will be considered for promotion during the next two years. Light has been with Pepperoni for a total of three years. During that period, the return on fixed assets in his region (the oldest in the firm) has increased dramatically. He is currently considering a proposal to open five new parlors in the Boston area. The total project involves an investment of $650,000 and will double the number of Pepperoni pizzas sold in the Northeast region to a total of 600,000 per year. At an average price of $6 each, total sales revenue will be $3,600,000.

The expenses of operating each of the new parlors include variable costs of $4 per pizza and fixed costs (excluding depreciation) of $80,000 per year. Because each of the new parlors has only a five-year life and no salvage value, yearly straight-line depreciation will be $26,000 [($650,000 ÷ 5 parlors) ÷ 5 years].

Required

a. Evaluate the desirability of the $650,000 investment in new pizza parlors by computing the internal rate of return and the net present value. Assume a time value of money of 14 percent. (Refer to Appendix 12B if you use the table approach.)

b. If Light is shrewd, will he approve the expansion? Why or why not? (Additional computations are suggested.)

LO2, 5, 6 **C12-40.** **NPV and Project Reevaluation with Taxes, Straight-Line Depreciation**

In 2012, the Bayside Chemical Company prepared the following analysis of an investment proposal for a new manufacturing facility:

	Predicted Cash Inflows (outflows) (A)	Year(s) of Cash Flows (B)	12% Present Value Factor (C)	Present Value of Cash Flows (A) × (C)
Initial investment				
Fixed assets.....................	$(810,000)	0	1.000	$ (810,000)
Working capital	(100,000)	0	1.000	(100,000)
Operations				
Annual taxable income				
without depreciation	310,000	1–5	3.605	1,117,550
Taxes on income				
($310,000 × 0.40)...............	(124,000)	1–5	3.605	(447,020)
Depreciation tax shield	64,800*	1–5	3.605	233,604
Disinvestment				
Site restoration..................	80,000	5	0.567	(45,360)
Tax shield of restoration				
($80,000 × 0.40)...............	32,000	5	0.567	18,144
Working capital	100,000	5	0.567	56,700
Net present value of all cash flows......................................				$ 23,618

*Computation of depreciation tax shield:

Annual straight-line depreciation ($810,000 ÷ 5).............	$162,000
Tax rate	× 0.40
Depreciation tax shield	$ 64,800

Because the proposal had a positive net present value when discounted at Bayside's cost of capital of 12 percent, the project was approved; all investments were made at the end of 2013. Shortly after production began in January 2014, a government agency notified Bayside of required additional expenditures totaling $200,000 to bring the plant into compliance with new federal emission regulations. Bayside has the option either to comply with the regulations by December 31, 2014, or to sell the entire operation (fixed assets and working capital) for $250,000 on December 31, 2014. The improvements will be depreciated over the remaining four-year life of the plant using straight-line depreciation. The cost of site restoration will not be affected by the improvements. If Bayside elects to sell the plant, any book loss can be treated as an offset against taxable income on other operations. This tax reduction is an additional cash benefit of selling.

Required

a. Should Bayside sell the plant or comply with the new federal regulations? To simplify calculations, assume that any additional improvements are paid for on December 31, 2014.

b. Would Bayside have accepted the proposal in 2013 if it had been aware of the forthcoming federal regulations?

c. Do you have any suggestions that might increase the project's net present value? (No calculations are required.)

LO1, 2, 5 **C12-41.** **Post-Audit and Reevaluation of Investment Proposal: NPV**

Anthony Company's capital budgeting committee is evaluating a capital expenditure proposal for the production of a high definition television receiver to be sold as an add-on feature for personal computers. The proposal calls for an independent contractor to construct the necessary facilities by December 31, 2014, at a total cost of $250,000. Payment for all construction costs will be made on that date. An additional $50,000 in cash will also be made available on December 31, 2014, for working capital to support sales and production activities.

Management anticipates that the receiver has a limited market life; there is a high probability that by 2021 all new PCs will have built-in high definition receivers. Accordingly, the proposal specifies that production will cease on December 31, 2020. The investment in working capital will be recovered on that date, and the production facilities will be sold for $30,000. Predicted net cash inflows from operations for 2015 through 2020 are as follows:

2015	$100,000
2016	100,000
2017	100,000
2018	40,000
2019	40,000
2020	40,000

Anthony Company has a time value of money of 14 percent. For capital budgeting purposes, all cash flows are assumed to occur at the end of each year.

Required

a. Evaluate the capital expenditure proposal using the net present value method. Should Anthony accept the proposal?

b. Assume that the capital expenditure proposal is accepted, but construction delays caused by labor problems and difficulties in obtaining the necessary construction permits delay the completion of the project. Payments totaling $200,000 were made to the construction company on December 31, 2014, for that year's construction. However, completion is now scheduled for December 31, 2015, and an additional $100,000 will be required to complete construction. If the project is continued, the additional $100,000 will be paid at the end of 2015, and the plant will begin operations on January 1, 2016.

Because of the cost overruns, the capital budgeting committee requests a reevaluation of the project in early 2015, before agreeing to any additional expenditures. After much effort, the following revised predictions of net operating cash inflows are developed:

2016	$120,000
2017	100,000
2018	40,000
2019	40,000
2020	40,000

The working capital investment and disinvestment and the plant salvage values have not changed, except that the cash for working capital would now be made available on December 31, 2015. Use the net present value method to reevaluate the initial decision to accept the proposal. Given the information currently available about the project, should it have been accepted in 2014? (Hint: Determine the net present value as of December 31, 2014, assuming management has not committed Anthony to the proposal.)

c. Given the situation that exists in early 2015, should management continue or cancel the project? Assume that the facilities have a current salvage value of $50,000. (Hint: Assume that the decision is being made on January 1, 2015.)

C12-42. **Post-Audit and Reevaluation of Investment Proposal: IRR**   LO1, 2, 5

Throughout his four years in college, Ronald King worked at the local Beef Burger Restaurant in College City. Although the working conditions were good and the pay was not bad, Ron believed he could do a much better job of managing the restaurant than the current owner-manager. In particular, Ron believed that the proper use of marketing campaigns and sales incentives, such as selling a second burger for a 25 percent discount, could increase annual sales by 40 percent.

Just before graduation in 2013, Ron inherited $500,000 from his great uncle. He seriously considered buying the restaurant. It seemed like a good idea because he liked the town and its college atmosphere, knew the business, and always wanted to work for himself. He also knew that the current owner wanted to sell the restaurant and retire to Florida. As part of a small business management course, Ron developed the following income statement for the restaurant's 2012 operations:

BEEF BURGER RESTAURANT: COLLEGE CITY
Income Statement
For Year Ended December 31, 2012

Sales		$450,000
Expenses		
Cost of food	$150,000	
Supplies	20,000	
Employee expenses.....................................	140,000	
Utilities	28,000	
Property taxes	20,000	
Insurance	10,000	
Advertising..	8,000	
Depreciation...	60,000	436,000
Net income..		$ 14,000

Ron believed that the cost of food and supplies were all variable, the employee expenses and utilities were one-half variable and one-half fixed in 2012, and all other expenses were fixed. If Ron purchased the restaurant and followed through on his plans, he believed there would be a 40 percent increase in unit sales volume and all variable costs. Of the fixed costs, only advertising would increase by $12,000. The use of discounts and special promotions would, however, limit the increase in sales revenue to only 30 percent even though sales volume increased 40 percent.

Required

a. Determine
  1. The current annual net cash inflow.
  2. The predicted annual net cash inflow if Ron executes his plans and his assumptions are correct.

b. Ron believes his plan would produce equal net cash inflows during each of the next 15 years, the period remaining on a long-term lease for the land on which the restaurant is built. At the end of that time, the restaurant would have to be demolished at a predicted net cost of $80,000. Assuming Ron would otherwise invest the money in stock expected to yield 12 percent, determine the maximum amount he should pay for the restaurant.

c. Assume that Ron accepts an offer from the current owner to buy the restaurant for $350,000. Unfortunately, although the expected increase in sales volume does occur, customers make much more extensive use of the promotions than Ron had anticipated. As a result, total sales revenues are 8 percent below projections. Furthermore, to improve employee attitudes, Ron gave a 10 percent raise immediately after purchasing the restaurant. Reevaluate the initial decision using the actual sales revenue and the increase in labor costs, assuming conditions will remain unchanged over the remaining life of the project. Was the investment decision a wise one? (Round calculations to the nearest dollar.)

d. Ron can sell the restaurant to a large franchise operator for $250,000. Alternatively, he believes that additional annual marketing expenditures and changes in promotions costing $20,000 per year could bring the sales revenues up to their original projections, with no other changes in costs. Should Ron sell the restaurant or keep it and make the additional expenditures? (Round calculations to the nearest dollar.) (*Hint:* Ron has just bought the restaurant.)

SOLUTIONS TO REVIEW PROBLEMS

<u>Mid-Chapter Review</u>

Solution

Basic computations:

Initial investment	
Depreciable assets	$(27,740)
Working capital	(3,000)
Total cash outflow..	$(30,740)
Operation	
Cash receipts...	$ 25,000
Cash expenditures..	(15,000)
Net cash inflow	$ 10,000
Disinvestment	
Sale of depreciable assets	$ 2,000
Recovery of working capital	3,000
Total cash inflow	$ 5,000

a. Net present value at a 10 percent discount rate:

	Predicted Cash Inflows (outflows) (A)	Year(s) of Cash Flows (B)	10% Present Value Factor (C)	Present Value of Cash Flows (A) × (C)
Initial investment	$(30,740)	0	1.000	$(30,740)
Operation.................................	10,000	1–4	3.170	31,700
Disinvestment	5,000	4	0.683	3,415
Net present value of all cash flows.				$ 4,375

b. Internal rate of return:

Using a spreadsheet, the proposal's internal rate of return is readily determined to be 16 percent:

	A	B
1	Year of cash flow	Cash flow
2	0	$(30,740)
3	1	10,000
4	2	10,000
5	3	10,000
6	4	15,000
7	IRR	0.16

The table approach requires additional analysis. Because the proposal has a positive net present value when discounted at 10 percent, its internal rate of return must be higher than 10 percent. Through a trial-and-error approach, the internal rate of return is determined to be 16 percent.

	Predicted Cash Inflows (outflows) (A)	Year(s) of Cash Flows (B)	16% Present Value Factor (C)	Present Value of Cash Flows (A) × (C)
Initial investment	$(30,740)	0	1.000	$(30,740)
Operation.	10,000	1–4	2.798	27,980
Disinvestment	5,000	4	0.552	2,760
Net present value of all cash flows.				$ 0

Chapter-End Review

Solution

Basic computations:

Initial investment	
Depreciable assets	$27,740
Working capital	3,000
Total	$30,740
Operation	
Cash receipts.	$25,000
Cash expenditures.	(15,000)
Net cash inflow	$10,000
Disinvestment	
Sale of depreciable assets	$ 2,000
Recovery of working capital	3,000
Total	$ 5,000

a. Payback period = $30,740 ÷ $10,000
$$= 3.074 \text{ years}$$

b. Accounting rate of return on initial and average investments:

Annual net cash inflow from operations.	$10,000
Less average annual depreciation [($27,740 − $2,000) ÷ 4].	(6,435)
Average annual increase in net income	$ 3,565

$$\text{Average investment} = (\$30,740 + \$5,000) \div 2$$
$$= \$17,870$$

$$\text{Accounting rate of return on initial investment} = \frac{\$ 3,565}{\$30,740}$$
$$= 0.1160, \text{ or } 11.6\%$$

$$\text{Accounting rate of return on average investment} = \frac{\$ 3,565}{\$17,870}$$
$$= 0.1995, \text{ or } 19.95\%$$

Managerial Analysis of Financial Statements

General purpose financial statements are designed to provide information to a large and diverse group of users, including stockholders, creditors, and managers. The objectives of financial statements are broad and, as such, they do not include certain financial measures that specific user groups often need. Through financial statement analysis, however, individual users are able to generate additional useful information and metrics from the statements.

Financial statement analysis is the process of interpreting and evaluating financial statements by using data and disclosures contained in them to produce additional financial measures. Financial statement analysis involves comparing financial statements for the current period with those of previous periods and/or other companies, assessing the internal composition of the financial statements, and measuring relations within and among the financial statements.

The purpose of this appendix is to describe basic measures of financial statement analysis and to consider how managers and others use these measures. For purposes of presentation, assume that the chief financial officer (CFO) of Columbia Corporation is reviewing the financial statements of Berkeley, Inc., a partially-owned subsidiary whose controlling interest is being considered for sale to another conglomerate. The CFO has read several newspaper and magazine articles critical of Berkeley's current operations and its position in the furniture industry. Although Berkeley's sales continue to increase, its profits are relatively flat. This concerns the CFO and she is in the process of gathering additional information about the company and the industry. Her final report will go to the board of directors of Columbia for a decision on the continuation of Berkeley as part of the conglomerate.

Financial statement analysis taps a large amount of useful information that otherwise is not immediately obvious. Credit analysts must evaluate the likelihood that a loan client will make its interest and principal payments on time, stockholders must evaluate the profitability of a firm's assets and the return on investment to various equity holders, and managers must evaluate their overall effectiveness in using the resources entrusted to them by creditors and stockholders.

Two measures often used in financial statement analysis, return on investment (ROI) and residual income, are common to profitability analysis, which was the theme of Chapter 11. Refer to that chapter for a detailed discussion of these measures and how they can also be used for evaluation purposes.

APPENDIX
ORGANIZATION

FINANCIAL STATEMENT ANALYSIS FOR MANAGERS

One of the most important reasons for managers to analyze their firm's financial statements is to evaluate the overall performance of the firm, especially as seen by those external to the firm. Managers should be aware of total company performance, not just the performance of their particular areas of responsibility. By analyzing the financial statements for the company as a whole, managers gain a perspective on how the organization is performing *and* how it is perceived.

LO1 Describe the importance of analyzing financial statements for managers.

General purpose financial statements provide the only overall measure of an organization's performance to some managers. The internal reporting system is often limited to reporting component performance, with no report of overall performance provided to managers below the executive level. This reporting limitation excludes many of the financial and nonfinancial sources of information discussed in this book. There is frequently no overall reporting of quality measures, value-added analysis, or activity-based costing between the component level and that of top management.

By evaluating the overall performance of the organization, managers are able to compare their firm with similar firms and to identify potential weaknesses that are worthy of management attention. For example, should managers be alarmed if their firm had a return on equity of 8 percent, while the industry norm is 15 percent? There can be good reasons for the below industry-average return; without financial analysis, however, management may not even be aware of the deficiency or the conditions causing it. Since internal reports of other companies are not available, the only basis for making comparisons with those companies is through their external financial statements and other published materials.

Financial analysis is also necessary for managers whose firms have lending agreements that impose financial restrictions on the organization. Analysis of financial statements is often necessary to determine if restrictions are being met. For example, an agreement may require the debt-to-equity ratio to be maintained below a specified level. Failure to comply could result in a call for immediate liquidation of the debt and could damage the firm's credit rating and its ability to obtain borrowed capital in the future.

A more subtle, but no less important, reason for managers to analyze financial statements is to see their firm as outsiders see it. The financial statements are, in effect, the only window through which many outsiders view the firm. By evaluating the firm's financial statements, managers can better understand outsiders' behavior and attitudes toward the firm and thereby develop a more realistic view of the firm.

FACTORS IMPACTING FINANCIAL STATEMENT ANALYSIS

LO2 Identify factors that influence financial statements and their analysis.

Before learning the procedures for financial statement analysis, it is important to consider several factors that influence the financial statements and the evaluation methods. First, no single financial statement analysis measure can summarize the performance of an organization. This is because each analysis measure is developed to evaluate an operating procedure or a specific area of the organization's performance. For example, sales ratios are used to measure various characteristics or conditions of sales. Although sales ratios help evaluate sales, they do not contribute to the analysis of operating expenses. Before drawing conclusions about the financial condition of an organization, the manager should select several evaluation measures that are germane to the organization being evaluated.

Second, the manager must know which alternative accounting procedures the firm uses. Also, if comparing the results with other companies or with industry standards, the manager must know the accounting procedures each uses. Alternative accounting procedures critical for financial statement analysis include methods of depreciation, inventory valuation (cost or lower of cost or market), and inventory cost flow method (FIFO, LIFO, or average costing). Each of these has an impact on various income statement, cash flow statement, and balance sheet amounts.

Third, inflation, or deflation, can distort the comparisons of financial statements between periods because the statements are based on historical dollars, not on dollars of the same value. Allowances must be made for these effects, or the analysis is distorted. To illustrate, assume that Etson Company has 2012 sales of $100,000 and cost of sales totaling $40,000. During 2013, when inflation is 5 percent, the company's selling prices increase by 5 percent, while its costs have a net increase of only 3 percent due to inventory available at 2012 prices. In 2014, both selling prices and costs go up by 5 percent. Therefore, the company has an increase in 2013 gross profit due primarily to inflation of $3,800 and an increase in 2014 gross profit of $3,190 due solely to inflation.

	2012	2013	2014
Sales.	$100,000	$105,000	$110,250
Cost of sales.	40,000	41,200	43,260
Gross profit.	$ 60,000	$ 63,800	$ 66,990

A manager must be careful to avoid stating that the company has increased operating efficiency when all it did was keep pace with inflation. As a general rule, ignoring inflation produces favorable results when other things remain equal. Inflation can even produce favorable results when actual, constant dollar results are unfavorable. We must remember that external financial statements are presented in historical dollars that have not been adjusted for inflation.

Fourth, changes in the product mix can distort a comparison of financial statements because most products have unique profit margins and their mix influences the firm's profit margin. Assume Wilson Company sells two products, CVT and GHK. During 2014, Wilson sold 100 units of each product; and in 2015, it sold 85 units of CVT and 125 units of GHK. The gross profit for CVT is $10 per unit; for GHK, it is $7 per unit. Total gross profit for 2014 and 2015 follows:

	2014			2015		
	CVT	GHK	Company	CVT	GHK	Company
Gross profit.	$1,000	$700	$1,700	$850	$875	$1,725

Without looking past the total numbers on the financial statements, the analyst might conclude that the company performed better in 2015 than it did in 2014. Total sales units went up from 200 to 210, and profit increased by $25. However, when the individual products are analyzed, another opinion might emerge. Although GHK had increased unit sales of 25 percent, CVT, the product with the higher profit per unit, declined 15 percent. This could signal problems if CVT unit sales continue to decline. For companies with large numbers of products, the changing product mix generally does not have a strong impact. However, companies with only a few products, or with some products that have large profit margins, can have financial results that are difficult to interpret unless the underlying facts are analyzed.

Fifth, changes in organizational structure should be reviewed as part of financial analysis. Today's business environment of mergers, acquisitions, and other changes creates many variations in the financial statements. As organizations are restructured, their accounting procedures change, new information systems are implemented, and many other changes take place that complicate financial analysis.

EVALUATIVE STANDARDS AND BENCHMARKS

Information obtained directly from financial statements and analytical measures derived from statements have little usefulness alone. To be interpreted effectively, this information must be evaluated against some standard. Depending on their objectives, managers can use several different standards. The most common financial analysis standards are: (1) **vertical analysis**, the restatement of amounts in the current financial statements as a percentage of some base measure such as sales; (2) **horizontal analysis**, the comparison of a firm's current financial measures to those of previous periods; (3) **competitor analysis**, the comparison of a firm's financial measures to similar measures for other firms in the industry or to industry averages; and (4) the comparison of a firm's financial measures to its budgeted measures.

LO3 Specify alternative standards useful in financial statement analysis.

Financial statement analysis often begins with an examination of the relations among various accounts. This is normally performed through vertical analysis, where one account, the base account, is set at 100 percent, and all other accounts are presented as a percentage of the base account. In an income statement, sales is typically the base account. After all accounts of a given financial statement are converted into percentages, the statement is known as a **common size statement**. Analysis of common size statements is useful for detecting items that are out of line, that deviate from some preset amount, or that are indicative of other problems. Vertical analysis can be improved by combining it with horizontal analysis and reviewing the common size statements of more than one year. Vertical and horizontal analyses are limited in that they involve comparisons of financial measures only for a single firm. If the firm's performance has been poor or mediocre in the past, these standards do not alert management or the analyst to the need for improvements.

Evaluating financial measures against comparable measures for other firms in the same industry is also beneficial to managers, especially to those in competitive industries. Several financial information services (including Dun and Bradstreet, Standard & Poors, and Moody's) publish averages for commonly used financial measures for all major industries. Failure to perform close to industry norms can signal difficulties in competing with other firms in the future.

When comparing a firm's financial measures with those of other firms, it is necessary to consider any significant differences that might exist among the firms. For example, if one firm is located farther from major suppliers than are other firms in the industry, higher freight costs and possibly lower profits can occur. Differences in accounting practices must also be taken into account in comparing firms; for example, allowances must be made in comparing two firms that use different methods of inventory valuation. Although there are limitations in making intercompany comparisons, looking at other firms' performances is a useful indicator of relative performance.

From management's perspective, the most realistic standard of performance is probably the firm's budgeted performance. Chapter 9 discussed operating budgets and pro forma financial statements, which represent management's most realistic expectations for the period. Managers should compare the analytical measures taken from these statements with the same measures derived from the actual financial statements for the period. For performance evaluation purposes, this comparison is likely to provide managers a useful evaluation of current financial statements.

APPLICATION OF FINANCIAL STATEMENT ANALYSIS

LO4 Describe vertical and horizontal analysis, and their difference.

In addition to the computation of common size statements for vertical and horizontal analysis, financial statement analysis measures include computations that measure the firm's solvency and performance. For a comprehensive analysis of a firm, these measures should be compared to industry norms if available. All of these concepts are illustrated using the 2012, 2013, and 2014 balance sheets and income statements for Berkeley, Inc., which are in Exhibit A.1. The only major economic change in Berkeley's operations during this period occurred in 2014 when it added a new product line. Financial statements for three successive periods are presented because several of the measures require multiple periods or averages. To obtain average information for a period, the beginning and ending balances are summed and divided by 2. Averages computed from values for only two points during the year (beginning and ending) should be used only if monthly or quarterly data are not available. In the following discussions, each analytical measure is presented in general form, along with the measure for Berkeley, Inc. All examples use Berkeley 2014 data unless otherwise noted.

Comparative and Common Size Statements

Converting balance sheets and income statements to common size statements is one of the most direct ways to analyze changes over time. Before the various ratios and account analyses are performed, the manager generally evaluates the income statement and balance sheet using common size statement measures such as sales and total assets. The percentages can also be related to some base period, a month or year, for example. The evaluation of trends in terms of financial statement percentages over time allows for analysis of the underlying movements and shifts in the firm's financial composition.

The percent columns of Exhibit A.1 provide the data needed for this initial evaluation for Berkeley, Inc., for 2014. The computation of common size statements for three to five years allows the manager or analyst to evaluate the activities of the company based on trends of prior periods.

Vertical Analysis

The vertical analysis of the common size statements for Berkeley uses sales from the income statement and total assets from the balance sheet as the bases; these are set at 100 percent. This analysis helps to identify significant changes that have taken place during the period and to determine whether the changes have favorable or unfavorable impacts on solvency and performance.

For example, in evaluating Berkeley's cash needs, the CFO might not be as concerned with the amount of cash as with the percentage of cash to total assets. For Berkeley, the relation of cash to total assets is approximately 17 percent in 2012 and 2013. The decline to 15.2 percent in 2014 could indicate a need to examine the status of cash flows. Before becoming overly concerned with the situation, the CFO would want to compare the status of the 2014 account balances with the company's guidelines or standards and available industry norms. Just because these items deviate from expectations does not indicate a problem. The deviation might indicate improved cash management or changes in credit sales or credit collection policies. The deviation should not be ignored, however, because it might indicate an undesirable trend leading to future difficulties.

Another useful application of common size balance sheet statements is the determination of where shifts occur within major categories. In current assets, for example, the decline in the percentage of cash is offset by increases in accounts receivable and inventories as a percent of total assets. Since the company experienced an increase in sales, it is logical for accounts receivable and inventories to increase. However, if these two accounts had increased and cash had decreased with no corresponding increases in sales, management should be concerned. The latter situation suggests excessive inventory investments and problems collecting accounts receivable.

Vertical analysis is also used with common size income statements. When evaluating the income statement, the manager can use common size measurements to determine quickly whether the company's operating goals are met. If Berkeley's target gross profit margin is 40 percent, attained in 2013 (39.7%), the manager can readily see that 2014 fell short of the goal by 2.5 percentage

EXHIBIT A.1	**Comparative Financial Statements**

BERKELEY, INC.
Comparative Balance Sheets with Common Size Statements
December 31, 2014, 2013, and 2012

($ thousands)	2014		2013		2012	
Assets						
Current assets						
Cash..	$1,335	15.2%	$1,341	17.7%	$1,295	17.0%
Marketable securities...........................	250	2.9	200	2.6	228	2.9
Accounts receivable...........................	1,678	19.2	1,386	18.3	1,371	18.0
Inventories....................................	1,703	19.5	1,439	19.1	1,437	18.9
Prepaid items.................................	280	3.2	156	2.1	150	2.0
Total current assets	5,246	60.0	4,522	59.8	4,481	58.8
Property, plant, and equipment	6,934	79.2	6,113	80.9	6,090	80.0
Less accumulated depreciation..................	3,426	39.2	3,080	40.7	2,955	38.8
Net property, plant and equipment	3,508	40.0	3,033	40.2	3,135	41.2
Total assets...................................	$8,754	100.0%	$7,555	100.0%	$7,616	100.0%
Liabilities and stockholders' equity						
Current liabilities						
Accounts payable	$1,564	17.9%	$1,228	16.3%	$1,243	16.3%
Taxes payable	482	5.5	336	4.4	380	5.0
Accrued expenses payable	202	2.3	178	2.4	152	2.0
Total current liabilities	2,248	25.7	1,742	23.1	1,775	23.3
Long-term Debt	1,208	13.8	1,422	18.8	1,976	25.9
Total liabilities................................	3,456	39.5	3,164	41.9	3,751	49.2
Stockholders' equity						
Common stock ($1 par)........................	414	4.7	404	5.3	404	5.3
Additional paid-in capital......................	531	6.1	270	3.6	270	3.5
Retained earnings	4,353	49.7	3,717	49.2	3,191	41.9
Total stockholders' equity	5,298	60.5	4,391	58.1	3,865	50.7
Total liabilities and equity......................	$8,754	100.0%	$7,555	100.0%	$7,616	100.0%

BERKELEY, INC.
Comparative Income Statements with Common Size Statements
For Years Ended December 31, 2014, 2013, and 2012

($ thousands, except per share)	2014		2013		2012	
Sales..	$9,734	100.0%	$8,028	100.0%	$7,841	100.0%
Cost of goods sold.............................	6,085	62.5	4,843	60.3	4,648	59.3
Gross profit....................................	3,649	37.5	3,185	39.7	3,193	40.7
Operating expenses						
Expenses, excluding depreciation.................	1,030	10.6	891	11.1	868	11.0
Depreciation.................................	602	6.2	527	6.6	500	6.4
Total expenses...............................	1,632	16.8	1,418	17.7	1,368	17.4
Operating income..............................	2,017	20.7	1,767	22.0	1,825	23.3
Other expenses (revenues)						
Dividend and interest revenue....................	(80)	(0.8)	(84)	(1.0)	(86)	(1.1)
Interest expense	345	3.5	314	3.9	342	4.4
Gain on sale of investments.....................	(45)	(0.5)	—	—	—	—
Loss on sale of PP&E..........................	35	0.4	—	—	—	—
Total expenses (revenues)	255	2.6	230	2.9	256	3.3
Income before income taxes	1,762	18.1	1,537	19.1	1,569	20.0
Provision for income taxes......................	599	6.2	523	6.5	533	6.8
Net income....................................	$1,163	11.9%	$1,014	12.6%	$1,036	13.2%
Basis earnings per share	$2.81		$2.51		$2.56	

points (40% − 37.5%). This suggests that lower prices or items within cost of goods sold were not kept in control. Although the income statement alone cannot provide the answer, it has helped identify the problem and given management a starting point in looking for the cause. Comparable evaluations can be performed on any of the income statement items and, as such, provide a different perspective of evaluation rather than simple reliance on dollar amounts.

Horizontal Analysis

Horizontal analysis is used to evaluate trends in the financial condition of an organization. This analysis allows current year common size statements to be compared to those of prior years and to the organization's goals and objectives. For companies that have few organizational changes and little growth, dollar amounts can be of use for horizontal analysis. However, for companies experiencing major economic changes during the period under evaluation (for example, new product lines, dropping product lines, new sales territories, mergers, or acquisitions), comparisons of dollar amounts are not meaningful. This is true for Berkeley when comparing dollar amounts for 2013 and 2014. Because sales increased substantially when Berkeley added a new product line, it is difficult to evaluate what the dollar amounts should be for most of the other income statement items. In this case, percentages are a better means for comparison.

Using inventories as an item for analysis, we examine how horizontal analysis helps in the evaluation process. From 2012 to 2013, inventories increased by $2,000 ($1,439,000 − $1,437,000), an acceptable change for such a large dollar amount and given that sales increased also. From 2013 to 2014, inventories increased $264,000 ($1,703,000 − $1,439,000), an increase of 18 percent over 2013, which can be alarming without further analysis. However, because the company added a new product line, some increase is expected—but how much of an increase? The current dollar amount seems large. Before rendering judgment, are the percentages from the common size statements just as large? From Exhibit A.1, we see that the percentages for inventory are 18.9%, 19.1%, and 19.5%, respectively, for 2012, 2013, and 2014. Although inventory as a percent of assets has increased, it does not appear unreasonable given the new product line and the overall increase in assets.

After the vertical and horizontal analyses are completed for the common size statements, the manager then begins to make computations concerning other relations within the company's financial reporting system. The most common financial analysis procedures used for financial statement evaluation are considered in the remainder of this appendix.

Solvency Analysis

LO5 Explain the analysis of a firm's solvency.

Solvency refers to the firm's ability to pay its debts as they come due. Primary measures of short-term solvency are the current ratio, acid test ratio, inventory turnover, and days sales in receivables. The debt-to-equity ratio and the times-interest-earned measures are useful in assessing long-term solvency. Information to compute these measures is available in corporate annual reports.

Current Ratio

The **current ratio** measures the relation between current assets and current liabilities. The general equation for the current ratio and the computation for Berkeley, as of December 31, 2014, follow:

$$\text{Current ratio} = \frac{\text{Current assets}}{\text{Current liabilities}}$$

$$\text{For Berkeley:} = \frac{\$5,246,000}{\$2,248,000}$$

$$= \underline{2.33}$$

Current assets represent cash and other assets that will be converted into cash (either directly or indirectly) through operations within a reasonably short period of time. Under normal operating conditions, cash is generated by sales of inventory and collection of accounts receivable. Current liabilities are financial obligations that will become due within a relatively short period of time and will be paid from cash currently available and from the pool of cash generated from current assets. Therefore, comparing current assets to current liabilities indicates the extent to which current assets are available to cover current liabilities. Berkeley's current ratio of 2.33 implies that it has $2.33 of current assets for each $1 of current liabilities.

There is no universal guideline for evaluating the current ratio. Although a current ratio of 1.5 is often considered to be the norm, using such an artificial guideline can lead to erroneous conclusions. For example, a current ratio of 1.5 is inadequate for a firm that has 90 percent of its current assets tied up in obsolete or slow-moving inventory, while most of its current liabilities are due in the near-term. The adequacy of a particular current ratio depends on (1) the composition of the current assets and how quickly they will convert to cash, and (2) how soon current liabilities must be paid.

Working Capital

The current asset and current liability accounts are often referred to as current operating, or current working, accounts because assets and liabilities related to operating revenues and expenses normally flow in and out of the balance sheet through these accounts. The difference between current assets and current liabilities is viewed as the net amount of working funds available in the short run. This fund is referred to as **working capital**. Berkeley's December 31, 2014, working capital follows:

Working capital	=	Current assets	−	Current liabilities
	=	$5,246,000	−	$2,248,000
	=	$2,998,000		

This means that Berkeley has $2,998,000 that it can use as operating funds in the near future. This working capital may be needed if accounts payable continues to increase as a result of the new product line started in 2014.

For a basic illustration as to how working capital is used, consider the following transaction. Assume that during January 2015, Berkeley needs to purchase equipment for $50,000 but does not want to incur a liability. The impact of this transaction is shown as follows:

Working capital	=	Current assets	−	Current liabilities
	=	$(50,000)	−	$0
	=	$(50,000)		

This leaves a net result of:

Working capital	=	Current assets	−	Current liabilities
	=	$5,196,000	−	$2,248,000
	=	$2,948,000		

Some transactions affect only current liabilities; others affect both current assets and current liabilities, but by different amounts; others affect both by the same amounts, resulting in no change in working capital; and some transactions have no effect on either. All of an organization's economic transactions—except those that deal solely with the long-term accounts; that is, property, plant and equipment, long-term liabilities, and equity—affect some aspect of the working capital equation.

Acid Test Ratio

Current liabilities are usually paid with cash, not with other current assets. The **acid test ratio** is more specific than is the current ratio as a test of short-term solvency. It measures the availability of cash and other current monetary assets that can be quickly converted into cash to pay current liabilities. Current monetary assets include cash, marketable securities, and current receivables. The general equation for the acid test ratio and the computation for Berkeley, as of December 31, 2014, follow:

$$\text{Acid test ratio} = \frac{\text{Cash} + \begin{array}{c}\text{Marketable} \\ \text{securities}\end{array} + \begin{array}{c}\text{Current accounts} \\ \text{receivable}\end{array}}{\text{Current liabilities}}$$

$$\text{For Berkeley:} = \frac{\$1,335,000 + \$250,000 + \$1,678,000}{\$2,248,000}$$

$$= \underline{1.45}$$

Berkeley's acid test ratio indicates that it has $1.45 of current monetary assets for each $1 of current liabilities. (This ratio is also referred to as the **quick ratio** because it shows the amount of cash that can be obtained relatively quickly for each $1 of current liabilities outstanding.) Many analysts consider an acid test ratio of near 1.0 to be adequate for most businesses. However, as stated earlier in discussing the current ratio, the composition of the ratio components must be considered before deciding what an adequate ratio is. When evaluating the current and acid test ratios, the manager must consider other factors such as seasonal characteristics of the business, the availability of short-term credit lines, the collection terms for accounts receivable, and the payment terms of accounts payable.

As a follow-up to the current and acid test ratios, most analysts evaluate the liquidity of the primary assets in the cash flow stream—namely, inventory and accounts receivable. The inventory turnover and days receivables outstanding are the measures ordinarily used for that purpose.

Inventory Turnover

Inventory turnover indicates the approximate number of times the average stock of inventory is sold and replenished during the year. Inventory turnover is often regarded as both a measure of solvency and a measure of performance. As a solvency measure, inventory turnover reveals how long it takes to convert inventory into current monetary assets. As a performance measure, inventory turnover reveals how well the firm is managing investments in inventory. Inventory turnover is computed as the total cost of the inventory sold during the year divided by the average inventory on hand during the year.

$$\text{Inventory turnover} = \frac{\text{Cost of goods sold}}{\text{Average inventory}}$$

$$\text{For Berkeley:} = \frac{\$6,085,000}{(\$1,703,000 + \$1,439,000)/2}$$

$$= \underline{3.87} \text{ times}$$

During 2014, Berkeley sold inventory costing $6,085,000, and the average inventory for the year was $1,571,000 ([$1,703,000 + $1,439,000]/2). Therefore, the average stock of inventory was sold and replenished 3.87 times during the year. Assuming a 365-day year, the average number of days required for each turnover of inventory was 94.3 days (365 days/3.87). That is, during the year, the average inventory available was sufficient to meet the average sales needs for 94.3 days. Since ending inventory is somewhat higher than is the average inventory for the year, inventory at year-end is sufficient to supply somewhat more than 94.3 days' average sales.

What constitutes an appropriate inventory turnover ratio varies from industry to industry and over time. Obviously, a fast-food restaurant should have a high inventory turnover, whereas a jewelry store typically has a low inventory turnover. Firms adopting just-in-time approaches to inventory management should have an increase in their inventory turnovers. If a firm's competitors' inventory turnovers are increasing, this could indicate that competitors changed their approach to inventory management. The nature of the firm's supply sources, the use of inventory display in selling merchandise, the quickness with which inventory is delivered to customers, and information on the industry should all be considered in interpreting the inventory turnover ratio.

Days Sales in Receivables

Next to cash and marketable securities, receivables are the most liquid assets. They are converted directly into cash in the normal course of business. The **days sales in receivables** ratio measures the number of days, on average, it takes to generate the credit sales uncollected at any point in time. Days sales in receivables is a measure of both solvency and performance. As a measure of solvency, it reveals how many days on average it takes to convert accounts receivable into cash. As a performance measure, days sales in receivables reveals how well the firm is managing the credit extended to customers. The longer the collection period the less cash is available for daily operations. Days sales in receivables is computed as receivables divided by average daily sales.

$$\text{Days sales in receivables} = \frac{\text{Accounts receivable}}{\text{Average daily credit sales}}$$

$$\text{For Berkeley:} = \frac{\$1,678,000}{\$9,734,000/365}$$

$$= \underline{\underline{62.9 \text{ days}}}$$

At year-end 2014, Berkeley had receivables equal to the average sales for 62.9 days (assuming all sales are on credit). In evaluating this measure, management should consider the terms under which credit sales are made. For example, if Berkeley sells goods and services on 30-day credit terms, a ratio of 62.9 days probably indicates serious receivables collection problems. This ratio, which is a broad average, is a reliable indicator only if the amount of daily sales was fairly even throughout the year. For more precise information, management should conduct a detailed analysis of year-end receivables to determine their ages and probable collection periods.

Debt-to-Equity Ratio

Most businesses have two basic sources of capital: debt and equity. The balance between the amounts of capital provided by creditors and owners is important in evaluating a business's long-term solvency. Creditors regard equity as a cushion against future operating losses and bankruptcy. The larger the percentage of total assets financed by equity capital, the more secure are the creditors. Aggressive, growth-oriented organizations tend to rely more heavily on debt than on equity, whereas stable, conservative organizations tend to have a larger proportion of equity. The **debt-to-equity ratio** is computed as total liabilities divided by total stockholders' equity.

$$\text{Debt-to-equity ratio} = \frac{\text{Total liabilities}}{\text{Total stockholders' equity}}$$

$$\text{For Berkeley:} = \frac{\$3,456,000}{\$5,298,000}$$

$$= \underline{\underline{0.65}}$$

Berkeley's December 31, 2014, debt-to-equity ratio of 0.65 indicates that its creditors have provided $0.65 of capital for each $1 that stockholders provided. Stated another way, for each $1.65 of asset book values, the company could suffer a $1 loss and still have total reported assets equal to total liabilities. Although the debt-to-equity ratio is useful as a general indicator of the adequacy of long-term solvency, the amount of long-term debt that a company can justify is primarily related to its ability to repay the funds plus interest.

Times-Interest-Earned

A financially sound business normally pays interest obligations out of current earnings. Accordingly, creditors are interested in the adequacy of earnings to provide payment of interest charges. **Times-interest-earned**, a measure of interest-paying ability, shows the relation between earnings available to pay interest and total interest expense.

$$\text{Times-interest-earned} = \frac{\text{Net income} + \text{Interest expense} + \text{Income taxes}}{\text{Interest expense}}$$

$$\text{For Berkeley:} = \frac{\$1,163,000 + \$345,000 + \$599,000}{\$345,000}$$

$$= \underline{\underline{6.11 \text{ times}}}$$

In the numerator, interest expense and income taxes are added to net income to determine the pool of earnings from which interest expense is paid. Since interest expense is deducted in computing taxable income, the earnings pool from which interest is paid is income before deductions for interest and taxes. For Berkeley, this pool of earnings for 2014 is 6.11 times the amount of the current year's interest charge on debt.

Performance Analysis

LO6 Explain the analysis of a firm's performance.

Operating performance is related to the broad objective of profitability. The basic activities that characterize a typical for-profit organization follow:

- Generating capital—equity and debt.
- Acquiring assets with capital.
- Using assets to generate sales and profits.
- Using profits to pay the cost of capital.

Primary measures of performance are asset turnover, return on sales, return on assets, return on equity, and earnings per share. Care must be taken when using ratios for performance evaluation. Several of the measures of solvency discussed previously are also used to assist in the evaluation of these activities. It is quite common to find inventory turnover and days sales in receivables as part of performance evaluation. Common measures of performance are discussed in this section.

Asset Turnover

The **asset turnover** ratio measures the firm's ability to use its assets to generate sales. Asset turnover is computed as sales divided by average total assets.

$$\text{Asset turnover} = \frac{\text{Sales}}{\text{Average total assets}}$$

$$\text{For Berkeley:} = \frac{\$9,734,000}{(\$8,754,000 + \$7,555,000)/2}$$

$$= \underline{\underline{1.19}} \text{ times}$$

For Berkeley, the asset turnover of 1.19 times indicates that, on the average, each $1 of assets generated $1.19 of sales during 2014. The interpretation of this measure depends largely on the nature of the business. Organizations that are capital-intensive, such as utilities or heavily automated manufacturers, typically have a lower asset turnover than do organizations that are labor-intensive, such as garment manufacturers. Also, firms that generate a small amount of sales with each dollar of assets usually must earn a higher percentage of profit on each sales dollar than do firms that produce a high amount of sales with each invested asset dollar.

Return on Sales

The ability of a firm to generate sales with available assets is important. To be profitable, however, these sales must exceed the cost of generating them. **Return on sales** is a measure of the firm's ability to generate profits from sales produced by the firm's assets. Return on sales is computed by dividing the sum of net income and net-of-tax interest expense by sales.

$$\text{Return on sales} = \frac{\text{Net income} + \text{Net-of-tax interest expense}}{\text{Sales}}$$

$$\text{For Berkeley:} = \frac{\$1,163,000 + \$345,000(1 - 0.34)}{\$9,734,000}$$

$$= \underline{\underline{0.143}}, \text{ or } \underline{\underline{14.3\%}}$$

Interest expense is added to net income because it is not considered an expense of using assets, but rather a cost of providing the capital invested in assets. Since interest expense reduces taxes, it is adjusted for taxes at the company's current effective tax rate of approximately 34 percent. This reveals that, on average, 14.3 percent of each $1 of Berkeley 2014 sales remained as profit after covering all expenses other than interest.

Return on Assets

The **return on assets** ratio combines asset turnover and return on sales to measure directly the firm's ability to use its assets to generate profits. The return on assets computation is derived from the asset turnover and return on sales ratios as follows:

Ratio derivation: Return on assets = Asset turnover × Return on sales

$$= \frac{\text{Sales}}{\text{Average total assets}} \times \frac{\text{Net income} + \text{Net-of-tax interest expense}}{\text{Sales}}$$

$$\text{Return on assets} = \frac{\text{Net income} + \text{Net-of-tax interest expense}}{\text{Average total assets}}$$

$$\text{For Berkeley:} \quad = \frac{\$1,163,000 + \$345,000(1 - 0.34)}{(\$8,754,000 + \$7,555,000)/2}$$

$$= \underline{0.171}, \text{ or } \underline{17.1\%}$$

Berkeley's 2014 return on assets is also approximated by multiplying the asset turnover of 1.19 times the return on sales of 14.3 percent. From the previous analyses, we conclude that, on average, each dollar of assets generates $1.19 of sales and $0.171 of income and that each dollar of sales results in $0.143 of income. Return on assets is an important indicator of management's overall performance because it measures management's effectiveness in using the total capital entrusted to them by both creditors and stockholders. A variation of this ratio (return on investment), discussed in Chapter 11, is commonly used for evaluating the performance of divisions in decentralized organizations.

The return on assets ratio measures profitability before deducting capital costs (interest and dividends). Thus, the adequacy of the profitability indicated by this ratio depends on the cost of debt and the return stockholders expect on their investments.

Return on Equity

Return on equity measures the profits attributable to shareholders as a percentage of their equity in the firm. This measure is more specific than is the return on assets ratio in measuring performance because return on equity focuses only on stockholders' profits and investment. The profits available to stockholders consist of net income after deducting all costs and expenses, including interest expense. Return on equity is computed as net income divided by average stockholders' equity.

$$\text{Return on equity} = \frac{\text{Net income}}{\text{Average stockholders' equity}}$$

$$\text{For Berkeley:} \quad = \frac{\$1,163,000}{(\$5,298,000 + \$4,391,000)/2}$$

$$= \underline{0.240}, \text{ or } \underline{24.0\%}$$

(If the company also has preferred stock outstanding, then return on equity is computed as the return on *common* equity; where net income is reduced by the amount of annual dividends on preferred stock, and stockholders' equity is reduced by the book value of preferred stock.)

The 2014 return attributable to Berkeley's shareholders was 24 percent, compared to a return on assets of 17.1 percent. The return to shareholders is higher than is its return on assets as a result of financial leverage. **Financial leverage** refers to the use of capital that has a fixed interest or dividend rate. Any time capital can be acquired at a fixed rate, and the return on assets is higher than that fixed rate, the return to the common shareholders is increased through favorable financial leverage. (The interest rate on a variable rate loan can change from period to period as the prime rate changes; however, even in this case, the interest is fixed for a short period of time, and management's ability to generate favorable leverage varies inversely with interest rate changes.) Conversely, if the fixed cost of capital is greater than the return it generates, the shareholders are subsidizing the cost of debt or other fixed rate capital, which reflects unfavorable financial leverage. Berkeley's favorable financial leverage occurred because the return on assets was 17.1 percent, whereas the interest rate as a percent of average total liabilities was 10.4 percent, computed as follows:

$$\text{Average interest rate} = \frac{\text{Interest expense}}{\text{Average total liabilities}}$$

$$\text{For Berkeley} = \frac{\$345,000}{(\$3,456,000 + \$3,164,000)/2}$$
$$= \underline{0.104}, \text{ or } \underline{10.4\%}$$

Berkeley's total debt required a return of only $345 (or 10.4 percent). Therefore, the return above 10.4 percent on the assets acquired with debt increased the return to the shareholders to 24.0 percent.

Earnings per Share

For external reporting purposes, earnings per share amounts are disclosed on the face of the income statement. If a company has gains or losses from extraordinary sources, such as from a natural disaster, or from other unusual and infrequent events, then income and earnings per share figures must be presented separately for income before extraordinary items and for net income. Berkeley's income statement in Exhibit A.1 reported earnings per share of $2.81 in 2014 and $2.51 in 2013. **Earnings per share** is defined as follows:

$$\text{Earnings per share} = \frac{\text{Net income}}{\text{Average number of common shares outstanding}}$$

$$\text{For Berkeley:} = \frac{\$1,163,000}{414,000}$$
$$= \underline{\$2.81}$$

Earnings per share for companies with simple capital structures is computed as net income divided by the average number of shares outstanding for the period. A *simple capital structure* is one consisting only of common stock. The computations are more difficult for a company with a *complex capital structure* that includes preferred stock, convertible bonds, or other types of equity securities. Also, changes in a company's capital structure during the year and over time make it more difficult to compare earnings per share from year to year.

Investors use earnings per share measures as a basis in evaluating the firm's overall profitability. The advantage of the earnings per share measure is that it is reported on the same basis as stock prices—that is, on an individual share basis. Investors often use the **price earnings ratio**, which is the ratio of the current market price divided by the earnings per share of the stock, to arrive at a multiple of earnings.

$$\text{Price earnings ratio} = \frac{\text{Market price per share}}{\text{Earnings per share}}$$

Some managers use earnings per share as a broad measure of overall performance. However, earnings per share should not be relied on too heavily, nor should it be substituted for other, more detailed profitability ratios that managers can obtain. Other profitability measures are often more useful to managers in evaluating overall management performance. Another reason why managers must monitor earnings per share is to better understand a measure that investors use in making decisions about buying or selling a company's capital stock.

Finally, some managers compute the *dividend payout ratio*, defined as dividends per common share divided by earnings per common share. Companies that have high reinvestment of their earnings would have low dividend payout ratios. Similarly, companies that have few investment opportunities and shareholders that seek dividends would have high dividend payout ratios. Another measure known as the *dividend yield ratio*, defined as dividends per common share divided by market price per common share, reflects the percent of the share market price paid out in cash. A complete summary of the ratios discussed in this chapter is provided at the end of the chapter in Exhibit A.3.

Horizontal Analysis of Solvency and Performance

Horizontal analysis, as already illustrated, provides good measures of performance over time. This analysis can be readily extended to the financial ratios of solvency and performance measures. The annual reports of most companies include several years' data for key items such as gross sales, operating profit margin, net income, earnings per share, dividends paid, and net changes to retained earnings. However, annual reports rarely include financial ratios that are important for evaluation purposes.

Horizontal analysis requires little additional computations because many of the items that provide input for other financial analysis techniques are already computed. A typical analysis often includes the current ratio. Although a measure of solvency in the short run, the current ratio can be a measure of performance when compared over a period of years. For example, if the information for Berkeley is extended back to 2010, a horizontal analysis of the current ratio reveals the following:

	2014	2013	2012	2011	2010
Current ratio	2.33	2.60	2.52	2.56	2.61

It appears that the ratio of current assets to current liabilities has been slowly declining. Such an analysis might alert the manager to take investigative action before the current ratio becomes undesirable. If creditors are using similar analysis, the decline might alert them to be cautious in extending credit to Berkeley.

Horizontal analysis can be performed using both dollars and common size units. However, care must be used when horizontal analysis is based only on dollar amounts. To illustrate, if we refer to Exhibit A.1 and use dollars, horizontal analysis of the income statement reveals that cost of goods sold in 2014 increased substantially over that of 2013 whereas in 2013 and 2012 cost of goods sold were about the same. Is this good or bad, considering 2014 sales also increased substantially? On the other hand, horizontal analysis with common size units reveals another picture—the increase is only 2.2 percent (62.5 percent − 60.3 percent).

Some types of analysis combine both dollars and common size units with two or more sets of data to make performance evaluations using horizontal analysis. Suppose the income statements for Berkeley appeared as follows:

	2014	2013	2012	2011	2010
Sales.	$9,734,000	$8,028,000	$7,841,000	$7,260,000	$7,000,000
Operating income.	2,017,000	1,767,000	1,825,000	1,670,000	1,610,000
Operating income as percent of sales	20.7%	22.0%	23.3%	23.0%	23.0%

If only the dollars are considered, the trend for Berkeley appears favorable, with sales increasing each year, including substantial growth in 2014. Dollars of operating income are also increasing, except for 2013, with 2014 again showing a substantial increase. However, after adding the common size data to the analysis, the company's performance appears less favorable. After several years of operating with a 23 percent margin, performance slipped to 20.7 percent, even with the large 2014 sales increase.

Another type of horizontal analysis is frequently used when a given point in time has been established as the base year or benchmark for comparison. Using the data above with 2010 as the base year (100%), a horizontal analysis using common size units follows:

	2014	2013	2012	2011	2010
Sales.	139%	115%	112%	104%	100%
Operating income.	125	110	113	104	100

| EXHIBIT A.2 | Base Year Common Size Statements |

BERKELEY, INC.
Common Size Comparative Income Statements
For Years Ended December 31, 2014, 2013, and 2012

	2014	2013	2012
Sales.	124.1%	102.4%	100.0%
Cost of goods sold.	130.9	104.2	100.0
Gross profit.	114.3	99.7	100.0
Operating expenses			
Expenses, excluding depreciation.	118.7	102.6	100.0
Depreciation.	120.4	105.4	100.0
Total operating expenses.	119.3	103.7	100.0
Operating income.	110.5	96.8	100.0
Other expenses and revenues			
Interest and dividend revenue	93.0	97.7	100.0
Interest expense	100.9	91.8	100.0
Gain on sale of investment*.	—	—	—
Loss on sale of PPE*	—	—	—
Total other expenses and revenues.	99.6	89.8	100.0
Income before income taxes	112.3	98.0	100.0
Provision for income taxes.	112.4	98.1	100.0
Net income.	112.2	97.9	100.0

*These items are reported only in 2014 and, thus, have no base in 2012.

When we add this information to the previous analysis, it appears that the first sign of declining profit was in 2013, when operating income increased much less than did sales. In fact, 2013 operating income was less than that of 2012 by 3 percentage points.

This application is frequently extended by converting an entire financial statement to a base period and computing the change in each account for several financial statements. This allows the manager to examine the movement of all items in relation to a single starting point. Exhibit A.2 reveals the results of holding 2012 as the base year for Berkeley and adjusting all subsequent income statement accounts against those of 2012. To illustrate this application, cost of goods sold showed an increase of 30.9 percent, whereas sales went up only 24.1 percent over the two-year period. Although gross profit increased 14.3 percent over the 2012 base, it did not improve at the same level as sales improved. Therefore, the manager might conclude that the increased sales attributable to the new product do not provide the same profit margin as the other products, or maybe the new product hindered the efficiency of producing existing products. This type of analysis is also applied to base-year comparisons of balance sheets.

Industry Benchmarking of Analysis Measures

Evaluation of a firm's financial condition and performance is incomplete without comparisons to, and benchmarking against, its industry (competitors) during the same operating period(s). Industry comparisons provide insight into the firm's relative financial condition and performance and show whether the firm is keeping pace, moving ahead, or lagging behind competitors. There are several sources, such as Moody's and Standard & Poors, that provide industry benchmarks on key financial analysis ratios and indexes.

Comparative evaluations must be made cautiously. First, avoid generalizations, such as every company should have a current ratio of 2 to 1. This caution was expressed in the section on current ratios. Second, avoid using industry averages or medians as absolute guidelines for performance measurement. Although industry benchmarks are better than rule-of-thumb generalizations, they do not apply equally to all firms within an industry. The industry benchmark is likely comprised of data from large firms, new firms, growing firms, diversified firms, and numerous other firms that do not match the case of the firm being evaluated. It is helpful if a distribution of the data statistics is provided within industry. (This is provided for many industries in the aforementioned publications.) For example, if the firm being evaluated has a current ratio of 1.6 and the industry average is 2.2, there may be cause for concern. However, if it is known that the firm fits into a

EXHIBIT A.3	Summary of Financial Analysis Ratios

Ratio	Formula	Reflects
Solvency		
Working capital	$=$ Current assets $-$ Current liabilities	Near-term debt-paying ability
Current ratio	$= \dfrac{\text{Current assets}}{\text{Current liabilities}}$	Near-term debt-paying ability
Acid test ratio	$= \dfrac{\text{Cash} + \text{Marketable Securities} + \text{Current receivables}}{\text{Current liabilities}}$	Near-term debt-paying ability
Accounts receivable turnover	$= \dfrac{\text{Net sales}}{\text{Average accounts receivable}}$	Efficiency of receivable collection
Inventory turnover	$= \dfrac{\text{Cost of goods sold}}{\text{Average inventory}}$	Efficiency of inventory management
Days sales in receivables	$= \dfrac{\text{Accounts receivable}}{\text{Credit sales}} \times 365$	Liquidity of receivables
Days sales in inventory	$= \dfrac{\text{Ending inventory}}{\text{Cost of goods sold}} \times 365$	Liquidity of inventory
Debt-to-equity ratio	$= \dfrac{\text{Total liabilities}}{\text{Total stockholders' equity}}$	Creditor versus owner financing
Times-interest-earned	$= \dfrac{\text{Net income} + \text{Interest expense} + \text{Income taxes}}{\text{Interest expense}}$	Interest-paying ability
Performance		
Asset turnover	$= \dfrac{\text{Net sales}}{\text{Average total assets}}$	Efficiency of total assets
Return on sales	$= \dfrac{\text{Net income} + \text{Net-of-tax interest expense}}{\text{Sales}}$	Profitability of sales given assets
Gross margin ratio	$= \dfrac{\text{Net income} - \text{Cost of goods sold}}{\text{Net sales}}$	Gross profit per sales dollar
Return on assets	$= \dfrac{\text{Net income} + \text{Net-of-tax interest expense}}{\text{Average total assets}}$	Profitability of assets
Return on equity	$= \dfrac{\text{Net income}}{\text{Average stockholders' equity}}$	Profitability of shareholder investment
Average interest rate	$= \dfrac{\text{Interest expense}}{\text{Average total liabilities}}$	Interest rate paid on debt
Book value per share	$= \dfrac{\text{Shareholders' equity of common shares}}{\text{Number of common shares outstanding}}$	Liquidation at reported values
Earnings per share	$= \dfrac{\text{Net income}}{\text{Average number of common shares outstanding}}$	Income per common share
Price earnings ratio	$= \dfrac{\text{Market price per common share}}{\text{Earnings per common share}}$	Market value multiple of earnings
Dividend yield	$= \dfrac{\text{Cash dividends per common share}}{\text{Market price per common share}}$	Cash return of market price
Dividend payout	$= \dfrac{\text{Cash dividends per common share}}{\text{Earnings per common share}}$	Payout percent of earnings

category of similar firms within the industry that have an average current ratio of 1.5, cause for concern is lessened.

A third caution relates to the overall industry performance. A firm that is slightly below average in a financially strong industry can be better than one at the top of a financially weak industry. Again, there are business publications that give periodic ratings by industry—for example, the *Wall Street Journal*.

Fourth, a firm must be analyzed as to its diversity or homogeneity. A firm with diversified product lines will often not fit into any group or industry. Various reporting requirements (via government agencies) force companies to classify themselves under some predefined industry classification whether they are diversified or not. Also, diversified firms tend to distort industry benchmarks of firms that have homogeneous product lines and that fit nicely into that particular industry category.

Fifth, size influences how a firm compares to industry benchmarks. Larger firms within an industry should probably be compared to industry benchmarks in a different way than are smaller firms. This is not to imply that large firms are better—in many industries, large firms are the weaker performers.

Each of these cautions should be considered as appropriate when analyzing a firm's financial condition and comparing that analysis to industry benchmarks. Comparing incompatible sets of data can result in managers making incorrect decisions, causing future performance to deteriorate.

Returning to the CFO's analysis of Berkeley, she must render a decision to the board of directors concerning the status of this subsidiary. Assuming her evaluation of Berkeley's position as related to the furniture industry is compatible with the newspaper and magazine articles she read before beginning her analysis, she is left with drawing conclusions about future trends of the company. While the existing current ratio, asset turnover ratio, return on sales, and most other measures are acceptable, the CFO is concerned about the trend evident from the horizontal analysis. That is, the current ratio has been declining, operating income as a percentage of sales has been declining, and the growth of operating income has not kept pace with the growth of sales. It is when faced with such decisions that executives such as this CFO demand timely and relevant information to recommend what is best for the long-run benefits of the company.

APPENDIX-END REVIEW: COMPARATIVE COMMON SIZE STATEMENTS AND RATIO ANALYSIS

Comparative 2013 and 2014 income statements and balance sheets for Oxford, Inc., follow.

OXFORD, INC.
Comparative Income Statements
For Years Ended December 31, 2014 and 2013

($ 000s)	2014	2013
Sales.	$3,000	$2,500
Cost of goods sold.	2,600	2,300
Gross profit.	400	200
Operating expenses		
Selling	125	105
General and administrative	70	60
Total operating expenses.	195	165
Operating income.	205	35
Other expenses (revenues)		
Interest income	(10)	(5)
Interest expense	40	20
Total other expenses	30	15
Income before income taxes	175	20
Provision for income taxes.	60	7
Net income.	$ 115	$ 13
Earnings per share	$ 1.28	$ 0.19

OXFORD, INC.
Comparative Balance Sheets
December 31, 2014 and 2013

($ 000s)	2014	2013
Assets		
Current assets		
Cash and cash equivalents	$ 375	$ 315
Accounts receivable.	325	280
Inventories	400	350
Interest receivable	60	55
Total current assets	1,160	1,000
Property, plant, and equipment	1,500	1,300
Less accumulated depreciation	800	750
Property, plant, and equipment, net.	700	550
Other assets	15	12
Total assets.	$1,875	$1,562
Liabilities and stockholders' equity		
Current liabilities		
Accounts payable	$ 435	$ 330
Income taxes payable	45	5
Interest payable	50	45
Total current liabilities	530	380
Long-term debt	300	250
Total liabilities	830	630
Stockholders' equity		
Common stock ($1 par)	90	70
Additional paid-in capital	15	10
Retained earnings	940	852
Total stockholders' equity	1,045	932
Total liabilities and equity	$1,875	$1,562

Additional information

- During 2014, operating expenses included $50,000 in depreciation expense.
- Cash dividends of $27,000 are declared and paid during 2014.
- Common stock of $15,000 is issued at par for cash in 2014.
- Equipment costing $200,000 is acquired during 2014 by paying cash of $190,000 and issuing 5,000 shares of common stock worth $10,000.
- During 2014, long-term debt of $20,000 is paid off with cash and new long-term debt of $70,000 is issued for cash.
- The company extended a $3,000 loan to the company president in 2014.

Required

a. Prepare common size statements for 2014 and 2013. Use sales as the base for the income statements and total assets as the base for the balance sheets.
b. What major changes are evident from 2013 to 2014 when horizontal analysis is performed? Explain.
c. Prepare a complete ratio analysis for 2014 including measures of solvency and performance.

The solution is on pages 498–500.

KEY TERMS

acid test ratio, 479	earnings per share, 484	return on assets, 483
asset turnover, 482	financial leverage, 483	return on equity, 483
common size statement, 475	financial statement analysis, 472	return on sales, 482
competitor analysis, 475	horizontal analysis, 475	solvency, 478
current ratio, 478	inventory turnover, 480	times-interest-earned, 481
days sales in receivables, 480	price earnings ratio, 484	vertical analysis, 475
debt-to-equity ratio, 481	quick ratio, 480	working capital, 479

DISCUSSION QUESTIONS

QA-1. What is the general purpose for conducting ratio analysis of financial statements?

QA-2. Name three reasons why managers should analyze their firm's financial statements.

QA-3. What is the purpose of evaluation standards (benchmarks) in financial analysis?

QA-4. What types of standards (benchmarks) are probably most relevant for financial analysis by managers?

QA-5. Explain how managers use vertical and horizontal analysis when evaluating financial statements. What changes are usually made in the statements before managers use these techniques?

QA-6. Explain and differentiate the terms solvency evaluation and performance evaluation.

QA-7. Explain the difference between the current ratio and the acid test ratio.

QA-8. Why is it useful to compute inventory turnover and the days sales in receivables? How is each of these measures computed?

QA-9. What are the primary measures of long-term solvency? How are they computed?

QA-10. Which financial statement analysis measure provides information concerning the sales output that a firm's assets produce?

QA-11. Why is interest expense added in the numerator in computing return on assets?

QA-12. Explain the concept of financial leverage. What causes financial leverage to be favorable? Unfavorable?

QA-13. Explain why comparisons to industry norms or averages are important when analyzing financial statements.

QA-14. What cautions should the manager take when using industry norms or benchmarks for comparison?

MINI EXERCISES

LO5   **MA-15.**   **Short-Term Solvency Ratios**

Following are financial data from year-end financial statements of York Company for 2014, 2013 and 2012.

	2014	2013	2012
Accounts receivable.	$ 153,000	$ 165,000	$ 150,000
Cost of goods sold.	1,680,000	1,450,000	1,600,000
Current assets	750,000	600,000	675,000
Current liabilities.	525,000	450,000	500,000
Inventory.	375,000	275,000	325,000
Sales.	1,850,000	2,000,000	1,750,000

Required

a. Compute the following financial ratios for 2013 and 2014. (Round calculations to two decimal places.)

1. Current ratio
2. Acid test ratio
3. Inventory turnover
4. Days receivables outstanding

b. Comment on the short-term solvency of York Company for 2013 and 2014. Did the company's short-term solvency improve or deteriorate during 2014? Explain.

MA-16. **Long-Term Solvency Ratios**   LO5

Summary data from year-end financial statements of Palo Alto Company for 2014 follow.

Summary Income Statement Data		
Sales.		$8,000,000
Cost of goods sold.	$3,425,000	
Selling expenses	625,000	
Administrative expenses	525,000	
Interest expense.	1,475,300	
Income tax expense.	50,250	6,100,550
Net income.		$1,899,450

Summary Balance Sheet Data			
Cash.	$ 60,000	Total liabilities.	$600,000
Noncash assets	790,000	Stockholders' equity	250,000
Total assets.	$850,000	Total liabilities and equity	$850,000

Required

a. Compute the ratio of times-interest-earned. (Round computations to two decimal places.)
b. Compute the debt-to-equity ratio.

MA-17. **Measures of Performance and Financial Leverage**   LO6

Following are selected data from year-end financial statements of Nelox Corporation for 2014 and 2013.

	2014	2013
Total assets.	$7,349,000	$6,553,000
Interest expense.	115,000	102,000
Long-term liabilities	1,220,000	1,239,000
Net income.	619,000	563,000
Sales.	8,196,000	6,996,000
Stockholders' equity	3,624,000	3,221,000

Required

a. Compute the following performance measurement ratios for 2014. (Round computations to three decimal places and ignore income taxes.)

1. Asset turnover
2. Return on sales
3. Return on assets
4. Return on equity

b. Is Nelox Company using financial leverage? If so, is the leverage favorable or unfavorable? Explain.

LO6 MA-18. **Financial Leverage**

Following are data from McClellan Company and McDonough Company for 2014:

	McClellan	McDonough
Net income.	$ 270,000	$ 405,000
Interest expense.	120,000	112,500
Total assets, beginning of 2014	3,750,000	6,375,000
Total assets, end of 2014	4,042,500	6,847,500
Stockholders' equity, beginning of 2014	1,594,500	3,703,500
Stockholders' equity, end of 2014	1,689,000	3,832,500

Required

a. Compute the following ratios for McClellan and McDonough Companies at the end of 2014. (Ignore taxes and round calculations to three decimal places.)

   1. Return on assets

   2. Return on equity

b. Comment on the use of financial leverage by these two companies. Which company is the more highly leveraged? Which company's stockholders are benefiting more from the use of leverage?

LO5 MA-19. **Changes in Working Capital**

Following is a list of typical financial, investing, and operating transactions. For each transaction indicate whether current assets, current liabilities, and working capital either increased, decreased, or are unchanged. Use the following column headings and relation: **Current assets − Current liabilities = Working capital**.

a. Sold capital stock for cash.

b. Purchased a building for cash.

c. Paid current liabilities with cash.

d. Issued long-term bonds payable for cash.

e. Purchased inventory on account.

f. Purchased a building site by issuing long-term bonds.

g. Sold equipment for a cash amount equal to book value.

h. Sold treasury stock for cash.

i. A long-term note matures next year is reported as a current payable at this year-end.

EXERCISES

LO2, 5 EA-20. **Effects of Financing Decisions**

Provo Company has total assets of $2,500,000 and total liabilities of $2,000,000. Provo is considering two alternatives for acquiring additional warehouse space. Under the first alternative, the building would be purchased for $300,000 and financed by issuing long-term bonds. Under the second alternative, the building would be rented with an annual lease cost of $30,000 per year.

Required

a. Compute the company's current debt-to-equity ratio.

b. What effect would the addition of warehouse space have on its debt-to-equity ratio

   1. Assuming the building is purchased by issuing bonds?

   2. Assuming the building is rented on an annual lease basis?

LO3, 4 EA-21. **Common Size Statements**

Comparative balance sheets for Albany, Inc., follow for year-end 2014 and 2013. Its president is concerned about the decline in total assets and wants to know where most of the decline took place.

	2014	2013
Cash.	$ 220,000	$ 230,000
Accounts receivable.	350,000	300,000
Inventory.	300,000	450,000
Property, plant, and equipment	1,200,000	1,200,000
Less accumulated depreciation	525,000	475,000
Total assets.	$1,545,000	$1,705,000
Accounts payable.	$ 260,000	$ 255,000
Long-term note payable.	280,000	350,000
Common stock.	500,000	500,000
Retained earnings	505,000	600,000
Total liabilities and equity	$1,545,000	$1,705,000

Required

Convert these comparative balance sheets to common size statements. Using the common size statements, explain to the president where the greatest changes occurred.

EA-22. **Changes in Working Capital**   LO5

Auckland Industries had a July 31 current asset balance of $31,200 and a current liability balance of $20,800. The following transactions took place in August:

- Sold land for $45,000 cash.
- Collected $80,000 cash on a long-term note receivable.
- Paid $47,000 cash toward outstanding payables.
- Purchased $65,000 of inventory on account.
- Paid $10,000 cash to settle long-term bonds payable two years prior to maturity.

Required

Determine the effects on working capital for each of those transactions and then compute ending working capital. Use the following format (the beginning balances are listed):

	Current assets	–	Current liabilities	=	Working capital
Beginning balance	$31,200		$20,800		$10,400

EA-23. **Assessing Inflationary Effects**   LO2, 5

The president of Townville Office Products is pleased with the progress her company has made in recent years, but she cannot understand why the company is always having to borrow funds when sales continually increase. Her office staff is small, and the largest cost outside of merchandise inventory is sales commissions, which are 20 percent of sales. As the cost of merchandise changes, she continually changes retail prices. Thus, she believes the profit margin should remain near the same percentage level for each period. However, even with her best efforts, the company continues to experience cash shortages. After gathering financial data, you prepare the following set of information for the past four years:

	2011	2012	2013	2014
Sales.	$240,000	$252,000	$264,600	$277,830
Cost of goods sold.	$150,000	$159,000	$168,540	$178,652
Current ratio	1.46	1.34	1.23	1.14
Inventory turnover	4.66	4.65	4.67	4.66
Inflation rate	6.00%	6.00%	6.00%	6.00%

Required

What conclusions can be drawn about the operating condition of Townville Office Products? Explain.

EA-24. **Assessing Inflationary Effects**   LO2, 6

The Nova Products Company wants to launch a new product to replace a current product that is technologically inferior. First-year sales for the replacement product are expected to be 100,000 units at a unit selling price of $4.00. The initial cost of the product is $3.00 per unit variable and

$100,000 fixed. The expected sales growth is 1,000 units per year, and the expected inflation rate is in a range of 4 to 5 percent for both sales and variable costs.

Required

a. Determine the anticipated profit margin for the new product for the first four years assuming:

1. No inflation
2. Inflation at 4 percent

b. Compute the profit margin difference between no inflation and 4 percent inflation. Would this information make a difference in your evaluation of the new product? Explain.

PROBLEMS

LO5, 6   PA-25.   **Comprehensive Financial Analysis**

Comparative income statements and balance sheets for Seneca Company follow for 2014 and 2013.

SENECA COMPANY Comparative Income Statements For Years Ended December 31, 2014 and 2013	2014	2013
Sales..	$11,778,070	$11,241,498
Cost of goods sold..............................	6,615,148	6,395,466
Gross profit....................................	5,162,922	4,846,032
Selling and administrative expenses	3,565,750	3,363,722
Operating income...............................	1,597,172	1,482,310
Other expenses (revenues)		
Interest revenue............................	(94,034)	(79,060)
Interest expense	76,698	70,204
Total other expenses (revenues)	(17,336)	(8,856)
Income before income taxes	1,614,508	1,473,454
Income taxes	720,368	660,818
Net income....................................	$ 894,140	$ 812,636

SENECA COMPANY Comparative Balance Sheets December 31, 2014 and 2013	2014	2013
Assets		
Cash..	$ 241,816	$ 259,370
Marketable securities...........................	437,268	202,802
Accounts receivable............................	966,982	1,046,246
Inventory......................................	1,501,438	1,620,470
Prepaid expenses..............................	124,988	115,618
Total current assets	3,272,492	3,244,506
Investments and other assets	774,836	604,368
Property, plant, and equipment, net.............	2,818,912	2,681,680
Trademarks and other intangibles	263,322	281,362
Total assets...................................	$7,129,562	$6,811,916

SENECA COMPANY Comparative Balance Sheets December 31, 2014 and 2013	2014	2013
Liabilities and stockholders' equity		
Notes payable	$ 179,294	$ 175,174
Current maturities of long-term debt	10,030	15,056
Accounts payable and accrued expenses	1,822,326	1,932,930
Total current liabilities	2,011,650	2,123,160
Long-term debt	556,368	539,280
Total liabilities	2,568,018	2,662,440
Common stock	124,778	124,744
Additional paid-in capital	228,388	226,344
Retained earnings	4,208,378	3,798,388
Total stockholders' equity	4,561,544	4,149,476
Total liabilities and equity	$7,129,562	$6,811,916

Required

a. Prepare a comprehensive financial analysis of Seneca for 2014, including the following measures (round all calculations to three decimal places):
   1. Short-term solvency ratios
   2. Long-term solvency ratios
   3. Performance measurement ratios
b. Comment on the financial condition of Seneca with respect to short-term solvency, long-term solvency, and performance.

PA-26. Comprehensive Common Size Statement Analysis   LO3, 4

After reviewing the financial analyses conducted in Problem A-25, the managers of Seneca Company are still uncertain about the performance of the company during 2014. They believe that common size statements might provide additional insights as to the company's performance.

Required

a. Using the data pertaining to Seneca Company from Problem A-25, prepare common size statements and evaluate the company's performance in 2014 as compared to 2013. For the balance sheets, use total assets as the base; for the income statements, make one set using sales of each year as the base for that year and another set using the year 2013 as the base for both years.
b. Comment on the condition of Seneca drawing on the common size statements.

PA-27. Comprehensive Financial Statement Analysis   LO4, 5, 6

You are part of the acquisitions committee of Witter Company and are asked to examine the potential acquisition of Dryds, Inc., a merchandising firm. Selected financial statement data from the past two years follow.

DRYDS, INC. Comparative Balance Sheets December 31, 2014 and 2013		
	2014	**2013**
Cash.	$ 130,000	$ 120,000
Accounts receivable.	430,000	370,000
Inventory.	400,000	400,000
Property, plant, and equipment	900,000	800,000
Less accumulated depreciation	325,000	250,000
Total assets.	$1,535,000	$1,440,000
Accounts payable.	$ 300,000	$ 260,000
Long-term note payable.	280,000	280,000
Common stock.	690,000	690,000
Retained earnings	265,000	210,000
Total liabilities and equity	$1,535,000	$1,440,000

DRYDS, INC. Income Statement For Year Ended December 31, 2014	
Sales.	$2,943,000
Cost of goods sold.	2,200,000
Wages expense	350,000
Supplies expense.	42,600
Depreciation expense.	100,000
Interest expense.	22,400
Loss on sale of fixed assets.	75,000
Net income before taxes	153,000
Income taxes	52,020
Net income.	$ 100,980

Required

a. Compute the following ratios for 2014. (Round calculations to three decimal places.)
1. Current ratio
2. Acid test
3. Inventory turnover
4. Days receivables outstanding
5. Debt-to-equity ratio
6. Times-interest-earned
7. Asset turnover
8. Return on sales
9. Return on assets
10. Return on equity
b. Prepare common size statements for each of the statements.
c. What is your recommendation regarding the acquisition of Dryds?

CASES AND PROJECTS

LO4, 5, 6 **CA-28. Financial Statement Analysis with Actual Annual Report**
Select a recent annual report or 10-K filing (or use one provided by your instructor) of a publicly held company and perform all of the financial analysis measures discussed in this appendix. Include vertical and horizontal analyses with common size statements. List any of the measures discussed in this appendix that you were unable to perform and state the reasons. Give your evaluation of the company's financial performance and trend, citing financial analysis measures

to support your interpretation. If industry data are available, make a comparison of the company under analysis with its industry norms and benchmarks. Evaluate the position the company holds within its industry.

CA-29. **Horizontal Analysis and Interpretation**   LO3, 4

Selected 5-year data for the Lexington Company, a manufacturing firm, follow:

	2010	2011	2012	2013	2014
Average cash balance . .	$ 12,500	$ 18,400	$ 25,600	$ 62,300	$ 88,600
Sales.	$432,000	$487,000	$539,000	$591,000	$642,000
Operating income.	$ 3,500	$ 7,850	$ 11,600	$ 94,400	$129,000
Current ratio	0.23	0.31	0.56	0.77	0.81
Asset turnover	0.80	0.90	1.00	1.09	1.19

Required

What assessments can be made about this company's performance and operating performance for this five-year period? Explain.

CA-30. **Horizontal Analysis and Interpretation**   LO3, 4

El Paso Investment Brokers is considering purchasing Rio Valley. The following data are from recent financial statements of Rio Valley ($ thousands):

	2010	2011	2012	2013	2014
Sales.	$4,000	$4,300	$4,900	$4,800	$5,100
Operating income.	$1,100	$1,150	$1,300	$1,285	$1,425
Net income.	$ 495	$ 520	$ 505	$ 490	$ 513
Current ratio	2.33	2.11	2.78	1.96	2.45
Asset turnover	1.01	1.34	1.68	1.73	2.07

Required

Determine the company's strengths and weaknesses as evident from the information provided. Identify one type of common size application for assessing the dollar amounts for your analysis. What do you recommend regarding the purchase of Rio Valley? Explain.

CA-31. **Interpreting Financial Analysis Ratios**   LO5, 6

Thorpe Company is a wholesale distributor of professional equipment and supplies. The company's sales averaged about $900,000 annually for the three-year period, 2012-2014. Its total assets at the end of 2014 were $850,000. The president of Thorpe Company asked the controller to prepare a report summarizing the financial aspects of the company's operations for the past three years. This report is to be presented to its Board of Directors at its next meeting. In addition to comparative financial statements, the controller decides to report a number of relevant financial ratios to assist in the identification and interpretation of trends. The controller computes the following ratios for the recent three-year period.

	2014	2013	2012
Current ratio	2.18	2.13	2.00
Acid test ratio	0.97	1.10	1.20
Days receivables outstanding	51.20	42.60	37.60
Inventory turnover	3.80	4.80	5.25
Debt-to-equity ratio	0.61	0.69	0.79
Asset turnover	1.99	1.88	1.75
Sales as a percentage of 2012 sales	1.06	1.03	1.00
Gross profit percent	38.50	38.60	40.00
Return on sales	8.0%	7.8%	7.8%
Return on assets	8.7%	8.6%	8.5%
Return on equity.	14.1%	14.6%	15.1%

In preparation of the report, the controller decides first to examine the financial ratios independently of any other data to determine if the ratios themselves reveal any significant trends over this three-year period.

Required

Answer the following questions. Indicate in each case which ratio(s) you used to arrive at your conclusion.

a. The current ratio is increasing, whereas the acid test ratio is decreasing. Using the ratios provided, identify and explain the contributing factor(s) for this apparently divergent trend.

b. In terms of the ratios provided, what conclusion(s) is drawn regarding the company's use of financial leverage during the 2012-2014 period? Explain.

c. Using the ratios provided, what conclusions are drawn regarding the company's ability to generate sales and profits from the assets available to management?

(CMA Adapted)

SOLUTIONS TO REVIEW PROBLEMS

Appendix-End Review

Solution

a.

OXFORD, INC.
Common Size Income Statements
For Years Ended December 31, 2014 and 2013

	2014	2013
Sales.	100.0%	100.0%
Cost of goods sold.	86.7	92.0
Gross profit.	13.3	8.0
Operating expenses		
Selling	4.2	4.2
General and administrative	2.3	2.4
Total operating expenses.	6.5	6.6
Operating income.	6.8	1.4
Other expenses (revenues)		
Interest income	(0.3)	(0.2)
Interest expense	1.3	0.8
Total other expenses	1.0	0.6
Income before income taxes	5.8	0.8
Provision for income taxes.	2.0	0.3
Net income.	3.8%	0.5%

OXFORD, INC.
Common Size Balance Sheets
December 31, 2014 and 2013

	2014	2013
Assets		
Current assets		
Cash and cash equivalents	20.0%	20.2%
Accounts receivable	17.3	17.9
Inventories	21.3	22.4
Interst receivable	3.2	3.5
Total current assets	61.8	64.0
Property, plant, and equipment:	80.0	83.2
Less accumulated depreciation	42.6	48.0
Net property, plant, and equipment	37.4	35.2
Other assets	0.8	0.8
Total assets	100.0%	100.0%
Liabilities and stockholders' equity		
Current liabilities		
Accounts payable	23.2%	21.1%
Income taxes payable	2.4	0.3
Interest payable	2.7	2.9
Total current liabilities	28.3	24.3
Long-term debt	16.0	16.0
Total liabilities	44.3	40.3
Stockholders' equity		
Common stock ($1 par)	4.8	4.5
Additional paid-in capital	0.8	0.6
Retained earnings	50.1	54.6
Total stockholders' equity	55.7	59.7
Total liabilities and equity	100.0%	100.0%

b. The common size statements reveal that current assets declined as a percentage of total assets, with the largest decline being inventories (1.1%). The largest change occurred with net property, plant, and equipment, which increased 2.1 percent.

Total liabilities as a group increased by 4.0 percent; taxes payable were the main driver. The primary change in stockholders' equity is retained earnings, which decreased by 4.4 percent.

The substantial increase in dollars of net income can be explained when reviewing the common size statements; cost of goods sold led the way with a 5.3 percent decline. The only items that increased were interest expense and provisions for taxes.

When a company experiences a major change in sales—such as the 20 percent increase for Oxford [($3,000,000 − $2,500,000)/$2,500,000]—it is difficult to assess dollar amounts and tell if every item maintained its proper contribution to the whole. Common size statements permit this analysis and provide evidence as to the degree of change of each item.

c.

Solvency measures:

Current ratio $= \dfrac{\text{Current assets}}{\text{Current liabilities}}$

$= \dfrac{\$1,160}{\$530}$

$= \underline{2.19}$

continued

Acid test ratio $= \dfrac{\text{Cash} + \text{Current receivables}}{\text{Current liabilities}}$

$= \dfrac{\$375 + \$325}{\$530}$

$= \underline{1.32}$

Inventory turnover $= \dfrac{\text{Cost of goods sold}}{\text{Average inventory}}$

$= \dfrac{\$2,600}{(\$350 + \$400)/2}$

$= \underline{6.93}$ times

Days sales in receivables $= \dfrac{\text{Ending receivables}}{\text{Average daily sales}}$

$= \dfrac{\$325}{\$3,000/365}$

$= \underline{39.54}$ days

Debt-to-equity ratio $= \dfrac{\text{Total liabilities}}{\text{Total stockholders' equity}}$

$= \dfrac{\$830}{\$1,045}$

$= \underline{0.79}$

Times-interest-earned $= \dfrac{\text{Net income} + \text{Interest expense} + \text{Income taxes}}{\text{Interest expense}}$

$= \dfrac{\$115 + \$40 + \$60}{\$40}$

$= \underline{5.38}$ times

Performance measures:

Asset turnover $= \dfrac{\text{Sales}}{\text{Average total assets}}$

$= \dfrac{\$3,000}{(\$1,562 + \$1,875)/2}$

$= \underline{1.75}$ times

Return on sales $= \dfrac{\text{Net income} + \text{Net-of-tax interest expense}}{\text{Sales}}$

$= \dfrac{\$115 + \$40(1 - 0.34)}{\$3,000}$

$= \underline{0.047}$, or $\underline{4.7\%}$

Return on assets $= \dfrac{\text{Net income} + \text{Net-of-tax interest expense}}{\text{Average total assets}}$

$= \dfrac{\$115 + \$40(1 - 0.34)}{(\$1,562 + \$1,875)/2}$

$= \underline{0.082}$, or $\underline{8.2\%}$

Return on equity $= \dfrac{\text{Net income}}{\text{Average stockholders' equity}}$

$= \dfrac{\$115}{(\$932 + \$1,045)/2}$

$= \underline{0.116}$, or $\underline{11.6\%}$

Glossary

A

absorption costing An approach to product costing that treats both variable and fixed manufacturing costs as product costs.

accelerated cost recovery system (ACRS, MACRS) A system of accelerated depreciation for tax purposes introduced in 1981 (ACRS) and modified starting in 1987 (MACRS); it prescribes depreciation rates by asset classification for assets acquired after 1980

accelerated depreciation method Any depreciation method under which the amounts of depreciation expense taken in the early years of an asset's life are larger than the amounts expensed in the later years; includes the double-declining balance method

access control matrix A computerized file that lists the type of access that each computer user is entitled to have to each file and program in the computer system

account A record of the additions, deductions, and balances of individual assets, liabilities, permanent stockholders' equity, revenues, and expenses

accounting cycle A series of basic steps followed to process accounting information during a fiscal year

accounting entity An economic unit that has identifiable boundaries and that is the focus for the accumulation and reporting of financial information

accounting equation An expression of the equivalency of the economic resources and the claims upon those resources of a specific entity; often stated as Assets = Liabilities + Stockholders' Equity

accounting period The time period, typically one year (or quarter), to which periodic accounting reports are related

accounting rate of return The average annual increase in net income that results from acceptance of a capital expenditure proposal divided by either the initial investment or the average investment in the project.

accounting system The structured collection of people, policies, procedures, equipment, files, and records that a company uses to collect, record, classify, process, store, report, and interpret financial data

accounting The process of measuring the economic activity of an entity in money terms and communicating the results to interested parties; the purpose is to provide financial information that is useful in making economic decisions

accounts payable turnover The ratio obtained by dividing annual cost of goods sold by average accounts payable

accounts receivable aging method A procedure that uses an aging schedule to determine the year-end balance needed in the allowance for uncollectible accounts account

accounts receivable turnover Annual net sales divided by average accounts receivable (net)

accounts receivable A current asset that is created by a sale on a credit basis; it represents the amount owed the company by the customer

accrual accounting Accounting procedures whereby revenues are recorded when they are earned and realized and expenses are recorded in the period in which they help to generate revenues

accruals Adjustments that reflect revenues earned but not received or recorded and expenses incurred but not paid or recorded

accrued expense An expense incurred but not yet paid; recognized with an adjusting entry

accrued revenue Revenue earned but not yet billed or received; recognized with an adjusting entry

accumulated depreciation The sum of all depreciation expense recorded to date; it is subtracted from the cost of the asset in order to derive the asset's net book value

acid test ratio More specific than the current ratio as a test of short-term solvency, the acid test ratio (also known as the quick ratio) measures the availability of cash and other current monetary assets that can be quickly generated into cash to pay current liabilities. The general equation for the acid test ratio is: (Cash + Marketable securities + Current receivables)/Current liabilities.

activities list *see* operations list.

activity cost drivers Specific units of work (activities) performed to serve customer needs that consume costly resources.

activity costing The determination of the cost of specific activities performed to fill customer needs.

activity dictionary A standardized list of processes and related activities.

activity A unit of work.

activity-based budgeting An approach to budgeting that uses an activity cost hierarchy to budget physical inputs and costs as a function of planned activity. It is mechanically similar to the output/input approach to budgeting where physical inputs and costs are budgeted as a function of planned activity.

activity-based costing (ABC) Used to develop cost information by determining the cost of activities and tracing their costs to cost objectives on the basis of the cost objective's utilization of units of activity.

activity-based management (ABM) The identification and selection of activities to maximize the value of the activities while minimizing their cost from the perspective of the final consumer.

adjusted trial balance A list of general ledger accounts and their balances taken after adjustments have been made

adjusting entries Entries made at the end of an accounting period under accrual accounting to ensure the proper matching of expenses incurred with revenues earned for the period

adjusting The process of adjusting the historical financial statements prior to the projection of future results; also called recasting and reformulating

aging schedule An analysis that shows how long customers' accounts receivable balances have remained unpaid

allowance for uncollectible accounts A contra asset account with a normal credit balance shown on the balance sheet as a deduction from accounts receivable to reflect the expected realizable amount of accounts receivable

allowance method An accounting procedure whereby the amount of uncollectible accounts expense is estimated and recorded in the period in which the related credit sales occur

Altman's Z-score A predictor of potential bankruptcy based on multiple ratios

amortization The periodic writing off of an account balance to expense; similar to depreciation and usually refers to the periodic writing off of an intangible asset

annuity A series of equal cash flows received or paid over equal intervals of time.

appraisal costs Quality costs incurred to identify nonconforming products or services before they are delivered to customers.

articles of incorporation A document prepared by persons organizing a corporation in the United States that sets forth the structure and purpose of the corporation and specifics regarding the stock to be issued

articulation The linkage of financial statements within and across time

assembly efficiency variance The difference between the standard cost of actual assembly inputs and the flexible budget cost for assembly.

assembly rate variance The difference between the actual cost and the standard cost of actual assembly inputs.

asset turnover A measure of performance, the asset turnover ratio measures the firm's ability to use its assets to generate sales. The general equation for asset turnover is: Net sales divided by Average total assets.

asset write-downs Adjustment of carrying value of assets down to their current salable value

assets The economic resources of an entity that are owned, will provide future benefits and can be reliably measured

audit report A report issued by independent auditors that includes the final version of the financial statements, accompanying notes, and the auditor's opinion on the financial statements

audit An examination of a company's financial statements by a firm of independent certified public accountants

authorized stock The maximum number of shares in a class of stock that a corporation may issue

automatic identification systems (AIS) The use of bar coding of products and production processes that allows inventory and production information to be entered into a computer without writing or keying.

available-for-sale securities Investments in securities that management intends to hold for capital gains and dividend income; although it may sell them if the price is right

average cash cycle Average collection period + modified average inventory days outstanding + modified average payable days outstanding

average collection period Determined by dividing accounts receivable by average daily sales, sometimes referred to as days sales outstanding or DSO

average inventory days outstanding (AIDO) An indication of how long, on average, inventories are on the shelves, computed as inventory divided by average daily cost of goods sold

B

backflush costing An inventory accounting system used in conjunction with JIT in which costs are assigned initially to cost of goods sold. At the end of the period, costs are backed out of cost of goods sold and assigned to appropriate inventory accounts for any inventories that may exist.

balance sheet A financial report based on the accounting equation that lists a company's assets, liabilities, and equity at a certain point in time

balanced scorecard A performance measurement system that includes financial and operational measures which are related to the organizational goals. The basic premise is to establish a set of indicators that can be used to monitor performance progress and then compare the goals that are established with the results.

batch level activity An activity performed for each batch of product produced.

bearer One of the terms that may be used to designate the payee on a promissory note; means the note is payable to whoever holds the note

benchmarking A systematic approach to identifying the best practices to help an organization take action to improve performance.

bill of materials A document that specifies the kinds and quantities of raw materials required to produce one unit of product.

bond A long-term debt instrument that promises to pay interest periodically and a principal amount at maturity, usually issued by the borrower to a group of lenders; bonds may incorporate a wide variety of provisions relating to security for the debt involved, methods of paying the periodic interest, retirement provisions, and conversion options

book value per share The dollar amount of net assets represented by one share of stock; computed by dividing the amount of stockholders' equity associated with a class of stock by the outstanding shares of that class of stock

book value The dollar amount carried in the accounts for a particular item; the book value of a depreciable asset is derived by deducting the contra account accumulated depreciation from the cost of the depreciable asset

borrows at a discount When the face amount of the note is reduced by a calculated cash discount to determine the cash proceeds

bottom-up budget A budget where managers at all levels—and in some cases even non-managers—become involved in the budget preparation.

break-even point The unit or dollar sales volume where total revenues equal total costs.

budget committee A committee responsible for supervising budget preparation. It serves as a review board for evaluating requests for discretionary cost items and new projects.

budget office An organizational unit responsible for the preparation, distribution, and processing of forms used in gathering budget data. It handles most of the work of actually formulating the budget schedules and reports.

budget A formal plan of action expressed in monetary terms.

budgetary slack Occurs when managers intentionally understate revenues or overstate expenses in order to produce favorable variances for the department.

budgeted financial statements Hypothetical statements that reflect the "as if" effects of the budgeted activities on the actual financial position of the organization. They reflect what the results of operations will be if all the predictions in the budget are correct.

budgeting Projecting the operations of an organization and their financial impact on the future.

C

calendar year A fiscal year that ends on December 31

call provision A bond feature that allows the borrower to retire (call in) the bonds after a stated date

capacity costs *see* committed fixed costs.

capital budgeting A process that involves the identification of potentially desirable projects for capital expenditures, the subsequent evaluation of capital expenditure proposals, and the selection of proposals that meet certain criteria.

capital expenditures Investments of significant financial resources in projects to develop or introduce new products or services, to expand current production or service capacity, or to change current production or service facilities. Expenditures that increase the book value of long-term assets; sometimes abbreviated as CAPEX.

capital lease A lease that transfers to the lessee substantially all of the benefits and risks related to ownership of the property; the lessee records the leased property as an asset and establishes a liability for the lease obligation

capital markets Financing sources, which are formalized when companies issue securities that are traded on organized exchanges; they are informal when companies are funded by private sources

capitalization of interest A process that adds interest to an asset's initial cost if a period of time is required to prepare the asset for use

capitalization The recording of a cost as an asset on the balance sheet rather than as an expense on the income statement; these costs are transferred to expense as the asset is used up

cash (operating) cycle The period of time from when cash is invested in inventories until inventory is sold and receivables are collected

cash and cash equivalents The sum of cash plus short-term, highly liquid investments such as treasury bills and money market funds; includes marketable securities maturing within 90 days of the financial statement date

cash budget Summarizes all cash receipts and disbursements expected to occur during the budget period.

cash discount An amount that a purchaser of merchandise may deduct from the purchase price for paying within the discount period

cash equivalents Short-term, highly liquid investments that are readily convertible into known amounts of cash and so near their maturity date that they present insignificant risk of change in value from interest or money market rate changes; generally, only investments with original maturities of three months or less are considered as possible cash equivalents.

cash An asset category representing the amount of a firm's available cash and funds on deposit at a bank in checking accounts and savings accounts

cash-basis accounting Accounting procedures whereby revenues are recorded when cash is received from operating activities and expenses are recorded when cash payments related to operating activities are made

centralization When top management controls the major functions of an organization (such as manufacturing, sales, accounting, computer operations, marketing, research and development, and management control).

certificate of deposit (CD) An investment security available at financial institutions generally offering a fixed rate of return for a specified period of time

chained target costing Bringing in suppliers as part of the coordination process to attain a competitively priced product that is delivered to the customer in a timely manner.

change in accounting estimate Modification to a previous estimate of an uncertain future event, such as the useful life of a depreciable asset, uncollectible accounts receivable, and warranty expenses; applied currently and prospectively only

changes in accounting principles Cumulative income or loss from changes in accounting methods (such as depreciation or inventory costing methods)

chart of accounts A list of all the general ledger account titles and their numerical code

clean surplus accounting Income that explains successive equity balances

closing procedures A step in the accounting cycle in which the balances of all temporary accounts are transferred to the retained earnings account, leaving the temporary accounts with zero balances

coefficient of determination (R2) A measure of the percent of variation in the dependent variable that is explained by variations in the independent variable when the least-squares estimation equation is used.

commitments A contractual arrangement by which both parties to the contract still have acts to perform

committed fixed costs (capacity costs) Costs required to maintain the current service or production capacity or to fill a previous legal commitment.

common cost A cost incurred for the benefit of two or more cost objectives—an indirect cost.

common segment costs Costs related to more than one segment and not directly traceable to a particular segment. These costs are referred to as common costs because they are incurred at one level for the benefit of two or more segments at a lower level.

common size statement A financial statement that has had all its accounts converted into percentages. As such, a common size statement is very useful for detecting items that are out of line, that deviate from some present amount, or that may be indications of other problems.

common stock The basic ownership class of corporate capital stock, carrying the rights to vote, share in earnings, participate in future stock issues, and share in any liquidation proceeds after prior claims have been settled

comparative financial statements A form of horizontal analysis involving comparison of two or more periods' financial statements showing dollar and/or percentage changes

compensating balance A minimum amount that a financial institution requires a firm to maintain in its account as part of a borrowing arrangement complex capital structure

competitor analysis The comparison of a firm's financial measures to similar measures or other firms in the industry or to industry averages

comprehensive income The total income reported by the company, including net profit and all other changes to stockholders' equity other than those arising from capital (stock) transactions; typical components of other comprehensive income (OCI) are unrealized gains (losses) on available-for-sale securities and derivatives, minimum pension liability adjustment, and foreign currency translation adjustments

computer-aided design (CAD) A method of design that involves the use of computers to design products.

computer-aided manufacturing (CAM) A manufacturing method that involves the use of computers to control the operation of machines.

computer-integrated manufacturing (CIM) The ultimate extension of the CAD, CAM, and FMS concepts to a completely automated and computer-controlled factory where production is self-operating once a product is designed and the decision to produce is made.

conceptual framework A cohesive set of interrelated objectives and fundamentals for external financial reporting developed by the FASB

conservatism An accounting principle stating that judgmental determinations should tend toward understatement rather than overstatement of net assets and income

consistency An accounting principle stating that, unless otherwise disclosed, accounting reports should be prepared on a basis consistent with the preceding period

consolidated financial statements Financial statements reflecting a parent company and one or more subsidiary companies and/or a variable interest entity (VIE) and its primary beneficiary

contingency A possible future event; significant contingent liabilities must be disclosed in the notes to the financial statements

contingent liabilities A potential obligation, the eventual occurrence of which usually depends on some future event beyond the control of the firm; contingent liabilities may originate with such events as lawsuits, credit guarantees, and environmental damages

continuous budgeting Budgeting based on a moving time frame that extends over a fixed period. The budget system adds an identical time period to the budget at the end of each period of operations, thereby always maintaining a budget of exactly the same time length.

continuous improvement (Kaizen) budgeting An approach to budgeting that incorporates a targeted improvement (reduction) in costs; management requests that a given process will be improved during the budgeting process. This may be applied to every budget category or to specific areas selected by management. Kaizen budgeting is based upon prior performance and anticipated operating conditions during the upcoming period.

continuous improvement (Kaizen) costing Establishing cost reduction targets for products or services that an organization is currently providing to customers.

continuous improvement An approach to activity-based management where the employees constantly evaluate products, services, and processes, seeking ways to do better.

contra account An account related to, and deducted from, another account when financial statements are prepared or when book values are computed

contract rate The rate of interest stated on a bond certificate

contributed capital The net funding that a company receives from issuing and acquiring its equity shares

contribution income statement An income statement format in which variable costs are subtracted from revenues to figure contribution margin, and fixed costs are then subtracted from contribution margin to calculate net income.

contribution margin ratio The portion of each dollar of sales revenue contributed toward covering fixed costs and earning a profit.

contribution margin The difference between total revenues and total variable costs; this amount goes toward covering fixed costs and providing a profit.

controlling The process of ensuring that results agree with plans.

conversion cost The combined costs of direct labor and manufacturing overhead incurred to convert raw materials into finished goods.

convertible bond A bond incorporating the holder's right to convert the bond to capital stock under prescribed terms

convertible securities Debt and equity securities that provide the holder with an option to convert those securities into other securities

copyright An exclusive right that protects an owner against the unauthorized reproduction of a specific written work or artwork

core income A company's income from its usual business activities that is expected to continue (persist) into the future

corporation A legal entity created by the granting of a charter from an appropriate governmental authority and owned by stockholders who have limited liability for corporate debt

cost allocation base A measure of volume of activity, such as direct labor hours or machine hours, that determines how much of a cost pool is assigned to each cost objective.

cost behavior How costs respond to changes in an activity cost driver.

cost center A responsibility center whose manager is responsible only for managing costs.

cost driver analysis The study of factors that influence costs.

cost driver A factor that causes or influences costs.

cost estimation The determination of the relationship between activity and cost.

cost method An investment is reported at its historical cost, and any cash dividends and interest received are recognized in current income

cost objective An object to which costs are assigned. Examples include departments, products, and services.

cost of capital The average cost of obtaining the resources necessary to make investments.

cost of goods sold percentage The ratio of cost of goods sold divided by net sales

cost of goods sold The total cost of merchandise sold to customers during the accounting period

cost of production report Used in a process costing system; summarizes unit and cost data for each department or process for each period.

cost pool A collection of related costs, such as departmental manufacturing overhead, that is assigned to one or more cost objectives, such as products.

cost prediction error The difference between a predicted future cost and the actual amount of the cost when, or if, it is incurred.

cost prediction The forecasting of future costs.

cost principle An accounting principle stating that asset measures are based on the prices paid to acquire the assets

cost reduction proposal A proposed action or investment intended to reduce the cost of an activity that the organization is committed to keeping.

cost-volume-profit (CVP) analysis A technique used to examine the relationships among total volume of some independent variable, total costs, total revenues, and profits during a time period (typically a month or a year).

cost-volume-profit graph An illustration of the relationships among activity volume, total revenues, total costs, and profits.

coupon (contract or stated) rate The coupon rate of interest is stated in the bond contract; it is used to compute the dollar amount of (semiannual) interest payments that are paid to bondholder during the life of the bond issue

coupon bond A bond with coupons for interest payable to bearer attached to the bond for each interest period; whenever interest is due, the bondholder detaches a coupon and deposits it with his or her bank for collection

covenants Contractual requirements put into loan or bond agreements by lenders

credit (entry) An entry on the right side (or in the credit column) of any account

credit card fee A fee charged retailers for credit card services provided by financial institutions; the fee is usually stated as a percentage of credit card sales

credit guarantee A guarantee of another company's debt by cosigning a note payable; a guarantor's contingent liability that is usually disclosed in a balance sheet footnote

credit memo A document prepared by a seller to inform the purchaser that the seller has reduced the amount owed by the purchaser due to a return or an allowance

credit period The maximum amount of time, usually stated in days, that the purchaser of merchandise has to pay the seller

credit terms The prescribed payment period for purchases on credit with discount specified for early payment

cumulative (preferred stock) A feature associated with preferred stock whereby any dividends in arrears must be paid before dividends may be paid on common stock

cumulative effect of a change in principle The cumulative effect on net income to the date of a change in accounting principle

cumulative translation adjustment The amount recorded in the equity section as necessary to balance the accounting equation when assets and liabilities of foreign subsidiaries are translated into \$US at the rate of exchange prevailing at the statement date

current assets Cash and other assets that will be converted to cash or used up during the normal operating cycle of the business or one year, whichever is longer

current liabilities Obligations that will require within the coming year or operating cycle, whichever is longer, (1) the use of existing current assets or (2) the creation of other current liabilities

current rate method Method of translating foreign currency transactions under which balance sheet amounts are translated using exchange rates in effect at the period-end consolidation date and income statement amounts using the average exchange rate for the period

current ratio A measure of solvency, the current ratio measures the relationship between current assets and current liabilities. The general equation for the current ratio is: Current assets divided by Current liabilities.

customer level activity An activity performed to obtain or maintain each customer.

customer profitability analysis A presentation showing the profits of individual or categories of customers net of the cost of serving and supporting those customers.

customer profitability profile A graphical presentation showing the cumulative profits from the most profitable to the least profitable customer

cycle efficiency The ratio of value-added to nonvalue-added manufacturing activities.

cycle time The total time required to complete a process. It is composed of the times needed for setup, processing, movement, waiting, and inspection.

D

dashboards Software programs that tabulate and display scorecard results using graphics that mimic the instrument displays on an automobile dashboard

days sales in receivables A measure of both solvency and performance, the days receivable outstanding tells how long it takes to convert accounts receivable into cash or how well the firm is managing the credit extended to customers. The general equation for days receivable outstanding is: Ending receivables/Average daily sales.

days sales in inventory Inventories divided by average cost of goods sold

debenture bond A bond that has no specific property pledged as security for the repayment of funds borrowed

debit (entry) An entry on the left side (or in the debit column) of any account

debt-to-equity ratio A measure of long-term solvency, the debt-to-equity ratio indicates the balance between the amounts of capital that creditors and owners provide. The general equation for the debt-to-equity ratio is: Total liabilities/Total stockholders' equity.

decentralization The delegation of decision-making authority to successively lower management levels in an organization. The lower in the organization the authority is delegated, the greater the decentralization.

declining-balance method An accelerated depreciation method that allocates depreciation expense to each year by applying a constant percentage to the declining book value of the asset

default The nonpayment of interest and principal and/or the failure to adhere to the various terms and conditions of the bond indenture

deferrals Adjustments that allocate various assets and revenues received in advance to the proper accounting periods as expenses and revenues

deferred revenue A liability representing revenues received in advance; also called unearned revenue

deferred tax liability A liability representing the estimated future income taxes payable resulting from an existing temporary difference between an asset's book value and its tax basis

deferred tax valuation allowance Reduction in a reported deferred tax asset to adjust for the amount that is not likely to be realized

defined benefit plan A type of retirement plan under which the company promises to make periodic payments to the employee after retirement

defined contribution plan A retirement plan under which the company makes cash contribution into an employee's account (usually with a third-party trustee like a bank) either solely or as a matching contribution

degree of operating leverage A measure of operating leverage, often computed as the contribution margin divided by income before taxes.

denominator variance *see* fixed overhead volume variance.

depletion The allocation of the cost of natural resources to the units extracted and sold or, in the case of timberland, the board feet of timber cut

depreciation accounting The process of allocating the cost of equipment, vehicles, and buildings (not land) to expense over the time period benefiting from their use

depreciation base The acquisition cost of an asset less estimated salvage value

depreciation rate An estimate of how the asset will be used up over its useful life—evenly over its useful life, more heavily in the early years, or in proportion to its actual usage

depreciation tax shield The reduction in taxes due to the deductibility of depreciation from taxable revenues.

depreciation The decline in economic potential (using up) of plant assets originating from wear, deterioration, and obsolescence

derivatives Financial instruments such as futures, options, and swaps that are commonly used to hedge (mitigate) some external risk, such as commodity price risk, interest rate risk, or risks relating to foreign currency fluctuations

descriptive model A model that merely specifies the relationships between a series of independent and dependent variables.

design for manufacture Explicitly considering the costs of manufacturing and servicing a product while it is being designed.

differential cost analysis An approach to the analysis of relevant costs that focuses on the costs that differ under alternative actions.

diluted earnings per share The earnings per share computation taking into consideration the effects of dilutive securities

dilutive securities Securities that can be exchanged for shares of common stock and, thereby, increase the number of common shares outstanding

direct costing *see* variable costing.

direct department cost A cost directly traceable to a department upon its incurrence.

direct labor Wages earned by production employees for the time they spend working on the conversion of raw materials into finished goods.

direct materials The costs of primary raw materials that are converted into finished goods.

direct method (for cost allocation) A method of allocating service department costs to producing departments based only on the amount of services provided to the producing departments; it does not recognize any interdepartmental services.

direct method (for statement of cash flow) A reporting format for the operating section of the statement of cash flows; where basically, the income statement is reconstructed on a cash basis so that the primary categories of cash inflows and outflows from operating activities are reported.

direct segment fixed costs Costs that would not be incurred if the segment being evaluated were discontinued. They are specifically identifiable with a particular segment.

discontinued operations Net income or loss from business segments that are up for sale or have been sold in the current period

discount bond A bond that is sold for less than its par (face) value

discount on notes payable A contra account that is subtracted from the Notes Payable amount on the balance sheet; as the life of the note elapses, the discount is reduced and charged to interest expense

discount period The maximum amount of time, usually stated in days, that the purchaser of merchandise has to pay the seller if the purchaser wants to claim the cash discount

discount rate The minimum rate of return required for the project to be acceptable.

discounted cash flow (DCF) model The value of a security is equal to the present value of the expected free cash flows to the firm, discounted at the weighted average cost of capital (WACC)

discounting The exchanging of notes receivable for cash at a financial institution at an amount that is less than the face value of the notes

discretionary cost center A cost center that does not have clearly defined relationships between effort and accomplishment.

discretionary fixed costs Costs set at a fixed amount each period at the discretion of management.

dividend discount model The value of a security today is equal to the present value of that security's expected dividends, discounted at the weighted average cost of capital

dividend payout ratio Annual dividends per share divided by the earnings per share

dividend yield Annual dividends per share divided by the market price per share

dividends account A temporary equity account used to accumulate owner dividends from the business

division margin The amount each division contributes toward covering common corporate expenses and generating corporate profits. It is computed by subtracting all direct fixed expenses identifiable with each division from the contribution margin.

double-entry accounting system A method of accounting that recognizes the duality of a transaction such that the analysis results in a recording of equal amounts of debits and credits

E

earned capital The cumulative net income (losses) retained by the company (not paid out to shareholders as dividends)

earned When referring to revenue, the seller's execution of its duties under the terms of the agreement, with the resultant passing of title to the buyer with no right of return or other contingencies

earnings per share A measure of performance, earnings per share are disclosed on the income statement. The general equation for basic earnings per share is: Net income less preferred stock dividends/ Weighted average number of common shares outstanding for the period.

earnings quality The degree to which reported earnings represent how well the firm has performed from an economic standpoint

earnings smoothing Earnings management with a goal to provide an earnings stream with less variability

economic profit The number of inventory units sold multiplied by the difference between the sales price and the replacement cost of the inventories (approximated by the cost of the most recently purchased inventories)

economic value-added (EVA) A variation of residual income calculated as income after taxes less the cost of capital employed; specifically, net operating profits after tax less a charge for the use of capital equal to beginning capital utilized in the business multiplied by the weighted average cost of capital.

effective interest method A method of amortizing bond premium or discount that results in a constant rate of interest each period and varying amounts of premium or discount amortized each period

effective interest rate The rate determined by dividing the total discount amount by the cash proceeds on a note payable when the borrower borrowed at a discount

effective rate The current rate of interest in the market for a bond or other debt instrument; when issued, a bond is priced to yield the market (effective) rate of interest at the date of issuance

efficient markets hypothesis Capital markets are said to be efficient if at any given time, current equity (stock) prices reflect all relevant information that determines those equity prices

electronic data interchange (EDI) The electronic communication of data between organizations.

employee severance costs Accrued (estimated) costs for termination of employees as part of a restructuring program

employee stock options A form of compensation that grants a select group of employees the right to purchase a fixed number of company shares at a fixed price for a predetermined time period

enterprise resource planning (ERP) Enterprise management information systems that provide organizations an integrated set of operating, financial, and management systems.

equity carve out A corporate divestiture of operating units

equity method The prescribed method of accounting for investments in which the investor company has a significant influence over the investee company (usually taken to be ownership between 20-50% of the outstanding common stock of the investee company)

equivalent completed units The number of completed units that is equal, in terms of production effort, to a given number of partially completed units.

ethics The moral quality, fitness, or propriety of a course of action that can injure or benefit people; also, the values, rules, and justifications that governs one's way of life.

expenses Decreases in stockholders' equity incurred by a firm in the process of earning revenues

external failure costs Quality costs incurred when nonconforming products or services are delivered to customers.

extraordinary items Revenues and expenses that are both unusual and infrequent and are, therefore, excluded from income from continuing operations

F

face amount The principal amount of a bond or note to be repaid at maturity

facility level activity An activity performed to maintain general manufacturing or marketing capabilities.

factoring Selling an account receivable to another company, typically a finance company or a financial institution, for less than its face value

file A collection of related records.

Financial Accounting Standards Board (FASB) The organization currently responsible for setting accounting standards for reporting financial information

financial accounting An information processing system that generates general-purpose reports of financial operations (income statement and cash flows statement) and financial position (balance sheet) for an organization.

financial assets Normally consist of excess resources held for future expansion or unexpected needs; they are usually invested in the form of other companies' stock, corporate or government bonds, and real estate

financial leverage The proportionate use of borrowed funds in the capital structure, computed as net financial obligations (NFO) divided by average equity; financial leverage is considered favorable if the return on assets is higher than the fixed rate on borrowed funds and unfavorable if the fixed rate is greater than the return it generates.

financial reporting objectives A component of the conceptual framework that specifies that financial statements should provide information (1) useful for investment and credit decisions, (2) helpful in assessing an entity's ability to generate future cash flows, and (3) about an entity's resources, claims to those resources, and the effects of events causing changes in these items

financial reporting The process of preparing financial statements (income statement, balance sheet, and statement of cash flows) for a firm in accordance with generally accepted accounting principles.

financial statement analysis The process of interpreting and evaluating financial statements by using the data contained in them to produce additional financial measures. Financial statement analysis involves comparing financial statements for the current period with those of the previous periods, studying the internal composition of the financial statements, and studying relationships within and among the financial statements.

financial statement elements A part of the conceptual framework that identifies the significant components—such as assets, liabilities, stockholders' equity, revenues, and expenses—used to put financial statements together

financing activities Business activities that involve (1) resource transfers between the entity and its owners and (2) the securement of loans from and the repayment of them to nonowners (creditors).

finished goods inventory The dollar amount of inventory that has completed the production process and is awaiting sale to customers

first-in, first-out (FIFO) method (in process costing) A costing method that accounts for unit costs of beginning inventory units separately from those started during the current period. The first costs incurred each period are assumed to have been used to complete the unfinished units left over from the previous period.

first-in, first-out (FIFO) method One of the prescribed methods of inventory costing; FIFO assumes that the first costs incurred for the purchase or production of inventory are the first costs relieved from inventory when goods are sold

fiscal year The annual accounting period used by a business firm

five forces of competitive intensity Industry competition, bargaining power of buyers, bargaining power of suppliers, threat of substitution, threat of entry

fixed assets An alternate label for long-term assets; may also be called property, plant, and equipment (PPE)

fixed costs Costs that do not change with changes in sales volume (over a reasonable range); with a unit level cost driver as the independent variable, fixed costs are a constant amount per period of time

fixed manufacturing overhead All fixed costs associated with converting raw materials into finished goods.

fixed overhead budget variance The difference between budgeted and actual fixed overhead.

fixed overhead volume variance The difference between total budgeted fixed overhead and total standard fixed overhead assigned to production.

fixed selling and administrative costs All fixed costs other than those directly associated with converting raw materials into finished goods.

flexible budget variance Computed for each cost as the difference between the actual cost and the flexible budget cost of producing a given quantity of product or service.

flexible budgets Budgets that are drawn up for a series of possible production and sales volumes or adjusted to a particular level of production after the fact. These budgets, based on cost-volume or cost-activity relationships, are used to determine what costs should have been for an attained level of activity.

flexible manufacturing systems (FMS) An extension of computer-aided manufacturing techniques through a series of manufacturing operations. These operations include the automatic movement of units between operations and the automatic and rapid setup of machines to produce each product.

forecast The projection of financial results over the forecast horizon and terminal periods

foreign currency transaction The $US equivalent of an asset or liability denominated in a foreign currency

foreign exchange gain or loss The gain (loss) recognized in the income statement relating to the change in the $US equivalent of an asset or liability denominated in a foreign currency

for-profit organization An organization that has profit as a primary mission.

franchise Generally, an exclusive right to operate or sell a specific brand of products in a given geographic area

free cash flow This excess cash flow (above that required to manage its growth and development) from which dividends can be paid; computed as NOPAT 2 Increase in NOA

full absorption cost *see* absorption costing.

full costing *see* absorption costing.

full costs Include all costs, regardless of their behavior patterns (variable or fixed) or activity level.

full disclosure principle An accounting principle stipulating the disclosure of all facts necessary to make financial statements useful to readers

fully diluted earnings per share *see* diluted earnings per share

functional currency The currency representing the primary currency in which a business unit conducts its operations

functional income statement A type of income statement where costs are classified according to function, rather than behavior. It is typically included in external financial reports.

fundamental analysis Uses financial information to predict future valuation and, hence, buy-sell stock strategies

funded status The difference between the pension obligation and the fair market value of the pension investments

future value The amount a current sum of money (or series of monies) earning a stated rate of interest will accumulate to at the end of a future period.

G

general and administrative expense budget Presents the expenses the organization plans to incur in connection with the general administration of the organization. Included are expenses for such things as the accounting department, the computer center, and the president's office.

general journal A journal with enough flexibility so that any type of business transaction can be recorded in it

general ledger A grouping of all of an entity's accounts that are used to prepare the basic financial statements

generally accepted accounting principles (GAAP) A set of standards and procedures that guide the preparation of financial statements

goal A definable, measurable objective.

going concern concept An accounting principle that assumes that, in the absence of evidence to the contrary, a business entity will have an indefinite life

goodwill The value that derives from a firm's ability to earn more than a normal rate of return on the fair market value of its specific, identifiable net assets; computed as the residual of the purchase price less the fair market value of the net tangible and intangible assets acquired

gross margin The difference between net sales and cost of goods sold: also called gross profit

gross profit margin (GPM) (percentage) The ratio of gross profit on sales divided by net sales

gross profit on sales The difference between net sales and cost of goods sold; also called gross margin

H

held-to-maturity securities The designation given to a portfolio of bond investments that are expected to be held until they mature

high-low method of cost estimation Utilizes data from two time periods, a representative high activity period and a representative low activity period, to estimate fixed and variable costs.

historical cost Original acquisition or issuance costs

holding company The parent company of a subsidiary

holding gain The increase in replacement cost since the inventories were acquired, which equals the number of units sold multiplied by the difference between the current replacement cost and the original acquisition cost

horizon period The forecast period for which detailed estimates are made, typically 5–10 years

horizontal analysis An evaluative standard, horizontal analysis is the comparison of a firm's current financial measures to those of previous periods. Horizontal analysis is used to evaluate trends in the firm's financial condition covering two or more years.

I

impairment loss A loss recognized on an impaired asset equal to the difference between its book value and current fair value

impairment A reduction in value from that presently recorded

imposed budget *see* top-down budget.

income statement A financial report on operating activities that lists revenues less expenses over a period of time, yielding a company's net income

incremental budgeting An approach to budgeting where costs for a coming period are budgeted as a dollar or percentage change from the amount budgeted for (or spent during) some previous period.

indirect department cost A cost reassigned, or allocated, to a department from another cost objective.

indirect method (for statement of cash flow) A reporting format for the operating section of the statement of cash flows; wherein net cash flow from operations is computed by entering adjustments to net income from the income statement.

indirect segment costs *see* common segment costs.

inspection time The amount of time it takes units to be inspected.

intangible assets A term applied to a group of long-term assets, including patents, copyrights, franchises, trademarks, and goodwill, that benefit an entity but do not have physical substance

integer programming A variation of linear programming that determines the solution in whole numbers.

interdepartmental services Services provided by one service department to other service departments.

interest cost (pensions) The increase in the pension obligation due to the accrual of an additional year of interest

internal auditing A company function that provides independent appraisals of the company's financial statements, its internal controls, and its operations

internal controls The measures undertaken by a company to ensure the reliability of its accounting data, protect its assets from theft or unauthorized use, make sure that employees are following the company's policies and procedures, and evaluate the performance of employees, departments, divisions, and the company as a whole

internal failure costs Quality costs incurred when materials, components, products, or services are identified as defective before delivery to customers.

internal rate of return (IRR) Often called the time-adjusted rate of return, the discount rate that equates the present value of a project's cash inflows with the present value of the project's cash outflows.

inventory carrying costs Costs of holding inventories, including warehousing, logistics, insurance, financing, and the risk of loss due to theft, damage, or technological or fashion change

inventory shrinkage The cost associated with an inventory shortage; the amount by which the perpetual inventory exceeds the physical inventory

inventory turnover (in dollars) Often regarded as a measure of both solvency and performance, inventory turnover tells how long it takes to convert inventory into current monetary assets and how well the firm is managing investments in inventory. The general equation for inventory turnover is: Cost of goods sold/Average inventory cost.

inventory turnover (in units) The annual demand in units divided by the average inventory in units.

investing activities Business activities that involve transactions related to acquiring and disposing of marketable securities, other long-term investments, and property, plant, and equipment, as well as making and collecting loans unrelated to the sale of goods or services; the acquiring and disposing of resources (assets) that a company uses to acquire and sell its products and services.

investing creditors Those who primarily finance investing activities

investment center A responsibility center whose manager is responsible for the relationship between its profits and the total assets invested in the center. In general, the management of an investment center is expected to earn a target profit per dollar invested.

investment returns The increase in pension investments resulting from interest, dividends, and capital gains on the investment portfolio

investment tax credit A reduction in income taxes of a percent of the cost of a new asset in the year the new asset is placed in service.

invoice price The price that a seller charges the purchaser for merchandise

invoice A document that the seller sends to the purchaser to request payment for items that the seller shipped to the purchaser

IOU A slang term for a receivable

irrelevant costs Costs that do not differ among competing decision alternatives.

issued stock Shares of stock that have been sold and issued to stockholders; issued stock may be either outstanding or in the treasury

J

job cost sheet A document used to track the status of and accumulate the costs for a specific job in a job cost system.

job order production The manufacturing of products in single units or in batches of identical units.

job production *see* job order production.

joint costs All materials and conversion costs of joint products incurred prior to the split-off point.

joint products Two or more products simultaneously produced by a single process from a common set of inputs.

journal A tabular record in which business transactions are analyzed in debit and credit terms and recorded in chronological order

just-in-time (JIT) inventory management A comprehensive inventory management philosophy that stresses policies, procedures, and attitudes by managers and other workers that result in the efficient production of high-quality goods while maintaining the minimum level of inventories.

just-in-time (JIT) inventory philosophy Receive inventory from suppliers into the production process just at the point it is needed

K

Kaizen costing *see* continuous improvement costing.

kanban system *see* materials pull system.

L

labor efficiency variance The difference between the standard cost of actual labor inputs and the flexible budget cost for labor.

labor rate (spending) variance The difference between the actual cost and the standard cost of actual labor inputs.

land improvements Improvements with limited lives made to land sites, such as paved parking lots and driveways

last-in, first-out (LIFO) method One of the prescribed methods of inventory costing; LIFO assumes that the last costs incurred for the purchase or production of inventory are the first costs relieved form inventory when goods are sold

lean accounting A system of product cost assignment where costs are assigned to value streams of multiple products rather than to individual products

lean production A philosophy of inventory production and management that emphasizes increased coordination throughout the value chain, reduced inventory, reduced production times, increased product quality, and increased employee involvement and empowerment

lease A contract between a lessor (owner) and lessee (tenant) for the rental of property

leasehold improvements Expenditures made by a lessee to alter or improve leased property

leasehold The rights transferred from the lessor to the lessee by a lease

least-squares regression analysis Uses a mathematical technique to fit a cost estimating equation to the observed data in a manner that minimizes the sum of the vertical squared estimating errors between the estimated and actual costs at each observation.

lessee The party acquiring the right to the use of property by a lease

lessor The owner of property who transfers the right to use the property to another party by a lease

leveraging The use of borrowed funds in the capital structure of a firm; the expectation is that the funds will earn a return higher than the rate of interest on the borrowed funds

liabilities The obligations, or debts, that an entity must pay in money or services at some time in the future because of past transactions or events

life-cycle budgeting An approach to budgeting when the entire life of the project represents a more useful planning horizon than an artificial period of one year.

life-cycle costs From the seller's perspective, all costs associated with a product or service ranging from those incurred with initial conception through design, pre-production, production, and after-production support. From the buyer's perspective, all costs associated with a purchased product or service, including initial acquisition costs and subsequent costs of operation, maintenance, repair, and disposal.

LIFO conformity rule IRS requirement to cost inventories using LIFO for tax purposes if they are costed using LIFO for financial reporting purposes

LIFO liquidation The reduction in inventory quantities when LIFO costing is used; LIFO liquidation yields an increase in gross profit and income when prices are rising

LIFO reserve The difference between the cost of inventories using FIFO and the cost using LIFO

linear algebra method (reciprocal) method A method of allocating service department costs using a series of linear algebraic equations, which are solved simultaneously, to allocate service department costs both interdepartmentally among service departments and to the producing departments.

linear programming An optimizing model used to assist managers in making decisions under constrained conditions when linear relationships exist between all variables.

liquidation value per share The amount that would be received by a holder of a share of stock if the corporation liquidated

liquidity How much cash the company has, how much is expected, and how much can be raised on short notice

list price The suggested price or reference price of merchandise in a catalog or price list

long-term liabilities Debt obligations not due to be settled within the normal operating cycle or one year, whichever is longer

lower of cost or market (LCM) GAAP requirement to write down the carrying amount of inventories on the balance sheet if the reported cost (using FIFO, for example) exceeds market value (determined by current replacement cost)

M

maker The signer of a promissory note

managed fixed costs *see* discretionary fixed costs.

management accounting A discipline concerned with financial and related information used by managers and other persons inside specific organizations to make strategic, organizational, and operational decisions.

management by exception An approach to performance assessment whereby management directs attention only to those activities not proceeding according to plan.

management discussion and analysis (MD&A) The section of the 10-K report in which a company provides a detailed discussion of its business activities

managerial accounting The accounting activities carried out by a firm's accounting staff primarily to furnish managers and other employees with accounting data for decisions related to the firm's operations

manufacturers Companies that convert raw materials and components into finished products through the application of skilled labor and machine operations

manufacturing cost budget A budget detailing the direct materials, direct labor, and manufacturing overhead costs that should be incurred by manufacturing operations to produce the number of units called for in the production budget.

manufacturing costs The costs of direct materials, direct labor, and manufacturing overhead incurred in the manufacture of a product

manufacturing margin The result when direct manufacturing costs (variable costs) are deducted from product sales.

manufacturing organizations Organizations that process raw materials into finished products for sale to others.

manufacturing overhead All manufacturing costs other than direct materials and direct labor.

margin of safety The amount by which actual or planned sales exceed the break-even point.

marginal cost The varying increment in total cost required to produce and sell an additional unit of product.

marginal revenue The varying increment in total revenue derived from the sale of an additional unit.

market (yield) rate This is the interest rate that investors expect to earn on the investment in this debt security; this rate is used to price the bond issue

market method accounting Securities are reported at current market values (marked-to-market) on the statement date

market segment level activity Performed to obtain or maintain operations in a market segment.

market value per share The current price at which shares of stock may be bought or sold

market value The published price (as listed on a stock exchange) multiplied by the number of shares owned

master budget The grouping together of all budgets and supporting schedules. This budget coordinates all the financial and operational activities and places them into an organization wide set of budgets for a given time period.

matching principle An accounting guideline that states that income is determined by relating expenses, to the extent feasible, with revenues that have been recorded

materiality An accounting guideline that states that transactions so insignificant that they would not affect a user's actions or perception of the company may be recorded in the most expedient manner

materials inventory The physical component of inventory; the other components of manufactured inventory are labor costs and overhead costs

materials price variance The difference between the actual materials cost and the standard cost of actual materials inputs.

materials pull system An inventory production flow system in which employees at each station work to replenish the inventory used by employees at subsequent stations. The building of excess inventories is strictly prohibited. When the number of units in inventory reaches a specified limit, work at the station stops until workers at a subsequent station pull a unit from the in-process storage area.

materials push system An inventory production flow system in which employees work to reduce the pile of inventory building up at their work stations. Workers at each station remove materials from an in-process storage area, complete their operation, and place the output in another in-process storage area. Hence, they push the work to the next work station.

materials quantity variance The difference between the standard cost of actual materials inputs and the flexible budget cost for materials.

materials requisition form A document used to record the type and quantity of each raw material issued to the factory.

maturity date The date on which a note or bond matures

measuring unit concept An accounting guideline noting that the accounting unit of measure is the basic unit of money

merchandise inventory A stock of products that a company buys from another company and makes available for sale to its customers

merchandising firm A company that buys finished products, stores the products for varying periods of time, and then resells the products

merchandising organizations Organizations that buy and sell goods without performing manufacturing operations.

method of comparables model Equity valuation or stock values are predicted using price multiples, which are defined as stock price divided by some key financial statement number such as net income, net sales, book value of equity, total assets, or cash flow; companies are then compared with their competitors

minimum level budgeting An approach to budgeting that establishes a base amount for all budget items and requires explanation or justification for any budgeted amount above the minimum (base).

minority interest The equity claim of a shareholder owning less than a majority or controlling interest in the company

mission The basic purpose toward which an organization's activities are directed.

mixed costs Costs that contain a fixed and a variable cost element.

model A simplified representation of some real-world phenomenon.

modified accelerated cost recovery system (MACRS) *see* accelerated cost recovery system

movement time The time units spend moving between work or inspection stations.

mutually exclusive investments Two or more capital expenditure proposals where the acceptance of one investment automatically causes the rejection of the other(s).

N

natural resources Assets occurring in a natural state, such as timber, petroleum, natural gas, coal, and other mineral deposits

net asset based valuation model Equity is valued as reported assets less reported liabilities

net assets The difference between an entity's assets and liabilities; net assets are equal to stockholders' equity

net book value (NBV) The cost of the asset less accumulated depreciation; also called carrying value

net financial obligations (NFO) Net total of all financial (nonoperating) obligations less financial (nonoperating) assets

net income The excess of a firm's revenues over its expenses

net loss The excess of a firm's expenses over its revenues

net operating assets (NOA) Current and long-term operating assets less current and long-term operating liabilities; or net operating working capital plus long-term net operating assets

net operating profit after tax (NOPAT) Sales less operating expenses (including taxes)

net present value The present value of a project's net cash inflows from operations and disinvestment less the amount of the initial investment.

net realizable value The value at which an asset can be sold, net of any costs of disposition

net sales volume variance Indicates the impact of a change in sales volume on the contribution margin, given the budgeted selling price and the standard variable costs. It is computed as the difference between the actual and the budgeted sales volumes times the budgeted unit contribution margin.

net sales The total revenue generated by a company through merchandise sales less the revenue given up through sales returns and allowances and sales discounts

net working capital Current assets less current liabilities

nominal rate The rate of interest stated on a bond certificate or other debt instrument

noncash investing and financing activities Significant business activities during the period that do not impact cash inflows or cash outflows

noncurrent liabilities Obligations not due to be paid within one year or the operating cycle, whichever is longer

nonoperating expenses Expenses that relate to the company's financing activities and include interest income and interest expense, gains and losses on sales of securities, and income or loss on discontinued operations

non-value-added activity An activity that does not add value to a product or service from the viewpoint of the customer.

no-par stock Stock that does not have a par value

NOPAT Net operating profit after tax

normal operating cycle For a particular business, the average period of time between the use of cash in its typical operating activity and the subsequent collection of cash from customers

note receivable A promissory note held by the note's payee

notes to financial statements Footnotes in which companies discuss their accounting policies and estimates used in preparing the statements

not-for-profit organization An organization that does not have profit as a primary goal.

not-sufficient-funds check A check from an individual or company that had an insufficient cash balance in the bank when the holder of the check presented it to the bank for payment

O

objective function In linear programming models, the goal to be minimized or maximized.

objectivity principle An accounting principle requiring that, whenever possible, accounting entries are based on objectively determined evidence

off-balance-sheet financing The structuring of a financing arrangement so that no liability shows on the borrower's balance sheet

operating activities Business activities that involve transactions that are related to a company's normal income-earning activity (research, develop, produce, purchase, market, and distribute company products and services) and that enter into the calculation of net income on the income statement.

operating asset turnover The ratio obtained by dividing sales by average net operating assets

operating budget Detailed plans to guide operations throughout the budget period.

operating cash flow to capital expenditures ratio A firm's net cash flow from operating activities divided by its annual capital expenditures

operating cash flow to current liabilities ratio A firm's net cash flow from operating activities divided by its average current liabilities

operating creditors Those who primarily finance operating activities

operating cycle The time between paying cash for goods or employee services and receiving cash from customers

operating expense margin (OEM) The ratio obtained by dividing any operating expense item or category by sales

operating expenses The usual and customary costs that a company incurs to support its main business activities; these include cost of goods sold, selling expenses, depreciation expense, amortization expense, research and development expense, and taxes on operating profits

operating lease A lease by which the lessor retains the usual risks and rewards of owning the property

operating leverage A measure of the extent that an organization's costs are fixed.

operating profit margin The ratio obtained by dividing NOPAT by sales

operational audit An evaluation of activities, systems, and internal controls within a company to determine their efficiency, effectiveness, and economy

operations list A document that specifies the manufacturing operations and related times required to produce one unit or batch of product.

opportunity cost The net cash inflow that could be obtained if the resources committed to one action were used in the most desirable other alternative.

optimal solution In linear programming models, the feasible solution than maximizes or minimizes the value of the objective function, depending on the decision maker's goal.

optimizing model A model that suggests a specific choice between decision alternatives.

order level activity An activity performed for each sales order.

order-filling costs Costs incurred to place finished goods in the hands of purchasers (for example, storing, packaging, and transportation).

order-getting costs Costs incurred to obtain customers' orders (for example, advertising, salespersons' salaries and commissions, travel, telephone, and entertainment).

organization chart An illustration of the formal relationships existing between the elements of an organization.

organization costs Expenditures incurred in launching a business (usually a corporation), including attorney's fees and various fees paid to the state

organization structure The arrangement of lines of responsibility within the organization.

organizational cost drivers Choices concerning the organization of activities and the involvement of persons inside and outside the organization in decision making.

organizational-based cost systems Used for financial reporting, these systems focus on organizational units such as a company, plant, or department rather than on processes and activities.

organizing The process of making the organization into a well-ordered whole.

outcomes assessment *see* performance measurement.

outlay costs Costs that require future expenditures of cash or other resources.

output/input budgeting An approach to budgeting where physical inputs and costs are budgeted as a function of planned unit level activities. The budgeted inputs are a function of the planned outputs.

outsourcing The external acquisition of services or components.

outstanding checks Checks issued by a firm that have not yet been presented to its bank for payment

outstanding stock Shares of stock that are currently owned by stockholders (excludes treasury stock)

owners' equity The interest of owners in the assets of an entity; equal to the difference between the entity's assets and liabilities; also called stockholders' equity

P

packing list A document that lists the items of merchandise contained in a carton and the quantity of each item; the packing list is usually attached to the outside of the carton

paid-in capital The amount of capital contributed to a corporation by various transactions; the primary source of paid-in capital is from the issuance of shares of stock

par (bonds) Face value of the bond

par value (stock) An amount specified in the corporate charter for each share of stock and imprinted on the face of each stock certificate, often determines the legal capital of the corporation

parent company A company owning one or more subsidiary companies

parsimonious method to multiyear forecasting Forecasting multiple years using only sales growth, net operating profit margin (NOPM), and the turnover of net operating assets (NOAT)

participation budget *see* bottom-up budget.

partnership A voluntary association of two or more persons for the purpose of conducting a business

password A string of characters that a computer user enters into a computer terminal to prove to the computer that the person using the computer is truly the person named in the user identification code

patent An exclusive privilege granted for 20 years to an inventor that gives the patent holder the right to exclude others from making, using, or selling the invention

payback period The time required to recover the initial investment in a project from operations.

payee The company or individual to whom a promissory note is made payable

payment approval form A document that authorizes the payment of an invoice

pension plan A plan to pay benefits to employees after they retire from the company; the plan may be a defined contribution plan or a defined benefit plan

percentage of net sales method A procedure that determines the uncollectible accounts expense for the year by multiplying net credit sales by the estimated uncollectible percentage

percentage-of-completion method Recognition of revenue by determining the costs incurred per the contract as compared to its total expected costs

performance measurement The determination of the extent to which actual outcomes correspond to planned outcomes.

period costs Expired costs not related to manufacturing inventory; they are recognized as expenses when incurred.

period statement A financial statement accumulating information for a specific period of time; examples are the income statement, the statement of stockholders' equity, and the statement of cash flows

permanent account An account used to prepare the balance sheet; that is, asset, liability, and equity capital (capital stock and retained earnings) accounts; any balance in a permanent account at the end of an accounting period is carried forward to the next period

physical inventory A year-end procedure that involves counting the quantity of each inventory item, determining the unit cost of each item, multiplying the unit cost times quantity, and summing the costs of all the items to determine the total inventory at cost

physical model A scaled-down version or replica of physical reality.

planning The process of selecting goals and strategies to achieve those goals.

plant assets Land, buildings, equipment, vehicles, furniture, and fixtures that a firm uses in its operations; sometimes referred to by the acronym PPE

pooling of interests method A method of accounting for business combinations under which the acquired company is recorded on the acquirer's balance sheet at its book value, rather than market value; this method is no longer acceptable under GAAP for acquisitions occurring after 2001

position statement A financial statement, such as the balance sheet, that presents information as of a particular date

post-closing trial balance A list of general ledger accounts and their balances after closing entries have been recorded and posted

postdated check A check from another person or company with a date that is later than the current date; a postdated check does not become cash until the date of the check

practical capacity The maximum possible activity, allowing for normal repairs and maintenance.

predetermined manufacturing overhead rate An overhead rate established at the start of each year by dividing the predicted overhead costs for the year by the predicted volume of activity in the overhead base for the year.

preemptive right The right of a stockholder to maintain his or her proportionate interest in a corporation by having the right to purchase an appropriate share of any new stock issue

preferred stock A class of corporate capital stock typically receiving priority over common stock in dividend payments and distribution of assets should the corporation be liquidated

premium bond A bond that is sold for more than its par (face) value

present value index The present value of the project's subsequent cash flows divided by the initial investment.

present value The current worth of a specified amount of money to be received at some future date at some specified interest rate.

prevention costs Quality costs incurred to prevent nonconforming products from being produced or nonconforming services from being performed.

price discrimination Illegally charging different purchasers different prices.

price earnings ratio A measure of performance, price earnings ratio compares the current market price with earnings per share of stock and arrives at a multiple of earnings represented by the selling price. Calculated as: Current market price per common share divided by Earnings per share

price fixing The organized setting of prices by competitors.

pro forma income A computation of income that begins with the GAAP income from continuing operations (that excludes discontinued operations, extraordinary items and changes in accounting principle), but then excludes other transitory items (most notably, restructuring charges), and some additional items such as expenses arising from acquisitions (goodwill amortization and other acquisition costs), compensation expense in the form of stock options, and research and development expenditures; pro forma income is not GAAP

process manufacturing A manufacturing environment where production is on a continuous basis.

process map (or process flowchart) A schematic overview of all the activities required to complete a process. Each major activity is represented by a rectangle on the map.

process reengineering The fundamental redesign of a process to serve internal or external customers.

process A collection of related activities intended to achieve a common purpose.

processing time The time spent working on units.

product costs All costs incurred in the manufacturing of products; they are carried in the accounts as an asset (inventory) until the product is sold, at which time they are recognized as an expense (cost of goods sold).

product level activity An activity performed to support the production of each different type of product.

product margin Computed as product sales less direct product costs.

production order A document that contains a job's unique identification number and specifies details for the job such as the quantity to be produced, the total raw materials requirements, the manufacturing operations and other activities to be performed, and perhaps even the time when each manufacturing operation should be performed.

productivity The relationship between outputs and inputs.

profit center A responsibility center whose manager is responsible for revenues, costs, and resulting profits. It may be an entire organization, but it is more frequently a segment of an organization such as a product line, marketing territory, or store.

profitability analysis An examination of the relationships between revenues, costs, and profits.

profit-volume graph Illustrates the relationship between volume and profits; it does not show revenues and costs.

project-level activity An activity performed to support the completion of each project.

promissory note A written promise to pay a certain sum of money on demand or at a determinable future time

purchase method The prescribed method of accounting for business combinations; under the purchase method, assets and liabilities of the acquired company are recorded at fair market value, together with identifiable intangible assets; the balance is ascribed to goodwill

purchase order A document that formally requests a supplier to sell and deliver specific quantities of particular items of merchandise at specified prices

purchase requisition An internal document that requests that the purchasing department order particular items of merchandise

purchases budget Indicates the merchandise or materials that must be acquired to meet current needs and ending inventory requirements.

Q

qualitative characteristics of accounting information The characteristics of accounting information that contribute to decision usefulness; the primary qualities are relevance and reliability

quality circles Groups of employees involved in the production of products who have the authority, within certain parameters, to address and resolve quality problems as they occur, without seeking management approval.

quality costs Costs incurred because poor quality of conformance does (or may) exist.

quality of conformance The degree of conformance between a product and its design specifications.

quality of design The degree of conformance between customer expectations for a product or service and the design specifications of the product or service.

quality Conformance to customer expectations.

quantitative model A set of mathematical relationships.

quarterly data Selected quarterly financial information that is reported in annual reports to stockholders

quick ratio *see* acid test ratio; Defined as quick assets (cash and cash equivalents, short-term investments, and current receivables) divided by current liabilities.

R

raw materials inventories The physical ingredients and components that will be converted by machines and/or human labor into a finished product.

realized (or **realizable**) When referring to revenue, the receipt of an asset or satisfaction of a liability as a result of a transaction or event

recognition criteria The criteria that must be met before a financial statement element may be recorded in the accounts; essentially, the item must meet the definition of an element and must be measurable

record A related set of alphabetic and/or numeric data items.

registered bond A bond for which the issuer (or the trustee) maintains a record of owners and, at the appropriate times, mails out interest payments

relational (cause-and-effect) cost center A cost center that has clearly defined relationships between effort and accomplishment (cause and effect).

relevance A qualitative characteristic of accounting information; relevant information contributes to the predictive and evaluative decisions made by financial statement users

relevant costs Future costs that differ between competing decision alternatives.

relevant range The range of activity within which a linear cost function is valid.

reliability A qualitative characteristic of accounting information; reliable information contains no bias or error and faithfully portrays what it intends to represent

remeasurement The computation of gain or loss in the translation of subsidiaries denominated in a foreign currency into $US when the temporal method is used

residual income for investment center Excess of investment center income over the minimum rate of return set by top management. The minimum dollar return is computed as a percentage of the investment center's asset base.

residual net operating income (ROPI) model An equity valuation approach that equates the firm's value to the sum of its net operating assets (NOA) and the present value of its residual operating income (ROPI)

residual operating income Net operating profits after tax (NOPAT) less the product of net operating assets (NOA) at the beginning of the period multiplied by the weighted average cost of capital (WACC)

responsibility accounting The structuring of performance reports addressed to individual (or group) members of an organization in a manner that emphasizes the factors they are able to control. The focus is on specific units within the organization that are responsible for the accomplishment of specific activities or objectives.

retailers Companies that buy products from wholesale distributors and sell the products to individual customers, the general public

retained earnings reconciliation The reconciliation of retained earnings from the beginning to the end of the year; the change in retained earnings includes, at a minimum, the net income (loss) for the period and dividends paid, if any, but may include other components as well; also called statement of retained earnings

retained earnings Earned capital, the cumulative net income and loss, of the company (from its inception) that has not been paid to shareholders as dividends

return on assets A financial ratio computed as net income divided by average total assets; sometimes referred to by the acronym ROA; as a measure of performance, return on assets combines the asset turnover and return on sales ratios to measure directly the firm's ability to use its assets to generate profits

return on common stockholders' equity A financial ratio computed as net income less preferred stock dividends divided by average common stockholders' equity; sometimes referred to by the acronym ROCE

return on equity A measure of performance, the return on equity measures the profits attributable to the shareholders as a percentage of their equity in the firm. The general equation for return on equity is: Net income/Average shareholders' equity; sometimes referred to by the acronym ROE.

return on investment for investment center A measure of the earnings per dollar of investment. The return on investment of an investment center is computed by dividing the income of the center by its asset base (usually average total assets). It can also be computed as investment turnover times the return-on-sales ratio.

return on investment The ratio obtained by dividing income by average investment; sometimes referred to by the acronym ROI

return on net operating assets (RNOA) The ratio obtained by dividing NOPAT by average net operating assets

return on sales A measure of performance, the return on sales measures the firm's ability to generate profits from sales produced by the firm's assets. The general equation for return on sales is: net income divided by net sales; sometimes referred to by the acronym ROS

return The amount earned on an investment; also called yield

revenue center A responsibility center whose manager is responsible for the generation of sales revenues.

revenue recognition principle An accounting principle requiring that revenue be recognized when earned and realized (or realizable)

revenue variance The difference between the budgeted sales volume at the budgeted selling price and the actual sales volume at the actual selling price.

revenues Inflows of earned resources from providing goods and services to customers; reflected as increases in stockholders' equity

Robinson-Patman Act Prohibits price discrimination when purchasers compete with one another in the sale of their products or services to third parties.

rolling budget *see* continuous budgeting.

S

sale on account A sale of merchandise made on a credit basis

sales budget A forecast of sales revenue for a future period. It may also contain a forecast of sales collections.

sales mix The relative portion of unit or dollar sales derived from each product or service.

sales price variance The impact on revenues of a change in selling price, given the actual sales volume. It is computed as the change in selling price times the actual sales volume.

sales volume variance Indicates the impact on revenues of change in sales volume, assuming there was no change in selling price. It is computed as the difference between the actual and the budgeted sales volumes times the budgeted selling price.

salvage value The expected net recovery when a plant asset is sold or removed from service; also called residual value

scatter diagram A graph of past activity and cost data, with individual observations represented by dots.

secured bond A bond that pledges specific property as security for meeting the terms of the bond agreement

Securities and Exchange Commission (SEC) The commission, created by the 1934 Securities Act, that has broad powers to regulate the issuance and trading of securities, and the financial reporting of companies issuing securities to the public

segment income All revenues of a segment minus all costs directly or indirectly charged to it.

segment margin The amount that a segment contributes toward the common (indirect) costs of the organization and toward profits. It is computed as segment sales less direct segment costs.

segment reports Income statements that show operating results for portions or segments of a business. Segment reporting is used primarily for internal purposes, although generally accepted accounting principles also require disclosure of segment information for some public corporations.

segments Subdivisions of a firm for which supplemental financial information is disclosed

selling expense budget Presents the expenses the organization plans to incur in connection with sales and distribution.

semi-variable costs *see* mixed costs.

sensitivity analysis The study of the responsiveness of a model to changes in one or more of its independent variables.

serial bond A bond issue that staggers the bond maturity dates over a series of years

service cost (pensions) The increase in the pension obligation due to employees working another year for the employer

service costing The process of assigning costs to services performed.

service department A department that provides support services to production and/or other support departments.

service organizations Nonmanufacturing organizations that perform work for others, including banks, hospitals, and real estate agencies.

setup time The time required to prepare equipment to produce a specific product.

Sherman Antitrust Act Prohibits price fixing.

significant influence The ability of the investor to affect the financing or operating policies of the investee

simplex method A mathematical approach to solving linear programming models containing three or more variables.

sinking fund provision A bond feature that requires the borrower to retire a portion of the bonds each year or, in some cases, to make payments each year to a trustee who is responsible for managing the resources needed to retire the bonds at maturity

solvency Refers to the firm's ability to pay its debts as they become due.

source document Any written document or computer record evidencing an accounting transaction, such as a bank check or deposit slip, sales invoice, or cash register tape

special purpose entity *see* variable interest entity

spin-off A form of equity carve out in which divestiture is accomplished by distribution of a company's shares in a subsidiary to the company's shareholders who then own the shares in the subsidiary directly rather than through the parent company

split-off point The point in the process where joint products become separately identifiable.

split-off A form of equity carve out in which divestiture is accomplished by the parent company's exchange of stock in the subsidiary in return for shares in the parent owned by its shareholders

spread The difference between the net financial return (NFR) and the return on net operating activities (RNOA)

standard cost variance analysis A system for examining the flexible budget variance, which is the difference between the actual cost and flexible budget cost of producing a given quantity of product or service.

standard cost A budget that indicates what it should cost to provide an activity or produce one batch or unit of product under efficient operating conditions.

stated value A nominal amount that may be assigned to each share of no-par stock and accounted for much as if it were a par value

statement of cash flows A financial statement that reports the major sources and uses of cash classified into operating, investing, and financing activities and that indicates the net increase or decrease in cash; the statement also includes a schedule of any significant noncash investing and financing activities that occur during the period.

statement of cost of goods manufactured A report that summarizes the cost of goods completed and transferred into finished goods inventory during the period.

statement of financial position A financial statement showing a firm's assets, liabilities, and stockholders' equity at a specific date; also called a balance sheet

statement of owner's equity A financial statement presenting information on the events causing a change in stockholders' equity during a period; the statement presents the beginning balance, additions to, deductions from, and the ending balance of stockholders' equity for the period

static budget A budget based on a prior prediction of expected sales and production.

step costs Costs that are constant within a narrow range of activity but shift to a higher level with an increased range of activity. Total step costs increase in a step-like fashion as activity increases.

step method A method of allocating service department costs that gives partial recognition to interdepartmental services by using a methodology that allocates service department costs sequentially to both the remaining service departments and the producing departments.

stock dividends The payment of dividends in shares of stock

stock split Additional shares of its own stock issued by a corporation to its current stockholders in proportion to their current ownership interests without changing the balances in the related stockholders' equity accounts; a formal stock split increases the number of shares outstanding and reduces proportionately the stock's per share par value

storyboard A process map developed by employees who perform the component activities within a process.

straight-line depreciation A depreciation procedure that allocates uniform amounts of depreciation expense to each full period of a depreciable asset's useful life

strategic business segment A segment that has its own mission and set of goals to be achieved. The mission of the segment influences the decisions that its top managers make in both short-run and long-run situations.

strategic cost management Making decisions concerning specific cost drivers within the context of an organization's business strategy, its internal value chain, and its place in a larger value chain stretching from the development and use of resources to the final consumers.

strategic plan A guideline or framework for making specific medium-range or short-run decisions.

strategic position analysis An organization's basic way of competing to sell products or services.

strategic position How an organization wants to place itself in comparison to the competition.

strategy A course of action that will assist in achieving one or more goals.

structural cost drivers Fundamental choices about the size and scope of operations and technologies employed in delivering products or services to customers. These choices affect the types of activities and the costs of activities performed to satisfy customer needs.

suboptimization When managers or operating units, acting in their own best interests, make decisions that are not in the best interest of the organization as a whole.

subsequent events Events occurring shortly after a fiscal year-end that will be reported as supplemental information to the financial statements of the year just ended

subsidiaries Companies that are owned by the parent company

subsidiary ledger A set of accounts or records that contains detailed information about the items included in the balance of one general ledger account

summary of significant accounting policies A financial statement disclosure, usually the initial note to the statements, which identifies the major accounting policies and procedures used by the firm

sum-of-the-years'-digits method An accelerated depreciation method that allocates depreciation expense to each year in a fractional proportion, the denominator of which is the sum of the years' digits in the useful life of the asset and the numerator of which is the remaining useful life of the asset at the beginning of the current depreciation period

sunk costs Costs resulting from past decisions that cannot be changed.

T

T-account An abbreviated form of the formal account in the shape of a T; use is usually limited to illustrations of accounting techniques and analysis

target costing Establishes the allowable cost of a product or service by starting with determining what customers are willing to pay for the product or service and then subtracting a desired profit on sales.

temporary account An account used to gather information for an accounting period; at the end of the period, the balance is transferred to a permanent stockholders' equity account; revenue, expense, and dividends accounts are temporary accounts

term loan A long-term borrowing, evidenced by a note payable, which is contracted with a single lender

terminal period The forecast period following the horizon period

theory of constraints Every process has a bottleneck (constraining resource), and production cannot take place faster than it is processed through the bottleneck. The theory's goal is to maximize throughput in a constrained environment.

throughput Sales revenue minus direct materials costs; *see also* theory of constraints.

time-adjusted rate of return *see* internal rate of return.

times interest earned ratio A measure of long-term solvency and interest-paying ability; measured as income before interest expense and income taxes divided by interest expense

top-down budget A budget where top management decides on the primary goals and objectives for the organization and communicates them to lower management levels.

total compensation cost The sum of gross pay, payroll taxes, and fringe benefits paid by the employer

trade credit Inventories purchased on credit from other companies

trade discount An amount, usually based on quantity of merchandise purchased, that the seller subtracts from the list price of merchandise to determine the invoice price

trade name An exclusive and continuing right to use a certain term or name to identify a brand or family of products

trademark An exclusive and continuing right to use a certain symbol to identify a brand or family of products

trading on the equity The use of borrowed funds in the capital structure of a firm; the expectation is that the funds will earn a return higher than the rate of interest on the borrowed funds

trading securities Investments in securities that management intends to actively trade (buy and sell) for trading profits as market prices fluctuate

transfer price The internal value assigned a product or service that one division provides to another.

transitory items Transactions or events that are not likely to recur

translation adjustment The change in the value of the net assets of a subsidiary whose assets and liabilities are denominated in a foreign currency

treasury stock Shares of outstanding stock that have been acquired (and not retired) by the issuing corporation; treasury stock is recorded at cost and deducted from stockholders' equity in the balance sheet

trend percentages A comparison of the same financial item over two or more years stated as a percentage of a base-year amount

trial balance A list of the account titles in the general ledger, their respective debit or credit balances, and the totals of the debit and credit amounts

U

unadjusted trial balance A list of general ledger accounts and their balances taken before adjustments have been made

uncollectible accounts expense The expense stemming from the inability of a business to collect an amount previously recorded as a receivable; sometimes called bad debts expense; normally classified as a selling or administrative expense

unearned revenue A liability representing revenues received in advance; also called deferred revenue

unit contribution margin The difference between the unit selling price and the unit variable costs.

unit level activity An activity performed for each unit of product produced or sold.

unit level approach An approach to analyzing cost behavior that assumes changes in costs are best explained by changes in the number of units or sales dollars of products or services provided for customers.

units-of-production method A depreciation method that allocates depreciation expense to each operating period in proportion to the amount of the asset's expected total production capacity used each period

useful life The period of time an asset is used by an entity in its operating activities, running from date of acquisition to date of disposal (or removal from service)

V

value chain analysis The study of value-producing activities, stretching from basic raw materials to the final consumer of a product or service.

value chain The set of value-producing activities stretching from basic raw materials to the final consumer.

value The worth in usefulness or importance of a product or service to the customer.

value-added activity An activity that adds value to a product or service from the viewpoint of the customer.

value stream Consists of the production processes for similar products. Each value stream in a lean company not only has lean processes; it also has a lean accounting system because most costs should be directly traceable to one of the value streams.

variable cost ratio Variable costs as a portion of sales revenue.

variable costing An approach to product costing that treats variable manufacturing costs as product costs and fixed manufacturing costs as period costs.

variable costs Those costs that change in proportion to changes in sales volume. Costs that are an identical amount for each incremental unit of activity. Their total amount increases as activity increases, equaling zero dollars when activity is zero and increasing at a constant amount per unit of activity.

variable interest entity (VIE) Any form of business organization (such as corporation, partnership, trust) that is established by a sponsoring company and provides benefits to that company in the form of asset securitization or project financing; VIEs were formerly known as special purpose entities (SPEs)

variable manufacturing overhead All variable costs, except direct labor and direct materials, associated with converting raw materials into finished goods.

variable overhead effectiveness variance The difference between the standard variable overhead cost for the actual inputs and the flexible budget cost for variable overhead based on outputs.

variable overhead spending variance The difference between the actual variable overhead cost and the standard variable overhead cost for the actual inputs.

variable selling and administrative costs All variable costs other than those directly associated with converting raw materials into finished goods.

variance A comparison of actual and budgeted (or allowed) costs or revenues which are usually identified in financial performance reports.

vertical analysis An evaluative standard that restates amounts in the current financial statements as a percentage of some base measure such as sales; focused on one period's statements.

virtual integration The use of information technology and partnership concepts to allow two or more entities along a value chain to act as if they were a single economic entity.

voucher Another name for the payment approval form

W

waiting time The time units spend in temporary storage waiting to be processed, moved, or inspected.

warranties Guarantees against product defects for a designated period of time after sale

wasting assets Another name for natural resources; *see* natural resources

weighted average cost of capital (WACC) The discount rate where the weights are the relative percentages of debt and equity in the capital structure and are applied to the expected returns on debt and equity respectively; an average of the after-tax cost of all long-term borrowings and the cost of equity

weighted average method In process costing, a costing method that spreads the combined beginning inventory cost and current manufacturing costs (for materials, labor, and overhead) over the units completed and those in ending inventory on an average basis.

work in process inventory The cost of inventories that are in the manufacturing process and have not yet reached completion

work ticket A document used to record the time a job spends in a specific manufacturing operation.

working capital A measure of solvency, working capital is the difference between current assets and current liabilities and is the net amount of working funds available in the short run. The general equation for working capital is: Current assets minus Current liabilities.

work-in-process inventories Partially completed goods consisting of raw materials that are in the process of being converted into a finished product.

Z

zero coupon bond A bond that offers no periodic interest payments but that is issued at a substantial discount from its face value

zero-based budgeting A variation of the minimum level approach to budgeting where every dollar of expenditure must be justified.

z-score The outcome of the Altman Z-score bankruptcy prediction model

Index